High-Performance
Parallel Database
Processing
and Grid Databases

**WILEY SERIES ON PARALLEL
AND DISTRIBUTED COMPUTING**

Editor: Albert Y. Zomaya

A complete list of titles in this series appears at the end of this volume.

High-Performance Parallel Database Processing and Grid Databases

David Taniar
Monash University, Australia

Clement H.C. Leung
Hong Kong Baptist University and Victoria University, Australia

Wenny Rahayu
La Trobe University, Australia

Sushant Goel
RMIT University, Australia

A John Wiley & Sons, Inc., Publication

Library of Congress Cataloging-in-Publication Data:

Taniar, David.
  High-performance parallel database processing and grid databases / by David
Taniar, Clement Leung, Wenny Rahayu.
       p. cm.
  Includes bibliographical references.
  ISBN 978-0-470-10762-1 (cloth : alk. paper)
1. High performance computing. 2. Parallel processing (Electronic computers)
3. Computational grids (Computer systems) I. Leung, Clement H. C. II. Rahayu,
  Johanna Wenny. III. Title.
  QA76.88.T36 2008
  004' .35 — dc22
                                        2008011010

10 9 8 7 6 5 4 3 2 1

Contents

Part III   Advanced Parallel Query Processing

6. Parallel GroupBy-Join   141

Preface

The sizes of databases have seen exponential growth in the past, and such growth is expected to accelerate in the future, with the steady drop in storage cost accompanied by a rapid increase in storage capacity. Many years ago, a terabyte database was considered to be large, but nowadays they are sometimes regarded as small, and the daily volumes of data being added to some databases are measured in terabytes. In the future, petabyte and exabyte databases will be common.

With such volumes of data, it is evident that the sequential processing paradigm will be unable to cope; for example, even assuming a data rate of 1 terabyte per second, reading through a petabyte database will take over 10 days. To effectively manage such volumes of data, it is necessary to allocate multiple resources to it, very often massively so. The processing of databases of such astronomical proportions requires an understanding of how high-performance systems and parallelism work. Besides the massive volume of data in the database to be processed, some data has been distributed across the globe in a Grid environment. These massive data centers are also a part of the emergence of Cloud computing, where data access has shifted from local machines to powerful servers hosting web applications and services, making data access across the Internet using standard web browsers pervasive. This adds another dimension to such systems.

Parallelism in databases has been around since the early 1980s, when many researchers in this area aspired to build large special-purpose database machines—databases employing dedicated specialized parallel hardware. Some projects were born, including Bubba, Gamma, etc. These came and went. However, commercial DBMS vendors quickly realized the importance of supporting high performance for large databases, and many of them have incorporated parallelism and grid features into their products. Their commitment to high-performance systems and parallelism, as well as grid configurations, shows the importance and inevitability of parallelism.

In addition, while traditional transactional data is still common, we see an increasing growth of new application domains, broadly categorized as data-intensive applications. These include data warehousing and online analytic processing (OLAP) applications, data mining, genome databases, and multiple media databases manipulating unstructured and semistructured data. Therefore, it is critical to understand the underlying principle of data parallelism, before specialized and new application domains can be properly addressed.

This book is written to provide a fundamental understanding of parallelism in data-intensive applications. It features not only the algorithms for database operations but also quantitative analytical models, so that performance can be analyzed and evaluated more effectively.

The present book brings into a single volume the latest techniques and principles of parallel and grid database processing. It provides a much-needed, self-contained advanced text for database courses at the postgraduate or final year undergraduate levels. In addition, for researchers with a particular interest in parallel databases and related areas, it will serve as an indispensable and up-to-date reference. Practitioners contemplating building high-performance databases or seeking to gain a good understanding of parallel database technology too will find this book valuable for the wealth of techniques and models it contains.

STRUCTURE OF THE BOOK

This book is divided into five parts. Part I gives an introduction to the topic, including the rationale behind the need for high-performance database processing, as well as basic analytical models that will be used throughout the book.

Part II, consisting of three chapters, describes parallelism for basic query operations. These include parallel searching, parallel aggregate and sorting, and parallel join. These are the foundation of query processing, whereby complex queries can be decomposed into any of these atomic operations.

Part III, consisting of the next four chapters, focuses on more advanced query operations. This part covers groupby-join operations, parallel indexing, parallel object-oriented query processing, in particular, collection join, and query scheduling and optimization.

Just as the previous two parts deal with parallelism of read-only queries, the next part, Part IV, concentrates on transactions, also known as write queries. We use the grid environment to study transaction management. In grid transaction management, the focus is mainly on grid concurrency control, atomic commitment, durability, as well as replication.

Finally, Part V introduces other data-intensive applications, including data warehousing, OLAP, business intelligence, and parallel data mining.

ACKNOWLEDGMENTS

The authors would like to thank the publisher, John Wiley & Sons, for agreeing to embark on this exciting journey. In particular, we would like to thank Paul Petralia, Senior Editor, for supporting this project. We would also like to thank Whitney Lesch and Anastasia Wasko, Assistants to the Editor, for their endless efforts to ensure that we remained on track from start to completion. Without their encouragement and reminders, we would not have been able to finish this book.

We also thank Bruna Pomella, who proofread the entire manuscript, for commenting on ambiguous sentences and correcting grammatical mistakes.

Finally, we would like to express our sincere thanks to our respective universities, Monash University, Victoria University, Hong Kong Baptist University, La Trobe University, and RMIT, where the research presented in this book was conducted. We are grateful for the facilities and time that we received during the writing of this book. Without these, the book would not have been written in the first place.

David Taniar
Clement H.C. Leung
Wenny Rahayu
Sushant Goel

Part I

Introduction

Chapter 1

Introduction

Parallel databases are database systems that are implemented on parallel computing platforms. Therefore, *high-performance query processing* focuses on query processing, including database queries and transactions, that makes use of parallelism techniques applied to an underlying parallel computing platform in order to achieve high performance.

In a Grid environment, applications need to create, access, manage, and distribute data on a very large scale and across multiple organizations. The main challenges arise due to the volume of data, distribution of data, autonomy of sites, and heterogeneity of data resources. Hence, *Grid databases* can be defined loosely as being data access in a Grid environment.

This chapter gives an introduction to parallel databases, parallel query processing, and Grid databases. Section 1.1 gives a brief overview. In Section 1.2, the motivations for using parallelism in database processing are explained. Understanding the motivations is a critical starting point in exploring parallel database processing in depth. This will answer the question of *why* parallelism is necessary in modern database processing.

Once we understand the motivations, we need to know the objectives or the goals of parallel database processing. These are explained in Section 1.3. The objectives will become the main aim of any parallel algorithms in parallel database systems, and this will answer the question of *what* it is that parallelism aims to achieve in parallel database processing.

Once we understand the objectives, we also need to know the various kinds of parallelism forms that are available for parallel database processing. These are described in Section 1.4. The forms of parallelism are the techniques used to achieve the objectives described in the previous section. Therefore, this section answers the questions of *how* parallelism can be performed in parallel database processing.

High-Performance Parallel Database Processing and Grid Databases,
by David Taniar, Clement Leung, Wenny Rahayu, and Sushant Goel
Copyright © 2008 John Wiley & Sons, Inc.

Without an understanding of the kinds of parallel technology and parallel machines that are available for parallel database processing, our introductory discussion on parallel databases will not be complete. Therefore, in Section 1.5, we introduce various parallel architectures available for database processing.

Section 1.6 introduces Grid databases. This includes the basic Grid architecture for data-intensive applications, and its current technological status is also outlined.

Section 1.7 outlines the components of this book, including parallel query processing, and Grid transaction management.

1.1 A BRIEF OVERVIEW: PARALLEL DATABASES AND GRID DATABASES

In 1965, Intel cofounder Gordon Moore predicted that the number of transistors on a chip would double every 24 months, a prediction that became known popularly as Moore's law. With further technological development, some researchers claimed the number would double every 18 months instead of 24 months. Thus it is expected that the CPU's performance would increase roughly by 50–60% per year. On the other hand, mechanical delays restrict the advancement of disk access time or disk throughput, which reaches only 8–10%. There has been some debate regarding the accuracy of these figures. Disk capacity is also increasing at a much higher rate than that of disk throughput. Although researchers do not agree completely with these values, they show the difference in the rate of advancement of each of these two areas.

In the above scenario, it becomes increasingly difficult to use the available disk capacity effectively. Disk input/output (I/O) becomes the bottleneck as a result of such skewed processing speed and disk throughput. This inevitable I/O bottleneck was one of the major forces that motivated parallel database research. The necessity of storing high volumes of data, producing faster response times, scalability, reliability, load balancing, and data availability were among the factors that led to the development of parallel database systems research. Nowadays, most commercial database management systems (DBMS) vendors include some parallel processing capabilities in their products.

Typically, a parallel database system assumes only a single administrative domain, a homogeneous working environment, and close proximity of data storage (i.e., data is stored in different machines in the same room or building). Below in this chapter, we will discuss various forms of parallelism, motivations, and architectures.

With the increasing diversity of scientific disciplines, the amount of data collected is increasing. In domains as diverse as global climate change, high-energy physics, and computational genomics, the volume of data being measured and stored is already scaling terabytes and will soon increase to petabytes. Data can be best collected locally for certain applications like earth observation and astronomy experiments. But the experimental analysis must be able to access the large volume of distributed data seamlessly. The above requirement emphasizes the need for Grid-enabled data sources. It should be easy and possible to quickly and automatically install, configure, and disassemble the data sources along with the need for data movement and replication.

The Grid is a heterogeneous collaboration of resources and thus will contain a diverse range of data resources. Heterogeneity in a data Grid can be due to the data model, the transaction model, storage systems, or data types. Data Grids provide seamless access to geographically distributed data sources storing terabytes to petabytes of data with proper authentication and security services.

The development of a Grid infrastructure was necessary for large-scale computing and data-intensive scientific applications. A Grid enables the sharing, selection, and aggregation of a wide variety of geographically distributed resources including supercomputers, storage systems, data sources, and specialized devices owned by different organizations for solving large-scale resource-intensive problems in science, engineering, and commerce. One important aspect is that the resources—computing and data—are owned by different organizations. Thus the design and evolution of individual resources are autonomous and independent of each other and are mostly heterogeneous.

Based on the above discussions, this book covers two main elements, namely, parallel query processing and Grid databases. The former aims at high performance of query processing, which is mainly read-only queries, whereas the latter concentrates on Grid transaction management, focusing on read as well as write operations.

1.2   PARALLEL QUERY PROCESSING: MOTIVATIONS

It is common these days for databases to grow to enormous sizes and be accessed by a large number of users. This growth strains the ability of single-processor systems to handle the load. When we consider a database of 10 terabyte in size, simple processing using a single processor with the capability of processing with a speed of 1 megabyte/second would take 120 days and nights of processing time. If this processing time needs to be reduced to several days or even several hours, parallel processing is an alternative answer.

$$10 \text{ TB} = 10 \times 1024 \times 1024 \text{ MB} = 1,048,576 \text{ MB}$$
$$10,048,576 \text{ MB}/1 \text{ MB/sec} \approx 10,048,576 \text{ seconds}$$
$$\approx 174,760 \text{ minutes}$$
$$\approx 2910 \text{ hours}$$
$$\approx 120 \text{ days and nights}$$

Because of the performance benefits, and also in order to maintain higher throughput, more and more organizations turn to parallel processing. Parallel machines are becoming readily available, and most RDBMS now offer parallelism features in their products.

But what is parallel processing, and why not just use a faster computer to speed up processing?

Computers were intended to solve problems faster than a human being could—this is the reason for their being invented. People continue to want computers to do more and more and to do it faster. The design of computers has now become more complex than ever before, and with the improved circuitry design, improved instruction sets, and improved algorithms to meet the demand for faster response times, this has been made possible by the advances in engineering. However, even with the advances in engineering that produce these complex, fast computers, there are speed limitations. The processing speed of processors depends on the transmission speed of information between the electronic components within the processor, and this speed is actually limited by the speed of light. Because of the advances in technology, particularly fiber optics, the speed at which the information travels is reaching the speed of light, but it cannot exceed this because of the limitations of the medium. Another factor is that, because of the density of transistors within a processor; it can be pushed only to a certain limit.

These limitations have resulted in the hardware designers looking for another alternative to increase performance. Parallelism is the result of these efforts. Parallel processing is the process of taking a large task and, instead of feeding the computer this large task that may take a long time to complete, the task is divided into smaller subtasks that are then worked on simultaneously. Ultimately, this divide-and-conquer approach aims to complete a large task in less time than it would take if it were processed as one large task as a whole. Parallel systems improve processing and I/O speeds by using multiple processors and disks in parallel. This enables multiple processors to work simultaneously on several parts of a task in order to complete it faster than could be done otherwise.

Additionally, database processing works well with parallelism. Database processing is basically an operation on a database. When the same operation can be performed on different fragments of the database, this creates parallelism; this in turn creates the notion of *parallel database processing*.

The driving force behind parallel database processing includes:

- Querying large databases (of the order of terabytes) and
- Processing an extremely large number of transactions per second (of the order of thousands of transactions per second).

Since parallel database processing works at the query or transaction level, this approach views the degree of parallelism as coarse-grained. Coarse-grained parallelism is well suited to database processing because of the lesser complexity of its operations but needs to work with a large volume of data.

1.3 PARALLEL QUERY PROCESSING: OBJECTIVES

The primary objective of parallel database processing is to gain performance improvement. There are two main measures of performance improvement. The first is *throughput*—the number of tasks that can be completed within a given time interval. The second is *response time*—the amount of time it takes to complete a single task from the time it is submitted. A system that processes a large number of small transactions can improve throughput by processing many transactions in parallel. A system that processes large transactions can improve response time as well as throughput by performing subtasks of each transaction in parallel.

These two measures are normally quantified by the following metrics: (*i*) speed up and (*ii*) scale up.

1.3.1 Speed Up

Speed up refers to performance improvement gained because of extra processing elements added. In other words, it refers to running a given task in less time by increasing the degree of parallelism. Speed up is a typical metric used to measure performance of read-only queries (data retrieval). Speed up can be measured by:

$$\text{Speed up} = \frac{\text{elapsed time on uniprocessor}}{\text{elapsed time on multiprocessors}}$$

A *linear speed up* refers to performance improvement growing linearly with additional resources—that is, a speed up of N when the large system has N times the resources of the smaller system. A less desirable *sublinear speed up* is when the speed up is less than N. *Superlinear speed up* (i.e., speed up greater than N) is very rare. It occasionally may be seen, but usually this is due to the use of a suboptimal sequential algorithm or some unique feature of the architecture that favors the parallel formation, such as extra memory in the multiprocessor system.

Figure 1.1 is a graph showing linear speed up in comparison with sublinear speed up and superlinear speed up. The resources in the x-axis are normally measured in terms of the number of processors used, whereas the speed up in the y-axis is calculated with the above equation.

Since superlinear speed up rarely happens, and is questioned even by experts in parallel processing, the ultimate goal of parallel processing, including parallel database processing, is to achieve linear speed up. Linear speed up is then used as an indicator to show the efficiency of data processing on multiprocessors.

To illustrate a speed up calculation, we give the following example: Suppose a database operation processed on a single processor takes 100 minutes to complete. If 5 processors are used and the completion time is reduced to 20 minutes, the speed up is equal to 5. Since the number of processors (5 processors) yields the same speed up (speed up = 5), a linear speed up is achieved.

If the elapsed time of the job with 5 processors takes longer, say around 33 minutes, the speed up becomes approximately 3. Since the speed up value is less than the number of processors used, a sublinear speed up is obtained.

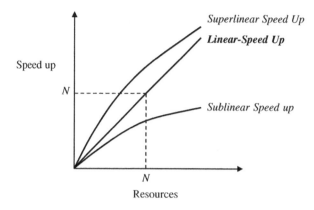

Figure 1.1 Speed up

In an extremely rare case, the elapsed time of the job with 5 processors may be less than 20 minutes—say, for example, 16.5 minutes; then the speed up becomes 6. This is a superlinear speed up, since the speed up (speed up = 6) is greater than the number of processors (processors = 5).

1.3.2 Scale Up

Scale up refers to the handling of larger tasks by increasing the degree of parallelism. Scale up relates to the ability to process larger tasks in the same amount of time by providing more resources (or by increasing the degree of parallelism). For a given application, we would like to examine whether it is viable to add more resources when the workload is increased in order to maintain its performance. This metric is typically used in transaction processing systems (data manipulation). Scale up is calculated as follows.

$$\text{Scale up} = \frac{\text{uniprocessor elapsed time on small system}}{\text{multiprocessor elapsed time on larger system}}$$

Linear scale up refers to the ability to maintain the same level of performance when both the workload and the resources are proportionally added. Using the above scale up formula, scale up equal to 1 is said to be linear scale up. A sublinear scale up is where the scale up is less than 1. A superlinear scale up is rare, and we eliminate this from further discussions. Hence, linear scale up is the ultimate goal of parallel database processing. Figure 1.2 shows a graph demonstrating linear/sublinear scale up.

There are two kinds of scale up that are relevant to parallel databases, depending on how the size of the task is measured, namely: (*i*) transaction scale up, and (*ii*) data scale up.

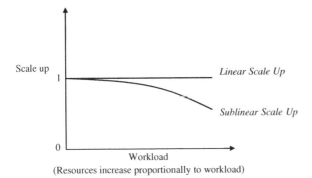

Figure 1.2   Scale up

Transaction Scale Up

Transaction scale up refers to the increase in the rate at which the transactions are processed. The size of the database may also increase proportionally to the transactions' arrival rate.

In transaction scale up, N-times as many users are submitting N-times as many requests or transactions against an N-times larger database. This kind of scale up is relevant in *transaction processing systems* where the transactions are small updates.

To illustrate transaction scale up, consider the following example: Assume it takes 10 minutes to complete 100 transactions on a single processor. If the number of transactions to be processed is increased to 300 transactions, and the number of processors used is also increased to 3 processors, the elapsed time remains the same; if it is 10 minutes, then a linear scale up has been achieved (scale up $= 1$).

If, for some reason, even though the number of processors is already increased to 3 it takes longer than 10 minutes, say 15 minutes, to process the 300 transactions, then the scale up becomes 0.67, which is less than 1, and hence a sublinear scale up is obtained.

Transaction processing is especially well adapted for parallel processing, since different transactions can run concurrently and independently on separate processors, and each transaction takes a small amount of time, even if the database grows.

Data Scale Up

Data scale up refers to the increase in size of the database, and the task is a large job whose runtime depends on the size of the database. For example, when sorting a table whose size is proportional to the size of the database, the size of the database is the measure of the size of the problem. This is typically found in *online analytical processing* (OLAP) in *data warehousing*, where the fact table is normally very large compared with all the dimension tables combined.

To illustrate data scale up, we use the following example: Suppose the fact table of a data warehouse occupies around 90% of the space in the database. Assume the job is to produce a report that groups data in the fact table according to some criteria specified by its dimensions.

For example, the processing of this operation on a single processor takes one hour. If the size of the fact table is then doubled up, it is sensible to double up the number of processors. If the same process now takes one hour, a linear scale up has been achieved.

If the process now takes longer than one hour, say for example 75 minutes, then the scale up is equal to 0.8, which is less than 1. Therefore, a sublinear scale up is obtained.

1.3.3   Parallel Obstacles

A number of factors work against efficient parallel operation and can diminish both speed up and scale up, particularly: (*i*) start up and consolidation costs, (*ii*) interference and communication, and (*iii*) skew.

Start Up and Consolidation Costs

Start up cost is associated with initiating multiple processes. In a parallel operation consisting of multiple processes, the start up time may overshadow the actual processing time, adversely affecting speed up, especially if thousands of processes must be started. Even when there is a small number of parallel processes to be started, if the actual processing time is very short, the start up cost may dominate the overall processing time.

Consolidation cost refers to the cost associated with collecting results obtained from each processor by a host processor. This cost can also be a factor that prevents linear speed up.

Parallel processing normally starts with breaking up the main task into multiple subtasks in which each subtask is carried out by a different processing element. After these subtasks have been completed, it is necessary to consolidate the results produced by each subtask to be presented to the user. Since the consolidation process is usually carried out by a single processing element, normally by the host processor, no parallelism is applied, and consequently this affects the speed up of the overall process.

Both start up and consolidation refer to sequential parts of the process and cannot be parallelized. This is a manifestation of the *Amdahl law*, which states that the compute time can be divided into the parallel part and the serial part, and no matter how high the degree of parallelism in the former, the speed up will be asymptotically limited by the latter, which must be performed on a single processing element.

For example, a database operation consists of a sequence of 10 steps, 8 of which can be done in parallel, but 2 of which must be done in sequence (such as start up and consolidation operations). Compared with a single processing element, an 8-processing element machine would attain a speed up of not 8 but somewhere around 3, even though the processing element cost is 8 times higher.

To understand this example, we need to use some sample figures. Assume that 1 step takes 1 minute to complete. Using a single processor, it will take 10 minutes, as there are 10 steps in the operation. Using an 8-processor machine, assume each step is allocated into a separate processor and it takes only 1 minute to complete the parallel part. However, the two sequential steps need to be processed by a single processor, and it takes 2 minutes. In total, it takes 3 minutes to finish the whole job using an 8-processor machine. Therefore, the speed up is 3.33, which is far below the linear speed up (speed up = 8). This example illustrates how the sequential part of the operations can jeopardize the performance benefit offered by parallelism.

To make matters worse, suppose there are 100 steps in the operation, 20 of which are sequential parts. Using an 80-processor machine, the speed up is somewhat under 5, far below the linear speed up of 80. This can be proven in a similar manner.

Using a single-processor machine, the 100-step job is completed in 100 minutes. Using an 80-processor machine, the elapsed time is 21 minutes (20 minutes for the sequential part and 1 minute for the parallel part). As a result, the speed up is equal to 4.8 (speed up = 100/21 = 4.76). Figure 1.3 illustrates serial and parallel parts in a processing system.

Interference and Communication

Since processes executing in a parallel system often access shared resources, a slowdown may result from the *interference* of each new process as it competes with existing processes for commonly held resources. Both speed up and scale up are affected by this phenomenon.

Very often, one process may have to communicate with other processes. In a synchronized environment, the process wanting to *communicate* with others may be forced to wait for other processes to be ready for communication. This waiting time may affect the whole process, as some tasks are idle waiting for other tasks.

Figure 1.4 gives a graphical illustration of the waiting period incurred during the communication and interference among parallel processes. This illustration uses the example in Figure 1.3. Assume there are four parallel processes. In Figure 1.4, all parallel processes start at the same time after the first serial part has been

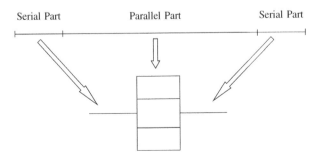

Serial Part   Parallel Part   Serial Part

Figure 1.3 Serial part vs. parallel part

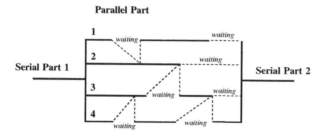

Figure 1.4   Waiting period

completed. After parallel part 1 has been going for a while, it needs to wait until parallel part 2 reaches a certain point in the future, after which parallel process 1 can continue. The same thing happens to parallel part 4, which has to wait for parallel part 3 to reach a certain point. The latter part of parallel part 4 also has to wait for parallel part 3 to completely finish. This also happens to parallel part 3, which has to wait for parallel part 2 to be completed. Since parallel part 4 finishes last, all other parallel parts have to wait until the final serial part finishes off the whole operation. All the waiting periods and their parallel part dependencies are shown in Figure 1.4 by dashed lines.

Skew

Skew in parallel database processing refers to the unevenness of workload partitioning. In parallel systems, equal workload (load balance) among all processing elements is one of the critical factors to achieve linear speed up. When the load of one processing element is heavier than that of others, the total elapsed time for a particular task will be determined by this processing element, and those finishing early would have to wait. This situation is certainly undesirable.

Skew in parallel database processing is normally caused by uneven data distribution. This is sometimes unavoidable because of the nature of data that is not uniformly distributed. To illustrate a skew problem, consider the example in Figure 1.5. Suppose there are four processing elements. In a uniformly distributed workload (Fig. 1.5(a)), each processing element will have the same elapsed time, which also becomes the elapsed time of the overall process. In this case, the elapsed time is t_1. In a skewed workload distribution (Fig. 1.5(b)), one or more processes finish later than the others, and hence, the elapsed time of the overall process is determined by the one that finishes last. In this illustration, processor 2 finishes at t_2, where $t_2 > t_1$, and hence the overall process time is t_2.

1.4   FORMS OF PARALLELISM

There are many different forms of parallelism for database processing, including (*i*) interquery parallelism, (*ii*) intraquery parallelism, (*iii*) interoperation parallelism, and (*iv*) intraoperation parallelism.

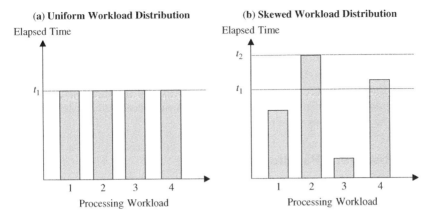

Figure 1.5 Balanced workload vs. unbalanced workload (skewed)

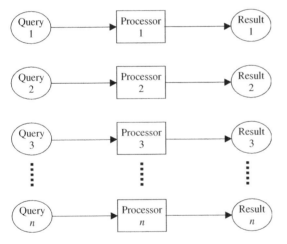

Figure 1.6 Interquery parallelism

1.4.1 Interquery Parallelism

Interquery parallelism is "parallelism among queries"—that is, different queries or transactions are executed in parallel with one another. The primary use of interquery parallelism is to scale up transaction processing systems (i.e., transaction scale up) in supporting a large number of transactions per second.

Figure 1.6 gives a graphical illustration of interquery parallelism. Each processor processes a query/transaction independently of other processors. The data that each query/transaction uses may be from the same database or from different databases.

In comparison with single-processor database systems, these queries/transactions will form a queue, since only one query/transaction can be processed at any given time, resulting in longer completion time of each query/transaction, even though the actual processing time might be very short. With interquery parallelism, the waiting time of each query/transaction in the queue is reduced, and subsequently the overall completion time is improved.

It is clear that transaction throughput can be increased by this form of parallelism, by employing a high degree of parallelism through additional processing elements, so that more queries/transactions can be processed simultaneously. However, the response time of individual transactions is not necessarily faster than it would be if the transactions were run in isolation.

1.4.2 Intraquery Parallelism

A query to a database, such as sort, select, project, join, etc, is normally divided into multiple operations. *Intraquery parallelism* is an execution of a single query in parallel on multiple processors and disks. In this case, the multiple operations within a query are executed in parallel. Therefore, intraquery parallelism is "parallelism within a query."

Use of intraquery parallelism is important for speeding up long-running queries. Interquery parallelism does not help in this task, since each query is run sequentially.

Figure 1.7 gives an illustration of an intraquery parallelism. A user invokes a query, and in processing this, the query is divided into n subqueries. Each subquery is processed on a different processor and produces subquery results. The results obtained with each processor need to be consolidated in order to generate final query results to be presented to the user. In other words, the final query results are the amalgamation of all subquery results.

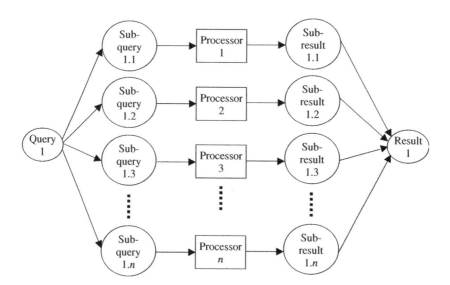

Figure 1.7 Intraquery parallelism

Execution of a single query can be parallelized in two ways:

- *Intraoperation parallelism.* We can speed up the processing of a query by parallelizing the execution of each individual operation, such as parallel sort, parallel search, etc.
- *Interoperation parallelism.* We can speed up the processing of a query by executing in parallel the different operations in a query expression, such as simultaneously sorting and searching.

1.4.3 Intraoperation Parallelism

Since database operations work on tables containing large data sets of records, we can parallelize the operations by executing them in parallel on different subsets of the table. Hence, intra-operation parallelism is often called *partitioned parallelism*—that is, parallelism due to the data being partitioned.

Since the number of records in a table can be large, the degree of parallelism is potentially enormous. Consequently, intra-operation parallelism is natural in database systems.

Figure 1.8 gives an illustration of intraoperation parallelism. This is a continuation of the previous illustration of intraquery parallelism. In intraoperation parallelism, an operation, which is a subset of a subquery, works on different data fragments to create parallelism. This kind of parallelism is also known as "Single Instruction Multiple Data" (SIMD), where the same instruction operation works on different parts of the data.

The main issues of intraoperation parallelism are (*i*) how the operation can be arranged so that it can perform on different data sets, and (*ii*) how the data is partitioned in order for an operation to work on it. Therefore, in database processing, intraoperation parallelism raises the need for formulating parallel versions of basic sequential database operations, including: (*i*) parallel search, (*ii*) parallel sort, (*iii*) parallel group-by/aggregate, and (*iv*) parallel join. Each of these parallel algorithms will be discussed in the next few chapters.

1.4.4 Interoperation Parallelism

Interoperation parallelism is where parallelism is created by concurrently executing different operations within the same query/transaction. There are two forms of interoperation parallelism: (*i*) *pipelined parallelism* and (*ii*) *independent parallelism.*

Pipeline Parallelism

In pipelining, the output records of one operation *A* are consumed by a second operation *B*, even before the first operation has produced the entire set of records

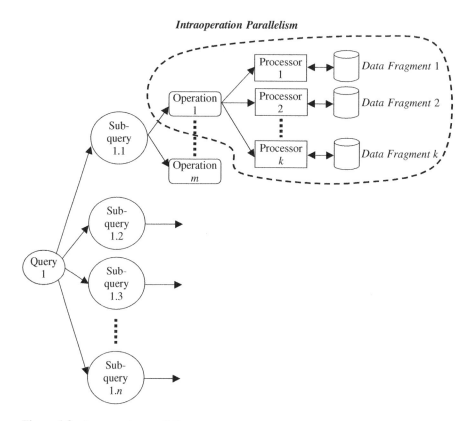

Figure 1.8   Intraoperation parallelism

in its output. It is possible to run *A* and *B* simultaneously on different processors, such that *B* consumes records in parallel with *A* producing them.

Pipeline parallelism is influenced by the practice of using an assembly line in the manufacturing process. In parallel database processing, multiple operations form some sort of assembly line to manufacture the query results.

The major advantage of pipelined execution is that we can carry out a sequence of such operations without writing any of the intermediate results to disk.

Figure 1.9 illustrates pipeline parallelism, where a subquery involving *k* operations forms in a pipe. The results from each operation are passed through the next operation, and the final operation will produce the final query results.

Bear in mind that pipeline parallelism is not sequential processing, even though the diagram seems to suggest this. Each operation works with a volume of data. The operation takes one piece of data at a time, processes it, and passes it to the next operation. Each operation does not have to wait to finish processing all data allocated to it before passing them to the next operation. The latter is actually a sequential processing. To emphasize the difference between sequential and

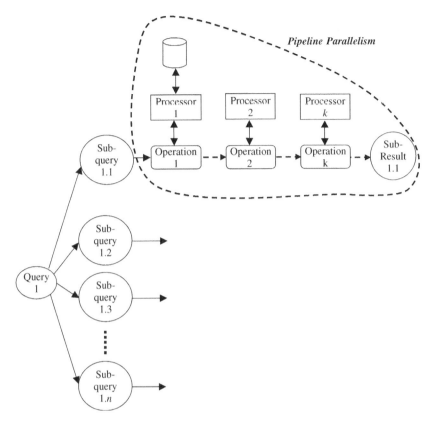

Figure 1.9   Pipeline parallelism

pipeline parallelism, we use a dotted arrow to illustrate pipeline parallelism, showing that each piece of data is passed through the pipe as soon as it has been processed.

Pipelined parallelism is useful with a small number of processors but does not scale up well for various reasons:

- Pipeline chains generally do not attain sufficient length to provide a high degree of parallelism. The degree of parallelism in pipeline parallelism depends on the number of operations in the pipeline chain. For example, a subquery with 8 operations forms an assembly line with 8 operators, and the maximum degree of parallelism is therefore equal to 8. The degree of parallelism is then severely limited by the number of operations involved.

- It is not possible to pipeline those operators that do not produce output until all inputs have been accessed, such as the set-difference operation. Some operations simply cannot pass temporary results to the next operation without having fully completed the operation. In short, not all operations are suitable for pipeline parallelism.

- Only marginal speed up is obtained for the frequent cases in which one operator's execution cost is much higher than that of the others. This is particularly true when the speed of each operation is not uniform. One operation that takes longer than the next operation will regularly require the subsequent operation to wait, resulting in a lower speed up. In short, pipeline parallelism is suitable only if all operations have uniform data unit processing time.

Because the above limitations, when the degree of parallelism is high, the importance of pipelining as a source of parallelism is secondary to that of partitioned parallelism.

Independent Parallelism

Independent parallelism is where operations in a query that do not depend on one another can be executed in parallel, for example, Table 1 *join* Table 2 *join* Table 3 *join* Table 4. In this case, we can process Table 1 *join* Table 2 in parallel with Table 3 *join* Table 4.

Figure 1.10 illustrates independent parallelism. Multiple operations are independently processed in different processors accessing different data fragments.

Like pipelined parallelism, independent parallelism does not provide a high degree of parallelism, because of the possibility of a limited number of independent operations within a query, and is less useful in a highly parallel system, although it is useful with a lower degree of parallelism.

1.4.5 Mixed Parallelism — A More Practical Solution

In practice, a mixture of all available parallelism forms is used. For example, a query joins 4 tables, namely, Table 1, Table 2, Table 3, and Table 4. Assume that the order of the join is Table 1 joins with Table 2 and joins with Table 3 and finally joins with Table 4. For simplicity, we also assume that the join attribute exists in the two consecutive tables. For example, the first join attribute exists in Table 1 and Table 2, and the second join attribute exists in Table 2 and Table 3, and the last join attribute exists in Table 3 and Table 4. Therefore, these join operations may form a bushy tree, as well as a left-deep or a right-deep tree.

A possible scenario for parallel processing of such a query is as follows.

- *Independent parallelism:*
  The first join operation between Table 1 and Table 2 is carried out in parallel with the second join operation between Table 3 and Table 4.
  Result1 = Table 1 join Table 2, in parallel with
  Result2 = Table 3 join Table 4.

- *Pipelined parallelism:*
  Pipeline Result1 and Result2 into the computation of the third join. This means that as soon as a record is formed by the first two join operations (e.g., Result1 and Result2), it is passed to the third join, and the third join can start

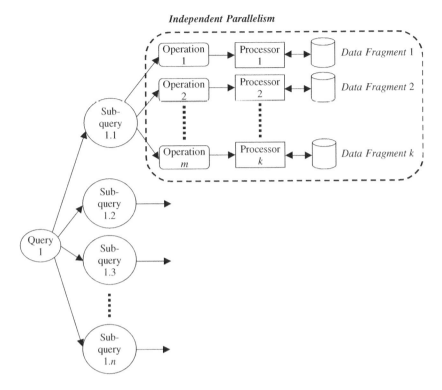

Figure 1.10 Independent parallelism

the operation. In other words, the third join operation does not wait until the first two joins produce their results.

- *Intraoperation parallelism:*
  Each of the three join operations above is executed with a partitioned parallelism (i.e., parallel join). This means that each of the join operations is by itself performed in parallel with multiple processors.

Figure 1.11 gives a graphical illustration of a mixed parallelism of the above example.

1.5 PARALLEL DATABASE ARCHITECTURES

The motivation for the use of parallel technology in database processing is influenced not only by the need for performance improvement, but also by the fact that parallel computers are no longer a monopoly of supercomputers but are now in fact available in many forms, such as systems consisting of a small number but powerful processors (e.g., SMP machines), clusters of workstations (e.g., loosely

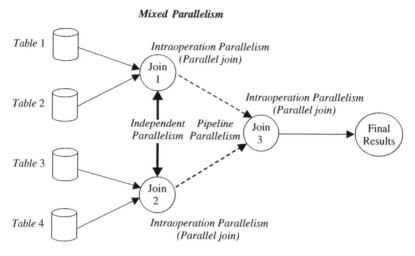

Figure 1.11   Mixed parallelism

coupled shared-nothing architectures), massively parallel processors (MPP), and clusters of SMP machines (i.e., hybrid architectures).

It is common for parallel architectures especially used for data-intensive applications to be classified according to several categories: (*i*) *shared-memory*, (*ii*) *shared-disk*, (*iii*) *shared-nothing*, and (*iv*) *shared-something*.

1.5.1   Shared-Memory and Shared-Disk Architectures

Shared-memory architecture is an architecture in which all processors share a common main memory and secondary memory. When a job (e.g., query/transaction) comes in, the job is divided into multiple slave processes. The number of slave processes does not have to be the same as the number of processors available in the system. However, normally there is a correlation between the maximum number of slave processes and the number of processors. For example, in Oracle 8 parallel query execution, the maximum number of slave processes is $10\times$ number of CPUs.

Since the memory is shared by all processors, processor load balancing is relatively easy to achieve, because data is located in one place. Once slave processes have been created, each of them can then request the data it needs from the central main memory. The drawback of this architecture is that it suffers from memory and bus contention, since many processors may compete for access to the shared data. Shared-memory architectures normally use a bus interconnection network. Since there is a limit to the capacity that a bus connection can handle, data/message transfer along the bus can be limited, and consequently it can serve only a limited number of processors in the system. Therefore, it is quite common for a shared-memory machine to be equipped with no more than 64 processors in a computer system box.

In *shared-disk* architecture, all processors, each of which has its own local main memory, share the disks. Shared-disk architecture is very similar to shared-memory architecture in the sense that the secondary memory is shared, not the main memory.

Because of the local main memory in each processor that keeps active data, data sharing problems can be minimized and load balancing can largely be maintained. On the other hand, this architecture suffers from congestion in the interconnection network when many processors are trying to access the disks at the same time.

The way a job is processed is also very similar. Once slave processes have been created, each process requests the data to be loaded from the shared disk. Once the data is loaded, it is kept in its processor's main memory. Therefore, the main difference between shared-disk and shared-memory architecture is the memory hierarchy that is being shared. From a memory hierarchy point of view, shared-memory and shared-disk architecture share the same principle. In shared-memory architecture, although "everything" (e.g., main memory and secondary memory) seems to be shared, each processor may have its own cache, which nowadays can be quite large (e.g., up to 4 megabytes). If we then assume that this cache acts similarly to main memory in a shared-disk architecture, then the difference between these two architectures is narrowed.

In the context of the computing platform, *shared-memory* and *shared-disk* architectures are normally found in *Symmetric Multi Processor* (*SMP*) machines. A typical SMP machine consists of several CPUs, ranging from 2 to 16 CPUs. A larger number of CPUs is not too common because of the scaling up limitation. Each CPU maintains its own cache, and the main-memory is shared among all the CPUs. The sizes of main-memory and caches may vary from machine to machine. Multiple disks may be attached to an SMP machine, and all CPUs have the same access to them. The operating system normally allocates tasks according to the schedule. Once a processor is idle, a task in the queue will be immediately allocated to it. In this way, balancing is relatively easy to achieve. Figure 1.12 gives an illustration of an SMP architecture.

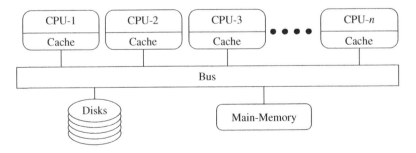

Figure 1.12 An SMP architecture

1.5.2   Shared-Nothing Architecture

A *shared-nothing* architecture provides each processor with a local main memory and disks. The problem of competing for access to the shared data will not occur in this system, but load balancing is difficult to achieve even for simple queries, since data is placed locally in each processor and each processor may have an unequal load. Because each processor is independent of others, it is often claimed that scaling up the number of processors without adversely affecting performance is achievable.

The way a shared-nothing architecture is used in parallel database processing is that when a job comes in, it comes into a processor in the system. Depending on the type of machine, this processor might be a host processor. In other cases, there is the notion of a host processor, meaning that any processor can receive a job. The processor that receives the job then splits the job into multiple processes to be allocated to each processor. Once each processor has its share of a piece of the job, it loads the data from its own local disk and starts (e.g., computation or data distribution when required) processing it.

The load imbalance problem is not only due to the size of local data in each processor that might be different from that of other processors, but also due to the need for data redistribution during processing of the job. Data redistribution is normally based on some distribution function, which is influenced by the value of the data, and this may further create workload imbalance. The skewness problem has been a major challenge in database processing using a shared-nothing architecture.

Shared-nothing architecture ranges from the workstation farm to *Massively Parallel Processing (MPP)* machines. The range is basically divided by the speed of the network, which connects the processing units (i.e., CPUs containing primary and secondary memory). For a workstation farm, the network is a slower Ethernet; whereas for MPP, the interconnection is done via a fast network or system bus. Whether it be a slow or fast network, the processing units communicate among each other via the network, as they do not share common data storage (i.e., main memory or secondary memory). Because the data storage is not shared but localized, shared-nothing architecture is often called *distributed-memory* architecture. Figure 1.13 shows a typical shared-nothing architecture.

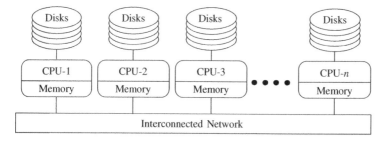

Figure 1.13   A shared-nothing architecture

1.5.3 Shared-Something Architecture

A *shared-something* architecture compromises the extensibility limitation of shared-memory architecture and the load balancing problem of shared-nothing architecture. This architecture is a mixture of shared-memory and shared-nothing architectures. There are a number of variations to this architecture, but basically each *node* is shared-memory architecture connected to an interconnection network a la shared-nothing architecture. As each shared-memory (i.e., SMP machine) maintains a group of processing elements, a collection of these groups is often called a "*cluster*," which in this case means *clusters of SMP* architecture. Figure 1.14 shows the architecture of clusters of SMP.

Obvious features of a shared-something architecture include flexibility in the configuration (i.e., number of nodes, size of nodes) and lower network communication traffic as the number of nodes is reduced. Intraquery parallelization can be isolated to a single multiprocessor shared-memory node, as it is far easier to parallelize a query in a shared-memory than in a distributed system and moreover, the degree of parallelism on a single shared-memory node may be sufficient for most applications. On the other hand, interquery parallelization is consequently achieved through parallel execution among nodes.

The popularity of cluster architectures is also influenced by the fact that processor technology is moving rapidly. This also means that a powerful computer today will be out of date within a few years. Consequently, computer prices are falling not only because of competitiveness but also because of the above facts. Therefore, it becomes sensible to be able to plug in new processing elements to the current system and to take out the old ones. To some degree, this can be done to an SMP machine, considering its scaling limitations and that only identical processors can be added into it. With MPP machines, although theoretically not imposing scaling limitations, their configurations are difficult to alter, and hence they cannot keep up with up-to-date technology, despite the high price of MPP machines. On the other hand, SMP machines are becoming popular because of

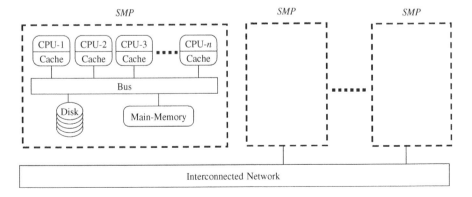

Figure 1.14 Cluster of SMP architectures

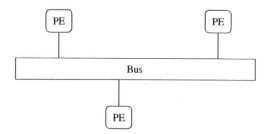

Figure 1.15 Bus interconnection network

their competitiveness in relative pricing and power, so it becomes easier and more feasible to add SMP machines to an interconnection network. Therefore, the cluster of SMP becomes demanding.

1.5.4 Interconnection Networks

Regardless of the kind of architectures, when several processors are connected, they are connected in an interconnection network. There are several types of interconnection networks for parallel computing systems. In this section, we cover the three most popular interconnection networks, namely, (*i*) bus, (*ii*) mesh, and (*iii*) hypercube.

Bus

A bus can be illustrated as a single communication line, which connects a number of processing elements (*PEs*). We use the notion of processing element here, as it can be a single processor or a processor with its own local memory. Figure 1.15 gives an illustration of a bus interconnection network.

With a bus interconnection network, all the system components can send data on and receive data from a single communication bus. Bus architectures work well for small numbers of processors. However, they do not scale well with increasing parallelism since the bus can handle communication from only one component at a time. A bus interconnection network is normally used in the SMP architectures.

Mesh

The processing elements are arranged as nodes in a Grid, and each processing element is connected to all its adjacent components in the Grid. Figure 1.16 gives an illustration of a mesh structure. In this example, the mesh is a 3 × 4 structure.

Processing elements that are not directly connected can communicate with one another by routing messages via a sequence of intermediate nodes that are directly connected to one another. For example, the processing element at the top left-hand corner wanting to send a message to the processing element at the bottom right hand corner in Figure 1.16 must pass through several intermediate processing elements.

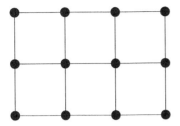

Figure 1.16   Mesh interconnection network

The number of communication links grows as the number of components grows, and the communication capacity of a mesh therefore scales better with increasing parallelism.

Hypercube

The processing elements are numbered in binary, and a processing element is connected to another if the binary representations of their numbers differ in exactly one. Thus each of the n components is connected to $\log(n)$ other components.

Figure 1.17 gives two examples of a hypercube interconnection network. In a 2-dimensional hypercube, it is exactly the same as a 2×2 mesh structure. In a 3-dimensional hypercube, the processing elements are connected as in a cube. Theoretically, the degree of dimension in a hypercube can be arbitrary. To visualize a higher degree of dimension, a 4-dimensional hypercube, it looks like a cube inside a bigger cube (possibly like a room), in which the corner of the inner cube is connected with the corner of the outer cube. In a 5-dimensional hypercube, the 4-dimensional hypercube is inside another bigger cube, and so on.

In a hypercube connection, a message from a processing element can reach any other processing element by going via at most $\log(n)$ links, where n is the number of processing elements connected in a hypercube interconnection network. For example, in a 2-dimensional hypercube, there are 4 processing elements, and

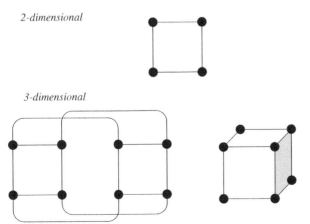

Figure 1.17   Hypercube interconnection network

therefore the longest route from one processing element to another is equal to $log(4) = 2$. In a 3-dimensional hypercube connecting 8 processing elements, the longest route takes only 3 links. It can be concluded that the degree of the dimension also determines the longest route from one processing element to the other.

1.6 GRID DATABASE ARCHITECTURE

Although the Grid technology has attracted much research attention during the last decade, it is only recently that data management in Grids including data Grid and Grid databases have attracted research attention. This was because the underlying middleware architecture, such as Globus, Legion, etc., had not been established.

Figure 1.18 shows the general architecture of databases working in a Grid environment. The Grid database architecture typically works in a wide area, spanning multiple institutions, and has autonomous and heterogeneous environment. Global data-intensive collaborative applications such as earth observation and simulation, weather forecasting, functional genomics, etc. will need to access geographically distributed data without being aware of the exact location of interesting data.

Various Grid services, for example, metadata repository services, lookup services, replica management services, etc., shown in Figure 1.18 will help to provide seamless access to data. Accounting services will be helpful in calculating the cost of using the resources held by other organizations. Authorization and security services will set the level of authorization and security required to access other organizations' resources. This depends on the extent to which the organizations are trusted. Various trust models have been developed for accessing resources. Apart from basic services, other application-specific services can be developed and plugged into the middleware. All these services together constitute the Grid middleware.

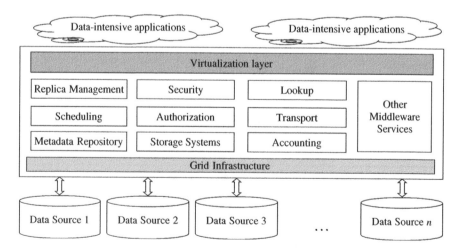

Figure 1.18 Data-intensive applications working in Grid database architecture

Grid middleware provides a complete suite of software for delivering various services, such as resource discovery, metadata management, job and queue management, security, encryption, authentication, file transfer, remote process management, storage access, Quality of Service, replica and coherency control, etc. Middleware toolkits are being developed to provide high-level services. The Globus toolkit is the most accepted Grid middleware, and is still evolving rapidly.

The middleware infrastructure is still evolving, but there is an understanding of the basic functionalities of existing middleware in the form of Globus, Condor, Legion, etc. Recent progress in data management in Grids is evident from the efforts of the Data Access and Integration Working-Group (DAIS-WG) and the Transaction Management Research-Group (TM-RG) of the GGF, a standardization body for Grids.

Apart from core Grid services mentioned above, user-level Grid middleware consists of programming tools and application development environment for managing global resources with the help of resource brokers. The transaction management protocols are lower-level correctness protocols, and they use some of the higher-level services from the middleware.

Most of the efforts in data management in Grid architecture have been focused on providing high-level services for locating the data, efficient access methods, transporting the data, making the replication decision, data caching, etc. This book introduces lower-level traditional transactional requirements and demonstrates how the Grid infrastructure affects the working of individual sites. It focuses on maintaining data consistency at individual data sites when these sites join the Grid infrastructure to make resources available to a wide and collaborative environment, while maintaining autonomy. It explores the lower-level transactional requirements of Grid databases rather than providing a higher-level service to the user.

All resources, for example, computational resources, storage resources, network, programs, etc., are represented as service in Open Grid Service Architecture (OGSA). A service-oriented approach is also used for the abstraction of underlying data stored in different types of data resources. *Data virtualization* is used to denote such abstraction of data resources. The Grid Data Distribution (GDD) model supports dynamic and efficient data distribution for providing data services. Figure 1.19 shows the data virtualization approach. The interfaces shown are OGSA's data service interface.

Data virtualization will help in accessing data stored on different physical media, maintained in different syntaxes, managed by different software systems, and made available by different protocols. Attempts to standardize the virtualization approach are being made by various Research- and Working-Groups of the GGF.

Referring to Figure 1.19, from the data management perspective, an important point is that Grids do not have Direct Attached Storage (DAS). Earlier computing infrastructures, such as monolithic, open, and distributed, all have DAS. A research survey carried out on storage systems shows that about 53% of businesses use DAS as their storage medium; 58% of organizations consider interoperability to be a

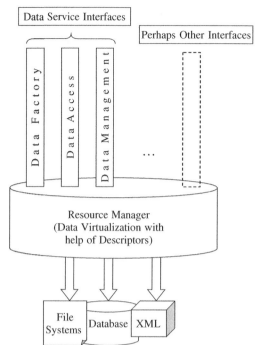

Figure 1.19 Data virtualization approach in Grid environment

critical issue. While interoperability and DAS have contradictory requirements, the good news is that more than 60% of organizations are considering moving toward network-based storage systems. This will make the integration of data sources convenient with the Grid.

Most of the work done in Data Grid infrastructure assumes the existence of file systems like Network File System (NFS) for data storage. Considering the global vision of Grids, it is believed that Grids must also integrate database systems into the infrastructure to support a wide range of applications. Hence, databases offer a much richer set of operations such as queries and transactions.

Oracle has launched its Grid-enabled database systems, denoted with a suffix *g* in its versions. Oracle's Real Application Cluster (RAC) can run the application workload on a cluster of servers. Two main distinct features are (*i*) integrated clusterware and (*ii*) automatic workload management. Integrated clusterware provides cluster connectivity, messaging and locking, recovery, etc. Automatic workload management provides the dynamic allocation of workloads to the servers. Allocation rules can be dynamically and automatically defined to allocate processing resources. Thus the main focus is on providing dynamic load balancing and allocation of workloads. It is greatly different from the autonomous, heterogeneous, and cross-institution working environment, or DAIS-WG or TM-RG. The earlier versions were not designed for heterogeneous and global Grids, but for intra-institutional dynamic workload management.

1.7 STRUCTURE OF THIS BOOK

This book covers two main elements, namely:

1. *Parallel Query Processing* and
2. *Grid Transaction Management*

The first element on parallel query processing mainly deals with real-only queries, whereas the second element on Grid databases deals with read as well as write transactions.

The book is structured in four parts: **Part I** gives an introduction to the topic, including this chapter. Since an analytical model is an important part of performance evaluation of any system, an introduction of analytical models will also be included in this part.

Part II and **Part III** concentrate on *Parallel Query Processing*. These parts feature parallel algorithms and approaches for all important database processing operations. This ranges from the very basic database operations, such as data searching and sorting, to the most complex database operations involving complex database computation, like universal quantifier, complex join, etc. Understanding these algorithms is critical in order to fully comprehend how parallel database processing works and enhances the performance of modern database applications. Basically, Part II describes the basic of query parallelism including parallel search, parallel sort, and parallel join, whereas Part III focuses on more complex query parallelism, such as groupby-join, indexing, universal quantification, and scheduling.

An understanding of the pseudocode of parallel algorithms is not enough to fully comprehend the behavior of each parallel algorithm and its contribution to performance improvement. We need to be able to describe their cost models. Analytical models for each parallel algorithm can be used to understand the internal components of each algorithm, to predict the performance of each algorithm, and to compare with other algorithms. Extensive cost models are also included in each chapter to describe the behavior of each parallel query processing method.

Part IV focuses on the second element of this book, namely, *Grid Transaction Management*. This covers the ACID properties of transactions as well as replication in a Grid environment. Transaction issues such as consistency, atomicity and recovery, which are more relevant in a database environment, are brought into focus. Data consistency issues are addressed in the presence of write transactions.

The final part, **Part V**, presents other data intensive applications in which parallelism might be applied in order to achieve high performance. These include parallel Online Analytical Processing (parallel OLAP) and parallel data mining techniques. The use of parallelism in these data-intensive applications is unavoidable because of the large volume of data to be processed.

1.8 SUMMARY

This chapter focuses on three fundamental questions in parallel query processing, namely, *why*, *what*, and *how*, plus one additional question based on the technological support. The more complete questions and their answers are summarized as follows.

- *Why is parallelism necessary in database processing?*
  Because there is a large volume of data to be processed and reasonable (improved) elapsed time for processing this data is required.

- *What can be achieved by parallelism in database processing?*
  The objectives of parallel database processing are (*i*) linear speed up and (*ii*) linear scale up. Superlinear speed up and superlinear scale up may happen occasionally, but they are more of a side effect, rather than the main target.

- *How is parallelism performed in database processing?*
  There are four different forms of parallelism available for database processing: (*i*) interquery parallelism, (*ii*) intraquery parallelism, (*iii*) intraoperation parallelism, and (*iv*) interoperation parallelism. These may be combined in parallel processing of a database job in order to achieve a better performance result.

- *What facilities of parallel computing can be used?*
  There are four different parallel database architectures: (*i*) shared-memory, (*ii*) shared-disk, (*iii*) shared-nothing, and (*iv*) shared-something architectures.

Distributed computing infrastructure is fast evolving. The architecture was monolithic in 1970s, and since then, during the last three decades, developments have been exponential. The architecture has evolved from monolithic, to open, to distributed, and lately virtualization techniques are being investigated in the form of Grid computing. The idea of Grid computing is to make computing a commodity. Computer users should be able to access the resources situated around the globe without knowing the location of the resource. And a pay-as-you-go strategy can be applied in computing, similar to the state-of-the-art gas and electricity distribution strategies. Data storages have reached petabyte size because of the increase in collaborative computing and the amount of data being gathered by advanced applications. The working environment of collaborative computing is hence heterogeneous and autonomous.

1.9 BIBLIOGRAPHICAL NOTES

The work in parallel databases began in around the late 1970s and the early 1980s. The term "Database Machine" was used, which focused on building special parallel machines for high-performance database processing. Two of the first papers in database machines were written by Su (*SIGMOD* 1978), entitled "Database Machines," and by Hsiao (*IEEE Computer* 1979), entitled "Database Machines are

Coming, Database Machine are Coming." A similar introduction was also given by Langdon (*IEEE TC* 1979) and by Hawthorn (*VLDB* 1980). A more complete survey on database machine was given by Song (*IEEE Database Engineering Bulletin* 1981). The work on the database machine was compiled and published as a book by Ozkarahan (1986). Although the rise of database machines was welcomed by many researchers, a critique was presented by Boral and DeWitt (1983). A few database machines were produced in the early 1980s. The two notable database machines were Gamma, led by DeWitt et al. (*VLDB* 1986 and *IEEE TKDE* 1990), and Bubba (Haran et al., *IEEE TKDE* 1990).

In the 1990s, the work on database machines was then translated into "Parallel Databases". One of the most prominent papers was written by DeWitt and Gray (*CACM* 1992). This was followed by a number of important papers in parallel databases, including Hawthorn (*PDIS* 1993) and Hameurlain and Morvan (*DEXA* 1996). A good overview on research problems and issues was given by Valduriez (*DAPD* 1993), and a tutorial on parallel databases was given by Weikum (*ICDT* 1995).

Ongoing work on parallel databases is supported by the availability of parallel machines and architectures. An excellent overview on parallel database architecture was given by Bergsten, Couprie, and Valduriez (*The Computer Journal* 1993). A thorough discussion on the shared-everything and shared-something architectures was presented by Hua and Lee (*PDIS* 1991) and Valduriez (*ICDE* 1993). More general parallel computing architectures, including SIMD and MIMD architectures, can be found in widely known books by Almasi and Gottlieb (1994) and by Patterson and Hennessy (1994).

A new wave of *Grid databases* started in the early 2000s. A direction on this area is given by Atkinson (*BNCOD* 2003), Jeffery (*EDBT* 2004), Liu et al. (*SIGMOD* 2003), and Malaika et al. (*SIGMOD* 2003). One of the most prominent works in Grid databases is the DartGrid project by Chen, Wu et al., who have reported their project in *Concurrency and Computation* (2006), at the *GCC* conference (2004), at the Computational Sciences conference (2004), and at the *APWeb* conference (2005).

Realizing the importance of parallelism in database processing, many commercial DBMS vendors have included some parallel processing capabilities in their products, including Oracle (Cruanes et al. *SIGMOD* 2004) and Informix (Weininger *SIGMOD* 2000). Oracle has also implemented some grid facilities (Poess and Othayoth *VLDB* 2005). The work on parallel databases continues with recent work on shared cache (Chandrasekaran and Bamford *ICDE* 2003).

1.10 EXERCISES

1.1. Assume that a query is decomposed into a serial part and a parallel part. The serial part occupies 20% of the entire elapsed time, whereas the rest can be done in parallel. Given that the one-processor elapsed time is 1 hour, what is the *speed up* if 10 processors are used? (For simplicity, you may assume that during the parallel processing of the parallel part the task is equally divided among all participating processors).

1.2. Under what conditions may *superlinear speed up* be attained?

1.3. Highlight the differences between *speed up* and *scale up*.

1.4. Outline the main differences between *transaction scale up* and *data scale up*.

1.5. Describe the relationship between the following:

- Interquery parallelism
- Intraquery parallelism

1.6. Describe the relationship between the following:

- Scale up
- Speed up

1.7. *Skewed workload distribution* is generally undesirable. Under what conditions that parallelism (i.e. the workload is divided among all processors) is not desirable.

1.8. Discuss the strengths and weaknesses of the following parallel database architectures:

- Shared-everything
- Shared-nothing
- Shared-something

1.9. Describe the relationship between parallel databases and Grid databases.

1.10. Investigate your favourite Database Management Systems (DBMS) and outline what kind of *parallelism* features have been included in their query processing.

1.11. For the database in the previous exercise, investigate whether the DBMS supports the *Grid* features.

Chapter 2

Analytical Models

Analytical models are cost equations/formulas that are used to calculate the elapsed time of a query using a particular parallel algorithm for processing. A cost equation is composed of variables, which are substituted with specific values at runtime of the query. These variables denote the cost components of the parallel query processing.

In this chapter, we briefly introduce basic cost components and how these are used in cost equations. In Section 2.1, an introduction to cost models including their processing paradigm is given. In Section 2.2, basic cost components and cost notations are explained. These are basically the variables used in the cost equations. In Section 2.3, cost models for skew are explained. Skew is an important factor in parallel database query processing. Therefore, understanding skew modeling is a critical part of understanding parallel database query processing. In Section 2.4, basic cost calculation for general parallel database processing is explained.

2.1 COST MODELS

To measure the effectiveness of parallelism of database query processing, it is necessary to provide cost models that can describe the behavior of each parallel query algorithm. Although the cost models may be used to estimate the performance of a query, it is the primary intention to use them to describe the process involved and for comparison purposes. The cost models also serve as tools to examine every cost factor in more detail, so that correct decisions can be made when adjusting the entire cost components to increase overall performance. The cost is primarily expressed in terms of the elapsed time taken to answer a query.

The processing paradigm is processor farming, consisting of a master processor and multiple slave processors. Using this paradigm, the master distributes the work to the slaves. The aim is to make all slaves busy at any given time, that is, the

High-Performance Parallel Database Processing and Grid Databases,
by David Taniar, Clement Leung, Wenny Rahayu, and Sushant Goel
Copyright © 2008 John Wiley & Sons, Inc.

workload has been divided equally among all slaves. In the context of parallel query processing, the user initiates the process by invoking a query through the master. To answer the query, the master processor distributes the process to the slave processors. Subsequently, each slave loads its local data and often needs to perform local data manipulation. Some data may need to be distributed to other slaves. Upon the completion of the process, the query results obtained from each slave are presented to the user as the answer to the query.

2.2 COST NOTATIONS

Cost equations consist of a number of components, in particular:

- Data parameters
- Systems parameters
- Query parameters
- Time unit costs
- Communication costs

Each of these components is represented by a variable, to which a value is assigned at runtime. The notations used are shown in Table 2.1.

Each cost component is described and explained in more detail in the following sections.

2.2.1 Data Parameters

There are two important data parameters:

- Number of records in a table ($|R|$) and
- Actual size (in bytes) of the table (R)

Data processing in each processor is based on the number of records. For example, the evaluation of an attribute is performed at a *record level*. On the other hand, systems processing, such as I/O (read/write data from/to disk) and data distribution in an interconnected network, is done at a *page level*, where a page normally consists of multiple records.

In terms of their notations, for the actual size of a table, a capital letter, such as R, is used. If two tables are involved in a query, then the letters R and S are used to indicate tables 1 and 2, respectively. Table size is measured in bytes. Therefore, if the size of table R is 4 gigabytes, when calculating a cost equation variable R will be substituted by $4 \times 1024 \times 1024 \times 1024$.

For the number of records, the absolute value notation is used. For example, the number of records of table R is indicated by $|R|$. Again, if table S is used in the query, $|S|$ denotes number of records of this table. In calculating the cost of an equation, if there are 1 million records in table R, variable $|R|$ will have a value of 1,000,000.

Table 2.1   Cost notations

Symbol	Description
Data parameters	
R	Size of table in bytes
R_i	Size of table fragment in bytes on processor i
$|R|$	Number of records in table R
$|R_i|$	Number of records in table R on processor i
Systems parameters	
N	Number of processors
P	Page size
H	Hash table size
Query parameters	
π	Projectivity ratio
σ	Selectivity ratio
Time unit cost	
IO	Effective time to read a page from disk
t_r	Time to read a record in the main memory
t_w	Time to write a record to the main memory
t_d	Time to compute destination
Communication cost	
m_p	Message protocol cost per page
m_l	Message latency for one page

In a multiprocessor environment, the table is fragmented into multiple processors. Therefore, the number of records and actual table size for each table are divided (evenly or skewed) among as many processors as there are in the system. To indicate fragment table size in a particular processor, a subscript is used. For example, R_i indicates the size of the table fragment on processor i. Subsequently, the number of records in table R on processor i is indicated by $|R_i|$. The same notation is applied to table S whenever it is used in a query.

As the subscript i indicates the processor number, R_1 and $|R_1|$ are fragment table size and number of records of table R in processor 1, respectively. The values of R_1 and $|R_1|$ may be different from (or the same as), say for example, R_2 and $|R_2|$. However, in parallel database query processing, the elapsed time of a query processing is determined by the longest time spent in a processor. In calculating the elapsed time, we are concerned only with the processors having the largest number of records to process. Therefore, for $i = 1 \ldots n$, we choose the largest R_i and $|R_i|$ to represent the longest elapsed time of the heaviest load processor. If table R is already divided evenly to all processors, then calculating R_i and $|R_i|$ is easy, that is, divide R and $|R|$ by number of processors, respectively. However, when the table is not evenly distributed (skewed), we need to determine the largest fragment of R to be used in R_i and $|R_i|$. Skew modeling is explained later in this chapter.

2.2.2 Systems Parameters

In parallel environments, one of the most important systems parameters is the number of processors. In the cost equation, the number of processors is symbolized by N. For example, $N = 16$ indicates that there are 16 processors to be used to process a query.

To calculate R_i and $|R_i|$, assuming the data is uniformly distributed, both R and $|R|$ are divided by N to get R_i and $|R_i|$. For example, there are 1 million records ($|R| = 1,000,000$) using 10 processors ($N = 10$). The number of records in any processors is $|R_i| = |R|/N$ ($|R_i| = 1,000,000/10 = 100,000$ records).

If the data is not uniformly distributed, $|R_i|$ denotes the largest number of records in a processor. Realistically, $|R_i|$ must be larger than $|R|/N$, or in other words, the divisor must be smaller than N. Using the same example as above, $|R_i|$ must be larger than 100,000 records (say for example 200,000 records). This shows that the processor having the largest record population is the one with 200,000 records. If this is the case, $|R_i| = 200,000$ records is obtained by dividing $|R| = 1,000,000$ by 5. The actual number of the divisor must be modeled correctly to imitate the real situation.

There are two other important systems parameters, namely:

- Page size (P) and
- Hash table size (H)

Page size, indicated by P, is the size of one data page in bytes, which contains a batch of records. When records are loaded from disk to main memory, it is not loaded record by record, but page by page.

To calculate the number of pages of a given table, divide the table size by the page size. For examples, $R = 4$ gigabytes ($= 4 \times 1024^3$ bytes) and $P = 4$ kilobytes ($= 4 \times 1024$ bytes), $R/P = 1024^2$ number of pages. Since the last page may not be a full page, the division result must normally be rounded up.

Hash table size, indicated by H, is the maximum size of the hash table that can fit into the main memory. This is normally measured by the maximum number of records. For example, $H = 10,000$ records.

Hash table size is an important parameter in parallel query processing of large databases. As mentioned at the beginning of this book, parallelism is critical for processing large databases. Since the database is large, it is likely that the data cannot fit into the main memory all at once, because normally the size of the main memory is much smaller than the size of a database. Therefore, in the cost model it is important to know the maximum capacity of the main memory, so that it can be precisely calculated how many times a batch of records needs to be swapped in and out from the main memory to disk. The larger the hash table, the less likely that record swapping will be needed, thereby improving overall performance.

2.2.3 Query Parameters

There are two important query parameters, namely:

- Projectivity ratio (π) and
- Selectivity ratio (σ)

Projectivity ratio π is the ratio between the projected attribute size and the original record length. The value of π ranges from 0 to 1. For example, assume that the record size of table R is 100 bytes and the output record size is 45 bytes. In this case, the projectivity ratio π is 0.45.

Selectivity ratio σ is a ratio between the total output records, which is determined by the number of records in the query result, and the original total number of records. Like π, selectivity ratio σ also ranges from 0 to 1. For example, suppose initially there are 1000 records ($|R_i| = 1000$ records), and the query produces 4 records. The selectivity ratio σ is then $4/1000 = 1/250 = 0.004$.

Selectivity ratio σ is used in many different query operations. To distinguish one selectivity ratio from the others, a subscript can be used. For example, σ_p in a parallel group-by query processing indicates the number of groups produced in each processor. Using the above example, the selectivity ratio σ of $1/250$ ($\sigma = 0.004$) means that each group in that particular processor gathers an average of 250 original records from the local processor.

If the query operation involves two tables (like in a join operation), a selectivity ratio can be written as σ_j, for example. The value of σ_j indicates the ratio between the number of records produced by a join operation and the number of records of the Cartesian product of the two tables to be joined. For example, $|R_i| = 1000$ records and $|S_i| = 500$ records; if the join produces 5 records only, then the join selectivity ratio σ_j is $5/(1,000 \times 500) = 0.00001$.

Projectivity and selectivity ratios are important parameters in query processing, as they are associated with the number of records before and after processing; additionally, the number of records is an important cost parameter, which determines the processing time in the main memory.

2.2.4 Time Unit Costs

Time unit costs are the time taken to process one unit of data. They are:

- Time to read from or write to a page on disk (IO),
- Time to read a record from main memory (t_r),
- Time to write a record to main memory (t_w),
- Time to perform a computation in the main memory, and
- Time to find out the destination of a record (t_d).

Time to read/write a page from/to disk is basically the time associated with an input/output process. The variable used in the cost equation is denoted by IO. Note that IO works at the page level. For example, to read a whole table from disk to main memory, divide table size and page size, and then multiply by the IO unit cost ($R/P \times IO$). In a multiprocessor environment, this becomes $R_i/P \times IO$.

The time to write the query results into a disk is very much reduced as only a small subset of R_i is selected. Therefore, in the cost equation, in order to reduce the number of records as indicated by the query results, R_i is normally multiplied by other query parameters, such as π and σ.

Times to read/write a record in/to main memory are indicated by t_r and t_w, respectively. These two unit costs are associated with reading records, which are already in the main memory. These two unit costs are also used when obtaining records from the data page. Note now that these two unit costs work at a record level, not at a page level.

The time taken to perform a computation in the main memory varies from one computation type to another, but basically, the notation is t followed by a subscript that denotes the type of computation. Computation time in this case is the time taken to compute a single process in the CPU. For example, the time taken to hash a record to a hash table is shown as t_h, and the time taken to add a record to current aggregate value in a group by operation is denoted as t_a.

Finally, the time taken to compute the destination of a record is denoted by t_d. This unit cost is used when a record needs to be distributed or transferred from one processor to another. Record distribution/transfer is normally dictated by a hash or a range function, depending on which data distribution method is being used. Therefore, in order for each record to be transferred, it needs to determine where this record should go, and t_d is used for this purpose.

2.2.5 Communication Costs

Communication costs can generally be categorized into the following elements:

- Message protocol cost per page (m_p) and
- Message latency for one page (m_l)

Both elements work at a page level, as with the disk. Message protocol cost is the cost associated with the initiation for a message transfer, whereas message latency is associated with the actual message transfer time.

Communication costs are divided into two major components, one for the sender and the other for the receiver. The sender cost is the total cost for sending records in pages, which is calculated by multiplying the number of pages to be sent and both communication unit costs mentioned above. For example, to send the whole table R, the cost would be $R/P \times (m_p + m_l)$. Note that the size of the table must be divided by the page size in order to calculate the number of pages being sent. The unit cost for the sending is the sum of the two communication cost components.

At the receiver end, the receiver cost is the total cost of receiving records in pages, which is calculated by multiplying number of pages received and the message protocol cost per page only. Note that in the receiver cost, the message latency is not included. Therefore, continuing the above example, the receiving cost would be $R/P \times m_p$.

In a multiprocessor environment, the sending cost is the cost of sending data from one processor to another. The sending cost will come from the heaviest loaded processor, which sends the largest volume of data. Assume the number of pages to be sent by the heaviest loaded processor is p_1; the sending cost is $p_1 \times (m_p + m_l)$. However, the receiving cost is not just simply $p_1 \times (m_p)$, since the maximum page size sent by the heaviest loaded processor may likely be different from the maximum page size received by the heaviest loaded processor. As a matter of fact, the heaviest loaded sending processor may also be different from the heaviest loaded receiving processor. Therefore, the receiving cost equation may look like $p_2 \times (m_p)$, where $p_1 \neq p_2$. This might be the case especially if $p_1 = |R|/N/P$ and p_2 involves skew and therefore will not equally be divided. However, when both p_1 and p_2 are heavily skewed, the values of p_1 and p_2 may be modeled as equal, even though the processor holding p_1 is different from that of p_2. But from the perspective of parallel query processing, it does not matter whether or not the processor is the same.

As has been shown above, the most important cost component is in fact p_1 and p_2, and these must be accurately modeled to reflect the accuracy of the communication costs involved in a parallel query processing.

2.3 SKEW MODEL

Skew has been one of the major problems in parallel processing. Skew is defined as the nonuniformity of workload distribution among processing elements. In parallel external sorting, there are two different kinds of skew, namely:

- Data skew and
- Processing skew

Data skew is caused by the unevenness of data placement in a disk in each local processor, or by the previous operator. Unevenness of data placement is caused by the fact that data value distribution, which is used in the data partitioning function, may well be nonuniform because of the nature of data value distribution. If initial data placement is based on a round-robin data partitioning function, data skew will not occur. However, it is common for database processing not to involve a single operation only. It sometimes involves many operations, such as selection first, projection second, join third, and sort last. In this case, although initial data placement is even, other operators may have rearranged the data—some data are eliminated, or joined, and consequently, data skew may occur when the sorting is about to start.

Processing skew is caused by the processing itself, and may be propagated by the data skew initially. For example, a parallel external sorting processing consists of several stages. Somewhere along the process, the workload of each processing element may not be balanced, and this is called processing skew. Note that even when data skew may not exist at the start of the processing, skew may exist at a later stage of processing. If data skew exists in the first place, it is very likely that processing skew will also occur.

Modeling skew is known to be a difficult task, and often a simplified assumption is used. A number of attempts to model skewness in parallel databases have been reported. Most of them use the *Zipf* distribution model.

Skew is measured in terms of different sizes of fragments that are allocated to the processors for the parallel processing of the operation. Given the total number of records $|R|$, the number of processors N, and a skew factor θ; the size of the ith fragment $|R_i|$ can be represented by:

$$|R_i| = \frac{|R|}{i^\theta \times \sum_{j=1}^{N} \frac{1}{j^\theta}} \qquad \text{where } 0 \leq \theta \leq 1 \qquad (2.1)$$

The symbol θ denotes the degree of skewness, where $\theta = 0$ indicates no skew and $\theta = 1$ highly skewed. Clearly, when $\theta = 0$, the fragment sizes follow a discrete uniform distribution with $|R_i| = \frac{|R|}{N}$. This is an ideal distribution, as there is no skew. In contrast, when $\theta = 1$ indicating a high degree of skewness, the fragment sizes follow a pure *Zipf* distribution. Here, the above equation becomes:

$$|R_i| = \frac{|R|}{i \times \sum_{j=1}^{N} \frac{1}{j}} = \frac{|R|}{i \times H_N} \approx \frac{|R|}{i \times (\gamma + \ln N)} \qquad (2.2)$$

where $\gamma = 0.57721$ (*Euler's constant*) and H_N is the *harmonic* number, which may be approximated by $(\gamma + \ln N)$. In the case of $\theta > 0$, the first fragment $|R_1|$ is always the largest in size, whereas the last one $|R_N|$ is always the smallest. (Note that fragment i is not necessarily allocated at processor i.) Here, the load skew is given by:

$$|R_{\max}| = \frac{|R|}{\sum_{j=1}^{N} \frac{1}{j^\theta}} \qquad (2.3)$$

For simplicity and generality of notation, we use $|R_i|$ instead of $|R_{\max}|$. When there is no skew,

$$|R_i| = \frac{|R|}{N} \qquad (2.4)$$

and when it is highly skewed, $|R_i| = \frac{|R|}{\sum_{j=1}^{N} \frac{1}{j^\theta}}$. To illustrate the difference between these two equations, we use the example shown in Figures 2.1 and 2.2. In this

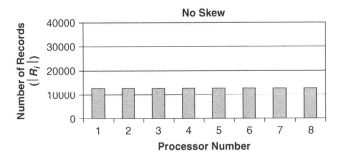

Figure 2.1   Uniform distribution (no skew)

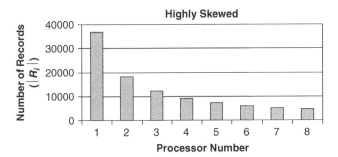

Figure 2.2   Highly skewed distribution

example, $|R| = 100,000$ records, and $N = 8$ processors. The x-axis indicates the load of each processor (processors are numbered consecutively), whereas the y-axis indicates the number of records ($|R_i|$) in each processor. In the no-skew graph (Fig. 2.1), θ is equal to zero, and as there is no skew the load of each processor is uniform as expected—that is, 12,500 records each.

In the highly skewed graph (Fig. 2.2), we use $0 - 1$ to model a high-skew distribution. The most heavily loaded processor holds more than 36,000 records, whereas the least loaded processor holds around 4500 records only. In the graph, the load decreases as the processor number increases. However, in real implementation, the heaviest load processor does not necessarily have to be the first processor, whereas the lightest load processor does not necessarily have to be the last processor. From a parallel query processing viewpoint, it does not matter which processor has the heaviest load. The important thing is that we can predict the heaviest load among all processors, as this will be used as the indicator for the processing time.

In extreme situations, the heaviest loaded processor can hold all the records (e.g., 100,000 records), whereas all other processors are empty. Although this is possible, in real implementation, it may rarely happen. And this is why a more

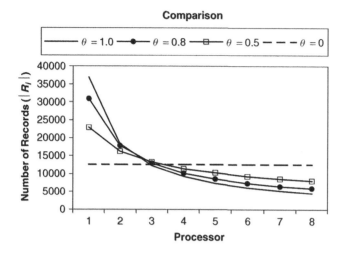

Figure 2.3   Comparison between highly skewed, less skewed, and no-skew distributions

realistic distribution model is used, such as the *Zipf* model, which has been well-regarded as being suitable for modeling data distribution in parallel database systems.

Figures 2.1 and 2.2 actually show the two extremes, namely highly skewed and no skew at all. In practice, the degree of skewness may vary between $\theta = 0$ and $\theta = 1$. Figure 2.3 shows a comparison of four distributions with skewness ratio of $\theta = 1.0$, 0.8, 0.5, and 0.0. From this graph, we note that the heaviest loaded processor holds from around 36,000 records to 12,500 records, depending on the skewness ratio. In modeling and analysis, however, it is normally assumed that when the distribution is skewed, it is highly skewed ($\theta = 1$), as we normally use the worst-case performance to compare with the no-skew case.

In the example above, as displayed in Figures 2.1–2.3, we use $N = 8$ processors. The heaviest load processor using a skew distribution is almost 3 times as much as that of the no-skew distribution. This difference will be widened as more processors are used. Figure 2.4 explains this phenomenon. In this graph, we show the load of the heaviest processor only. The x-axis indicates the total number of processors in the system, which varies from 4 to 256 processors (N), whereas the y-axis shows the number of records in the heaviest load processor ($|R_i|$). From this graph, it clearly shows that when there are 4 processors, the highly skewed load is almost double that of the no-skew load. With 32 processors, the difference is almost 8 times as much (the skewed load is 8 times as much as the no-skew load). This gap continues to grow—for example with 256 processors, the difference is more than 40 times.

In terms of their equations, the difference between the no-skew and highly skewed distributions lies in the divisor of the equation. Table 2.2 explains the divisor used in the two extreme cases. This table shows that in the no-skew distribution, $|R|$ is divided by N to get $|R_i|$. On the other hand, in a highly skewed

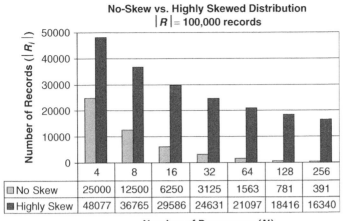

Figure 2.4   Comparison between the heaviest loaded processors using no-skew and highly skewed distributions

Table 2.2   Divisors (with vs. without skew)

N	4	8	16	32	64	128	256
Divisor without skew	4	8	16	32	64	128	256
Divisor with skew	2.08	2.72	3.38	4.06	4.74	5.43	6.12

distribution, $|R|$ is divided by a corresponding divisor shown in the last row in order to obtain $|R_i|$.

The divisor with the high skew remains quite steady compared with the one without skew. This indicates that skew can adversely affect the performance to a great extent. For example, the divisor without skew is 256 when the total number of processors is 256, whereas that with the high skew is only 6.12. Assuming that the total number of records is 100,000, the workload of each processor when the distribution is uniform (i.e., $\theta = 0$) is around 390 records. In contrast, the most overloaded processor in the case of highly skewed distribution (i.e., $\theta = 1$) holds more than 16,000 records. Our data skew and processing skew models adopt the above *Zipf* skew model.

2.4   BASIC OPERATIONS IN PARALLEL DATABASES

Operations in parallel database systems normally follow these steps:

- Data loading (scanning) from disk,
- Getting records from data page to main memory,

- Data computation and data distribution,
- Writing records (query results) from main memory to data page, and
- Data writing to disk

2.4.1 Disk Operations

The first step corresponds to the last step, where data is read from and written to the disk. As mentioned above in this chapter, disk reading and writing is based on page (i.e., I/O page). Several records on the same page are read/written as a whole.

The cost components for disk operations are the size of database fragment in the heaviest loaded processor (R_i or a reduced version of R_i), page size (P), and the I/O unit cost (IO). R_i and $|P|$ are needed to calculate the number of pages to be read/written, whereas IO is the actual unit cost.

If all records are being loaded from a disk, then we use R_i to indicate the size of the table read. If the records have been initially stored and distributed evenly to all disks, then we use a similar equation to Equation (2.4) to calculate R_i, where $R_i = R/N$.

However, if the initial records have not been stored evenly in all disks, then it is skewed, and a skew model must be used. As aforementioned, in performance modelling, when it is skewed, we normally assume it is highly skewed with $\theta = 1.0$. Therefore, we use an equation similar to Equation 2.3 to determine the value of R_i, which gives $R_i = R/(\gamma + \ln N)$.

Once the correct value of R_i has been determined, we can calculate the total cost of reading the data page from the disk as follows:

$$scanning\ cost = R_i/P \times IO \qquad (2.5)$$

The disk writing cost is similar. The main difference is that we need to determine the number of pages to be written, and this can be far less than R_i, as some or many data have been eliminated or summarized by the data computation process.

To adjust Equation (2.5) for the writing cost, we need to introduce cost variables that imitate the data computation process in order to determine the number of records in the query results. In this case, we normally use the selectivity ratio σ and the projectivity ratio π. The use of these parameters in the disk writing cost depends on the algorithms, but normally the writing cost is as follows:

$$writing\ cost = (data\ computation\ variables \times R_i)/P \times IO \qquad (2.6)$$

where the value of the data computation variables is between 0.0 and 1.0. The value of 0.0 indicates that no records exist in the query results, whereas 1.0 indicates that all records are written back.

Equations 2.5 and 2.6 are general and basic cost models for disk operations. The actual disk costs depend on each parallel query operation, and will be explained in due course in relevant chapters.

2.4.2 Main Memory Operations

Once the data has been loaded from the disk, the record has to be removed from the data page and placed in main memory (the cost associated with this activity is called *select cost*). This step also corresponds to the second last step—that is, before the data is written back to the disk, the data has to be transferred from main memory to the data page, so that it will be ready for writing to the disk (this is called *query results generation cost*).

Unlike disk operations, main memory operations are based on records, not on pages. In other words, $|R_i|$ is used instead of R_i.

The select cost is calculated as the number of records loaded from the disk times the reading and writing unit costs to the main memory (t_r and t_w). The reading unit cost is used to model the reading operation of records from the data page, whereas the writing unit cost is to actually write the record, which has been read from the data page, to main memory. Therefore, a select cost is calculated as follows:

$$select\ cost = |R_i| \times (t_r + t_w) \tag{2.7}$$

Equations 2.3 and 2.4 can be used to estimate $|R_i|$, in the case of skew and no-skew data distribution, respectively.

The query results generation cost is similar to the select cost, like the disk writing cost is to the disk reading cost. In the query results generation cost, there are two main important differences in particular. One is that the unit time cost is the writing cost (t_w) only, and no reading cost (t_r) is involved. The main reason is that the reading time for the record is already part of the computation, and only the writing to the data page is modeled. The other important element, which is the same as for the disk writing cost, is that the number of records in the query results must be modeled correctly, and additional variables must be included. A general query results generation cost is as follows:

$$query\ results\ generation\ cost = (data\ computation\ variables \times |R_i|) \times t_w \tag{2.8}$$

The query results generation operation may occur many times depending on the algorithm. The intermediate query results generation cost in this case is the cost associated with the temporary query results at the end of each step of data computation operations. The cost of generating the final query results is the cost associated with the final query results.

2.4.3 Data Computation and Data Distribution

The main process in any parallel database processing is the middle step, consisting of data computation and data distribution. What we mean by data computation is the performance of some basic database operations, such as searching, sorting, grouping, filtering of data. Here, the term computation is used in the context of database operation. Data distribution is simply record transmission from one processor to another.

There is no particular order for data computation and data distribution. It depends on the algorithms. Some algorithms do not perform any processing once the data has been loaded from its local disk and redistribute the data immediately to other processors depending on some distribution function. Some other algorithms perform initial data computation on the local data before distributing it to other processors for further data computation. Data computation and data distribution may be carried out in several steps, also depending on the algorithms.

Data Computation

As data computation works in main memory, the cost is based on the number of records involved in the computation and the unit computation time itself. Each data computation operation may involve several basic costs, such as unit costs for hashing, for adding the current record to the aggregate value, and so on. However, generally, the data computation cost is a product of the number of records involved in the computation ($|R_i|$) and the data computation unit costs (t_x, where x indicates the total costs for all operations involved). Hence, a general data computation cost takes the form:

$$data\ computation\ cost = |R_i| \times (t_x) \qquad (2.9)$$

Equation (2.9) assumes that the number of records involved in the data computation is $|R_i|$. If the number of records has been reduced because of previous data computation, then we must insert additional variables to reduce $|R_i|$. Also, the data computation unit cost t_x must be spelled out in the equation, which may be a sum of several unit costs. If skew or no skew is assumed, $|R_i|$ can be calculated by the previous Equations (2.3) and (2.4) as appropriate.

Data Distribution

Data distribution involves two costs: the cost associated with determining where each record goes and the actual data transmission itself. The former, as it works in main memory, is based on the number of records, whereas the latter is based on the number of pages.

The destination cost is calculated by the number of records to be transferred ($|R_i|$) and the unit cost for calculating the destination (t_d). The value of t_d depends on the complexity involved in calculating the destination, which is usually influenced by the complexity of the distribution function (e.g., hash function). A general cost equation for determining the destination is as follows:

$$determining\ the\ destination\ cost = |R_i| \times (t_d) \qquad (2.10)$$

Again, if $|R_i|$ has been reduced, additional cost variables must be included. Also, an appropriate assumption must be made whether $|R_i|$ involves skew or no skew.

The data transmission itself, which is explained above in Section 2.2.5, is divided into the sending cost and the receiving cost.

2.5 SUMMARY

This chapter is basically centered on the basic cost models to analytically model parallel query processing. The basic elements of cost models include:

- *Basic cost notations*, which includes several important parameters, such as data parameters, systems parameters, query parameters, time unit costs, and communication costs
- *Skew model*, using a *Zipf* distribution model
- *Basic parallel database processing costs*, including general steps of parallel database processing, such as disk costs, main memory costs, data computation costs, and data distribution costs

2.6 BIBLIOGRAPHICAL NOTES

Two excellent books on performance modeling are Leung (1988) and Jain (1991). Although the books are general computer systems performance modeling and analysis books, some aspects may be used in parallel database processing. A general book on computer architecture is Hennessy and Patterson (1990), where the details of a low-level architecture are discussed.

Specific cost models for parallel database processing can be found in Hameurlain and Morvan (*DEXA* 1995), Graefe and Cole (*ACM TODS* 1995), Shatdal and Naughton (*SIGMOD* 1995), and Ganguly, Goel, and Silberschatz (*PODS* 1996). Different authors use different cost models to model and analyze their algorithms. The analytical models covered in this book are based on those by Shatdal and Naughton (1995). In any database performance modeling, the use of certain distributions is inevitable. Most of the work in this area uses the Zipf distribution model. The original book was written by Zipf himself in 1949.

Performance modeling, analysis, and measurement are tightly related to benchmarking. There are a few benchmarking books, including Gray (1993) and O'Neil (1993). A more specific benchmarking for parallel databases is presented by Jelly et al. (*BNCOD* 1994).

2.7 EXERCISES

2.1. When are R and $|R|$ used?
Explain the difference between the two notations.

2.2. If the processing cost is dependent on the number of records, why is P used, instead of just using the number of records in the processing cost calculation?

2.3. When is H used in the processing cost calculation?

2.4. When calculating the communication costs, why is R used, instead of $|R|$?

2.5. If 150 records are retrieved from a table containing 50,000 records, what is the selectivity ratio?

2.6. If a query displays (projects) 4 attributes (e.g., employee ID, employee last name, employee first name, and employee DOB), what is the projectivity ratio of this query, assuming that the employee table has 20 attributes in total?

2.7. Explain what the *Zipf* model is, and why it can be used to model skew in parallel database processing.

2.8. If the number of processors is $N = 100$, using the *Zipf* model, what is the divisor when the skewness degree $\theta = 1$?

2.9. What is the *select cost*, and why is it needed?

2.10. Discuss why analytical models are useful to examine the query processing cost components. Investigate your favorite DBMS and find out what kind of tools are available to examine the query processing costs.

Part II

Basic Query Parallelism

Chapter 3

Parallel Search

Searching is a common task in our everyday lives and may involve activities such as searching for telephone numbers in a directory, locating words in a dictionary, checking our appointment diary for a given day/time, etc., etc. Searching is also a key activity in *database applications*. Searching is the task of locating a particular record within a collection of records. Searching is one of the most primitive, yet most of the time the most accessed, operations in database applications. In this chapter, we focus on search operations.

In Section 3.1, search queries are expressed in SQL. A search classification is also given based on the searching predicate in the SQL. As parallel search is very much determined by data partitioning, in Section 3.2 various data partitioning methods are discussed. These include single-attribute-based data partitioning methods, no-attribute-based data partitioning methods, and multiattribute-based partitioning methods. The first two are categorized as basic data partitioning, whereas the latter is called complex data partitioning.

Section 3.3 studies serial and parallel search algorithms. Serial search algorithms, together with data partitioning, form parallel search algorithms. Therefore, understanding these two key elements is an important aspect of gaining a comprehensive understanding of parallel search algorithms.

3.1 SEARCH QUERIES

The *search* operation in databases is represented by the *selection* operation. Selection is one of the most common *relational algebra* operations. It is a unary operation in which the operator takes one operand only—a table. Selection is an operation that selects specified records based on a given criteria. The result of the selection is a horizontal subset (records) of the operand. Figure 3.1 gives a

Input Table   Result Table

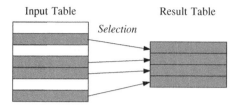

Figure 3.1 Selection operation

graphical illustration of a selection operation. The selected records are indicated with shading.

In SQL, a selection operation is implemented in a Where clause where the selection criteria (predicates) are specified. Queries having a selection operation alone are then called *"selection queries."* In other words, selection queries are nothing but search queries—queries that serve the purpose of searching records from single tables. In this book, we refer to selection queries as *"search queries."* Depending on the search predicates, we categorize search queries into (*i*) exact match search, (*ii*) range search, and (*iii*) multiattribute search.

3.1.1 Exact-Match Search

An *exact match Search query* is a query where the selection predicate on attribute *attr* is to check for an exact match between a search attribute *attr* and a given value. An example of an exact match query is "retrieve student details with student identification number 23." The input table in this case is table Student, and the selection predicate is Student ID Sid = 23. The query written in SQL for the above query is given as follows.

Query 3.1:
```
Select *
From STUDENT
Where Sid = 23;
```

The resulting table of an exact match query can contain more than one record, depending on whether there are duplicate values in the search attribute. In this case, since the search predicate is on the primary key, the resulting table contains one record only. However, if the search predicate is on a nonprimary key attribute in which duplicate values are allowed, it is likely that the resulting table will contain more than one record. For example, the query "retrieve student details with last name Robinson" may return multiple records. The SQL is expressed as follows:

Query 3.2:
```
Select *
From STUDENT
Where Slname = 'Robinson';
```

3.1.2 Range Search Query

A *range search query* is a query where the search attribute `attr` value in the query result may contain more than single unique values. Range queries fall into two categories:

- Continuous range search query and
- Discrete range search query

In the *continuous range search query*, the search predicates contain a continuous range check, normally with continuous range-checking operators, such as $<$, $\leq$, $>$, $\geq$, !=, Between, Not, and Like operators. On the other hand, the *discrete range search query* uses discrete range check operators, such as In and Or operators.

An example of a *continuous range search query* is "retrieve student details for students having GPA more than 3.50". The query in this case uses a $>$ operator to check the Sgpa. The SQL of this query is given below.

Query 3.3:
```
Select *
From STUDENT
Where Sgpa > 3.50;
```

An example of a *discrete range search query* is "retrieve student details of students doing Bachelor of Computer Science (BCS) or Bachelor of Information Systems (BInfSys)". The search operator used in this query is an In operator, which basically checks whether the degree is either BCS or BInfSys. The SQL is written as follows.

Query 3.4:
```
Select *
From STUDENT
Where Sdegree IN ('BCS', 'BInfSys');
```

Note the main difference between the two range queries—the continuous range search query checks for a particular range and the values within this range are continuous, whereas the discrete range search query checks for multiple discrete values that may or may not be within a particular range. Both these queries are called range queries simply because the search operation checks for multiple values, as opposed to a single value as in the exact match queries.

A general range search query may contain the property of both continuous and discrete range search queries; that is, the search predicates contain some discrete range search predicates, such as

Query 3.5:
```
Select *
From STUDENT
Where Sdegree IN ('BCS', 'BinfSys')
And Sgpa > 3.50;
```

In this case (Query 3.5), the first predicate is a discrete range predicate as in Query 3.4, whereas the second predicate is a continuous range predicate as in

Query 3.3. Therefore, the resulting table contains only those excellent BCS and BInfSys students (measured by greater than 3.50 in their GPAs).

3.1.3   Multiattribute Search Query

Both exact match and range search queries as given in Queries 3.1–3.4 involve single attributes in their search predicates. If multiple attributes are involved, we call this query a *multiattribute search query*. Each attribute in the predicate can be either an exact match predicate or a range predicate.

Multiattribute search query can be classified into two types, depending on whether AND or OR operators are used in linking each of the simple predicates. Complex predicates involving AND operators are called *conjunctive predicates*, whereas predicates involving OR operators are called *disjunctive predicates*. When AND and OR operators exist, it is common for the predicate to be normalized in order to form a *conjunctive prenex normal form (CPNF)*.

An example of a multiattribute search query is "retrieve student details with the surname 'Robinson' enrolled in either BCS or BInfSys". This query is similar to Query 3.2 above, with further filtering in which only BCS and BInfSys are selected. The first predicate is an exact match predicate on attribute Slname, whereas the second predicate is a discrete range predicate on attribute Sdegree. These simple predicates are combined in a form of CPNF. The SQL of the above query is as follows.

Query 3.6:
```
Select *
From STUDENT
Where Slname = 'Robinson'
And Sdegree IN ('BCS', 'BInfSys');
```

3.2   DATA PARTITIONING

Data partitioning is used to distribute data over a number of processing elements. Each processing element is then executed simultaneously with other processing elements, thereby creating parallelism. Data partitioning is the basic step of parallel query processing, and this is why, before we discuss in detail how parallel searching algorithms can be done, an understanding of data partitioning is critical.

Depending on the architecture, data partitioning can be done physically or logically. In a *shared-nothing architecture*, data is placed permanently over several disks, whereas in a *shared-everything* (i.e., shared-memory and shared-disk) *architecture*, data is assigned logically to each processor. Regardless of the adopted architecture, data partitioning plays an important role in parallel query processing since parallelism is achieved through data partitioning.

Basically, there are two data partitioning techniques: (*i*) basic data partitioning and (*ii*) complex data partitioning. Both of them will be discussed next.

3.2.1 Basic Data Partitioning

There are two basic types of data partitioning:

- *Vertical data partitioning* and
- *Horizontal data partitioning*

Figure 3.2 gives a graphical illustration of both of these.

Vertical partitioning partitions the data vertically across all processors. Each processor has a full number of records of a particular table, but with partial attributes. Because each processor has different fields/attributes, when searching a particular field/attribute value, only those processors that hold that field/attribute will participate in the searching process. Therefore, processors that do not hold that particular field/attribute become idle. This model is more common in *distributed database systems*, where the network/communication is slow, than in *parallel database systems*, where processing elements are more tightly coupled through a fast interconnection network. The rationale for using parallelism in database systems is to distribute the processing tasks among all processors, so that the query elapsed time is reduced to a minimum. Processor participation in the whole process is crucial. Even more important, the degree of participation must be as even as possible.

Horizontal partitioning is a model in which each processor holds a partial number of complete records of a particular table. A query that evaluates a particular attribute value will require all processors to participate. Hence, the degree of parallelism improves. This model is more common to parallel database systems, where communication is fast and processor participation in the whole process is often crucial to performance. The horizontal method has been used by most existing parallel relational database systems. There are a number of well-known horizontal partitioning strategies, namely:

- *Round-robin data partitioning,*
- *Hash data partitioning,*
- *Range data partitioning,* and
- *Random-unequal data partitioning*

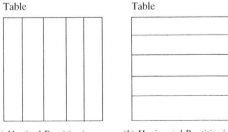

Table   Table

(a) Vertical Partitioning   *(b) Horizontal Partitioning*

Figure 3.2 Vertical and horizontal data partitioning

Round-Robin

Round-robin data partitioning is the simplest data partitioning method, whereby each record in turn is allocated to a processing element in a clockwise manner. This means that the first record of a table to be partitioned is distributed to the first processing element, the second record to the second processing element, and so on. Once the last processing element has obtained a record, the record distribution will start again in the first processing element. At the end of data distribution, each processing element will receive a roughly equal partition, except that the last round of record distribution might not reach the last processing element, if the total number of records is not divisible by the number of processing elements. Figure 3.3 gives an illustration of round-robin data partitioning.

Since round-robin data partitioning distributes the data evenly among all processing elements, it is also known as *"equal partitioning."* Round-robin is a special case of a more general *"random-equal partitioning,"* where each processor receives an equal share of the original table, regardless of the way the partitioning is actually done; for example, divide the table into equal subtables and then distribute each subtable to a separate processing element.

The main advantages of round-robin or random-equal partitioning are that the data is distributed evenly. Since the aim of parallel processing, especially parallel database processing, is to achieve load balance in order to reduce the elapsed time of a job, then this data partitioning supports that objective.

Although the division of the records is equal, records within one partition are not grouped semantically. The records are grouped simply to achieve equal partitions in each processor. This is the main drawback of round-robin. Say, for example, that we want to find records with a particular property such as students with the surname "Brown", then all processors must be activated, although probably only a few of the processing elements will produce the desired results. There is no way to tell in advance which processing elements hold these records. As start-up costs and processor involvement costs are expensive, especially if these processing elements at the end do not produce anything, these will incur unnecessary overheads. It would be convenient if only those processing elements that were likely to produce results were involved in the processing. However, this is certainly unachievable with round-robin as the data partitioning does not have any semantics.

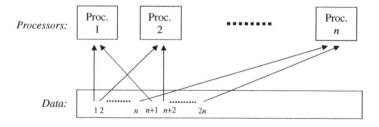

Figure 3.3   *Round-robin* data partitioning

Hash

In order to make a partition more meaningful (by grouping records having the same semantics or features), partitioning must be based on a particular attribute. One type of attribute-based partitioning is *hash partitioning*, where a hash function is applied. The result of this hash function determines the processor where the record will be placed. As a result, records within one partition have the same hash value. Figure 3.4 gives a graphical illustration of a hash data partitioning.

This arrangement is best for exact match retrieval based on the partitioning attribute, where the processor containing the desired records can be accessed directly, provided that the hash function is based on the attribute that is also the same attribute of the exact retrieval. In this case, only selected processing elements are activated as they hold the candidate records, while other processing elements are not required to work, thereby reducing the total cost. Those processing elements that are idle during this particular job may be available to process other jobs.

An example of an exact match retrieval using a hash data partitioning is as follows. For example, the hash function is based on attribute Student ID, and the search is to find the student with Student ID 98555. This Student ID is hashed, using the same hash function for the data partitioning. The result of this hashing determines where the record is located, and the processing element that holds this record will be activated and the desired record searched. This is an example of an exact match retrieval using a hash data partitioning.

A problem of hash partitioning involves processing records of a certain range, where hash partitioning cannot directly detect the location of a record. Suppose the above search is modified in order to find all students with Student IDs ranging from 98555 to 99555. With a hashing method, it is not possible to hash each individual Student ID value within that range, and we do not have prior knowledge about the maximum value for a Student ID starting with 98. Even if we did, it would be time consuming to hash each individual Student ID just to determine in which processor each record is located. Consequently, hash data partitioning is not suitable for range searching.

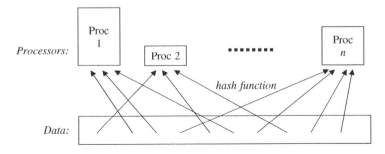

Figure 3.4 *Hash* data partitioning

Another disadvantage is exhibited in the graphical illustration of hash partitioning in Figure 3.4. Note that the load of each processing element might likely be skewed, because of the data value distribution, which is very likely to be non-uniform. From a searching operation point of view, it might not be a great deal as explained above. But from the perspective of other operations, it may have an adverse impact on performance, because the initial data allocated is already skewed.

Range

Range partitioning spreads records based on a given range of the partitioning attribute. For example, the student table is partitioned based on Student Last Name according to the following range distribution: last names starting with letters *A* to *C* go to the first processing element, last names starting from *D* to *G* to the second processing element, and so on. Figure 3.5 gives a graphical illustration of range data partitioning.

A consequence of this range data partitioning is that the processing of records on a particular range of the partitioning attribute can be directed to a small subset of processors containing the desired range of records. For example, retrieval of students with last name Robert something (e.g., Roberts, Robertson, Roberton, Roberta, etc.) can be directed to the processing element that holds records starting with an "R". Another example might be a retrieval of students whose last names start with letters *A* to *F*, and this query can be directed to processors 1 and 2 only.

It can be seen here that range partitioning is particularly suitable for range retrieval. However, both hash and range partitioning risk data skew. In the illustration in Figure 3.5 (as well as Fig. 3.4 for hash partitioning), the load of each processing element might not be balanced and uniform. This may impact negatively upon the performance of some other operations, as the initial data placement is already skewed.

Furthermore, retrieval processing based on a nonpartitioning attribute cannot make use of hash/range partitioning. For example, if the partitioning (either in range or hash) is based on attribute Student ID and the query is based on Student Name, then the query will not be able to make use of the benefits offered by range

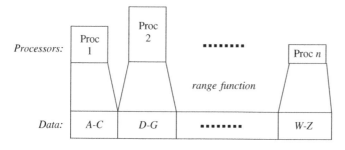

Figure 3.5   *Range* data partitioning

or hash partitioning, because the attribute used in data partitioning is different from that in the query. In this case, all processors must be activated and used to process the query. As a matter of fact, both range and hash partitioning in this case produce more disadvantages, as the initial data allocation in each processing element is nonuniform. In other words, all processors are used for processing, and since the load of each processor is different, the completion time of each processor will not be equal, and the longest finishing time becomes the query elapsed time.

Random-Unequal

The last basic data partitioning method is *random-unequal* data partitioning. As its name states, there are two important facts about the random-unequal data partitioning method:

- The partitioning is not based on the same attribute as the retrieval processing is based on (the partitioning might be a hash or a range partitioning method on a nonretrieval processing attribute, or the partitioning method is just simply unknown) and

- The size of each partition is likely to be unequal. The word "random" in the name indicates that the records within each partition are not grouped semantically, but are randomly allocated.

Random-unequal partitioning method is common, especially when the operation is actually an operation based on temporary results obtained from the previous operations. The initial partitioning method used may have lost its semantics through a pipeline of operators. Figure 3.6 gives an illustration of a random-unequal data partitioning.

Comparative Summary

The above four basic data partitioning methods can actually be categorized into (*i*) attribute-based data partitioning and (*ii*) non-attribute-based data partitioning. Attribute-based data partitioning uses hash and range data partitioning methods, whereas non-attribute-based data partitioning uses random-equal (round-robin)

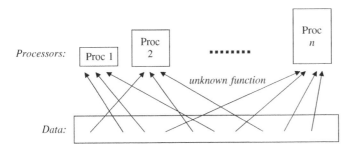

Figure 3.6 *Random-unequal* data partitioning

Table 3.1   *Attribute-based* versus *non-attribute-based* data partitioning

Attribute-Based Partitioning	Non-Attribute-Based Partitioning
Based on a particular attribute	Not based on any attribute
Has grouping semantics	No grouping semantics
Skew	Balanced

and random-unequal data partitioning methods. Table 3.1 gives a comparative summary of the attribute-based and non-attribute-based data partitioning methods.

A general conclusion from Table 3.1 is that if the search is based on the same attribute as the data partitioning (attribute-based partitioning), then the search can benefit from some advantages offered by the attribute-based partitioning, such as an exact match search using a hash data partitioning or a range search using a range data partitioning. If the search attribute is different from that of the partitioning attribute, then a non-attribute-based partitioning, especially the random-equal (round-robin) is the best option. Random-unequal is explained here because, in many cases, the data is already partitioned and the query has to pick up from wherever the data is already located.

3.2.2 Complex Data Partitioning

The basic data partitioning methods above either are based on a single attribute or no attribute is used as the basis of the partitioning. A more complex data partitioning, which is still based on a single attribute, is to combine several basic data partitioning methods. One is based on a variation of the range partitioning, called *hybrid-range partitioning strategy (HRPS)*. This partitioning technique attempts to compromise the features of range partitioning with hash and round-robin partitioning, resulting in all small partitions being distributed in a round-robin fashion. This technique uses a grid file structure to store partitions, where rows and columns of the grid file use hash and range partitioning techniques. This method is capable of supporting both range and exact match retrievals

The problem of data placement that is based on a single attribute is that when a query includes any operations based on anything other than the partitioning attribute, the features of the used partitioning technique will not apply, since the query must be directed to all processors. To overcome this problem, multiattribute partitioning is used. In this section, two multiattribute data partitioning methods are introduced, namely *MAGIC* (Multiattribute Grid Declustering), and *BERD* (Bubba's Extended Range Declustering).

Hybrid-Range Partitioning Strategy (HRPS)

HRPS strikes a compromise between the sequential execution paradigm of range partitioning and the load balancing/intraquery parallelism characteristics of the hash and round-robin partitioning methods. With the hybrid-range partitioning strategy, a table is partitioned into many small logical fragments so that each fragment contains a distinct range of the partitioning attribute value. The number of fragments is independent of the number of processors in the configuration. The HRPS partitions a table into fragments based on the following criteria:

- Each fragment contains approximately *FC* records.
- Each fragment contains a unique range of values of the partitioning attribute.

The variable *FC* is determined based on the processing capability of the system and the resource requirements of the queries that access the table, rather than the number of processors in the configuration. Variable *FC* is calculated by the following equation:

$$FC = \frac{RecordsPerQ_{Ave}}{M} \tag{3.1}$$

where $RecordsPerQ_{Ave}$ is the average number of records retrieved and processed by each query, and M is the number of processors that should participate in the execution of an average query.

The general steps of the HRPS are as follows:

- The table must be sorted on the partitioning attribute.
- The table can then be partitioned such that each fragment contains approximately *FC* records.
- The fragments are distributed among the processors in a round-robin fashion, ensuring that M adjacent fragments will be assigned to different processors.

For example, assume there are 10,000 student records, the partitioning attribute is Student ID, which is unique for each student, and the value of the Student ID ranges from 1 to 10,000. Assume that the average query accessing this table uses a range predicate on the partitioning attribute to retrieve and process 500 records ($RecordsPerQ = 500$). Queries on the student table normally access students per year enrolment, and we assume it averages around 500 records. Assume that the optimal performance is achieved when 5 processors are used ($M = 5$). Therefore,

$$FC = \frac{RecordsPerQ_{Ave}}{M} = 100$$

Therefore, the table will be partitioned into 100 fragments. The next step is the distribution the fragments to the participating processors. Here, there are three possibilities (cases):

- $M = N$
- $M > N$
- $M < N$

where N is the number of processors in the configuration and M is the number of processors participating in the query execution.

- Case 1: $M = N$

  For example, $M = N = 5$ processors. Since fragments of the table are assigned in a round-robin fashion among processors, the query will overlap either 5 or 6 fragments. In either case, all processors will be used to execute the query.

  Comparing the HRPS with hash partitioning, the hash partitioning method will also use all N processors, since it cannot localize the execution of a range query.

  Comparing this with range partitioning, the range partitioning method will also partition the table into 5 fragments. For example, range 1–2000 goes to processing element 1, range 2001–4000 goes to processor 2, and so on. Figure 3.7 illustrates the way in which the fragments are distributed among the 5 processing elements and provides a comparison with the range partitioning method.

  Since the range of a query falls within the range of a single fragment, and most of the tile overlaps the range of two fragments some of the time, the query will be directed to either 1 or 2 processors only. For example, a query retrieving students with Student ID between 1250 and 1750 will need only processor 1 to work, whereas a different query retrieving Student ID between 5900 and 6400 will need only processors 3 and 4 to work.

  On the other hand, with the HRPS, a query retrieving 500 students will be evenly spread among the five processors, and hence a shorter elapsed time can be expected.

- Case 2: $M > N$

  For example, $M = 5$ and $N = 2$. In this case, the first fragment goes to processor 1, the second to processor 2, the third back to processor 1, and so on. Since, on average, the query will retrieve 500 consecutive records, the query using a HRPS method will still use all N processors (e.g., 2 processors in this case) because it enforces the constraint that the M adjacent fragments be assigned to different processors whenever possible.

  Conversely, the range partitioning method in this case partitions the table into two fragments, significantly increasing the probability of a query being directed to only one processor.

HRPS	1-100	101-200	201-300	301-400	401-500
	. . .	. . .	. . .	. . .	. . .
	. . .	. . .	. . .	. . .	. . .
	. . .	. . .	. . .	. . .	. . .
	9501-9600	9601-9700	9701-9800	9801-9900	9901-10000
Range	1-2000	2001-4000	4001-6000	6001-8000	8001-10000

Figure 3.7   Case 1 ($M = N$) and a comparison with the range partitioning method

HRPS	1-100	101-200
	201-300	301-400
	. . .	. . .
	. . .	. . .
	9801-9900	9901-10000
Range	1-5000	5001-10000

Figure 3.8   Case 2 ($M > N$) and a comparison with the range partitioning method

Figure 3.8 gives a comparative illustration of HRPS and range partitioning methods. Say, for example, to retrieve records 1250 to 1750, with the range method only the first processor is used, whereas with the HRPS method the two processors will be used. Hence, the latter will reduce the elapsed time of the query.

- Case 3: $M < N$

  For example, $M = 5$ but $N = 10$ processors. The HRPS will distribute the 100 fragments of the table across all N processors in order to ensure that all available resources are used so as to maximize the throughput of the system when executing multiple queries concurrently. However, since the range of query will overlap only 5 or 6 fragments, each individual query is localized to almost the optimal number of processors. For example, a query retrieving Student IDs ranging from 1250 to 1750 will require 6 processors to work—that is processors 3 to processors 8 (see Fig. 3.9).

  Conversely, the hash partitioning strategy will send the query to all N processors, incurring the start up, communication, and termination overheads associated with executing the query on more processors than absolutely necessary.

  The range partitioning strategy will again execute the query on only 1 or 2 processors, again using fewer than the optimal number of processors. In the above case (see Figure 3.9 again), the query will make use of processor 2 only, which contains values ranging from 1001 and 2000.

Based on the three cases above, the advantages of the HRPS can be summarized as follows.

- *Support for Small Tables*

  Because the number of fragments created by the HRPS method is dependent on the processing capability of the system and the resource requirements of the workload and is independent of the number of processors in the multiprocessors, if the number of fragments of a table is less than the number of processors, then the table will automatically be partitioned across a subset of the processors.

HRPS	1-100	101-200	201-300	301-400	401-500	501-600	601-700	701-800	801-900	901-1000
	: :	: :	: :	: :	: :	: :	: :	: :	: :	: :
	9001-9100	9101-9200	9201-9300	9301-9400	9401-9500	9501-9600	9601-9700	9701-9800	9801-9900	9901-10000
Range	1-1000	1001-2000	2001-3000	3001-4000	4001-5000	5001-6000	6001-7000	7001-8000	8001-9000	9001-10000

Figure 3.9 Case 3 ($M < N$) and a comparison with the range partitioning method

- *Support for Tables with Nonuniform Distributions of the Partitioning Attribute Values*
  Because the cardinality of each fragment is not based on the value of the partitioning attribute value, once the HRPS determines the cardinality of each fragment, it will partition a table based on that value.

  For example, assume a table has a cardinality of 100,000 records and assume that 4000 of these records have 2 as their partitioning attribute value. Assume also that the cardinality of each fragment should be 1000 records. After sorting the table on the partitioning attribute, the records with a partitioning attribute value of 2 will be distributed among 4–5 fragments, which will each be assigned to a different processor. Thus, if the query is an exact match query looking for a value 2, the query will be directed to 4 processors (rather than 1 processor, had the table been partitioned with either hash or range partitioning methods).

MAGIC (Multiattribute Grid Declustering)

MAGIC is a data partitioning method based on multiple attributes. MAGIC can use two or more attributes of a table to partition its records across multiple processors and disks. The main idea behind a multiattribute data partitioning is that it can support search queries based on either of the data partitioning attributes. In single-attribute data partitioning, search queries must also be based on the same attribute in order to make use of the benefits offered by the data partitioning. With multiattribute data partitioning, search queries can be broadened as more attributes are available for the search. Another benefit of MAGIC is that it is able to support range search as well as exact match on each of the partitioning attributes.

To understand how MAGIC works, assume there are two very frequent queries. The first query retrieves student details based on the student's last name, whereas the second query is a range query to retrieve students with a range of Student ID values. For example:

Query 1 (one-half of the accesses):
  Equality predicate on the Student Last Name attribute, such as
  Slname = 'Roberts'

Query 2 (the other half):
  Range predicate on the Student ID attribute, such as
  Sid > 98555 AND *Sid* < 98600

Assume both queries produce only a few records. MAGIC partitioning works as follows:

- Create a two-dimensional grid with the two partitioning attributes as its dimension (e.g., *Slname* for the column and *Sid* for the row).
- Depending on the number of processing elements available in the system, the number of cells in the grid must be equal to the number of processing elements.

Table 3.2   MAGIC data partitioning

		Slname					
		A–D	**E–H**	**I–L**	**M–P**	**Q–T**	**U–Z**
	98000–98100	1	2	3	4	5	6
	98101–98200	7	8	9	10	11	12
Sid	**98201–98300**	13	14	15	16	17	18
	98301–98400	19	20	21	22	23	24
	98401–98500	25	26	27	28	29	30
	98501–98600	31	32	33	34	35	36

- Determine the range value for each column and row.
- Allocate a processor in each cell in the grid.

Table 3.2 illustrates the MAGIC partitioning method. In this example, there are 36 processing elements, and the *Slname* range partitioning is based on the first letter of the student's last name, whereas the *Sid* range partitioning is based on the Student ID. The number in each cell determines the processor number, which contains student records that fall into the category determined by the column (*Slname* range) and the row (*Sid* range). For simplicity, the range of *Sid* used in this example is limited from 98000 to 98600, and there are 36 processing elements in the system. In this example, for instance, processor 8 holds student records with *Slname* between "E" and "H" and *Sid* between 98101 and 98200.

In order to evaluate the efficiency of MAGIC, let us compare it with hash partitioning. The comparison is based on the above two queries, which dominate the query accesses. Since the hash partitioning method is a single-attribute-based data partitioning, we assume that the hash partitioning is based on the *Slname* attribute.

- Query 1 (exact match on *Slname*)

  The *hash partitioning* method can localize the execution of this query to a single processor, since this is an exact match query and hash partitioning is very suitable for exact matching of queries. Therefore, the queries on "Roberts" will need to use a single processor, as the "Roberts" records have been hashed and placed in a single location.

  The *MAGIC* partitioning method will use 6 processors to execute this query because its selection predicate maps to one column of the two-dimensional directory. In this case, the query will use processing numbers 5, 11, 17, 23, 29, and 35 (see Table 3.2)—that is, those in the second last column of the grid directory.

- Query 2 (range query on *Sid*)

  Since the *hash partitioning* method is based on *Slname* and this query is based on a different attribute, namely *Sid*, the hash partitioning method must direct this query to all 36 processing elements.

  The *MAGIC* partitioning method directs this query to 6 processors since its predicate value maps to 1 row of the grid directory and the entries of each row have been assigned to 6 different processors. In this case, the predicate

$98555 < Sid < 98600$ will use processors 31 to 36 (the last row of the grid directory).

In order to make a comparison with *range partitioning*, suppose the STUDENT table has been range partitioned on the *Sid* attribute. In this case, the second query would have used one processor. However, the first query would have been executed by all 36 processors, since the query is not based on the partitioning attribute.

Therefore, the use of a single-attribute-based partitioning like range or hash partitioning favors only one of the two queries and is not suitable for the other query. In contrast, MAGIC does not favor any particular query, but on average it uses fewer processors for both queries. In the above example, *MAGIC* uses an average of 6 processors, while the *range* and the *hash* partitioning methods both use an average of 18.5 processors.

Ideally, however, a single processor should have been used for each query since they both have minimal resource requirements. Approximating the optimal number of processors by a closer margin has two important benefits:

- The average response time of both queries is reduced because query initiation overhead is reduced.

- Using fewer processors increases the overall throughput of the system since the "freed" processors can be used to execute additional queries.

BERD (Bubba's Extended Range Declustering)

BERD is another multiattribute partitioning method. The method is used in the Bubba Database Machine. BERD uses two levels of data partitioning, called *primary* and *secondary* data partitioning. Therefore, two attributes must be nominated as the partitioning attributes.

The first step of the BERD partitioning method is to partition the table based on the primary partitioning attribute, and the partitioning method used is a range partitioning. Table 3.3 gives an example of primary partitioning in BERB. Here, the *Sid* attribute is used as the primary partitioning attribute. For simplicity, we provide only a few records in each partition, and each partition is based on a certain range.

The second step is that each fragment above is scanned and an auxiliary "table" is constructed from the attribute value of the secondary partitioning attribute and a list of processors containing the original records. In this example, the *Slname*

Table 3.3 Primary partitioning in BERD

Sid	Slname	Sid	Slname	Sid	Slname
98001	Robertson	98105	Black	98250	Chan
98050	Williamson	98113	White	98270	Tan

98001–98100   98101–98200   98201–98300

Table 3.4 Auxiliary table in the secondary partitioning

Slname	Processor
Robertson	1
Black	2
Chan	3
Williamson	1
White	2
Tan	3

attribute is used as a secondary partitioning attribute. Table 3.4 depicts the auxiliary table (called Table *IndexB*)

The third step is that this auxiliary table is range partitioned on the secondary partitioning attribute (e.g., *Slname*). For example, $A-K$ goes to processor 1, $L-T$ to processor 2, and the rest to processor 3. Therefore, Students Black and Chan go to processor 1, Robertson and Tan to processor 2, and Williamson and White to the last processor.

The final step is to place the fragments resulting from the first step above (fragments of the Student Table) and the fragments resulting from the third step above (fragments of the auxiliary table). Table 3.5 shows the result of this step. Each processor now has two portions: a fragment of *IndexB* and a fragment of table *Student*.

The number of processors actually used by a query depends on the correlation between the primary and secondary partitioning attribute values. A high correlation between primary and secondary partitioning attribute values means that there is a large portion where the auxiliary fragment located at one processor has entries pointing to the same processor where this fragment is located. If there is a high

Table 3.5 BERD partitioning combining the primary partitions and the secondary partitions

IndexB	
Black	2
Chan	3

Student	
98001	Robertson
98050	Williamson

IndexB	
Robertson	1
Tan	3

Student	
98005	Black
98113	White

IndexB	
Williamson	1
White	2

Student	
98250	Chan
98270	Tan

correlation, then the query is directed to only a few processors. Otherwise, the query may be directed to all processors.

For queries with an exact match predicate on the secondary partitioning attribute, the auxiliary table provides enough information to direct the execution of a query to at least one (high correlation between the two partitioning attribute values) and at most two processors (two correlation). For example, an exact match for student "Chan" will direct the first process to the first processor, and then goes to the third processor, where record "Chan" is actually located.

For range queries, such as *Sid* between 98150 and 98170, the primary partitioning provides enough information to direct the query to the necessary fragments.

3.3 SEARCH ALGORITHMS

Before discussing parallel search, it is important to know how searching is done serially. Serial search algorithms, plus data partitioning, will become the basis for parallel search algorithms.

3.3.1 Serial Search Algorithms

Depending on how the records are arranged, there are two kinds of serial search: (i) linear search and (ii) binary search.

Linear Search

Linear search is the simplest and most direct approach to searching. Given an unsorted table of records, linear search scans the entire table, one record at a time, searching for a given record. Since this is performed for each record one by one until either the desired record is found or the end of table is reached, linear search is also known as an "*exhaustive search.*"

To facilitate an understanding of a linear search algorithm, Figure 3.10 shows a Java code for linear search. For simplicity of the program, an integer array will serve as data records, and each element in the array will represent one key.

The complexity of the algorithm is normally calculated by counting the number of comparisons. The number of comparisons can then be used as an indication of the length of time that the program will run. There are several cases, in particular for unsuccessful search, successful search, and average search.

- *Unsuccessful Search: n* comparisons, where *n* is the number of records.
- *Successful Search: k* comparisons, where *k* is the position where the desired record is found in the table. Thus the best time for a successful search is 1 comparison, and the worst is *n* comparisons.
- *Average:* Total number of comparisons of linear search running for *n* times is: $1 + 2 + 3 + \cdots + n = \frac{1}{2}n(n + 1)$

Algorithm: Linear Search

```
int position = -1;          /* Not Found position */
public int linear_search (int []data, int key)
{
  /* Java arrays have a 0 offset */
  for (int i = 0; i < data.length; i++)
    if (data[i] == key)
    {
      position = i;
      break;
    }
  return position;
}
```

Figure 3.10 Linear search

Thus the average number of comparisons is: $\dfrac{\frac{1}{2}n(n+1)}{n} = \frac{1}{2}(n+1)$. Since $(n+1)$ and n do not differ significantly for large n, the complexity of a linear search is roughly equal to $O(n/2)$, where the O symbol is normally used to measure the complexity of an algorithm.

In terms of cost models for estimating the elapsed time of a linear search, these can be expressed as follows.

- *Scanning cost*: the cost of loading half of the records (on average) from disk to main memory:

$$\frac{1}{2} \times R/P \times IO$$

- *Select cost*: the cost of obtaining a record from data page:

$$\frac{1}{2} \times |R| \times (t_r + t_w)$$

- *Comparison cost*: the cost of comparing a record with the search predicate:

$$\frac{1}{2} \times |R| \times t_c$$

where t_c is a time unit cost for search predicate comparison.

- *Result generation cost*: the cost to write records found to the data page:

$$\sigma \times |R| \times t_w$$

where σ is the search query selection ratio. The product of σ and $|R|$ is equal to one for an exact match query and the search attribute values are unique. In other words, the product of these two variables estimates the number of records in the query result.

- *Disk writing cost*: the cost to write query results into the disk:

$$\sigma \times R/P \times IO$$

The total cost is the sum of the costs of scanning, selecting the data page, making a comparison, generating results, and disk writing.

Binary Search

Binary search requires that the list be already completely in order. A binary search starts by comparing the key with the middle entry of an ordered table. If they match, it returns the index of this element. Otherwise, processing continues, using either the lower or upper half of the table (depending on the value of the key). In essence, we eliminate half the table with only one comparison.

Figure 3.11 shows a simple Java code for a binary search. Again, for simplicity, the input table is represented as an array of integers, and the record to be searched for is indicated by the variable *key*. The program first initializes three variables, namely *lower*, *middle*, and *upper*, each of which points to the respective elements in the array. The main comparison is done between the *key* and the *middle* element. Further comparisons are done by updating the values of *lower* or *upper* depending on the result of the previous unsuccessful comparison.

The complexity of a binary search can be explained as follows. If the algorithm fails to locate the desired record during the first iteration of its loop, it divides the list in half and repeats the process. At this point, the comparison cost is 1 plus the cost of processing the remaining half. This is $O(1 + O(n/2))$, where n represents the number of elements in the table.

The cost of a failed second pass is much the same: 1 plus the cost of processing half of the remaining entries, that is, $O(1 + 1 + O(n/4))$. We can continue in this manner building upon each successive term. In other words, with each failed iteration, we add 1 to our formula and divide n again by the next power of 2. Hence, the complexity of a binary search is:

$$f(1) = 1 \qquad \text{if } n = 1 \text{ then } f(1) = 1$$
$$f(n) = 1 + f(n/2)$$

The second formula can be expanded to:

$$\begin{aligned} f(n) &= 1 + f(n/2) \\ &= 1 + 1 + f(n/2^2) \\ &= 1 + 1 + 1 + f(n/2^3) \\ &= \ldots\ldots\ldots \\ f(n) &= \log_2(n) + 1 \end{aligned}$$

The additional 1 term is to compensate for the fact that in general $\log_2(n)$ might not compute to an even integer. As a result, a binary search might perform one additional comparison. Thus this yields a complexity of $O(\log_2(n))$.

Algorithm: Binary Search

```
int position = -1; /* Not Found position */
public int binary_search (int []data, int key)
{
  int lower = 0;
  int middle = 0;
  int upper = data.length - 1;

  while (lower <= upper)
  {
    middle = (lower + upper) / 2;
    if (key == data[middle])
    {
      /* successful search */
      position = middle;
      break;
    }
    else if (key > data[middle])
      /* reduce to the top half of the list */
      lower = middle + 1;
    else
      /* reduce to the bottom half of the list */
      upper = middle - 1;
  }
  return position;
}
```

Figure 3.11   Binary search

The cost models for binary search are very similar to those of linear search. The main difference is actually already indicated by the O notation, where the linear search has a component of $1/2$, whereas the binary search is $\log_2$. Therefore, the complete cost models for a binary search are as follows.

$$Scanning\ cost = \log_2(R)/P \times IO$$
$$Select\ cost = \log_2(|R|) \times (t_r + t_w)$$
$$Comparison\ cost = \log_2(|R|) \times t_c$$
$$Result\ generation\ cost = \sigma \times |R| \times t_w$$
$$Disk\ writing\ cost = \sigma \times R/P \times IO$$

The $\log_2$ cost component in the first three cost equations above indicates the worst case of a binary search, in which $\log_2(|R|)$ number of records should be read and evaluated. The last two cost equations are the same as those for a linear search, since, whatever searching method is used, the number of records generated by the query should be the same; hence, result generation and disk writing costs should be the same for both linear search and binary search.

3.3.2 Parallel Search Algorithms

Parallel search algorithms have three main elements: (*i*) processor activation or involvement, (*ii*) local searching method, and (*iii*) key comparison.

Processor Activation or Involvement

Processor activation or *involvement* indicates the number of processors to be used by the algorithm. This can be illustrated as follows. If one already knows where the data to be sought are stored, then there is no point in activating all other processors in the searching process, since most of them will not produce the requested data anyway. However, if one does not know in which processor the requested data is stored, then there is no option but to search all processors.

Processor activation or involvement is dependent upon the data partitioning method that is used to partition the data. Note that here data parallelism is used, whereby a parallel search algorithm is applied to different portions of the data, and the final results are consolidated from all processors that produce the requested data.

Processor activation or involvement is also dependent upon the type of selection query that is performed, that is, whether it is an exact match or a range selection.

Table 3.6 shows the processor activation or involvement of parallel search algorithms. Note that in some cases, only one processor is all that is needed, for example, if the search is an exact match query and the data is already partitioned with a range partitioning. In other words, the location of the data to be searched for is already known. Consequently, only the processor that holds the data needs to be used. In this case, there is no parallelism. In fact, parallelism will not be of any use, since the involvement of other processors will only be an additional burden because they will not produce any results anyway.

Local Searching Method

The local searching method is the searching method to be applied to the processor(s) involved in the searching process. The local searching method to be used is dependent upon the data ordering. If the data has already been sorted, then a binary search is applied, or if the data has not been sorted, then a linear search must be conducted. This is applicable regardless of the type of search query, that

Table 3.6 Processor activation or involvement of parallel search algorithms

		Data Partitioning Methods			
		Random-Equal	Hash	Range	Random-Unequal
Exact Match		All	1	1	All
Range Selection	**Continuous**	All	All	Selected	All
	Discrete	All	Selected	Selected	All

Table 3.7   Local searching method of parallel search algorithms

		Records Ordering	
		Ordered	Unordered
Exact Match		Binary Search	Linear Search
Range Selection	Continuous	Binary Search	Linear Search
	Discrete	Binary Search	Linear Search

is, whether it is an exact match or a range selection. Table 3.7 shows the local searching method for parallel search algorithms.

It can be deduced from the local searching method above that parallelism in the search algorithm is based on data parallelism, whereby parallelism is achieved because the data is partitioned, and the same search algorithm is applied to different parts of the data. The final results are consolidated from those processors which produce the requested data.

Key Comparison

Searching basically consists of comparing the data from the table with the condition specified by the user. When a match is found, there are two options: whether to continue the comparison process in order to find more matches, or whether to stop the entire process. It is obvious that the key comparison is dependent upon whether the search attribute values are, or are not, unique. If the attribute values to be searched are not unique, it is imperative to continue the searching process since further matches might be found. Table 3.8 shows the key comparison based on whether or not the requested data is unique.

Note that the comparison will stop when a match is found if the query is an exact match and the attribute values are unique. For example, if a certain student ID is searched, and assuming that there is no duplicate of the student ID, then if the requested student ID is already found, there is no need to continue with the searching process. For all other types of search queries, the comparison process will not stop until all data has been examined.

3.4 SUMMARY

This chapter addresses the most basic parallel database operation, namely parallel search. Some key points from this chapter include:

Table 3.8   Key comparison of parallel search algorithms

		Search Attribute Values	
		Unique	Duplicate
Exact Match		Stop	Continue
Range Selection	Continuous	Continue	Continue
	Discrete	Continue	Continue

- *Searching in SQL* is provided through the *Where* clause in the SQL's *Select-From-Where* queries.

- *Search predicates* indicate the type of search operation, whether it is an exact match, range (continuous or discrete), or multiattribute search.

- *Data partitioning* is a basic mechanism of parallel search, whereby the search operator can concentrate on different data fragments. Data partitioning methods can be single-attribute-based partitioning, no-attribute-based partitioning, or multiattribute-based partitioning.

- *Parallel search algorithms* have three main components: processor involvement, local searching method, and key comparison. Processor involvement in the search is determined by the type of data partitioning of the table, the local searching method is decided by the ordering of the table, and key comparison may or may not continue after one match has been found.

3.5 BIBLIOGRAPHICAL NOTES

Bell (1984) describes the complexity and difficulties of data placement problems. Ghandeharizadeh et al. proposed a number of data partitioning methods for parallel databases, including hybrid-range (*VLDB* 1990), multiattribute partitioning (*SIGMOD* 1992), and MAGIC (*IEEE TPDS* 1994). Other data partitioning methods for parallel databases have been reported by Hua and Lee (*VLDB* 1990) and Ibá nez-Espiga and Williams (*DEXA* 1992). Data placement used by the Bubba Database Machine was presented by Copeland (*SIGMOD* 1988).

In recent years, data partitioning and placement have been adopted by new database domains, such as data warehouses and multidimensional, XML data, and the Grid. Furtado (2004) discussed data partitioning the context of data warehouses; Stöhr et al. (2000) and Sun et al. (1998) presented data partitioning for multidimensional databases. The work on XML data partitioning can be found in Tang et al. (2005) and Zhu and Lü (2001), whereas Kido et al. (2006) focused on XPath. Watson (2005) discussed data locality and distribution in the context of grid databases.

The basic searching techniques can be found in the classic book by Knuth (1973). Most recent work in searching exists in nontraditional database systems, such as spatial and geo-spatial databases (Gao et al. 2006; Tamura et al. 2001), video databases (Geisler 2003), and time series databases (Duan et al. 2006; Qiao et al. 2006).

3.6 EXERCISES

3.1. Why is *horizontal data partitioning* more appropriately used in parallel database systems?

3.2. Why is *random-unequal* data partitioning categorized as a non-attribute-based data partitioning? Illustrate your answer with an example.

3.3. Explain why *attribute-based data partitioning* methods do not directly help parallel search in most cases.

3.4. *HRPS* combines range and round-robin (i.e., random-equal) data partitioning. One of the advantages of HRPS is that the method is capable of supporting both range and exact match retrievals. Explain this statement. Use an example to illustrate your points.

3.5. *MAGIC* also supports both range and exact match retrievals. Explain this statement and use an example to illustrate how it works.

3.6. Given a data set $D = \{55, 30, 68, 39, 1, 4, 49, 90, 34, 76, 82, 56, 31, 25, 78, 56, 38, 32, 88, 9, 44, 98, 11, 70, 66, 89, 99, 22, 23, 26\}$, three processors, and a *random-equal* data partitioning, illustrate how the parallel searching of data item 78 is carried out.

3.7. Use the same data set D as in the previous exercise, also with three processors. Let us now adopt *range* data partitioning. Illustrate how the parallel searching of data items between 70 and 79 can be carried out.

3.8. Use the same data set D as in Exercise 3.6 above, but now use a *hash* data partitioning. Illustrate how to do a parallel search of data items $10, 20, 30, \ldots, 90$.

3.9. Given the same data set D as in Exercise 3.6 above, suppose a *binary search* algorithm is to be used. Assume that there are three processors available. What is the most suitable data partitioning for this operation? Show step by step how parallel binary search works in finding data item 78.

3.10. Investigate your favorite DBMS that supports parallelism, and see how parallel search is expressed in SQL.

Chapter 4

Parallel Sort and GroupBy

Apart from searching, sorting is one of the most common operations in database processing. Sorting is also widely known in various forms in computer science. The topic of sorting in traditional data structure and algorithm subjects is divided into two areas, namely, *internal* and *external sorting*.

Internal sorting is where sorting takes place totally within main memory. The data to be sorted is assumed to be small and fits into main memory. A number of internal sorting methods, both serial and parallel, have been explored, including parallel quick sort, parallel heap sort, etc.

External sorting on the other hand is where the volume of data to be sorted is large and resides in secondary memory. Thus external sorting is also known as file sorting. In databases, since data is stored in tables (or files) and its volume is normally very large, database sorting is therefore mostly external sorting. Therefore, in this chapter, we focus on parallel external sorting methods for parallel database systems.

The second part of this chapter concentrates on GroupBy queries. GroupBy queries involving aggregates are very common in database processing, especially in Online Analytical Processing (OLAP), and data warehouse. Queries containing aggregate functions summarize a large set of records based on the designated grouping. These queries are often used as a tool for strategic decision making. As the data repository containing data for integrated decision making grows, aggregate queries are required to be executed efficiently.

The structure of this chapter is as follows: In Section 4.1, an introduction to sorting and duplicate removal is given. The section also includes a basic introduction to aggregate queries involving GroupBy. In order to understand how a parallel sorting operation works, it is essential to understand the basic concept of sorting in a serial environment. This is explained in Section 4.2. Following this, five parallel sorting algorithms for parallel database systems are described in Section 4.3. This is then

High-Performance Parallel Database Processing and Grid Databases,
by David Taniar, Clement Leung, Wenny Rahayu, and Sushant Goel
Copyright © 2008 John Wiley & Sons, Inc.

followed by parallelism of GroupBy queries in Section 4.4. The analytical models for the sorting and GroupBy are given in Sections 4.5 and 4.6, respectively.

4.1 SORTING, DUPLICATE REMOVAL, AND AGGREGATE QUERIES

4.1.1 Sorting and Duplicate Removal

Sorting is a typical operation that places the records in a particular order based on one or more nominated attribute(s). Sorting is instigated by the need to have a more efficient searching technique other than linear search. This then gave rise to binary search, which outperforms linear search but requires the input data to have been sorted. Therefore, the sorting operation becomes critically important.

In terms of query retrieval, sorting is often explicitly requested by users in order to present the query results in a particular order. This is achieved through the use of an Order By clause in SQL. The Order By clause basically requires the query results to be ordered on the designated attributes in ascending or descending order. The following query shows an example of the use of the Order By clause in an SQL query. The resulting table from this query is sorted based on attribute Sdegree.

Query 4.1:
```
Select *
From STUDENT
Order By Sdegree;
```

Sorting, in SQL, can be based on multiattributes—by listing the attributes following the Order By. In the above example, sorting is based on a single attribute only, that is, attribute Sdegree. By default, sorting is always ascending. Descending sorting is also possible when indicated by Desc following the attribute. For example:

Query 4.2:
```
Select *
From STUDENT
Order By Sdegree Desc, Sname;
```

Sorting may also be required in join operations through the use of the sort-merge join algorithm. This is less explicit than the use of Order By and Distinct clauses in SQL. However, some query optimizers allow users to specify any join algorithms to be used when invoking an SQL query.

Duplicate removal is closely associated with sorting. When sorting a list of data, duplicate removal can also be concurrently carried out. Therefore, algorithms for sorting often incorporate duplicate removal. The need for duplicate removal in databases is driven by both user requirements and relational theory. The former is a typical requirement by users, whereas the latter is influenced by the fact that a relation in relational databases must not contain duplicate records.

In SQL, duplicate removal is carried out by the `Distinct` clause in the `Select` clause. The `Distinct` operation basically removes all duplicates found in the query result. This can be achieved by first sorting the query results, followed by removing duplicates through scanning. In an optimized scenario, both operations are carried out at the same time during the sorting process. The following is an example whereby duplicate values of `Sdegree` have been removed, resulting in a unique list of degrees in the `Student` table.

Query 4.3:

```
Select Distinct Sdegree
From STUDENT;
```

4.1.2 Scalar Aggregate

Basic aggregate queries are normally categorized into:

- Scalar aggregates and
- Aggregate functions

Scalar aggregate queries produce single values for a given set of records (i.e., table), whereas *aggregate function queries* generate a set of values for a given table. The former is like grouping the whole table and producing a single value, whereas the latter is like grouping the table into several groups, and for each group a single value is produced.

SQL queries in the real world are replete with scalar aggregates and aggregate functions. These queries are often used for strategic decision making because of the nature of group-by queries, where raw information is grouped according to the designated groups and within each group aggregate functions are normally carried out.

In SQL, scalar aggregates are available through the use of built-in functions, such as `Max` for maximum, `Sum` for summing numerical attributes, etc. For the aggregate function queries, generating a set of groups for a given table is done through the use of the `Group By` clause. Therefore, aggregate function queries are also known as "*GroupBy*" queries.

An example of a *scalar aggregate query* is "retrieve students having the highest GPA". The input table in this case is table `Student`, and the single value to be produced is the largest value in attribute `Sgpa`. The SQL and a sample result of the above query are given below.

Query 4.4:

```
Select MAX(Sgpa)
From STUDENT;
```

The above query produces a single value, and this value is generated by the MAX function. Other basic functions, such as COUNT, SUM, AVG and MIN, may also be used. Apart from these basic functions, most commercial relational database management systems (RDBMS) also include other advanced functions, such as advanced statistical functions, etc. From a query processing point of view, these functions take a set of records (i.e., a table) as their input and produce a single value as the result.

4.1.3   GroupBy

An example of a *GroupBy query* is "retrieve number of students for each degree". The student records are grouped according to specific degrees, and for each group the number of records is counted. These numbers will then represent the number of students in each degree program. The SQL and a sample result of this query are given below.

Query 4.5:

```
Select Sdegree, COUNT(*)
From STUDENT
Group By Sdegree;
```

It is also worth mentioning that the input table may have been filtered by using a Where clause (in both scalar aggregate and GroupBy queries), and additionally for GroupBy queries the results of the grouping may be further filtered by using a Having clause.

4.2   SERIAL EXTERNAL SORTING METHOD

Serial external sorting is external sorting in a uniprocessor environment. The most common serial external sorting algorithm is based on sort-merge. The underlying principle of sort-merge algorithm is to break the file up into unsorted subfiles, sort the subfiles, and then merge the sorted subfiles into larger and larger sorted subfiles until the entire file is sorted. Note that the first stage involves sorting the first lot of subfiles, whereas the second stage is actually the merging phase. In this scenario, it is important to determine the size of the first lot of subfiles that are to be sorted. Normally, each of these subfiles must be small enough to fit into the main memory, so that sorting of these subfiles can be done in the main memory with any internal sorting technique. In other words, the size of these subfiles is usually determined by the buffer size in main memory, which is to be used for sorting each subfile internally. A typical algorithm for external sorting using B buffers is presented in Figure 4.1.

The algorithm presented in Figure 4.1 is divided into two phases: *sort* and *merge*. The merge phase consists of loops and each run in the outer loop is called a pass; subsequently, the merge phase contains i passes, where $i = 1, 2, \ldots$. For consistency, the sort phase is named pass 0.

To explain the sort phase, consider the following example. Assume the size of the file to be sorted is 108 pages and we have 5 buffer pages available ($B = 5$

Algorithm: Serial External Sorting

```
// Sort phase – Pass 0
1. Read B pages at a time into memory
2. Sort them, and Write out a sub-file
3. Repeat steps 1-2 until all pages have been processed

// Merge phase – Pass i = 1, 2, ...
4. While the number of sub-files at end of previous pass
   is > 1
5. While there are sub-files to be merged from
   previous pass
6.    Choose B-1 sorted sub-files from the previous pass
7.    Read each sub-file into an input buffer page
      at a time
8.    Merge these sub-files into one bigger sub-file
9.    Write to the output buffer one page at a time
```

Figure 4.1   External sorting algorithm based on sort-merge

pages). First read 5 pages from the file, sort them, and write them as one subfile into the disk. Then read, sort, and write another 5 pages. In the last run, read, sort, and write 3 pages only. As a result of this sort phase, $\lceil 108/B \rceil = 22$ subfiles, where the first 21 subfiles are of size 5 pages each and the last subfile is only 3 pages long.

Once the sorting of subfiles is completed, the merge phase starts. Continuing the example above, we will use $B - 1$ buffers (i.e., 4 buffers) for input and 1 buffer for output. The merging process is as follows. In pass 1, we first read 4 sorted subfiles that are produced in the sort phase. Then we perform a 4-way merging (because only 4 buffers are used as input). This 4-way merging is actually a k-way merging, and in this case $k = 4$, since the number of input buffers is 4 (i.e., $B - 1$ buffers = 4 buffers). An algorithm for a k-way merging is explained in Figure 4.2.

The above 4-way merging is repeated until all subfiles (e.g., 22 subfiles from pass 0) are processed. This process is called pass 1, and it produces $\lceil 22/4 \rceil = 6$ subfiles of 20 pages each, except for the last run, which is only 8 pages long.

The next pass, pass 2, repeats the 4-way merging to merge the 6 subfiles produced in pass 1. We then first read 4 subfiles of 20 pages long and perform a 4-way merge. This results in a subfile 80 pages long. Then we read the last 2 subfiles, one of which is 20 pages long while the other is only 8 pages long, and merge them to become the second subfile in this pass. So, as a result, pass 2 produces $\lceil 6/4 \rceil = 2$ subfiles.

Finally, the final pass, pass 3, is to merge the 2 subfiles produced in pass 2 and to produce a sorted file. The process stops as there are no more subfiles.

In the above example, using an 108-page file and 5 buffer pages, we need to have 4 passes, where pass 0 is the sort phase and passes 1 to 3 are the merge phase. The

---

Algorithm: k-way merging

```
input files f₁, f₂, ..., fₙ;
output file f₀
/* Sort files f₁, f₂, ..., fₙ, based on the attributes a₁
   of all files */
1. Open files f₁, f₂, ..., fₙ.
2. Read a record from files f₁, f₂, ..., fₙ.
3. Find the smallest value among attributes a₁ of the
   records from step 2. Store this value to aₓ and the
   file to fₓ (f₁≤fₓ≤fₙ).
4. Write aₓ to an output file f₀.
5. Read a record from file fₓ.
6. Repeat steps 3-5, until no more record in all files
   f₁, f₂, ..., fₙ.
```

Figure 4.2 k-Way merging algorithm

number of passes can be calculated as follows. The number of passes needed to sort a file with B buffers available is $\lceil \log_{B-1} \lceil file\ size/B \rceil \rceil + 1$, where $\lceil file\ size/B \rceil$ is the number of subfiles produced in pass 0 and $\lceil \log_{B-1} \lceil file\ size/B \rceil \rceil$ is the number of passes in the merge phase. This can be seen as follows. In general, the number of passes x in the merge phase of α items satisfies the relationship: $\alpha/(B-1)^x = 1$, from which we obtain $x = \log_{B-1}(\alpha)$.

In each pass, we read and write all the pages (e.g., 108 pages). Therefore, the total I/O cost for the overall serial external sorting can be calculated as $2 \times file\ size \times number\ of\ passes = 2 \times 108 \times 4 = 864$ pages. More comprehensive cost models for serial external sort are explained below in Section 4.4.

As shown in the above example, an important aspect of serial external sorting is the buffer size, where each subfile comfortably fits into the main memory. The bigger the buffer (main memory) size, the fewer number of passes taken to sort a file, resulting in performance gain. Table 4.1 illustrates how performance is improved when the number of buffers increases.

In terms of total I/O cost, the number of passes is a key determinant. For example, to sort 1 billion pages, using 129 buffers is 6 times more efficient than using 3 buffers (e.g., 30:5 = 6:1).

There are a number of variations to the serial external sort-merge explained above, such as using a double buffering technique or a blocked I/O method. As our concern is not with the serial part of external sorting, our assumption of serial external sorting is based on the above sort-merge technique using B buffers.

As stated in the beginning, serial external sort is the basis for parallel external sort. Particularly in a shared-nothing environment, each processor has its own

Table 4.1   Number of passes in serial external sorting as number of buffer increases

R	B = 3	B = 5	B = 9	B = 17	B = 129	B = 257
100	7	4	3	2	1	1
1,000	10	5	4	3	2	2
10,000	13	7	5	4	2	2
100,000	17	9	6	5	3	3
1 million	20	10	7	5	3	3
10 million	23	12	8	6	4	3
100 million	26	14	9	7	4	4
1 billion	30	15	10	8	5	4

data, and sorting this data locally in each processor is done as per serial external sort explained above. Therefore, the main concern in parallel external sort is not on the local sort but on when the local sort is carried out (i.e., local sort is done first or later) and how merging is performed. The next section describes different methods of parallel external sort by basically considering the two factors mentioned above.

4.3   ALGORITHMS FOR PARALLEL EXTERNAL SORT

In this section, five parallel external sort methods for parallel database systems are explained; (*i*) parallel merge-all sort, (*ii*) parallel binary-merge sort, (*iii*) parallel redistribution binary-merge sort, (*iv*) parallel redistribution merge-all sort, and (*v*) parallel partitioned sort. Each of these will be described in more detail in the following.

4.3.1   Parallel Merge-All Sort

The *Parallel merge-all sort* method is a traditional approach, which has been adopted as the basis for implementing sorting operations in several database machine prototypes (e.g., Gamma) and some commercial Parallel DBMS. Parallel merge-all sort is composed of two phases: *local sort* and *final merge*. The *local sort phase* is carried out independently in each processor. Local sorting in each processor is performed as per a normal serial external sorting mechanism. A serial external sorting is used as it is assumed that the data to be sorted in each processor is very large and cannot be fitted into the main memory, and hence external sorting (as opposed to internal sorting) is required in each processor.

After the local sort phase has been completed, the second phase, *final merge phase*, starts. In this final merge phase, the results from the local sort phase are

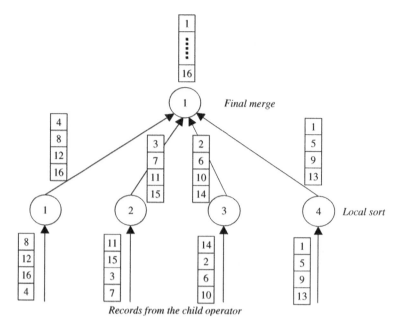

Figure 4.3   Parallel merge-all sort

transferred to the host for final merging. The final merge phase is carried out by one processor, namely, the host. An algorithm for a k-way merging is explained in Figure 4.2.

Figure 4.3 illustrates a parallel merge-all sort process. For simplicity, a list of numbers is used and this list is to be sorted. In the real world, the list of numbers is actually a list of records from very large tables.

Figure 4.3 shows that a parallel merge-all sort is simple, because it is a one-level tree. Load balancing in each processor at the local sort phase is relatively easy to achieve, especially if a round-robin data placement technique is used in the initial data partitioning. It is also easy to predict the outcome of the process, as performance modeling of such a process is relatively straightforward.

Despite its simplicity, the parallel merge-all sort method incurs an obvious problem, particularly in the final merging phase, as merging in one processor is heavy. This is true especially if the number of processors is large and there is a limit to the number of files to be merged (i.e., limitation in number of files to be opened). Another factor in merging is the buffer size as mentioned above in the discussion of serial external sorting.

Another problem with parallel merge-all sort is network contention, as all temporary results from each processor in the local sort phase are passed to the host. The problem of merging by one host is to be tackled by the next sorting scheme, where merging is not done by one processor but is shared by multiple processors in the form of hierarchical merging.

4.3.2   Parallel Binary-Merge Sort

The first phase of *parallel binary-merge sort* is a *local sort* similar to the parallel merge-all sort. The second phase, the *merging phase*, is pipelined instead of concentrating on one processor. The way the merging phase works is by taking the results from two processors and then merging the two in one processor. As this merging technique uses only two processors, this merging is called "binary merging." The result of the merging between two processors is passed on to the next level until one processor (the host) is left. Subsequently, the merging process forms a hierarchy. Figure 4.4 illustrates the process.

The main reason for using parallel binary-merge sort is that the merging workload is spread to a pipeline of processors instead of one processor. It is true, however, that final merging still has to be done by one processor.

Some of the benefits of parallel binary-merge sort are similar to those of parallel merge-all sort. For instance, balancing in local sort can be done if a round-robin

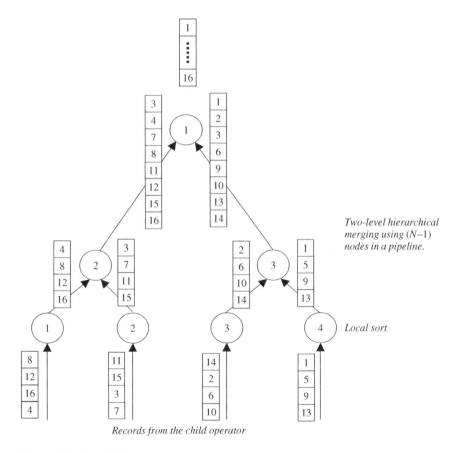

Figure 4.4   Parallel binary-merge sort

Parallel Merge-All Sort   *Parallel Binary-Merge Sort*

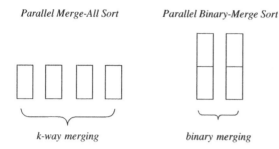

k-way merging   *binary merging*

Figure 4.5 Binary-merge vs. k-way merge in the merging phase

data placement is initially used for the raw data to be sorted. Another benefit, as stated above, is that by merging the workload it is now shared among processors.

However, problems relating to the heavy merging workload in the host still exist, even though now the final merging merges only a pair of lists of sorted data and is not a k-way merging like that in parallel merge-all sort. Binary merging can still be time consuming, particularly if the two lists to be merged are very large. Figure 4.5 illustrates binary-merge versus k-way merge, which is carried out by the host.

The main difference between k-way merging and binary merging is that in k-way merging, there is a searching process in the merging; that is, it searches the smallest value among all values being compared at the same time. In binary merging, this searching is purely to obtain a comparison between two values simultaneously.

Regarding the system requirement, k-way merging requires a sufficient number of files to be opened at the same time. This requirement is trivial in binary merging, as it requires only a maximum of two files to be opened, and this is easily satisfied by any operating systems.

The pipeline system, as in the binary merging, will certainly produce extra work through the pipe itself. The pipeline mechanism also produces a higher tree, not a one-level tree as with the previous method. However, if there is a limit to the number of opened files permitted in the k-way merging, parallel merge-all sort will incur merging overheads.

In parallel binary-merge sort, there is still no true parallelism in the merging because only a subset, not all, of the available processors are used.

In the next three sections, three possible alternatives using the concept of redistribution or repartitioning are described. The first approach is a modification of parallel binary-merge sort by incorporating redistribution in the pipeline hierarchy of merging. The second approach is an alteration to parallel merge-all sort, also through the use of redistribution. The third approach differs from the others, as local sorting is delayed after partitioning is done.

4.3.3 Parallel Redistribution Binary-Merge Sort

Parallel redistribution binary-merge sort is motivated by parallelism at all levels in the pipeline hierarchy. Therefore, it is similar to parallel binary-merge sort, because both methods use a hierarchy pipeline for merging local sort results, but differs in terms of the number of processors involved in the pipe. With parallel redistribution binary-merge sort, all processors are used at each level in the hierarchy of merging.

The steps for parallel redistribution binary-merge sort can be described as follows. First, carry out a local sort in each processor similar to the previous sorting methods. Second, redistribute the results of the local sort to the same pool of processors. Third, do a merging using the same pool of processors. Finally, repeat the above two steps until final merging. The final result is the union of all temporary results obtained in each processor. Figure 4.6 illustrates the parallel redistribution binary-merge sort method.

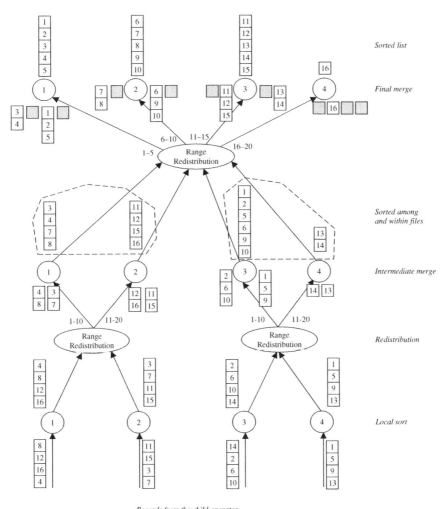

Figure 4.6 Parallel redistribution binary-merge sort

Note from the illustration that in the final merge phase, some of the boxes are empty (i.e., gray boxes). This indicates that they do not receive any values from the designated processors. For example, the first box on the left is gray because there are no values ranging from 1 to 5 from processor 2. Practically, in this example, processor 1 performs the final merging of two lists, because the other two lists are empty.

Also, note that the results produced by the intermediate merging in the above example are sorted within and among processors. This means that, for example, processors 1 and 2 produce a sorted list each, and the union of these results is also sorted where the results from processor 2 are preceded by those from processor 1. This is applied to other pairs of processors. Each pair of processors in this case forms a pool of processors. At the next level of merging, two pools of processors use the same strategy as in the previous level. Finally, in the final merging, all processors will form one pool, and therefore results produced in each processor are sorted, and these results united together are then sorted based on the processor order. In some systems, this is already a final result. If there is a need to place the results in one processor, results transfers are then carried out.

The apparent benefit of this method is that merging becomes lighter compared with those without redistribution, because merging is now shared by multiple processors, not monopolized by just one processor. Parallelism is therefore accomplished at all levels of merging, even though the performance benefits of this mechanism are restricted.

The problem of the redistribution method still remains, which relates to the height of the tree. This is due to the fact that merging is done in a pipeline format. Another problem raised by the redistribution is skew. Although initial placement in each disk is balanced through the use of round-robin data partitioning, redistribution in the merging process is likely to produce skew, as shown in Figure 4.6. Like the merge-all sort method, final merging in the redistribution method is also dependent upon the maximum number of files opened.

4.3.4   Parallel Redistribution Merge-All Sort

Parallel redistribution merge-all sort is motivated by two factors, namely, reducing the height of the tree while maintaining parallelism at the merging stage. This can be achieved by exploiting the features of parallel merge-all and parallel redistribution binary-merge methods. In other words, parallel redistribution is a two-phase method (local sort and final merging) like parallel merge-all sort, but does a redistribution based on a range partitioning. Figure 4.7 gives an illustration of parallel redistribution merge-all sort.

As shown in Figure 4.7, parallel redistribution merge-all sort is a two-phase method, where in phase one, local sort is carried out as is done with other methods, and in phase two, results from local sort are redistributed to all processors based on a range partitioning, and merging is then performed by each processor.

Similar to parallel redistribution binary-merge sort, empty (gray) boxes are actually empty lists as a result of data redistribution. In the above example, processor

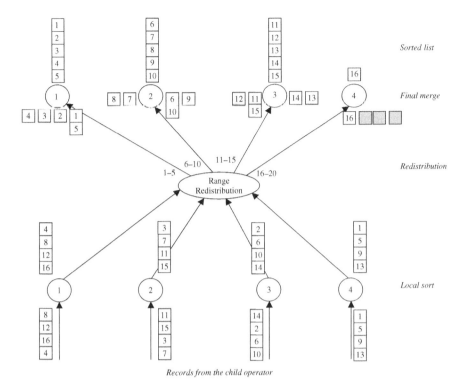

Figure 4.7   Parallel redistribution merge-all sort

4 has three empty lists coming from processors 2, 3, and 4, as they do not have values ranging from 16 to 20 as specified by the range partitioning function.

Also, note that the final results produced in the final merging phase in each processor are sorted, and these are also sorted among all processors based on the order of the processors specified by the range partitioning function.

The advantage of this method is the same as that of parallel redistribution binary-merge sort, including true parallelism in the merging process. However, the tree of parallel redistribution merge-all sort is not a tall tree as in the parallel redistribution binary-merge sort. It is, in fact, a one-level tree, the same as in parallel merge-all sort.

Not only do the advantages of parallel redistribution merge-all sort mirror those in parallel merge-all sort and parallel redistribution binary-merge sort, so also do the problems. Skew problems found in parallel redistribution binary-merge sort also exist with this method. Consequently, skew modeling needs some simplified assumptions as well. Additionally, a bottleneck problem in merging, which is similar to that of parallel merge-all sort is also common here, especially if the number of processors is large and exceeds the limit of the number of files that can be opened at once.

4.3.5 Parallel Partitioned Sort

Parallel partitioned sort is influenced by the techniques used in parallel partitioned join, where the process is split into two stages: partitioning and independent local work. In parallel partitioned sort, first we partition local data according to range partitioning used in the operation. Note the difference between this method and others. In this method, the first phase is not a local sort. Local sort is not carried out here. Each local processor scans its records and redistributes or repartitions according to some range partitioning.

After partitioning is done, each processor will have an unsorted list whose values come from various processors (places). It is then that local sort is carried out. Thus local sort is carried out after the partitioning, not before. It is also noted that merging is not needed. The results produced by the local sort are already the final results. Each processor will have produced a sorted list, and all processors in the order of the range partitioning method used in this process are also sorted. Figure 4.8 illustrates this method.

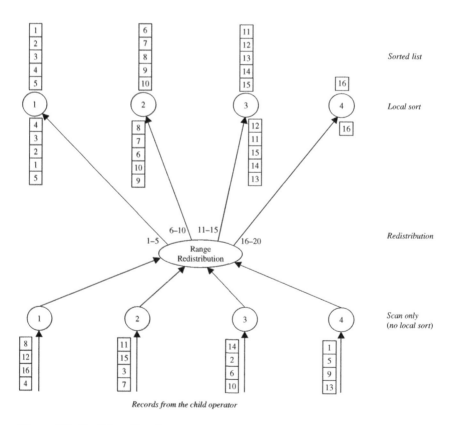

Figure 4.8 Parallel partitioned sort

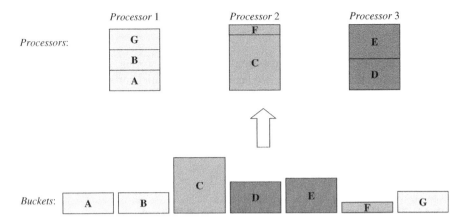

Figure 4.9   Bucket tuning load balancing

The main benefit of parallel partitioned sort is that no merging is necessary, and hence the bottleneck in merging is avoided. It is also a true parallelism, as all processors are being used in the two phases. And most importantly, it is a one-level tree, reducing unnecessary overheads in the pipeline hierarchy.

Despite these advantages, the problem that still remains outstanding is skew that is produced by the partitioning. This is a common problem even in the partitioned join. Load balancing in this situation is often carried out by producing more buckets than there are available processors, and the workload arrangement of these buckets can then be carried out by evenly distributing buckets among processors. For example, in Figure 4.9, seven buckets have been created for three processors. The size of each bucket is likely to be different, and after the buckets are created bucket placement and arrangement are performed to make the workload of the three processors balanced. For example, buckets *A*, *B*, and *G* go to processor 1, buckets *C* and *F* to processor 2, and the rest to processor 3. In this way, the workload of these three processors will be balanced.

However, bucket tuning in the original form as shown in Figure 4.9 is not relevant to parallel sort. This is because in parallel sort the order of the processors is important. In the above example, bucket *A* will have values that are smaller than those in bucket *B*, and values in bucket *B* are smaller than those in bucket *C*, etc. Then buckets *A* to *G* are in order. The values in each bucket are to be sorted, and once they are sorted the union of values from each bucket, together with the bucket order, produces a sorted list. Imagine that bucket tuning as shown in Figure 4.9 is applied to parallel partitioned sort. Processor 1 will have three sorted lists, from buckets *A*, *B*, and *G*. Processors 2 and 3 will have 2 sorted lists each. However, since the buckets in the three processors are not in the original order (i.e., *A* to *G*), the union of sorted lists from processors 1, 2, and 3 will not produce a sorted list, unless a further operation is carried out.

4.4 PARALLEL ALGORITHMS FOR GROUPBY QUERIES

Parallel aggregate processing is very similar to parallel sorting, described in the previous section. From the lessons we learned from parallel sorting, we focus on three parallel aggregate query algorithms;

- ◦ *Traditional* methods including merge-all and hierarchical merging,
- ◦ *Two-phase* method, and
- ◦ *Redistribution* method

4.4.1 Traditional Methods (Merge-All and Hierarchical Merging)

The *traditional* method was first used in Gamma, one of the first parallel database system prototypes. This method consists of two steps, which are explained as follows.

The first step is a *local aggregation* step. In this step, each node groups local records according to the designated group-by attribute and performs the aggregate function. Using Query 4.5 as an example, one node may produce, for example, (Math, 300) and (Science, 500) and another node (Business, 100) and (Science, 100). The numerical figures indicate the number of students in that degree.

The second step is a *global aggregation* step, in which all the temporary results obtained in each node are passed to the host for consolidation in order to produce the global aggregate values. Continuing the above example, (Science, 500) from the first node and (Science, 100) from the second are merged into one record, that is, (Science, 600). This global aggregation step can be very tricky depending on the complexity of the aggregate functions used in the actual query. If, for example, an AVG function were used instead of COUNT in the above query, when calculating an average value based on temporary averages, one must take into account the actual raw records involved in each node. Therefore, for these kinds of aggregate functions, the local aggregate must also produce the number of raw records in each node, although they are not specified in the query. This is needed in order for the global aggregation to produce correct values.

Query 4.6:

```
Select Sdegree, AVG(SAge)
From STUDENT
Group By Sdegree;
```

For example, one node may produce (Science, 21.5, 500) and the other (Science, 22, 100). The host calculates the global average by dividing the sum of the two SAge by the total number of students. The total number of students in each degree needs to be determined in each node, although it is not specified in the SQL.

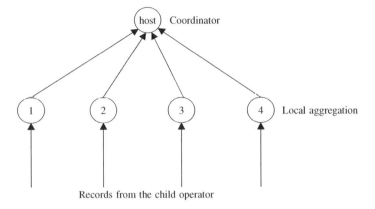

Figure 4.10   Traditional method

As the host coordinates all temporary results from each node, intuitively this method works well if the number of nodes is small and the number of resulting records is also very small. But as soon as the groups size becomes moderate, the host starts becoming a bottleneck. In general, the use of a single node for global aggregation forms a serial bottleneck at that node. Figure 4.10 shows the traditional parallel aggregate method.

The *hierarchical merging* method is introduced in order to overcome the bottleneck of the host as in the traditional method. Instead of using one node to do the global aggregation, it utilizes a binary merging scheme to off-load some of the work from the host node. This binary merging scheme can be explained as follows. For each pair of nodes, the local aggregation results of one of the nodes are sent to the other, where a second level of local aggregates is computed. Once all pairs have been processed, all the nodes holding the second-level aggregates are then processed in the same manner, until there is only one processor left, the top node of which coordinates the final aggregate results. Figure 4.11 shows the hierarchical merging method.

Like the traditional method, the hierarchical merging method works well with a small number of results. Although it may handle medium-sized results well, when the number of records becomes sufficiently large, its performance will decline. This is simply because the final merging phase still creates a bottleneck.

4.4.2   Two-Phase Method

As the name states, the *two–phase* method consists of two phases: *local aggregation* and *global aggregation*. The *first* phase is the *local aggregation phase*, where each processor calculates its local aggregate values. Local aggregation is calculated based on the records on the local processor. In this phase, each processor groups local records according to the designated group-by attribute and performs the aggregate function. Using the same query as an example, one processor

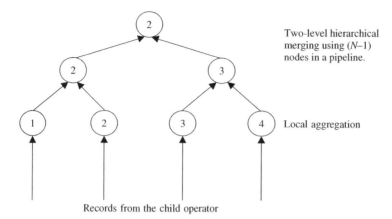

Two-level hierarchical merging using (*N*–1) nodes in a pipeline.

Local aggregation

Records from the child operator

Figure 4.11 Hierarchical merging method

may produce, for instance, (Math, 300) and (Science, 500) and another processor (Business, 100) and (Science, 100). The numerical figures indicate the number of students in these degrees.

The *second phase* is a *global aggregation phase*, in which all the temporary results obtained in each processor are redistributed to all processors to produce the global aggregate values. The way global aggregation works is as follows. After local aggregates are formulated in each processor, each processor distributes each of the groups to another processor depending on the adopted distribution function. A possible distribution function is, for example, that degrees beginning with *A–G* are to be distributed to processor 1, *H–M* to processor 2, *N–T* to processor 3, and the rest to processor 4. With this range distribution function, the processor that produces (Math, 300) and (Science, 500) will distribute its (Math, 300) to processor 2 and (Science, 500) to processor 3. This distribution scheme is commonly used in parallel join, where raw records are partitioned into buckets based on an adopted partitioning scheme like the above range partitioning.

Once the distribution of local results based on a particular distribution function has been completed, global aggregation in each processor is done by simply merging all identical degrees into one aggregate value. For example, processor 3 will merge (Science, 500) from one processor and (Science, 100) from the other to produce (Science, 600), which is the final aggregate value for this degree. The global aggregation operation for different groups is done in parallel by distributing local aggregates, so as to avoid the bottleneck produced by the traditional method. Figure 4.12 illustrates this method. The circles indicate processors, and the directed arrows show data flow.

4.4.3 Redistribution Method

The *redistribution* method is influenced by the practice of parallel join algorithms, where raw records are first partitioned and allocated to each processor and then

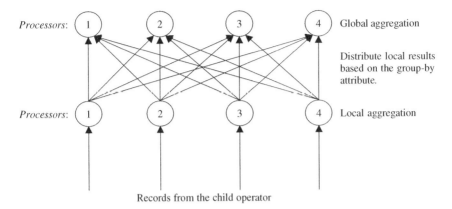

Figure 4.12 Two-phase method

each processor performs its operation. In the context of parallel aggregates, the difference between the redistribution method and other methods is that this method does not process local aggregates. The redistribution method is motivated by the fast message passing of multiprocessor systems.

The *first* phase (i.e., *partitioning phase*) in the Redistribution method is partitioning of raw records based on the group-by attribute according to a distribution function. An example of a partitioning function is, as for the previous example, to allocate to each processor degrees ranging from certain letters as their first letter and certain letters as their last letter. Using the same range partitioning as described in the previous sections, a processor will have all records that have degrees from letter *A* to *G*. Other processors will follow on the basis of alphabet division, such as processor 2 from *H* to *M*.

Once the partitioning has been completed, each processor will have records within certain groups identified by the group-by attribute. Subsequently, the *second* phase (the *aggregation phase*), which calculates the aggregate values of each group, can proceed. Aggregation in each processor can be carried out with a sort or a hash function. As a result of the second phase, each processor will have one aggregate value for each group; for example, processor 3 will have (Science, 600). Since each processor has distinct aggregate groups as a result of partitioning of the group-by attribute, the final query result is a union of all subresults produced by each processor.

Figure 4.13 illustrates the redistribution method. Note that partitioning is done to the raw records, and the aggregate operation on each processor is carried out after the partitioning phase. Also, observe that if the number of groups is less than the number of available processors, not all processors can be utilized, thereby reducing the capability of parallelism.

The cost components for the redistribution method are different from those of two-phase method, particularly in the first phase, in which the redistribution method does not perform a local aggregation. In the first phase of the redistribution

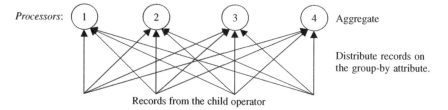

Figure 4.13   Redistribution method

method, the raw records are simply distributed to other processors. Hence, the main cost component of the first phase of the redistribution method is the distribution cost.

4.5   COST MODELS FOR PARALLEL SORT

In addition to the cost notations described in Chapter 2, there are a few new cost notations, which are particularly relevant for parallel sort. These are listed in Table 4.2.

Before presenting the cost models for each of the five parallel external sortings discussed in the previous section, we will first study the cost models for serial external sort, which are the foundation of cost models for the parallel versions; understanding these is important in the context of parallel external sort.

4.5.1   Cost Models for Serial External Merge-Sort

There are two main cost components for serial external sort, the costs relating to I/O and those relating to CPU processing. The I/O costs are the disk costs, which consist of load cost and save cost. These I/O costs are as follows.

Table 4.2   Additional cost notations for parallel sort

Symbol	Description
System parameters	
B	Buffer size
Time unit costs	
t_m	Time to merge
t_s	Time to compare and swap two keys
t_v	Time to move a record

- *Load cost* is the cost of loading data from disk to main memory. Data loading from disk is done by pages.

Load cost = Number of pages × Number of passes × Input/output unit cost

where *Number of pages* $= (R/P)$ and

$$Number\ of\ passes = (\lceil log_{B-1}(R/P/B)\rceil + 1) \qquad (4.1)$$

Hence, the above load cost becomes:

$$(R/P) \times (\lceil log_{B-1}(R/P/B)\rceil + 1) \times IO$$

- *Save cost* is the cost of writing data from the main memory back to the disk. The save cost is actually identical to the load cost, since the number of pages loaded from the disk is the same as the number of pages written back to the disk. No filtering to the input file has been done during sorting.

The CPU cost components are determined by the costs involved in getting records out of the data page, sorting, merging, and generating results, which are as follows.

- *Select cost* is the cost of obtaining a record from the data page, which is calculated as the number of records loaded from the disk times reading and writing unit cost to the main-memory. The number of records loaded from the disk is influenced by the number of passes, and therefore equation 4.1 above is being used here to calculate the number of passes.

$$|R| \times Number\ of\ passes \times (t_r + t_w)$$

- *Sorting cost* is the internal sorting cost, which has a $O(N \times log_2 N)$ complexity. Using the cost notation, the $O(N \times log_2 N)$ complexity has the following cost.

$$|R| \times \lceil log_2(|R|)\rceil \times t_s$$

The sorting cost is the cost of processing a record in pass 0 only.

- *Merging cost* is applied to pass 1 onward. It is calculated based on the number of records being processed, which is also influenced by the number of passes in the algorithm, multiplied by the merging unit cost. The merging unit cost is assumed to involve a k-way merging where searching for the lowest value in the merging is incorporated in the merging unit cost. Also, bear in mind that 1 must be subtracted from the number of passes, as the first pass (i.e., pass 0) is used by sorting.

$$|R| \times (Number\ of\ passes - 1) \times t_m$$

- *Generating result cost* is the number of records being generated or produced in each pass before they are written to disk multiplied by the writing unit cost.

$$|R| \times Number\ of\ passes \times t_w$$

4.5.2   Cost Models for Parallel Merge-All Sort

The cost models for parallel merge-all sort are divided into two categories: *local merge-sort costs* and *final merging costs*. *Local merge-sort costs* are the costs of local sorting in each processor using a merge-sort technique, whereas the *final merging costs* are the costs of consolidating temporary results from all processing elements at the host.

The *local merge-sort costs* are similar to the serial external merge-sort cost models explained in the previous section, except for two major differences. One difference is that for the local merge-sort costs in parallel merge-all sort the fragment size to be sorted in each processor is determined by the values of R_i and $|R_i|$, instead of just R and $|R|$. This is because in parallel merge-all sort the data has been partitioned to all processors, whereas in the serial external merge-sort only one processor is being used. Since we now use R_i and $|R_i|$, these two cost elements may involve *data skew*. When skew is involved, the values of R_i and $|R_i|$ are calculated not by a straight division with N, but with a much lower value than N due to skewness.

The second difference is that the local merge-sort costs of parallel merge-all sort involve communication costs, which do not appear in the original serial external sort cost models. The communication costs are the costs associated with the data transfer from each processor to the host at the end of the local sorting phase.

The local merge-sort costs, consisting of I/O costs, CPU costs, and communication costs, are summarized as follows.

- *I/O costs*, which consist of *load* and *save costs*, are as follows:

$$Save\ cost = Load\ cost = (R_i/P) \times Number\ of\ passes \times IO \quad (4.2)$$

  where $Number\ of\ passes = (\lceil \log_{B-1}(R_i/P/B) \rceil + 1)$

- CPU costs, which consist of *select cost, sorting cost, merging cost*, and *generating results cost*, are as follows:

$$Select\ cost = |R_i| \times Number of passes \times (t_r + t_w)$$
$$Sorting\ cost = |R_i| \times \lceil log_2(|R_i|) \rceil \times t_s$$
$$Merging\ cost = |R_i| \times (Number of passes - 1) \times t_m$$
$$Generating\ result\ cost = |R_i| \times Number of passes \times t_w$$

  where *Number of passes* is as shown in equation 4.2 above.

- *Communication costs* for sending local sorted results to the host are given by the number of pages to be transferred multiplied by the message unit cost, as follows:

$$Communication\ cost = (R_i/P) \times (m_p + m_l)$$

The *final merging costs* involve communication costs, I/O costs, and CPU costs. The communication costs are the costs involved when the host receives data from all other processors. The I/O and CPU costs are the costs associated directly with the merging process at the host. The three cost components for the final merging costs are given as follows.

- *Communication cost*, which is the receiving record cost from local sorting operators, is calculated by the number of records being received (in this case the total number of records from all processors) multiplied by the message unit cost.

$$Communication\ cost = (R/P) \times m_p$$

- *I/O cost*, which consists of *load* and *save costs*, is influenced by two factors, the total number of records being received and processed and the number of passes in the merging of N subfiles. When the data is first received from the local sorting operator, the data has to be written out to the disk in the host. After this, the host starts the k-way merging process by first loading the data from the local host disk, processing them, and saving the results back to the local host disk.

  As the k-way merging process may be done at a number of passes, data loading and saving are carried out as many times as the number of passes in the merging process. Moreover, the total number of data savings is one more than the total number of data loadings, as the first data saving must be done when the data is first received by the host.

$$Save\ cost = (R/P) \times (Number\ of\ merging\ passes + 1) \times IO$$
$$Load\ cost = (R/P) \times Number\ of\ merging\ passes \times IO \qquad (4.3)$$

where *Number of merging passes* $= \lceil \log_{B-1}(N) \rceil$

Note that the *Number of merging passes* is determined by the number of processors N and the number of buffers. The number of processors N is served as the number of streams in the k-way merging, and each stream contains a sorted list of data, which is obtained from the local sorting phase. Since all processors participate in the local sorting phase, the value of N is not influenced by skew. Whether or not there is data skew in the local sorting phase, all processors will have at least one record to work with, and subsequently when these data are transferred to the host, none of the stream is empty.

- *CPU cost* consists of the select costs, merging costs, and generating results costs only. Sorting costs are not included since the host does not sort data but only merges. CPU costs are determined by the total number of records being merged, the number of merging passes, and the unit cost.

$$Select\ cost = |R| \times Number\ of\ merging\ passes \times (t_r + t_w)$$
$$Merging\ cost = |R| \times Number\ of\ merging\ passes \times t_m$$
$$Generating\ result\ cost = |R| \times Number\ of\ merging\ passes \times t_w$$

where *Number of merging passes* is as shown in equation 4.3 above.

There are two things to mention regarding the above final merging costs. First, the host processes all records, and hence R and $|R|$ are used in the cost equations, not R_i and $|R_i|$. Second, since only one processor, namely the host, is working, the notion of skew does not exist in the cost equation. In other words, data skew may occur in the local sorting phase, but in the final merging phase only the host performs its work.

4.5.3   Cost Models for Parallel Binary-Merge Sort

The cost models for parallel binary-merge sort are divided into two parts: *local merge-sort costs* and *pipeline merging costs*. The *local merge-sort costs* are exactly the same as those of parallel merge-all sort, since the local sorting phase in both parallel sorting methods is the same. Therefore, we focus on the cost models for pipeline merging only.

In pipeline merging, we first need to determine the number of levels in the pipeline. Since we use binary-merge, where each merging takes the results from two processors, the number of levels in the pipeline is $\lceil log_2(N) \rceil$. Level numbers start from 1, which is the immediate level after local sort, to the last level $\lceil log_2(N) \rceil$, which is basically a final merging done by one processor, namely the host.

In *level* 1 in the pipeline, the number of processors used is basically up to half, and we use a notation of N', where $N' = \lceil N/2 \rceil$. The implication to the skew equation is that $|R_i'| = \dfrac{|R|}{\sum_{j=1}^{N'} \frac{1}{j^\theta}}$. Note that we use the notations $|R_i'|$ and N', where $|R_i'|$ indicates the number of records being processed at a node in a level of pipeline merging and N' is the number of processors involved. If no skew is involved, $|R_i'| = \frac{|R|}{N'}$.

The process in level 1 basically follows the following order. First, receive records from the local sort operator. Second, save and load these records on local disks. This I/O process is particularly needed especially when the data being transferred is very large, and hence storing it on local disk upon arrival is necessary. The actual merging process starts with data loading from the local disk. Third, merge the data, which incurs costs in selecting, merging, and generating result. And fourth, transfer the merging results to the next level of the pipeline, possibly to a different processor. The cost models for these processes are as follows.

$$Receiving\ cost = (R_i'/P) \times m_p$$
$$Save\ cost = (R_i'/P) \times IO$$
$$Load\ cost = (R_i'/P) \times IO$$
$$Select\ cost = |R_i'| \times (t_r + t_w)$$
$$Merging\ cost = |R_i'| \times t_m$$
$$Generating\ result\ cost = |R_i'| \times t_w$$
$$Data\ transfer\ cost = (R_i'/P) \times (m_p + m_l)$$

In the subsequent levels, the number of processors involved is further reduced by half, because of binary merging. With the N' notation, the new N' value becomes $N' = \lceil N'/2 \rceil$. This also impacts upon the skew equation where N' is used. Apart from the number of processors involved in the next level of pipeline merging, the process is the same, and therefore the above cost equations can be used.

At the last level of pipeline merging where the host performs a final binary merging, $N' = 1$. Another main difference between the last level and previous levels is that, in the last level of pipeline merging, the data transfer cost is substituted with another save cost, since the final results are not transferred but are saved in the host disks.

To summarize, the total pipeline binary merging costs are as follows.

$$Receiving\ cost = (R'_i/P) \times \lceil log_2(N) \rceil \times m_p$$
$$Save\ cost = (R'_i/P) \times (\lceil log_2(N) \rceil + 1) \times IO$$
$$Load\ cost = (R'_i/P) \times \lceil log_2(N) \rceil \times IO$$
$$Select\ cost = |R'_i| \times \lceil log_2(N) \rceil \times (t_r + t_w)$$
$$Merging\ cost = |R'_i| \times \lceil log_2(N) \rceil \times t_m$$
$$Generating\ result\ cost = |R'_i| \times \lceil log_2(N) \rceil \times t_w$$
$$Data\ transfer\ cost = (R'_i/P) \times (\lceil log_2(N) \rceil - 1) \times (m_p + m_l)$$

It must be stressed that the values of R'_i and $|R'_i|$ are not constant throughout the pipeline but increase from level to level as the number of processors N' used is reduced by half when progressing from one level to another. Another point is that R'_i and $|R'_i|$ may be affected by processing skew.

4.5.4 Cost Models for Parallel Redistribution Binary-Merge Sort

Like those for parallel binary-merge sort, parallel redistribution binary-merge sort costs have two main components: *local merge-sort costs* and *pipeline merging costs*.

The local sort operation in parallel redistribution binary-merge sort is similar to parallel merge-all sort and parallel binary-merge sort. The main difference is that, in parallel redistribution binary-merge sort, temporary results are being redistributed to processors in the next level of operations. This redistribution operation incurs additional overhead, particularly for each record being redistributed. The destination of this record needs to be determined based on the partitioning method used. We call this overhead *compute destination cost*

$$Compute\ destination\ cost = |R_i| \times t_d$$

Similar to parallel merge-all sort and parallel binary-merge sort, R_i in the above equation may involve data skew. Other than the compute destination cost, the local merge-sort costs in parallel redistribution binary-merge sort are the same as those in parallel merge-all sort.

The *pipeline merging costs* in parallel redistribution binary-merge sort are similar to those in parallel "without redistribution" binary-merge sort. We first mention a couple of similarities. First, the number of levels of the pipeline is $\lceil log_2(N) \rceil$, where level 1 is the first level after the local sorting phase. Second, the order of the process is similar, starting from data received from the network to data transferred to the next level of the pipeline.

However, there are a number of principal differences. One relates to the number of processors participating at each level. In parallel redistribution binary-merge sort, all processors participate. Hence, in the cost equations, we should use R_i and $|R_i|$, not R'_i and $|R'_i|$. Another main difference relates to the compute destination costs, which are absent in the parallel "without redistribution" binary-merge sort costs. Compute destination costs are applicable here at all levels of the pipeline except the last one, where the results are written back to disk, not redistributed over the network.

In summary, the *pipeline merging costs* for parallel redistribution binary-merge sort are as follows.

$$Receiving\ cost = (R_i/P) \times \lceil log_2(N) \rceil \times m_p$$
$$Save\ cost = (R_i/P) \times (\lceil log_2(N) \rceil + 1) \times IO$$
$$Load\ cost = (R_i/P) \times \lceil log_2(N) \rceil \times IO$$
$$Select\ cost = |R_i| \times \lceil log_2(N) \rceil \times (t_r + t_w)$$
$$Merging\ cost = |R_i| \times \lceil log_2(N) \rceil \times t_m$$
$$Generating\ result\ cost = |R_i| \times \lceil log_2(N) \rceil \times t_w$$
$$\boldsymbol{Compute\ destination\ cost = |R_i| \times (\lceil log_2(N) \rceil - 1) \times t_d}$$
$$Data\ transfer\ cost = (R_i/P) \times (\lceil log_2(N) \rceil - 1) \times (m_p + m_l)$$

4.5.5 Cost Models for Parallel Redistribution Merge-All Sort

Like the other parallel sort methods, parallel redistribution merge-all sort has two main cost components: *local merge-sort costs* and *merging costs*.

The *local merge-sort costs* are the same as those of parallel redistribution binary-merge sort. Both have the compute destination costs, as both redistribute data from the local sort phase to the merging phase.

The *merging costs* are somewhat similar to those of parallel merge-all sort, except for one main difference, that is, here we use R_i and $|R_i|$, not R and $|R|$ in parallel merge-all sort. The reason is simple—in parallel redistribution merge-all sort, all processors are being used in the merging phase, whereas in parallel "without redistribution" merge-all sort, only the host is used in the merging phase. As now R_i and $|R_i|$ are used in the merging costs, both may be affected by processing skew, and hence, the previously explained skew model is applied.

The merging costs for parallel redistribution merge-all sort are given as follows.

$$Communication\ cost = (R_i/P) \times m_p$$
$$Save\ cost = (R_i/P) \times (Number\ of\ merging\ passes + 1) \times IO$$
$$Load\ cost = (R_i/P) \times Number\ of\ merging\ passes \times IO$$
$$Select\ cost = |R_i| \times Number\ of\ merging\ passes \times (t_r + t_w)$$
$$Merging\ cost = |R_i| \times Number\ of\ merging\ passes \times t_m$$
$$Generating\ result\ cost = |R_i| \times (Number\ of\ merging\ passes) \times t_w$$

where *Number of merging passes* $= \lceil log_{B-1}(N) \rceil$

Despite the similarity between the above merging costs for parallel redistribution merge-all sort and those for parallel redistribution binary-merge sort, there are major differences. The first relates to the number of levels in the pipeline, which is $\lceil log_2(N) \rceil$ for parallel redistribution binary-merge sort and 1 for parallel redistribution merge-all sort. The second concerns the number of merging passes involved in the *k*-way merging. In parallel redistribution binary-merge sort the merging is binary, and hence the number of merging passes is 1. In contrast, merging in parallel redistribution merge-all sort is multiple depending on the number of processors N and number of buffers B, and hence the number of merging passes is calculated as $\lceil log_{B-1}(N) \rceil$.

4.5.6 Cost Models for Parallel Partitioned Sort

Parallel partitioned sort costs have two components as well; these are not local merge-sort costs and merging costs, but *scanning and partitioning costs* and *local merge-sort costs*. As explained previously, in parallel partitioned sort, local sorting is done after the partitioning.

The *scanning and partitioning costs* involve I/O costs, CPU costs, and communication costs. The I/O cost is basically a load cost during the scanning of all records. The CPU costs mainly involve the select costs and compute destination costs. The communication cost is a data transfer cost from each processor in the scanning/partitioning phase to processors in the sorting phase.

- *I/O costs*, which consist of *load costs*, are as follows:

$$(R_i/P) \times IO$$

- *CPU costs* consist of *select cost*, which is the cost associated with obtaining a record from the data page and computing destination.

$$|R_i| \times (t_r + t_w + t_d)$$

- *Communication costs* consist of data transfer costs, which are given as follows.

$$(R_i/P) \times (m_p + m_l)$$

The first phase costs, like the others, may be affected by data skew. The *local merge-sort costs* are to some degree similar to other local merge-sort costs, except the communication costs are associated with data received from the first phase of processing, not with data transfer as in other local sort-merge costs.

- *Communication costs* consist of data receiving costs, which are given as follows.

$$Data\ receiving\ costs = (R_i/P) \times m_p$$

- *I/O costs* consist of *load* and *save costs*. The save costs are double those of the load costs as data saving is done twice: once after the data has arrived from the network and again when final results are produced and saved to disk.

$$Save\ cost = (R_i/P) \times (Number\ of\ passes + 1) \times IO$$
$$Load\ cost = (R_i/P) \times Number\ of\ passes \times IO \qquad (4.4)$$

where *Number of passes* $= (\lceil log_{B-1}(R_i/P/B) \rceil + 1)$

- CPU costs, which consist of select cost, sorting cost, merging cost, and generating results cost, are as follows:

$$Select\ cost = |R_i| \times Number\ of\ passes \times (t_r + t_w)$$
$$Sorting\ cost = |R_i| \times \lceil log_2(|R_i|) \rceil \times t_s$$
$$Merging\ cost = |R_i| \times (Number\ of\ passes - 1) \times t_m$$
$$Generating\ result\ cost = |R_i| \times Number of passes \times t_w$$

where *Number of passes* is as shown in equation 4.4

The above CPU costs are identical to the CPU costs of local merge-sort in parallel merge-all sort.

4.6 COST MODELS FOR PARALLEL GROUPBY

In addition to the cost notations described in Chapter 2, Table 4.3 presents the additional cost notations. They are basically comprised of parameters known by the system as well as the data—parameters related to the query, unit time costs, and communication costs.

4.6.1 Cost Models for Parallel Two-Phase Method

The cost components in the first phase (local aggregation phase) of the two-phase method are as follows.

- *Scan cost* is the cost for loading data from local disk in each processor. Since data loading from disk is done page by page, the fragment size of the table residing in each disk is divided by the page size in order to obtain the number of pages.

$$(R_i/P) \times IO$$

Table 4.3 Cost notations

Symbol	Description
Query parameters	
σ_p	Selectivity ratio of local aggregate in a processor
σ_n	Selectivity ratio of local aggregate in a node
σ_g	Selectivity ratio of global aggregate
Time unit costs	
t_h	Time to compute hash value
t_a	Time to add a record to current aggregate value

- *Select cost* is the cost to obtain records from the data page, which is calculated as the number of records loaded from the disk times the reading and writing unit cost to the main-memory.

$$|R_i| \times (t_r + t_w)$$

- *Local aggregation* involves reading, hashing, and computing the cumulative value, which is given by the number of records in each processor's main-memory times the reading, hashing, and computation unit costs.

$$|R_i| \times (t_r + t_h + t_a)$$

The hashing process is very much determined by the size of the hash table that can fit into the main-memory. If the memory size is smaller than the hash table size, we normally partition the hash table into multiple buckets so that each bucket can perfectly fit into main-memory. A hashing technique can be roughly explained as follows.

a. The records are read and hashed into a hash table based on the *Group By* attribute. The first record hashing to a new value adds an entry to the hash table, and the subsequent matches update the cumulative result as appropriate.

b. If the entire hash table cannot be fitted into the allocated memory, the records are hash partitioned into multiple buckets, and all but the first bucket are spooled to the disk.

c. The overflow buckets are processed one by one as in step a above.

In this scenario, we must include the I/O cost for reading and writing overflow buckets, which is as follows.

- *Reading/Writing of overflow buckets* cost is the I/O cost associating with the limitation of main-memory to accommodate the entire hash table. This cost includes the costs of reading and writing records not processed in the first pass of hashing.

$$\left(1 - \min\left(\frac{H}{\sigma_p \times |R_i|}, 1\right)\right) \times \left(\pi \times \frac{R_i}{P} \times 2 \times IO\right)$$

The first term of the above equation can be explained as follows. For example, if the maximum hash table size H is 10 records, selectivity ratio σ_p is $1/4$, and there are 200 records ($|R_i|$), the number of groups in the query result will be equal to 50 ($\sigma_p \times |R_i|$). Since only 10 groups can be processed at a time, we need to break the hash table into 5 buckets. All buckets but the first are spooled to disk. Hence, 80% of the groups $(1 - (10/50))$ is overflow. Should there be only fewer or equal to 10 groups in the query result, the first term of the above equation would be equal to 0 (zero), and hence there would be no overhead.

The second term of the above equation is explained as follows. The constant 2 refers to two input/output accesses: one is for spooling of the overflow buckets to disk and two is for reading the overflow buckets from disk. Note that the record size is reduced by the projectivity ratio π, because in the hash table only the projected attributes are kept, not the whole record.

- *Generating result records cost* is the number of selected records multiplied by the writing unit cost.

$$|R_i| \times \sigma_p \times t_w$$

- *Determining the destination cost* is the cost of calculating the destination of each aggregate record from the processor in phase one to phase two. This overhead is given by the number of selected aggregate records in each fragment times the destination computation unit cost, which is given as follows.

$$|R_i| \times \sigma_p \times t_d$$

- *Data transfer cost* for sending local results to other processors is given by the number of pages to be sent multiplied by the message unit cost, which is given as follows.

$$(\pi \times R_i \times \sigma_p / P) \times (m_p + m_l)$$

The sum of the above equations gives the total cost for phase one of the two-phase method.

The cost component for the second phase (consolidation phase) is the merging cost, which is influenced by the number of records arriving at a processor and is given as follows

$$|R_i| \times \sigma_p \quad \text{and} \quad \pi \times R_i \times \sigma_p$$

The first term of the above equation is the number of selected records from the first phase, whereas the second term is the table size of the selected records. Based on the number of records arriving in each processor, the cost components of the coordinator are given as follows.

- *Receiving records cost* from local aggregation operators is calculated by the number of projected values from local aggregation multiplied by the message unit cost.

$$(\pi \times R_i \times \sigma_p/P) \times (m_p)$$

- *Computing final aggregate value cost* for each group involves reading and computing the cumulative values, which is given as follows.

$$|R_i| \times \sigma_p \times (t_r + t_a)$$

- *Generating final result cost* is the number of projected records from local aggregation multiplied by the writing unit cost. Remember that the final result is obtained by further filtering the local aggregate results. Note that we use the symbol σ_g where $\sigma_p \geq \sigma_g$.

$$|R_i| \times \sigma_g \times t_w$$

- *Disk cost* of storing the final result is the number of pages needed to store the final aggregate values times disk unit cost, which is:

$$(\pi \times R_i \times \sigma_g/P) \times IO$$

The total cost of phase two of the two-phase method is sum of the above.

4.6.2   Cost Models for Parallel Redistribution Method

The cost components for the first phase (distribution phase) of the redistribution method are as follows. The *scan costs* and the *select costs* are the same as for those in the two-phase method, which are:

- *Scan cost* for loading data from local disk in each processor is:

$$(R_i/P) \times IO$$

- *Select cost* for getting record out of data page is:

$$|R_i| \times (t_r + t_w)$$

Apart from these two costs, the finding destination cost and the data transfer cost are added to this model, which are as follows.

- *Finding destination cost* is:
$$|R_i| \times (t_d)$$

- *Data transfer cost* is:

$$(\pi \times R_i/P) \times (m_p + m_l)$$

The sum of the above equations gives the total partitioning cost of the redistribution method.

If the number of groups is less than the number of processors, $R_i = R/$ *(Number of groups)*, instead of $R_i = R/N$ (i.e., assuming uniform distribution), because not all processors are used. Consequently, when the number of groups is smaller than the available number of processors, performance can be expected to be poor.

The second phase (aggregation phase) cost components for the redistribution method are composed of the receiving cost, which is the cost of receiving records from the first phase, the actual aggregation cost, which covers reading and computing the aggregate value, generating result records, and disk cost for storing query results.

To some degree, the cost components of the redistribution method are somewhat similar to those of the second phase of the two-phase method. The main difference is that with the two-phase method the number of records processed in the second phase has been reduced in the local aggregation phase, whereas the number of records received at the second phase of the redistribution method is the total number of records. We consider the total records for the redistribution method, simply because the first phase of this method does not do any filtering, therefore ALL records from the first phase proceed to the second phase.

In terms of the cost equation, they are as follows.

- *Receiving records cost* from processors in the first phase is:

$$(\pi \times R_i/P) \times (m_p)$$

When redistributing the records during the first phase, only those attributes relevant to the query are redistributed. This factor is depicted by the projectivity factor of the group-by query, which is shown by π.

- *Computing aggregate value cost* for each group is:

$$|R_i| \times (t_r + t_h + t_a)$$

The above equation does not include π, because we take into account the number of records, not the total record size.

- *Reading/writing of overflow buckets cost* is:

$$\left(1 - \min\left(\frac{H}{\sigma \times |R_i|}, 1\right)\right) \times \left(\pi \times \frac{R_i}{P} \times 2 \times IO\right)$$

Where σ is the overall GroupBy selectivity ratio, which is calculated as $\sigma = \sigma_p \times \sigma_g$.

- *Generating final result cost* is:

$$|R_i| \times \sigma \times t_w$$

- *Disk cost* for storing final result is:

$$(\pi \times R_i \times \sigma/P) \times IO$$

4.7 SUMMARY

Sorting and duplicate removal are tightly coupled database operations, in which the duplicate removal operation is normally incorporated into the sorting algorithm. Some key points in this chapter include:

- *Sorting and duplicate removal* in SQL are expressed in the *Order By* and *Distinct* clauses.
- *Five parallel algorithms for database sorting* are studied. These include (*i*) parallel merge-all sort, (*ii*) parallel binary-merge sort, (*iii*) parallel redistribution binary-merge sort, (*iv*) parallel redistribution merge-all sort, and (*v*) parallel partitioned sort. The third and fourth algorithms are the redistribution versions of the second and first, respectively.
- *Cost models for each parallel sort algorithm* are studied. The unique features of these cost models include external sorting cost, which depends on the size of the available buffer, and data redistribution to bridge the first and second steps of parallel sorting.
- The *redistribution versions* of parallel sorting algorithms, which are normally better than the non-redistribution version, are prone to *processing skew*, even though the initial data placement is uniformly distributed. Solving processing skew in parallel sorting is a challenge without which performance degradation can be expected, especially when a high degree of skewness is involved.
- As a *rule of thumb* for selecting an appropriate parallel sorting algorithm, the following rules can be adopted:
  - If *processing skew* degree is high, then use parallel redistribution merge-all sort.
  - If both *data skew* and *processing skew* degrees are high OR *no skew*, then use parallel partitioned sort.

In this chapter, three parallel algorithms for processing GroupBy queries in high-performance parallel database systems have also been studied. These algorithms are the *traditional* method covering merge all and hierarchical merging, the *two-phase* method, and the *redistribution* method. The last two methods differ in the order when aggregate processing is done, either before data redistribution or after data redistribution.

In general, the performance of two-phase and redistribution methods are better than those of the traditional and hierarchical merging methods. These two methods reduce the global aggregation phase, because the global aggregation operation is divided into all participating processors. This is not the case with the traditional method, as only one processor is used with the hierarchical-merging because the overhead of hierarchical pipeline merging is more expensive than the two-phase and redistribution methods.

The two-phase method works well when the number of groups is small, whereas the redistribution method works well when the number of groups is large.

In the middle ranges, both methods show comparable performance. The two-phase method is not able to do enough reduction in the number of records through local aggregation in the first phase if the selectivity is very small. Therefore, the second phase has to do a lot of work in global aggregation, thus significantly increasing the overhead. In other words, the two-phase method is good when there is enough filtering done in the local aggregation process, but not feasible when the selectivity does not filter the original records greatly. On the other hand, the redistribution method is good when the selectivity ratio between the original number of records and the groups produced by the query is large, possibly close to 1.0.

4.8 BIBLIOGRAPHICAL NOTES

The classical *The Art of Computer Programming, vol 3* by Knuth (1973) describes various sorting techniques. Bitton et al. (*ACM Comp Surv* 1984) present various parallel sorting techniques, whereas Iyer and Dias (*ICDE* 1990) and DeWitt et al. (1992) discuss systems issues in parallel database sorting.

Parallel sorting for databases uses external sorting methods. Yamane and Take (1987) and Zhao et al. (2000) proposed a parallel partition sort. Lorie and Young (*VLDB* 1999) concentrated on the communication costs of parallel sorting, whereas Lo and Huang (2002) focused on the skew aspects.

Recent work on parallel sorting is reported by Govindaraju et al. (*SIGMOD* 2006) on GPUTeraSort using graphics coprocessors, and Cérin et al. (*FGCS* 2006) on parallel sorting using heterogenous clusters.

4.9 EXERCISES

4.1. What is the commonality between *sort* and *group-by* operations?

4.2. Outline why *internal sorting* methods may not be directly used by *external sorting*.

4.3. Given a data set $D = \{55, 30, 68, 39, 1, 4, 49, 90, 34, 76, 82, 56, 31, 25, 78, 56, 38, 32, 88, 9, 44, 98, 11, 70, 66, 89, 99, 22, 23, 26\}$ and four processors, show step by step how the following parallel sorting methods work:

    a. Parallel merge-all sort

    b. Parallel binary-merge sort

    c. Parallel redistribution binary-merge sort

    d. Parallel redistribution merge-all sort

    e. Parallel partitioned sort

4.4. Given a data set $D = \{(A,55), (A,30), (D,68), (D,39), (D,1), (C,4), (C,49), (B,90), (D,34), (C,76), (D,82), (B,56), (B,31), (B,25), (B,78), (D,56), (B,38), (D,32), (D,88), (D,9), (A,44), (C,98), (A,11), (D,70), (D,66), (D,89), (D,99), (A,22), (D,23), (B,26)\}$ and three processors, the query is to calculate the sum of all the numerical attribute values in each group denoted by the alphabet. Show step by step how the following parallel group-by methods work:

a. Traditional methodas (merge-all and hierarchical merging)

b. Two-phase method

c. Redistribution method

4.5. The *overflow buckets cost* is used in the processing cost calculation especially when the hash table grows bigger than the allocated main-memory. Discuss the possibility for achieving a superlinear speed up, when more processors arc added to the system with the consequence that each processor may now be responsible for a smaller partition of the data.

4.6. Give a proof for the following rule: If *processing skew* degree is high, then use parallel redistribution merge-all sort, whereas if both *data skew* and *processing skew* degrees are high or *no skew*, then use parallel partitioned sort.

4.7. Investigate your favourite parallel DBMS, and show how parallel sort and parallel group-by are expressed in SQL.

Chapter 5

Parallel Join

The join operation is one of the most common operations in relational databases where information is split into multiple tables because of normalization. Consequently, when the information needs to be assembled for presentation to users, the data needs to be gathered from multiple tables through join operations.

The join operation is also considered to be one of the most expensive operations in relational database processing as it is a binary operation that requires two tables for processing. Many algorithms have been proposed to reduce the complexity of join operations. Since the tables to be joined may involve a large number of records, parallel processing of a join operation is a sensible solution.

This chapter focuses on parallel algorithms for join queries. It starts with Section 5.1 describing the nature of join operations. Section 5.2 describes serial algorithms for join operations. Section 5.3 focuses on various parallel algorithms for join queries using different kinds of data partitioning. Section 5.4 discusses the cost models, while Section 5.5 describes options available for optimizing parallel join algorithms.

5.1 JOIN OPERATIONS

A join operation is used to link two tables based on the nominated attribute—one from each table. The link is created because of the equality of the values from the two designated attributes. Because of this equality element, this type of join query is called an *equi-join* query. Figure 5.1 gives an illustration of a join query between two tables, table *R* and table *S*, based on attribute *attr2* of table *R* and attribute *attr1* of table *S*. The results are the matched records from the two tables.

A typical equi-join query would be a join between two tables through a link from the primary key (*PK*) of one table to the foreign key (*FK*) of the other table. This link between two tables is often necessary when assembling information, since the desired information is often split during the design as a result of the normalization process.

High-Performance Parallel Database Processing and Grid Databases,
by David Taniar, Clement Leung, Wenny Rahayu, and Sushant Goel
Copyright © 2008 John Wiley & Sons, Inc.

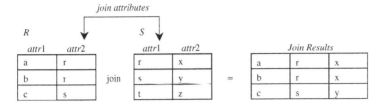

Figure 5.1   The join operation

An example of a *PK-FK* equi-join is "retrieve each student together with their enrolment details". This query joins table `Enrolment` and table `Student`. The SQL of this query is shown below.

Query 5.1:
```
Select *
From STUDENT S, ENROLMENT E
Where S.Sid = E.Sid;
```

The attribute that links both tables, `Student` and `Enrolment`, is attribute `Sid` that exists in both tables.

Joining can also be performed on two unrelated tables. The join operation is often required by users, even though there is no obvious relationship between these two tables. The join must, however, also be based on a designated attribute of both tables. In other words, the relationship between the two tables is not established through the design, but through the join query.

An example of a non-PK-FK equi-join query is "retrieve pairs of lecturers and courses from the same department". The query joins table `Lecturer` and table `Course`, and the join attribute is `Ldept` of `Lecturer` and attribute `Cdept` of `Course`. In our database schema, both tables `Lecturer` and `Course` are not directly related, apart from a nondirect relationship through table `Enrolment`. However, in this query, we explicitly join the two tables. The SQL statement for the above query is as follows.

Query 5.2:
```
Select *
From LECTURER L, COURSE C
Where L.Ldept = C.Cdept;
```

An example of two-PK equi-join is "retrieve lecturers who are also students". This can be obtained by joining tables `Student` and `Lecturer` on their PKs. Assume the value of a person's ID (e.g., student ID and lecturer ID) is unique in the university, and therefore a lecturer who already has an ID when enrolling in a program (e.g., graduate program) maintains his/her ID. The SQL statement for this query is as follows:

Query 5.3:
```
Select *
```

```
From LECTURER L, STUDENT S
Where L.Lid = S.Sid;
```

From the query point of view, there is no difference among these three equi-join queries, as all of these queries join two tables and the join predicates are clearly defined. However, when processing these equi-join queries, the difference is escalated because of the presence of an index for every PK.

5.2 SERIAL JOIN ALGORITHMS

To study parallel join algorithms, it is necessary to first understand serial join algorithms, that is, join algorithms implemented in nonparallel machines. The rationale is that parallel join algorithms adopt a data partitioning parallelism approach, whereby parallelism is achieved through data partitioning. In this case, the same algorithm is applied to different parts of the data. Consequently, a join operation implemented on each processor would employ a serial join algorithm.

There have been many join algorithms proposed in the literature. However, they fall into one of the three categories:

- Nested-loop join algorithm,
- Sort-merge join algorithm, and
- Hash-based join algorithms

The next three sections will study each of these. As an ongoing example throughout this chapter, the sample data in Figure 5.2 will be used. For simplicity, the two tables are named table *R* and table *S*, each of which has two attributes: one is an alphabetical attribute, and the other is a numerical attribute. The join attribute is the numerical attribute. Table *R* has 15 records, whereas table *S* has 9 records. To make the alphabetical attributes more meaningful and easy to remember, the value is an alphabetical value starting from letter "A" following the order of the alphabet (e.g., table *R* has records *A*dele, *B*ob, *C*lement, *D*ave, etc, whereas table *S* has records *A*rts, *B*usiness, *C*ompSc, *D*ance, etc; we can therefore assume that table *R* is related to students and table *S* to courses). The numerical attributes have random numerical values. Note that in this case, the join operation produces three records.

5.2.1 Nested-Loop Join Algorithm

Nested-loop join is the simplest form of join algorithm—for each record of the first table, it goes through all records of the second table. This is repeated for all records of the first table. It is called a nested loop because it consists of two levels of loops: *inner loop* (looping for the second table) and *outer loop* (looping for the first table).

Using the sample data in Figure 5.2, first take the first record of table *R* (record Adele) and then examine table *S* record by record to see whether there is a match

Table R			Table S			Join Results		
Adele	8		Arts	8		Adele	8	Arts
Bob	22		Business	15		Ed	11	Health
Clement	16		CompSc	2		Joanna	2	CompSc
Dave	23		Dance	12	
Ed	11		Engineering	7	
Fung	25		Finance	21	
Goel	3		Geology	10	
Harry	17		Health	11	
Irene	14		IT	18	
Joanna	2	
Kelly	6	
Lim	20	
Meng	1	
Noor	5	
Omar	19	

Figure 5.2   Sample data

based on the join attribute. In this case, it happens that the match is found in the first record of table S (record Arts). Assuming that the join attribute is based on unique attributes, once a match is found in table S, there is no need to continue searching for other matches for Adele. The same process is repeated for the second record of table R (record Bob). In this case, the worst scenario happens, where none of the records in table S matches Bob. This process continues until all records from table R are processed. The results as shown in Figure 5.2 produce three matches. A nested-loop join algorithm is summarized in Figure 5.3.

In terms of its efficiency, note that in general every record in table S has to be visited (read) as many times as there are records in table R. If there are N records in table R and M records in table S, the efficiency of a nested-loop join algorithm is basically $O(NM)$. Although the algorithm is very simple, it is definitely not efficient, because of repeated I/O scans of one of the tables.

Algorithm: Nested-loop join

```
Input: Tables R and S
Output: Query Result Qr
1. Let Qr = {}
2. For each record of table R
3.    Read record from table R
4.    For each record of table S
5.       Read record from table S
6.       Compare the join attributes
7.       If matched Then
8.          Store the records into Qr
```

Figure 5.3   Nested-loop join algorithm

5.2.2   Sort-Merge Join Algorithm

Sort-merge join is based on sorting and merging operations. The first step of joining is to sort the two tables based on the joining attribute in an ascending order, and the second step is merging the two sorted tables. If the value of the joining attribute in *R* is smaller than that in *S*, it skips to the next value of the joining attribute in *R*. On the other hand, if the value of the joining attribute in *R* is greater than that in *S*, it skips to the next value of the joining attribute in *S*. When the two values match, the two corresponding records are concatenated and placed into the query result. This process continues until one of the tables runs out of records.

Using the sample data from Figure 5.2, the two sorted tables are shown in Figure 5.4. The sorting is based on the join attributes, which are the numerical attributes from the two tables.

After the two tables have been sorted based on the join attributes, the merging process starts. Using the sample data in Figure 5.4, first take the first record of table *R* (record Meng), compare this with the first record of table *S* (record CompSc), and see whether the two numerical attribute values are the same. If they are not the same, then the record that has a smaller value has to move on. In this case, we need to move on to the second record of table *R* (record Joanna). Then we compare again with the same record of table *S* (record CompSc). Since they match, we put them into the result.

If the join attribute values are unique, when a match is found the next process is to take the next records from both tables. In this case, after record Joanna and CompSc are matched, we take record Goel from table *R* and record Engineering from table *S*. The process is then repeated until one of the tables has exhausted all the records. Figure 5.4 shows that the next match after Joanna/CompSc is Adele/Arts, followed by Ed/Health.

Table R			Table S			Join Results		
Meng	1		CompSc	2		Joanna	2	CompSc
Joanna	2		Engineering	7		Adele	8	Arts
Goel	3		Arts	8		Ed	11	Health
Noor	5		Geology	10				
Kelly	6		Health	11				
Adele	8		Dance	12				
Ed	11		Business	15				
Irene	14		IT	18				
Clement	16		Finance	21				
Harry	17							
Omar	19							
Lim	20							
Bob	22							
Dave	23							
Fung	25							

Figure 5.4   Sorted tables

Algorithm: Sort-merge join

Input: Tables R and S
Output: Query Result Qr
1. Let Qr = {}
2. Sort records of table R based on the join attribute
3. Sort records of table S based on the join attribute
4. Let i = 1 and j = 1
5. Repeat
6.   Read record $R(i)$
7.   Read record $S(j)$
8.   If join attribute $R(i)$ < join attribute $S(j)$ Then
9. $i++$
10.   Else
11.   If join attribute $R(i)$ > join attribute $S(j)$ Then
12. $j++$
13.   Else
14.   Put records $R(i)$ and $S(j)$ into the Qr
15. $i++$; $j++$
16.   If either $R(i)$ or $S(j)$ is EOF Then
17.   Break

Figure 5.5   Sort-merge join algorithm

The sort-merge join algorithm is also quite simple. The main task is basically sorting, which is done first to the two tables. The merging itself is then quite straightforward. Figure 5.5 summarizes the sort-merge join algorithm, where the join attributes are assumed to be unique.

The sort-merge join algorithm shown in Figure 5.5 needs to be revised slightly if the join attributes are not unique. In this case, there is a small nested loop among duplicate values of the matched join attributes. For example, if there is another record after Joanna that has the same number as Joanna (e.g., Jon/2) and also there is another record after CompSc that has the same number as CompSc (e.g., CompEng/2), then there will be a small nested loop among these records to produce four records, namely Joanna/2/CompSc, Joanna/2/CompEng, Jon/2/CompSc, and Jon/2/CompEng.

In terms of its efficiency, the sort-merge join algorithm is an improvement compared with the nested-loop join. Sorting is generally $O(NlogN)$ for one table (and $O(MlogM)$ for the other table), whereas merging the two sorted tables is linear (i.e., $O(N+M)$). This is considerably better than the nested loop of $O(NM)$, especially if N and M are very large.

5.2.3 Hash-Based Join Algorithm

A number of hash-based join algorithms such as hybrid-hash and Grace hash join, have been proposed in the literature. A hash-based join is basically made up of two processes: *hashing* and *probing*. A hash table is created by hashing all records of the first table using a particular hash function. Records from the second table are also hashed with the same hash function and probed. If any match is found, the two records are concatenated and placed in the query result.

A decision must be made about which table is to be hashed and which table is to be probed. Since a hash table has to be created, it would be better to choose the smaller table for hashing and the larger table for probing. For the sample data in Figure 5.2, table *S* is to be hashed. Figure 5.6 illustrates how table *S* is hashed into a hash table. In this example, assume that the hash function used in the hashing process works by summing the first and second digits of the hashed attribute, which in this case is the join attribute. The hashing is done record by record. First, record Arts/8 is hashed to hash table index entry 8, and then record Business/15 is hashed to hash index 6.

In any hashing process, collision must be taken care of. For example, record CompSc/2 is hashed to index entry 2 in the hash table, and record Health/11 is hashed to the same hash table index. In this example, collision is handled by creating additional entries in the same index entry. From the sample in Figure 5.6, there are several collisions, as well as several empty index spots.

After the hashing is complete, the next stage is probing. In the probing stage, take the other table and hash record by record with the same hashing function. If it is hashed to a nonempty index entry, then examine each record in that entry to determine whether a match has been found.

Continuing the example in Figure 5.7, record Adele/8 is hashed and probed into index entry 8, and a match with Arts/8 is found. Another example is record Ed/11, which is hashed and probed into index entry 2. Since there is more than one record on that index entry, conduct a traversal of each of the records and examine whether it is matched with Ed/2. In this case, Ed/11 found a match with Health/11. The same is the case with Joanna/2, which found a match with CompSc/2.

Other records in table *R* were hashed either into an empty index entry or hashed into a non-empty index entry, but did not find a match. An example of the former

Table S

Arts	8
Business	15
CompSc	2
Dance	12
Engineering	7
Finance	21
Geology	10
Health	11
IT	16

hashed into →

Hash Table

Index	Entries	
1	Geology/10	
2	CompSc/2	Health/11
3	Dance/12	Finance/21
4		
5		
6	Business/15	
7	Engineering/7	
8	Arts/8	
9	IT/18	
10		
11		
12		

Figure 5.6   Hashing table *S*

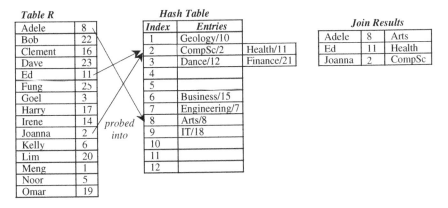

Figure 5.7   Probing table *R*

is record Bob/22, which is hashed into index entry 4 which is empty. An example of the latter is Clement/16 hashed into index entry 7 but which did not find any match with the record in that index entry.

Figure 5.8 summarizes an algorithm for a hash-based join (assume table *S* is used for hashing, whereas table *R* is used for probing). Note from the hashing and probing process mentioned above that each record from the above two tables are scanned only once. Consequently, there is no repeat scan as in the

---

Algorithm: Hash-based join

```
Input: Tables R and S
Output: Query Result Qr
1. Let Qr = {}
2. Let H be a hash function
3. For each record in table S
4.    Read a record from table S
5.    Hash the record based on join attribute value using
      hash function H into hash table
6. For each record in table R
7.    Read a record from table R
8.    Hash the record based on join attribute value
      using H
9.    Probe into the hash table
10.   If an index entry is found Then
11.      Compare each record on this index entry
         with the record of table S
12.      If matched Then
13.         Put the pair into Qr
```

Figure 5.8   Hash-based join algorithm

N	M	O(NM)	O(NlogN+MlogM+N+M)	O(N+M)
10	10	100	40	20
100	100	10,000	600	200
1000	1000	1,000,000	8000	2000
10,000	10,000	100,000,000	100,000	20,000
100,000	100,000	10,000,000,000	1,200,000	200,000
1,000,000	1,000,000	1,000,000,000,000	14,000,000	2,000,000

Figure 5.9   Complexity comparison of the three serial join algorithms

nested-loop and sort-merge join algorithms. Therefore, hash-based join, which has a linear complexity of $O(N + M)$, is considered more efficient than nested-loop and sort-merge join.

5.2.4 Comparison

The complexity of join algorithms is normally dependent on the number of times that a disk scan needs to be performed. Disk scan is considered to be the most expensive operation in computer systems, as it requires disk arm movement, which is very slow in comparison with CPU operations. Therefore, minimizing disk scan is the ultimate objective not only in join algorithms, but also in any query processing algorithms.

The complexity of the three join algorithms as discussed above is as follows:

- Nested-loop join algorithm $= O(NM)$
- Sort-merge join algorithm $= O(NlogN + MlogM + N + M)$
- Hash-based join algorithm $= O(N + M)$

The hash-based join algorithm is widely accepted as the most efficient join algorithm, as proven by the complexity listed above. To illustrate how well a hash-based join algorithm performs, Figure 5.9 shows the complexity of the three algorithms in various data sizes N and M.

In Figure 5.9, we note that the complexity of $O(NM)$ grows exponentially. When N and M are large, $O(NM)$ grows massively. On the other hand, linear complexity like $O(N + M)$ is quite good. $O(NlogN)$ is not that bad compared with nested loop, but linear complexity $O(N + M)$ is the best. On the basis of this simplified comparison, it is obvious that the hash-based join algorithm is the best choice.

5.3 PARALLEL JOIN ALGORITHMS

Parallelism of join queries is achieved through data parallelism, whereby the same task is applied to different parts of the data. In other words, after data partitioning has been completed, each processor will have its own data to work with. Subsequently, each processor will apply any serial join algorithm. Once this is carried out in each processor, the final results of the join operation are consolidated from the results obtained from different processors. Based on this, the parallel join algorithm is determined by the type of data partitioning used in parallel join.

There are generally two kinds of data partitioning that can be used in any parallel join algorithms. They are:

○ Divide and broadcast and
○ Disjoint data partitioning

The first data partitioning method has some degree of replication, whereas the second one has no replication. For the local join itself, as already mentioned above, any serial join algorithm may be used. However, because of the superiority of the hash-based join algorithm, it is desirable to use a hash-based join algorithm in each processor. Therefore, the local join uses a hash-based serial join algorithm.

In the next two sections, the two data partitioning methods for parallel join algorithms will be described separately.

5.3.1 Divide and Broadcast-Based Parallel Join Algorithms

"Divide and broadcast"-based parallel join algorithms are composed of two stages: data partitioning using the divide and broadcast method and a local join.

The divide and broadcast data partitioning method consists of dividing one table into multiple disjoint partitions, where each partition is allocated a processor, and broadcasts the other table to all available processors. Dividing one table may be done simply by using equal division, so that each partition will have the same size, whereas broadcasting is actually replicating the content of the second table to all processors. Thus it is preferable for the smaller table to be broadcast and the larger table to be divided.

Using the sample data presented above in Figure 5.2, assume that a shared-nothing architecture is used, whereby three processors are available in the system. The data is already partitioned and stored in each processor. Figure 5.10 shows the initial data placement on each processor. Assume that table R is equally partitioned into three tables using simple table division whereby the first five records go to processor 1, the next five to processor 2, and the last five to processor 3. For table S, assume that a simple round-robin partitioning of the table has been used.

Since the data is already initially partitioned, what needs to be done is the broadcasting. Since table S is smaller than table R, it is desirable that table S be broadcast and table R be left partitioned. Therefore, each processor loads its table S partition (e.g., partition $S1$, partition $S2$, and partition $S3$, respectively) and broadcasts it to all other processors. For example, processor 1 will broadcast partition $S1$ to processors 2 and 3, and processor 2 will broadcast partition $S2$ to

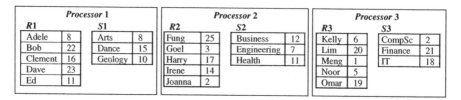

Figure 5.10   Initial data placement

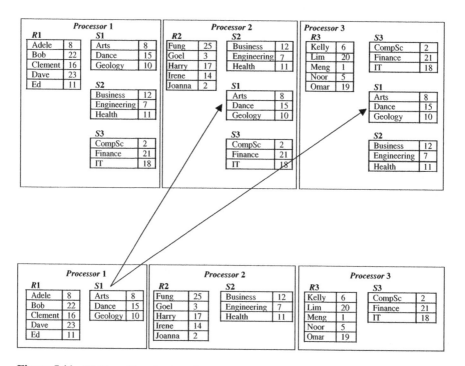

Figure 5.11   Divide and broadcast result

processors 1 and 3, etc. Partitions from table R are left untouched since table R is already initially partitioned.

Figure 5.11 shows the position after the broadcast stage, which is the end of the divide and broadcast data partitioning. Note that on each processor there is one partition from table R and the complete table S. To clarify the picture, the arrows show that partition $S1$ is broadcast to processors 2 and 3.

Once the divide and broadcast partitioning is complete, each processor may work independently to join one partition of table R with the complete table S. Any serial join algorithm may be used. However, for efficiency purposes, a hash-based serial join may be applied. Figure 5.12 shows the results from each processor.

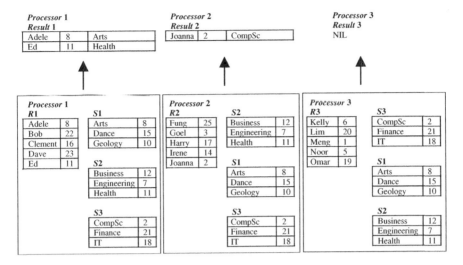

Figure 5.12   Join results based on divide and broadcast

The final result from all processors is consolidated. Not all processors may produce some results. In contrast, some other processors may dominate the results. In the above example, processor 3 does not produce any result, whereas processor 1 produces two-thirds of the overall results.

From the load balancing point of view, the load of each processor in terms of the number of records processed is the same; that is, in each processor there will be an equal fragment of the first table and the whole second table, and hence there is no load imbalance problem. However, the processing method imposed by the broadcast of one of the tables causes inefficiency that includes not only the broadcasting overhead but also the storage overhead.

However, the problem of workload imbalance will occur if the table that is partitioned is not partitioned equally. For example, if table R in the above example is already partitioned in each processor but the partitioning is not balanced, then workload imbalance will occur.

The load balancing problem theoretically might still occur even when table R is partitioned equally, as in the above example. This problem arises from the imbalance of the result production. Note that in the sample shown in Figure 5.12, the results are not balanced in each processor. Some processors that produce more results than others might work a little harder than others. However, this problem is not as bad as it would be if the partitioned table were not partitioned equally in the first place.

If a shared-memory architecture is used, then there is no replication of the broadcast table. Consequently, each processor will access the entire table S and access a portion of table R. However, if each processor does not have enough working space, then the local join might not be able to use a hash-based join.

Algorithm: Parallel nested-loop join

Input: Tables R and S
Output: Query Result Qr
1. **Parallel** For each record of table R
2.   Read record from table R
3.   **Serial** For each record of table S
4.   Comparison between two records to find a match
5.   Store the match in Qr

Figure 5.13   Parallel nested-loop join algorithm

A nested-loop serial join would be used as a local join instead. This would incur another inefficiency problem.

Basically a parallel nested-loop join algorithm works as follows. The outer for loop uses a parallel for loop, in which a parallel round-robin can be used. The inner for loop, on the other hand, is a serial for loop. This has the implication that the inner loop is executed as a whole by each processor. Therefore, the outer loop is the divide part, whereas the inner loop is the broadcast part. Figure 5.13 illustrates a parallel nested-loop join algorithm, which has a manifestation of the divide and broadcast partitioning.

Nevertheless, the bottom line of the "divide and broadcast"-based parallel join algorithm is that one table is partitioned, whereas the other is replicated/broadcast. The limiting element of this type of parallel join algorithm is the replication/broadcast.

5.3.2 Disjoint Partitioning-Based Parallel Join Algorithms

Disjoint partitioning-based parallel join algorithms also consist of two stages: a data partitioning stage using a disjoint partitioning and a local join. For the data partitioning, a disjoint partitioning, such as range partitioning or hash partitioning, may be used.

In range partitioning, both tables are partitioned based on the join attributes with the same range partitioning function. If a shared-nothing architecture is used, whereby the table is already partitioned, each processor has to redistribute the records following a range function. This is similar to the parallel redistribution sort discussed in Chapter 4.

Figure 5.14 illustrates range partitioning based on the sample data presented in Figure 5.10. In this case, assume that the range is that processor 1 will get records with join attribute value between 1 and 9, processor 2 between 10 and 19, and processor 3 between 20 and 29. To simplify the illustration, one arrow shows that record Adele/8 stays in processor 1, whereas record Bob/22 goes from processor 1 to processor 3.

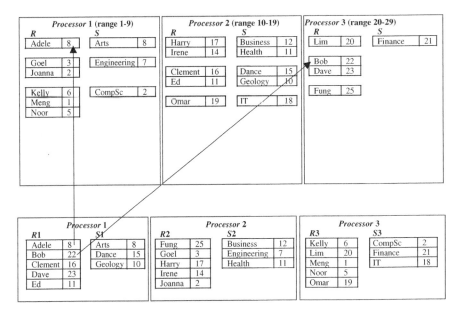

Figure 5.14   Range partitioning

Note that, as a result of range partitioning, the load of each processor may differ, thereby creating a load imbalance problem. For example, processor 2 has 10 records in total from the two tables, whereas processor 3 has only 5 records from the two tables. Therefore, it can be expected that processor 3 will require only half the time to complete the job compared with that taken by processor 2.

As for the local join, any serial join algorithm might be used. Figure 5.15 shows the results of the join. Since range partitioning is used, the results on each processor will also be according to the range partitioning. For example, processor 1 produces 2 results: one is Adele/8/Arts and the other is Joanna/2/CompSc; processor 2 produces Ed/11/Health. Note that in this case, the results composition is slightly different from that of divide and broadcast as shown in Figure 5.12 (where processor 1 produces Adele and Ed and processor 2 produces Joanna). Nevertheless, the overall results that are amalgamated from all processors are the same with both parallel join methods.

If a shared-memory architecture is used instead of a shared-nothing architecture, the sorting will be carried out using parallel sorting as discussed in Chapter 4. Once the two tables have been sorted, a parallel merge can be performed.

Another disjoint data partitioning might be used, that is, hash partitioning, as shown in the following example. In this example, assume that the hash partitioning function is the sum of each digit of the partitioning attribute value. For example, record Bob/22 will be hashed to 4(= 2+2), whereas record Clement/16 will be hashed to 7(= 1+6). Once each record has been hashed based on the join attribute, the record will be distributed to a particular processor. For example, assume that processor 1 will take hash 1, 4, 7, etc; processor 2 hashed to 2, 5, 8, etc; and

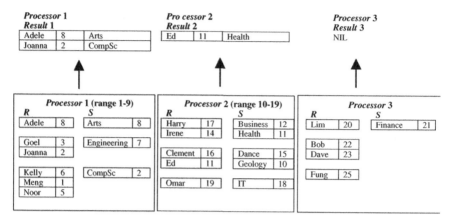

Figure 5.15 Join results based on range partitioning

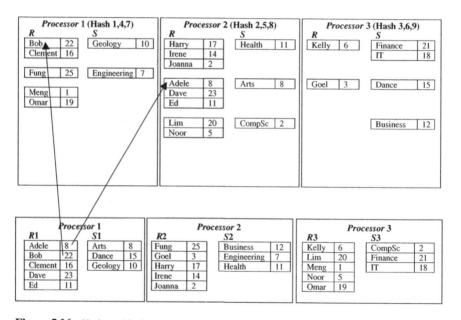

Figure 5.16 Hash partitioning

processor 3 to 3, 6, 9, etc. Figure 5.16 shows the hash partitioning of the same data used in Figure 5.10. For clarity of presentation, in Figure 5.16 the arrow from record Adele/8 shows that it is hashed into processor 2, whereas record Bob/22 is hashed to processor 1.

Similar to range partitioning, hash partitioning also produces some skew in the distribution. Basically, in any disjoint data partitioning, skew distribution is inevitable, because of the nature of the distribution of the data itself.

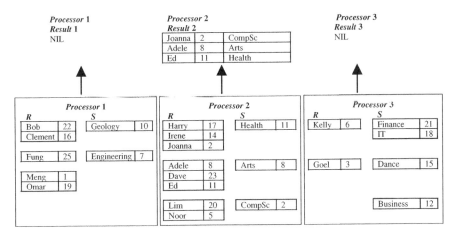

Figure 5.17 Join results based on hash partitioning

For the local join, any serial join algorithm may be used. However, it is appropriate to use a hash join algorithm. Figure 5.17 shows the join results based on hash partitioning. In this example, only processor 2 produces the query results, whereas the other two processors do not produce anything.

For a shared-memory version, the hash partitioning is done in parallel. Once the hash table has been built, the probing is also done in parallel. In other words, it applies a parallel hash join algorithm.

Figure 5.18 shows a high level pseudo-code of a parallel hash join algorithm. Parallelism is achieved through the two parallels for loop, one for the hashing and the other for the probing. The hash table itself, which is created during the hashing process, is shared among all processors.

In summary, for shared-memory architecture, the hash partitioning-based parallel join algorithm is based on hash join (called parallel hash join algorithm), whereas the range partitioning based parallel join algorithm is based on

---

Algorithm: Parallel hash join

Input: Tables R and S
Output: Query Result Qr
1. **Parallel** For each record of table R
2.   Read record from table R and hash into a hash table
3. **Parallel** For each record of table S
4.   Read record S, hash, and probe
5.   Put the match in Qr

Figure 5.18 Parallel hash join algorithm

sort-merge join (hence the name parallel sort-merge join algorithm). The divide and broadcast-based parallel join algorithm is based on nested-loop join and hence is called a parallel nested-loop join algorithm.

5.4 COST MODELS

Cost notations were previously listed in Chapter 2. The cost models to be discussed in this section are mainly the two data partitionings for parallel join and the local join processing.

5.4.1 Cost Models for Divide and Broadcast

It is assumed that the tables have already been partitioned and placed in each processor. In this case, a shared-nothing architecture is used. Figure 5.10 above gives an illustration of the initial data placement. Based on this scenario, there is no cost for the divide phase of the divide and broadcast partitioning parallel join. The cost component is applied only to the broadcast stage (as in Figure 5.11).

The cost components for the broadcast stage can be divided into three phases according to the order of the broadcasting process. The first phase is the data loading by each processor, followed by the broadcasting (replication) in the second phase. The final phase is storing the replicated data in each processor.

The first phase of data loading consists of the *scan costs* and the *select costs*, which are as follows. In this case, it is assumed that table S is broadcast, and therefore, variable S is used in the cost equations, instead of R.

- *Scan cost* for loading data from local disk in each processor is:

$$(S_i/P) \times IO$$

- *Select cost* for getting record out of data page is:

$$|S_i| \times (t_r + t_w)$$

The second phase is the broadcast cost, which is done by each processor broadcasting its fragment to all other processors. Subsequent to this, all other processors must receive all other fragments from all other processors. Therefore, the main costs for this phase are data transfer and receiving costs, which are as follows:

- *Data transfer cost* is:

$$(S_i/P) \times (N - 1) \times (m_p + m_l)$$

The $(N - 1)$ indicates that each processor must broadcast to all other processors. Note that broadcasting from one processor to the others has to be done one processor at a time, although all processors send the broadcast in parallel.

The above cost equation would be the same as

$$(S - S_i) \times (m_p + m_l)$$

where $(S - S_i)$ indicates the size of other fragments, which is the total table size minus the fragment that each processor has.

- *Receiving records cost* is:

$$(S - S_i) \times (m_p)$$

The receiving cost is similar to the sending cost. The only difference is the transfer cost, whereby the sending cost induces an extra cost m_l for each byte sent across the network.

Finally, in the third phase, each processor after receiving all other fragments of table S must store the table on local disk.

- *Disk cost* for storing the table is:

$$(S - S_i) \times IO$$

5.4.2 Cost Models for Disjoint Partitioning

The disjoint partitioning costs also comprise three main elements according to the three phases of the disjoint partitioning. These are loading costs, distribution costs, and finally storing costs.

The loading costs include scan costs and select costs. Since both tables R and S need to be loaded, these are reflected in the cost components:

- *Scan cost* for loading tables R and S from local disk in each processor is:

$$((R_i/P) + (S_i/P)) \times IO$$

- *Select cost* for getting record out of data page is:

$$(|R_i| + |S_i|) \times (t_r + t_w)$$

The distribution cost also includes the cost of determining the destination of each record. If a hash partitioning method is used, then the destination determination cost is related to the hashing function cost to determine the processor to which each record will be sent. Then this will be followed by the actual sending and receiving costs.

- *Finding destination cost* is:

$$(|R_i| + |S_i|) \times (t_d)$$

- *Data transfer cost* is:

$$((R_i/P) + (S_i/P)) \times (m_p + m_l)$$

R_i and S_i in the cost equation indicate the fragment size of both tables in each processor.

- *Receiving records cost* is:

$$((R_i/P) + (S_i/P)) \times (m_p)$$

Both data transfer and receiving costs look similar, as also mentioned above for the divide and broadcast cost. However, for disjoint partitioning the size of R_i and S_i in the data transfer cost is likely to be different from that of the receiving cost. The reason is as follows. Following the example in Figures 5.14 and 5.16, R_i and S_i in the data transfer cost are the size of each fragment of both tables in each processor. Again, assuming that the initial data placement is done with a round-robin or any other equal partitioning, each fragment size will be equal. Therefore, R_i and S_i in the data transfer cost are simply dividing the total table size by the available number of processors.

However, R_i and S_i in the receiving cost are most likely skewed (as already mentioned in Chapter 2 on analytical models). As shown in Figures 5.14 and 5.16, the spread of the fragments after the distribution is not even. Therefore, the skew model must be taken into account, and consequently the values of R_i and S_i in the receiving cost are different from those of the data transfer cost.

Finally, the last phase is data storing, which involves storing all records received by each processor.

- *Disk cost* for storing the result of data distribution is:

$$((R_i/P) + (S_i/P)) \times IO$$

5.4.3 Cost Models for Local Join

For the local join, since a hash-based join is the most efficient join algorithm, it is assumed that a hash-based join is used in the local join. The cost of the local join with a hash-based join comprises three main phases: data loading from each processor, the joining process (hashing and probing), and result storing in each processor.

The data loading consists of scan costs and select costs. These are identical to those of the disjoint partitioning costs, which are:

- *Scan cost* $= ((R_i/P) + (S_i/P)) \times IO$
- *Select cost* $= (|R_i| + |S_i|) \times (t_r + t_w)$

It has been emphasized that $(|R_i| + |S_i|)$ as well as $((R_i/P) + (S_i/P))$ correspond to the values in the receiving and disk costs of the disjoint partitioning.

The join process itself is basically incurring hashing and probing costs, which are as follows:

- *Join costs* involve reading, hashing, and probing:

$$(|R_i| \times (t_r + t_h)) + (|S_i| \times (t_r + t_h + t_j))$$

The process is basically reading each record R and hashing it to a hash table. After all records R have been processed, records S can be read, hashed, and probed. If they are matched, the matching records are written out to the query result.

The hashing process is very much determined by the size of the hash table that can fit into main memory. If the memory size is smaller than the hash table size, we normally partition the hash table into multiple buckets whereby each bucket can perfectly fit into main memory. All but the first bucket are spooled to disk.

Based on this scenario, we must include the I/O cost for reading and writing overflow buckets, which is as follows.

- *Reading/writing of overflow buckets* cost is the I/O cost associated with the limited ability of main memory to accommodate the entire hash table. This cost includes the costs for reading and writing records not processed in the first phase of hashing.

$$\left(1 - \min\left(\frac{H}{|S_i|}, 1\right)\right) \times \left(\frac{S_i}{P} \times 2 \times IO\right)$$

Although this looks similar to that mentioned in other chapters regarding the overhead of overflow buckets, there are two significant differences. One is that only S_i is included in the cost component, because only the table S is hashed; and the second difference is that the projection and selection variables are not included, because all records S are hashed.

The final cost is the query results storing cost, consisting of generating result cost and disk cost.

- *Generating result records cost* is the number of selected records multiplied by the writing unit cost.

$$|R_i| \times \sigma_j \times |S_i| \times t_w$$

Note that the cost is reduced by the join selectivity factor σ_j, where the smaller the selectivity factor, the lower the number of records produced by the join operation.

- *Disk cost* for storing the final result is the number of pages needed to store the final aggregate values times the disk unit cost, which is:

$$(\pi_R \times R_i \times \sigma_j \times \pi_S \times S_i/P) \times IO$$

As not all attributes from the two tables are included in the join query result, both table sizes are reduced by the projectivity ratios π_R and π_S.

The total join cost is the sum of all cost equations mentioned in this section.

5.5   PARALLEL JOIN OPTIMIZATION

The main aim of query processing in general and parallel query processing in particular is to speed up the query processing time, so that the amount of elapsed time may be reduced. In terms of parallelism, the reduction in the query elapsed time can be achieved by having each processor finish its execution as early as possible and all processors spend their working time as evenly as possible. This is called the problem of load balancing. In other words, load balancing is one of the main aspects of parallel optimization, especially in query processing.

In parallel join, there is another important optimization factor apart from load balancing. Remember the cost models in the previous section, especially in the disjoint partitioning, and note that after the data has been distributed to the designated processors, the data has to be stored on disk. Then in the local join, the data has to be loaded from the disk again. This is certainly inefficient. This problem is related to the problem of managing main memory.

In this section, the above two problems will be discussed in order to achieve high performance of parallel join query processing. First, the main memory issue will be addressed, followed by the load balancing issue.

5.5.1   Optimizing Main Memory

As indicated before, disk access is widely recognized as being one of the most expensive operations, which has to be reduced as much as possible. Reduction in disk access means that data from the disk should not be loaded/scanned unnecessarily. If it is possible, only a single scan of the data should be done. If this is not possible, then the number of scans should be minimized. This is the only way to reduce disk access cost.

If main memory size is unlimited, then single disk scan can certainly be guaranteed. Once the data has been loaded from disk to main memory, the processor is accessing only the data that is already in main memory. At the end of the process, perhaps some data need to be written back to disk. This is the most optimal scenario. However, main memory size is not unlimited. This imposes some requirements that disk access may be needed to be scanned more than once. But minimal disk access is always the ultimate aim. This can be achieved by maximizing the usage of main memory.

As already discussed above, parallel join algorithms are composed of data partitioning and local join. In the cost model described in the previous section, after the distribution the data is stored on disk, which needs to be reloaded by the local join. To maximize the usage of main memory, after the distribution phase not all data should be written on disk. They should be left in main memory, so that when the local join processing starts, it does not have to load from the disk. The size of the data left in the main memory can be as big as the allocated size for data in the main memory.

Assuming that the size of main memory for data is M (in bytes), the disk cost for storing data distribution with a disjoint partitioning is:

$$((R_i/P) + (S_i/P) - M) \times IO$$

and the local join scan cost is then reduced by M as well.

$$((R_i/P) + (S_i/P) - M) \times IO$$

When the data from this main memory block is processed, it can be swapped with a new block. Therefore, the saving is really achieved by not having to load/scan the disk for one main memory block.

5.5.2   Load Balancing

Load imbalance is one of the main obstacles in parallel query processing. This problem is normally caused by uneven data partitioning. Because of this, the processing load of each processor becomes uneven, and consequently the processors will not finish their processing time uniformly. This data skew further creates processing skew. This skew problem is particularly common in parallel join algorithms.

The load imbalance problem does not occur in the divide and broadcast-based parallel join, because the load of each processor is even. However, this kind of parallel join is unattractive simply because one of the tables needs to be replicated or broadcast. Therefore, it is commonly expected that the parallel join algorithm adopts a disjoint partitioning-based parallel join algorithm. Hence, the load imbalance problem needs to be solved, in order to take full advantage of disjoint partitioning. If the load imbalance problem is not taken care of, it is likely that the divide and broadcast-based parallel join algorithm might be more attractive and efficient. To maximize the full potential of the disjoint partitioning-based parallel join algorithm, there is no alternative but to resolve the load imbalance problem. Or at least, the load imbalance problem must be minimized. The question is how to solve this processing skew problem so that all processors may finish their processing time as uniformly as possible, thereby minimizing the effect of skew.

In disjoint partitioning, each processor processes its own fragment, by evaluating and hashing record by record, and places/distributes each record according to the hash value. At the other end, each processor will receive some records from other processors too. All records that are received by a processor, combined with the records that are not distributed, form a fragment for this processor. At the end of the distribution phase, each processor will have its own fragment and the content of this fragment is all the records that have already been correctly assigned to this processor. In short, one processor will have one fragment.

As discussed above, the sizes of these fragments are likely to be different from one another, thereby creating processing skew in the local join phase. Load balancing in this situation is often carried out by producing more fragments than the

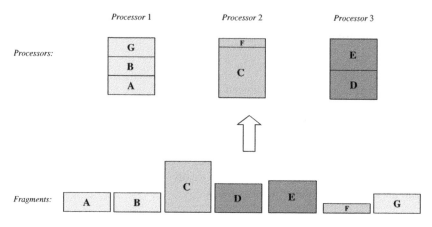

Figure 5.19   Load balancing

available number of processors. For example, in Figure 5.19, seven fragments are created; meanwhile, there are only three processors and the size of each fragment is likely to be different.

After these fragments have been created, they can be arranged and placed so that the loads of all processors will be approximately equal. For example, fragments A, B, and G should go to processor 1, fragments C and F to processor 2, and the rest to processor 3. In this way, the workload of these three processors will be more equitable.

The main question remains that is concerning the ideal size of a fragment, or the number of fragments that need to be produced in order to achieve optimum load balancing. This is significant because the creation of more fragments incurs an overhead. The smallest fragment size is actually one record each from the two tables, whereas the largest fragment is the original fragment size without load balancing. To achieve an optimum result, a correct balance for fragment size needs to be determined. And this can be achieved through further experimentation, depending on the architecture and other factors.

5.6 SUMMARY

Parallel join is one of the most important operations in high-performance query processing. The join operation itself is one of the most expensive operations in relational query processing, and hence the parallelizing join operation brings significant benefits. Although there are many different forms of parallel join algorithms, parallel join algorithms are generally formed in two stages: data partitioning and local join. In this way, parallelism is achieved through data parallelism whereby each processor concentrates on different parts of the data and the final query results are amalgamated from all processors.

There are two main types of data partitioning used for parallel join: one is with replication, and the other is without replication. The former is divide and broadcast, whereby one table is partitioned (divided) and the other is replicated (broadcast). The latter is based on disjoint partitioning, using either range partitioning or hash partitioning.

For the local join, three main serial join algorithms exist, namely: nested-loop join, sort-merge join, and hash join. In a shared-nothing architecture, any serial join algorithm may be used after the data partitioning takes place. In a shared-memory architecture, the divide and broadcast-based parallel join algorithm uses a nested-loop join algorithm, and hence is called a parallel nested-loop join algorithm. However, the disjoint-based parallel join algorithms are either parallel sort-merge join or parallel hash join, depending on which data partitioning is used: sort partitioning or hash partitioning.

5.7 BIBLIOGRAPHICAL NOTES

Join is one of the most expensive database operations, and subsequently, parallel join has been one of the main focuses in the work on parallel databases. There are hundreds of papers on parallel join, mostly concentrated on parallel join algorithms, and others on skew and load balancing in the context of parallel join processing.

To list a few important work on parallel join algorithms, Kitsuregawa et al. (*ICDE* 1992) proposed parallel Grace hash join on a shared-everything architecture, Lakshmi and Yu (*IEEE TKDE* 1990) proposed parallel hash join algorithms, and Schneider and DeWitt (*VLDB* 1990) also focused on parallel hash join. A number of papers evaluated parallel join algorithms, including those by Nakano et al. (*ICDE* 1998), Schneider and DeWitt (*SIGMOD* 1989), and Wilschut et al. (*SIGMOD* 1995). Other methods for parallel join include the use of pipelined parallelism (Liu and Rundensteiner *VLDB* 2005; Bamha and Exbrayat *Parco* 2003), distributive join in cube-connected multiprocessors (Chung and Yang *IEEE TPDS* 1996), and multiway join (Lu et al. *VLDB* 1991). An excellent survey on join processing is presented by Mishra and Eich (*ACM Comp Surv* 1992).

One of the main problems in parallel join is skew. Most parallel join papers have addressed skew handling. Some of the notable ones are Wolf et al. (two papers in *IEEE TPDS* 1993—one focused on parallel hash join and the other on parallel sort-merge join), Kitsuregawa and Ogawa (*VLDB* 1990; proposing bucket spreading for parallel hash join) and Hua et al. (*VLDB* 1991; *IEEE TKDE* 1995; proposing partition tuning to handle dynamic load balancing). Other work on skew handling and load balancing include DeWitt et al. (*VLDB* 1992) and Walton et al (*VLDB* 1991), reviewing skew handling techniques in parallel join; Harada and Kitsuregawa (*DASFAA* 1995), focusing on skew handling in a shared-nothing architecture; and Li et al. (*SIGMOD* 2002) on sort-merge join.

Other work on parallel join covers various join queries, like star join, range join, spatial join, clone and shadow joins, and exclusion joins. Aguilar-Saborit et al. (*DaWaK* 2005) concentrated on parallel star join, whereas Chen et al. (1995) concentrated on parallel range join and Shum (1993) reported parallel exclusion join. Work on spatial join can be found in Chung et al. (2004), Kang et al. (2002), and Luo et al. (*ICDE* 2002). Patel and DeWitt (2000) introduced clone and shadow joins for parallel spatial databases.

5.8 EXERCISES

5.1. Serial join exercises—Given the two tables shown (e.g., Tables *R* and *S*) in Figure 5.20, trace the result of the join operation based on the numerical attribute values using the following serial algorithms:

Table R

Austria	7
Belgium	20
Czech	26
Denmark	13
Ecuador	12
France	8
Germany	9
Hungary	17
Ireland	1
Japan	2
Kenya	16
Laos	28
Mexico	22
Netherlands	18
Oman	19

Table S

Amsterdam	18
Bangkok	25
Cancun	22
Dublin	1
Edinburgh	27
Frankfurt	9
Geneva	11
Hanoi	10
Innsbruck	7

Figure 5.20   Sample tables

a. Serial *nested-loop* join algorithm,
b. Serial *sort-merge* join algorithm, and
c. Serial *hash-based* join algorithm

5.2. Initial data placement:

a. Using the two tables above, partition the tables with a round-robin (random-equal) data partitioning into three processors. Show the partitions in each processor.

5.3. Parallel join using the *divide and broadcast partitioning* method exercises:

a. Taking the partitions in each processor as shown in exercise 5.2, explain how the divide and broadcast partitioning works by showing the partitioning results in each processor.

b. Now perform a join operation in each processor. Show the join results in each processor.

5.4. Parallel join using the *disjoint partitioning* method exercises:

a. Taking the initial data placement partitions in each processor as in exercise 5.2, show how the *disjoint partitioning* works by using a range partitioning.

b. Now perform a join operation in each processor. Show the join results in each processor.

5.5. Repeat the disjoint partitioning-based join method in exercise 5.4, but now use a hash-based partitioning rather than a range partitioning. Show the join results in each processor.

5.6. Discuss the load imbalance problem in the two disjoint partitioning questions above (exercises 5.4 and 5.5). Describe how the load imbalance problem may be solved. Illustrate your answer by using one of the examples above.

5.7. Investigate your favorite DBMS and see how parallel join is expressed in SQL and what parallel join algorithms are available.

Part III

Advanced Parallel Query Processing

Chapter 6

Parallel GroupBy-Join

In this chapter, parallel algorithms for queries involving group-by and join operations are described. First, in Section 6.1, an introduction to GroupBy-Join query is given. Sections 6.2 and 6.3 describe parallel algorithms for GroupBy-*Before*-Join queries, in which the group-by operation is executed before the join, and parallel algorithms on GroupBy-*After*-Join queries, in which the join is executed first, followed by the group-by operation. Section 6.4 presents the basic cost notations, which are used in the following two sections (Sections 6.5 and 6.6) describing the cost models for the two parallel GroupBy-Join queries.

6.1 GROUPBY-JOIN QUERIES

SQL queries in the real world are replete with group-by clauses and join operations. These queries are often used for strategic decision making because of the nature of group-by queries where raw information is grouped according to the designated groups and within each group aggregate functions are normally carried out. As the source information to these queries is commonly drawn from various tables, joining tables—together with grouping—becomes necessary. These types of queries are often known as "*GroupBy-Join*" queries. In strategic decision making, parallelization of GroupBy-Join queries is unavoidable in order to speed up query processing time.

It is common for a GroupBy query to involve multiple tables. These tables are joined to produce a single table, and this table becomes an input to the group-by operation. We call these kinds of queries *GroupBy-Join* queries; that is, queries involving join and group-by. For simplicity of description and without loss of generality, we consider queries that involve only one aggregate function and a single join.

High-Performance Parallel Database Processing and Grid Databases,
by David Taniar, Clement Leung, Wenny Rahayu, and Sushant Goel
Copyright © 2008 John Wiley & Sons, Inc.

Since two operations, namely group-by and join operations, are involved in the query, there are two options for executing the queries: group-by first, followed by the join; or join first and then group-by. To illustrate these two types of GroupBy queries, we use the following tables from a suppliers-parts-projects database:

```
SUPPLIER (S#, Sname, Status, City)
PARTS (P#, Pname, Color, Weight, Price, City)
PROJECT (J#, Jname, City, Budget)
SHIPMENT (S#, P#, J#, Qty)
```

These two types of group-by join queries will be illustrated in the following two sections.

6.1.1   Groupby Before Join

A *GroupBy Before Join* query is when the join attribute is also one of the group-by attributes. For example, the query to "retrieve project numbers, names, and total number of shipments for each project having the total number of shipments of more than 1000" is shown by the following SQL:

Query 6.1:
```
Select PROJECT.J#, PROJECT.Jname, SUM(Qty)
From PROJECT, SHIPMENT
Where PROJECT.J# = SHIPMENT.J#
Group By PROJECT.J#, PROJECT.Jname
Having SUM(Qty) > 1000
```

In the above query, one of the group-by attributes, namely, PROJECT.J# of table Project becomes the join attribute. When this happens, it is expected that the group-by operation will be carried out first, and then the join operation. In processing this query, all Project records are grouped based on the J# attribute. After grouping, the result is joined with table Shipment.

As is widely known, join is a more expensive operation than group-by, and it would be beneficial to reduce the join relation sizes by applying the group-by first. Generally, a group-by operation should always precede join whenever possible. In real life, early processing of the group-by before join reduces the overall execution time, as stated in the general query optimization rule where unary operations are always executed before binary operations if possible. The semantic issues of group-by and join, and the conditions under which group-by would be performed before join, can be found in the literature.

6.1.2   Groupby After Join

A *GroupBy After Join* query is where the join attribute is totally different from the group-by attributes, for example: "group the part shipment by their city locations and select the cities with average number of shipments between 500 and 1000". The query written in SQL is as follows.

```
Query 6.2:
    Select PARTS.City, AVG(Qty)
    From PARTS, SHIPMENT
    Where PARTS.P# = SHIPMENT.P#
    Group By PARTS.City
    Having AVG(Qty) > 500 AND AVG(Qty) < 1000
```

The main difference between queries 6.1 and 6.2 lies in the join attributes and group-by attributes. In query 6.2, the join attribute is totally different from the group-by attribute. This difference is a critical factor, particularly in processing GroupBy-Join queries, as there are decisions to be made as to which operation should be performed first: the group by or the join operation. When the join attribute and the group-by attribute are different, there will be no choice but to invoke the join operation first, and then the group-by operation.

6.2 PARALLEL ALGORITHMS FOR GROUPBY-BEFORE-JOIN QUERY PROCESSING

Depending on how the data is distributed among processors, parallel algorithms for *GroupBy-Before-Join* queries exist in three formats:

- *Early distribution* scheme,
- *Early GroupBy with partitioning* scheme, and
- *Early GroupBy with replication* scheme

6.2.1 Early Distribution Scheme

The *early distribution scheme* is influenced by the practice of parallel join algorithms, where raw records are first partitioned/distributed and allocated to each processor, and then each processor performs its operation. This scheme is motivated by fast message-passing multiprocessor systems. For simplicity of notation, the table that becomes the basis for GroupBy is called table R, and the other table is called table S.

The early distribution scheme is divided into two phases:

- *Distribution* phase and
- *GroupBy-Join* phase.

In the *distribution* phase, raw records from both tables (i.e., tables R and S) are distributed based on the join/group-by attribute according to a data partitioning function. An example of a partitioning function is to allocate each processor with project numbers ranging from and to certain values. For example, project numbers (i.e., attribute $J\#$) $p1$ to $p99$ go to processor 1, project numbers $p100-p199$ to processor 2, project numbers $p200-p299$ to processor 3, and so on. We need to emphasize that the two tables R and S are both distributed. As a result, for

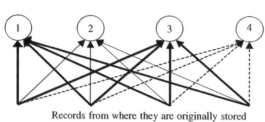

Perform *group-by* (aggregate function) of table *R*, and then *join* with table *S*.

Distribute the two tables (*R* and *S*) on the group-by/join attribute.

Records from where they are originally stored

Figure 6.1 Early distribution scheme

example, processor 1 will have records from the Shipment table with *J#* between *p1* and *p99*, inclusive, as well as records from the Project table with *J# p1–p99*. This distribution scheme is commonly used in parallel join, where raw records are partitioned into buckets based on an adopted partitioning scheme like the above range partitioning.

Once the distribution has been completed, each processor will have records within certain groups identified by the group-by/join attribute. Subsequently, the *second* phase (the *group-by-join* phase) groups records of table *R* based on the group-by attribute and calculates the aggregate values of each group. Aggregating in each processor can be carried out through a sort or a hash function. After table *R* has been grouped in each processor, it is joined with table *S* in the same processor. After joining, each processor will have a local query result. The final query result is a union of all subresults produced by each processor.

Figure 6.1 illustrates the early distribution scheme. Note that partitioning is done to the raw records of both tables *R* and *S*, and the aggregate operation of table *R* and join with table *S* in each processor is carried out after the distribution phase.

Several things need to be highlighted from this scheme.

- *First*, the grouping is still performed before the join (although after the distribution). This is to conform to an optimization rule for such kinds of queries: A group-by clause must be carried out before the join in order to achieve more efficient query processing time.

- *Second*, the distribution of records from both tables can be expensive, as all raw records are distributed and no prior filtering is done to either table. It becomes more desirable if grouping (and aggregation function) is carried out even before the distribution, in order to reduce the distribution cost, especially of table *R*.

This leads to the next schemes, called *Early GroupBy* schemes, for reducing the communication costs during the distribution phase. There are two variations of the *Early GroupBy* schemes, which are discussed in the following two sections.

6.2.2 Early GroupBy with Partitioning Scheme

As the name states, the *Early GroupBy* scheme performs the group by operation first before anything else (e.g., distribution). The *early GroupBy with partitioning* scheme is divided into three phases:

- Local grouping phase,
- Distribution phase, and
- Final grouping and join phase

In the *local grouping* phase, each processor performs its group-by operation and calculates its local aggregate values on records of table *R*. In this phase, each processor groups local records *R* according to the designated group-by attribute and performs the aggregate function. With the same example as that used in the previous section, one processor may produce (*p1*, 5000) and (*p140*, 8000), and another processor may produce (*p100*, 7000) and (*p140*, 4000). The numerical figures indicate the SUM(Qty) of each project.

In the second phase (i.e., *distribution* phase), the results of local aggregates from each processor, together with records of table *S*, are distributed to all processors according to a partitioning function. The partitioning function is based on the join/group-by attribute, which in this case is an attribute *J#* of tables Project and Shipment. Again using the same partitioning function in the previous section, *J#* of *p1–p99* are to go to processor 1, *J#* of *p100–p199* to processor 2, and so on.

In the third phase (i.e., *final grouping and join* phase), two operations in particular are carried out: final aggregate or grouping of *R* and then joining it with *S*. The final grouping can be carried out by merging all temporary results obtained in each processor. The way this works can be explained as follows. After local aggregates are formulated in each processor, each processor then distributes each of the groups to another processor depending on the adopted distribution function. Once the distribution of local results based on a particular distribution function is completed, global aggregation in each processor is done by simply merging all identical project numbers (*J#*) into one aggregate value. For example, processor 2 will merge (*p140*, 8000) from one processor and (*p140*, 4000) from another to produce (*p140*, 12000), which is the final aggregate value for this project number.

Global aggregation can be tricky depending on the complexity of the aggregate functions used in the actual query. If, for example, an AVG function was used as an aggregate function, calculating an average value based on temporary averages must take into account the actual raw records involved in each node. Therefore, for these kinds of aggregate functions, the local aggregate must also produce the number of raw records in each processor although they are not specified in the query. This is needed for the global aggregation to produce correct values. For example, one processor may produce (*p140*, 8000, 5) and the other (*p140*, 4000, 1). After distribution, suppose processor 2 received all *p140* records. The average for project *p140* is calculated by dividing the sum of the two quantities (e.g., 8000

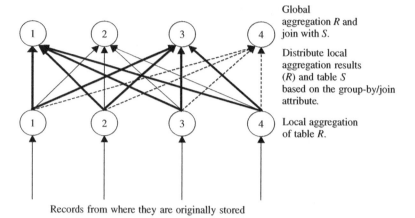

Global aggregation R and join with S.

Distribute local aggregation results (R) and table S based on the group-by/join attribute.

Local aggregation of table R.

Records from where they are originally stored

Figure 6.2   Early GroupBy with *partitioning* scheme

and 4000) and the total shipment records for that project. (i.e., $(8000 + 4000)/(5 + 1) = 2000$). The total shipments in each project need to be determined by each processor, although it is not specified in the query.

After global aggregation results are obtained, it is then joined to table S in each processor. Figure 6.2 illustrates this scheme.

There are several things worth noting.

- *First*, records R in each processor are aggregated/grouped before distributing them. Consequently, communication costs associated with table R can be expected to reduce depending on the group-by selectivity factor. This scheme is expected to improve the *early distribution* scheme.

- *Second*, we observe that if the number of groups is less than the number of available processors; not all processors can be exploited, thereby reducing the capability of parallelism.

- And *finally*, records from table S in each processor are all distributed during the second phase. In other words, no filtering mechanism is applied to S before distribution. This can be inefficient, particularly if S is very large. To avoid the problem of distributing S, we will introduce another scheme in the next section.

6.2.3   Early GroupBy with Replication Scheme

The *early GroupBy with replication* scheme is similar to the early GroupBy with partitioning scheme. The similarity is due to the group-by processing to be done before the distribution phase. However, the difference is indicated by the keyword *"with replication"* in this scheme, as opposed to *"with partitioning."* The early GroupBy with replication scheme, which is also divided into three phases, works as follows.

The first phase, that is, the *local grouping* phase, is exactly the same as that of the early GroupBy with partitioning scheme. In each processor, the local aggregate is performed to table R.

The main difference is in phase two. With the "*with replication*" scheme, the local aggregate results obtained from each processor are replicated to all processors. Table S is not at all moved from where they are originally stored.

In the third phase, the *final grouping and join* phase, is basically similar to that of the "*with partitioning*" scheme. That is, local aggregates from all processors are merged to obtain the global aggregate and then joined with S. With further detailed examination, we can find a difference between the two early GroupBy schemes. In the "*with replication*" scheme, after the replication phase each processor will have local aggregate results from all processors. Consequently, processing global aggregates in each processor will produce the same results, and this can be inefficient as no parallelism is employed. However, joining and global aggregation processes can be done at the same time. First, hash local aggregate results from R to obtain global aggregate values, and then hash and probe the fragment of table S to produce the final query result. The waste lies in the fact that many of the global aggregate results will have no match with local table S in each processor.

Figure 6.3 gives a graphical illustration of the scheme. It looks very similar to Figure 6.2, except that in the replication phase the arrows are thicker to emphasize the fact that local aggregate results from each processor are replicated to all processors, not distributed.

Apart from the fact that the non-group-by table (table S) is not distributed and the local aggregate results of table R are replicated, assuming that table S is uniformly distributed to all processors initially (that is, round-robin data placement is adopted in storing records S), there will be no skew problem in the joining phase. This is not the case with the previous two schemes, as distribution is done during the process, and this can create skewness depending on the partitioning attribute values.

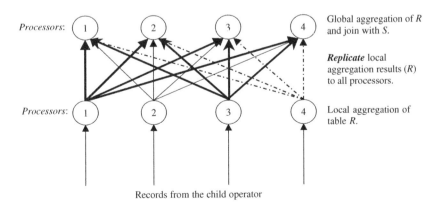

Figure 6.3 Early GroupBy with *replication* scheme

6.3   PARALLEL ALGORITHMS FOR GROUPBY-AFTER-JOIN QUERY PROCESSING

An important decision needs to be made in processing *GroupBy-After-Join* queries, namely, choosing the partitioning attribute. Selecting a proper partitioning attribute plays a crucial role in performance. Although in general any attributes of the operand relations may be chosen, two particular attributes (i.e., *join attribute* and *group-by attribute*) are usually considered.

If the *join attribute* is chosen, both relations are partitioned into N fragments by employing a partitioning function (e.g., a hash/range function) where N is the number of processors. The cost of a parallel join operation can therefore be reduced compared with a single-processor system. However, after join and local aggregation at each processor, a global aggregation is required at the data consolidation phase, since local aggregation is performed on a subset of the group-by attribute.

If the *group-by attribute* is used for data partitioning, the relation with the group-by can be partitioned into N fragments, while the other relation needs to be broadcasted to all processors for the join operation.

Comparing the two methods above, in the second method (partitioning based on the group-by attribute), the join cost is not reduced as much as in the first method (partitioning based on the join attribute). However, no global aggregation is required after local join and local aggregation, because records with identical values of the group-by attribute have been allocated to the same processor.

In parallel processing of GroupBy-After-Join queries, it must be decided which attribute is to be used as a partitioning attribute, particularly the join attribute or the group-by attribute. Based on the partitioning attribute, there are two parallel processing methods for *GroupBy-After-Join* queries, namely:

- *Join partitioning* scheme and
- *GroupBy partitioning* scheme

6.3.1   Join Partitioning Scheme

Given the two tables R and S to be joined, and the result grouped-by according to the group-by attribute and possibly filtered through a Having predicate, parallel processing of such query with the *Join Partitioning* scheme can be stated as follows.

Step 1:   *Data Partitioning.* The relations R and S are partitioned into N fragments in terms of join attribute; that is, the records with the same join attribute values in the two relations fall into a pair of fragments. Each pair of the fragments will be sent to one processor for execution.

Using query 6.2 as an example, the partitioning attribute is attribute *P#* of both tables Parts and Shipment, which is the join attribute. Suppose we use 4 processors, and the partitioning method is a range partitioning, whose part numbers (*P#*) *p1–p99, p100–p199, p200–p299,* and *p300–399* are distributed to processors 1, 2, 3, and 4, respectively. This partitioning function is applied to both Parts and Shipment tables. Consequently, a processor such as processor 1 will have Parts and Shipment records where the values of its *P#* attribute are between *p1–p99*, and so on.

Step 2: *Join Operation.* Upon receipt of the fragments, the processors perform in parallel the join operation on the allocated fragments. The joins in each processor are done independently of each other. This is possible because the two tables have been disjointly partitioned based on the join attribute.

Using the same example as above, a join operation in a processor like processor 1 will produce a join result consisting of Parts-Shipment records having *P#* between *p1* and *p99*.

It is worth mentioning that any sequential join algorithm (i.e., nested-loop join, sort-merge join, nested index join, hash join) may be used in performing a local join operation in each processor.

Step 3: *Local Aggregation.* After the join is completed, each processor then performs a local aggregation operation. Join results in each processor is grouped-by according to the group-by attribute.

Continuing the same example as the above, each city found in the join result will be grouped. If, for example, there are three cities, Beijing, Melbourne, and Sydney, found in processor 1, the records will be grouped according to these three cities. The same aggregate operation is applied to other processors. As a result, although each processor has distinct part numbers, some of the cities, if not all of those distributed among the processors, may be identical (duplicated). For example, processor 2 may have three cities, such as London, Melbourne, and Sydney, whereas Melbourne and Sydney are also found in processor 1 as mentioned above, but not London.

Step 4: *Redistribution.* A global aggregation operation is to be carried out by redistributing the local aggregation results across all processors such that the result records with identical values of the group-by attribute are allocated to the same processors.

To illustrate this step, range partitioning is again used to partition the group-by attribute so that processors 1, 2, 3, and 4 are allocated cities beginning with letters *A–G*, *H–M*, *N–T*, and *U–Z*, respectively. With this range partitioning, processor 1 will distribute its Melbourne record to processor 2, the Sydney record to processor 3, and leave the Beijing record in processor 1. Processor 2 will do the same to its Melbourne and Sydney records, whereas the London record will remain in processor 2.

Step 5: *Global Aggregation.* Each processor performs an *N*-way merging of the local aggregation results, followed by performing a restriction operation for the Having clause if required by the query.

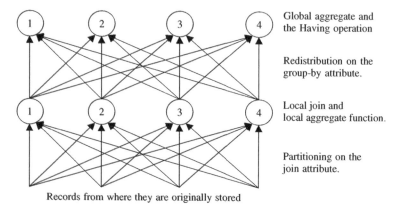

Global aggregate and
the Having operation

Redistribution on the
group-by attribute.

Local join and
local aggregate function.

Partitioning on the
join attribute.

Records from where they are originally stored

Figure 6.4   Join partitioning scheme

The result of this global aggregate in each processor is a subset of
the final results, meaning that each record in each processor has a different city, and furthermore, the cities in each processor will not appear
in any other processors. For example, processor 1 will produce one Beijing record in the query result, and this Beijing record does not appear
in any other processors. Additionally, some of the cities may then be
eliminated through the Having clause.

Step 6:   *Consolidation.* The host simply amalgamates the partial results from the
processors by a union operation and produces the query result.

Figure 6.4 gives a graphical illustration of the *join partitioning* scheme. The
circles represent processing elements, whereas the arrows denote data flow through
data partitioning or data redistribution.

6.3.2 GroupBy Partitioning Scheme

The *GroupBy partitioning* scheme relies on partitioning based on the group-by
attribute. As the group-by attribute belongs to just one of the two tables, only the
table having the group-by attribute will be partitioned. The other table has to be
broadcasted to all processors. The processing steps of this scheme are explained as
follows.

Step 1:   *Data Partitioning.* The table with the group-by attribute, say R, is partitioned into N fragments in terms of the group-by attribute, that is, the
records with identical attribute values will be allocated to the same processor. The other table, S, needs to be broadcasted to all processors in
order to perform the join operation.

Using query 6.2 as an example, table Parts is partitioned according to
the group-by attribute, namely City. Assuming that a range partitioning

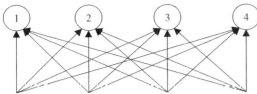

Join, Group-By (Aggregation), and Having operations.

Partitioning one table on the group-by attribute and broadcast the other table.

Records from where they are originally stored

Figure 6.5   GroupBy partitioning scheme

method is used, processors 1, 2, 3, and 4 will have Parts records having cities beginning with letters A–G, H–M, N–T, and U–Z, respectively. On the other hand, table Shipment is replicated to all four processors.

Step 2:   *Join Operations.* After data distribution, each processor carries out the joining of one fragment of R with the entire table S.

Using the same example, each processor joins its Parts fragment with the entire table Shipment. The results of this join operation in each processor are pairs of Parts-Shipment records having the same $P\#$ (join attribute) and the value of its City attribute must fall into the category identified by the group-by partitioning method (e.g., processor $1 = A$–G, processor $2 = H$–M, etc).

Step 3:   *Aggregate Operations.* The aggregate operation is performed by grouping the join results based on the group-by attribute, followed by a Having restriction if it exists on the query.

Continuing the above example, processor 1 will group the records based on the city and the cities are in the range of A to G. The other processors will, of course, have a different range. Therefore, each group in each processor is distinct from the others both within and among processors.

Step 4:   *Consolidation.* Since table R is partitioned on group-by attribute, the final aggregation result can be obtained simply by a union of the local aggregation results from the processors.

Figure 6.5 illustrates the *GroupBy partitioning* scheme. Note the difference between the join partitioning and the GroupBy partitioning schemes. The former imposes a "two-phase" partitioning scheme, whereas the latter is a "one-phase" partitioning scheme.

6.4   COST MODEL NOTATIONS

For completeness, the notations used by the cost models are presented in Table 6.1. They are basically comprised of parameters known by the system as well as the data—the parameters are related to the query, unit time costs, and communication costs.

Table 6.1   Cost notations

Symbol	Description
System and data parameters	
N	Number of processors
R and S	Size of table R and table S
$|R|$ and $|S|$	Number of records in table R and table S
$|R_i|$ and $|S_i|$	Number of records in table R and table S on node i
P	Page size
H	Hash table size
Query parameters	
π_R and π_S	Projectivity ratios of table R and table S
σ_R and σ_S	GroupBy selectivity ratios of table R and table S
σ_j	Join selectivity ratio
Time unit cost	
IO	Effective time to read a page from disk
t_r	Time to read a record
t_w	Time to write a record
t_h	Time to compute hash value
t_a	Time to add a record to current aggregate value
t_j	Time to compare a record with a hash table entry
t_d	Time to compute destination
Communication cost	
m_p	Message protocol cost per page
m_l	Message latency for one page

The *projectivity* and *selectivity* ratios (i.e., π and σ) in the query parameters have values ranging from 0 to 1.

The *projectivity* ratio π is the ratio between the projected attribute size and the original record length. Since two tables are involved (i.e., tables R and S), we use the notations of π_R and π_S to distinguish between the projectivity ratio of one table and the other. Using query 6.1 as an example, assume that the record size of table Project is 100 bytes and the output record size is 45 bytes. In this case, the projectivity ratio π_R is 0.45.

There are two different kinds of *selectivity* ratio: one is related to the group-by operation, whereas the other is related to the join operation. The *group-by selectivity* ratio σ_R is a ratio between the number of groups in the aggregate result and the original total number of records. Since table R is aggregated (grouped-by), the selectivity ratio σ_R is applicable to table R only. To illustrate how σ_R is determined, we again use query 6.1 as an example. Suppose there are 1000 projects (1000 records in the table Project R), and it produces 4 groups only. The selectivity ratio σ_R is then $4/1000 = 1/250 = 0.004$. This selectivity ratio σ_R of $1/250$ ($\sigma_R = 0.004$) also means that each group will gather on average 250 original records R.

The *join selectivity* ratio σ_j is also similar—that is, the ratio between the join query result and the product of the two tables R and S. For example, if there are 100 and 200 records from table R and table S, respectively, and the join between R and S produces 50 records, the join selectivity ratio σ_j can be calculated as $(50/(100 \times 200)) = 0.0025$. We must stress that the table sizes of R and S are not necessarily the original table sizes of the respective tables, but the table sizes of the join operation. So, in our case, if table R has been filtered by the previous operation, namely the group-by operation, the above example that shows that table R has 100 records, this is not the original size of table R but the number of groups produced by the previous group-by operation, which then needs to be joined with table S.

6.5 COST MODEL FOR GROUPBY-BEFORE-JOIN QUERY PROCESSING

6.5.1 Cost Models for the Early Distribution Scheme

Since there are two phases in the early distribution scheme, we describe the cost components of the two phases.

Cost Models for Phase One (Distribution Phase)

Cost components of the first phase (*distribution* phase) of the early distribution scheme are the sum of scan cost, select data cost, finding destination cost, and data transfer cost. These are presented in more detail as follows.

- *Scan cost* is the cost of loading data from local disk in each processor. Since data loading from disk is done page by page, the fragment size of the table residing in each disk is divided by the page size to obtain number of pages.

$$((R_i/P) \times IO) + ((S_i/P) \times IO) \tag{6.1}$$

    The term on the left is the data loading cost of table R in processor i, whereas the term on the right is the associated loading cost of table S. Note that both tables need to be loaded from the disk where they reside.

- *Select cost* is the cost of getting the record out of the data page, which is calculated as the number of records loaded from the disk times reading and writing unit cost to the main memory.

$$(|R_i| \times (t_r + t_w)) + (|S_i| \times (t_r + t_w)) \tag{6.2}$$

    The select cost also involves both records from tables R and S in each processor.

- *Determining the destination cost* is the cost of calculating the destination of each record to be distributed from the processor in phase one to phase two. This overhead is given by the number of records in each fragment times the destination computation unit cost, which is given as follows.

$$(|R_i| \times t_d) + (|S_i| \times t_d) \qquad (6.3)$$

- *Data transfer cost* of sending records to other processors is given by the number of pages to be sent multiplied by the message unit cost, which is given as follows.

$$((\pi_R \times R_i/P) \times (m_p + m_l)) + ((\pi_S \times S_i/P) \times (m_p + m_l)) \qquad (6.4)$$

When distributing the records during the first phase, only those attributes relevant to the query are redistributed. This factor is depicted by the projectivity factor, denoted by π.

Cost Models for Phase Two (GroupBy-Join Phase)

The second phase (*GroupBy-Join* phase) cost components of the early distribution scheme include the receiving cost, which is the cost of receiving records from the first phase, actual group-by cost, joining cost, generating result records, and disk cost of storing query results.

- *Receiving records cost* from processors in the first phase is calculated by the number of projected values of the two tables multiplied by the message unit cost.

$$((\pi_R \times R_i/P) \times m_p) + ((\pi_S \times S_i/P) \times m_p) \qquad (6.5)$$

If the number of groups is less than the number of processors, $R_i = R$ /(*Number_of_Groups*), instead of $R_i = R/N$ (i.e., assume uniform distribution), because not all processors are used. Consequently, when the number of groups is small, smaller than the available number of processors, performance can be expected to be poor.

- *Aggregation and join costs* involve reading, hashing, computing the cumulative value, and probing. The costs are as follows:

$$(|R_i| \times (t_r + t_h + t_a)) + (|S_i| \times (t_r + t_h + t_j)) \qquad (6.6)$$

The aggregation process basically consists of reading each record R, hashing it to a hash table, and calculating the aggregate value. After all records R have been processed, records S can be read, hashed, and probed. If they are matched, the matching records are written out to the query result.

The hashing process is very much determined by the size of the hash table that can fit into main memory. If the memory size is smaller than the hash table size, we normally partition the hash table into multiple buckets whereby each bucket can perfectly fit into main memory. All but the first bucket are spooled to disk.

Given such a scenario, we must include the I/O cost for reading and writing overflow buckets, which is as follows.

- *Reading/writing of overflow buckets cost* is the I/O costs associated with the limitation of main memory to accommodate the entire hash table. This cost includes the costs for reading and writing records not processed in the first pass of hashing.

$$\left(1 - \min\left(\frac{H}{\sigma_R \times |R_i|}, 1\right)\right) \times \left(\pi_R \times \frac{R_i}{P} \times 2 \times IO\right) \qquad (6.7)$$

The first term of the above equation can be explained as follows. For example, if the maximum hash table size H is 10 records, selectivity ratio σ_R is $\frac{1}{4}$, and there are 200 records ($|R_i|$), the number of groups in the query result will be equal to 50 groups ($\sigma_R \times |R_i|$). Since only 10 groups can be processed at a time, we need to break the hash table into 5 buckets. All buckets but the first are spooled to disk. Hence, 80% of the groups $(1 - (10/50))$ is overflow. Should there be only less or equal to 10 groups in the query result, the first term of the above equation would be equal to 0 (zero), and hence there would no overhead.

The second term of the above equation is explained as follows. The constant 2 refers to two input/output accesses: one is for spooling of the overflow buckets to disk and two is for reading the overflow buckets from disk. Note that the record size is reduced by the projectivity ratio π_R, because in the hash table only the projected attributes are kept, not the whole record.

The overflow buckets associated with table S are very similar. Assuming that the percentage of overflowing records is the same as that of for table R, the overflow buckets for table S becomes:

$$\left(1 - \min\left(\frac{H}{\sigma_R \times |R_i|}, 1\right)\right) \times \left(\pi_S \times \frac{S_i}{P} \times 2 \times IO\right) \qquad (6.8)$$

The term on the left defines the percentage of overflow, whereas the term on the right is the I/O cost associated with rewriting and reloading table S.

- *Generating result records cost* is the number of selected records multiplied by the writing unit cost.

$$|R_i| \times \sigma_R \times |S_i| \times \sigma_j \times t_w \qquad (6.9)$$

- *Disk cost* of storing final result is the number of pages to store the final aggregate values times disk unit cost, which is:

$$(\pi_R \times R_i \times \sigma_R \times \pi_S \times S_i \times \sigma_j / P) \times IO \qquad (6.10)$$

The total cost of the early distribution scheme is the sum of equations 6.1 to 6.10.

6.5.2 Cost Models for the Early GroupBy with Partitioning Scheme

Like the early distribution scheme cost models, we describe the cost model for the early GroupBy with partitioning scheme in term of the phases.

Cost Models for Phase One (Grouping Phase)

The cost components of the first phase (*grouping* phase) consist of scan cost, select data page cost, local aggregation cost, and generating local aggregation writing cost.

- *Scan cost* is associated with both tables R and S, which is the same as that of the "early distribution" scheme, and therefore **equation** 6.1 in the previous section can be used.

- *Select cost* is also associated with both tables R and S, and it is identical to **equation** 6.2 in the early distribution scheme.

- *Local aggregation cost* covers the reading, hashing, and accumulating aggregate values costs, which are as follows.

$$|R_i| \times (t_r + t_h + t_a) \tag{6.11}$$

  Note that the cost equation involves R only, not S, since table S has not yet been processed. equation 6.11 is similar to the left-hand side term of equation 6.6 presented in the previous section. The only difference is that equation 6.6 involves the hashing/probing cost of table S. In equation 6.11, only the aggregation cost is involved.

- *Reading/writing of overflow buckets cost* is similar to equation 6.7 in the early distribution scheme. The main difference is that the group-by selectivity factor used here is now identified by σ_{R1} instead of σ_R because in the early GroupBy with partitioning scheme, there are two group-by operations: local group-by and final/global group-by. Here σ_{R1} indicates the first group-by selectivity ratio.

$$\left(1 - \min\left(\frac{H}{\sigma_{R1} \times |R_i|}, 1\right)\right) \times \left(\pi_R \times \frac{R_i}{P} \times 2 \times IO\right) \tag{6.12}$$

- *Generating final result cost* is:

$$|R_i| \times \sigma_{R1} \times t_w \tag{6.13}$$

The sum of equations 6.11 to 6.13 gives the total cost for phase one of the early GroupBy with partitioning scheme.

Cost Models for Phase Two (Distribution Phase)

Cost components of the second phase (*distribution* phase) are comprised of finding destination costs, actual data transfer, and receiving costs.

- *Determining the destination cost* is associated with both tables R and S, since both tables are distributed.

$$(|R_i| \times \sigma_{R1} \times t_d) + (|S_i| \times t_d) \qquad (6.14)$$

  Note that R has been reduced by the group-by selectivity ratio of σ_{R1} whereas S is not yet filtered.

- *Data transfer cost* is the cost of sending local aggregate results and fragment of table S from each processor.

$$((\pi_R \times R_i \times \sigma_{R1}/P) \times (m_p + m_l)) + ((\pi_S \times S_i/P) \times (m_p + m_l)) \quad (6.15)$$

  Also note that R has been reduced by both the projectivity factor of π_R and the group-by selectivity factor of σ_{R1}, whereas S is reduced by the projectivity factor π_S only.

- *Receiving records cost* is similar to the data transfer cost, but without the message latency overhead.

$$((\pi_R \times R_i \times \sigma_{R1}/P) \times m_p) + ((\pi_S \times S_i/P) \times m_p) \qquad (6.16)$$

  We must reiterate that if the number of groups is less than the number of processors, $R_i = R/(Number\_of\_Groups)$, instead of $R_i = R/N$ (i.e., assume uniform distribution).

The sum of equations 6.14 to 6.16 gives the total cost for phase two of the early GroupBy with partitioning scheme.

Cost Models for Phase Three (GroupBy-JoinPhase)

Cost components of the third phase (*grouping and joining* phase) are as follows.

- *Aggregation and Join* costs involve reading, hashing, computing the cumulative value, and probing. The costs are as follows:

$$(|R_i| \times \sigma_{R1} \times (t_r + t_h + t_a)) + (|S_i| \times (t_r + t_h + t_j)) \qquad (6.17)$$

- *Reading/Writing of overflow buckets cost* is similar to equations 6.7 and 6.8 described above. The overflow percentage is determined by the maximum hash table size and the table to be hashed. Note that $|R_i|$ has been reduced by σ_{R2} and this is determined by the second group-by selectivity ratio. We assume that $\sigma_{R1} \geq \sigma_{R2}$, meaning that the second group-by selectivity ratio is a further filtering of the first group-by selectivity. Note also that the I/O cost associated with $|R_i|$ has been reduced by the first group-by selectivity ratio σ_{R1}.

$$\left(1 - \min\left(\frac{H}{\sigma_{R2} \times |R_i|}, 1\right)\right) \times \left(\pi_R \times \sigma_{R1} \times \frac{R_i}{P} \times 2 \times IO\right) +$$
$$\left(1 - \min\left(\frac{H}{\sigma_{R2} \times |R_i|}, 1\right)\right) \times \left(\pi_S \times \frac{S_i}{P} \times 2 \times IO\right) \qquad (6.18)$$

- *Generating result records cost* is the number of selected records multiplied by the writing unit cost, which is identical to **equation** 6.9. In the early GroupBy with partitioning scheme, we also use equation 6.9. Note that equation 6.9 uses σ_R. Here σ_R is calculated as the product of σ_{R1} and σ_{R2}.

- *Disk cost* for storing final result is the number of pages to store the final aggregate values times the disk unit cost, which is identical to **equation** 6.10. Similar to the above (i.e., generating result records cost), σ_R is used to indicate the overall group-by selectivity ratio.

The total cost of the early GroupBy with partitioning scheme is the sum of equations 6.11 to 6.18.

6.5.3   Cost Models for the Early GroupBy with Replication Scheme

Cost Models for Phase One (Grouping Phase)

The cost component of the first phase of the early GroupBy with replication scheme is identical to that of the first phase of the early GroupBy with partitioning scheme.

Cost Models for Phase Two (Replication Phase)

The cost component of the second phase shows a major difference, since now we replicate local aggregate results. This cost component is associated solely with table R, as table S has not moved at all from where it was stored. Also, in the replication, no cost is associated with finding destination, since no hashing/ranging operation is performed in order to find the processor to which each record was sent.

- *Data transfer cost* is the cost of sending local aggregate results of each processor to all processors.

$$((\pi_R \times R_i \times \sigma_{R1} \times (N - 1)/P) \times (m_p + m_l)) \qquad (6.19)$$

In the above equation, R_i is reduced by two factors, namely π_R and σ_{R1}. However, the replication cost is increased by the number of processors $N - 1$.

- *Receiving records cost* is as follows.

$$((\pi_R \times R_i \times \sigma_{R1} \times (N - 1)/P) \times m_p) \qquad (6.20)$$

The sum of the above two equations gives the total cost for phase two of the early GroupBy with replication scheme.

Cost Models for Phase Three (Grouping/Joining Phase)

Cost components for the third phase (*grouping and joining* phase) are as follows

- *Aggregation and Join costs* are as follows:

$$(|R| \times \sigma_{R1} \times (t_r + t_h + t_a)) + (|S_i| \times (t_r + t_h + t_j)) \qquad (6.21)$$

  Note that number of records $|R|$ is used, instead of $|R_i|$, because of the replication done in the previous phase. If $|S_i|$ is initially placed in each local disk with a round-robin data placement method, there will be no skew associated with $|S_i|$ and $|S_i| = |S|/N$.

- *Reading/writing of overflow buckets cost* is very similar to equation 6.18 except that now we use R, not R_i, because of the replication.

$$\left(1 - \min\left(\frac{H}{\sigma_{R2} \times |R|}, 1\right)\right) \times \left(\pi_R \times \sigma_{R1} \times \frac{R}{P} \times 2 \times IO\right)$$
$$+ \left(1 - \min\left(\frac{H}{\sigma_{R2} \times |R|}, 1\right)\right) \times \left(\pi_S \times \frac{S_i}{P} \times 2 \times IO\right) \qquad (6.22)$$

The *generating result records cost* and *disk cost* are the same as those of the early GroupBy with partitioning scheme, which are also identical to those of the early distribution scheme. Hence, **equations** 6.9 and 6.10 can be used.

6.6   COST MODEL FOR "GROUPBY-AFTER-JOIN" QUERY PROCESSING

6.6.1   Cost Models for the Join Partitioning Scheme

Since there are four phases in the join partitioning scheme, we describe the cost components of the four phases.

Cost Models for Phase One (Data Partitioning Phase)

Cost components in the first phase (*data partitioning* phase) of the join partition method are the sum of scan cost, select data cost, and local partitioning cost. These are presented in more detail as follows.

- *Scan cost*, which is the cost of loading data from local disk in each processor, is identical to **equation** 6.1 given for the GroupBy-before-join schemes.
- *Select cost*, which the cost of getting a record out of the data page, is identical to **equation** 6.2 given for the GroupBy-before-join schemes.

- *Determining the local partitioning cost* is the cost of the relations of tables R and S being partitioned into N fragments in terms of join attribute. This cost is given in **equation** 6.3 given for the GroupBy-before-join schemes.

Cost Models for Phase Two (Join and Local Aggregation Phase)

The second phase (*join and local aggregation* phase) cost components for the join partition method are comprised of the receiving cost, which is the cost of receiving records from the first phase, and the joining cost of joining the allocated fragments.

- *Join costs* involve reading, hashing, and probing. The costs are as follows:

$$(|R_i| \times (t_r + t_h + t_j)) + (|S_i| \times (t_r + t_h + t_j)) \qquad (6.23)$$

- *Local aggregation costs* are as follows:

$$(|R_i| \times \sigma_j \times (t_r + t_h + t_a)) + (|S_i| \times \sigma_S \times (t_r + t_h + t_a)) \qquad (6.24)$$

- *Reading/writing of overflow buckets cost* is the I/O costs associated with the limitation of main memory to accommodate the entire hash table. This cost includes the costs for reading and writing records not processed in the first pass of hashing. This cost is similar to equation 6.7. However, the main difference is that here the size of table R is already reduced by the join selectivity factor σ_j.

$$\left(1 - \min\left(\frac{H}{\sigma_j \times |R_i|}, 1\right)\right) \times \left(\pi_R \times \frac{R_i}{P} \times 2 \times IO\right) \qquad (6.25)$$

The overflow buckets associated with table S are very similar. Assuming that the percentage of records overflowing is the same as that for table R, the overflow buckets for table S become:

$$\left(1 - \min\left(\frac{H}{\sigma_j \times |R_i|}, 1\right)\right) \times \left(\pi_S \times \frac{S_i}{P} \times 2 \times IO\right) \qquad (6.26)$$

The left-hand term defines the percentage of overflow, whereas the right-hand term is the I/O cost associated with rewriting and reloading table S.

- *Generating result records cost* is the number of selected records multiplied by the writing unit cost.

$$|R_i| \times \sigma_j \times |S_i| \times \sigma_S \times t_w \qquad (6.27)$$

Cost Models for Phase Three (Redistribution Phase)

The third phase (*redistribution* phase) cost components for the join partition method are comprised of the joining cost, which is the cost of joining records from the second phase, generating result records, and disk cost of storing query results.

- *Determining the destination cost* is associated with both tables R and S, since both tables are distributed.

$$(|R_i| \times \sigma_j \times t_d) + (|S_i| \times \sigma_S \times t_d) \tag{6.28}$$

- *Data transfer cost* is the cost for sending local aggregate results.

$$((\pi_R \times R_i \times \sigma_j / P) \times (m_p + m_l)) + ((\pi_S \times S_i \times \sigma_S / P) \times (m_p + m_l)) \tag{6.29}$$

Cost Models for Phase Four (Global Aggregation Phase)

Cost components for the fourth phase (*global aggregation* phase) are comprised of receiving costs, aggregation costs, generating result costs, and disk costs.

- *Receiving records cost* is similar to the data transfer cost, but without the message latency overhead.

$$((\pi_R \times R_i \times \sigma_j / P) \times m_p) + ((\pi_S \times S_i \times \sigma_S / P) \times m_p) \tag{6.30}$$

- *Aggregation costs* involve reading, hashing, computing the cumulative value, and probing. The costs are as follows:

$$(|R_i| \times \sigma_j \times (t_r + t_h + t_a)) + (|S_i| \times \sigma_S \times (t_r + t_h + t_a)) \tag{6.31}$$

- *Generating result records cost* is the number of selected records multiplied by the writing unit cost.

$$|R_i| \times \sigma_j \times |S_i| \times \sigma_S \times t_w \tag{6.32}$$

- *Disk cost* of storing final result is the number of pages to store the final aggregate values times disk unit cost, which is:

$$(\pi_R \times R_i \times \sigma_j \times \pi_S \times S_i \times \sigma_S / P) \times IO \tag{6.33}$$

6.6.2 Cost Models for the GroupBy Partitioning Scheme

Like the join partitioning scheme cost models, we shall describe the cost model for the GroupBy partitioning scheme in terms of the phases.

Cost Models for Phase One (Data Partitioning and Broadcasting Phase)

The cost components in the first phase (*data partitioning* phase) consist of scan cost, select data page cost, local aggregation cost, and generating local aggregation writing cost.

- *Scan cost* is associated with both tables R and S, which is the same as that of the join partitioning scheme, and therefore **equation** 6.1 presented in the previous section can be used.

- *Select cost* is also associated with both tables R and S, and it is identical to **equation** 6.2 in the join partitioning scheme.

- *Determining the local partitioning cost* is the cost for the relations of tables R is partitioned into N fragments in terms of group-by attribute.

$$(|R_i| \times t_d) \tag{6.34}$$

- *Data transfer cost* for sending records to other processors is given by the number of pages to be sent multiplied by the message unit cost, which is given as follows.

$$((\pi_S \times S_i \times (N - 1)/P) \times (m_p + m_l)) \tag{6.35}$$

The sum of all costs described above (for phase one) is the total cost of the first phase of the GroupBy partitioning scheme.

Cost Models for Phase Two (Join and Aggregation Phase)

The second phase (*join and aggregation* phase) cost components for the GroupBy partitioning scheme are comprised of the receiving cost, which is the cost of receiving records from the first phase, and the joining cost for joining the allocated fragments.

- *Receiving records cost* is similar to the data transfer cost, but without the message latency overhead.

$$((\pi_S \times S_i \times \sigma_S/P) \times m_p) \tag{6.36}$$

- *Join costs* involve reading, hashing, computing the cumulative value, and probing. The costs are as follows:

$$(|R_i| \times \sigma_R \times (t_r + t_h + t_j)) + (|S_i| \times (t_r + t_h + t_j)) \tag{6.37}$$

The aggregation process basically involves reading each record R, hashing it to a hash table, and calculating the aggregate value. After all records R have been processed, records S can be read, hashed, and probed. If they are matched, the matching records are written out to the query result.

The hashing process is very much determined by the size of the hash table that can fit into main memory. If the memory size is smaller than the hash table size, we normally partition the hash table into multiple buckets whereby each bucket can perfectly fit into main memory. All but the first bucket are spooled to disk.

Given this scenario, we must include the I/O cost for reading and writing overflow buckets, which is as follows.

- *Aggregation costs* involve reading, hashing, computing the cumulative value, and probing. The costs are as follows:

$$(|R_i| \times \sigma_R \times (t_r + t_h + t_a)) + (|S_i| \times \sigma_j \times (t_r + t_h + t_a)) \quad (6.38)$$

- *Reading/writing of overflow buckets cost* is the I/O costs associated with the limitation of main memory to accommodate the entire hash table. This cost includes the costs for reading and writing records not processed in the first pass of hashing.

$$\left(1 - \min\left(\frac{H}{\sigma_R \times |R_i|}, 1\right)\right) \times \left(\pi_R \times \frac{R_i}{P} \times 2 \times IO\right) \quad (6.39)$$

For table S, assuming that the percentage of records overflowing is the same as that of for table R, the overflow buckets for table S becomes:

$$\left(1 - \min\left(\frac{H}{\sigma_R \times |R_i|}, 1\right)\right) \times \left(\pi_S \times \frac{S_i}{P} \times 2 \times IO\right) \quad (6.40)$$

The left-hand term defines the percentage of overflow, whereas the right-hand term is the I/O cost associated with rewriting and reloading table S.

The *generating result records cost* and *disk cost* are the same as those of the join partitioning scheme. Hence, **equations** 6.9 and 6.10 can be used.

6.7 SUMMARY

The focus of this chapter is parallelism of queries involving join and group-by operations.

The first query is where the join attribute is identical with the group-by attribute. This is called the *GroupBy-before-join* query. In this query, the group-by operation is carried out first and is then followed by the join operation. There are three parallel algorithms to process this type of queries, namely, the *Early Distribution scheme*, the *Early GroupBy with partitioning scheme*, and the *Early GroupBy with replication scheme*. The early distribution scheme is preferred when the number of groups produced has grown to be large, but is not favored when the number of groups produced is small. On the other hand, the Early-GroupBy with replication is preferable when the number of groups produced is small, but it gives rise to serious performance problems once the number of groups produced by the query is large.

The second query is where the join attribute is different from the group-by attribute. Consequently, the group-by operation has to be carried out after the join operation. This is called *GroupBy-after-join* query. There are two methods of parallel processing of such a query, depending on which attribute is chosen as a partitioning attribute: the join attribute or the group-by attribute. The former is called the *join partitioning scheme*, whereas the latter is called the *GroupBy partitioning scheme*. For efficiency, when the join selectivity factor is small and the degree of skewness is low, the join partitioning scheme leads to less cost; otherwise, the GroupBy partitioning scheme is desirable. In addition, it can be observed that the partitioning with the group-by attribute scheme is insensitive to the group-by factor and thus the scheme will simplify algorithm design and implementation.

6.8 BIBLIOGRAPHICAL NOTES

Group-by and aggregate functions are tightly related. Early work on aggregate functions and group-by operations include optimization SQL queries having aggregates (Bultzingsloewen *VLDB* 1987; Muralikrishna *VLDB* 1992), and group-by operation in relational algebra (Gray *BNCOD* 1981). Yan and Larson (*ICDE* 1994) worked on group-by before join, where they proposed to perform early reduction through early grouping.

In the parallelism area, Shatdal and Naughton (*SIGMOD* 1995) pioneered the work on parallel aggregate algorithms. Spiliopoulou et al. (*IEEE TKDE* 1996) later proposed parallel join with set operators and aggregates. Liang and Orlowska (1996) focused on parallel multidimensional aggregates, whereas Hassan and Bamha (2006) later proposed parallel group-by-join queries processing on shared-nothing architectures.

Other work on group-by, aggregates, and join focuses on the data streams applications, including those by Ganguly et al. (*EDBT* 2004 and *PODS* 2005), Jiang et al. (*DEXA* 2006), and Wang et al. (*ADBIS* 2004). Recent work has emerged in XQueries employing a groupby operation (Deutsch et al. *ICDE* 2004).

6.9 EXERCISES

6.1. Given the following initial data placement of tables Project and Shipment in three processors, assume the query is expressed in the following SQL command:

Processor 1		Processor 2		Processor 3	
Project.J#	**Shipment.J#**	**Project.J#**	**Shipment.J#**	**Project.J#**	**Shipment.J#**
P1	P2	P2	P1	P3	P1
P4	P2	P5	P2	P6	P3
P7	P3	P8	P4	P9	P3
	P4		P4		P3
	P5		P5		P4

```
Select PROJECT.J#, SUM(Qty)
From PROJECT, SHIPMENT
Where PROJECT.J# = SHIPMENT.J#
Group By PROJECT.J#;
```

Show how the following *parallel GroupBy-before-join* algorithms work, using the above tables.

(a) *Early distribution* scheme

(b) *Early GroupBy with partitioning* scheme

(c) *Early GroupBy with replication* scheme

6.2. Write the pseudo-code algorithms for the above-mentioned three parallel schemes for parallel GroupBy-before-join algorithms.

6.3. Given the following initial data placement of tables Parts and Shipment in three processors, assume the query is expressed in the following SQL command:

Processor 1		Processor 2		Processor 3	
Parts.P#, Parts.City	**Shipment.P#**	**Parts.P#, Parts.City**	**Shipment.P#**	**Parts.P#, Parts.City**	**Shipment.P#**
A1, Sydney	A2	A2, Adelaide	A1	A3, Adelaide	A1
A4, Melbourne	A2	A5, Adelaide	A2	A6, Melbourne	A3
A7, Sydney	A3	A8, Melbourne	A4	A9, Sydney	A3
	A4		A4		A3
	A5		A5		A4

```
Select PARTS.City, AVG(Qty)
From PARTS, SHIPMENT
Where PARTS.P# = SHIPMENT.P#
Group By PARTS.City;
```

Show how the following *parallel GroupBy-after-join* algorithms work, using the above tables.

(a) *Join partitioning* scheme

(b) *GroupBy partitioning* scheme

6.4. Write the pseudo-code algorithms for the above-mentioned two parallel schemes for parallel GroupBy-after-join.

6.5. Looking at the cost notations in Table 6.1, explain two categories of *selectivity ratios* σ_R and σ_j.

6.6. Explain the main difference between equations 6.7 and 6.12 in terms of the selectivity ratio σ_R in equation 6.7 and σ_{R1} in equation 6.12.

6.7. Explain the similarity and difference between equations 6.7 and 6.8. Illustrate your answer with an example.

6.8. Investigate how parallel GroupBy-before-join and parallel GroupBy-after-join are expressed in SQL. Examine how these queries are executed in parallel by the query engine. Is there any difference between their parallel execution by the query engine and the parallel schemes described in this chapter, especially in terms of the sequence of the join operation and the group-by operation?

Chapter 7

Parallel Indexing

Index is an important element in databases, and the existence of index is unavoidable. Because of the importance of index in database systems, in this chapter we focus solely on parallel indexing. Three important elements in parallel indexing are studied, namely, parallel index structures, parallel index maintenance, and parallel index storage.

In Section 7.1, a classification of parallel indexing for parallel databases is outlined. The details of parallel indexing structures are explained in Section 7.2. Section 7.3 focuses on parallel index maintenance, including insertion and deletion of a node from a parallel index tree. The next issue on parallel indexing is storage. Since there are different kinds of parallel index structures, we need to understand the storage requirements for each of them. These are discussed in Section 7.4.

When an index has been built on a particular attribute, database operations (e.g., selection, join) on this attribute will become more efficient by utilizing the index. Here, we also present parallel search and parallel join query processing whereby one or more indexes based on the attribute involved in the query exist. Therefore, parallel search and parallel join may need to make use of this already existing index.

In Sections 7.5 and 7.6, we look at the algorithms for parallel search and parallel join query processing involving indexes. As there are many different parallel indexing structures and parallel algorithms for search and join, a comparative analysis is given. The aim of this comparative analysis is to examine each parallel indexing structure in terms of its support for efficient parallel query processing, particularly for parallel search and parallel join. For this purpose, Section 7.7 is included in this chapter, where a full comparison is given.

High-Performance Parallel Database Processing and Grid Databases,
by David Taniar, Clement Leung, Wenny Rahayu, and Sushant Goel
Copyright © 2008 John Wiley & Sons, Inc.

7.1 PARALLEL INDEXING – AN INTERNAL PERSPECTIVE ON PARALLEL INDEXING STRUCTURES

To understand parallel indexing support of parallel query processing, it is critical to know how a parallel index is structured in a parallel environment. Parallel indexing structure is essentially data partitioning, which focuses on how indexes are partitioned in parallel environments.

Data partitioning methods for parallel database systems are studied in Chapter 6. Since the table structure is flat, data partitioning for tables is relatively straightforward. This is not the case for indexes. Because of their complex structure, index partitioning is not as straightforward as table partitioning, and a comprehensive study in index partitioning becomes challenging. In this section, a classification for index partitioning is provided.

There are various data structures for indexing in database systems. One of the most popular data structures for index is based on B+ trees. With a B+ tree, each nonleaf node may consist of up to k keys and $k+1$ pointers to the nodes on the next level on the tree hierarchy (i.e., child nodes). All child nodes, which are on the left-hand side of the parent node, have key values less than, or equal to, the key of their parent node. On the other hand, keys of child nodes on the right-hand side of the parent node are greater than the key of their parent node. The structure of leaf nodes is slightly different from that of nonleaf nodes. Each leaf node consists of up to k keys, where each key has a pointer (called data pointer) to the actual record; and each node has one node pointer to a right-side neighboring leaf node. Having all data pointers stored on the leaf nodes is considered better than storing data pointers in the nonleaf nodes like the original B trees. Furthermore, by having node pointers on the leaf level, it becomes possible to trace all leaf nodes from the left-most to the right-most nodes, producing a sorted list of keys.

As a running example, in this chapter we provide a table with some sample records in it (see Figure 7.1). The sample table consists of records of IDs and Names. The index is inserted based on the order of the records in the table. Assume that in the index tree the maximum number of node pointers from any nonleaf node is 4, and the maximum number of data pointers from any leaf node is 3.

In parallel index partitioning or parallel indexing structures, given a network of processing elements, each with its own processor, disk, and main memory (i.e., shared-nothing architecture), various partitioning methods exist. In general, there are three parallel indexing structures, namely:

1. Nonreplicated index (**NRI**),
2. Partially replicated index (**PRI**), and
3. Fully replicated index (**FRI**)

For the first two parallel indexing structures (i.e., NRI and PRI), three different variations are considered, which depend on two factors, namely, *index partitioning attributes* and *table partitioning attributes*. The first variation is where the index

Table (ID, Name):

23	Adams		18	Kathy		39	Uma
65	Bernard		21	Larry		43	Vera
37	Chris		10	Mary		47	Wenny
60	David		74	Norman		50	Xena
46	Eric		78	Oprah		69	Yuliana
92	Fred		15	Peter		75	Zorro
48	Greg		16	Queen		8	Agnes
71	Harold		20	Ross		49	Bonnie
56	Ian		24	Susan		33	Caroline
59	Johanna		28	Tracey		38	Dennis

Index (B+ Tree):

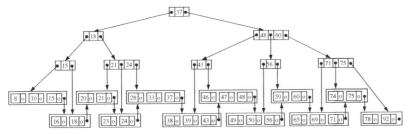

Figure 7.1   A sample table and index

partitioning attribute is the same as the table partitioning attribute. The second variation is where no index partitioning attribute is used. The last option is where the index partitioning attribute is different from that of the table. For the FRI structure, only two variations are available, that is, the first and the third variations above. This classification gives a complete possibility of indexing in parallel database systems, even though only a few of these categories have been applied to commercial database management systems, such as Oracle.

To give the reader a better view of these different structures, Figure 7.2 shows a matrix of the three parallel indexing structures and their various options. The details of each parallel indexing structure are discussed in the next section.

7.2 PARALLEL INDEXING STRUCTURES

7.2.1 Nonreplicated Indexing (NRI) Structures

A *nonreplicated indexing (NRI)* structure, as the name suggests, is where the global index is partitioned into several disjoint and smaller indices. Each of these small indices is placed in a separate processing element. When partitioning the index, we need to consider partitioning of the table as well. This explains the background of the three variations of NRI as described in the previous section.

	Indexed Attribute = Table Partitioning Attribute	No Index Partitioning Attribute	Indexed Attribute ≠ Table Partitioning Attribute
Nonreplicated Index NRI	NRI-1	NRI-2	NRI-3
Partially Replicated Index PRI	PRI-1	PRI-2	PRI-3
Fully Replicated Index FRI	FRI-1		FRI-3

Figure 7.2   Parallel indexing structures

The first model of NRI, abbreviated as **NRI-1**, is where the index partitioning attribute is the same as the table partitioning attribute. Using the sample data shown in Figure 7.1, if the table (consisting of ID and Name fields) is range partitioned based on the ID, the global index is also partitioned with the same attribute. Suppose that there are three processing elements, and the adopted range partitioning indicates that processor 1 is between IDs 1 and 30, processor 2 is between 31 and 60, and the last processor is between 60 and 100. After the table has been partitioned according to this range partitioning strategy, each processing element then builds its local index on the ID field. Figure 7.3 shows the composition of each

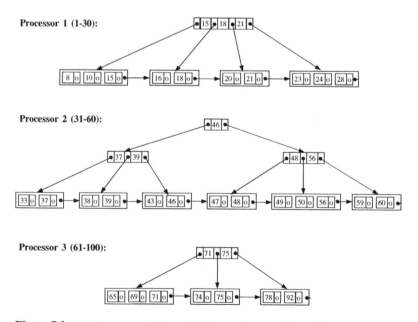

Figure 7.3   NRI-1 structure (index partitioning attribute = table partitioning attribute)

processing element with its local index. The partial table is now shown, but each key in the local index has a corresponding record locally.

The second model of NRI, abbreviated as *NRI-2*, is where local indices are built on whatever data already exists in each processing element. The table partitioning attribute can be unknown, a different attribute is used in table partitioning, or even a nonrange partitioning applied to the indexed attribute. For example, the table is partitioned based on attribute Name. Suppose the partitioning strategy for the table is to take the second letter of each Name and to apply the following rules. If the second letter of the Name is a consonant, place it in processing element 1. If it is a vowel of letter *a* or *e*, place it in processing element 2, and finally if it is the other vowel (i.e., letter *i*, *o*, or *u*), place it in processing element 3. Once the table is partitioned with these rules, local indices based on the ID field are then built. Because the local index has no global semantics, we describe this indexing method as not having an index partitioning attribute. NRI-2 structure assumes that each processor is like an independent single processor, and an index is built on the local data without considering the global picture of a multiprocessor environment. Figure 7.4 shows the composition of each processing element with its local data and index.

The last model of NRI, abbreviated as *NRI-3*, is where there is an attribute used in the index partitioning, but it is different from that of the table partitioning. For example, the index is partitioned based on the ID field, whereas the table is partitioned according to the Name field. This structure is quite common in parallel database systems, since parallel searching on the table partitioning attribute can use the information on table partitioning, whereas parallel searching on the indexed attribute may use the information on index partitioning.

Because of the difference in attribute partitioning, it becomes impossible to locate all of the records at the same place as its indices. For example, record (10, Mary) is allocated to processing element 2 because "Mary" has letter *a* as its second character and letter *a* is a vowel of either *a* or *e*, and hence record (10, Mary) should be placed in processing element 2 according to the partitioning rules set for NRI-2. However, ID 10 for Mary will be allocated in processing element 1 because processing element 1 is ranged between IDs 1 and 30. Therefore, it will be necessary to have a data pointer from the leaf node containing key ID 10 in processor 1 to the actual record of (10, Mary) in processor 2. In other words, the data pointer crosses between processors. Figure 7.5 shows an illustration of NRI-3 (dashed arrows are the data pointers). For simplicity of the diagram, not all data pointers are shown.

In summary, NRI-1 and NRI-2 are where the index is local and built on the local data, whereas NRI-3 is where the index is not built on the local data but is partitioned based on the index partitioning attribute.

7.2.2 Partially Replicated Indexing (PRI) Structures

There are two major differences between a *partially replicated indexing* (**PRI**) structure and the NRI structures. The first is suggested by the name itself, where PRI has some degree of replication, while NRI has not. The second difference is

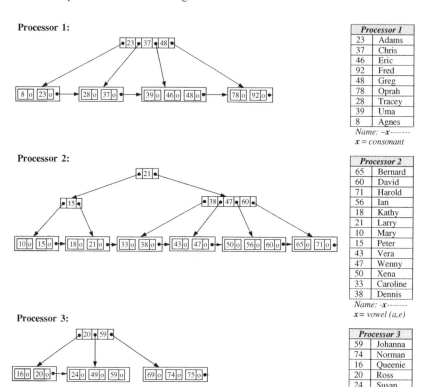

Figure 7.4   NRI-2 (no index partitioning attribute is used)

related to the composition of the index itself. Unlike in NRI, where the global index is physically partitioned, in PRI the global index is maintained. In other words, each processing element has a different part of the global index, and the overall structure of the global index is still preserved. The ownership rule of each index node is that the processor owning a leaf node also owns all nodes from the root to that leaf. Consequently, the root node is replicated to all processors, and nonleaf nodes may be replicated to some processors. Additionally, if a leaf node has several keys belonging to different processors, this leaf node is also replicated to the processors owning the keys.

Like NRI, PRI has three variations: the index partitioning attribute is the same as the table partitioning attribute; no index partitioning attribute is used; and the index partitioning attribute is different from the table partitioning attribute. Using the same example shown previously, **PRI-1** is exhibited in Figure 7.6. In this example, PRI-1 uses the ID field as the index partitioning attribute, which is the same as for the table partitioning. Assume the range partitioning rules used are that processor

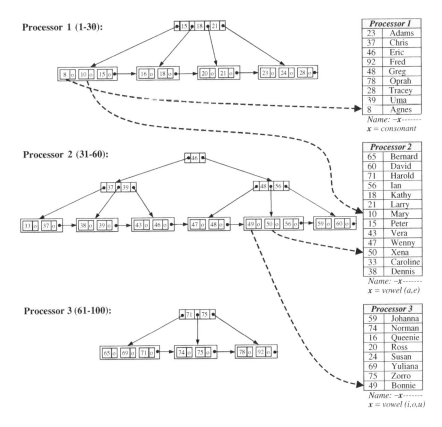

Figure 7.5 NRI-3 (index partitioning attribute ≠ table partitioning attribute)

1 holds IDs between 1 and 30, processor 2 holds IDs between 31 and 60, and the rest go to processor 3. Note in Figure 7.6 that the fifth leaf node (28, 33, 37) is replicated to processors 1 and 2 because key 28 belongs to processor 1 while keys 33 and 37 belong to processor 2. Also, note that some nonleaf nodes are replicated whereas others are not. For example, nonleaf node 15 is not replicated and is located only in processor 1, whereas nonleaf node 18 is replicated to processors 1 and 2. It is also clear that the root node is fully replicated.

Data structure for the PRI structures can be rather problematic in implementation. To illustrate our point, consider the root node 37, which is replicated to all processors. Since the child node 18 is located in processor 1 as well as processor 2, the root node 37 in both processors would have to maintain two node pointers each, one to the node 18 locally and the other to the copy of node 18 located at the other place. The structure of each node will need to be altered to allow multiple data pointers. Furthermore, the left node pointers coming out from node 37 located at processor 3 are linked to nodes 18 at processors 1 and 2. Figure 7.7 gives a diagrammatic illustration of this matter. It shows only the first two levels of the index tree as previously displayed in Figure 7.6.

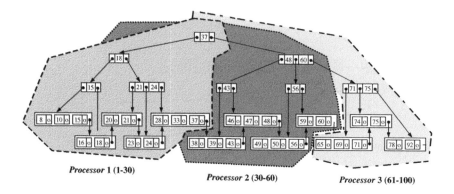

Processor 1 (1-30)   Processor 2 (30-60)   Processor 3 (61-100)

Figure 7.6 PRI-1 (index partitioning attribute = table partitioning attribute)

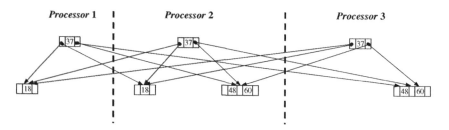

Figure 7.7 Multiple node pointers model for PRI

Since the multiple node pointers model for PRI raises node pointer complexity, this model is not practical. Rather, a single node pointer model is more efficient and practical. In the single node pointer model, each node pointer has only one outgoing node pointer.

If the child node exists locally, the node pointer points to this local node only, even when this child node is also replicated to other processors. For example, from node 37 at processor 1 there is only one node pointer to the local node 18. The child node 18 at processor 2 will not receive an incoming node pointer from the root node 37 at processor 1; instead, it will receive one node pointer from the local root node 37 only.

If the child node does not exist locally, the node pointer will choose one node pointer pointing to the nearest child node (in case multiple child nodes exist somewhere else). For example, from the root node 37 at processor 1 there is only one outgoing right node pointer to child node (48,60) at processor 2. In this case, we assume that processor 2 is the nearest neighbor of processor 3. Child node (48,60), which also exists at processor 3, will not receive a node pointer from root node 37 at processor 1.

With this single node pointer model, it is always possible to trace a node from any parent node, and consequently there is no crucial need to have multiple node pointers. For example, it is possible to trace to node (71,75) from the root node 37 at processor 1, although there is no direct link from root node 37 at processor 1 to its direct child node (48,60) at processor 3. Tracing to node (71,75) can still be done through node (48,60) at processor 2.

A more formal proof for the single node pointer model of PRI is as follows. First, given that a parent node is replicated when its child nodes are scattered at multiple locations, there is always a direct link from the copy of this parent node to any of its child nodes. Second, using the same methodology as the first statement above, given a replicated grandparent node, there is always a direct link from whichever copy of this grandparent node to any of the parent nodes. Considering the first and the second statements above, we can conclude that there is always a direct link from the copy of the grandparent node to any of its child nodes.

Figure 7.8 shows an example of a single node pointer model for PRI. It shows only the top three levels of the index tree depicted previously in Figure 7.6.

Apart from the issue of a node pointer at a nonleaf level, that of node pointers being at a leaf level is also worth mentioning. As some leaf nodes are replicated, and leaf nodes are chained from the left to the right, it is also important to maintain a node pointer from the right-most leaf node of one processor to the first leaf node of the next processor, which does not exist in the previous processor. For example, Figure 7.9 shows that leaf node (28, 33, 37), which is replicated at processors 1 and 2, has a node pointer coming from processor 1 to node (38, 39 43) at processor 2.

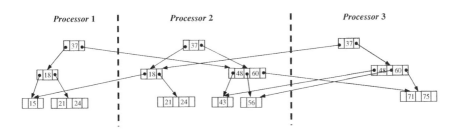

Figure 7.8 Single node pointer model for PRI

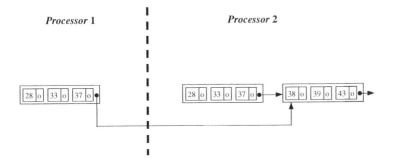

Figure 7.9 Node pointers at a leaf node level crossing from one processor to another

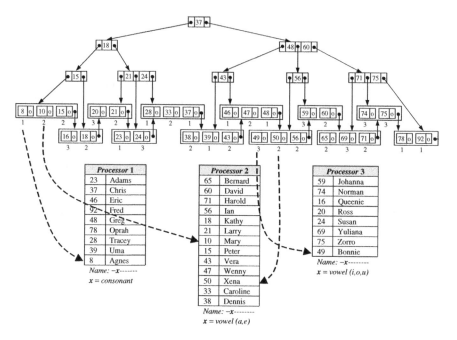

Figure 7.10(a) PRI-2 (no index partitioning attribute is used)

PRI-2 structure has a concept similar to NRI-2; that is, the leaf node and its pointed record are located at the same place. The main difference between PRI-2 and NRI-2 is the fact that the PRI structures have one global index whereas the NRI structures use local indexes. Figure 7.10(a) gives an illustration of PRI-2. In this diagram, not all data pointers are shown in order to improve the readability of the diagram. We use numbers 1, 2 and 3 to correspond to the processor number (instead of arrows to represent data pointers).

In this example, the table is partitioned on the Name field according to the same rule applied to NRI-2. The global index is subsequently partitioned based on the location of the partial table. For example, record Agnes (8,Agnes) is located in processor 1 according to the rule as stated in NRI-2, and so is leaf node 8 (the first key of the first leaf node on the left side of the index tree). The data pointer of leaf node 8 points to record Agnes. Since a leaf node consists of *k* keys, and each key may be located at a different processor, replication exists at the leaf node level. For example, the first leaf node of (8,10,15) is replicated in processors 1 and 2, since key 8 is located at processor 1 and the other two keys are located at processor 2.

The replication is propagated at the nonleaf node levels. Figure 7.10(b) gives an illustration of this replication. As the replication becomes more complex, as it does in this example, it is probably difficult to visualize it because of overlapping. To help readers visualize each processor, we use a dashed line for processor 1, a dotted line for processor 2, and a dashed-dotted line for processor 3. The figure

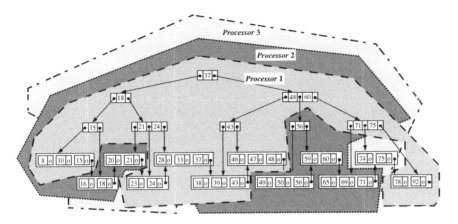

Figure 7.10(b) Replication in PRI-2

shows that most of the nonleaf nodes are replicated to all three processors, except for nonleaf node (43), where processor 3 is excluded, and nonleaf node (56), where processor 1 is excluded.

Comparing PRI-1 and PRI-2, we can closely examine Figure 7.9 and Figure 7.10(b). They clearly show that replication at both leaf and nonleaf node levels exists more in PRI-2 than in PRI-1. This is mainly caused by leaf node replication in PRI-2. In PRI-1, replication at the leaf node level exists at the neighboring leaf nodes only; that is, the right-most leaf node in one processor may be overlapped with the left-most leaf node in the other processor. Leaf node replication in PRI-2 may happen anywhere, depending on the value of the keys in each leaf node.

PRI-3 structure is analogous to NRI-3; that is, the table is partitioned according to some rule on an attribute, which is different from the index partitioning attribute, or the partitioning rule for the table is not a range partitioning. Using the same example in NRI-3, in PRI-3 the table is partitioned based on the Name field, whereas the index is based on the ID field. As a result of this partitioning strategy, not only do we have data pointers crossing the processor boundary as in NRI-3, but also we increase the chance of leaf nodes to be replicated as in PRI-2, for the same reason. Figure 7.11 shows an illustration of PRI-3.

Comparing PRI-1 and PRI-3 (see Fig. 7.9 and Fig. 7.11), note that the global index tree for PRI-3 is the same as that for PRI-1. The main difference between PRI-1 and PRI-3 lies in the data pointers, where data pointers in PRI-3 may cross the boundary of the processor since the location of the record and its leaf node may be different. This is not the case with PRI-1.

Comparing PRI-2 and PRI-3 (see Fig. 7.10(b) and Fig. 7.11), the difference is mainly in the replication degree, which is likely to be higher in PRI-2. Replication in PRI-3 is the same as that for PRI-1, since the global index tree itself is the same for both PRI-1 and PRI-3.

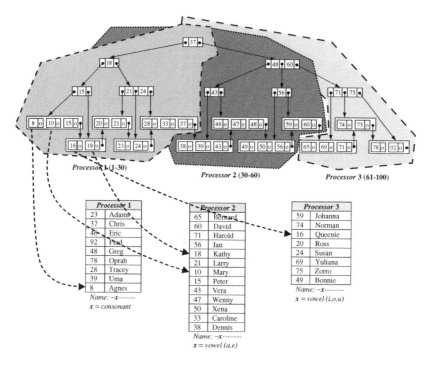

Figure 7.11   PRI-3 (index partitioning attribute ≠ table partitioning attribute)

In summary, PRI structures are very similar to NRI structures except that the global index is preserved in PRI. As a consequence, replication of index nodes has to be carefully maintained.

7.2.3   Fully Replicated Indexing (FRI) Structures

A *fully replicated indexing (FRI)* structure is where the global index is fully replicated to all available working processors. Because of the simplicity of this parallel indexing structure, there are only two different variations: the table partitioning attribute is the same as the indexed attribute, and the table partitioning attribute is different from the indexed attribute. In the context of NRI and PRI, only variations 1 and 3 are available to FRI structures. To make the naming convention uniform across the three parallel indexing structures, the two variations for the FRI structures are numbered as 1 and 3, leaving variation 2 as not applicable.

FRI-1 has a similar concept as the other two variations 1 (i.e., NRI-1 and PRI-1). For example, the table is partitioned on the ID field, and the index is built on the same field. Since the global index is fully replicated, leaf nodes that do not have the base data located at the same place must have their data pointers crossing the processor boundaries. As a result, all records will have *n* incoming data pointers from the leaf nodes, where *n* is the number of processors. Figure 7.12 illustrates

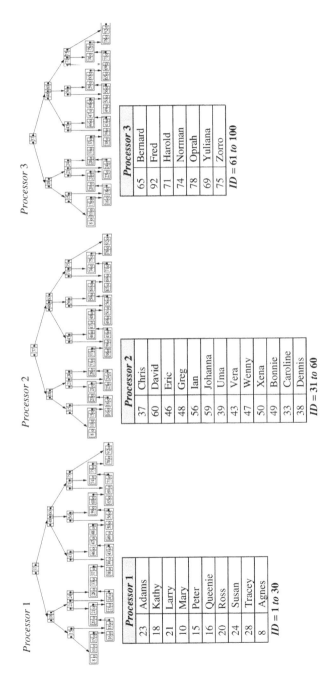

Figure 7.12 FRI-1 (index partitioning attribute = table partitioning attribute)

the FRI-1 structure. Note that the global index is replicated to the three processors. In the diagram, the data pointers are not shown. However, one can imagine that each key in the leaf nodes has a data pointer going to the correct record, and each record will have three incoming data pointers.

FRI-3 is quite similar to PRI-1, except that the table partitioning for FRI-3 is not the same as the indexed attribute. For example, the table partitioning is based on the Name field and uses a range partitioning, whereas the index is on the ID field. However, the similarity is that the index is fully replicated, and each of the records will also have *n* incoming data pointers, where *n* is the number of replication of the index. Figure 7.13 shows an example of the FRI-3. Once again, the data pointers are not shown in the diagram.

It is clear from the two variations discussed above (i.e., FRI-1 and FRI-3) that variation 2 is not applicable for FRI structures, because the index is fully replicated. Unlike the other variations 2 (i.e., NRI-2 and PRI-2), they exist because the index is partitioned, and part of the global index on a particular processor is built upon the records located at that processor. If the index is fully replicated, there will not be any structure like this, because the index located at a processor cannot be built purely from the records located at that processor alone. This is why FRI-2 does not exist.

7.3 INDEX MAINTENANCE

In this section, we examine the various issues and complexities related to maintaining different parallel index structures. Index maintenance covers insertion and deletion of index nodes. The general steps for index maintenance are as follows:

- Insert/delete a record to the table (carried out in processor p_1),
- Insert/delete an index node to/from the index tree (carried out in processor p_2), and
- Update the data pointers.

In the last step above, if it is an insertion operation, a data pointer is created from the new index key to the new inserted record. If it is a deletion operation, a deletion of the data pointer takes place.

Parallel index maintenance essentially concerns the following two issues:

- Whether $p_1 = p_2$. This relates to the data pointer complexity.
- Whether maintaining an index (insert or delete) involves multiple processors. This issue relates to the restructuring of the index tree itself.

The simplest form of index maintenance is where $p_1 = p_2$ and the insertion/deletion of an index node involves a single processor only. These two issues for each of the parallel indexing structures are discussed next.

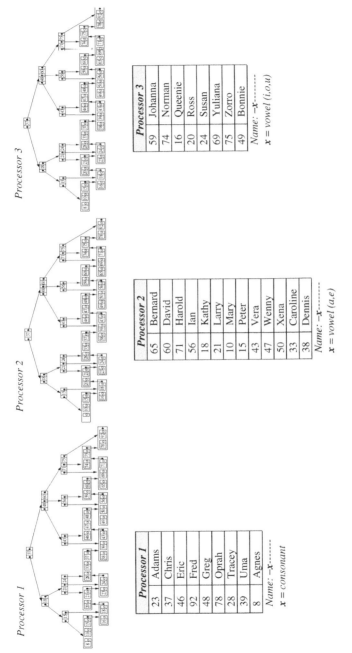

Processor 1

23	Adams
37	Chris
46	Eric
92	Fred
48	Greg
78	Oprah
28	Tracey
39	Uma
8	Agnes

Name: –x--------

x = consonant

Processor 2

65	Bernard
60	David
71	Harold
56	Ian
18	Kathy
21	Larry
10	Mary
15	Peter
43	Vera
47	Wenny
50	Xena
33	Caroline
38	Dennis

Name: –x--------

x = vowel (a,e)

Processor 3

59	Johanna
74	Norman
16	Queenie
20	Ross
24	Susan
69	Yuliana
75	Zorro
49	Bonnie

Name: –x--------

x = vowel (i,o,u)

Figure 7.13 FRI-3 (index partitioning attribute ≠ table partitioning attribute)

181

7.3.1 Maintaining a Parallel Nonreplicated Index

Maintenance of the NRI structures basically involves a single processor. Hence, the subject is really whether p_1 is equal to p_2. For the NRI-1 and NRI-2 structures, $p_1 = p_2$. Accordingly, these two parallel indexing structures are the simplest form of parallel index. The mechanism of index maintenance for these two parallel indexing structures is carried out as per normal index maintenance on sequential processors. The insertion and deletion procedures are summarized as follows.

After a new record has been inserted to the appropriate processor, a new index key is inserted to the index tree also at the same processor. The index key insertion steps are as follows. First, search for an appropriate leaf node for the new key on the index tree. Then, insert the new key entry to this leaf node, if there is still space in this node. However, if the node is already full, this leaf node must be split into two leaf nodes. The first half of the entries are kept in the original leaf node, and the remaining entries are moved to a new leaf node. The last entry of the first of the two leaf nodes is copied to the nonleaf parent node. Furthermore, if the nonleaf parent node is also full, it has to be split again into two nonleaf nodes, similar to what occurred with the leaf nodes. The only difference is that the last entry of the first node is not copied to the parent node, but is moved. Finally, a data pointer is established from the new key on the leaf node to the record located at the same processor.

The deletion process is similar to that for insertion. First, delete the record, and then delete the desired key from the leaf node in the index tree (the data pointer is to be deleted as well). When deleting the key from a leaf node, it is possible that the node will become underflow after the deletion. In this case, try to find a sibling leaf node (a leaf node directly to the left or to the right of the node with underflow) and redistribute the entries among the node and its sibling so that both are at least half full; otherwise, the node is merged with its siblings and the number of leaf nodes is reduced.

Maintenance of the NRI-3 structure is more complex because $p_1 \neq p_2$. This means that the location of the record to be inserted/deleted may be different from the index node insertion/deletion. The complexity of this kind of index maintenance is that the data pointer crosses the processor boundary. So, after both the record and the index entry (key) have been inserted, the data pointer from the new index entry in p_1 has to be established to the record in p_2. Similarly, in the deletion, after the record and the index entry have been deleted (and the index tree is restructured), the data pointer from p_1 to p_2 has to be deleted as well. Despite some degree of complexity, there is only *one* data pointer for each entry in the leaf nodes to the actual record.

7.3.2 Maintaining a Parallel Partially Replicated Index

Following the first issue on $p_1 = p_2$ mentioned in the previous section, maintenance of PRI-1 and PRI-2 structures is similar to that of NRI-1 and NRI-2 where

$p_1 = p_2$. Hence, there is no additional difficulty to data pointer maintenance. For PRI-3, it is also similar to NRI-3; that is, $p_1 \neq p_2$. In other words, data pointer maintenance of PRI-3 has the same complexity as that of NRI-3, where the data pointer may be crossing from one processor (index node) to another processor (record).

The main difference between the PRI and NRI structures is very much related to the second issue on single/multiple processors being involved in index restructuring. Unlike the NRI structures, where only single processors are involved in index maintenance, the PRI structures require multiple processors to be involved. Hence, the complexity of index maintenance for the PRI structures is now moved to index restructuring, not so much on data pointers.

To understand the complexity of index restructuring for the PRI structures, consider the insertion of entry 21 to the existing index (assume the PRI-1 structure is used). In this example, we show three stages of the index insertion process. The stages are (*i*) the initial index tree and the desired insertion of the new entry to the existing index tree, (*ii*) the splitting node mechanism, and (*iii*) the restructuring of the index tree.

The initial index tree position is shown in Figure 7.14(a). When a new entry of 21 is inserted, the first leaf node becomes overflow. A split of the overflow leaf node is then carried out. The split action also causes the nonleaf parent node to be overflow, and subsequently, a further split must be performed to the parent node (see Fig. 7.14(b)).

Not that when splitting the leaf node, the two split leaf nodes are replicated to processors 1 and 2, although the first leaf node after the split contains entries of the first processor only (18 and 21—the range of processor 1 is 1–30). This is because the original leaf node (18, 23, 37) has already been replicated to both processors 1 and 2. The two new leaf nodes have a node pointer linking them together.

When splitting the nonleaf node (37, 48, 60) into two nonleaf nodes (21; 48, 60), processor 3 is involved because the root node is also replicated to processor 3. In the implementation, this can be tricky as processor 3 needs to be informed that it must participate in the splitting process. An algorithm is presented at the end of this section.

The final step is the restructuring step. This step is necessary because we need to ensure that each node has been allocated to the correct processors. Figure 7.14(c) shows a restructuring process. In this restructuring, the processor allocation is updated. This is done by performing an in-order traversal of the tree, finding the range of the node (min, max), determining the correct processor(s), and reallocating to the designated processor(s). When reallocating the nodes to processor(s), each processor will also update the node pointers, pointing to its local or neighboring child nodes. Note that in the example, as a result of the restructuring, leaf node (18, 21) is now located in processor 1 only (instead of processors 1 and 2).

Next, we present an example of a deletion process, which affects the index structure. In this example, we would like to delete entry 21, expecting to get the original tree structure shown previously before entry 21 is inserted. Figure 7.15 shows the current tree structure and the merge and collapse processes.

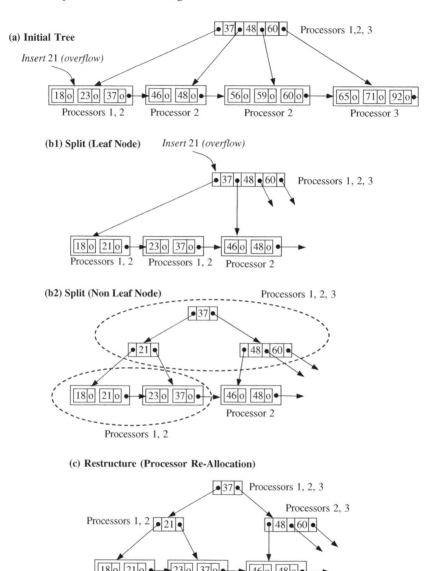

Figure 7.14 Index entry insertion in the PRI structures

As shown in Figure 7.15(a), after the deletion of entry 21, leaf node (18) becomes underflow. A merging with its sibling leaf node needs to be carried out. When merging two nodes, the processor(s) that own the new node are the union of all processors owning the two old nodes. In this case, since node (18) is located in processor 1 and node (23, 37) is in processors 1 and 2, the new merged node

(a) Initial Tree

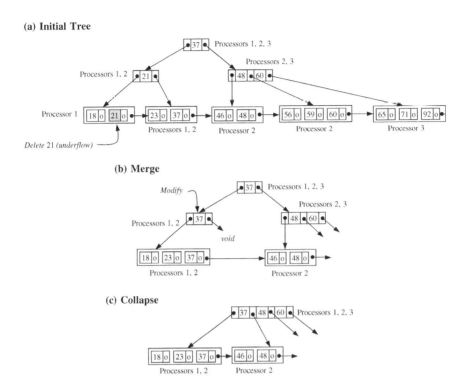

Figure 7.15   Index entry deletion in PRI structures

(18, 23, 37) should be located in processors 1 and 2. Also, as a consequence of the merging, the immediate nonleaf parent node entry has to be modified in order to identify the maximum value of the leaf node, which is now 37, not 21. As shown in Figure 7.15(b), the right node pointer of the nonleaf parent node (37) becomes *void*. Because nonleaf node (37) has the same entry as its parent node (root node (37)), they have to be collapsed together, and consequently a new nonleaf node (37, 48, 60) is formed (see Fig. 7.15(c)).

The restructuring process is the same as for the insertion process. In this example, however, processor allocation has been done correctly and hence, restructuring is not needed.

Maintenance Algorithms

As described above, maintenance of the PRI structures relates to splitting and merging nodes when performing an insertion or deletion operation and to restructuring and reallocating nodes after a split/merge has been done. The insertion and deletion of a key from an index tree are preceded by a searching of the node where the desired key is located. Algorithm find_node illustrates a key searching procedure on an index tree. The find_node algorithm is a recursive algorithm. It basically starts from a root node and traces into the desired leaf node either at the local or neighboring processor by recursively calling the find_node algorithm and passing a child tree to the same processor or following the trace to a different processor. Once the node has been found, an operation insert or delete can be performed.

After an operation has been carried out to a designated leaf node, if the node is overflow (in the case of insertion) or underflow (in the case of deletion), a split or a merge operation must be done to the node. Splitting or merging nodes are performed in the same manner as splitting or merging nodes in single-processor systems (i.e., single-processor B + trees).

The difficult part of the find_node algorithm is that when splitting/merging nonleaf nodes, sometimes more processors need to be involved in addition to those initially used. For example, in Figure 7.14(a) and (b), at first processors 1 and 2 are involved in inserting key 21 into the leaf nodes. Inserting entry 21 to the root node involves processor 3 as well, since the root node is also replicated to processor 3. The problem is how processor 3 is notified to perform such an operation while only processors 1 and 2 were involved in the beginning. This is solved by activating the find_node algorithm in each processor. Processor 1 will ultimately find the desired leaf node (18,23,37) in the local processor, and so will processor 2. Processor 3 however, will pass the operation to processor 2, as the desired leaf node (18,23,37) located in processor 2 is referenced by the root node in processor 3. After the insertion operation (and the split operation) done to the leaf nodes (18,23,37) located at processors 1 and 2 has been completed, the program control is passed back to the root node. This is due to the nature of a recursive algorithm, where the initial copy of the algorithm is called back when the child copy of the process has been completed. Since all processors were activated in the beginning of the find node operation, each processor now can perform a split process (because of the overflow to the root node). In other words, there is no special process whereby an additional processor (in this case processor 3) needs to be invited or notified to be involved in the splitting of the root node. Everything is a consequence of the recursive nature of the algorithm which was initiated in each processor. Figure 7.16 lists the find_node algorithm.

After the find_node algorithm (with an appropriate operation: insert or delete), it is sometimes necessary to restructure the index tree (as shown in Fig. 7.14(c)). The restructure algorithm (Fig. 7.17) is composed of three algorithms. The main restructure algorithm calls the inorder algorithm where the traversal is done. The inorder traversal is a modified version of the traditional inorder traversal, because an index tree is not a binary tree.

For each visit to the node in the inorder algorithm, the proc_alloc algorithm is called, for the actual checking of whether the right processor has been allocated to each node. The checking in the proc_alloc algorithm basically checks whether or not the current node should be located at the current processor. If not, the node is deleted (in the case of a leaf node). If it is a nonleaf node, a careful checking must be done, because even when the range of (min,max) is not

---

Algorithm: Find a node initiated in each processor

---

find_node (tree, key, operation)
1. if (key is in the range of local node)
2.   if (local node is leaf)
3.   execute operation insert or delete on local node
4.   if (node is overflow or underflow)
5.   perform split or merge on leaf
6.   else
7.   locate child tree
8.   perform **find_node** (child, key, operation)
9.   if (node is overflow or underflow)
10.   perform split or collapse on non-leaf
11. else
12.   locate child tree in neighbour
13.   perform **find_node** (neighbour, key, operation)

Figure 7.16   Find a node algorithm

Algorithm: Index restructuring algorithms

---

restructure (tree)   // Restructure in each local
processor
1. perform **inorder** (tree)

inorder (tree)   // Inorder traversal for non-binary
                            // trees (like B+ trees)
1. if (local tree is not null)
2.   for i=1 to number of node pointers
3.   perform **inorder** (tree→node pointer i)
4.   perform **proc_alloc** (node)

proc_alloc (node)   // Processor allocation
1. if (node is leaf)
2.   if ((min,max) is not within the range)
3.   delete node
4. if (node is non-leaf)
5.   if (**all** node pointers are either void or
     point to non local nodes)
6.   delete node
7.   if (a node pointer is void)
8.   re-establish node pointer to a neighbor

Figure 7.17   Index restructuring algorithms

exactly within the range of the current processor, it is not necessary that the node should not be located in this processor, as its child nodes may have been correctly allocated to this processor. Only in the case where the current nonleaf node does not have child nodes should the nonleaf node be deleted; otherwise, a correct node pointer should be reestablished.

7.3.3 Maintaining a Parallel Fully Replicated Index

As an index is fully replicated to all processors, the main difference between NRI and FRI structures is that in FRI structures, the number of data pointers coming from an index leaf node to the record is equivalent to the number of processors. This certainly increases the complexity of maintenance of data pointers.

In regard to involving multiple processors in index maintenance, it is not as complicated as in the PRI structures, because in the FRI structures the index in each processor is totally isolated and is not coupled as in the PRI structures. As a result, any extra complication relating to index restructuring in the PRI structures does not exist here. In fact, index maintenance of the FRI structures is similar to that of the NRI structures, as all indexes are local to each processor.

7.3.4 Complexity Degree of Index Maintenance

The order of the complexity of parallel index maintenance, from the simplest to the most complex, is as follows.

- The simplest forms are NRI-1 and NRI-2 structures, as $p_1 = p_2$ and only single processors are involved in index maintenance (insert/delete).
- The next complexity level is on data pointer maintenance, especially when index node location is different from based data location. The simpler one is the NRI-3 structure, where the data pointer from an index entry to the record is 1-to-1. The more complex one is the FRI structures, where the data pointers are N-to-1 (from N index nodes to 1 record).
- The highest complexity level is on index restructuring. This is applicable to all three PRI structures.

7.4 INDEX STORAGE ANALYSIS

Even though disk technology and disk capacity are expanding, it is important to analyze space requirements of each parallel indexing structure. When examining index storage capacity, we cannot exclude record storage capacity. Therefore, it becomes important to include a discussion on the capacity of the base table, and to allow a comparative analysis between index and record storage requirement.

In this section, the storage cost models for uniprocessors is first described. These models are very important, as they will be used as a foundation for indexing the storage model for parallel processors. The storage model for each of the three parallel indexing structures is described next.

7.4.1 Storage Cost Models for Uniprocessors

There are two storage cost models for uniprocessors: one for the record and the other for the index.

Record Storage

There are two important elements in calculating the space required to store records of a table. The first is the length of each record, and the second is the blocking factor. Based on these two elements, we can calculate the number of blocks required to store all records.

The length of each record is the sum of the length of all fields, plus one byte for deletion marker (Equation 7.1). The latter is used by the DBMS to mark records that have been logically deleted but have not been physically removed, so that a rollback operation can easily be performed by removing the deletion code of that record.

$$Record\ length = Sum\ of\ all\ fields + 1\ byte\ Deletion\ marker \qquad (7.1)$$

The storage unit used by a disk is a block. A blocking factor indicates the maximum number of records that can fit into a block (Equation 7.2).

$$Blocking\ factor = \text{floor}(Block\ size/Record\ length) \qquad (7.2)$$

Given the number of records in each block (i.e., blocking factor), the number of blocks required to store all records can be calculated as follows.

$$Total\ blocks\ for\ all\ records = \text{ceiling}(Number\ of\ records/Blocking\ factor) \qquad (7.3)$$

Index Storage

There are two main parts of an index tree, namely *leaf* nodes and *nonleaf* nodes. Storage cost models for *leaf nodes* are as follows. First, we need to identify the number of entries in a leaf node. Then, the total number of blocks for all leaf nodes can be determined. Each leaf node consists of a number of indexed attributes (i.e., key), and each key in a leaf node has a data pointer pointing to the corresponding record. Each leaf node has also one node pointer pointing to the next leaf node. Each leaf node is normally stored in one disk block. Therefore, it is important to find out the number of keys (and their data pointers) that can fit into one disk block (or one leaf node). Equation 7.4 shows the relationship between number of keys in a leaf node and the size of each leaf node.

$$(p_{leaf} \times (Key\ size + Data\ pointer)) + Node\ pointer \leq Block\ size \qquad (7.4)$$

where p_{leaf} is the number of keys in a leaf node, *Key size* is the size of the indexed attribute (or key), *Data pointer* is the size of the data pointer, *Node pointer* is the size of the node pointer, and *Block size* is the size of the leaf node.

The number of leaf nodes can be calculated by dividing the number of records by the number of keys in each leaf node. Since it is likely that a node can be partially full, an additional parameter to indicate an average percentage that each node is full must be incorporated. The number of leaf nodes (we use the symbol of b_1) can then be calculated as follows.

$$b_1 = \texttt{ceiling}(\textit{Number of records}/(\textit{Percentage} \times p_{leaf})) \qquad (7.5)$$

where *Percentage* is the percentage that indicates by how much percentage a node is full.

The storage cost models for *non-leaf nodes* are as follows. Like that of leaf nodes, we need to identify the number of entries in a nonleaf node. The main difference between leaf and nonleaf nodes is that nonleaf nodes do not have data pointers but have multiple node pointers. The number of node pointers in a nonleaf node is always one more than the number of indexed attributes in the nonleaf node. Hence, the number of entries in each nonleaf node (indicated by p; as opposed to p_{leaf}) can be calculated as follows.

$$(p \times \textit{Node pointer}) + ((p - 1 \times \textit{Key size}) \leq \textit{Block size} \qquad (7.6)$$

Each nonleaf node has a number of child nonleaf nodes. This is called *fanout* of nonleaf node (we called it *fo* for short). Since the index tree is likely to be nonfull, a *Percentage* must be used to indicate the percentage of an index tree to be full.

$$fo = \texttt{ceiling}(\textit{Percentage} \times p) \qquad (7.7)$$

The number of levels in an index tree can be determined by incorporating the fanout degree (fo) in a *log* function; it is actually a *fo*-based *log* function of b_1. This will actually give the number of levels above the leaf node level. Hence, the total number of levels, including the leaf node level, is one extra level.

$$x = \texttt{ceiling}(\log_{fo}(b_1)) + 1) \qquad (7.8)$$

where x is the number of levels of an index tree.

Since b_1 is used to indicate the leaf nodes, the next level up is the first nonleaf node level, indicated by symbol b_2. The level number goes up and the last level that is a root node level is b_x, where x is the number of levels. The total number of nonleaf nodes in an index tree is the sum of number of nonleaf nodes of all nonleaf node levels, which is calculated as follows.

$$\textit{Total nonleaf nodes} = \sum_{i=2}^{x} b_i \qquad (7.9)$$

where $b_i = \texttt{ceiling}\ (b_{i-1}/fo)$

Total index space for an index tree is the sum of leaf nodes (b_1) and all nonleaf nodes ($b_2..b_x$).

$$Total\ index\ blocks = b_1 + Total\ nonleaf\ nodes \qquad (7.10)$$

7.4.2 Storage Cost Models for Parallel Processors

In this section, the storage cost models for the three parallel indexing structures are studied.

NRI Storage

The same calculation applied to uniprocessor indexing can be used by NRI. The only thing in NRI is that the number of records is smaller than that of the uniprocessors. Hence, equations 7.1 to 7.10 above can be used directly.

PRI Storage

The space required by the records is the same as that of NRI storage, since the records are uniformly distributed to all processors. In fact, the record storage cost models for NRI, PRI, and FRI are all the same, that is, divide the number of records evenly among all processors, and calculate the total record blocks in each processor.

For the index using a PRI structure, since there is only one global index shared by all processors, the height of the tree index is higher than local NRI index trees. Another difference lies in the overlapping of nodes in each level. For the leaf node level, the worst case is where one leaf node on the left-hand side is replicated to the processor on the left and one leaf node on the right-hand side is also replicated. Assuming that the index entry distribution is uniform, the number of leaf nodes in each processor (we call this c_1, instead of b_1) can be calculated as follows.

$$c_1 = \texttt{ceiling}(b_1/Number\ of\ processors) + 2 \qquad (7.11)$$

The same method of calculation can also be applied to the nonleaf nodes ($c_2..c_x$, corresponding with $b_2..b_x$), except for the root node level, where c_x must be equal to b_x. Total index space is the sum of c_1 (leaf node level), c_i where $i = 2, \ldots,$ $x - 1$ (non-leaf node level, except root level), and c_x (root node level).

$$Total\ non\text{-}leaf\ nodes = c_1 + \sum_{i=2}^{x-1} c_i + c_x \qquad (7.12)$$

FRI Storage

As mentioned earlier, the record storage is the same for all indexing structures, as the records are uniformly partitioned to all processors. Therefore, the main difference lies in the index storage. The index storage model for the FRI structures is very similar to that of the NRI structures, except for the following two aspects. First, the number of records used in the calculation of the number of entries in leaf nodes is not divided by the number of processors. This is because the index is fully replicated in FRI, not partitioned like in NRI. Therefore, it can be expected that the height of the index tree is higher, which is similar to that of the PRI structures. Second, the sizes of data pointers and node pointers must incorporate information on processors. This is necessary since both data and node pointers may go across to another processor.

7.5 PARALLEL PROCESSING OF SEARCH QUERIES USING INDEX

In this section, we consider the parallel processing of search queries involving index. Search queries where the search attributes are indexed are quite common. This is especially true in the case where a search operation is based on a primary key (PK) or secondary key (SK) on a table. Primary keys are normally indexed to prevent duplicate values that exist in that table, whereas secondary keys are indexed to speed up the searching process.

As the search attributes are indexed, parallel algorithms for these search queries are very much influenced by the indexing structures. Depending on the number of attributes being searched for and whether these attributes are indexed, parallel processing of search queries using parallel index can be categorized into two types of searches, namely (*i*) *parallel one-index search* and (*ii*) *parallel multi-index search*. The former deals with queries on the search operation of one indexed attribute. This includes exact match or range queries. The latter deals with multiattribute queries, that is, queries having search predicates on multiple indexed attributes.

7.5.1 Parallel One-Index Search Query Processing

Parallel processing of a one-index selection query exists in various formats, depending on the query type, whether exact-match, continuous-range, or discrete-range queries. In the next two sections, important elements in parallelization of these search queries are examined. These are then followed by a complete parallel algorithm.

Parallel Exact-Match Search Queries

There are three important factors in parallel exact-match search query processing: *processor involvement, index tree traversal,* and *record loading.*

- **Processor Involvement:** For exact match queries, ideally parallel processing may isolate into the processor(s) where the candidate records are located. Involving more processors in the process will certainly not do any good, especially if they do not produce any result. Considering that the number of processors involved in the query is an important factor, there are two cases in parallel processing of exact match search queries.

  Case 1 (selected processors are used): This case is applicable to all indexing structures, except for the NRI-2 structure. If the indexing structure of the indexed attribute is NRI-1, PRI-1, or FRI-1, we can direct the query into the specific processors, since the data partitioning scheme used by the index is known. The same case applies with NRI-3, PRI-3, and FRI-3. The only difference between NRI/PRI/FRI-1 and NRI/PRI/FRI-3 is that the records may not be located at the same place as where the leaf nodes of the index tree are located. However, from the index tree searching point of view they are the same, and hence it is possible to activate selected processors that will subsequently perform an index tree traversal.

  For PRI-2 indexing structure, since a global index is maintained, it becomes possible to traverse to any leaf node from basically anywhere. Therefore, only selected processors are used during the traversing of the index tree.

  The processor(s) containing the candidate records can be easily identified with NRI-1/3, PRI-1/3, or FRI-1/3 indexing structures. With the PRI-2 indexing structure, searching through an index tree traversal will ultimately arrive at the desired processor.

  Case 2 (all processors are used): This case is applicable to the NRI-2 indexing structure only, because with the NRI-2 indexing structure there is no way to identify where the candidate records are located without searching in all processors. This is because there is no partitioning semantics in NRI-2. NRI-2 basically builds a local index based on whatever data it has from the local processor without having global knowledge.

- **Index Tree Traversal:** Searching for a match is done through index tree traversal. The traversal starts from the root node and finishes either at a matched leaf node or no match is found. Depending on the indexing scheme used, there are two cases:

  Case 1 (traversal is isolated to local processor): This case is applicable to all indexing structures but PRI-2. When any of the NRI indexing structures is used, index tree traversal from the root node to the leaf node will stay at the same processor.

  When PRI-1 or PRI-3 is used, even though the root node is replicated to all processors and theoretically traversal can start from any node, the host processor will direct the processor(s) containing the candidate results to initiate the searching. In other words, index tree traversal will start from the processors that hold candidate leaf nodes. Consequently, index tree traversal will stay at the same processor.

For any of the FRI indexing structures, since the index tree is fully replicated, it becomes obvious that there is no need to move from one processor to another during the traversal of an index tree.

Case 2 (traversal crosses from one processor to another): This case is applicable to PRI-2 only, where searching that starts from a root node at any processor may end up on a leaf node at a different processor. For example, when a parent node at processor 1 points to a child node at processor 2, the searching control at processor 1 is passed to processor 2.

- **Record Loading:** Once a leaf node containing the desired data has been found, the record pointed by the leaf node is loaded from disk. Again here there are two cases:

    Case 1 (local record loading): This case is applicable to NRI/PRI/FRI-1 and NRI/PRI-2 indexing structures, since the leaf nodes and the associated records in these indexing schemes are located at the same processors. Therefore, record loading will be done locally.

    Case 2 (remote record loading): This case is applicable to NRI/PRI/FRI-3 indexing structures where the leaf nodes are not necessarily placed at the same processor where the records reside. Record loading in this case is performed by trailing the pointer from the leaf node to the record and by loading the pointed record. When the pointer crosses from one processor to another, the control is also passed from the processor that holds the leaf node to the processor that stores the pointed record. This is done similarly to the index traversal, which also crosses from one processor to another.

Parallel Range Selection Query

For *continuous-range* queries, possibly more processors need to be involved. However, the main importance is that it needs to determine the lower and/or the upper bound of the range. For open-ended continuous-range predicates, only the lower bound needs to be identified, whereas for the opposite, only the upper bound of the range needs to be taken into account. In many cases, both lower and upper bounds of the range need to be determined. Searching for the lower and/or upper bounds of the range can be directed to selected processors only because of the same reasons as those for the exact match queries.

With the selected attribute being indexed, once these boundaries are identified it becomes easy to trace all values within a given range, by traversing leaf nodes of the index tree. If the upper bound is identified, leaf node traversal is done to the left, whereas if the lower bound is identified, all leaf nodes to the right are traversed. We must also note that record loadings within each processor are performed sequentially. Parallel loading is possible only among processors, not within each processor.

For *discrete-range* queries, each discrete value in the search predicate is converted into multiple exact-match predicates. Further processing follows the processing method for exact-match queries.

Parallel Algorithm for One-Index Search Query Processing

The algorithm for parallel one-index search query processing consists of four modules: (*i*) *initialization*, (*ii*) *processor allocation*, (*iii*) *parallel searching*, and (*iv*) *record loading*. The last three modules correspond to the three important factors discussed above, whereas the first module does the preliminary processing, including variable declaration and initialization, and transformation of discrete-range queries.

The algorithm is listed in Figure 7.18.

7.5.2 Parallel Multi-Index Search Query Processing

When multiple indexes on different selection attributes are used, there are two methods in particular used to evaluate such selection predicates: one is through the use of an *intersection operation*, and the other is *to choose one index* as the processing base and ignore the others.

Intersection Method

With the *intersection method*, all indexed attributes in the search predicate are first searched independently. Each search predicate will form a list of index entry results found after traversing each index. After all indexes have been processed, the results from one index tree will be intersected with the results of other index trees to produce a final list. Once this has been formed, the pointed records are loaded and presented to the user as the answer to the query. This intersection method is a materialization of *CPNF* in a form of AND operations on the search predicates.

Since multiple indexes are used, there is a possibility that different indexing structures are used by each indexed attribute. For instance, the first attribute in the search predicate might be indexed with the NRI-2 structure and the second attribute uses PRI-3, and so on. However, there is a restriction whereby if one index is NRI-1, PRI-1, or FRI-1, other indexes cannot be any of these three. Bear in mind that these three indexing structures have one thing in common—that is, the index partitioning attribute is the same as the record partitioning attribute. For example, the table is partitioned based on EmployeeID and the index is also based on EmployeeID. Therefore, it is just not possible that one index is based on NRI-1 and another index is based on PRI-1. This is simply because there is only one partitioning attribute used by the table and the index. Other than this restriction, it is possible to mix and match with other indexing structures.

Algorithm: Parallel-One-Index-Selection (Query Q
and Index I)

```
// Initialization - in the host processor processor:
1.  Let P be all available processors
2.  Let P_Q be processors to be used by query Q
3.  Let V_exact be the search value in Q_exact_match
4.  Let V_lower and V_upper be the range lower and upper values
5.  If Q is discrete range
6.      Convert Q_discrete into Q_exact_match
7.      Establish an array of V_exact []

// Processor Allocation - in the host processor
   processor:
8.  If index I is NRI-2
9.      P_Q = P                          // use all processors
10. Else
11.     Select P_Q from P based on Q    // use selected proc

// Parallel Search - using processor P_Q:
12. For each searched value V in query Q
13.     Search value V in index tree I
14.     If a match is found in index tree I
15.         Put index entry into an array of index entry
            result
16.     If Q is continuous range
17.          Trace to the neighboring leaf nodes
18.     Put the index entry into the array of index entry
        result

// Record Loading - using processor P_Q:
19. For all entries in the array of index entry result
20.     Trace the data pointer to the actual record r
21.     If record r is located at a different processor
22.         Load the pointed remote record r thru message
            passing
23.     Else
24.         Load the pointed local record r
25.     Put record r into query result
```

Figure 7.18 Parallel one-index search query processing algorithm

Since the indexes in the query may be of different indexing structures, three cases are identified.

- **Case 1 (one index is based on NRI-1, PRI-1, or FRI-1):** This case is applicable if one of the indexes is either NRI-1, PRI-1, or FRI-1. Other attributes in the search predicates can be any of the other indexing structures, as long as it is not NRI-1, PRI-1, or FRI-1. For clarity of our discussions here, we refer the first selection attribute as indexed based on NRI-1, PRI-1, or FRI-1, and the second selection attribute as indexed based on non-NRI/PRI/FRI-1.

Based on the discussion in the previous section on parallel one-index selection, one of the key factors in determining the efficiency of parallel selection processing is processor involvement. Processor involvement determines whether all or only selected processors are used during the operation. In processor involvement, if the second indexing structure is NRI-2, PRI-2, or FRI-3, only those processors used for processing the first search attribute (which uses either NRI/PRI/FRI-1) will need to be activated. This is because other processors, which are not used by the first search attribute, will not produce a final query result anyway. In other words, NRI/PRI/FRI-1 dictate other indexed attributes to activate only the processors used by NRI/PRI/FRI-1. This process is a manifestation of an early intersection.

Another important factor, which is applicable only to multiattribute search queries, is the intersection operation. In the intersection, particularly for NRI-3 and PRI-3, the leaf nodes found in the index traversal must be sent to the processors where the actual records reside, so that the intersection operation can be carried out there. This is particularly required because NRI-3 and PRI-3 leaf nodes and their associated records may be located differently. Leaf node transfer is not required for NRI-2, PRI-2, or even FRI-3. The former two are simply because the leaf nodes and the records are collocated, whereas the last is because the index is fully replicated, and no physical leaf node transfer is required.

- **Case 2 (one index is based on NRI-3, PRI-3, or FRI-3):** This is applicable to the first index based on NRI/PRI/FRI-3 and the other indexes based on any other indexing structures, including NRI/PRI/FRI-3, but excluding NRI/PRI/FRI-1. The combination between NRI/PRI/FRI-3 and NRI/PRI/FRI-1 has already been covered by case 1 above.

  Unlike case 1 above where *processor involvement* is an important factor, case 2 does not perform any early intersection. This is because, in this case, there is no way to tell in advance which processors hold the candidate records. Therefore, processor involvement will depend on each individual indexing structure, and does not influence other indexing structures.

  The *intersection operation*, particularly for NRI/PRI-3, will be carried out as for case 1 above; that is, leaf nodes found in the searching process will need to be sent to where the actual records are stored and the intersection will be locally performed there.

- **Case 3 (one index is based on NRI-2 or PRI-2):** This case is applicable for multiattribute search queries where all indexes are either NRI-2 or PRI-2. The main property of these two indexing structures is that the leaf nodes and pointed records are collocated, and hence there is no need for leaf node transfer.

  In terms of processor involvement, like case 2 above, there will be no early intersection, since none of NRI/PRI/FRI-1 is used.

Algorithm:Parallel-Multi-Index-Selection-*Intersection-Version* (Query *Q* and Index *I*)

```
// Initialization - in host processor
1.  Let Pₒ be all processors to be used by Q
2.  Let Psₖ be processors to be used by S[k] where (k≥1)
3.  Let S[1] be the first index and S[2] be other indexes
4.  If S[1] is NRI-1 or PRI-1 or FRI-1 Then
5.     If S[2] is NRI-2 or PRI-2 or FRI-2 Then
6.        Let Ps₁₁ be processors to be used by all
          predicates S
7.  Pₒ = Ps₁₁

// Individual Index Access - using processor Pₒ:
8.  Call Parallel-One-Index-Selection
    (selection predicate S, index I)

// Intersection -  using processor Pₒ:
9.  If record r is located at different processor as
    the found leaf node Then
10.    Send leaf node to processor r
11.    Intersect all found index entry leaf nodes
       in each proc.
12.    Put the index entry into array of index entry result

// Record Loading -  using processor Pₒ:
13. For all entries in the array of index entry result
14.    Load the pointed local record r
15.    Put record r into query result
```

Figure 7.19   Parallel multi-index search query processing algorithm (*intersection version*)

An algorithm for parallel multi-index search query processing is presented in Figure 7.19.

In the *initialization* module, the processors and the search predicates are initialized. If one index is based on NRI/PRI/FRI-1 and the other is based on NRI/PRI-2 or FRI-3, then all selected processors are used.

In the *individual index access* module, a parallel one-index search query algorithm is called, where each search predicate is processed independently.

In the *intersection* module, the actual intersection of results obtained by each individual search is performed. If, in a particular searching, a leaf node points to a remote record, the index entry in this leaf node has to be transferred to where the remote record is located, so that the intersection operation can be done independently in each processor.

Finally, in the *record loading* module, the results of the intersection operation, which is a list of index entries that satisfy all the search predicate of the query pointing to the associated records, are loaded and placed into the query results to be presented to users.

One-Index Method

The second method for processing multi-index search queries is by using just one of the indexes. With this method, one indexed attribute that appears in the search predicates is chosen. The processing follows the parallel one-index search query processing. Once the found records are identified, other search predicates are evaluated. If all search predicates are satisfied (i.e., *CPNF*), the records are selected and put in the query result.

There are two main factors in determining the efficiency of this method: (*i*) the selectivity factor of each search predicate and (*ii*) the indexing structure that is used by each search predicate. Regarding the former, it will be ideal to choose a search predicate that has the lowest selectivity ratio, with a consequence that most records have already been filtered out by this search predicate and hence less work will be done by the rest of the search predicates. In the latter, it will be ideal to use an indexing structure that uses selected processors, local index traversals, and local record loading. Thorough analysis is needed to correctly identify a search predicate that delivers the best performance.

An algorithm for parallel multi-index search query processing using a one-index method is presented in Figure 7.20.

Algorithm: Parallel-Multi-Index-Selection-*One-Index-Access-Version* (Query Q and Index I)

```
// Initialization - in host processor
1. Let S[k] be all selection predicates
2. Choose a selection attribute S[m] where (1≤ m≤ k)
3. Let P_Q be the processors to be used by S[m]

// One-Index Access - using processor P_Q:
4. Call Parallel-One-Index-Selection
   (selection predicate S[m], index I[m])

// Other Predicates Evaluation - using processor P_Q:
5. For all entries in the array of index entry result
6.    Load the pointed local record r
7.    Perform all other selection predicate S[k] on
      record r
8.    If record r satisfies S[k]
9.       Put record r into query result
```

Figure 7.20   Parallel multi-index search query processing algorithm (*one-index version*)

In the *initialization* module, the most efficient predicate is chosen as the basis of the search operation. Then in the *one-index access* module, the parallel one-index search algorithm is called upon to process this search predicate. Finally, in the *other predicates evaluation* module, the records obtained from the one-index access module are evaluated against all other predicates.

7.6 PARALLEL INDEX JOIN ALGORITHMS

In this section, the central focus is on index-join queries. Index-join queries are join queries involving index. It is common to expect that one or both join attributes are indexed. This is especially true in the case where a join between two tables is based on a primary key (PK) on one table and a foreign key (FK) on the other table. Primary keys are normally indexed to prevent duplicate values that exist in that table. PK-FK join is common in relational databases because a database is composed of many tables and the tables are linked between each other through PK-FK relationships, in which referential integrity is maintained. Such join queries are called "*index-join*" queries (not to be confused with "join indices," which is a specialized data structure for efficient access path).

There are two categories of index-join queries: (*i*) *one-index join* and (*ii*) *two-index join*, depending on the existence of an index on one or two tables to be joined.

A *one-index join query*, as the name states, is a join query whereby one join attribute is indexed while the other is not. This is typical of a primary key—foreign key (PK-FK) join, in which the primary key is normally indexed, while the foreign key may not be. Processing a one-index join query can be done through a nested block index; that is, for each record of the non-index join attribute, search for a match in the index attribute.

A *two-index join query* is a join query on two indexed attributes. The main characteristic of a two-index join query is that processing such a query can be done by merging the two indexes. In other words, joining is carried out by a matching scan of the leaf nodes of the two indexes.

The main difference in processing the two index join query types is that the two-index join is mainly concerned with leaf node scanning, whereas the one-index join focuses primarily on index searching. Details of parallel processing of both index-join queries are discussed next.

7.6.1 Parallel One-Index Join

Parallel one-index join processing, involving one nonindexed table (say table *R*) and one indexed table (say table *S*), adopts a nested index block processing, whereby for each nonindexed record *R*, we search for a matching index entry of table *S*. Like other parallel join processing methods, parallel one-index join query processing is divided into *data partitioning* and *local join* steps.

In the *data partitioning* step, depending on which parallel indexing scheme is used by table S, data partitioning to table R may or may not be conducted. Four different cases are identified and explained as follows.

Case 1 (NRI-1 and NRI-3)

This case is applicable if table S is indexed with either the NRI-1 or NRI-3 structures. Suppose the index of table S uses a range partitioning function *rangefunc()*. At the initial stage of processing, table R, as well as table S, has already been partitioned and placed into each processor. This is called data placement. A number of data placement methods have been discussed in Chapter 3 on parallel search.

In the data partitioning step of parallel one-index join algorithm, records of table R are repartitioned according to the same range partitioning function already used by table S, namely, *rangefunc()*. Both the records and index tree of table S are not at all mutated. At the end of the data partitioning step, each processor will have records R and index tree S having the same range of values of the join attribute. Subsequently, the local join step can start.

Case 2 (NRI-2)

If table S is indexed with the NRI-2 structure, the above data partitioning method used by Case 1 will not work, since NRI-2 does not have a partitioning function for the index. The partitioning function is in fact not for the index, but for the table, which is not applicable to one-index join processing. Consequently, the nonindexed table R has to be broadcasted to all processors. It is not possible to partition the nonindexed table.

Case 3 (PRI)

If table S is indexed with any of the PRI structures (i.e., PRI-1, PRI-2, or PRI-3), the nonindexed table R does not need to be redistributed, since by using a PRI structure, the global index is maintained and, more importantly, the root index node is replicated to all processors so that tracing to any leaf node can be done from any root node at any processor. In the case where the location of the root node is different from that of the requested leaf node, the traversal of the index tree must cross the processor boundary in which the traversal moves from one parent node on one processor to a child node on another processor.

Case 4 (FRI)

If table S is indexed with any of the FRI structures (i.e., FRI-1 or FRI-3), like Case 3 above, the nonindexed table R is not redistributed either. The reason for not redistributing records R is, however, different from that of Case 3. The main reason is quite obvious: the global indexed table has been fully replicated. Each record R will now be compared with a full global index s in each processor.

According to the four cases above, it can be summarized that data/record partitioning is applicable to Case 1, and data/record broadcasting to Case 2. Other cases do not require the data partitioning step.

In the local join step, each processor performs its joining operation independently of the others. Using a nested block index join method as described earlier, for each record R, search for a matching index entry of table S. If a match is found, depending on the location of the record (i.e., whether it is located at the same place as the leaf node of the index), record loading is performed. An algorithm for parallel one-index join processing is described in Figure 7.21.

In the implementation, there are two technical elements that need mentioning: one is when record S is located at a different place from the index entry, particularly if table S is indexed with either NRI-3, PRI-3, or FRI-3. When a match is found in the searching, a message has to be sent to the processor holding the actual record S. This is performed by sending a message from the processor holding the index entry to the processor that stores the record. After this, the latter processor loads the requested record S and sends it to the former processor to be placed in the query result. The main concern of this process is that the searching process should not wait for record S to be retrieved, either locally or even through a message passing to load a remote record S. The searching process should continue.

Algorithm: Parallel-One-Index-Join (table R and index S)

```
// Data Partitioning - in each processor:
1.  If index S is NRI-1 or NRI-3            -- Case 1
2.     Let range partitioning for index tree S is
       called rangefunc()
3.     For each record r
4.        Redistribute record R according to rangefunc()
5.  If index S is NRI-2                      -- Case 2
6.     For each record R
7.        Broadcast record R to all processors

// Local Join - in each processor:
8.  For each record R
9.     Load record R and read join attribute value av
10.    Search value av of record R in index tree
       of table S
11.    If a match is found in index tree S Then
12.       Trace the data pointer to the actual record S
13.       If record S is located at a different processor
14.          Load pointed remote record S thru message
             passing
15.       Else
16.          Load the pointed local record S
17.       Concatenate records R and S into query results
```

Figure 7.21   Parallel one-index-join query processing algorithm

Practically speaking, this can be achieved by creating a separate thread from the searching thread every time a match is found. This thread sends a message to the corresponding processors that hold the record, waits until the record is sent back, and puts it into the query results together with record R. By using this approach, searching is not halted.

Another technical element in the searching is when any of the PRI structures is involved. The searching that starts from a root node at any processor may end up with a leaf node at a different processor. When a parent node at processor 1 points to a child node at processor 2, the searching control at processor 1 is passed to processor 2, in which a new searching thread at processor 2 is created. If later, processor 2 passes its control to processor 3 and a leaf node is found there, data loading as described in the previous paragraph can be applied. The main concern is that the retrieved record S needs to be passed back to the original processor where the searching started in order to be concatenated with the record R. As a result, the retrieved record S needs to return to the original processor. This can be implemented with a similar threading technique whereby, when searching control is passed from one processor to another, a new searching thread at the new processor is created. When the desired record has been retrieved, the retrieved record travels in a reverse direction.

Figure 7.22 shows an architecture of a processor in which the processor consists of two thread groups: one is for the searching process, and the other is for the data loading to serve either another processor or the same processor. The first thread in the first thread group is the searching thread. If a traversal from the current processor to another processor is necessary, the thread control is passed to another processor. If a match is found, it creates a new thread to handle the data retrieval. This thread actually sends a message to another thread, which may be located at a different processor. This thread informs the I/O thread to actually load the requested data. Once it has been loaded from a disk, it is sent to the requested thread.

7.6.2 Parallel Two-Index Join

Parallel two-index join processing is where each processor performs an independent merging of the leaf nodes, and the final query result is the union of all temporary results gathered by each processor. Because there are a number of parallel indexing schemes, it is possible that the two tables to be joined may have adopted different parallel indexing schemes. For example, one table uses NRI-1, whereas the other uses FRI-3. In this circumstance, two cases are available.

Case 1

Case 1 is applicable to all parallel indexing structures except NRI-2 and PRI-2. For example, the case of two tables to be joined, where one of the tables is indexed with NRI-3 and the other is indexed with PRI-1, falls into this category. It may also be true that both indexes may use the same indexing structure, such as both using

Processor:

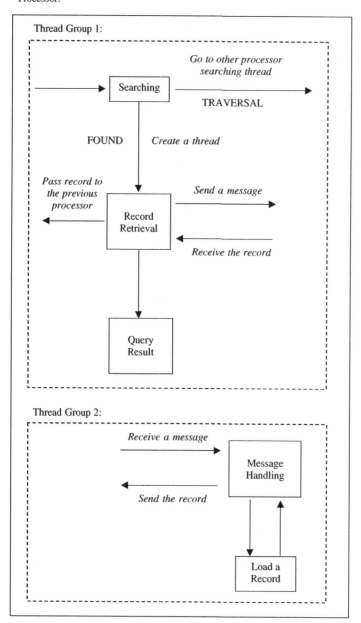

Figure 7.22   A searching architecture

FRI-1. Whichever parallel indexing structure is used, they must adopt the same index partitioning function. For instance, if the join attribute is based on ID field, both tables must adopt the same partitioning function for the ID field, such as IDs 0–99 go to processor 1, IDs 100–199 go to processor 2, and so on.

Basically, the main processing in parallel two-index join processing is a merging operation of the leaf nodes of the two index trees in each processor. Merging all leaf nodes in each processor can be performed by first scanning the left-most leaf node and then following the node pointer to the next leaf node on the right until all leaf nodes have been scanned. As merging involves leaf nodes only, nonleaf nodes contribute very little to the overall performance of the operation.

If one or both indexes are NRI-1 or NRI-3, leaf node scanning can be quite simple, as the local index in one processor has no overlap with the local index in other processors. Local merging is simply done as for normal merging in uniprocessors. This is also similar to PRI-1 and PRI-3, even through the first and/or the last leaf nodes in each processor may be replicated in the neighboring processors.

Merging that involves FRI-1 or FRI-3 can be a little more complex, as the full global index exists in each processor. One simplistic merging method is to merge all leaf nodes. A better merging is achieved by setting up a range for merging in each processor, so that each processor does not merge the whole global index but only part of the global index, as in that of PRI structures. Workload division can be accomplished by consulting the range function used in the base table partitioning or simply by dividing the workload equally. In either case, the range of the two extremes, the starting and ending values of each range, must be determined. Once these values have been obtained, each processor knows where to start and where to stop when merging.

An algorithm for parallel two-index join processing is presented in Figure 7.23. Step 2 in the algorithm is to find out the starting and ending nodes for the merging process. In particular, this is needed especially if one or both of the indexes are fully replicated indexes. For nonreplicated and partially replicated indexes, the starting and ending nodes for merging are obvious; that is, the left-most leaf nodes and the right-most leaf nodes.

Case 2

This case assumes that the join attributes are indexed with either NRI-2 or PRI-2. Unfortunately, parallel two-index join query processing cannot make use of these indexes. Therefore, NRI-2 and PRI-2 are useless for parallelizing two-index join query processing.

Imagine that two tables (say table Employee and table Student) are to be joined based on their ID fields, and the indexes are based on their Name fields with either NRI-2 or PRI-2. Suppose that the base table partitioning function is a simple range partitioning whereby names starting from A to G go to processor 1, H–M to processor 2, and so on. NRI-2 and PRI-2 build their local indexes on the ID

Algorithm: Parallel-Two-Index-Join-Category-1
(indexes *R* & *S*)

```
// In each processor:
1. Let starting and ending values of the range
   partitioning used are startval and endval
2. If FRI-1 or FRI-3 is used Then
      Determine startval by searching a startval in
      index tree
      And
      the last node visited in this index tree becomes
      the starting node of the index in the merging
      process
   Else
      Starting node for comparison is the left most
      leaf node
      And ending node for comparison is the right
      most leaf node in each processor
3. Merge leaf nodes of indexes R and S from the
   respective starting leaf nodes
4. If matched Then
      Trace the data pointer to the base record.
      If the base record is located at a different
      processor
        Load the pointed remote record thru message
        passing
      Else
        Load the pointed local record
      Concatenate the two records into query results
5. Repeat steps 3-4 until one of the indexes' leaf nodes
   have run out or contain index entry greater or equal
   to endval
```

Figure 7.23 Parallel two-index-join query processing algorithm (category 1)

fields based on the local data. A possible scenario for ID distribution is such that Employee IDs 7, 188, are located in processor 1, Employee IDs 9, 155 are in processor 2, Student IDs 7, 9 are located in processor 1, and Student IDs 155, 188 are in processor 2. It is impossible for each processor to perform an independent merging of the indexes on the ID field, as the indexes of both tables located at one processor bear no identical semantics on the ID field. This is because data placement (records and index nodes) is done based on a nonjoin attribute.

If table *R* is indexed with either NRI-2 or PRI-2, and table *S* is indexed with neither NRI-2 nor PRI-2, the index is ignored and table *R* is assumed to be not indexed. Join processing then follows parallel one-index join processing as described in the previous section.

If table R and table S are indexed with either NRI-2 or PRI-2 but the indexing structure of both tables are different, the index NRI-2 is ignored, and join processing follows that of parallel one-index join. The reason for ignoring NRI-2 and using PRI-2 instead is that with PRI-2 in parallel one-index join, the nonindexed table does not need to be redistributed. If, for example, NRI-2 is used instead, the other table needs to be broadcasted. Broadcasting all records is expensive and therefore is avoided.

If both indexes use the same indexing structure, either NRI-2 or PRI-2, both indexes cannot be used, as described earlier. Hence, common parallel join processing without indexes (e.g., parallel hash join) is applied instead.

7.7 COMPARATIVE ANALYSIS

As there are different kinds of parallel indexing structures and consequently various parallel algorithms for search and join queries involving index, as studied in the previous sections, it becomes important to analyze the efficiency of each parallel indexing structure in the context of parallel search and join query processing.

7.7.1 Comparative Analysis of Parallel Search Index

In this section, parallel one-index and multi-index search query processing are examined, followed by some discussions.

Analyzing Parallel One-Index Search Query Processing

As mentioned previously, in *parallel one-index search query processing* there are three main elements: (i) processor involvement, (ii) index traversal, and (ii) record loading. In processor involvement, it is either selected or involves all processors. In index traversal, traversal may be localized in each processor or it may sometimes be required to traverse to a different processor. Meanwhile, the record loading may be done locally at the same processor or remotely at a different processor where searching is performed.

Based on these three factors, Figure 7.24 presents a matrix to show a comparison among parallel indexing structures. The shaded cells show more expensive operations in comparison with others within the same operation, whereas the nonshaded cells indicate cheaper operations.

Based on this table comparison, each parallel indexing structure shows some advantages as well as disadvantages in supporting parallel index search query processing. It is clear from the table in Figure 7.24 that NRI/PRI/FRI-1 indexing structures provide more advantages than others, since only selected processors are used and index traversal and record loading are locally done.

Less attractive indexing structures are offered by NRI/PRI/FRI-3 where record loading may be done remotely. The efficiency of remote data loading is very much determined by the selectivity factor of the query. The higher the selectivity,

	NRI Schemes			PRI Schemes			FRI Schemes	
	NRI-1	**NRI-2**	**NRI-3**	**PRI-1**	**PRI-2**	**PRI-3**	**FRI-1**	**FRI-3**
Processor Involvement	Selected processors	All processors	Selected processors	Selected processors	Selected processors	Selected processors	Selected processors	Selected processors
Index Traversal	Local search	Local search	Local search	Local search	Remote search	Local search	Local search	Local search
Record Loading	Local record load	Local record load	Remote record load	Local record load	Local record load	Remote record load	Local record load	Remote record load

Figure 7.24 A comparative table for parallel one-index selection query processing

the more records to be loaded, and there is a great chance the records need to be loaded remotely and this incurs overhead. In contrast, if the selectivity ratio is very small, overheads for record loading can be minimal. Consequently, NRI/PRI/FRI-3 can be as good as NRI/PRI/FRI-1 indexing structures particularly for parallel one-index selection query processing.

The other option is the NRI/PRI-2 indexing structure. NRI-2 requires all processors to be used. If the selectivity ratio is very small, most processors will not produce any results. From an elapsed time point of view (speed up), it may not be a problem, but from a throughput point of view (scale up), those processors that do not bring any results may waste a lot of unnecessary processing time. PRI-2, on the other hand, may isolate into selected processors, but traversal may need to move from one processor to another, thereby increasing communication overhead.

Analyzing Parallel Multi-Index Search Query Processing

In *parallel multi-index search query processing*, two main methods are considered: (*i*) the intersection method and (*ii*) the one-index access method.

Analyzing the Intersection Method

There are two important key factors to consider when determining the efficiency of the *intersection method*: (*i*) individual index searching and (*ii*) the intersection operation. In individual index searching, basically processor involvement is critical, as this can identify whether or not early intersection can be carried out. In the intersection operation, the focus is on whether the found leaf nodes in each individual search predicate evaluation need to be sent from one processor to another for an intersection operation with other found leaf nodes.

Figure 7.25 illustrates these two key factors. Since each factor is further categorized into two possibilities, a matrix 2×2 is conveniently drawn (see Fig. 7.25(a)). Figure 7.25(b) to (d) shows the three cases explained above.

Figure 7.25(b) shows the properties of case 1 (one index is based on NRI/PRI/FRI-1 and the other is not) in terms of their processor involvement in each individual index attribute searching and the intersection operation that intersects all results obtained from each individual index attribute searching. The selected processor involvement cells explain an early intersection mechanism imposed in this case, whereas the intersection operation may or may not involve leaf node transfer depending on whether or not NRI/PRI-3 is used.

Case 2 (Fig. 7.25(c)) shows that no early intersection is carried out since there is no effect on individual searching in terms of their processor involvement. In other words, processor involvement is dictated by individual index attribute searching.

Case 3 (Fig. 7.25(d)) is a subset of case 2, where in the intersection operation leaf node transfer is unnecessary since the records and their leaf nodes in the index tree are collocated.

An ideal situation is clearly displayed in Figure 7.25(e), where an early intersection is enforced through the use of selected processors as dictated by

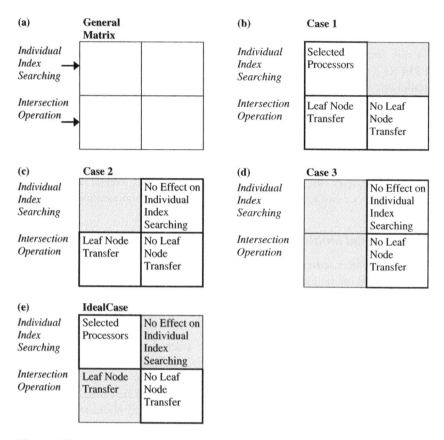

Figure 7.25   A comparative table for parallel multi-index selection query processing using an *intersection method*

NRI/PRI/FRI-1, and record loading is done locally as in NRI/PRI/FRI-1 and NRI/PRI-2.

Analyzing the One-Index Access Method

The main aim of the one-index access method is to minimize as much I/O as possible, so that further search predicate evaluations based on the records that have been selected through one-index access may evaluate as small a number of records as possible. In other words, the first search predicate, which uses an index, should have the smallest selectivity ratio.

Another important factor following this is that when a set of records have been initially selected by the index attribute searching, it would be ideal for these records to be spread to multiple processors, so that further search predicate evaluation can be done in parallel on multiple processors.

	NRI Schemes			PRI Schemes			FRI Schemes	
	NRI-1	**NRI-2**	**NRI-3**	**PRI-1**	**PRI-2**	**PRI-3**	**FRI-1**	**FRI-3**
Exact-Match Search Queries	Isolated record loading	Record loading possibly spread (if nonunique)	Record loading possibly spread (if nonunique)	Isolated record loading	Record loading possibly spread (if nonunique)	Record loading possibly spread (if nonunique)	Isolated record loading	Record loading possibly spread (if nonunique)
Continuous-Range Search Queries	Record loading possibly spread, but not random	Record loading possibly spread randomly	Record loading possibly spread randomly	Record loading possibly spread, but not random	Record loading possibly spread randomly	Record loading possibly spread randomly	Record loading possibly spread, but not random	Record loading possibly spread randomly

Figure 7.26 A comparative table for parallel multi-index selection query processing using a *one-index access method*

Both of these factors determine the efficiency of parallel multi-index search query processing based on the one-index access method. The selectivity factor is greatly determined by the type of the search query, whereas the spread of records is influenced by the indexing scheme used. Figure 7.26 shows a comparative table for parallel multi-index search query processing based on the one-index access method.

In the *exact-match search queries*, the selected records might be either unique or nonunique. In the case of unique results, the selectivity must be very low, as low as one record selected. With NRI/PRI/FRI-1 indexing structure, record loading is isolated to a single processor only. Even when the records are not unique, I/O is still isolated to a single processor. However, the objective of spreading the I/O for further search predicate evaluation is not met. If the other indexing structure is used instead, record loading is randomly spread if the records are not unique.

In the *continuous-range search queries*, record loading will likely be spread to multiple processors, unless the range is quite small and fits into one processor, especially when NRI/PRI-FRI-1 is used. When NRI/PRI-FRI-1 is used, the spread is likely to be nonrandom, meaning that the spread is, for example, from one processor to the neighboring processors only. This is because the records are sorted within and among other processors. However, if the other indexing structure is used, the spread will most likely be more random.

Discrete-range search queries are not included in the comparison chart, since they can be regarded as a combination of exact-match selection and continuous-range search, in terms of record loading and its spread.

From the table in Figure 7.26, a few lessons can be learned. One is that the smallest selectivity ratio is given by an exact-match search predicate with unique records, and the most efficient indexing structure is NRI/PRI/FRI-1. Therefore, this is the most preferable indexing structure. The next preferable option will be exact-match search predicates of nonunique records or continuous-range search predicates depending on the selectivity ratio with NRI-2/3 or PRI-2/3 or FRI-3. In this case, it is hard to predefine which one is better unless performance measurement is conducted.

Discussions

In wrapping up the comparison, it can be clearly seen that NRI/PRI/FRI-1 offer much benefit for parallel search query processing involving index. These indexing structures clearly offer the best performance, especially for parallel one-index search query processing. The main difference between these three indexing structures is the structure of the index, where NRI-1 is purely local index, PRI-1 maintains a global index that is spread among processors, and FRI-1 replicates the whole index. Since extra benefits of PRI-1 and FRI-1 are not obvious, at least in parallel one-index search query processing, maintaining global index as in PRI-1 and replicating the whole index as in FRI-1 do not offer extra benefits. In fact, the drawback of PRI-1 and FRI-1 is quite clear, as PRI-1 needs to maintain the link from one index node of one processor to another node in another processor and

FRI-1 needs enormous extra space to maintain the index. On the other hand, NRI-1 is sufficient to provide support for parallel one-index search query processing.

The second preferable indexing structure to support parallel search query processing cannot be easily identified. NRI/PRI/FRI-3 indexing structures are quite favorable, particularly in parallel one-index search query processing. On the other hand, NRI/PRI-2 indexing structures are favorable in the intersection method of parallel multi-index search query processing. Therefore, further performance analysis, incorporating storage space analysis and other operation analysis, is necessary in order to identify the efficiency of these indexing structures.

7.7.2 Comparative Analysis of Parallel Index Join

In this section, parallel one-index and multi-index join query processing are examined.

In *parallel one-index join processing*, there are two main elements in particular: (i) data partitioning of the nonindexed table and (ii) local join. Data partitioning is either to partition, to broadcast, or to do nothing to the nonindexed table. In local join, two major factors, searching of the indexed table and data/record loading pointed by an index entry, are highlighted. In the searching process, the searching may be localized in each processor or it may sometimes be required to traverse to a different processor. Meanwhile, the record loading may be done locally at the same processor or remotely at a different processor where searching is performed.

In *parallel two-index join processing*, two main factors are considered: (i) determining merge starting and ending points through searching and (ii) data/record loading. The starting and ending points in merging can be determined either directly in each processor or by a searching process. The record loading factor is the same as that of parallel one-index join processing, that is, record loading locally or remotely.

Based on the above-mentioned factors, a matrix is drawn to show a comparison among parallel indexing structures. This is shown in Figure 7.27. The heavily shaded cells show more expensive operations in comparison with others within the same operation, whereas the lightly shaded cells indicate operations that are not as expensive as those of the heavily shaded cells. The nonshaded cells indicate the cheapest operations.

Based on the above table comparison, each parallel indexing structure has advantages and disadvantages in supporting parallel index-join processing. There is no single parallel indexing structure that is the most efficient in all aspects. However, it is noted that NRI-2 and PRI-2 do not support parallel index-join processing efficiently. Therefore, the use of these parallel indexing structures is not suggested.

The comparison shows that NRI-1 requires data partitioning of the nonindexed table, whereas NRI-3 adds remote data loading of the indexed table in both parallel one-index and parallel two-index join processing. The efficiency of remote data loading is very much determined by the selectivity factor of the query. The higher

Parallel One-Index Join			NRI Schemes			PRI Schemes			FRI Schemes	
			NRI-1	**NRI-2**	**NRI-3**	**PRI-1**	**PRI-2**	**PRI-3**	**FRI-1**	**FRI-3**
	Data partitioning		Partition	Broadcast	Partition	No Partition	No Partition	No Partition	No Partition	No Partition
	Local join	Indexed table searching	Local search	Local search	Local search	Remote search	Remote search	Remote search	Local search	Local search
		Indexed table record loading	Local data load	Local data load	Remote data load	Remote data load	Remote data load	Remote data load	Remote data load	Remote data load
Parallel Two-Index Join	Merging	Searching start and end values	Not necessary	N/A	Not necessary	Not necessary	N/A	Not necessary	Searching needed	Searching needed
		Data loading	Local data load		Remote data load	Local data load		Remote data load	Local data load	Remote data load

Figure 7.27 A comparative table for parallel index-join query processing

the selectivity, the more records to be loaded, and there is a great chance the records need to be loaded remotely and this incurs overhead. Comparing PRI-1 with PRI-3, both seek remote index searching and data loading in parallel one-index join. Additionally, PRI-3 needs remote record loading in parallel two-index join. FRI-1 and FRI-3 are similar, since both require remote data loading in parallel one-index join and searching for starting and ending values for merging in parallel two-index join. However, in parallel two-index join FRI-3 needs remote data loading as well.

When designing a parallel database system, especially when building a parallel index, we are left with two options: The first is to construct an index based on the partitioning attribute used in the table partitioning, and the second is to build an index totally based on a nonpartitioning attribute. The first option is to choose whether to adopt NRI-1, PRI-1, or FRI-1, whereas the second option is between NRI-3, PRI-3, and FRI-3 (not that NRI-2 and PRI-2 have been eliminated from the options). Consequently, it is reasonable to determine which parallel indexing structure is suitable for each of the two situations above.

Let us compare NRI-1, PRI-1, and FRI-1 first. Based on parallel one-index join operation, NRI-1 and FRI-1 are quite comparable, in that NRI-1 requires data partitioning of the nonindexed table, whereas FRI-1 does not require data partitioning but imposes remote data loading. Also, note that FRI-1 for parallel one-index join is not as expensive as PRI-1, because PRI-1, in addition to what FRI-1 requires, needs remote index searching. Based on parallel two-index join operation, NRI-1 is the best, as data loading is local and does not need searching for starting/ending points like FRI-1. On a whole, it can be said that NRI-1 is quite promising for parallel index-join processing. FRI-1 seems to be very good, while PRI-1, on the other hand, is less attractive.

Comparing NRI-3, PRI-3, and FRI-3, based on parallel one-index join operation FRI-3, which requires remote data loading, offers the best option, compared with PRI-3, which additionally needs to do a remote index searching, and with NRI-3, which additionally needs data partitioning. NRI-3 and PRI-3 are the same in parallel two-index join, where both require remote data loading. On the other hand, FRI-3 requires an additional searching for starting/ending values for merging. Depending on which is more expensive, data partitioning or remote searching in parallel one-index join, the efficiency of NRI-3 and PRI-3 are quite comparable. FRI-3 seems to be good for both parallel index-join processing, as it needs only a small overhead for searching of starting/ending values in the merging process.

To conclude our comparison, it is generally expected that fully replicated systems offer a great number of benefits in parallel processing, which in this case is confirmed in parallel one-index join and parallel two-index join processing. An obvious drawback is storage overhead, which can be enormously large. If storage overhead is to be minimized, the nonreplicated parallel indexing structures, in particular NRI-1 and NRI-3, are favorable. On the other hand, the PRI structures do not seem to provide any advantages in addition to those already offered by NRI and FRI.

7.8 SUMMARY

Indexing is important in database systems, and consequently operations involving index are significant and need comprehensive examination. First, three aspects of parallel indexing are discussed: parallel indexing structures, parallel indexing maintenance, and parallel indexing storage.

- **Parallel Indexing Structures**

  Three parallel indexing structures are presented and discussed. They are *nonreplicated indexing* structures (NRI), *partially replicated indexing* structures (PRI), and *fully replicated indexing* structures (FRI). Both NRI and PRI structures have three different variations: the index attribute is also the record partitioning attribute: the local index is built from its local data: and the indexed partitioning attribute is different from the record partitioning attribute (the record partitioning may be unknown or different from the indexed attribute). For the FRI structures, only two variations are known, these being the first and the third of the above.

- **Parallel Indexing Maintenance**

  Index maintenance, including insertion and deletion operations, focuses on the complexity/simplicity of each of the parallel index structures. This chapter has described how maintenance of the PRI structures can be done and discussed to some degree the complexity involved in splitting, merging, and index restructuring. Data pointer maintenance for NRI and FRI structures is also explained.

- **Parallel Indexing Storage**

  There are two important components of storage: storage for tables and storage for indexes. Parallel indexing storage is similar to indexing storage for uniprocessors. This chapter has also studied both indexing storage for uniprocessors and for parallel environments.

  Further, the use of parallel index is applied to two operations: search and join operations.

- **Parallel Index-Search Query Processing**

  Parallel index-search query processing algorithms exists in two forms: *one-index search queries* and *multiple-index search queries*. Parallel one-index selection queries are for search queries on a single attribute and this attribute is indexed, whereas parallel multiple-index search queries are for search queries on multiple attributes and consequently on multiple indexes.

  The comparison among these parallel indexing structures particularly in supporting the efficiency of parallel index-search query algorithms shows clearly that NRI/PRI/FRI-1 are the most supportive. Others offer various advantages and disadvantages. Examining this matter in more detail, it appears that PRI/FRI structures do not add extra benefits. The decision to choose another index for other attributes is determined by the balance between storage versus performance.

- **Parallel index-join query processing**

     Parallel index-join algorithms exist in two forms: parallel one-index join and two-index join queries. Parallel one-index join focuses more on index node searching, as for nested block index join algorithms, whereas parallel two-index join is mainly concerned with leaf node merging. We have considered how the two parallel index join might use the available parallel indexing structures.

The comparison among these parallel indexing structures, particularly in supporting the efficiency of parallel index-join algorithms, shows clearly that NRI-2 and PRI-2 indexing structures are not supportive. Others offer various advantages and disadvantages. Looking into this matter in more detail, it appears that PRI structures do not add extra benefits, and therefore only NRI-1/3 and FRI-1/3 are left as plausible options. The decision is determined by striking a balance between storage versus performance.

7.9 BIBLIOGRAPHICAL NOTES

Standard database textbooks, like Elmasri and Navathe (2007) and Ramakrishnan and Gehrke (2000) cover basic indexing structures (e.g., B^+ trees) for database systems.

     Indexing for parallel database systems was covered in Honishi et al. (1992). Index structures for shared-nothing architecture were presented by Achyutuni et al (*SIGMOD* 1996), presenting techniques for online index modification, and Feelifl et al. (*DEXA* 2000), proposing an online heat-balancing. Index structures to improve query performance were presented by Berchtold et al. (*EDBT* 1998), where the performance of high-dimensional index is improved by bulk-load operations, and Omiecinski et al. (1990), focusing on parallel join processing using nonclustered indexes.

     Newer work on parallel indexing includes parallel indexing for multidimensional data (Ali et al. *DAPD* 2005; Bok et al. *WAIM* 2005 and *DASFAA* 2006; Dehne et al. 2003) and semistructured data (Cooper et al. 2002).

7.10 EXERCISES

7.1. Given a data set $D = \{55, 30, 68, 39, 1, 4, 49, 90, 34, 76, 82, 56, 31, 25, 78, 56, 38, 32, 88, 9, 44, 98, 11, 70, 66, 89, 99, 22, 23, 26\}$, construct an index tree of this data set with a B^+ tree structure. Assume that the maximum number of pointers in each node is 4.

7.2. Using the index tree built in the exercise 7.1, and assuming that there are three processors, construct parallel indexes with the following parallel indexing schemes:

  a. NRI-1 scheme
  b. PRI-1 scheme

7.3. Using the PRI-1 results from exercise 7.2, show step by step how data item 33 is inserted into the index tree.

7.4. Using the PRI-1 results from exercise 7.2, show how data item 33 can be deleted.

7.5. Compare the storage size of parallel indexes using the NRI-1 scheme and the NRI-2 scheme. Also compare the storage size of NRI-1 and NRI-3 schemes.

7.6. Using the PRI-1 index tree in exercise 7.2, show step by step how the following parallel search works:

   a. Search data item 78.

   b. Search a range of data items from 70 to 79, inclusive.

   c. Search data items ending with a zero between 10 and 90, inclusive (e.g., 10, 20, 30, . . . , 90).

7.7. For parallel one-index search query processing, list in order of preference the parallel indexing structures according to their efficiency.

7.8. For parallel one-index join query processing in Figure 7.27, explain why data partitioning is not needed for the PRI and FRI schemes.

7.9. Explain why NRI-2 and PRI-2 are useless for parallelizing two-index join query processing.

7.10. Investigate how parallel indexes are expressed in SQL.

Chapter 8

Parallel Universal Qualification—Collection Join Queries

The birth of the collection join is due to two things: one is an extension to relational division, which is a manifestation of universal quantification, and the other is the existence of collection types and collection attributes in database systems, particularly in object-based databases. This chapter focuses on the issues surrounding collection join queries—including collection join query types and their parallel algorithms.

In Section 8.1, collection join queries in association with relational division are highlighted. In Section 8.2, different kinds of collection types and collection join queries are described. Section 8.3 outlines parallelism for collection join queries. This is elaborated in more detail in the following three sections.

Section 8.4 studies parallel algorithms for collection-equi join queries. This includes disjoint data partitioning and several local join techniques, including double sort-merge, sort-hash, and hash.

Section 8.5 focuses on parallel algorithms for collection-intersect join queries. Several non-disjoint data partitioning methods become the central focus. The local join makes use of a combination of sort, merge, and hash.

Finally, Section 8.6 describes parallel algorithms for subcollection join queries. The properties of these algorithms are very much influenced by the previous two parallel algorithms.

High-Performance Parallel Database Processing and Grid Databases,
by David Taniar, Clement Leung, Wenny Rahayu, and Sushant Goel
Copyright © 2008 John Wiley & Sons, Inc.

8.1 UNIVERSAL QUANTIFICATION AND COLLECTION JOIN

A relational division operation is a manifestation of a universal quantifier. The collection join query is actually an extension of the concept of relational division. To illustrate this concept, let us see how relational division operation works.

Figure 8.1 shows an example of a relational division operation. In this case, the dividend table is a union of **all** editors-in-chief, and the divisor table is the program-chairs of **a** conference object p. The editor-in-chief table consists of two attributes: the first attribute is the journal name and the second attribute is the editor-in-chief ID. Assume that each person identified in this table has a unique ID that is associated with the details of each person. The conference table also consists of two attributes: the conference name and the ID of its program-chair. The result of this division is the combination of b and p.

Now assume that there are many conferences, and we would like to repeat the division process; then we would have repeated relational division operations for each conference. Figure 8.2 gives this illustration. The results of this repeated relational division is b–p and i–w (the results are based on this incomplete data).

all editors-in-chief			program-chairs of **a** conference			division result	
a	250						
a	75	dividedby	p	123	giving	b	p
b	210		p	210			
b	123						
c	125						
c	181						
...	...						
...	...						
...	...						
i	80						
i	70						

Figure 8.1 Relational division

all editors-in-chief			program-chairs of **all** conference			division results	
a	250						
a	75	dividedby	p	123	giving	b	p
b	210		p	210			
b	123						
c	125		r	50			
c	181		r	40			
d	4						
d	237		w	80		i	w
e	289		w	70			
...	...						
...	...						
...	...						
i	80						
i	70						

Figure 8.2 Repeated relational division

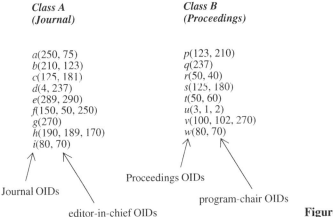

Figure 8.3 Sample data

The example in Figure 8.2 can be redrawn so that each journal and conference is represented as a unit (record). Each journal may consist of multiple editors-in-chief, and each conference may also consist of multiple program-chairs. Figure 8.3 shows a different look at Figure 8.2 (with a more complete journal and conference data).

The sample data shown in Figure 8.3 is not a relational structure, since multiple values (editors-in-chief and program-chairs) exist in each journal and conference records. However, this is possible in object-based databases as an attribute can be of a collection type, not only an atomic type. Therefore, the data shown in Figure 8.3 is more relevant to object-based databases. However, since the concept is very similar to relational division, it is also interesting to include a discussion on possible queries arising from this new data structure.

The sample data in Figure 8.3 above will be used as a running example throughout this chapter. Suppose class *A* and class *B* are *Journal* and *Proceedings*, respectively. Both classes contain a few objects, shown by their OIDs (e.g., objects *a* to *i* are Journal objects and objects *p* to *w* are Proceedings objects). The join attributes are *editor-in-chief* of Journal and *program-chair* of Proceedings and are of type collection *Person*. The OIDs of each person in these attributes are shown in brackets. For example, $a(250, 75)$ denotes a Journal object with OID *a*, and the editors of this journal are Persons with OIDs *250* and *75*. The elements *250* and *75* form a collection for journal *a*. This collection attribute consists of multiple elements of the same type, in this case Persons' OIDs. Depending on how the elements are arranged, whether they are in a particular order, and whether the elements can be repeated within a collection, there are many different kinds of collection types. Because there are various collection types available, there are many different kinds of join queries involving collection attributes. In the next sections, various collection types and collection join queries are discussed.

8.2 COLLECTION TYPES AND COLLECTION JOIN QUERIES

The Object Database Standard *ODMG* has formulated four kinds of collection types, namely:

- Set
- List
- Array
- Bag

Sets are basically unordered collections that do not allow duplicates. Each object that belongs to a set is unique. *Lists* are ordered collections that allow duplicates. The order of the elements in a list is based on the insertion order or the semantic of the elements. *Arrays* are one-dimensional arrays with variable length, and they allow duplicates. The main difference between a list and an array is in the method used to store the pointers that assign the next element in the list/array. Because this difference is mainly from the implementation point of view, lists and arrays will have the same treatment in this book. A *bag* is similar to a set except for allowing duplicate values to exist. Thus, it is an unordered collection that allows duplicates.

For example, an attribute *author* of class *Book* has a collection of *Person* as its domain. Because the order of persons in the attribute *author* is significant, the collection must be of type *list*. In other words, the type of the attribute *author* is *list of Person*. This shows that the domain can be a collection, not only a single value or a single object.

Based on these collection types, three collection-join queries are defined, namely, (*i*) *collection-equi*, (*ii*) *collection-intersect*, and (*iii*) *subcollection* joins.

8.2.1 Collection-Equi Join Queries

Collection-equi join queries contain join predicates in the form of a standard comparison using a relational operator, particularly the equality operator (i.e., the = operator). The operands of these queries are attributes of any collection types.

A typical collection-equi join query is used to compare two collections for a full equality. Suppose the attribute *editor-in-chief* of class *Journal* and the attribute *program-chair* of class *Proceedings* are of type arrays of *Person*. To retrieve conferences chaired by *all* editors-in-chief of a journal, the join predicate becomes (editor-in-chief = program-chair). Only pairs having an exact match between the join attributes will be retrieved. The query expressed in OQL (Object Query Language) can be written as follows:

Query 8.1:

```
Select A, B
From A in Journal, B in Proceedings
Where A.editor-in-chief = B.program-chair
```

The query results using the sample data shown in Figure 8.3 depend on the collection type adopted by the join attributes. If the attributes are of type *array* or *list*, the query results are a concatenation between object *i* of class *Journal* and object *w* of class *Proceedings*, since both have the exact match not only on the OIDs of all elements but also in that order. However, if the join attributes are of type *set*, the query results also include objects *b–p*.

Relational operators, like the = operator, are overloaded functions. This feature is not new to object-oriented join queries, because long before object-oriented databases existed, relational operators in relational joins have shown this capability. For example, it is permitted to compare an integer with a real number. One of the operands is automatically converted to the type of the other operand (in this case, *integer* to *real*). Casting a collection, however, must be done explicitly in the join predicate. Using the previous example, if *editor-in-chief* is a *list* and *program-chair* is a *set*, the equality predicate becomes (`listtoset(editor-in-chief)` = `program-chair`), where the editor-in-chief is converted from a list to a set. Comparing two sets/bags can then be done easily by sorting them before the actual comparison.

8.2.2   Collection–Intersect Join Queries

Collection-intersect join queries contain a join predicate where one collection attribute of the join predicate is compared against another collection attribute and the predicate checks for an intersection. An *intersect* predicate can be written by applying an intersection between the two sets and comparing the intersection result with an empty set. Collection-intersect join predicates have to use two operators, namely an `intersect` operator and a `! =` (not equal) operator. The reason is that according to ODMG, an `intersect` operator is a binary operator, not a Boolean operator. On the other hand, predicates are Boolean, not binary. To solve this mismatch, checking whether there is an intersection between two collections or not must obtain intersection results through the use of the `intersect` operator first, and then it checks whether or not these results are empty.

An example of a collection-intersect join is to retrieve pairs of Journal and Proceedings, where the program-chairs of a conference intersect with the editors-in-chief of a journal. The query expressed in OQL can be written as follows:

Query 8.2:

```
Select A, B
From A in Journal, B in Proceedings
Where (A.editor-in-chief intersect B.program-chair)
!= set(nil)
```

Note that the join predicate is in a form of (`attr1 intersect attr2`) `! =` `set(nil)`, and both attributes `attr1` and `attr2` are of type set. Seven pairs of Journal-Proceedings objects are formed as a result of the above query. They are: *b–p, c–s, d–q, f–r, f–t, g–v,* and *i–w*.

Bag intersection is similar to set intersection as shown in the above example, but it has a distinctive feature, which is different from that of set intersection, that is, intersection of 2 bags yields a bag that contains the maximum for each of the duplicate values. For example, `bag(1,2,2,3) intersect bag(2,3,3,4) = bag (2,2,3,3)`, not just `bag(2,3)` as one might expect. Despite this unique feature of bag intersection as defined by ODMG, there is no difference in the context of join predicates used in a collection-intersect join, as the predicates check whether or not the result of the intersection is nil.

List or array intersection is not yet defined by ODMG, and hence the semantics of list/array intersection is still unclear. One simple way to deal with collections of type list or array is done simply by converting them into bags in which duplicates are reserved but the order of the elements is lost.

8.2.3 Subcollection Join Queries

Subcollection join queries contain a join predicate where one collection attribute of the join predicate is compared against another collection attribute and the predicate evaluates for a subset, sublist, proper subset, or proper sublist. The difference between *proper* and *nonproper* is that the proper predicates require both join operands to be a proper subcollection. This means that if both operands are the same they do not satisfy the predicate, and hence return a false result. The difference between subset and sublist originated from the basic difference between sets and lists. In other words, subset predicates are applied to sets/bags, whereas sublists are applied to lists/arrays.

A *subset* predicate can be written by applying an intersection between the two sets and comparing the intersection result with the smaller set. It is normally in a form of `(attr1 intersect attr2) = attr1`. Attributes `attr1` and `attr2` are of type set. If one or both of them are of type bag, they must be converted to sets. An example of a subcollection join is to retrieve pairs of Journal and Proceedings, where the program-chairs of a conference are a *subset* of the editors-in-chief of a journal. The query expressed in OQL can be written as follows:

Query 8.3:

```
Select A, B
From A in Journal, B in Proceedings
Where (A.editor-in-chief intersect B.program-chair)
= B.program-chair
```

Using the previous sample data, there are three pairs of objects produced by the query, namely, $b–p$, $d–q$, and $i–w$. The first and the last pairs are produced because both collections within each pair are the same, whereas the second pair is produced because the collection in q is a subset of that of d. If a *proper subset* predicate is required instead, a further process is needed to eliminate the pairs in which both collections are identical. In this case, the final query result will be just $d–q$.

If the join predicate is a *proper subset*, the Where clause of the above query must be ANDed with **A.editor-in-chief !=B.program-chair**. This is necessary to enforce that both operands are not identical.

The *sublist* predicate checks whether the first list is a sublist of the second. Two identical lists are regarded as one list being a sublist of the other. If the predicate is a *proper sublist* instead, identical lists are not allowed. The difference between sublist and subset predicate is determined by the type of the operand.

The *sublist* predicate is very complex in its original form. Suppose a *sublist* expression is available that builds all possible sublists of a given list. For example,

```
sublist (list(1, 2, 3)) = list(list(1), list(2),
list(3), list(1,2), list(2,3), list(1,2,3))
```

By combining an *in* operator with the *sublist* operator, a predicate to check for a sublist can be constructed. The sublist join predicate may look like the following: (attr2 in sublist(attr1)), where attr1 and attr2 are of type list. To implement a proper sublist predicate, it must further check that the two lists are not identical.

8.3 PARALLEL ALGORITHMS FOR COLLECTION JOIN QUERIES

As there are three types of collection join queries, parallel algorithms for each of these collection join queries are studied, particularly:

- Parallel collection-equi join algorithms,
- Parallel collection-intersect join algorithms, and
- Parallel subcollection join algorithms

Parallel join algorithms are normally decomposed into two steps: *data partitioning* and *local join*. Data partitioning creates parallelism, as it divides the data to multiple processors so that the join can then be performed locally in each processor without interfering with others.

General data partitioning exists in two forms: disjoint and overlap (non-disjoint). Disjoint partitioning is available to parallel collection-equi join algorithms, whereas the other two parallel algorithms have to adopt a non-disjoint data partitioning.

The local join processing exists in various forms, such as sort-merge, hash, and sort-hash. When hashing is used for collection, multiple hash tables may need to be employed.

8.4 PARALLEL COLLECTION-EQUI JOIN ALGORITHMS

Parallel algorithms for collection-equi join queries exist in three forms, depending on the techniques used in the local joining process. They are:

- Parallel double sort-merge algorithm,
- Parallel sort-hash algorithm, and
- Parallel hash algorithm

The first algorithm is based on the sort-merge technique, whereas the other two parallel algorithms are based on a hashing technique.

Similar to any other parallel join algorithms, these algorithms proceed in two steps. The data partitioning step produces disjoint partitions, whereas the joining step is the local join operation. In this section, we study the disjoint data partitioning first, followed by the three parallel algorithms for collection-equi join queries.

8.4.1 Disjoint Data Partitioning

The *data partitioning* method for parallel collection-equi join is highly influenced by common practices of array/set comparison in programming. An array can be compared with another array by evaluating each pair of elements from the same position of the two arrays. A characteristic of array comparison is that once an element is found to be different from its counterpart (i.e., element of the same position from the other array), the comparison stops and returns a negative result. Unlike array comparison, set comparison is not based on the position of each element in the collection, since the order of the elements is not significant. For example, $array(2,3,1) \neq array(3,2,1)$, but $set(2,3,1) = set(3,2,1)$. In comparing two sets, it will become easier if the two sets are alphabetically/numerically presorted. For instance, $set(2,3,1)$ is sorted to be $set(1,2,3)$, and so is the second set. Comparison can then be carried out as per array comparison.

It is clear that an array comparison very much depends on the position of each element in an array. The first element will open the gate for further element comparisons only if the first pair is evaluated to be true. In contrast, set comparison depends on the smallest element in a set, which is the first element after sorting. This element acts like the first element in the array. Based on these characteristics, the first element of an array and the smallest element of a set play an important role in data partitioning. Common horizontal data partitioning methods, such as range or hash, can be used to produce disjoint (non-overlap) partitions. If the collection is an array or a list, partitioning is based solely on the first element of the list/array, since a list/array comparison operates on the original element composition of the collection. If the partitioning attribute is a set or a bag, partitioning is based on the smallest element of the collection, because a set/bag comparison requires the collections to be sorted.

Figure 8.4 shows the data partitioning for parallel collection-equi join based on the sample data shown in Figure 8.3. Two cases are presented as an example. Case 1 is where the two collections are arrays, and case 2 is where the collections are sets. Note the difference that determines which element in each collection is chosen as the basis for data partitioning (the chosen elements are given in bold).

CASE 1: ARRAYS

Processor **1** (Range 0-99)	d(**4**, 237) i(**80**, 70)	r(**50**, 40) t(**50**, 60) u(**3**, 1, 2) w(**80**, 70)
Processor **2** (Range 100-199)	c(**125**, 181) f(**150**, 50, 250) h(**190**, 189, 170)	p(**123**, 210) s(**125**, 180) v(**100**, 102, 270)
Processor **3** (Range 200-299)	a(**250**, 75) b(**210**, 123) e(**289**, 290) g(**270**)	q(**237**)

Notes:
- Collections 1 and 2 are arrays,
- 3 processors are used,
- Range partitioning is used (processor 1 = 0-99, processor 2 = 100-199, and processor 3 = 200-299)
- Partitioning is based on the **first element** in each collection
- Collections are sorted based on their first elements.

CASE 2: SETS

Processor **1** (Range 0-99)	a(250, **75**) d(**4**, 237) f(150, **50**, 250) i(80, **70**)	r(50, **40**) t(**50**, 60) u(3, **1**, 2) w(80, **70**)
Processor **2** (Range 100-199)	b(210, **123**) c(**125**, 181) h(190, 189, **170**)	p(**123**, 210) s(**125**, 180) v(**100**, 102, 270)
Processor **3** (Range 200-299)	e(**289**, 290) g(**270**)	q(**237**)

Notes:
- Collections 1 and 2 are sets,
- 3 processors are used,
- Range partitioning is used (processor 1 = 0-99, processor 2 = 100-199, and processor 3 = 200-299)
- Partitioning is based on the **smallest element** in each collection
- Each collection is sorted first, and then all collections are sorted based on their first elements.

Figure 8.4   Disjoint data partitioning

8.4.2 Parallel Double Sort-Merge Collection-Equi Join Algorithm

The joining step is decomposed into the *sorting* and *merging* phases. The sorting operation is applied twice: to the collections and to the class. A sorting of each collection is needed only if the collection is a set or a bag, and sorting the objects

---

Algorithm: Parallel-Double-Sort-Merge-Collection-
Equi-Join

```
// step 1: partitioning step
   Partition the objects of both classes based on their
   first elements (for lists/arrays), or their minimum
   elements (for sets/bags).

// step 2: joining step (in each processor)
   // a. sort phase
       (i) Sort elements of each collection (sets/bags
           only)
      (ii) Sort the objects based on the 1st element of
           the collection.

   // b. merge phase
     (iii) Merge the objects of both classes based on
           their first element on the join attribute.
      (iv) If matched, merge the two collection
           attributes based on their individual
           elements (starting from the second
           element).
```

Figure 8.5   Parallel double sort-merge collection-equi join algorithm

is based on the first element (if it is an array or a list) or on the smallest element (if it is a set or a bag). The sorting phase is not carried out before data partitioning, as sorting that is done in parallel in each processor after data partitioning will minimize the elapsed time.

Like the sorting phase, the merging phase consists of two operations: class-level merging and collection-level merging. Merging the objects of the two classes is based on the first element of each collection. If they are matched, a subsequent element comparison can proceed.

The complete parallel algorithm based on double sort-merge for collection-equi join queries is shown in Figure 8.5. Figure 8.6 gives an illustration of the result of the algorithm. Two cases are presented as examples. Case 1 is where the two collections are arrays, and case 2 is where the collections are sets.

8.4.3   Parallel Sort-Hash Collection-Equi Join Algorithm

Parallel sort-hash algorithm is based on a combination of both sort and hashing techniques. Since the join attributes are of type collections, hashing on a collection necessitates multiple hash tables. Each hash table contains all elements of the same position of all collections. For example, entries in hash table 1 contain all first elements in the collections. The number of hash tables is determined by the largest

CASE 1: ARRAYS

Processor **1** (Range 0-99) *Results = (i, w)*	d(**4**, 237) i(**80**, 70)	u(**3**, 1, 2) r(**50**, 40) t(**50**, 60) w(**80**, 70)
Processor **2** (Range 100-199) *Results = nil*	c(**125**, 181) f(**150**, 50, 250) h(**190**, 189, 170)	v(**100**, 102, 270) p(**123**, 210) s(**125**, 180)
Processor **3** (Range 200-299) *Results = nil*	b(**210**, 123) a(**250**, 75) g(**270**) e(**289**, 290)	q(**237**)

Notes: Collections are sorted based on their first elements.

CASE 2: SETS

Processor **1** (Range 0-99) *Results = (i, w)*	d(**4**, 237) f(**50**, 150, 250) i(**70**, 80) a(**75**, 250)	u(1, 2, 3) r(**40**, 50) t(**50**, 60) w(**70**, 80)
Processor **2** (Range 100-199) *Results = (b, p)*	b(**123**, 210) c(**125**, 181) h(**170**, 189, 190)	v(**100**, 102, 270) p(**123**, 210) s(**125**, 180)
Processor **3** (Range 200-299) *Results = nil*	g(**270**) e(**289**, 290)	q(**237**)

Notes: Each collection is sorted first, and then all collections are sorted based on their first elements.

Figure 8.6 Results of parallel double sort-merge algorithm

collection among objects of the class to be hashed. If the collection is a *list/array*, the position of the element is similar to the original element composition in each collection. If the collection is a *set/bag*, the smallest element within each collection will be hashed into the first hash table, the second smallest element is hashed to the second hash table, and so on.

Set/bag hashing will be enhanced if the set/bag is *preprocessed* by means of *sorting*, so that the hashing process will not have to search for the order of the elements within the set/bag. Figure 8.7 shows an example in which three objects are hashed into multiple hash tables. Case 1 is where the objects are arrays, and case 2 is where the objects are sets.

In the case of collision, it will be resolved as per normal collision handling. However, it must be noted that the same element value and position in another collection (especially set) may not necessary result in a collision. For example, a new collection $h(150,50,25)$ is to be hashed. If collection h is a *set*, the elements 150, 50, and 25 will be hashed to the hash tables 3, 2, and 1, respectively. No

Case 1: ARRAYS

$a(250, 75)$
$b(210, 123)$
$f(150, 50, 250)$

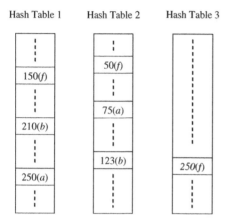

Case 2: SETS

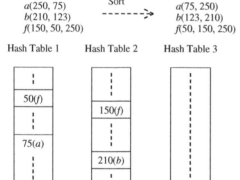

Figure 8.7   Multiple hash tables

collision will occur between $h(150,50,25)$ and collection $f(150,50,250)$. Collision will occur, however, if collection h is a list. The element $150(h)$ will be hashed to hash table 1 and will collide with $150(f)$. Subsequently, the element $150(h)$ will go to the next available entry in hash table 1, as a result of the collision.

Once the multiple hash tables have been built, the probing process begins. The probing process is basically the central part of collection join processing. The probing function for collection-equi join is called a *function universal*. It recursively checks whether a collection exists in the multiple hash table and the elements belong to the same collection. Since this function acts like a universal quantifier where it checks only whether all elements in a collection exist in another collection, it does not guarantee that the two collections are equal. To check for the equality of two collections, it has to check whether collection of class *A* (collection in the multiple hash tables) has reached the end of collection. This can be done by checking whether the size of the two matched collections is the same. Figure 8.8 shows the algorithm for the parallel sort-hash collection-equi join algorithm.

Algorithm: Parallel-Sort-Hash-Collection-Equi-Join

```
// step 1 (disjoint partitioning):
   Partition the objects of both classes based on their
   first elements (for lists/arrays), or their minimum
   elements (for sets/bags).

// step 2 (local joining):
   In each processor, for each partition
   // a. preprocessing (sorting)      // sets/bags only
      For each collection of class A and class B
        Sort each collection
   // b. hash
      For each object of class A
        Hash the object into multiple hash tables
   // c. hash and probe
      For each object of class B
        Call universal (1, 1)  // element 1,hash table 1
        If TRUE AND the collection of class A has
        reached end of collection
          Put the matching pair into the result

Function universal (element i, hash table j): Boolean
  Hash and Probe element i to hash table j
  If matched              // match the element and the
    object Increment i and j
    // check for end of collection of the probing class.
    If end of collection is reached
      Return TRUE
    If hash table j exists     // check for the hash
      table result = universal (i, j)
    Else
      Return FALSE
  Else
    Return FALSE
  Return result
```

Figure 8.8   Parallel sort-hash collection-equi join algorithm

8.4.4 Parallel Hash Collection-Equi Join Algorithm

Unlike the parallel sort-hash explained in the previous section, the algorithm described in this section is purely based on hashing only. No sorting is necessary. Hashing collections or multivalues is different from hashing atomic values. If the join attributes are of type list/array, all of the elements of a list can be concatenated and produce a single value. Hashing can then be done at once. However, this method is applicable to lists and arrays only. When the join attributes are of type set or bag, it is necessary to find new ways of hashing collections.

To illustrate how hashing collections can be accomplished, let us review how hashing atomic values is normally performed. Assume a hash table is implemented as an array, where each hash table entry points to an entry of the record or object. When collision occurs, a linear linked-list is built for that particular hash table entry. In other words, a hash table is an array of linear linked-lists. Each of the linked-lists is connected only through the hash table entry, which is the entry point of the linked-list.

Hash tables for collections are similar, but each node in the linked-list can be connected to another node in the other linked-list, resulting in a "two-dimensional" linked-list. In other words, each collection forms another linked-list for the second dimension. Figure 8.9 shows an illustration of a hash table for collections. For example, when a collection having three elements 3, 1, 6 is hashed, the gray nodes create a circular linked-list. When another collection with three elements 1, 3, 2 is hashed, the white nodes are created. Note that nodes 1 and 3 of this collection collide with those of the previous collection. Suppose another collection having duplicate elements (say elements 5, 1, 5) is hashed; the black nodes are created. Note this time that both elements 5 of the same collection are placed within the same collision linked-list. Based on this method, the result of the hashing is always sorted.

When probing, each probed element is tagged. When the last element within a collection is probed and matched, a traversal is performed to check whether the matched nodes form a circular linked-list. If so, it means that a collection is successfully probed and is placed in the query result.

Figure 8.10 shows the algorithm for the parallel hash collection-equi join algorithm, including the data partitioning and the local join process.

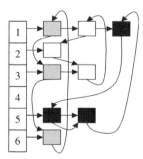

Figure 8.9 Hashing collections/multivalues

Algorithm: `Parallel-Hash-Collection-Equi-Join`

```
// step 1 (data partitioning)
   Partition the objects of both classes to be joined
   based on their first elements (for lists/arrays), or
   their smallest elements (for sets/bags) of the
   join attribute.

// step 2 (local joining): In each processor
   // a. hash
      Hash each element of the collection.
      Collision is handled through the use of linked-
      list within the same hash table entry.
      Elements within the same collection are linked
      in a different dimension using a circular
      linked-list.

   // b. probe
      Probe each element of the collection.
      Once a matched is not found:
         Discard current collection, and
         Start another collection.

      If the element is found Then
         Tag the matched node

      If the element found is the last element in the
      probing collection Then
         Perform a traversal
      If a circle is formed Then
         Put into the query result
      Else
         Discard the current collection
         Start another collection
      Repeat until all collections are probed.
```

Figure 8.10   Parallel hash collection-equi join algorithm

8.5   PARALLEL COLLECTION-INTERSECT JOIN ALGORITHMS

Parallel algorithms for collection-intersect join queries also exist in three forms, like those of collection-equi join. They are:

- Parallel sort-merge nested-loop algorithm,
- Parallel sort-hash algorithm, and
- Parallel hash algorithm

There are two main differences between parallel algorithms for collection-intersect and those for collection-equi. The first difference is that for collection-intersect, the simplest algorithm is a combination of sort-merge and nested-loop, not double-sort-merge. The second difference is that the data partitioning used in parallel collection-intersect join algorithms is non-disjoint data partitioning, not disjoint data partitioning.

8.5.1   Non-Disjoint Data Partitioning

Unlike the collection-equi join, for a collection-intersect join, it is not possible to have non-overlap partitions because of the nature of collections, which may be overlapped. Hence, some data needs to be replicated. There are three non-disjoint data partitioning methods available to parallel algorithms for collection-intersect join queries, namely:

- Simple replication,
- Divide and broadcast, and
- Divide and partial broadcast.

Simple Replication

With a *Simple Replication* technique, each element in a collection is treated as a single unit and is totally independent of other elements within the same collection. Based on the value of an element in a collection, the object is placed into a particular processor. Depending on the number of elements in a collection, the objects that own the collections may be placed into different processors. When an object has already been placed at a particular processor based on the placement of an element, if another element in the same collection is also to be placed at the same place, no object replication is necessary.

Figure 8.11 shows an example of a simple replication technique. The bold printed elements are the elements, which are the basis for the placement of those objects. For example, object $a(250, 75)$ in processor 1 refers to a placement for object a in processor 1 because of the value of element 75 in the collection. And also, object $a(250, 75)$ in processor 3 refers to a copy of object a in processor 3 based on the first element (i.e., element 250). It is clear that object a is replicated to processors 1 and 3. On the other hand, object $i(80, 70)$ is not replicated since both elements will place the object at the same place, that is, processor 1.

Divide and Broadcast

The *divide and broadcast* partitioning technique basically divides one class into a number of processors equally and broadcasts the other class to all processors. The performance of this partitioning method will be strongly determined by the size of the class that is to be broadcasted, since this class is replicated on all processors.

Class A	Class B	
a(250, **75**) *d*(**4**, 237) *f*(150,**50**, 250) *i*(**80**, **70**)	*r*(**50**, **40**) *t*(**50**, **60**) *u*(**3**, **1**, **2**) *w*(**80**, **70**)	Processor 1 (range 0–99)
b(210, **123**) *c*(**125**, **181**) *f*(**150**, 50, 250) *h*(**190**, **189**, **170**)	*p*(**123**, 210) *s*(**125**, **180**) *v*(**100**, **102**, 270)	Processor 2 (range 100–199)
a(**250**, 75) *b*(**210**, 123) *d*(4, **237**) *e*(**289**, **290**) *f*(150, 50, **250**) *g*(**270**)	*p*(123, **210**) *q*(**237**) *v*(100, 102, **270**)	Processor 3 (range 200–299)

Figure 8.11   Simple replication technique for parallel collection-intersect join

There are two scenarios for data partitioning using divide and broadcast. The first scenario is to divide class *A* and to broadcast class *B*, whereas the second scenario is the opposite. With three processors, the result of the first scenario is as follows. The division uses a round-robin partitioning method.

Processor 1: class *A* (*a*, *d*, *g*) and class *B* (*p*, *q*, *r*, *s*, *t*, *u*, *v*, *w*)

Processor 2: class *A* (*b*, *e*, *h*) and class *B* (*p*, *q*, *r*, *s*, *t*, *u*, *v*, *w*)

Processor 3: class *A* (*c*, *f*, *i*) and class *B* (*p*, *q*, *r*, *s*, *t*, *u*, *v*, *w*)

Each processor is now independent of the others, and a local join operation can then be carried out. The result from processor 1 will be the pair $d - q$. Processor 2 produces the pair $b - p$, and processor 3 produces the pairs of $c - s$, $f - r$, $f - t$, and $i - w$. With the second scenario, the divide and broadcast technique will result in the following data placement.

Processor 1: class *A* (*a*, *b*, *c*, *d*, *e*, *f*, *g*, *h*, *i*) and class *B* (*p*, *s*, *v*).

Processor 2: class *A* (*a*, *b*, *c*, *d*, *e*, *f*, *g*, *h*, *i*) and class *B* (*q*, *t*, *w*).

Processor 3: class *A* (*a*, *b*, *c*, *d*, *e*, *f*, *g*, *h*, *i*) and class *B* (*r*, *u*).

The join results produced by each processor are as follows. Processor 1 produces *b–p* and *c–s*, processor 2 produces *d–q*, *f–t*, and *i–w*, and processor 3 produces *f–r*. The union of the results from all processors gives the final query result.

Both scenarios will produce the same query result. The only difference lies in the partitioning method used in the join algorithm. It is clear from the examples that the division should be on the larger class, whereas the broadcast should be on the smaller class, so that the cost due to the replication will be smaller.

Another way to minimize replication is to use a variant of divide and broadcast called "*divide and partial broadcast*". The name itself indicates that broadcasting is done *partially*, instead of completely.

Algorithm: Divide and Partial Broadcast

```
// step 1 (divide)
1. Divide class B based on largest element in each
   collection
2. For each partition of B (i = 1, 2, ..., n)
     Place partition Bi to processor i

// step 2 (partial broadcast)
3. Divide class A based on smallest element in each
   collection
4. For each partition of A (i = 1, 2, ..., n)
     Broadcast partition Ai to processor i to n
```

Figure 8.12 Divide and partial broadcast algorithm

Divide and Partial Broadcast

The *divide and partial broadcast* algorithm (see Fig. 8.12) proceeds in two steps. The first step is a *divide* step, and the second step is a *partial broadcast* step. We divide class B and partial broadcast class A.

The *divide* step is explained as follows. Divide class B into n number of partitions. Each partition of class B is placed in a separate processor (e.g., partition $B1$ to processor 1, partition $B2$ to processor 2, etc). Partitions are created based on the largest element of each collection. For example, object $p(123, 210)$, the first object in class B, is partitioned based on element 210, as element 210 is the largest element in the collection. Then, object p is placed on a certain partition, depending on the partition range. For example, if the first partition is ranging from the largest element 0 to 99, the second partition is ranging from 100 to 199, and the third partition is ranging from 200 to 299, then object p is placed in partition $B3$, and subsequently in processor 3. This is repeated for all objects of class B.

The *partial broadcast* step can be described as follows. First, partition class A based on the smallest element of each collection. Then for each partition Ai where $i = 1$ to n, broadcast partition Ai to processors i to n. This broadcasting technique is said to be partial, since the broadcasting decreases as the partition number increases. For example, partition $A1$ is basically replicated to all processors, partition $A2$ is broadcast to processor 2 to n only, and so on.

The result of the divide and partial Broadcast of the sample data shown earlier in Figure 8.3 is shown in Figure 8.13.

In regard to the load of each partition, the load of the last processor may be the heaviest, as it receives a full copy of A and a portion of B. The load goes down as class A is divided into smaller size (e.g., processor 1). To achieve more load balancing, we can apply the same algorithm to each partition but with a reverse role of A and B; that is, *divide A and partial broadcast B* (previously it was *divide*

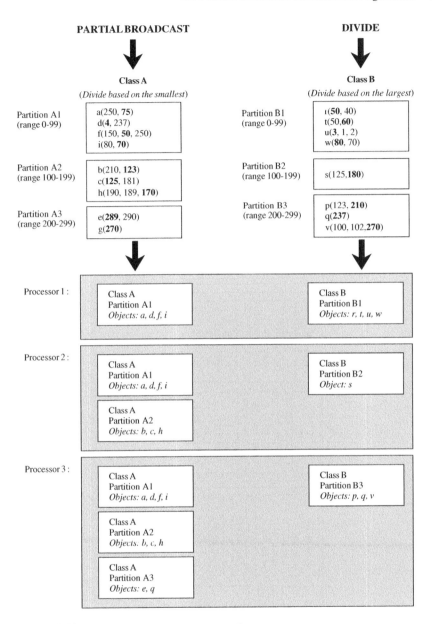

Figure 8.13   Divide and partial broadcast example

B and *partial broadcast A*). This is then called a "two-way" divide and partial broadcast.

Figure 8.14(a and b) shows the results of reverse partitioning of the initial partitioning. Note that from processor 1, class *A* and class *B* are divided into three

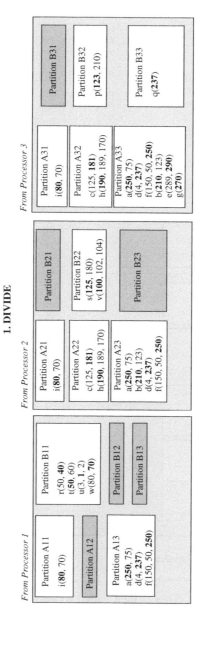

1. DIVIDE

Figure 8.14(a) Two-way divide and partial broadcast (divide)

2. PARTIAL BROADCAST

Figure 8.14(b) Two-way divide and partial broadcast (partial broadcast)

239

partitions each (i.e., partitions 11, 12, and 13). Partition A12 of class A and partitions B12 and B13 of class B are empty. Additionally, at the broadcasting phase, bucket 12 is "half empty" (contains collections from one class only), since partitions A12 and B12 are both empty. This bucket can then be eliminated. In the same manner, buckets 21 and 31 are also discarded.

Further load balancing can be done with the conventional bucket tuning approach, whereby the buckets produced by the data partitioning are redistributed to all processors to produce more load balanced. For example, because the number of buckets is more than the number of processors (e.g., 6 buckets: 11, 13, 22, 23, 32 and 33, and 3 processors), load balancing is achieved by spreading and combining partitions to create more equal loads. For example, buckets 11, 22 and 23 are placed at processor 1, buckets 13 and 32 are placed at processor 2, and bucket 33 is placed at processor 3. The result of this placement, shown in Figure 8.15, looks better than the initial placement.

In the implementation, the algorithm for the *divide and partial broadcast* is simplified by using decision tables. Decision tables can be constructed by first understanding the ranges (smallest and largest elements) involved in the divide and partial broadcast algorithm. Suppose the domain of the join attribute is an integer from 0–299, and there are three processors. Assume the distribution is divided into three ranges: 0–99, 100–199, and 200–299. The result of one-way divide and partial broadcast is given in Figure 8.16.

There are a few things that we need to describe regarding the example shown in Figure 8.16.

First, the range is shown as two pairs of numbers, in which the first pairs indicate the range of the smallest element in the collection and the second pairs indicate the range of the largest element in the collection.

Second, in the first column (i.e., class A), the first pairs are highlighted to emphasize that collections of this class are partitioned based on the smallest element in each collection, and in the second column (i.e., class B), the second pairs are printed in bold instead to indicate that collections are partitioned according to the largest element in each collection.

Third, the second pairs of class A are basically the upper limit of the range, meaning that as long as the smallest element falls within the specified range, the range for the largest element is the upper limit, which in this case is 299. The opposite is applied to class B, that is, the range of the smallest element is the base limit of 0.

Finally, since class B is divided, the second pairs of class B are disjoint. This conforms to the algorithm shown above in Figure 8.12, particularly the divide step. On the other hand, since class A is partially broadcast, the first pairs of class A are overlapped. The overlapping goes up as the number of bucket increases. For example, the first pair of bucket 1 is [0–99], and the first pair of bucket 2 is [0–199], which is essentially an overlapping between pairs [0–99] and [100–199]. The same thing is applied to bucket 3, which is combined with pair [200–299] to

Processor Allocation

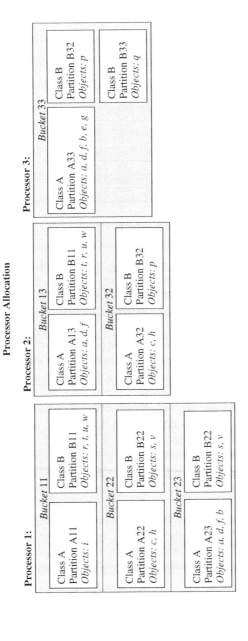

Figure 8.15 Processor allocation

241

	Class A	Class B
Bucket 1	**[0-99]** .. [0-299]	[0-99] .. **[0-99]**
Bucket 2	**[0-199]** .. [0-299]	[0-199] .. **[100-199]**
Bucket 3	**[0-299]** .. [0-299]	[0-299] .. **[200-299]**

Figure 8.16 "One-way" divide and partial broadcast

	Class A	Class B
Bucket 11	[0-99] .. **[0-99]**	**[0-99]** .. [0-99]
Bucket 12	[0-99] .. **[100-199]**	**[0-199]** .. [0-99]
Bucket 13	[0-99] .. **[200-299]**	**[0-299]** .. [0-99]
Bucket 21	[0-199] .. **[0-99]**	**[0-99]** .. [100-199]
Bucket 22	[0-199] .. **[100-199]**	**[0-199]** .. [100-199]
Bucket 23	[0-199] .. **[200-299]**	**[0-299]** .. [100-199]
Bucket 31	[0-299] .. **[0-99]**	**[0-99]** .. [200-299]
Bucket 32	[0-299] .. **[100-199]**	**[0-199]** .. [200-299]
Bucket 33	[0-299] .. **[200-299]**	**[0-299]** .. [200-299]

Figure 8.17 "Two-way" divide and partial broadcast

produce pair [0–299]. This kind of overlapping is a manifestation of partial broadcast as denoted by the algorithm, particularly the partial broadcast step. Figure 8.17 shows an illustration of a "two-way" divide and partial broadcast.

There are also a few things that need clarification regarding the example shown in Figure 8.17.

First, the second pairs of class A and the first pairs of class B are now printed in bold to indicate that the partitioning is based on the largest element of collections in class A and on the smallest element of collections in class B. The partitioning model has now been reversed.

Second, the nonhighlighted pairs of classes A and B of buckets xy (e.g., buckets 11, 12, 13) in the "two-way" divide and partial broadcast shown in Figure 8.17 are identical to the highlighted pairs of buckets x (e.g., bucket 1) in the "one-way" divide and partial broadcast shown in Figure 8.16. This explains that these pairs have not mutated during a reverse partitioning in the "two-way" divide and partial broadcast, since buckets 11, 12, and 13 basically come from bucket 1, and so on.

Finally, since the roles of the two classes have been reversed, in that class A is now divided and class B is partially broadcast, note that the second pairs of class A originated from the same bucket in the "one-way" divide and partial broadcast are disjoint, whereas the first pairs of class B originated from the same buckets are overlapped.

Now the decision tables, which are constructed from the above tables, can be explained, First the decision tables for the "one-way" divide and partial broadcast, followed by those for the "two-way" version. The intention is to outline the difference between the two methods, particularly the load involved in the process, in

Class A

Range		Buckets		
Smallest	Largest	1	2	3
0-99	0-99			
0-99	100-199			
0-99	200-299			
100-199	100-199			
100-199	200-299			
200-299	200-299			

Figure 8.18(a)   "One-way" divide and partial broadcast decision table for class *A*

Class B

Range		Buckets		
Smallest	Largest	1	2	3
0-99	0-99			
0-99	100-199			
0-99	200-299			
100-199	100-199			
100-199	200-299			
200-299	200-299			

Figure 8.18(b)   "One-way" divide and partial broadcast decision table for class *B*

which the "two-way" version filters out more unnecessary buckets. Based on the division tables, implementing a "two-way" divide and partial broadcast algorithm can also be done with multiple checking.

Figures 8.18(a) and (b) show the decision table for class *A* and class *B* for the original "one-way" divide and partial broadcast. The shaded cells indicate the applicable ranges for a particular bucket. For example, in bucket 1 of class *A* the range of the smallest element in a collection is [0–99] and the range of the largest element is [0–299]. Note that the load of buckets in class *A* grows as the bucket number increases. This load increase does not happen that much for class *B*, as class *B* is divided, not partially broadcast. The same bucket number from the two different classes is joined. For example, bucket 1 from class *A* is joined only with bucket 1 from class *B*.

Figures 8.19(a) and (b) are the decision tables for the "two-way" divide and partial broadcast, which are constructed from the ranges shown in Figure 8.17. Comparing decision tables of the original "one-way" divide and partial broadcast and that of the "two-way version", the lighter shaded cells are from the "one-way" decision table, whereas the heavier shaded cells indicate the applicable range for

Class A

Range		Buckets								
Smallest	Largest	11	12	13	21	22	23	31	32	33
0-99	0-99	■	▓	▓	■	▓	▓	■	▓	▓
0-99	100-199	▓	■	▓		■	▓		■	▓
0-99	200-299	▓		■		▓	■		▓	■
100-199	100-199				▓	■	▓		■	
100-199	200-299				▓		■		▓	■
200-299	200-299							▓		■

Figure 8.19(a) "Two-way" divide and partial broadcast decision table for class A

Class B

Range		Buckets								
Smallest	Largest	11	12	13	21	22	23	31	32	33
0-99	0-99	▓	▓	▓						
0-99	100-199				▓	▓	▓			
0-99	200-299							▓	▓	▓
100-199	100-199				▓	▓	▓			
100-199	200-299							▓	▓	▓
200-299	200-299							▓	▓	▓

Figure 8.19(b) "Two-way" divide and partial broadcast decision table for class B

each bucket with the "two-way" method. It is clear that the "two-way" version has filtered out ranges that are not applicable to each bucket. In terms of the difference between the two methods, class A has significant differences, whereas class B has marginal ones.

8.5.2 Parallel Sort-Merge Nested-Loop Collection-Intersect Join Algorithm

The join algorithms for the collection-intersect join consist of a simple sort-merge and a nested-loop structure. A sort operator is applied to each collection, and then a nested-loop construct is used in join-merging the collections. The algorithm uses a nested-loop structure, not only because of its simplicity, but also because of the need for all-round comparisons among objects.

There is one thing to note about the algorithm: To avoid a repeated sorting especially in the inner loop of the nested-loop, sorting of the second class is taken out from the nested loop and is carried out before entering the nested-loop.

Algorithm: Parallel-Sort-Merge-Collection-Intersect-Join

```
// step 1 (data partitioning):
   Call DivideBroadcast or DividePartialBroadcast

// step 2 (local joining): In each processor
   // a sort class B
      For each object b of class B
         Sort collection bc of object b

   // b merge phase
      For each object a of class A
         Sort collection ac of object a
         For each object b of class B
            Merge collection ac and collection bc
            If matched Then
               Concatenate objects a and b into query result
```

Figure 8.20   Parallel sort-merge collection-intersect join algorithm

In the merging, it basically checks whether there is at least one element that is common to both collections. Since both collections have already been sorted, it is relatively straightforward to find out whether there is an intersection. Figure 8.20 shows a parallel sort-merge nested-loop algorithm for collection-intersection join queries.

Although it was explained in the previous section that there are three data partitioning methods available for parallel collection-intersect join, for parallel sort-merge nested-loop we can only use either divide and broadcast or divide and partial broadcast. The simple replication method is not applicable.

8.5.3 Parallel Sort-Hash Collection-Intersect Join Algorithm

A parallel sort-hash collection-intersect join algorithm may use any of the three data partitioning methods explained in the previous section. Once the data partitioning has been applied, the process continues with local joining, which consists of hash and hash probe operations.

The hashing step is to hash objects of class A into multiple hash tables, like that of parallel sort-hash collection-equi join algorithms. In the hash and probe step, each object from class B is processed with an *existential procedure* that checks whether an element of a collection exists in the hash tables.

Figure 8.21 gives the algorithm for parallel sort-hash collection-intersect join queries.

Algorithm: `Parallel-Sort-Hash-Collection-Intersect-Join`

```
// step 1 (data partitioning):
   Choose any of the data partitioning methods:
     Simple Replication, or
     Divide and Broadcast, or
     Divide and Partial Broadcast

// step 2 (local joining): In each processor
   // a. hash
      For each object of class A
        Hash the object into the multiple hash tables
   // b hash and probe
      For each object of class B
        Call existential procedure

Procedure existential (element i, hash table j)
  For each element i
    For each hash table j
      Hash element i into hash table j
      If TRUE
        Put the matching objects into query result
```

Figure 8.21 Parallel sort-hash collection-intersect join algorithm

8.5.4 Parallel Hash Collection-Intersect Join Algorithm

Like the parallel sort-hash algorithm, parallel hash may use any of the three non-disjoint data partitioning available for parallel collection-intersect join, such as simple replication, divide and broadcast, or divide and partial broadcast.

The local join process itself, similar to those of conventional hashing techniques, is divided into two steps: hash and probe. The hashing is carried out to one class, whereas the probing is performed to the other class. The hashing part basically runs through all elements of each collection in a class. The probing part is done in a similar way, but is applied to the other class. Figure 8.22 shows the pseudocode for the parallel hash collection-equi join algorithm.

8.6 PARALLEL SUBCOLLECTION JOIN ALGORITHMS

Parallel algorithms for subcollection join queries are similar to those of parallel collection-intersect join, as the algorithms exist in three forms:

- Parallel sort-merge nested-loop algorithm,

Algorithm: `Parallel-Hash-Collection-Intersect-Join`

```
// step 1 (data partitioning):
   Choose any of the data partitioning methods:
      Simple Replication, or
      Divide and Broadcast, or
      Divide and Partial Broadcast

// step 2 (local joining): In each processor
   // a. hash
      For each object a(c1) of class R
         Hash collection c1 to a hash table

   // b. probe
      For each object b(c2) of class S
         Hash and probe collection c2 into the hash table
         If there is any match
            Concatenate object B and the matched object A
            into query result
```

Figure 8.22 Parallel hash collection-intersect join algorithm

- Parallel sort-hash algorithm, and
- Parallel hash algorithm

The main difference between parallel subcollection and collection-intersect algorithms is, in fact, in the data partitioning method. This is explained in the following section.

8.6.1 Data Partitioning

In the data partitioning, parallel processing of subcollection join queries has to adopt a non-disjoint partitioning. This is clear, since it is not possible to determine whether one collection is a subcollection of the other without going through full comparison, and the comparison result cannot be determined by just a single element of each collection, as in the case of collection-equi join, where the first element (in a list or array) and the smallest element (in a set or a bag) plays a crucial role in the comparison. However, unlike parallelism of collection-intersect join, where there are three options for data partitioning, parallelism of subcollection join can only adopt two of them, *divide and broadcast* partitioning and its variant *divide and partial broadcast* partitioning.

The simple replication method is simply not applicable. This is because with the simple replication method each collection may be split into several processors because of the value of each element in the collection, which may direct the placement of the collection into different processors, and consequently each processor will not be able to perform the subcollection operations without interfering with other processors. The idea of data partitioning in parallel query processing, including parallel collection-join, is that after data partitioning has been completed, each processor can work independently to carry out a join operation without communicating with other processors. The communication is done only when the temporary query results from each processor are amalgamated to produce the final query results.

8.6.2 Parallel Sort-Merge Nested-Loop Subcollection Join Algorithm

Like the collection-intersect join algorithm, the parallel subcollection join algorithm also uses a sort-merge and a nested-loop construct. Both algorithms are similar, except in the merging process, in which the collection-intersect join uses a simple merging technique to check for an intersection but the subcollection join utilizes a more complex algorithm to check for subcollection.

The parallel sort-merge nested-loop subcollection join algorithm, as the name suggests, consists of a simple sort-merge and a nested-loop structure. A sort operator is applied to each collection, and then a nested-loop construct is used in join-merging the collections. There are two important things to mention regarding the sorting: One is that sorting is applied to the *is_subset* predicate only, and the other is that to avoid a repeated sorting especially in the inner loop of the nested loop, sorting of the second class is taken out from the nested loop. The algorithm uses a nested-loop structure, not only for its simplicity but also because of the need for all-round comparisons among all objects.

In the merging phase, the *is_subcollection* function is invoked, in order to compare each pair of collections from the two classes. In the case of a subset predicate, after converting the sets to lists the *is_subcollection* function is executed. The result of this function call becomes the final result of the subset predicate. If the predicate is a sublist, the *is_subcollection* function is directly invoked, without the necessity to convert the collection into lists, since the operands are already lists.

The *is_subcollection* function receives two parameters: the two collections to compare. The function first finds a match of the first element of the smallest list in the bigger list. If a match is found, subsequent element comparisons of both lists are carried out. Whenever the subsequent element comparison fails, the process has to start finding another match for the first element of the smallest list again (in case duplicate items exist). Figure 8.23 shows the complete parallel sort-merge-nested-loop join algorithm for subcollection join queries.

Using the sample data in Figure 8.3, the result of a subset join is $(g, v),(i, w)$, and (b, p). The last two pairs will not be included in the results, if the join predicate is a proper subset, since the two collections in each pair are equal.

Regarding the sorting, the second class is sorted outside the nested loop similar to the collection-intersect join algorithm. Another thing to note is that sorting is applied to the *is_subset* predicate only.

Algorithm: `Parallel-Sort-Merge-Nested-Loop-Subcollection`

```
// step 1 (Data Partitioning):
   Call DivideBroadcast or DividePartialBroadcast

// step 2 (Local Join in each processor)
   // a sort class B (is_subset predicate only)
      For each object of class B
         Sort collection b of class B.

   // b nested loop and sort class A
      For each collection a of class A
         For each collection b of class B
            If the predicate is subset or proper subset
               Convert a and b to list type
            // c merging
            If is_subcollection(a,b)
               Concatenate the two objects into query
               result

Function is_subcollection (L1, L2: list): Boolean
   Set i to 0
   For j=0 to length(L2)
     If L1[i] = L2[j]
        Set Flag to TRUE
        If i = length(L1)-1        // end of L1
          Break
        Else
        i++                        // find the next match
     Else
        Set Flag to FALSE          // reset the flag
        Reset i to 0
   If Flag = TRUE and i = length(L1)-1
      Return TRUE
        (for is_proper predicate:
          If len(L1) != len(L2)
             Return TRUE
          Else
             Return FALSE
   Else
      Return FALSE
```

Figure 8.23   Parallel sort-merge-nested-loop sub-collection join algorithm

8.6.3 Parallel Sort-Hash Subcollection Join Algorithm

In the local join step, if the collection attributes where the join is based are sets or bags, they are sorted first. The next step would be hash and probe.

In the hashing part, the supercollections (e.g., collection of class *B*) are hashed. Once the multiple hash tables have been built, the probing process begins. In the probing part, each subcollection (e.g., collection of class *A* in this example) is probed one by one. If the join predicate is an *is _ proper* predicate, it has to make sure that the two matched collections are not equal. This can be implemented in two separate checkings with an XOR operator. It checks either the first matched element is *not* from the first hash table, or the collection of the first class has not been reached. If either condition (not both) is satisfied, the matched collections are put into the query result. If the join predicate is a normal subset/sublist (i.e., nonproper), apart from the probing process, no other checking is necessary. Figure 8.24 gives the pseudocode for the complete parallel sort-hash subcollection join algorithm.

The central part of the join processing is basically the probing process. The main probing function for subcollection join queries is called *function some*. It recursively checks for a match for the first element in the collection. Once a match has been found, another function called *function universal* is called. This function checks recursively whether a collection exists in the multiple hash table and the elements belong to the same collection. Figure 8.25 shows the pseudocode for the two functions for the sort-hash version of the parallel subcollection join algorithm.

Algorithm: Parallel-Sort-Hash-Sub-Collection-Join

```
// step 1 (data partitioning):
    Call DivideBroadcast or
    Call DivideAndPartialBroadcast partitioning

// step 2 (local joining): In each processor
    // a preprocessing (sorting) (set/bags only)
        For each object a and b of class A and class B
            Sort each collection ac and bc of object a and b

    // b hash
        For each object b of class B
            Hash the objectinto multiple hash tables

    // c probe
        For each object of class A
            Case is_proper predicate:
                If some(1,1)        // element 1, hash table 1
                    If first match is not from the first hash
                    table
                    XOR not end of collection of the first class
                        Put the matching pairs into the result
            Case is_non_proper predicate:
                If some(1,1) Then
                    Put the matching pair into the result
```

Figure 8.24   Parallel sort-hash sub-collection join algorithm

---

Algorithm: Probing Functions

```
Function some (element i, hash table j) Return Boolean
  Hash and Probe element i to hash table j
  // match the element and the object
  If matched
    Increment i and j
    //check for end of collection of the probing class
    If end of collection reached
      Return TRUE
    // check for the hash table
    If hash table j exists Then
      Result = universal (i, j)
    Else
      Return FALSE
  Else
      Increment j
      // continue searching the next hash table
        (recursive)
      Result = some (i, j)
  Return result
End Function

Function universal (element i, hash table j) Return
Boolean
  Hash and Probe element i to hash table j
  // match the element and the object
  If matched Then
    Increment i and j
    //check for end of collection of the probing class
    If end of collection is reached
      Return TRUE
    // check for the hash table
    If hash table j exists
      Result = universal (i, j)
    Else
      Return FALSE
  Else
    Return FALSE
  Return result
```

Figure 8.25   Probing functions

8.6.4 Parallel Hash Subcollection Join Algorithm

The features of a subcollection join are actually a combination of those of collection-equi and collection-intersect join. This can be seen in the data partitioning and local join adopted by the parallel hash subcollection join algorithm.

The data partitioning is based on *DivideBroadcast* or *DividePartialBroadcast* partitioning, which is a subset of data partitioning methods available for parallel collection-intersection join.

Local join of subcollection join queries is similar to that of collection-equi, since the hashing and probing are based on collections, not on atomic values as in parallel collection-intersect join. The difference is that, when probing, a circle does not become a condition for a result. The condition is that as long as all elements probed are in the same circular linked-list, the result is obtained. The circular condition is only applicable if the subcollection predicate is a *nonproper* subcollection predicate, where the predicate checks for the nonequality of both collections. Figure 8.26 shows the pseudocode for parallel hash subcollection join algorithm.

8.7 SUMMARY

This chapter focuses on universal quantification found in object-based databases, namely, collection join queries. Collection join queries are join queries based on collection attributes (i.e., nonatomic attributes), which are common in object-based databases. There are three collection join query types: *collection-equi* join, *collection-intersect* join, and *subcollection* join. Parallel algorithms for these collection join queries have also been explained.

- **Parallel Collection-Equi Join Algorithms**
  Data partitioning is based on disjoint partitioning. The local join is available in three forms, double sort-merge, sort-hash, and purely hash.

- **Parallel Collection-Intersect Join Algorithms**
  Data partitioning methods available are *simple replication, divide and broadcast*, and *divide and partial broadcast*. These are non-disjoint data partitioning. The local join process uses sort-merge nested-loop, sort-hash, or pure hash. When sort-merge nested-loop is used, the simple replication data partitioning is not applicable.

- **Parallel Subcollection Join Algorithms**
  Data partitioning methods available are *divide and broadcast* and *divide and partial broadcast*. The simple replication method is not applicable to subcollection join processing. The local join uses techniques similar to those of collection-intersect, namely, sort-merge nested-loop, sort-hash, and pure hash. However, the actual usage of these techniques differs, since the join predicate is now checking for one collection being a subcollection of the other, not one collection intersecting with the other.

8.8 BIBLIOGRAPHICAL NOTES

One of the most important works in parallel universal quantification was presented by Graefe and Cole (*ACM TODS* 1995), in which they proposed and evaluated

---

Algorithm: Parallel-Hash-Sub-Collection-Join

```
// step 1 (data partitioning)
   Call DivideBroadcast or
   Call DivideAndPartialBroadcast partitioning

// step 2 (local joining): In each processor
   // a. hash
      Hash each element of the collection.
      Collision is handled through the use of linked-
      list within the same hash table entry.
      Elements within the same collection are linked in
      a different dimension using a circular
      linked-list.

   // b. probe
      Probe each element of the collection.
      Once a matched is not found
         Discard current collection, and
         Start another collection.

      If the element is found Then
         Tag the matched node

      If the element found is the last element in the
      probing collection Then
         Perform a traversal
         If all elements probed are matched with nodes
         from the same circular linked-list Then
            Put the matched objects into the query result
      Else
         Discard the current collection
         Start another collection.
      Repeat until all collections are probed
```

Figure 8.26   Parallel hash sub-collection join algorithm

parallel algorithms for relational division using sort-merge, aggregate, and hash-based methods.

The work in parallel object-oriented query started in the late 1980s and early 1990s. The two most early works in parallel object-oriented query processing were written by Khoshafian et al. (*ICDE* 1988), followed by Kim (*ICDE* 1990). Leung and Taniar (1995) described various parallelism models, including intra- and interclass parallelism. The research group of Sampaio and Smith et al. published various papers on parallel algebra for object databases (1999), experimental results (2001), and their system called Polar (2000).

Table R	
A	7, 202, 4
B	20, 111, 66
C	260, 98
D	13
E	12, 17
F	8, 75, 88
G	9, 200
H	170
I	100, 205
J	112
K	160, 161
L	228
M	122, 55
N	18, 75
O	290, 29

Table S	
P	75, 18
Q	25, 95
R	220
S	100, 205
T	270, 88, 45, 3
U	99, 199, 299
V	11
W	100, 200
X	4, 7
Y	60, 161, 160
Z	88, 2, 117, 90

Figure 8.27 Sample data

One of the features of object-oriented queries is path expression, which does not exist in the relational context. Path expression in parallel object-oriented query processing is discussed in Wang et al. (*DASFAA* 2001) and Taniar et al. (1999).

8.9 EXERCISES

8.1. Using the sample tables shown in Figure 8.27, show the results of the following collection join queries (assume that the numerical attributes are of type set):

　a. Collection-equi join,

　b. Collection-intersect join, and

　c. Subcollection join.

8.2. Assuming that the numerical attributes are now of type array, repeat exercise 8.1.

8.3. *Parallel collection-equi* join query exercises:

　a. Taking the sample data shown in Figure 8.27 where the numerical attributes are of type set, perform an initial disjoint data partitioning using a range partitioning method over three processors. Show the partitions in each processor.

　b. Perform a *parallel double sort-merge* algorithm on the partitions. Using the sample data, show the steps of the algorithm from the initial data partitioning to the query results.

8.4. *Parallel collection-intersect* join query exercises:

　a. Using the sample data shown in Figure 8.27 (numerical attribute of type set), show the results of the following partitioning methods:

　　○ Simple replication technique,

　　○ Divide and broadcast technique,

　　○ *One-way* divide and partial broadcast technique, and

　　○ *Two-way* divide and partial broadcast technique.

　b. Adopting the *two-way* divide and partial broadcast technique, show the results of the collection-intersect join query using the *parallel sort-merge nested-loop* algorithm.

8.5. *Parallel subcollection* join query exercises:

a. Adopting the *two-way* divide and partial broadcast technique in exercise 8.4, show the result of the subcollection join query using the *parallel sort-merge nested-loop algorithm.*

8.6. Discuss why parallel collection-equi join uses a disjoint data partitioning, whereas the other two parallel collection joins (i.e., parallel collection-intersect join and parallel subcollection join) use non-disjoint data partitioning.

8.7. Should the above sample data be written in a relational table structure, how can collection join queries be expressed in SQL?

Chapter 9

Parallel Query Scheduling and Optimization

A query in a database system is conveniently expressed in a nonprocedural language such as SQL, where the user does not specify the precise algorithm for retrieving the information, but only the requirements of the desired information. Therefore, it is possible to have many different access paths in executing a query. The optimization technique becomes significant as it formulates and chooses the most efficient way to deliver the query results to the user.

Query optimization in database systems is a classical problem and has been recognized as one of the most difficult problems to solve, since it has proven to be NP-complete; that is, there is no polynomial time algorithm to solve the problem, and therefore more realistic approaches, such as heuristic, cost-based, or semantic optimization, must be employed. The main task of query optimization is to find the most efficient access so that the query response time can be reduced.

A query, before it is executed, is usually scanned and parsed into some internal representation. A typical form used is some kind of query tree or query decomposition. This internal representation is then transformed into an optimized query tree. The rules that transform the initial tree into the final tree must preserve the equivalence. This final query tree is sometimes known as a query access plan, which will be executed to obtain the query result.

Figure 9.1 shows the steps for query processing and optimization. The tasks of parallel query optimization can be divided into two major areas, *parallel query optimization* and *parallel query execution*. Parallel query optimization includes access plan formulation and execution scheduling. Access plan formulation is for developing the best sequential query access plan, whereas execution scheduling is for incorporating parallelism scheduling into the query access plans. Parallelization models

High-Performance Parallel Database Processing and Grid Databases,
by David Taniar, Clement Leung, Wenny Rahayu, and Sushant Goel
Copyright © 2008 John Wiley & Sons, Inc.

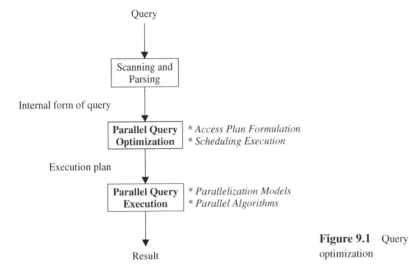

Query

Scanning and
Parsing

Internal form of query

**Parallel Query
Optimization** | *Access Plan Formulation*
Scheduling Execution

Execution plan

**Parallel Query
Execution** | *Parallelization Models*
Parallel Algorithms

Result

Figure 9.1   Query
optimization

and parallel algorithms contain the basic form of parallelism for basic query operations. Complex queries are normally decomposed into multiple basic operations, and for each basic operation an appropriate parallelism algorithm is applied. Execution scheduling deals with managing execution plans among these parallelizable basic operations.

All of the previous chapters deal with parallel query execution, focusing on efficient formulation of parallel algorithms of each query operation. This chapter, on the other hand, concentrates on parallel query optimization, and in particular parallel subquery scheduling and dynamic parallel query optimization.

This chapter starts with a query execution plan to be described in Section 9.1. Section 9.2 describes subquery scheduling. Section 9.3 compares and contrasts the two subquery scheduling mechanisms, namely, serial subquery scheduling and parallel subquery scheduling, and Section 9.4 presents the scheduling rules. Section 9.5 introduces the cluster query processing model, and Section 9.6 describes dynamic cluster query optimization. Finally, Section 9.7 briefly discusses other approaches to dynamic query optimization.

9.1 QUERY EXECUTION PLAN

A query execution may consist of a number of subqueries, and a subquery is the basic processing unit that involves one or more operations to be processed together. The query execution plan is expressed by a query tree with each node representing a subquery and an arc between two nodes specifying the execution order of the subqueries. A node may have one or more incoming arcs and one outgoing arc, except for the root of the tree, which gives the final result of the query.

Each node with incoming arc(s) cannot be executed until its predecessor node(s) finish.

A typical execution method follows a *phase-oriented* paradigm, whereby the operations of a query plan are performed by several execution phases. The first phase involves the operations that require only base tables. The next phase may then contain the operations that become ready to process after the completion of the previous phase. The last phase produces the result of the query. Within an execution phase, each of the operations is allocated to one or more processors such that all operations in the phase are processed in parallel and are expected to finish at about the same time.

The execution of a query may be divided into a number of sequential phases. Within each phase, a number of operations are executed in parallel, and the results from one phase will be passed to the next for further processing. Depending on how the results need to be finally presented, a consolidation operator may be required to arrange the results in an appropriate final form. If necessary, the consolidation operator will redistribute the output objects for further processing. However, the final consolidation operation is not parallelizable, so it involves the bringing together of parallel results for final presentation.

The task of the consolidation operator can vary from collecting the result of two operators at a time to collecting the result of all operators at once. Thus, the degree of parallelization can be classified into four categories: *left-deep tree* parallelization, *bushy-tree* parallelization, *right-deep tree* parallelization, and *flat-tree* parallelization. Figure 9.2 illustrates these four types of trees, where a node represents a predicate evaluation of a class. In this example, node A can be regarded as the first predicate evaluation, node B as the second, and so on. Furthermore, the result of each predicate is subsequently joined. For example, AB indicates the result of joining process (implicitly or explicitly) between the first and the second predicates.

It is obvious from the parallelization trees shown in Figure 9.2 that the purpose of parallelization is to reduce the height of the tree. The height of a balanced bushy

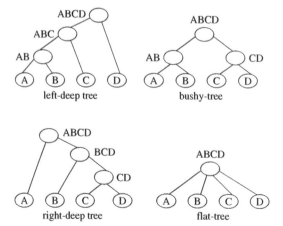

Figure 9.2   Parallelization trees

tree is equal to $log_2 N$, where N is the number of nodes. When each predicate evaluation is independent of the others, bushy-tree parallelization is the best, since the reduction of the height of the tree is quite significant. However, in the case where each predicate evaluation is dependent on the previous ones (e.g., in path expressions), bushy-tree parallelization is inapplicable.

Left-deep tree and right-deep tree are similar to sequential processing with a reduction of one phase only. These parallelization techniques are suitable for predicate evaluations that must follow a sequential order; that is, the result of a predicate evaluation will become an input to the next predicate evaluation. This mechanism is like a pipeline-style parallelization. Left-deep trees are not much different from right-deep trees, except for the order of processing the predicates. When a query follows a particular direction to process the predicates for efficiency reasons, only one of these methods can be used. In contrast, when the query disregards the direction, the query optimizer must be able to decide which method will be used that will produce a minimum cost.

Flat-tree parallelization is a tree of height one. Here, the consolidation operator can be very heavily loaded, since the results of all predicate evaluations are collected at the same time. Hence, parallelization may not have much improvement. However, this technique works well for queries with a single table and many predicates, because no join operation is needed.

In a simpler parallelization, a query tree (or indeed part of a query tree) consists of two main subqueries, which may be processed simultaneously since each of them is independent of the others. In this scenario, the main objective is to complete all subqueries as early as possible, since the operation of the next phase cannot start before the completion of all subqueries. In the following sections, two subqueries scheduling strategies are discussed in greater detail.

9.2 SUBQUERIES EXECUTION SCHEDULING STRATEGIES

Apart from the availability of parallel algorithms for each basic operation in the query, scheduling subqueries execution plays an important role. There are two existing approaches to the subqueries execution scheduling: One way is to process each subquery one by one (*serial* scheduling). The other way is to process all subqueries concurrently (*parallel* scheduling). Performance of these scheduling strategies is much influenced by the presence of load skew in each subquery.

9.2.1 Serial Execution Among Subqueries

In *serial* scheduling, the operations in a given query access plan are carried out one after another, proceeding from the leaf operations to the root operation that produces the query result. When a subquery is being processed, all resources are allocated to it. For each operation, parallel processing is exploited by partitioning and distributing objects over all available processors, followed by an execution of

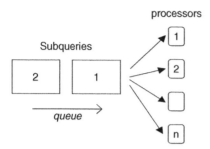

Figure 9.3   Serial execution among subqueries

the operation in parallel. If multiple subqueries exist in a phase, the order of the execution of these subqueries does not matter, as they do not have any interdependence. One essential element is that these subqueries must be completed before the next phase can start. Figure 9.3 gives an illustration of serial execution among subqueries.

When the operands of each operation are uniformly distributed to the processors, that is no load skew, maximum speed up of the operation is achieved, since no processors are idle when others are busy working. However, if load skew occurs, some processors may have heavier loads than others and require more time to complete the portion of the assigned operation. The completion time of the whole operation therefore would be much higher than expected since it is determined by the time required for the heaviest loaded processor.

Skewness has been one of the major problems in parallel database systems. Load skew refers to the nonuniform distribution of workload among the processors. Load skew is a main obstacle to achieving load balancing and linear speed up. In the presence of skew, query execution time depends on the most heavily loaded processors, and those processors finishing early would have to wait.

Load skew in single-table queries is mainly caused by nonuniform data partitioning (e.g., hash or range partitioning). With nonuniform data partitioning, an exact-match or range query on the partitioning attribute can be localized to a small subset of processors containing the desired data. This kind of query normally requires minimal resources (depending on the range for range queries). Hence, activating all processors, most of which will not produce any result, is often a waste. However, choosing a correct partitioning attribute is similar to an index selection problem, which is known to be difficult. Moreover, exact-match or range queries on a nonpartitioning attribute make the initial partitioning meaningless, as the data partitioning does not offer any benefit to processing these queries. Since the partitioning is nonuniform, the processing of these queries will produce a skew problem.

Load skew in join queries is a result of partitioning on the join attribute. Parallel processing of join queries is normally made up of two stages: partitioning and local joining. In the partitioning stage, data from the two classes to be joined are partitioned based on the joining attribute. The results of this partitioning are disjoint partitions. Subsequently, these partitions are processed locally in each processor. The partitioning method used is a nonuniform data partitioning method (normally

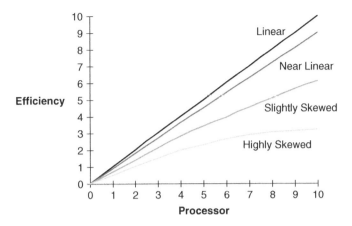

Figure 9.4   Linear speed up vs. skewed performance

hash partitioning is used). Depending on the partitioning function and the actual data distribution in the joining attributes, load skew may vary from lightly to heavily skewed.

The biggest impact of load skew is performance degradation. If linear speed up is drawn as a linear function $f(x) = x$, performance of a skewed operation is lower than the desired speed up. Figure 9.4 shows a performance comparison between linear speed up and skew.

In situations where there is a high degree of skew, adding more resources will not improve the efficiency significantly. This fact is known as the *skew principle*, which states that allocating a large number of resources to a skewed operation will not improve performance significantly, and may lead to degradation in performance under certain circumstances.

9.2.2 Parallel Execution Among Subqueries

In *parallel* scheduling, multiple subqueries within one phase are executed simultaneously. The execution of the phases is still carried out in sequence, as this follows a phased-oriented paradigm. Figure 9.5 illustrates parallel execution among subqueries.

When executing multiple subqueries within one phase the resources must be efficiently divided, so that all of these subqueries may finish at the same time and, most importantly, they are expected to complete the jobs as early as possible, so that the execution of the next phase can proceed as early as possible. Intuitively, one would allocate more resources to a larger subquery. However, if this subquery contains a high degree of skewness, the allocation of more resources may not improve performance significantly. Hence, one might allocate fewer resources than initially planned and give away some of the resources to the other subqueries whenever possible.

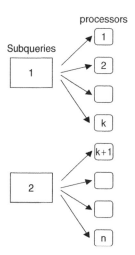

Figure 9.5   Parallel execution among subqueries

Given two subqueries in a phase, where subquery 1 is large but skewed and subquery 2 is small but not skewed, a dilemma of the *parallel* approach can be explained as follows. One method is to allocate fewer resources to subquery 1 (because it is skewed), which will result in the subquery taking more time to finish the job, while subquery 2 finishes very early. Another method is to allocate more resources to subquery 1, although subquery 1 is expected to improve just slightly. Subquery 2 with fewer resources will finish more slowly as compared to the previous method. Hence, it is necessary to find a trade-off between these two approaches.

Resource division has been recognized as one of the most difficult problems in scheduling and processor allocation. Basically, there are two main approaches to resource division, *static* and *dynamic* resource division. The *static* resource division is based on the precomputed workload. This is often estimated with cost models. Suppose that N is the number of processors to be divided among two subqueries ($S1$ and $S2$); the algorithm in Figure 9.6 can be used to divide resources to the two subqueries. The algorithm basically runs through all possible processor configurations for the two subqueries, from one extreme case (1 processor for subquery 1 and $N - 1$ processors for subquery 2) to the other extreme case ($N - 1$ processor for subquery 1 and 1 processor for subquery 2). The most optimal configuration will be between these two extremes.

With the static method, the workload of $S1$ and $S2$ must be known before the execution at runtime. This is sometimes unreasonable, since workload estimation is difficult most of the time. This is one of the reasons that researchers prefer the second method, that is, the *dynamic* resource division. The *dynamic* resource division is basically to divide the resources at runtime.

The main aims of resource division are to achieve an equal finishing time of the parallel tasks and to reduce the total execution time, which is determined by the latest-finished task. To achieve these goals, a number of approaches have been taken. The first approach is to use an algorithm to calculate the load of each task

---

Algorithm: Function CalculateResourceDivision
          (S1, S2: subqueries; N: number of processors)
Return: processors_for_S1

```
Initialize: Total_Time = max number
For i = 1 To (N-1)
  Calculate max (S1/i)
  Calculate max (S2/(N-i))
  If time (S1) > time (S2) Then
    Store time (S1) to Temp
  Else
    Store time (S2) to Temp
  If Temp < Total_Time Then
    Store Temp to Total_Time
    Processor for S1 = i
Return Processors_for_S1
```

Figure 9.6 Static resource division

and to do an adjustment afterwards. The algorithm usually receives the load of each task and determines the load distribution. The load distribution calculation is normally a polynomial-time algorithm. The estimation of the load of each task is acknowledged to be difficult, and assumptions are often made to simplify the problem.

The second approach is to use a *time equalization* method. Based on a target time taken to be efficient for a given query phase, each operation in that phase is given a number of processors that will enable it to complete the task within that time.

Other methods include *task stealing* and *partition tuning*. *Task stealing* is a dynamic load balancing, where load balancing is achieved by tackling the skew problem when it occurs at the joining phase. Based on the global information, an idle processor determines the donor (the overloaded processor) and the amount of load to be transferred. This process of stealing is repeated until some criterion, which indicates that the minimum completion time has been achieved, has been satisfied.

Partition tuning is accomplished by producing more partitions than the number of available processors. Processor allocation is done by distributing several partitions to each processor, so that the load of each processor is equal. The simplest tuning algorithm is one where each processor sorts its local partitions and retains a number of its largest partitions. The coordinator then receives a report from each processor regarding its load and reallocates the excess partitions from the overloaded processors to the underloaded processors. Partition tuning is a static load balancing, in which load balancing is achieved by pre-estimating that the load will be balanced during the join operation.

9.3 SERIAL VS. PARALLEL EXECUTION SCHEDULING

Execution scheduling for subqueries in a query is influenced particularly by two factors: *skewness* and the *size* of the subqueries. Three cases are considered:

(i) Both subqueries are not skewed.

(ii) Both subqueries are skewed.

(iii) One of them is skewed.

9.3.1 Nonskewed Subqueries

Consider a query having two subqueries. The two subqueries involve selection operations on single tables. If a round-robin partitioning is used, neither subquery will produce load skew. The number of objects per processor of the first subquery can be represented as a function $f(x) = \frac{r_1}{x}$, where r_1 is the number of records and x is the number of processors used to process the subquery. If n processors are available, then $1 \leq x \leq n$. Likewise, the number of objects per processor of the second subquery can be represented as: $g(x) = \frac{r_2}{x}$. We note that both $f(x)$ and $g(x)$ are decreasing functions of x.

When a *serial* execution of subqueries is used, the total elapsed time for phase 1 is calculated by adding $f(n)$ and $g(n)$. If a *parallel* execution method is used, it is essential to locate the intersection between $f(x)$ and $g(x)$ to find the most efficient processor configuration, since the intersection represents equal finishing times for both subqueries without any idleness. This can be done by mirroring $g(x)$ and shifting as far as $n - 1$, resulting in $g(n - x)$. Subsequently, the intersection between the two subqueries can be found by equating:

$$f(x) = g(n - x)$$
$$\frac{r_1}{x} = \frac{r_2}{n - x}$$
$$x = \left(\frac{r_1}{r_1 + r_2}\right) n \qquad (9.1)$$

By using this value for x, we can show that $f(n) + g(n) = f(x)$. This is true because

$$f(n) + g(n) = f(x)$$
$$\frac{r_1}{n} + \frac{r_2}{n} = f\left(\frac{r_1 \cdot n}{r_1 + r_2}\right)$$
$$\frac{r_1 + r_2}{n} = \frac{r_1}{\frac{r_1 \cdot n}{r_1 + r_2}}$$
$$\frac{r_1 + r_2}{n} = r_1 \frac{r_1 + r_2}{r_1 \cdot n}$$
$$\frac{r_1 + r_2}{n} = \frac{r_1 + r_2}{n}$$

which is obviously true. Likewise, $f(n) + g(n) = g(n - x)$, which is true because

$$f(n) + g(n) = g(n - x)$$

$$\frac{r_1}{n} + \frac{r_2}{n} = g\left(n - \frac{r_1 \cdot n}{r_1 + r_2}\right)$$

$$\frac{r_1 + r_2}{n} = \frac{r_2}{n - \frac{r_1 \cdot n}{r_1 + r_2}}$$

$$\frac{r_1 + r_2}{n} = \frac{r_2}{\frac{(r_1 + r_2)n}{r_1 + r_2} - \frac{r_1 \cdot n}{r_1 + r_2}}$$

$$\frac{r_1 + r_2}{n} = \frac{r_2}{\frac{r_1 \cdot n + r_2 \cdot p - r_1 \cdot n}{r_1 + r_2}}$$

$$\frac{r_1 + r_2}{n} = r_2 \cdot \frac{r_1 + r_2}{r_2 \cdot n}$$

$$\frac{r_1 + r_2}{n} = \frac{r_1 + r_2}{n}$$

which is obviously true. Since x is not always an integer, it needs to be rounded off. Hence, the intersection of $f(x)$ and $g(x)$ is actually either $ceil(x)$ or $floor(x)$. The most efficient parallel scheduling time is determined by the minimum of either $f(ceil(x))$ or $g(n - floor(x))$. Hence, we need to prove that:

$$f(n) + g(n) = \min(f(ceil(x)), g(n - floor(x))) \tag{9.2}$$

Condition 9.2 can be proven by showing that

$$f(x) < f(ceil(x)) \text{ and } g(n - x) < g(n - floor(x))$$

Noting that both $f(x)$ and $g(x)$ are decreasing functions, and since $x < ceil(x)$, hence $f(x) < f(ceil(x))$, and since $x > floor(x)$, hence $n - x < n - floor(x)$, and $g(n - x) < g(n - floor(x))$.

As condition 9.2 has been proven, it means that when there is no skew involved in the two subqueries, serial scheduling is better than parallel scheduling to the two subqueries.

This can also be shown with a graphical representation. Suppose the second subquery time is reflected; $g(x)$ becomes $g(n - x) = \frac{r_2}{n - x}$, where $g(n - x)$ is a reflection along $x = 2/n$. The new curve shows that the number of processors used in the second subquery is $n - x$ processors, where x is the number of processors for the first subquery. Figure 9.7c shows the curve for $g(n - x)$. Figure 9.7d shows an intersection between $f(x)$ and $g(n - x)$, which can be calculated by equation 9.1.

9.3.2 Skewed Subqueries

If each subquery is partitioned with a hash or a range data partitioning, load skew may occur as the result of an imbalance in data partitioning. Load skew is frequently modelled by means of the *Zipf* distribution. Incorporating the *Zipf*

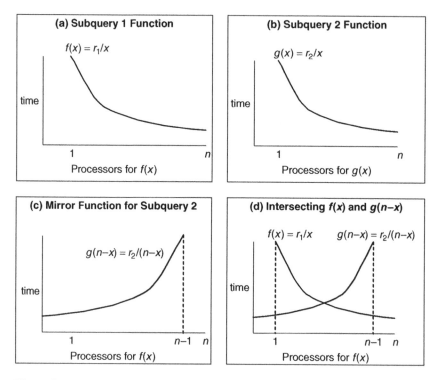

Figure 9.7 Performance graphs of nonskewed subqueries

distribution to model skew, the function for a subquery with the class size r_1 is indicated by $f(x) = \frac{r_1}{H_x}$, where x is the number of processors used to process the subquery. This function represents the most overloaded processor and determines the total execution time for this subquery. Figure 9.8a shows the shape of the function $f(x)$ from $x = 1$ (1 processor used) to $x = n$ (n processors used).

For the second subquery, the function is $g(x)$, which is given by $g(x) = \frac{r_2}{H_x}$, where the class size for the second subquery is r_2. The similarity between $f(x)$ and $g(x)$ is that the function uses the same skew model, that is, the *Zipf* model (as indicated by the denominator H_x), and the number of processors used is x. The main difference between $f(x)$ and $g(x)$, however, is the table size, that is, r_1 and r_2, respectively. Hence, the shape of both functions drawn in a graph should be the same (see Fig. 9.8a). The actual line graph for $f(x)$ and $g(x)$ can go up or down depending on the value of the numerator, which is indicated by either r_1 and r_2.

The difference between $f(x) = \frac{r_1}{H_x}$ and $g(x) = \frac{r_2}{H_x}$ is analogous to that of the functions for nonskewed subqueries $f(x) = \frac{r_1}{x}$ and $g(x) = \frac{r_2}{x}$. In other words, the distribution, whether it is normal or skewed, is determined by the denominator (i.e., x for normal distribution or nonskewed or H_x for skewed distribution modeled with the *Zipf* model). Compared with nonskewed subqueries, the shape of the functions

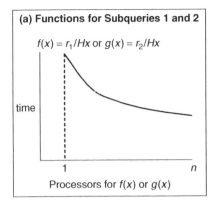
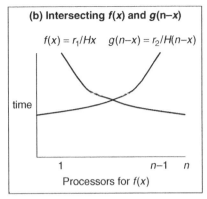

Figure 9.8 Performance graphs of skewed subqueries

for skewed subqueries is different. The shape of the function for a skewed subquery does not go down as steeply as that of a nonskewed subquery.

Likewise for the nonskewed subqueries, an intersection between the two functions $f(x)$ and $g(x)$ can be determined by making a mirror function for one of the two subqueries. If $g(x)$ is mirrored and shifted as far as $n - 1$, $g(n - x)$ becomes: $g(n - x) = \frac{r_2}{H_{n-x}}$. This does not admit an analytical solution since

$$\frac{r_1}{H_x} = \frac{r_2}{H_{n-x}}$$
$$\frac{r_1}{\gamma + \ln x} = \frac{r_2}{\gamma + \ln(n - x)}$$
$$r_1 \cdot \gamma - r_2 \cdot \gamma = \ln x^{r_2} - \ln(n - x)^{r_1}$$
$$e^{r_1 \cdot \gamma - r_2 \cdot \gamma} = \frac{x^{r_2}}{(n - x)^{r_1}}$$

Solving for x in closed form in this is generally not possible. It is difficult to show analytically that $f(n) + g(n) > max(f(x), g(n - x))$. Even a solution in an approximate form is difficult to obtain. Since the objective is to find an intersection point that is indicated by x, we can obtain an approximate value for x through a graphical solution. Figure 9.8b shows an intersection between $f(x)$ and $g(n - x)$. The intersection determines the most efficient processor configuration for both subqueries where these subqueries do not overlap when occupying the resources.

9.3.3 Skewed and Nonskewed Subqueries

If one of the subqueries is not skewed and the other one is skewed, the sizes of the subqueries play an important role in deciding the execution scheduling strategy. In this section, three cases are considered. Case 1 is where the two subqueries are approximately equal in size. Case 2 is where the skewed subquery is larger, and

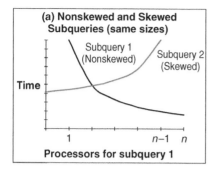
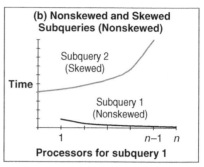
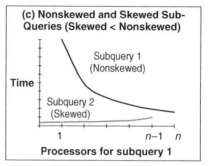

Figure 9.9   Intersection of nonskewed subquery and skewed subquery

case 3 is where the nonskewed subquery is larger. The intersection of the three cases is illustrated in Figure 9.9.

Assume that the first subquery is not skewed and the second subquery is skewed. Using the functions $f(x)$ and $g(x)$ to represent the subqueries, the functions for the first and the second subqueries are:

$$f(x) = \frac{r_1}{x} \text{ and } g(x) = \frac{r_2}{H_x} \tag{9.3}$$

The intersection between the two subquery functions is shown by equating

$$\frac{r_2}{H_x} = \frac{r_1}{n - x}$$

$$\frac{r_2}{\gamma + \ln x} = \frac{r_1}{n - x}$$

$$r_2 \cdot n - r_2 \cdot x = r_1 \cdot \gamma + \ln x^{r_1}$$

$$r_1 \cdot \ln x + r_2 \cdot x = r_2 \cdot n - r_1 \cdot \gamma$$

In x can be expanded in a form of series, which is as follows: $\ln x = \left(\frac{x-1}{x}\right) + \frac{1}{2}\left(\frac{x-1}{x}\right)^2 + \frac{1}{3}\left(\frac{x-1}{x}\right)^3 + \frac{1}{4}\left(\frac{x-1}{x}\right)^4 + \cdots$. The longer the terms, the more accurate is the result for $\ln x$. The value of x is determined by the number of processors, which can be a few (possibly 2, 4, or 8) to large (particularly in massively parallel systems). Therefore, the first term $\left(\frac{x-1}{x}\right)$ is just less than 1. Since $(x-1)/x < 1$, the values for the second and subsequent terms must be $< 0.5, < 0.33, < 0.25, \ldots$. To obtain a rough approximation, we may omit the second and subsequent terms from the $\ln x$ expansion. The final result may not be that accurate, but at least it is shown that a closed form for x is rather difficult to obtain. In omitting the second and subsequent terms from the $\ln x$ expansion:

$$r_1 \left(\frac{x-1}{x}\right) + r_2 \cdot x = r_2 \cdot n - r_1 \cdot \gamma$$

$$r_1 \cdot x - r_1 + r_2 \cdot x^2 = r_2 \cdot n \cdot x - r_1 \cdot \gamma \cdot x$$

$$r_2 \cdot x^2 + (r_1 + r_1 \cdot \gamma - r_2 \cdot n) \cdot x - r_1 = 0$$

$$x \approx \frac{r_2 \cdot n - r_1(1+\gamma)}{\pm \sqrt{(r_2 \cdot n - r_1(1+\gamma))^2 + 4 \cdot r_1 \cdot r_2}}{2 \cdot r_2}$$

Better, but slightly more cumbersome, approximations may be obtained by taking more terms from the $\ln x$ expansion, giving rise to cubic, quartic, etc. expansions that still admit direction solution. Since an analytical solution is difficult to obtain, a graphical solution is necessary.

It can be concluded from Figure 9.9 that in some cases there is no solution to the problem of optimally allocating a processor. The same lesson is also learned from Figure 9.8. In general, if one or both of the subqueries involve any degree of skewness (i.e., $0 < \theta \leq 1$), an advance estimation (before runtime) of optimal processor configuration is difficult. However, it does not mean that at runtime optimal processor configuration cannot be obtained. An optimal processor configuration is still achievable through dynamically allocating processors at runtime.

9.4 SCHEDULING RULES

Processor allocation in parallel query processing is to assign resources (i.e., processors) to incoming queries with possible multiple subqueries in such a way that the query execution times are minimized. Three rules are developed around the two execution scheduling strategies. Two factors in particular are considered: *skewness* and the *size* of each subquery.

Rule 1: Given two subqueries in a phase, if both subqueries do *not* involve any skewness, *serial* execution of the subqueries may be usefully adopted.

Since the subqueries are not skewed, linear speed up may be attainable. In other words, the addition of resources to the operation will proportionally increase performance. Because of the potential of linear speed up, the two subqueries can be viewed as one large subquery consisting of the two smaller subqueries running one after another. Should the two subqueries be run concurrently instead, without a careful resource division, it will be likely that these subqueries may not finish at the same time, causing some processors to be idle.

> *Rule 2:* Given two subqueries in a phase, if both subqueries involve a certain degree of skewness, the *parallel* execution of the subqueries may be usefully adopted.

Using the skew principle, it is known that adding new processors to a skewed operation will not always make a significant impact on performance improvement. Since the resources are limited, it will be better to keep the number of processors minimal for a particular operation. Hence, the resources are divided into multiple operations (e.g., two subqueries). Although the execution time of each operation is increased because of fewer resources being allocated to it, the overall performance of the two subqueries is improved because the operations are executed in parallel.

> *Rule 3:* Given two subqueries in a phase, if one subquery involves skewness and the other does not, the decision on the appropriate execution scheduling depends on the largest subquery. If the largest subquery is skewed, the *parallel* execution of the subqueries is preferred. Otherwise, the *serial* execution of the subqueries is preferable. In the case where the two subqueries are roughly equal in size, the skewed subquery is more dominant, and hence *parallel* execution is more desirable.

The largest subquery makes the biggest impact on overall performance, since the average performance of the smallest subquery is usually smaller than that of the largest subquery. Incorporating the skew principle, execution scheduling is also determined by the presence of skewness in the case when the two subqueries are equal in size.

9.5 CLUSTER QUERY PROCESSING MODEL

The motivation to use parallelism for performance benefits is also influenced by the fact that parallel architecture is no longer a monopoly of supercomputers. As already mentioned in Chapter 1, parallel architectures are now available in many forms, such as systems consisting of a small number but powerful processors (i.e., SMP machines), massively parallel processors (i.e., MPP), and clusters of SMP machines (i.e., hybrid architectures).

As described in Chapter 1, the "shared-something" architecture compromises the extensibility limitation of shared-memory and the load balancing problem of shared-nothing. Basically, each *node* is a shared-memory architecture connected to an interconnection network a la shared-nothing. Each node maintains a group of processing elements. The entire cluster architecture is then composed of a set of *SMP* nodes. In other words, a node consists of a number of shared-memory processors, and a cluster architecture consists of a number of shared-memory nodes.

Obvious features of a cluster architecture include flexibility in the configuration (i.e., number of nodes, size of nodes) and lower network communication traffic as the number of nodes is reduced. Intraquery parallelization can be isolated to a single multiprocessor shared-memory node, as it is far easier to parallelize a query in a shared-memory than a distributed system, and moreover, the degree of parallelism on a single shared-memory node may be sufficient for most applications. On the other hand, interquery parallelization is consequently achieved through parallel execution among nodes.

The popularity of cluster architectures is also influenced by the fact that processor technology is moving rapidly. This also means that a powerful computer today will be out of date within a few years. Consequently, computer pricing is falling not only because of competitiveness, but also because of the facts presented above. Therefore, it makes sense to be able to plug in new processing elements to the current system and to take out the old ones. To some degree, this can be done to *SMP machines* (e.g., shared-memory machines), considering scaling limitations and that only identical processors can be added. Although, theoretically, *MPP machines* (shared-nothing machines) do not impose scaling limitations, their configurations are difficult to alter, and hence they cannot keep pace with up-to-date technology, not to mention the high cost of *MPP* machines. On the other hand, since *SMP* machines are becoming popular because of their competitiveness in pricing and power, it becomes easier and more feasible to add *SMP* machines to an interconnection network. Therefore, the cluster of *SMP* becomes demanding. In the following sections, the cluster technology is used as the basic architecture for parallel query optimization.

9.5.1 Overview of Dynamic Query Processing

An example of a query execution plan is shown in Figure 9.10. The query consists of five subqueries P_1 to P_5 including three join subqueries P_2, P_3, P_5 and two restriction subqueries P_1, P_4. The query involves four relations, namely R_1, R_2, R_3, and R_4, located at processing nodes 1, 2, 3 and 4, respectively. Associated with each node are its processing node, processing method, and the estimated execution cost.

To choose an optimal query plan, the cost associated with each possible query plan needs to be estimated. To estimate such costs, it is necessary to estimate the sizes of the intermediate result relations in the query. The estimation methods can be based on (*i*) perfect knowledge, (*ii*) statistical model or histograms, or (*iii*) a combination of both. With a perfect knowledge method, exact information about all parameters required in an estimation formula is known. Thus the size of the result of an operation can be calculated accurately. However, if such information is not available, a statistical method may be used. With a statistical method, the parameters in the estimation formula are first characterized by some statistical model. The expected values of the parameters are then estimated based on the model.

An optimal query plan that minimizes the execution cost or execution time of the query can be formulated statically at compile time. In practice, however, a statically formulated query plan may not have a guaranteed expected performance

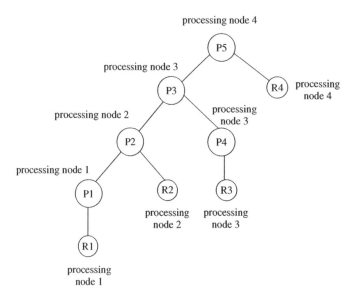

Figure 9.10   Query execution plan

since the plan formulation uses estimates of dynamic parameters. Dynamic parameters are those for which actual values can be obtained only during query execution, such as intermediate result sizes of the query and site loads of the system. Dynamic query plan formulation attempts to ensure the good performance of a query plan either by delaying important optimization decisions until the query is ready to be executed or by modifying, during execution, any decisions made in static plan formulation that are found to be wrong. As the query execution proceeds and up-to-date information about dynamic parameters becomes available, better optimization decisions can be made.

9.5.2 A Cluster Query Processing Architecture

Queries can arrive at any one of the processing nodes, and hence a decentralized processing control scheme must be used. The processing architecture consists of a set of nodes with identical configurations and processing capacities. The nodes are connected by a high-bandwidth network, and the database is partitioned over the processing nodes with the possibility of some degree of replication. A single processing node model is shown in Figure 9.11.

Each processing node has a *ready queue* and a *suspended queue*. The ready queue stores the ready-to-process subqueries, whereas the suspended queue stores the subqueries waiting for the completion of other subqueries. When a query is initiated, the query, possibly consisting of subqueries, is sent to the processing nodes assigned by the query plan, entering ready queues or suspended queues depending

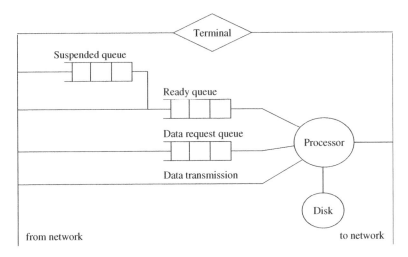

Figure 9.11   A processing node

on whether they have predecessor tasks. Each of the processing nodes chooses the subquery(s) in the ready queue to run and produces an intermediate result of the query. During the execution, the subqueries in the suspended queue will be moved to the ready queue as soon as its operand relations are available. A query is done when all the subqueries involved have been completed. In the case of parallel processing of a subquery, the fragments of the subquery are sent to several processing nodes. The processing nodes do not need to treat the subquery or the fragments differently in terms of the execution, although the full intermediate result of the subquery must be consolidated after the parallel execution.

9.5.3   Load Information Exchange

Based on the above processing model, one way to measure the processing node load is to take the sum of the estimated subquery costs in each queue, thereby giving accurate load information. However, since the algorithm is concerned primarily with the subqueries that may be migrated or partitioned, such information is not critical. Therefore, the number of subqueries in the ready queue determines the processing node load. Given a predefined constant N, a processing node is categorized into:

- *Low load processing node*, if the ready queue is empty (a subquery may, however, be being processed), or
- *Medium load processing node*, if the number of subqueries in the ready queue is less than a predefined constant N, or
- *High load processing node* otherwise.

The constant N serves as a design parameter for the migration process described in the following section. A small N leads to frequent subquery migration because many processing nodes would be classified as high load. By increasing N, the attempt for migrations will certainly reduce. Therefore, the selection of N depends on the possible performance gains and the overhead of the migration algorithm on the underlying system configurations.

Every processing node maintains a load table that stores the most recent load information of all processing nodes. The entry for each node in the load table contains:

- *Load level,*
- *Complete time*, the estimated time that the processing node will take to complete the subquery under processing, used only when the node is at low load level,
- *Parallel group*, the group with which the processing node is participating in parallel processing, and
- *Update time*, the time when the last update is made.

The complete and update times are useful in the algorithm to estimate the delay of the next subquery execution. This delay is taken into account when a subquery is considered for parallel processing.

The load table at each processing node is updated when the load level of any node changes. This can be simply done by every node with load change broadcasting a load update message. However, this simple scheme may be improved to reduce the messages across the network. Since the query processing is carried out in a cooperative manner, the processing node that initiates a query or coordinates parallel execution of a subquery may send the load update message on behalf of all nodes involved in the execution. Therefore, the following rules are used for message broadcast in the algorithm:

- The processing node that initiates a new query updates the load levels for every node that is assigned with some subqueries and broadcasts a load update message including all updated load information. The new load level for each of the processing nodes is determined by the current load level plus the number of new subqueries allocated to the node.
- Each processing node that receives a load update message checks its update load level made by the query initiating node against the actual load level. If it is incorrect, a load message is sent to all processing nodes.
- The processing node that relocates a subquery to a low load processing node updates the load levels for both the reallocated node and itself, and sends a load update message.
- The processing node that parallelizes a subquery with a set of low load processing nodes updates the load levels for all the nodes involved and sends a load update message including information about parallel group and data partitioning.

- The processing node that has completed a subquery updates its load level and, if the level reduces, sends a load update message.

To increase the performance, "*correction, migration, and partition*" approaches can be adopted. Correction is used to alter the initial query execution plan based on dynamic information that states that the initial query execution plan is no longer feasible because of some errors in the initial estimate. Migration is used to reallocate the whole query/subquery from one node to another, whereas partition is used to partition a query/subquery originated from one node into a number of nodes for parallel processing. The details are explained in the following sections.

9.6 DYNAMIC CLUSTER QUERY OPTIMIZATION

The steps for dynamic query processing in clusters are as follows:

(i) *Static Query Plan Formulation:* A query execution plan is first statically formulated at compile time without using dynamic load information. The subqueries involved in the plan are distributed to the processing nodes initially assigned by the plan with the objective of minimizing total query execution costs.

(ii) *Load Information Exchange:* The processing nodes that participate in query processing communicate with each other whenever their load levels are changed.

(iii) *Query Plan Correction:* During execution, the intermediate results produced by the subqueries defined in the query execution plan are monitored. If the actual result size of a completed subquery is found to be far different from its expected value, the processing node will report this error to the query coordinator node, which then starts a plan correction process. A new query plan for the so far unexecuted subqueries will be formulated and replace the existing plan.

(iv) *Subquery Migration:* During this process, subqueries that are assigned to the processing nodes with medium to high level loads will be reallocated to lightly loaded nodes.

(v) *Subquery Partition:* When there is no high load of processing nodes across the system, a processing node with medium load may initiate a parallelization process to probe some low load processing nodes. If some or all these nodes agree, the subquery at the initiating node will be processed in parallel by the nodes obtained.

Static plan formulation and load exchange information (i.e., steps (*i*) and (*ii*)) have been explained in the previous sections. This section focuses on steps (*iii*) to (*v*), which are query execution plan correction, subquery migration, and subquery partition.

A biased load balancing and parallelizing strategy is used; that is, the query plan correction and subquery migration takes place whenever it is needed, while subquery partition is carried out only when the overall system load is relatively low. There are several observations. First, the subquery migration is simple and involves fewer overheads than parallel processing in a distributed environment. Second, when parallel processing of a subquery is applied, the reduction in execution time is gained in a trade of increase in the sum of the processing costs over the clusters. Such cost increase is not desirable when the overall system loads are already high. Parallel processing improves the query response time significantly, as the system load is low to medium, but does not perform well for a high system load. In addition, the parallel processing may suffer from the problem of data partitioning skew, which causes uneven distribution of operand relations over the processing nodes and thus delays the completion time of the subquery. Therefore, a biased scheme appears to be a promising approach.

In designing a decentralized dynamic algorithm, it would be desirable to reduce to a minimum the changes that the introduction of migration will make to a query plan. An algorithm that uses a static plan formulation and dynamic correction scheme will not introduce new complexity into the query optimization process and will keep the dynamic mechanism in a simple form. In addition, the overheads of subquery migration and partition are kept small since (*i*) an initial subquery allocation is done at compile time and this may not change significantly during execution; (*ii*) migration and partition are attempted only when there exist low load processing nodes.

9.6.1 Correction

The process first formulates a static query execution plan at compile time, followed by *correcting* the plan when a significant estimation error is found during query execution. Several decisions need to be made in the plan correction procedure.

- *Triggering:* A decision on whether a plan correction process should be initiated. The primary concern in selecting the strategy is its efficiency since the overheads of the correction mechanism are often significant. A plan correction should be triggered only when a better plan is expected, that is, the cost reduction expected from the correction is larger than the overheads.

- *Correcting:* A method for query plan correction after error occurrence and correction triggering. A part of the query plan is chosen to be corrected if the corrected plan is likely better than the current plan. The method is also known as *partial plan correction*. The objective of the partial plan correction method is to maximize overall performance improvement of the query plan.

- *Deferring:* A strategy to defer query plan correction until some more subqueries in the query plan are processed. The strategy is an enhancement of the partial plan correction method.

- *Discarding:* A strategy to decide whether a subquery with estimation error should be abandoned. The main concern in discarding is the trade-off between

---

Algorithm: Correction Algorithm

Input: a query plan (in the form of tree) Q, and
       a subquery node P that is completed most recently
1. Replace the estimated result size of P by the actual
   size obtained, and update the costs of affected nodes
   in Q;

2. If the difference between the estimated and actual
   result sizes of P is less than a pre-defined threshold
   λ, terminate;

3. Determine a subplan Q_c of Q which is affected by the
   estimation error at node P;

4. Invoke the underlying query optimizer to formulate a
   new execution plan Q_c for the unexecuted subqueries
   involved in Q_c;

5. Q_c is replaced by Q_c
   if it leads to a reduction in the cost,
   otherwise no correction is made, and terminates.

6. If there exists at least one low load cluster,
   invoke **Subquery Migration** process to change
   the processing node allocation if further performance
   gain is expected.

Figure 9.12 Correction algorithm

savings that might be achieved by avoiding large intermediate result relations and the penalty of redoing the subquery.

The procedure for query plan correction is outlined in Figure 9.12. The corrected plan is always expected to perform no worse than the original plan, but the corrected plan may perform worse than the plan it replaces if further errors occur in the corrected plan since the corrected plan is also based on inaccurate estimates. A number of different approaches for partial plan correction are possible. If we wanted to ensure that no performance degradation was caused by future errors, the subplan to be corrected should involve only the operations whose result sizes can be computed accurately. If this approach is followed, the performance improvement might not be drastic since any operation whose result size could not be computed accurately would not be included in plan correction and only a small part of the query plan is likely to be corrected. On the other hand, we might choose to correct a large portion of the query plan hoping to obtain a much better improvement but take the risk that future errors may lead to performance degradation. Below are three different plan correction methods.

Optimistic Plan Correction (OPC)

In the optimistic plan correction method, the subplan Q_c includes all operations that have not been processed. The *OPC* method therefore takes an optimistic approach by assuming that the estimates for all the remaining operations are accurate and needs no information on the accuracy of the remaining estimates. When the estimates of the remaining operations are accurate or close to accurate, the *OPC* method is expected to perform well. However, when there are one or more large errors in the estimates used in the corrected plan, the *OPC* method may suffer performance degradation.

We consider an example of the *OPC* method using the query plan shown in Figure 9.10. Assume that an estimation error is found after operation P_1 finishes. Let the actual result size of P_1 be three times the estimated size. Figure 9.13 shows a reformulated plan for the unexecuted operations P_2, P_3, and P_5 using the same cost model and plan formulation algorithm. Since P_2 encounters a much larger than expected operand relation, its execution is pushed back to the last in the new plan. Consequently, P_3 and P_5 will be performed first. The execution order of the original query plan can be expressed algebraically as $((\sigma_{p1}(R_1) \times_{p2} R_2) \times_{p3} \sigma_{p4}(R_3)) \times_{p5} R_4$, and the new plan is $\sigma_{p1}(R_1) \times_{p2} ((R_2 \times_{p3} \sigma_{p4}(R_3)) \times_{p5} R_4)$, where σ_p stands for restriction and $\times_p$ for join operation.

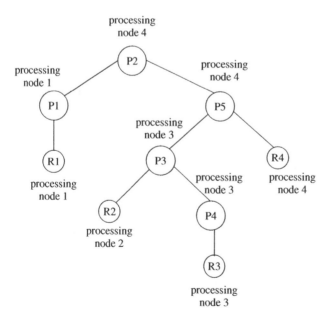

Figure 9.13 Corrected query execution plan

Pessimistic Plan Correction (PPC)

In contrast to the *OPC* method, the *PPC* method is based on the pessimistic assumption that an estimation error will occur in all operations unless the estimates are known to be accurate. Therefore, the *PPC* method limits plan correction only to operations whose estimates are close to the actual values. The cost of the corrected plan may then be guaranteed to be no higher than the cost of the original plan.

The *PPC* method requires accuracy information to identify good estimates. Assume that the size estimate of an operation P is given by a pair of values (s, d), where s is the size estimate and d is the deviation of s. If d is equal or close to zero, we say that s is a good estimate. The correctable condition for the *PPC* method can be stated as:

An operation node in a query plan is correctable if

(a) its size estimate is good; or

(b) the actual result size of the operation is known.

For example, consider again the example query shown in Figure 9.10, where an error is found at P_1. Assuming that the operation P_5 is not good in the sense of estimate of result size, the plan correction will then include unexecuted operation P_2 and P_3 but does not include P_5. Therefore, whatever the estimation error at P_5, the cost of the corrected plan will be less than the cost of the statically formulated plan.

Adaptive Plan Correction (APC)

In the adaptive plan correction method, the subplan Q_c to be corrected is determined according to both the current error and the errors that are likely to occur in the remaining query plan. Q_c is proposed to include those operations that have not yet been executed and are expected not to have large errors. An error is considered large if it is greater than the current error. The reason for choosing this heuristic is based on the desirability of correcting all of the plan if a very large estimation error has been found and not correcting very much of the plan if the current error is small.

Given a query plan Q, let P be the node of Q with the current estimation error. Let a and s be the actual and the estimated result size of P. The absolute estimation error at P therefore is $|a - s|$. Correctable nodes should be those where the estimation errors are not expected to be larger than $|a - s|$. Assume that the error for each operation P_i in Q is in the range of $(s_i - d_i, s_i + d_i)$, where s_i is the size estimate and d_i is the deviation of s_i. Therefore, the *APC* correctable condition can be defined as follows:

An operation node P_i in a query plan Q is correctable if

(a) $d_i < \gamma |a - s|$, where γ is a constant; or

(b) the actual result size of P_i is known.

The constant γ can be used as a design parameter to determine the operations that will be corrected. When γ takes a large value, the operations with large potential estimation errors will be involved in the plan correction. A small value of γ implies that the plan correction is limited to the operations whose result sizes can be estimated more accurately. In fact, when $\gamma = 0$, the *APC* method becomes the *PPC* method, while for sufficiently large γ the *APC* method becomes the *OPC* method.

9.6.2   Migration

Subquery migration is based on up-to-date load information available at the time when the query plan is corrected. Migration process is activated by a high load processing node when it finds at least one low load processing node from the load table. The process interacts with selected low load processing nodes, and if successful, some ready-to-run subqueries are migrated. Two decisions need to be made on which node(s) should be probed and which subquery(s) is to be reallocated. Alternatives may be suggested from simple random selection to biased selection in terms of certain benefit/penalty measures. A biased migration strategy is used that attempts to minimize the additional cost of the migration.

In the migration process described in Figure 9.14, each subquery in the ready queue is checked in turn to find a current low load processing node, migration to which incurs the smallest cost. If the cost is greater than a constant threshold α, the subquery is marked as *nonmigratable* and will not be considered further. Other subqueries will be attempted one at a time for migration in an ascending order of the additional costs. The process stops when either the node is no longer at high load level or no low load node is found.

The threshold α determines which subquery is migratable in terms of additional data transfer required along with migration. Such data transfer imposes a workload on the original subquery cluster that initiates the migration and thus reduces or even negates the performance gain for the cluster. Therefore, the migratable condition for a subquery q is defined as follows: Given a original subquery processing node S_i and a probed migration node S_j, let $C(q, S_i)$ be the cost of processing q at S_i and let $D(q, S_i, S_j)$ be the data transmission cost for S_i migrating q to $S_j \cdot q$ is said to be migratable from S_i to S_j if $\Delta C_{i,j} = \frac{D(q, S_i, S_j)}{C(q, S_i)} < \alpha$.

It can be seen from the definition that whether or not a subquery is migratable is determined by three main factors: the system configuration that determines the ratio of data transmission cost to local processing cost, the subquery operation(s) that determines the total local processing cost, and the data availability at the probed migration processing node. If the operand relation of the subquery is available at the migration processing node, no data transfer is needed and the additional cost $\Delta C_{i,j}$ is zero.

The value of threshold α is insensitive to the performance of the migration algorithm. This is because the algorithm always chooses the subqueries with minimum additional cost for migration. Moreover, the subquery migration takes place only when a query plan correction has already been made. In fact, frequent changes

---

Algorithm: Migration Algorithm

---

1. The process is activated by any high load processing
   node when there exists a low load processing node.

2. For each subquery Q_i in the ready queue, do
      For each low load processing node j, do
         Calculate cost increase $\Delta C_{i,j}$ for migrating Q_i to j
      Find the node $s_{i,min}$ with the minimum cost
      increase $\Delta C_{i,min}$
      If $\Delta C_{i,min} < \alpha$, mark Q_i as migratable,
      otherwise it is non-migratable

3. Find the migratable subquery Q_i with minimum cost
   increased

4. Send a migration request message to processing
   node $s_{i,min}$

5. If an accepted message is received,
      Q_i is migrated to node $s_{i,min}$
   Else
      Q_i is marked as non-migratable

6. If processing node load level is still high
   and there is a migratable subquery, go to step 3,
   otherwise go to **Subquery Partition**.

Figure 9.14 Migration algorithm

in subquery allocation are not desirable because the processing node's workloads change time to time. A node that has a light load at the time of plan correction may become heavily loaded shortly because of the arrival of new queries and reallocated queries. The case of *thrashing*, that is, some subqueries are constantly reallocated without actually being executed, must be avoided.

9.6.3 Partition

The *partition process* is invoked by a medium load processing node when there is at least one low load processing node but no high load processing node. The medium load node communicates with a set of selected low load nodes and waits for a reply from the nodes willing to participate in parallel processing. Upon receipt of an accept message, the processing node partitions the only subquery in its ready queue and distributes it to the participating nodes for execution. The subquery is performed when all nodes complete their execution.

The subquery parallelization proceeds in several steps as shown in Figure 9.15. The first thing to note is that a limit is imposed on the number of processing nodes

---

Algorithm: Partition Algorithm

---

1. The process is activated by a medium load processing node, when there are more than one low load processing nodes (Note that a medium load node is assumed to have only one ready subquery). Let the subquery in ready queue be Q and initially the parallel group $G = 0$.

2. Determine the maximum number of nodes to be considered in parallel execution, i.e., $K = num\_of\_low\_clusters/num\_of\_medium\_clusters + 1$;

3. For $i = 0$ to K do
    Find a low load node with the largest relation operand of Q and put the node into group G (if no clusters have relation operand of Q, random selection is made)

4. Sort the processing nodes selected in S in an ascending order of the estimated complete time.

5. $i = 1$; T_0 = initial execution time of Q

6. Estimate Q's execution time T_i by using first i nodes in G for parallel processing

7. If $T_i < T_{i-1}$, then $i = i+1$; If $i < K$ then go to step 6
8. Send parallel processing request to the first i nodes in G
9. Distribute Q to these nodes that accept the request, and stop

---

Figure 9.15 Partition algorithm

to be probed. When there is more than one medium load node, each of them may initiate a parallelization process and therefore compete for low load nodes. To reduce unsuccessful probing and to prevent one node obtaining all low load nodes, the number of nodes to probe is chosen as $K = \frac{num\_of\_low\_cluster}{num\_of\_medium\_cluster} + 1$. Second, a set of nodes called parallel group G has to be determined. Two types of nodes are preferred for probing:

- Nodes that have some or all operand objects of the subquery to be processed since the data transmission required is small or not required, and
- Nodes that are idle or have the earliest complete time for the current subquery under execution because of a small delay to the start of parallel execution

In the process, therefore, choose K low load nodes that have the largest amount of operand data and put them in parallel group G. The processing nodes in G are then sorted according to the estimated complete time. The execution time of the subquery is calculated repeatedly by adding one processing node of G at a time for processing the subquery until no further reduction in the execution time is achieved or all clusters in G have been considered. The final set of processing nodes to be probed is subsequently determined.

Once a subquery is assigned to more than one processing node, a parallel processing method needs to be determined and used for execution. The selection of the methods mainly depends on what relational operation(s) is involved in the subquery and where the operand data are located over the processing clusters. To demonstrate the effect of the parallel methods, consider a single join subquery as an example because it is one of the most time-consuming relational operations.

There are two common parallel join methods, *simple join* and *hash join*. The hash join method involves first the hash partitioning of both join relations followed by distribution of each pair of the corresponding fragments to a processing node. The processing nodes then conduct join in parallel on the pair of the fragments allocated. Assuming m nodes participate in join operation, $i = 1, 2 \ldots, m$, the join execution time can then be expressed as

$$T_{join} = T_{init} + \max(T_{hash}^i) + \delta \sum T_{data}^i + \max(T_{join}^i)$$

where T_{init}, T_{hash}, T_{data}, and T_{join} are the times for initiation, hash partitioning, data transmission, and local join execution, respectively. The parameter δ accounts for the effect of the overlapped execution time between the data transmission and local join processing and thus varies in the range $(0,1)$. A simple partitioned join first partitions one join relation into a number of equal-sized fragments, one for a processing node (data transmission occurs only when a node does not have the copy of the assigned fragment). The other join relation is then broadcasted to all nodes for parallel join processing. Since the partitioning time is negligible, the execution time of the join is given as

$$T_{simple\_join} = T_{init} + \delta \sum T_{data}^i + \max(T_{local}^i)$$

The use of the two parallel join methods depends on the data fragmentation and replication as well as the ratio of local processing time to the communication time. When the database relations are fragmented and the data transmission is relatively slow, the simple partitioned join method may perform better than the hash partitioned join method. Otherwise, the hash method usually outperforms the simple method. For example, consider a join of two relations R and S using four processing nodes. Assume that the relation R consists of four equal size fragments and each fragment resides at a separate node, whereas S consists of two fragments allocated at two nodes. The cardinality of both relations are assumed to be the same, that is, $|R| = |S| = k$. According to the above cost model, the execution times of the join with two join methods are given as

$$T_{part\_join} = T_{init} + |S|T_{data} + \left(\frac{|R|}{4} + |S|\right)T_{join} \quad T_{join} = T_{init} + kT_{data} + \frac{5}{4}kT_{join}$$

$$T_{hash\_join} = T_{init} + \left(\frac{|R|}{4} + \frac{|S|}{2}\right)T_{hash} + \frac{3}{4}(|R| + |S|)T_{data} + \frac{1}{4}(|R| + |S|)T_{join}$$

$$= T_{init} + \frac{3}{4}kT_{hash} + \frac{3}{2}kT_{data} + \frac{1}{2}kT_{join}$$

It can be seen that the simple partitioned join involves less data transmission time since the relation R is already available at all processing nodes. However, the local join processing time for the simple partitioned join is obviously larger than the hash partitioned join. If we assume $T_{hash} = \frac{1}{4}T_{join}$, the simple join will be better than the hash join only when $T_{join} < \frac{1}{2}T_{data}$, that is, data transmission time is large compared with local processing time.

9.7   OTHER APPROACHES TO DYNAMIC QUERY OPTIMIZATION

In dynamic query optimization, a query is first decomposed into a sequence of irreducible subqueries. The subquery involving the minimum cost is then chosen to be processed. After the subquery finishes, the costs of the remaining subqueries are recomputed and the next subquery with the minimum cost is executed, and so forth. Similar strategies were also used by other researchers for semijoin-based query optimization. However, the drawback of such step-by-step plan formulation is that the subqueries have to be processed one at a time and thus parallel processing may not be explored. Moreover, choosing one subquery at a time often involves large optimization overhead.

Query plan correction is another dynamic optimization technique. In this algorithm, a static query execution plan is first formulated. During query execution, comparisons are made on the actual intermediate result sizes and the estimates used in the plan formulation. If the difference is greater than a predefined threshold, the plan is abandoned and a dynamic algorithm is invoked. The algorithm then chooses the remaining operations to be processed one at a time. First, when the static plan is abandoned, a new plan for all unexecuted operations is formulated. The query execution then continues according to the new plan unless another inaccurate estimate leads to abandonment of the current plan. Second, multiple thresholds for correction triggering are used to reduce nonbeneficial plan reformulation. There are three important issues regarding the efficiency of midquery reoptimization: (i) the point of query execution at which the runtime collection of dynamic parameters should be made, (ii) the time when a query execution plan should be reoptimized, and (iii) how resource reallocation, memory resource in particular, can be improved.

Another approach is that, instead of reformulating query execution plans, a set of execution plans is generated at compile time. Each plan is optimal for a given set of values of dynamic parameters. The decision about the plan to be used is made at the runtime of the query.

Another approach to query scrambling applied dynamic query processing is to tackle a new dynamic factor: unexpected delays of data arrival over the network. Such delays may stall the operations that are read-to-execute or are already under execution. The query scrambling strategy attempts to first reschedule the execution order of the operations, replacing the stalled operations by the data-ready ones. If the rescheduling is not sufficient, a new execution plan is generated. Several query scrambling algorithms have been reported that deal with different types of data delays, namely, initial delays, bursty arrival, and slow delivery.

Unlike query scrambling, dynamic query load balancing attempts to reschedule query operations from heavily loaded sites to lightly loaded sites whenever performance improvement can be achieved. A few early works studied dynamic load balancing for distributed databases in the light of migrating subqueries with minimum data transmission overhead. However, more works have shifted their focus to balancing workloads for parallel query processing on shared-disk, shared-memory, or shared-nothing architectures. Most of the algorithms were proposed in order to handle load balancing at single operation level such as join. Since the problem of unbalanced processor loads is usually caused by skewed data partitioning, a number of specific algorithms were also developed to handle various kinds of skew.

Another approach is a dynamic load balancing for a hierarchical parallel database system NUMA. The system consists of shared-memory multiprocessor nodes interconnected by a high-speed network and therefore, both intra- and interoperator load balancing are adopted. Intraoperator load balancing within each node is performed first, and if it is not sufficient, interoperator load balancing across the nodes is then attempted. This approach considers only parallel hash join operations on a combined shared-memory and shared-nothing architecture. Query plan reoptimization is not considered.

9.8 SUMMARY

Parallel query optimization plays an important role in parallel query processing. This chapter basically describes two important elements, (*i*) subquery scheduling and (*ii*) dynamic query optimization.

Two execution scheduling strategies for subqueries have been considered, particularly *serial* and *parallel* scheduling. The serial scheduling is appropriate for nonskewed subqueries, whereas the parallel scheduling with a correct processor configuration is suitable for skewed subqueries. Nonskew subqueries are typical for a single class involving selection operation and using a round-robin data partitioning. In contrast, skew subqueries are a manifest of most path expression queries. This is due to the fluctuation of the fan-out degrees and the selectivity factors.

For dynamic query optimization, a cluster architecture is used as an illustration. The approach deals in an integrated way with three methods, *query plan correction*, *subquery migration*, and *subquery partition*. Query execution plan correction is needed when the initial processing time estimate of the subqueries exceeds a threshold, and this triggers a better query execution plan for the rest of the query. Subquery migration happens when there are high load processing nodes whose workloads are to be migrated to some low load processing nodes. Subquery partition is actually used in order to take advantage of parallelization, particularly when there are available low load processing nodes that like to share some of the workloads of medium load processing nodes.

9.9 BIBLIOGRAPHICAL NOTES

A survey of some of the techniques for parallel query evaluation, valid at the time, may be found in Graefe (1993). Most of the work on parallel query optimization has concentrated on query/operation scheduling and processor/site allocation, as well as load balancing. Chekuri et al. (*PODS* 1995) discussed scheduling problems in parallel query optimization. Chen et al. (*ICDE* 1992) presented scheduling and processor allocation for multijoin queries, whereas Hong and Stonebraker (*SIGMOD* 1992 and *DAPD* 1993) proposed optimization based on interoperation and intraoperation for XPRS parallel database. Hameurlain and Morvan (*ICPP* 1993, *DEXA* 1994, *CIKM* 1995) also discussed interoperation and scheduling of SQL queries. Wolf et al. (*IEEE TPDS* 1995) proposed a hierarchical approach to multiquery scheduling.

Site allocation was presented by Frieder and Baru (*IEEE TKDE* 1994), whereas Lu and Tan (*EDBT* 1992) discussed dynamic load balancing based on task-oriented query processing. Extensible parallel query optimization was proposed by Graefe et al. (*SIGMOD* 1990), which they later revised and extended in Graefe et al. (1994). Biscondi et al. (*ADBIS* 1996) studied structured query optimization, and Bültzingsloewen (*SIGMOD Rec* 1989) particularly studied SQL parallel optimization.

In the area of grid query optimization, most work has focused on resource scheduling. Gounaris et al. (*ICDE* 2006 and *DAPD* 2006) examined resource scheduling for grid query processing considering machine load and availability. Li et al. (*DKE* 2004) proposed an on-demand synchronization and load distribution for grid databases. Zheng et al. (2005, 2006) studied dynamic query optimization for semantic grid database.

9.10 EXERCISES

9.1. What is meant by a *phase-oriented* paradigm in a parallel query execution plan?

9.2. The purpose of query parallelization is to reduce the height of a parallelization tree. Discuss the difference between *left-deep/right-deep* and *bushy-tree* parallelization, especially in terms of their height.

9.3. *Resource division* or *resource allocation* is one of the most difficult challenges in parallel execution among subqueries. Discuss the two types of resource division and outline the issues each of them faces.

9.4. Discuss what will happen if two nonskewed subqueries adopt a parallel execution between these two subqueries, and not a serial execution of the subqueries.

9.5. Explain what *dynamic query processing* is in general.

9.6. How is cluster (*shared-something*) query optimization different from *shared-nothing* query optimization?

9.7. Discuss the main difference between *subquery migration* and *partition* in dynamic cluster query optimization.

9.8. Explore your favorite DBMS and investigate how the query tree of a given user query can be traced.

Part IV

Grid Databases

Chapter 10

Transactions in Distributed and Grid Databases

The architecture of distributed computing has evolved rapidly during the last three decades. At the same time, the nature of applications using computing, and the amount of data being produced and stored, have also increased dramatically. Applications are already producing terabytes of data each day and need to store up to petabytes of data. The latest computing infrastructural development is moving toward Grid computing. Grid infrastructure aims to provide widespread access to both autonomous and heterogeneous computing and data resources.

Advanced scientific and business applications are data intensive. These applications are collaborative in nature, and data is collected at geographically distributed sites. Databases have an important role in storing, organizing, accessing, and manipulating data in numerous applications, and its importance cannot be underestimated. The traditional distributed database management systems assume a homogeneous and tightly synchronized (with help of global management layer) working environment. Individual sites in Grid architecture are geographically distributed and belong to independent institutions. Design decisions of individual databases are completely dependent on the owning institution, unlike traditional distributed database systems where the global management system is built at the top of all participating sites. Thus the scaling of traditional distributed databases is also a major concern because of tight integration among participating database sites. The global behavior of Grid databases is inherently heterogeneous, autonomous, asynchronous, and dynamic.

In data management, especially in a distributed environment, the most important requirement is to maintain the correctness of data. In an asynchronous Grid environment, the chances of data being corrupted are high because of the lack of a global management system. Various relaxed consistency requirements have been

High-Performance Parallel Database Processing and Grid Databases,
by David Taniar, Clement Leung, Wenny Rahayu, and Sushant Goel
Copyright © 2008 John Wiley & Sons, Inc.

proposed for data management in Grids. High-precision data-centric scientific applications cannot tolerate any inconsistency. This chapter focuses on maintaining the consistency of data in presence of write transactions in Grids.

Section 10.1 outlines the design challenges of grid databases. Section 10.2 discusses distributed and multidatabase systems and their suitability for the Grids. Section 10.3 presents the fundamental definition of the terms related to transaction management. Properties of transactions are also presented in Section 10.4. Section 10.5 examines various transaction management models in different distributed database systems. Section 10.6 summarizes the requirements for the Grids. Section 10.7 discusses the concurrency control protocols followed by atomic commit protocols in Section 10.8. Section 10.9 describes the replica synchronization protocols.

10.1 GRID DATABASE CHALLENGES

In this section, a sample application is outlined to show that applications with high data consistency are also required in a Grid environment.

EXAMPLE

Consider a group of people gathering data to study earth movement or weather forecasting. The group is a collaboration of a number of diverse institutes and universities from all over the globe. Data for such a project can best be collected locally, but to run an experiment, it is necessary to access data collected by other organizations situated at globally distributed sites. Hence, individual organizations collect data in their databases (or other data source) locally and are connected to other organizations by the Grid infrastructure. Considering the huge amount of data gathered, databases are replicated at participating database sites for performance reasons. It is assumed that security and authentication requirements are taken care of by services provided by Grid middleware, and the correctness of data is the main focus. If any site runs an experiment and forecasts a cyclone or earthquake, then the result must be updated in, and by, all the participants in a synchronous manner. If the result of the forecast is not strictly serialized between sites, then other database sites may override or may never know about the forecast, which may lead to disaster.

From the above example, it is clear that certain applications need strict synchronization and a high level of data consistency within the replicated copies of the data as well as in the individual data sites. Considering the requirements of different applications, the following design challenges are identified from the perspective of data consistency:

- Transactional requirements may vary depending on the application requirement, for example, the applications can have read-only queries or write transactions. On the one hand, read queries will not corrupt the data and thus can be executed in any order, while on the other hand, write transactions need to be scheduled carefully so that the distributed data is not corrupted.

- Since the individual data sites are in different administrative domains and are autonomous, the resulting sites are heterogeneous. Heterogeneity can occur at various levels, including transaction and data models. The effect of heterogeneity in scheduling policies of sites and in maintaining correctness of data is a major design challenge.

- Traditional distributed DBS uses either centralized or decentralized consensus-based (e.g., 2-phase commit) policies for transaction scheduling. How do these scheduling schemes fit into globally distributed and independently managed sites in the Grid infrastructure?

- Looking at the nature of applications and the vastness of the infrastructure, replication of data is an important feature from the performance perspective. How does data replication affect the data consistency?

10.2 DISTRIBUTED DATABASE SYSTEMS AND MULTIDATABASE SYSTEMS

Management of distributed data has evolved with continuously changing computing infrastructures. Many transaction models are available for different distributed architectures. In a broad sense, distributed architecture that leads to different transaction models can be classified as follows:

- Homogeneous distributed architecture: Distributed database systems
- Heterogeneous distributed architecture: Multidatabase systems.

Although many different protocols have been proposed for each individual architecture, the underlying architectural assumption is the same for all protocols in one category. For example, all protocols in the homogeneous distributed architecture assume the existence of global information such as global logs; or all protocols in the heterogeneous distributed architecture assume the existence of a two-level (one local and another global) system.

This section gives an overview of distributed and multidatabase systems, and evaluates their suitability for the Grids.

10.2.1 Distributed Database Systems

Distributed database systems store data at geographically distributed sites, but the distributed sites are typically in the same administrative domain. For example, an organization has four branch offices located in four different cities, and they want to generate a combined report. In the above scenario, technology and policy decisions still lie in one administrative domain. Thus the design strategy typically used is a bottom-up strategy. The basic idea is that the communication between sites is done over a network instead of through shared memory. One of the major advantages of using distributed processing of data is to effectively manage a large volume of data by using a well-known divide-and-conquer rule. It has been shown that processing bigger tasks in smaller, more manageable units has cost benefits in software development. The concept of a distributed DBMS is best suited to individual institutions operating at geographically distributed locations, for example, banks, universities, etc.

Distributed Database Architectural Model

A distributed database system in general has three major dimensions: (*i*) autonomy, (*ii*) distribution, and (*iii*) heterogeneity.

Autonomy.   When a database is developed independently of other DBMS, it is not aware of design decisions and control structures adopted at those sites. Thus a top-level management system is required to manage these databases. Individual databases still have their identity and are not affected by joining or leaving the global structure. The autonomy dimension deals with distribution of control, not data. Different levels of autonomy have been identified as *tight integration, semi-autonomous*, and *total isolation*. Total isolation leads to multidatabase systems.

Distribution.   The distribution dimension deals with the physical distribution of data over multiple sites while still maintaining the conceptual integrity of the data. Two major types of distribution have been identified: client/server distribution and peer-to-peer distribution. In client/server distribution, data managing and processing responsibility is delegated only to those servers and clients that have the user interface. In peer-to-peer distribution strategy, each site has full database functionality and can communicate with other peers for transaction execution or query processing.

Heterogeneity.   Heterogeneity may occur at the hardware as well as data/transaction model level. Heterogeneity is one of the important factors that needs careful consideration in a distributed environment because any transaction that spans more than one database may need to map one data/transaction model to another. Although theoretically the heterogeneity dimension has been identified, a lot of research work and applications have focused only on the homogeneous environment.

Distributed Database Working Model

The architecture shown in Figure 10.1 is the general architecture that is used in the literature in one form or another. Transactions $(T_1, T_2, \ldots T_n)$ from different sites are submitted to the global transaction monitor (GTM). The global data dictionary is used to build and execute the distributed queries. Each subquery is then transported to local transaction monitors via the communication network, checked for local correctness, and then passed down to the local database management system (LDBMS). The results are sent back to the GTM. Any potential problem, for example, global deadlock, is resolved by GTM after gathering information from all the participating sites.

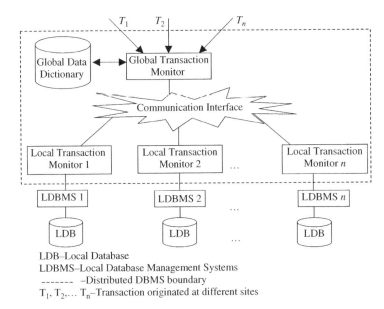

LDB–Local Database
LDBMS–Local Database Management Systems
------- –Distributed DBMS boundary
$T_1, T_2, \dots T_n$–Transaction originated at different sites

Figure 10.1   A conceptual schema of distributed database systems

The GTM has the following components: global transaction request module, global request semantic analyzer module, global query decomposer module, global query object localizer module, global query optimizer module, global transaction scheduler module, global recovery manager module, global lock manager module, and transaction dispatcher module.

The global transaction request module is responsible for receiving the distributed transactions from different sites and putting them in the queue for processing. The semantic analyzer then consults the global data dictionary to verify the semantics of the transaction. The semantically correct query is then divided into subtransactions with the query decomposer module, according to the fragments of the distributed database, so that they can be sent to the respective remote sites. The query decomposer works together with the query object localizer to build a simple relational algebra query that contains communication primitives that will aid in moving around the intermediate table relations used to solve the transaction. Global query optimization techniques are then applied, removing any redundant predicates. Information from the global data dictionary is used for this purpose.

The first five components are mostly query-based, while the last four modules deal with transactions and maintain the consistency of the data. An optimized query is submitted to the global transaction scheduler. The transaction scheduler is responsible for managing the correct serialization order of multiple concurrent transactions. The global scheduler achieves this with the help of the global recovery manager and the global lock manager module. The global recovery manager maintains the global transaction log. The global transaction log maintains the before and after images of database objects. It also manages the commit and abort list that helps the system to recover under failure (or transaction abort) conditions and is very similar to a centralized log.

The global lock manager maintains the list of all the locks allocated to different data objects residing at multiple sites. This information is maintained in the global lock table. The transaction scheduler and concurrency control protocols use information stored in the global lock table. The global lock table stores the type of operation being executed (read/write) against that transaction ID and uses this information to schedule operations from different transactions in a serializable manner. Lock information is also helpful in a deadlock situation to decide which transaction to abort. This lock-based concept is equally applicable for other concurrency control protocols, such as timestamp ordering and optimistic protocols. The last component of the global monitor is the transaction dispatcher that transports query fragments to the distributed sites and accepts the results. Messages like commit/abort can also be passed back and forth from the distributed sites.

Suitability of Distributed DBMS in Grids

The major advantages offered by distributed database systems are transparent data access of physically distributed data, replicating the data at local sites for efficient access, and fast processing of data by divide-and-conquer technique, and at times distributed processing is computationally and economically cheaper. It is easy to monitor the modular growth of systems rather than monitoring one big system. Although distributed databases have numerous advantages, their design presents many challenges to developers.

Partitioning and Replication.   Data partitioning is one of the major factors that affects the performance of distributed database systems. The database is divided into a number of disjoint partitions, each of which is placed at a different site. Major design issues include fragmenting the database and distributing it optimally. Replication may be used to increase the access efficiency of the data. If all partitions are stored at each site, it is known as full replication, while partial replication is the storing of each partition at more than one site, but not at all sites.

The implementation of concepts of distributed DBMS is not practical in the Grid environment because of the following challenges. By examining the conceptual schema, it is noted that the distributed DBMS design has a global data dictionary and a transaction monitor. All design requirements of the database system are available to the designer before the system is built. This encourages a bottom-up design strategy. Under these circumstances, as the size of the database grows, it becomes increasingly difficult to manage huge amounts of global information such as the global lock table, global directory, etc.

Another challenge is that the distributed DBMS model assumes that the use of uniform protocols among distributed sites, such as concurrency control protocols, will require that all database sites support a locking protocol (or timestamp or optimistic). This is undesirable in the Grid architecture as individual sites have different administrators and they may choose to implement different protocols independently. That having been said, however, distributed DBMSs will play an important role in global Grid architecture.

10.2.2 Multidatabase Systems

In a broader sense, a multidatabase system can be defined as an interconnected collection of autonomous databases. The fundamental concept of a multidatabase system is autonomy. Autonomy refers to the distribution of control and indicates the degree to which individual DBMSs can operate independently. Levels of autonomy are as follows:

Design Autonomy: Individual DBMSs can use the data models and transaction management techniques without intervention of any other DBMS.

Communication Autonomy: Each DBMS can decide on the information it wants to provide to other databases.

Execution Autonomy: Individual databases are free to execute the transactions according to their scheduling strategy.

Multidatabase systems have a combined top-down and bottom-up design strategy, as individual sites are considered to be autonomous and evolve independently (top-down). On the other hand, a global layer of multidatabase management system (MDMS) has to be designed (bottom-up) for a specific set of databases. The component-based architectural model of MDMS manages full-fledged individual DBMSs. The MDMS allows users to access various independent databases with the help of a top-layer management system (Fig. 10.2).

Multidatabase Architecture

Figure 10.2 shows the general architecture of a multidatabase system. Each database in a multidatabase environment has its own transaction processing components such as a local transaction manager, local data manager, local scheduler, etc. Transactions submitted to individual databases are executed independently, and the local DBMS is completely responsible for their correctness. MDMS is not aware of any local execution at the local database. A global transaction that needs to access data from multiple sites is submitted to MDMS, which in turn forwards the request to, and collects the result from, the local DBMS on behalf of the global transaction. The components of MDMS are called global components and include the global transaction manager, global scheduler, etc.

Suitability of Multidatabase in Grids

Architecturally, multidatabase systems are close to Grid databases as individual database systems are autonomous. But the ultimate applications' requirements separate the two database systems. Local database systems in multidatabase systems

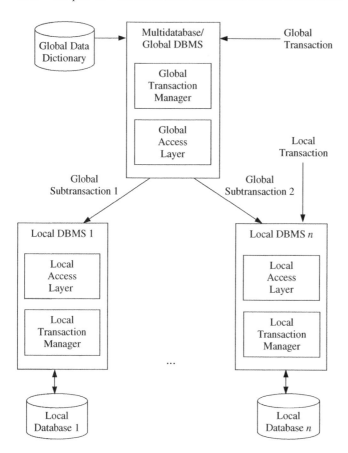

Figure 10.2   Multidatabase architecture

are not designed for sharing the data. Hence, issues related to efficient sharing of data between sites, for example, replication, are not addressed in multidatabase systems.

The multidatabase system is the preferred option when individual databases have to be combined logically for specific purposes and a short duration. If a large volume of data has to be managed and data distribution is an important factor in performance statistics, then a multidatabase may not be the preferred design option.

The design strategy of a multidatabase is a combination of top-down and bottom-up strategies. Individual database sites are designed independently, but the development of MDMS requires an underlying working knowledge of sites. Thus virtualization of resources is not possible in multidatabase architecture. Furthermore, maintaining consistency for global transactions is the responsibility of MDMS. This is undesirable in a Grid setup.

Depending on the level of heterogeneity and the type of underlying protocols used by individual participating sites, the top layer of MDMS can change significantly. Although the multidatabase design supports evolution and collaboration of autonomous databases, the MDMS layer is specific to the constituting databases. Thus, adding and removing participants in the multidatabase is not transparent and needs modification in the MDMS layer, a scenario not suitable for Grid architecture. Furthermore, a distributed multidatabase is required to replicate the MDMS layer at each local DBMS site that participates in the multidatabase.

10.3 BASIC DEFINITIONS ON TRANSACTION MANAGEMENT

Transactions, interleaving of operations in different transactions (*schedule* or *history*) and correctness criteria of schedules, such as serializability, are defined below.

Definition 10.1 (Transaction): A transaction T_i is a set of read (r_i), write (w_i), abort (a_i), and commit (c_i). T_i is a partial order with ordering relation $\prec_i$ where:

(1) $T_i \subseteq \{r_i[x], w_i[x] | x$ is a data item$\} \cup \{a_i, c_i\}$

(2) $a_i \in T_i$ iff $c_i \notin T_i$

(3) If t is a_i or c_i, for any other operation $p \in T_i$, $p \prec_i t$

(4) If $r_i[x], w_i[x] \in T_i$, then either $r_i[x] \prec_i w_i[x]$ or $w_i[x] \prec_i r_i[x]$

Condition 1 states that transactions have read and write operations followed by a termination condition (commit or abort) operation. Condition 2 says that a transaction can have only one termination operation, namely, either commit or abort, but not both. Condition 3 defines that the termination operation is the last operation in the transaction. Finally, condition 4 defines that if the transaction reads and writes the same data item, it must be strictly ordered.

A history or schedule indicates the order in which the operations of the transactions were executed relative to each other. Formally, let $T = \{T_1, T_2, \ldots T_n\}$ be a set of transactions.

Definition 10.2 (Schedule or history): A complete history H over T is a partial order with ordering relation $\prec_H$ where:

(1) $H = \cup_{i=1}^{n} T_i$;

(2) $\prec_H \supseteq \cup_{i=1}^{n} \prec_i$; and

(3) For any two conflicting operations $p, q \in H$, either $p \prec_H q$ or $q \prec_H p$

A pair (op_i, op_j) is called conflicting pair iff (if and only if):

(1) Operations op_i and op_j belong to different transactions,

(2) Two operations access the same database entity, and

(3) At least one of them is a *write* operation.

Condition 1 of definition 10.2 states that a history H represents the execution of all operations of the set of submitted transactions. Condition 2 emphasizes that the execution order of the operations of an individual transaction is respected in the schedule. Condition 3 is clear by itself.

A history represents concurrent execution of the transactions with interleaved operations. Interleaving of operations from different transactions may lead to corruption of data. Hence, the history must follow certain rules that will ensure the consistency of data being accessed (read or written) by different transactions. The theory is popularly known as *serializability theory*. The basic idea of serializability theory is that concurrent transactions are isolated from one another in terms of their effect on the database. In theory, all transactions, if executed in a serial manner, that is, one after another, will not corrupt the data.

Definition 10.3 (Serial history): A database history H_s is serial iff

$$(\exists p \in T_i, \exists q \in T_j \text{ such that } p \prec_{H_s} q) \text{ then } (\forall r \in T_i, \forall s \in T_j, r \prec_{H_s} s)$$

Definition 10.3 states that if any operation, p, of a transaction T_i precedes any operation, q, of some other transaction T_j in a serial history H_s, then all operations of T_i must precede all operations of T_j in H_s. Serial execution of transactions is not feasible for performance reasons; hence, the transactions are interleaved. The serializability theory ensures the correctness of data if the transactions are interleaved. A history is *serializable* if it is equivalent to a serial execution of the same set of transactions.

Definition 10.4 (Serializable history): A history H is *serializable (SR)* if its committed projection, $C(H)$, is equivalent to a serial execution H_s.

Equivalence ($\equiv$) of two histories H and H_1 is defined as follows:

(1) Both histories should be defined over the same set of transactions and have the same operations.

(2) Both H and H' order conflicting operations of nonaborted transactions in the same way. For example, for any two conflicting operations $p_i \in T_i$ and $q_j \in T_j$, where $a_i, a_j \notin H$, if $p_i \prec_H q_j$ then $p_i \prec_{H'} q_j$.

A serialization graph (SG) is the most popular way to examine the serializability of a history. A history will be serializable if, and only if (iff) the SG is acyclic.

Definition 10.5 (Serialization graph): The SG for history H over a set of transactions $T = \{T_1, T_2, \ldots T_n\}$, denoted SG($H$), is a directed graph whose nodes are the transactions in T that are committed in H and whose edges are all $T_i \rightarrow T_j$ such that one of T_i's operations precedes and conflicts with one of T_j's operations in H.

Consider the following transactions:

$$T_1 : r_1[x]w_1[x]r_1[y]w_1[y]c_1$$
$$T_2 : r_2[x]w_2[x]c_2$$

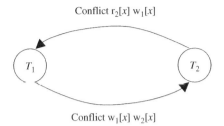

Conflict $r_2[x]\, w_1[x]$

T_1 T_2

Conflict $w_1[x]\, w_2[x]$

Figure 10.3   A conflict SG for history H

Consider the following history:

$$H = r_1[x]\, r_2[x]\, w_1[x]\, r_1[y]\, w_2[x]\, w_1[y]c_1c_2$$

The SG for the history, H, is shown in Figure 10.3.

The SG in Figure 10.3 contains a cycle; hence, the history H is not serializable. From the above example, it is clear that the outcome of the history depends only on the conflicting transactions. Ordering of nonconflicting operations either way has the same computational effect. View serializability has also been proposed in addition to conflict serializability for maintaining correctness of the data. But from a practical point of view, almost all concurrency control protocols are conflict-based.

10.4 ACID PROPERTIES OF TRANSACTIONS

The ultimate goal of a transaction is to preserve the consistent state of the database after its execution (successful or unsuccessful). The database may be in a temporarily inconsistent state during the execution of the transaction. If the transaction executes successfully, then the effects of the transaction are made permanent in the database and if the transaction fails, then the database regains its previous consistent state. Transaction management protocols ensure that the database is in a consistent state in the presence of concurrent accesses or failures. A generic transaction model is shown in Figure 10.4. Thus the transaction management protocols should ensure consistency for successfully completed transactions, and reliability for unsuccessful transactions.

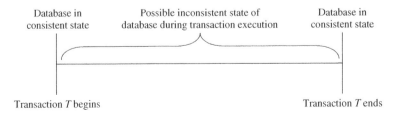

Database in consistent state   Possible inconsistent state of database during transaction execution   Database in consistent state

Transaction T begins   Transaction T ends

Figure 10.4   A generic transaction model

The concurrent execution of transactions may encounter problems such as *dirty-read problem*, *lost update problem*, *incorrect summary problem*, and *unrepeatable read problem* that may corrupt the data in the database. As these are standard database problems, only the lost update problem is presented here for the sake of brevity.

The lost update problem occurs when two transactions access the same data item in the database and the operations of the two transactions are interleaved in such a way that the database is left with incorrect value. Suppose data item D_1 is accessed by two simultaneously executing transactions, T_1 and T_2. The initial value of $D_1 = 100$.

Let us assume that D_1 is a bank account, with a balance of 100 dollars, and two transactions are modifying the account concurrently: One is depositing 50 dollars, and the other is withdrawing 50 dollars. Correct execution for this scenario will leave the account balance of 100 dollars. After the execution of the schedule with interleaving as shown in Figure 10.5, the account balance will be 150 dollars. This is because the update done by T_1 that had withdrawn 50 dollars from the account was lost. Concurrency control algorithms are used in order to avoid such an incorrect interleaving.

To obtain consistency and reliability, a transaction must have the following four properties, which are known as ACID properties.

(1) Atomicity

(2) Consistency

(3) Isolation

(4) Durability

The *atomicity* property is also known as the all-or-nothing property. This ensures that the transaction is executed as one unit of operations, that is, either all of the transaction's operations are completed or none at all. Thus if the transaction execution is interrupted by a failure, the transaction management protocol decides

T_1	T_2
$r_1[D_1]$	
$D_1 := D_1 - 50$	
	$r_1[D_1]$
	$D_1 := D_1 + 50$
$w_1[D_1]$	
	$w_1[D_1]$

Time

Figure 10.5 Lost update problem

whether to undo all operations of the transaction executed thus far or complete the remaining operations of the transaction.

A transaction will preserve the ***consistency***, if complete execution of the transaction takes the database from one consistent state to another. A transaction is a program or set of instructions. A database programmer coding these instructions should ensure that if the database is in a consistent state before executing the transaction, it will also be in a consistent state after completion of the transaction.

The ***isolation*** property requires that all transactions see a consistent state of the database. It ensures that concurrent transactions do not reveal their intermediate inconsistent results to each other. Four levels of isolation include: at level 0 isolation, a transaction does not overwrite *dirty* data of other transactions (i.e., no *dirty read problem*); at level 1 isolation, transactions do not have *lost update problem*; at level 2 isolation level, transactions do not have a lost update and dirty read problem. Finally, at level 3 isolation (true isolation), in addition to level 2 properties, other transactions do not dirty any data read by a transaction before it completes its execution (i.e., no *unrepeatable read problem*).

The ***durability*** property of the database is responsible for ensuring that once the transaction commits, its effects are made permanent within the database. The results of the committed transactions will survive any subsequent system failure. Recovery protocols are responsible for ensuring the durability property.

The above discussion applies to both a centralized database system and a distributed database system.

10.5 TRANSACTION MANAGEMENT IN VARIOUS DATABASE SYSTEMS

This section discusses how the ACID properties are obtained in various DBMSs. These strategies are critically analyzed from the perspective of Grid database systems.

10.5.1 Transaction Management in Centralized and Homogeneous Distributed Database Systems

Transaction management in centralized DBMSs and homogeneous distributed DBMSs are similar in the way that both database management systems operate under a single administrative domain. This discussion is true for centralized and distributed DBMSs, because these DBMSs use a centralized management system and are in the same administrative domain.

Lock tables, timestamps, commit/abort decisions, hardware, software, etc. can be easily shared in centralized and homogeneous DBMSs. A central management system is implemented to maintain the ACID properties of the transaction. The management system is known as the global transaction manager (GTM) in a distributed database system. The transactions are submitted to the GTM, and results are returned to the database site via the GTM. The transaction properties are discussed below for homogeneous distributed DBMSs.

Atomicity

For a global transaction, the atomicity property requires that the transaction succeed at all sites or abort at all sites. All sites participate and collaborate with the GTM to help achieve the atomicity. Sites can communicate with the GTM or with other sites synchronously to achieve the uniform global decision. Thus consensus-based protocols are implemented to achieve atomicity in homogeneous distributed DBMS.

Popularly, a prepare-to-commit message is sent to the GTM to help achieve the consensus. After sending the prepare message, the local transaction manager cannot make a decision. The prepare-to-commit operation may force the site to hold the resources for an unspecified period of time. 2PC is implemented to reach an atomic decision. 2PC is a blocking protocol, which is one of the main disadvantages. Various commit protocols for homogeneous distributed DBMS have been proposed, but essentially all of these commit protocols require the existence of GTM and are consensus-based, and not applicable in a Grid database environment.

Consistency

The local transaction managers are responsible for maintaining the consistency of data in individual databases. Consistency of the global transaction is enforced in the GTM. The global data dictionary, global lock table, global logs, and other information required to maintain the global consistency are stored in the GTM. Implementation of GTM in a homogeneous distributed DBMS is easy because all databases are in a single administrative domain. Thus the GTM can be designed in a bottom-up fashion to prevent any consistency anomalies being introduced by global transactions.

The sites in a homogeneous distributed DBMS are tightly coupled and can communicate synchronously. This makes the implementation of the GTM easy and feasible in homogeneous systems. Concurrency control protocols are responsible for ensuring consistency. Concurrency control protocols such as the locking protocol use the global lock table stored at the GTM to ensure the consistency property.

Isolation

The isolation property requires that an executing transaction cannot reveal its intermediate results to other transactions before its completion. Enforcing the isolation property helps to prevent lost update and cascading abort anomalies. The isolation property is directly related to the consistency of the database and is addressed by concurrency control protocols. Serializability is the most widely accepted correctness criterion for ensuring transaction isolation. Serializability requires that the effects of concurrently executing a set of transactions are equivalent to some serial execution over the same set of transactions. Concurrency control protocols are broadly classified into pessimistic and optimistic categories. Mainly, two types of concurrency control algorithms are proposed: (i) locking and (ii) timestamp ordering (TO). In distributed database systems, global transactions will access multiple database sites. Thus global serializability is used as the concurrency control criterion.

Locking protocols may lead to deadlocks. Particularly in distributed databases, global deadlocks can occur. Distributed deadlocks are identified and resolved with the use of a global wait-for-graph, constructed by using information available in the global lock table. From this perspective, all the serializability algorithms (concurrency control protocols) are centralized in nature, as they need to access the information stored in the GTM. Furthermore, to maintain global serializability, the global serializability algorithm must be aware of the global as well as local transactions executing at all sites. This is not feasible in a Grid environment because of the autonomy of sites.

Durability

Durability is the property that ensures that results of the committed transactions are made permanent in the database. The effects of the transactions will sustain any subsequent failure. Every individual database site has a local recovery manager (LRM). The LRM must maintain some information about the database state. This information is used during failure recovery. Each write transaction updates a log file, which will help the LRM during the recovery process to restore the database state to what it was before failure. The log file maintains the before-image and after-image of all write transactions. Recovery algorithms are based on two main types of updating: in-place updating and out-of-place updating. In-place updating directly changes the value of the data item in the database; as a result, the previous database value is lost. On the other hand, out-of-place updating maintains the new value separately. Write-ahead logging is used to store the before- and after-image of the data item in the log. The before-image facilitates the Undo operation and the after-image facilitates the Redo operations to restore the stable database state before system failure.

Recovery of global transactions needs to access multiple sites and also the information stored in the global recovery manager. Thus the recovery of global transactions is centralized and uses global information. In a Grid environment, global information such as the global recovery manager, global logs, etc. is absent, thereby making failure of recovery in a Grid environment a challenging issue.

10.5.2 Transaction Management in Heterogeneous Distributed Database Systems

The discussion in this section is especially relevant for multidatabase systems. Heterogeneous distributed DBMSs emerge because of the collaboration of pre-existing, autonomous database systems. They are commonly known as multidatabase systems. These DBMSs clearly distinguish between local transactions and global transactions. Local and global transactions are used in the same sense as those of homogeneous DBMSs, that is, a local transaction accesses the data from a single DBMS and a global transaction accesses data from multiple

DBMSs. Transaction management in the heterogeneous DBMS is hierarchical. A local transaction manager (LTM) is responsible for correct scheduling of all local transactions and the subtransactions of the global transactions executing at its site. The LTM ensures serializable execution at that individual database site.

The global software layer (multidatabase management system) manages global transactions and ensures global serializability. The global serializability criterion guarantees the correct concurrent execution of global transactions. Global serializability requires that the LTMs at all database sites, where the subtransactions of the global transactions are executing, serialize the subtransactions in the same way. Unlike homogeneous distributed DBMS, heterogeneous DBMS is collection of independent DBMS. Autonomy of sites is preserved in such a collection. Thus, the information available at one local DBMS cannot be shared with other local DBMSs or the global DBMS. Maintaining transaction properties in the heterogeneous environment is more complicated than for its homogeneous counterpart. The transaction properties are discussed below for heterogeneous distributed DBMS. The terms "heterogeneous DBMSs" and "multidatabase systems" are used interchangeably. The transaction properties are addressed below:

Atomicity

In the multidatabase environment, the participating sites are autonomous and the DBMS maintains complete control over the databases. Thus the decision to commit/abort the local transactions and subtransactions of the global transaction completely depend on the LTM. The GTM of multi-DBMS is unaware of existence of any local transaction. To address such a situation, a top-level global management layer is designed and implemented. This layer is known as a multidatabase management system (MDBS). The MDBS consists of a GTM and a set of *servers* or *agents*. Servers are associated with each local DBMS. A global transaction is submitted to the MDBS, and thus it is the responsibility of the GTM to correctly schedule the global transactions.

The prepare-to-commit operation cannot be implemented in the multidatabase environment, because it holds the local resources for some external process, which interferes with the local autonomy of the sites. Autonomy is one of the prime requirements of multidatabase systems, and cannot be compromised. That having been said, there is no standard position accepted by the research community on whether or not to support prepare-to-commit operation. Nevertheless, all multidatabase systems need a global management layer (like homogeneous DBMS). The MDMS software varies with the different composition of the multidatabases. Thus it is difficult to virtualize multidatabase systems (as required by Grid databases).

Consistency

Each individual LTM ensures that the transactions (local and subtransactions of global transaction) do not violate any consistency constraints. Since the sites are autonomous, there are no integrity constraints defined on data items residing at different sites. Thus there are no global integrity constraints in multidatabase systems. Hence, all global transactions will meet the consistency property.

Isolation

Global serializability, in addition to local serializability, is required in multidatabase systems. Any information regarding global transaction is stored at the global layer. A ticket is maintained at each local database site to ensure global serializability. Any global transaction is required to read the ticket value, increment the value, and write the new value into the database. The ticket value indicates the serialization order of the global transactions at the site. The GTM also keeps a serialization graph for all active global transactions. It should be noted that the concurrency control protocols in multidatabase systems need to make a clear distinction between global and local transactions. In a Grid environment, although local and global transactions exist, a strict distinction between the two is not essential. Furthermore, the responsibility of scheduling for the global transactions needs to be designated to multiple participants, in the absence of a global management layer.

Durability

The durability property requires modification of the data values stored at databases after the failure recovery. Global transactions access multiple local DBMSs, and thus after the failure recovery the GTM will need to restore values at more than one database. Because of the autonomy of sites, the durability property cannot be directly implemented by the GTM. Although execution autonomy (three types of autonomy are (i) design, (ii) execution, and (iii) control autonomy) could be preserved during failure recovery, it is necessary to infringe upon the control autonomy of the local DBMSs to maintain the durability property. The recovery process must ensure that the desired correctness is maintained. Thus the durability property is closely associated with atomicity and consistency. Most recovery approaches require that the local transactions not be allowed to access the DBMS resources until the global (MDMS) layer has completed the recovery process. Effectively, the recovery process is hierarchical, with local and multi-DBMS executing their recovery processes separately. This setup is unsuitable for a Grid database, because it needs a transparent recovery process.

10.6 REQUIREMENTS IN GRID DATABASE SYSTEMS

Considering the requirement of Grid architecture and the correctness protocols available for distributed DBMSs, a comparison of traditional distributed DBMSs and Grid databases for various architectural properties is shown in Table 10.1.

Table 10.1 emphasizes that, because of different architectural requirements, traditional DBMS techniques will not suffice for Grid databases. Specifically, the

Table 10.1 Architectural comparison matrix for distributed data management systems

	Distributed DBMS	Multidatabase	Grid Database
Heterogeneity	Maybe	Yes	Yes
Autonomy	No	Yes	Yes
Distribution	Yes	Yes	Yes
Replication	Yes	No	Yes
Design philosophy	Bottom-up	Combined top-down/bottom-up	Top-down
Global DBMS	Yes	Yes	No (service oriented)
Resource transparency	No	No	Yes
Data transparency	No	No	Yes

design philosophy of a Grid database is top-down, which is different from any other distributed DBMSs because of the absence of a global management layer. Thus it emphasizes the need for revisiting distributed database standards in order to meet the requirements of the Grid database. The bottom-up design strategy indicates that the global system can be analyzed before it is built. But the top-down design strategy indicates that because of the heterogeneity, dynamic nature and autonomy of sites, the global system cannot be analyzed as a whole. Although Grid databases are architecturally close to multidatabase systems in the heterogeneity, autonomy, and distribution dimensions, both are very different in the aspects of design philosophy, global data management, and transparency. Thus, in such a loosely coupled Grid infrastructure, maintaining data consistency becomes a challenging task.

Therefore, the main objectives of Grid database transaction management can be summarized as follows:

- To address the transaction management issues in Grid database systems including:
  - Atomicity
  - Consistency
  - Isolation
  - Durability
- To address the replica synchronization issues at a protocol level (not at service level)
- To study multiple levels of operations to take advantage of replication

Weaker consistency requirements for data management in the Grid environment are common. However, high-precision applications such as earth simulation, astronomical systems, weather forecasting, and biomedical engineering cannot work at weaker consistency levels. Hence, absolute consistency is crucial.

10.7 CONCURRENCY CONTROL PROTOCOLS

Mostly, the concurrency control protocols are classified based on synchronization criterion. The concurrency control protocols are broadly classified as (*i*) pessimistic and (*ii*) optimistic. Pessimistic algorithms provide mutually exclusive access-shared data and thus synchronize the process early in the execution. Optimistic algorithms assume that there are very few conflicts during the execution and do the synchronization toward the transaction termination. The complete set of classification is shown in Figure 10.6.

Locking-based algorithms act as semaphores. A transaction physically or logically locks a particular *granule* of the database (lock unit) and does not allow access to that locked unit to any other transaction until it finishes execution. In a distributed environment, the locking protocol typically tends to designate one site to store global information such as lock tables, responsibility of granting and releasing locks, etc. A basic lock compatibility matrix for granting locks is shown in Table 10.2. Another assumption is that all sites use locking protocols. The design strategy for distributed databases is bottom-up, and hence the basic assumption is

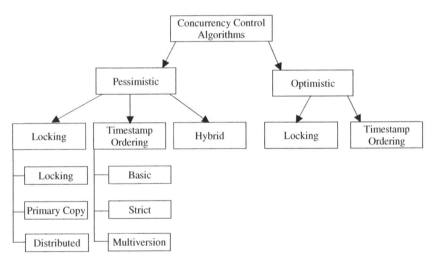

Figure 10.6 Taxonomy of concurrency control algorithms

Table 10.2 A basic lock compatibility matrix

		Lock held by a transaction	
		Read	**Write**
Lock requested by another transaction	**Read**	Yes	No
	Write	No	No

homogeneity among participating sites (the design strategy of distributed databases is discussed in more detail in Chapter 11). Other variants of locking protocols are certify locks, intension locks, altruistic locks etc., but from the design perspective, the common feature of all variants is homogeneity.

Timestamp ordering algorithms assign timestamps to transactions and data items stored in the database to maintain consistency. A transaction can be identified uniquely with the help of the timestamp. Timestamp ordering algorithms order the transactions based on their timestamps. The schedule generated by timestamp ordering protocols is equivalent to the *particular serial order* corresponding to the order of the timestamps. Timestamp ordering algorithms have three main variants: (*i*) basic, (*ii*) strict, and (*iii*) multiversion. Timestamps are sometimes associated with locking-based protocols to improve performance and concurrency. These protocols are known as hybrid protocols.

These locking and timestamp-based protocols are either conservative or pessimistic because they perform some type of checking before the operation is performed. This imposes an overhead on the concurrency control protocols. On the other hand, optimistic protocols do not perform any validation or checking during transaction execution and expect that there will be no conflict between transactions. During the transaction execution, all updates are stored temporarily in local copies. At the time of transaction termination, the protocol checks whether the updates made by the transaction violate any requirement of serializability. If the serializability requirements are not violated, then the updates in the temporary copies may be made permanent; otherwise the transaction is aborted. Optimistic protocols have better performance if the application does not have much conflict between transactions.

10.8 ATOMIC COMMIT PROTOCOLS

Atomic commitment is an important requirement of transactions running in a distributed environment. All cohorts of distributed transactions should either commit or abort in order to maintain the atomicity property of the transactions and, consequently, maintain the correctness of stored data. Other approaches like workflow and business process have been studied widely, and they need weaker consistency and atomicity requirements. But, as discussed in the example above in this chapter, the importance of conserving ACID properties in a Grid environment cannot be denied. Distributed DBMS are broadly classified into two categories to study ACPs: (*i*) homogeneous and (*ii*) heterogeneous.

10.8.1 Homogeneous Distributed Database Systems

A distributed transaction has subtransactions executing at more than one site. To achieve the all-or-nothing property of the transaction, each of the subtransactions of the distributed transaction must either commit or abort. An ACP helps the processes/subtransactions to reach decision such that:

- All subtransactions that reach a decision reach the same one.
- A process cannot reverse its decision after it has reached one.
- A commit decision can be reached only if all subtransactions are ready to commit.
- If there are no failures and all subtransactions are ready to commit, then the decision will be to commit.

Two-Phase Commit (2PC) is the simplest and most popular ACP proposed in the literature to achieve atomicity in homogeneous DBS.

A coordinator is typically the site where the transaction is submitted or any other site that keeps all the global information regarding the distributed transaction. Participants are all the other sites where the subtransaction of the distributed transaction is executing. 2PC works as follows:

(1) The coordinator sends *vote_request* to all the participating sites.

(2) After receiving the request to vote, the site responds by sending its vote, either *yes* or *no*. If the participant voted *yes*, it enters into *prepared* or *ready* state and waits for final decision from the coordinator. If the vote was *no*, the participant can abort its part of the transaction.

(3) The coordinator collects all votes from the participants. If all votes including the coordinator's vote are *yes*, then the coordinator decides to *commit* and sends the message accordingly to all the sites. If even one of the votes is *no*, the coordinator decides to abort the distributed transaction.

(4) After receiving either a *commit* or an *abort* decision from the coordinator, the participant commits or aborts accordingly from the prepared state.

Figure 10.7 shows the state diagram of 2PC for coordinator and the participants.

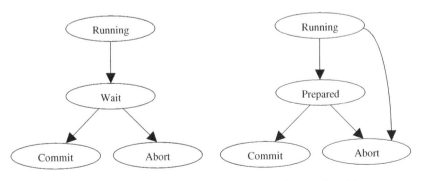

State Diagram of coordinator   State Diagram of participant

Figure 10.7   State diagram of 2PC

There are two phases (hence the name 2-phase commit) in the commit procedure: the voting phase (step 1 and step 2) and the decision phase (step 3 and step 4).
At step 2, the participant enters the prepared state and is waiting for the final decision from the coordinator. The participant cannot make a final decision during this
state and must wait for the final response from the coordinator. During this period
of uncertainty, the participant holds all the resources of the site despite finishing its
part of the transaction execution. This limitation, in particular, may hinder the performance (and sometimes, impossible to implement) of the applications in the Grid
environment, where applications are long-running and asynchronous in nature.

In 2PC, if the coordinator fails while the participant is in the prepared state
(i.e., in the uncertainty period), the progress of the transaction is blocked. Consequently, the participant cannot unilaterally decide whether to commit or to abort
and may be blocked for an unlimited period of time, holding local site resources
such as locks on data items indefinitely. *Three-phase commit* (3PC) was proposed
as a nonblocking protocol, but it incurs an extra round of message delays and is
not suitable for high-performance distributed systems. 3PC needs a prepared state
and a precommit state in order to reach atomic commitment decision. Figure 10.8
shows the state diagram of the coordinator and participants in the 3PC protocol.

In 2PC, after the participant sends a "yes" vote, it is in an uncertain state but in
3PC the participants expect a "pre-commit" message from the coordinator. If all the
participants' votes were "yes," then the coordinator sends a pre-commit message
to all participants and waits for an *acknowledgment* from participants. This extra
round of messages removes the uncertainty period from the participants. If the
participant is in the pre-commit state, then it can unilaterally decide to go into the
commit state; and the participant can decide to abort unilaterally from the prepared
state (unlike 2PC), thus avoiding the uncertainty period.

Some of the commit protocols are briefly analyzed in view of their applicability
to Grid infrastructure. The Implicit Yes Vote (IYV) protocol was proposed with
the intention of eliminating the voting phase and capitalizing on the *early prepare*

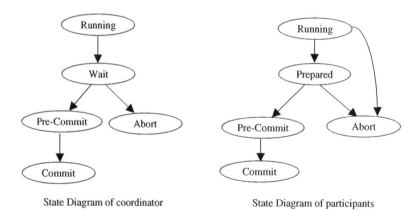

State Diagram of coordinator   State Diagram of participants

Figure 10.8   State diagram of 3PC

concept. Two basic assumptions behind the IYV protocol that make it unsuitable for the Grid environment are: (1) each site employs a strict *two-phase locking* protocol, and (2) the coordinator should have a partial image of the participant. Assumption 1 is not practical in Grids because of the heterogeneity of participants, and assumption 2 will violate the autonomy of participants, which is not acceptable to many participants in the Grid environment.

The 3PC protocol discussed above is a nonblocking protocol, but it incurs an extra cost of two rounds of messages to reach a final decision even in a failure-free environment. Although the 3PC does not block the transaction in the case of coordination failure, it still implements the *prepared* state for all the participants and also holds the lock for the time of two extra rounds of messages. The 3PC protocol is more expensive in terms of time complexity, programming, understanding, and implementing. Most importantly, the basic assumption of 3PC is the same as for 2PC, namely, homogeneity among distributed sites and synchronous communication between sites, which are not possible in the Grid environment.

Other nonblocking optimization protocols like *uniform reliable broadcast* and *uniform timed reliable broadcast* also assume a synchronous model, that is, the process execution and message delays are synchronized. For the above-mentioned reasons, they cannot be used in Grids.

More recently, the Paxos commit algorithm has been proposed. The Paxos commit protocol is based on the Paxos algorithm and is consensus-based. The Paxos commit protocol tries to eliminate a single point of failure of the coordinator in 2PC. It uses $(2F+1)$ coordinators and makes progress if at least $(F+1)$ of them are working, where F is the number of failure of processes. Thus the protocol has interdependent communications and assumes a homogeneous working environment.

10.8.2 Heterogeneous Distributed Database Systems

Multidatabase systems assume an autonomous environment for transaction execution. They typically execute a top layer of multidatabase management systems for transaction management. These systems are designed for certain application specific requirements and mostly for short-running transactions. Because of the high design and execution autonomy requirements in multidatabase systems, the ACPs are not designed for replicated data. Considering the distributed nature of the applications, replication is a major design decision in Grid infrastructure. Strategies used in multidatabase systems are also not suitable for virtual Grid environments as they focus on a small set of databases and the design philosophy is a combination of top-down and bottom-up strategies. For example, an organization may want to communicate between its two databases located at two different locations. The two sites may have been designed and developed independently. But when the top management decides to communicate between the two databases, they can be combined with multidatabase techniques, and thus they do not need any virtualization techniques. This scenario is different from a typical Grid application, where the databases are in completely different administrative domains and virtualization of resources is a necessity. Three major strategies are discussed for atomic commitment of distributed transaction in heterogeneous database environment: (1) redo, (2) retry, and (3) compensate.

Since all sites may not support the prepare-to-commit state, even if a global distributed transaction decides to commit, some local subtransaction may decide to abort because of a local conflict (as sites are autonomous) while others may decide to commit. Hence, those subtransactions that decided to abort must *redo* the write operation to reach a consistent global decision. This strategy imposes a requirement that all local schedulers should be at least cascade-less. The *redo* strategy also imposes certain restrictions on data access for transactions—for instance, global transactions may read local data items but cannot update them. These restrictions limit the applicability of the redo approach in the Grid environment.

Another approach for dealing with the above problem is the *retry* approach. In this approach, the whole subtransaction is retried rather than *redo*ing only the write operations. The inherent limitation of this approach is that the subtransaction must be *retriable*. For example, if a subtransaction fails because of insufficient funds in a fund-transfer application, the failed transaction may keep on retrying forever. Also, a subtransaction is retriable only if the top layer of the multidatabase system has saved the execution state of the aborted subtransaction, which is not the case in Grids. Again, these limitations make the retry approach unsuitable for a Grid database.

If the global decision is to abort and any local subtransaction decides to commit, then *compensating* transactions can be executed to semantically undo the effects of the committed subtransaction. Since the results may have been externalized to other transactions, the resulting state may not be the same as if the transaction in question never executed, but will be semantically equivalent to it. Certain transactions, such as firing of a missile, can be noncompensatable. This approach is most suitable for a Grid infrastructure, as the decision of an individual site is independent of other sites. Although compensation may lead to cascading aborts, considering the architectural requirement of Grids this seems unavoidable.

10.9 REPLICA SYNCHRONIZATION PROTOCOLS

Grid databases store a large volume of data at geographically distributed sites. The large amount of data and its worldwide distribution make data management a challenging task. There is a wide range of scientific experimentations, such as astronomical analysis, high-energy physics (HEP), weather forecasting, earth simulation, etc., that will require gathering a huge amount of data. These experiments generate, gather, process, and store huge volume of data everyday. Particle physics experiments, for example, *Babar*, may need to store up to 500 GB of data each day and are among the world's largest databases. Applications will soon be managing petabytes of data. The data will be accessed by institutions and scientists around the globe. For instance, the particle physics experiment is a collaboration of 75 institutions in 10 countries. For easy access to the data and for performance improvement, the data need to be replicated at multiple sites. Having replicas of data items at various sites also improves the system's availability. Thus the replication of data has two major goals: (i) increasing availability and (ii) improving performance. Since the data is available at multiple sites, it is likely that a transaction may find a copy locally or at a site close to it.

If the replica protocols are not designed carefully, the purpose of replication may be defeated because of the overhead of maintaining multiple copies. Another issue concerning replicated data is maintaining the correctness of data. The replicated data remains transparent to the user, and the database management system should ensure the data consistency among replicas. The user has a one-copy view of the database, and thus the correctness criterion is known as 1-copy serializability (1SR). Various replica synchronization protocols such as write-all, write-all-available, primary copy, etc. have been proposed.

The problem of replica synchronization becomes significant especially when the data can be modified. Recent research and prototype proposals for Grids deal with replication of read-only files and do not address the replica synchronization problem. Looking at the critical nature of the applications discussed above, replica synchronization becomes a challenging task.

10.9.1 Network Partitioning

Network partitioning is a phenomenon that prevents communication between two sets of sites in distributed architecture. Communication failures are the major reason for network partitioning. Broadly, the network partitioning can be of two types, depending on the communicating set of sites: (i) simple partitioning and (ii) multiple partitioning. If the network is divided into two compartments, then it is known as simple partitioning, and if there are more than two compartments, then it is called multiple partitioning.

Definition 10.6 (Network Partitioning): Two set of operational sites, $P_1 = \{A_1, A_2, \ldots, A_n\}$ and $P_2 = \{B_1, B_2, \ldots, B_n\}$, are partitioned if the following two conditions hold:

Condition 1: $\forall A_i \in P_1$ can communicate with $\forall A_i \in P_1$.

Condition 2: $\exists A_i \in P_1$ cannot communicate with $\exists B_i \in P_2$ because of communication failure.

In read-only queries, network partitioning does not have much impact because the data is not modified by the queries. But network partitioning has a greater impact in the presence of write transactions because transactions can access replicas in one partition and update them independently while other partitions are not aware of the update. Thus network partitioning may lead to inconsistent data values, and replica synchronization protocols must be equipped to address network partitioning issues. The following section discusses some of the common replica synchronization protocols.

10.9.2 Replica Synchronization Protocols

Replica synchronization protocols can broadly be classified as (*i*) pessimistic and (*ii*) optimistic, also known as *eager* and *lazy* protocols, respectively. Pessimistic protocols are *eager* to update all replicated copies in a synchronous way and avoid any inconsistency in the replicated system. The pessimistic approach ensures serializable execution (and thus is 1SR) but reduces the performance of write transactions by increasing the number of updates. The availability of the system is restricted in the pessimistic approach in case of any site failure because all replicas are not available for update. The read-one-write-all (ROWA) approach is an example of the pessimistic replica control protocol.

On the other hand, an optimistic protocol allows any transaction to be executed in any partition. The optimistic replica control protocol increases the availability, but has a serious limitation in that it jeopardizes the consistency of the replicated data. Thus the replica control protocols are a trade-off between maintaining the consistency of data and increasing availability and performance of the replicated system. Below we discuss some of the replica control protocols.

Read-One-Write-All (ROWA)

The ROWA protocol is the simplest of all replica control protocols. The read operation may be executed at any arbitrary copy, but the write operation has to be executed on all replicated copies of the data. In this scenario, if any data item fails, then any transaction that writes the data item cannot be executed and must wait for the replicated site to recover. Thus, in the presence of any site failure, the ROWA protocol limits the availability of the replicated system, which may be unsatisfactory for many real-time applications.

ROWA-Available (ROWA-A)

ROWA-A was proposed to provide more flexibility to the ROWA algorithm in the presence of failures. The read operation of ROWA-A can be performed similar to ROWA, that is, on any replicated copy. But to provide more flexibility, write operations are performed only on the *available* copies, and it ignores any failed replicas. ROWA-A solves the availability problem, but the correctness of the data may have been compromised. After the failed site has recovered, it stores the stale value of the data. Any transaction reading that replica reads an out-of-date copy of the replica, and thus the resulting execution is not 1SR. Deploying ROWA or ROWA-A in a Grid infrastructure is thus an impractical proposition.

Primary Copy

This approach assigns one copy of the replicated data as a primary copy. All read and write requests are redirected to the primary site. This approach works well only if site failures are distinguishable from the network failure. In the case of network partitioning, only the partition having the primary copy can execute. In case of failure of the primary site, no request can be processed. Dependence on a single site in a global Grid environment is not a feasible idea. Most importantly, the primary copy protocol violates the autonomy requirement of Grid databases since it depends on other sites to process the request.

Quorum-Based Protocols

Quorum- or voting-based protocols have been of interest to the replication community because of their flexibility. Every copy of the replica is assigned a nonnegative vote (quorum). Read and write thresholds are defined for each data item. The sum of read and write thresholds as well as twice the write threshold must be greater than the total vote assigned to the data. These two conditions ensure that there is always a nonnull intersection between any two quorum sets. The nonnull set between read quorum and write quorum guarantees at least one latest copy of the data item in any set of sites. A timestamp or a version number is used to determine the latest copy of the data item. This constraint guarantees that in case of site failure or network partitioning, a transaction will never read stale data. The nonnull intersection between two write quorums ensures that no two writes can happen in parallel. All transactions must collect a read (write) quorum to read (write) any data item. A read (write) quorum of a data is any set of copies of the data with a weight of at least read (write) threshold. Quorum-based protocols maintain the consistency of data despite operating only on a subset of the replicated database. For any data item it is assumed:

Q = Total number of votes (maximum quorum) = Number of sites in the
replicated system (assuming each site has equal weight)

Q_R and Q_W = Read and write quorum, respectively

To read an item a transaction must collect a quorum of at least Q_R votes, and to write it must collect a quorum of Q_W votes. The overlapping of the read and write quorums ensures that a reading transaction will get at least one up-to-date copy of the replica. The quorums must satisfy the following two threshold constraints:

(i) $Q_R + Q_W > Q$

(ii) $Q_W + Q_W > Q$

A quorum-based replicated system may continue to operate even in the case of site or communication failure if it is successful in obtaining the quorum for the data item. This makes quorum-based protocols promising candidates for replica control in Grid databases. However, a challenging problem in implementing the traditional quorum-based protocols in Grid databases is that they are designed for homogeneous database systems, and therefore cannot be implemented in Grids as they are. Thus these protocols need to be revisited before being implemented in the Grid infrastructure.

In a homogeneous system, protocols depend on communication between distributed sites. Grid databases will, most of the time, be heterogeneous and autonomous, thereby making communication between replicated sites difficult and sometimes even impossible. Unlike Grids, synchronization between sites is easy to achieve in homogeneous systems. Typically, replication strategies for homogeneous systems leverage the fact that they can use the prepared state of the transaction at all replicated sites. Furthermore, the quorum values assigned in homogeneous systems are static, which limits the implementation of quorum-based protocols in Grids, especially in the presence of multiple network partitioning.

Although various semantic approaches like log-transformations and general quorum consensus have been proposed, they depend on the semantics of the application and are not general-purpose protocols. Other approaches like epidemic and independent approaches increase the availability of data, but only at the cost of inconsistency. Only general-purpose replica synchronization protocols, which ensure that schedules are 1SR, are discussed in this book.

10.10   SUMMARY

In this chapter, an introduction of three protocols of traditional distributed database systems is presented, which includes (*i*) concurrency control protocols, (*ii*) atomic commitment protocols, and (*iii*) replica synchronization protocols. In view of the evolving Grid infrastructure, these protocols are discussed in detail in the following chapters. These protocols are crucial in maintaining the correctness of the distributed data. Figure 10.9 shows the structure of the rest of Part IV of this book focusing on the ACID properties and replication in Grid databases. The advantage of replication in reducing aborts is also demonstrated.

10.11   BIBLIOGRAPHICAL NOTES

Two of the early works on parallel transaction management are by Weikum and Hasse (*VLDB J* 1993), who introduced parallelism in multilevel transactions, and Burger et al. (*BNCOD* 1994), who presented branching transactions for parallel

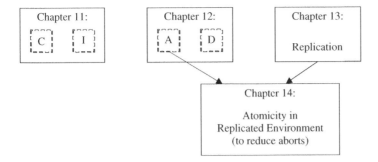

Figure 10.9   General framework of Grid transaction management

database systems. Machado and Collet (*DASFAA* 1997) described a parallel execution model for database transactions, and Wang et al. (*Parallel Computing* 1997) focused on concurrency control in parallel transaction processing. After the turn of the century, Brayner (*DEXA* 2001) presented lock downgrading for intertransaction parallelism, and Colohan et al. (*VLDB* 2005) focused on intratransaction parallelism.

In the area of Grid transaction management, Qi et al. (*Concurrency and Computation* 2006) presented a membrane calculus, a formal method for grid transactions, whereas Tang et al. (2004) used a Petri-net based coordination for grid transactions. Leymann and Güntzel (2003) concentrated on the business process.

10.12 EXERCISES

10.1. Outline the main differences between *distributed databases* and *parallel databases*.

10.2. Outline the main differences between *distributed databases* and *multidatabase systems*.

10.3. Discuss the suitability of parallel databases, distributed databases, and multidatabase systems in the Grids.

10.4. Describe the following terminologies:

    a. Transaction

    b. Schedule or history

    c. Serial history

    d. Serializable history

    e. Serialization graph

10.5. Give an example of a *dirty read problem* in transaction management.

10.6. Describe the ACID properties of a transaction in a centralized environment. Illustrate your answer with examples.

10.7. Table 10.1 states that the Grid databases adopt a top-down design philosophy. Describe this property and highlight the primary difference between a top-down approach in Grid databases and a bottom-up approach in distributed databases.

10.8. Compare and contrast two-phase commit (2PC) and three-phase commit (3PC) in a homogenous distributed database system.

10.9. Explain the concept of network partitioning.

10.10. Discuss why ROWA and ROWA-Available are impractical for Grid databases.

Chapter 11

Grid Concurrency Control

The concurrency control protocol helps to maintain the consistency of data in a database. It helps to achieve the "C" and "I" of ACID properties. *Serializability* is the most widely accepted correctness criterion in any database management system (DBMS). Protocols implemented to achieve serializability may depend on the database architecture. For example, the serializability theory for a centralized DBMS will be different from that for a distributed DBMS. The Grid database is also a distributed database, but because of architectural differences, it cannot implement the same concurrency control protocols.

This chapter describes the concurrency control algorithm for Grid databases. Before discussing the concurrency control protocol, it is necessary to provide the working environment of a Grid database and the motivation behind the work. Section 11.1 presents the general working environment of the Grid database. Section 11.2 discusses the motivation of addressing the concurrency issue in Grid databases, followed by the details of the Grid concurrency control protocol in Section 11.3. Section 11.4 shows the correctness of the protocol, whereas Section 11.5 discusses some features of the concurrency control protocol.

11.1 A GRID DATABASE ENVIRONMENT

Data is geographically distributed in Grid databases. A typical working of databases in Grid architecture is shown in Figure 11.1. For simplicity, a system with only three database sites is shown. Without loss of generality, originator sites (where transactions are submitted) and participant sites (where transactions are executed) are also distinguished. The same database site may act as an originator for some transactions, and at the same time it may act as a participant

High-Performance Parallel Database Processing and Grid Databases,
by David Taniar, Clement Leung, Wenny Rahayu, and Sushant Goel
Copyright © 2008 John Wiley & Sons, Inc.

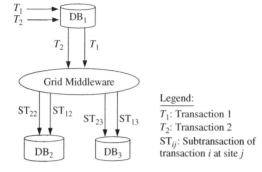

Legend:

T_1: Transaction 1

T_2: Transaction 2

ST_{ij}: Subtransaction of transaction i at site j

Figure 11.1 Distributed database systems communicating with Grid middleware

for some other transactions. The originator is sometimes also referred to as the coordinator.

Figure 11.1 shows three geographically distributed database sites DB_1, DB_2 and DB_3 connected via the Grid middleware. Assume that two transactions, T_1 and T_2, are submitted to DB_1. Both transactions also need to access data from the other two databases, DB_2 and DB_3. Hence, DB_1 is the originator or coordinator, and both DB_2 and DB_3 act as participants. DB_1 forwards the request of T_1 and T_2 to the Grid middleware. Grid middleware, with the help of metadata service, forms subtransactions of each transaction and submits them to respective participants. The transaction identifier and site identifier are suffixed to represent subtransactions; for example, a subtransaction of transaction 1 executing at site 2 will be denoted as ST_{12}. Since both transactions need to access DB_2 and DB_3, the subtransactions would be (ST_{12} and ST_{13}) and (ST_{22} and ST_{23}) for T_1 and T_2, respectively.

Data access must be synchronized to maintain the correctness of the data. Generally, global management of data with the help of global lock table or global logs cannot be implemented in a Grid database, unlike traditional distributed DBMS. Another challenge in maintaining consistency is the heterogeneity of concurrency control protocols implemented by different participants. For example, one site might use the locking protocol for concurrency control, while another site might use an optimistic concurrency control protocol. This makes maintaining the consistency of data in Grid databases a difficult task. Since sites in Grid databases are autonomous and the design process is top-down, heterogeneity among sites is unavoidable. The following example shows that, because of heterogeneity and the absence of a global management layer, it becomes impossible to maintain consistent data by using traditional concurrency control protocols.

11.2 AN EXAMPLE

Consider the sites from Figure 11.1; the following example shows how the use of traditional concurrency control protocols in a Grid environment may potentially corrupt the data. Say that four data objects (for simplicity sake only four items are considered), O_1, O_2, O_3, and O_4, are stored in two databases, DB_2 and DB_3, with following distribution:

$$DB_2 = O_1 \text{ and } O_2$$
$$DB_3 = O_3 \text{ and } O_4$$

Now, consider two transactions submitted to the database DB_1, as shown below.

$$T_1 = r_1(O_1)r_1(O_2)w_1(O_3)w_1(O_1)C_1$$
$$T_2 = r_2(O_1)r_2(O_3)w_2(O_4)w_2(O_1)C_2$$

DB_1 submits T_1 and T_2 to Grid middleware. The metadata service of the Grid middleware locates data objects to be accessed by the transaction and thus helps in forming subtransactions of T_1 and T_2. The following subtransactions are obtained for T_1:

$$ST_{12} = r_{12}(O_1)r_{12}(O_2)w_{12}(O_1)C_{12} \tag{11.1}$$
$$ST_{13} = w_{13}(O_3)C_{13} \tag{11.2}$$

The following subtransactions are obtained for T_2:

$$ST_{22} = r_{22}(O_1)w_{22}(O_1)C_{22} \tag{11.3}$$
$$ST_{23} = r_{23}(O_3)w_{23}(O_4)C_{23} \tag{11.4}$$

The subtransactions can then be submitted to their respective database sites, that is, (ST_{12} and ST_{22}) are submitted to DB_2 and (ST_{13} and ST_{23}) are submitted to DB_3. All participants are autonomous, and no global information is available to any participant. Thus participants have to schedule subtransactions locally and independently. Say that DB_2 produces the following history (H_2):

$$H_2 = r_{12}(O_1)r_{12}(O_2)w_{12}(O_1)C_{12}r_{22}(O_1)w_{22}(O_1)C_{22} \tag{11.5}$$

and DB_3 produces the following history (H_3):

$$H_3 = r_{23}(O_3)w_{23}(O_4)C_{23}w_{13}(O_3)C_{13} \tag{11.6}$$

Assume that each individual local database site implements a serializable scheduler. H_2 and H_3 both are locally serializable with the following serialization order:

> Serialization order of $H_2 : T_1 \prec T_2$
>
> (transaction 1 executes before transaction 2)
>
> Serialization order of $H_3 : T_2 \prec T_1$
>
> (transaction 2 executes before transaction 1)

In the absence of a global management system, the execution of H_2 and H_3 is possible. Although H_2 and H_3 are serializable (serial in the above example) at local sites, execution of both histories simultaneously is undesirable because the combined effect of both histories produces a cycle in the serialization graph. The serialization graph has the following execution order of transactions, which produces a cycle: $T_1 \rightarrow T_2 \rightarrow T_1$. Traditional distributed databases handle this problem by implementing a global management system, which stores global information, such as global lock tables and logs. If global information on transactions is available, it is easy to avoid execution of H_2 and H_3 and thus avoid formation of a cycle in the serialization graph. But, because of their service-oriented nature, heterogeneity, autonomy, and security requirements, Grid databases cannot store global information. Thus maintaining consistency of data in the absence of a global management layer is a challenging job.

11.3 GRID CONCURRENCY CONTROL

The example mentioned above shows that even if an individual site produces serial (or serializable) histories, because of the unavailability of a global management system in the Grid database, the overall execution may produce an incorrect serialization order. In this section, a *grid concurrency control* (GCC) protocol is used to maintain the correct serialization order of transactions in Grid databases, that is, in the absence of a global management layer.

11.3.1 Basic Functions Required by GCC

The following are some of the functions used by the GCC protocol to ensure the correct interleaving of transactions. These functions are helpful in forming subtransactions of global transactions, finding active transactions at any database site, and appending a unique timestamp to all subtransactions of any transaction. Some of the functions need the assistance of the Grid middleware and some do not. These functions are explained below:

(1) *DB_accessed(T_i)*: This function takes the global transaction as argument. When a global transaction is submitted to any database, the transaction is redirected to the Grid middleware. The data location service of the Grid middleware locates other database sites to be accessed by the global transaction. The function returns the *set of databases* where the subtransactions are submitted.

(2) *split_trans(T_i)*: This function takes the global transaction as argument and returns the *set of subtransactions*. Subtransactions are formed based on data accessed by the global transaction. Each database site where the global transaction needs to access the data will have one subtransaction.

(3) *active_trans(DB)*: This function returns the *set of global transactions* having any subtransaction running in the database. The database, where the active global transactions have to be found, is supplied as an argument to the function. The local database's log file is used to collect this information.

(4) *cardinality(Any_set)*: This function takes any set, e.g., a set of databases or a set of subtransactions, as argument and returns the number of elements in the set.

(5) *append_TS(ST$_{ij}$)*: All subtransactions of a global transaction are appended with a unique timestamp before being submitted to their respective sites. The subtransaction is supplied as an argument to the function, which appends the timestamp generated by the Grid middleware. Subtransactions belonging to the same global transaction will have the same timestamp value.

11.3.2 Grid Serializability Theorem

The traditional serializability theory, for example, conflict serializability, is not sufficient to ensure data consistency (the "C" of ACID properties) and transaction isolation (the "I" of ACID properties) in Grid databases. The Grid serializability theorem is needed to ensure correct interleaving of the concurrent transactions in the absence of a global management layer.

Broadly, global transactions are classified in two categories: (*a*) having only a single subtransaction and (*b*) having more than one subtransaction. Global transactions with only one subtransaction do not pose any threat to Grid serializability because only a local conflict may arise, which is taken care of by the local scheduler. *Total-order* is defined below, before we proceed with the Grid serializability theorem.

Definition 11.1 (Total-order): Two global transactions T_i and T_j are in total-order if $\exists p \in T_i$ precedes execution of $\exists q \in T_j$ at any database site then $\forall p \in T_i$ must precede execution of $\forall q \in T_j$ at all database sites where they both appear.

The Grid serialization theorem follows the steps of traditional serializability theorems to maintain uniformity of the proposed theorem in keeping with existing literature. In traditional serializability theory, serial history is considered correct. On the same grounds, *Grid-serial* history is considered correct in Grid architecture.

Definition 11.2 (Grid-serial history): A history in Grid architecture is considered correct if it is Grid-serial. A history is considered Grid-serial if:

(1) Every individual database produces a serial history.

(2) Any global transaction having more than one subtransaction, i.e., accessing more than one database, executes the transaction according to total-order.

Condition 1 of definition 11.2 does not allow interleaving of operations of the local transactions. This is a very strict criterion. If the consistency of data is not compromised, interleaving of the local transactions is perfectly valid. Hence, a more practical approach for maintaining correctness of data is to use a history that interleaves operations from different transactions.

Definition 11.3 (Grid-serializable history): A history in Grid architecture is Grid-serializable iff it is equivalent ($\equiv$) to Grid-serial history.

Grid-serializability is analyzed by the *Grid-serializability graph*. If the graph is acyclic, the history is known as a Grid-serializable history. The graph shows only the committed projection of transactions.

Definition 11.4 (Grid-serializability graph): At any given instance, histories of individual database sites can be represented by a directed graph defined by the ordered three (T_l, T_g, A). The graph created is referred to as a Grid-serializability graph. Elements of the ordered three are defined below:

(1) T_l is the set of local transactions forming the nodes of the directed graph.

(2) T_g is the set of global transactions having more than one *subtransaction* forming the nodes of the directed graph.

(3) A is the set of arcs representing the ordering of two conflicting transaction in any database where at least one of the two transactions is a global transaction.

Condition 1 in definition 11.4 considers local transactions in the Grid-serializability graph. Condition 2 considers only those global transactions having more than one subtransaction. Since transactions with one subtransaction do not pose any threat to the concurrency control protocol, they will be ignored in any subsequent discussion, unless otherwise mentioned. Condition 3 shows the arc between conflicting transactions. The local concurrency control protocol can resolve conflicts among local transactions, but is unable to resolve conflicts involving global transactions. Hence, a Grid-serializability graph considers those conflicts where at least one transaction is a global transaction.

The major difference between the Grid-serializability graph and the serializability graphs of a traditional distributed database (and multidatabase) is the location where the graph is stored. Traditional serializability graphs are stored in the global management system, but because of autonomy restrictions and the absence of the global management layer, the Grid-serializability graphs are stored in individual database sites.

The following types of conflicts among transactions are possible in the Grid database environment:

(1) Conflict between global transactions (global-global conflict);

(2) Conflict between global transaction and local transaction (global-local conflict); and

(3) Conflict between local transactions (local-local conflict).

The local scheduler resolves the conflict between local transactions and hence does not need special attention. But local schedulers cannot resolve conflicts involving global transactions. An acyclic Grid-serializability graph is used to resolve global-local conflict, and total-order is used to resolve global-global conflict, based on the definition of Grid-serializability graph and total-order.

Theorem 11.1 (Grid-serializability theorem): A schedule in the Grid database is Grid-serializable iff the Grid-serializability graph is acyclic at all participating database sites and is in total-order.

Proof (if part): Suppose the committed projection $(C(H))$ of the history (H) at any site has $\{T_1, T_2, \ldots, T_n\}$ transactions. Transactions can be global or local. $T_1, T_2, \ldots, T_n$ are all represented as nodes in the Grid-serializability graph. Since Grid-serializability graph is acyclic it can be topologically sorted. A topological sort in a graph is a sequence of (all) the nodes of the graph, such that if T_1 appears before T_2 in a sequence, there is no path from T_2 to T_1. Let $T_{i1}, T_{i2}, \ldots, T_{in}$ be a topological sort of the Grid-serializability graph, where $i_1, i_2, \ldots, i_n$ is permutation of $1, 2, \ldots, n$. Let the corresponding Grid-serial history be $T_{i1}, T_{i2}, \ldots, T_{in}$. We need to prove the equivalence $(\equiv)$ of committed projection $(C(H))$ and the Grid-serial history. To prove this, let $p \in T_i$ and $q \in T_j$, where $T_i, T_j \in C(H)$. Suppose p and q are conflicting operations, and $p \prec_H q$. Two possibilities exist with respect to location of conflicting operations: (i) both can reside in the same site or (ii) different sites. If the conflicting operations are in the same site, it will be reflected in the Grid-serializability graph, but it is difficult to represent conflicting operations (and thus conflicting transactions) in the Grid-serializability graph if they reside in different sites. Thus total-order is implemented to handle conflicting operations residing in different sites.

An arc exists in the Grid-serializability graph from T_i to T_j if the conflicting transactions are in same site. And transactions are in total-order if the conflicting transactions are in different sites. Therefore in any topological sort of serializability graph, at all sites, T_i must precede T_j. Thus in Grid-serial history all operations of T_i appear before any operation of T_j at all participating sites. Hence, any two conflicting operations are ordered in the same way, at all sites, in $C(H)$ as in the Grid-serial history. Thus $C(H) \equiv Grid - serial$, and from definition 11.3 H is Grid-serializable, as was to be proved.

Proof (only if part): Given that the history (H) is Grid-serializable, it will be sufficient to show that Grid-serializable graph must be acyclic at all sites and must be in total-order. Let H_s be a Grid-serial history equivalent to commit projection of H. Consider that an arc, $T_i \rightarrow T_j$, exists in the Grid-serializability graph at any site. This implies that there exist two conflicting operations $p \in T_i$ and $q \in T_j$ such that $p \prec_H q$ at some database site DB_i. Since $C(H) \equiv Grid - serial$ history, $p \prec q$ in Grid-serial history also, which implies $T_i \prec T_j$ in Grid-serial history. Thus if T_i precedes T_j in Grid-serializable graph, then T_i precedes T_j in Grid-serial history as well. Following are two possible cases which will be discussed separately:

(1) *Cyclic Grid-serializability graph*: Suppose there is a cycle in the Grid-serializability graph. Without loss of generality let the cycle be $T_i \rightarrow \ldots \rightarrow$

$T_n \rightarrow \ldots \rightarrow T_i$. With the above cycle, in Grid-serial history, it could be deduced that T_i precedes and conflicts with T_n, which in turn precedes and conflicts with T_i. This means T_i appears before itself in Grid-serial history, which is an absurdity. This also implies that the local scheduler is generating incorrect schedules, a contradiction of the earlier assumption. Thus the Grid-serializability graph cannot contain any cycle.

(2) *Absence of Total-order*: Suppose the transactions are not in total order. Without loss of generality, let $T_i \rightarrow T_j$ in site 1 and $T_j \rightarrow T_i$ in site 2. With the above precedence order of transactions at two different sites, it could be deduced that T_i precedes itself in the Grid-serial history (from the global perspective), which is an absurdity. Thus all participating sites in Grid database must follow total-order.

Thus, while the Grid-serializability graph resolves the global-local conflict and the global-global conflict for transactions (or subtransactions) executing in the same database site, the total-order resolves the conflict between two global transactions having subtransactions executing in different database sites.

EXAMPLE

In addition to global transactions in the example shown earlier in this chapter, consider additional local transactions as follows:

Local transaction at DB_2, $LT_{12} = lr_{12}(O_1)lw_{12}(O_2)lC_{12}$ (LT_{12} is read as local transaction 1 at database site DB_2)

Local transaction at DB_3, $LT_{13} = lw_{13}(O_3)lC_{13}$

Consider the following modified histories:

$$H_2 = lr_{12}(O_1)r_{12}(O_1)r_{12}(O_2)w_{12}(O_1)C_{12}r_{22}(O_1)w_{22}(O_1)lw_{12}(O_2)C_{22}lC_{12}$$
$$H_3 = r_{23}(O_3)w_{23}(O_4)lw_{13}(O_3)C_{23}w_{13}(O_3)C_{13}lC_{13}$$

Figure 11.2 shows the Grid-serializability graph at sites DB_2 and DB_3. The three possible types of conflicts are discussed below.

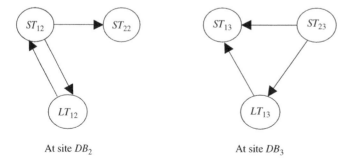

At site DB_2 At site DB_3

Figure 11.2   Grid serializability graph constructed from Grid serializability theorem

(1) *Global-global conflict*: At site DB_2, an arc exists from global subtransaction ST_{12} to ST_{22}, i.e., the arc is from global transaction T_1 to T_2. In site DB_3, the arc is from global subtransaction ST_{23} to ST_{13}, i.e., the arc is from global transaction T_2 to T_1. Thus transactions T_1 to T_2 form a cycle at distributed sites. In traditional distributed database systems, the arc can be easily detected by the use of a global management system. But in the absence of the global layer, it is impossible to detect the cycle being created at distributed sites. The total-order used in the Grid serializability theorem avoids formation of cycles at distributed sites.

(2) *Global-local conflict*: Since global-local conflicts can only occur in single sites, they can be resolved by the Grid-serializability graph. For example, at site DB_2, the conflict between the subtransaction of the global transaction, T_2, and the local transaction, LT_1, is represented by the cycle. The cycle can be identified and resolved by the local DBMS.

(3) *Local-local conflict*: Conflicts between local transactions can be resolved with the traditional DBMS, and do not need special attention.

11.3.3 Grid Concurrency Control Protocol

The Grid concurrency control (GCC) criterion is used to maintain the correctness of data (the "C" and "I" of ACID properties), while strictly following the autonomy and heterogeneity limitations of Grid architecture. In this section, the GCC protocol is described that is used as a concurrency control protocol for Grid databases.

The GCC protocol has two phases: (*i*) the submission phase and (*ii*) the termination phase. The site where the transaction is submitted is known as the *originator*. If the transaction needs to access data other than the originator site, it uses the metadata service of the Grid middleware to form multiple subtransactions. The split_trans(T_i) function is used to generate multiple subtransactions from the global transaction (T_i). Subtransactions are then submitted to their respective *participating sites*. The middleware appends a unique timestamp to each subtransaction before submitting them to the corresponding databases. Subtransactions at the local databases are executed in total-order. The timestamp attached to the subtransaction is helpful in enforcing the total-order. The scheduler does not distinguish between a local transaction and a subtransaction of a global transaction executing in the same database site. Global transactions with only one subtransaction need not follow total-order, as they cannot conflict with other global transactions at more than one site simultaneously (unlike the example presented above in this chapter).

Submission Phase

The submission phase of the GCC protocol has the following steps:

(1) As soon as the transaction arrives at any database site, it checks whether data from multiple sites is to be accessed. If the transaction needs to access data only from the originator, it acts as a local transaction. But if the transaction needs to access data from multiple data sites, it is submitted to the metadata service of the Grid middleware and is treated as a global transaction. The split_trans(T_i) function is used to form multiple subtransactions.

(2) The global transactions currently executing are added to a set, which stores all active transactions. The set of active transactions is represented as **Active_Trans**.

(3) The middleware appends a timestamp to every subtransaction of the global transaction before submitting it to the corresponding database.

(4) If there are two active global transactions that access more than one database site simultaneously, this creates a potential threat that local databases may schedule the subtransactions in conflicting order. The subtransactions are therefore executed strictly according to the timestamp attached to the subtransaction. Total-order is achieved by executing the conflicting subtransactions according to the timestamp.

(5) When all subtransactions of any global transaction complete the execution at all the sites, the transaction terminates and is removed from **Active_Trans** set (see details in *Termination Phase*).
Note: Active_trans and *Active_Trans(DB)* are different. The former is the set of currently active global transactions, and the latter is a function that takes the database site as an argument and returns the set of active transactions running at that database site.

Explanation of Figure 11.3. Line 1 of Figure 11.3 checks the number of subtransactions of the submitted transaction. If there is only a single subtransaction, then the global transaction can start executing immediately. The global transaction is added in the active set (line 2) and is submitted immediately to the database for execution (line 3). If the global transaction has more than one subtransaction, that is, the transaction accesses more than one database site, then total-order must be followed. Hence, the timestamp must be appended to all subtransactions of the global transaction. The global transaction is added in the active set (line 4). Global transactions having only one subtransaction are filtered out from the active set, and the new set (**Conflict_Active_trans**) of the conflicting global transactions is formed (line 5). Timestamps are then appended to all subtransactions of the global transaction (line 6 and line 7). If the global transaction being submitted conflicts with other active global transactions, it must be submitted to the participant site's queue to be executed in total-order. Conflict of a submitted global transaction (T_i) with some other active global transaction (T_j) (having more than one active subtransaction) is checked in line 8. If two global transactions having more than one active subtransaction (i.e., global-global conflict) exist, then the global transaction is added in all participating sites' active transaction sets (*Active_Trans(DB_i)*) (line 13) and the subtransactions are submitted to the participants' queue (line 14), to be strictly executed according to the total-order. If the submitted global transaction does not conflict with any other active global transaction (i.e., line 8 is true), then the global transaction is added in the active transaction set of all the participant sites (line 10), and the subtransaction is immediately submitted for scheduling (line 11).

Global transactions are said to be conflicting if two global transactions have more than two active subtransactions executing in different participating sites

---

Algorithm: Grid Concurrency Control Algorithm for the
submission phase

---

input T_i: Transaction
var **Active_trans**: set of active transactions
var **Conflict_Active_trans**: set of active transactions
that conflict with global transaction being submitted
var **Database_accessed** [T_i]: database sites being accessed
by global transaction T_i
Generate timestamp ts: unique timestamp is generated

> $Split\_trans(T_i)$
> **Database_accessed** [T_i] $\leftarrow$ $DB\_accessed(T_i)$
> 1. if $Cardinality($**Database_accessed** [T_i]$) = 1$
> 2. $Active\_Trans(DB_i) \leftarrow Active\_Trans(DB_i) \cup T_i$
>   // T_i has only one subtransaction
> 3.   **submit** subtransaction to DB_i
>   else
> 4.   **Active_trans** $\leftarrow \bigcup Active\_Trans(DB_i)$
> 5.   **Conflict_Active_trans** $\leftarrow \{T_i \mid T_i \in$ **Active_trans** $\wedge$
> $Cardinality(DB\_accessed(T_j)) > 1\}$
> 6.   for each subtransaction of T_i
> 7. $Append\_TS(Subtransaction)$
> 8.   if $Cardinality($**Database_accessed**$[T_i] \cap (\bigcup_{T \in Conflict\_Active\_trans}$
> $DB\_accessed(T_j)) \leq 1)$
> 9.   **for each** $DB_i \in$ **Database_accessed** [T_i]
> 10. $Active\_Trans(DB_i) \leftarrow Active\_Trans(DB_i) \cup T_i$
> 11.   **submit** subtransaction to DB_i
>   // Subtransaction executes immediately
>   else
> 12.   for each $DB_i \in$ **Database_accessed** [T_i]
> 13. $Active\_Trans(DB_i) \leftarrow Active\_Trans(DB_i) \cup T_i$
> 14.   submit subtransaction to participant's DB
> $Queue$
>   // Signifies that subtransaction must follow
>   // total-order

Figure 11.3   Grid concurrency control algorithm for submission phase

simultaneously. This is different from the definition of conflicting transaction in definition 11.2. The use of these two terms will be easily distinguished by the context.

Termination Phase

The global transaction is considered active until a response from all subtransactions is received. Because of the atomicity property of the transaction, the global transaction cannot reach a final decision (i.e., commit or abort) until it has received a decision from all the subtransactions. The steps of the transaction termination phase are explained as follows:

(1) When any subtransaction finishes execution, the originator site of the global transaction is informed.

(2) Active transactions, conflicting active transactions, and databases accessed (by the global transaction) set are adjusted to reflect the recent changes due to completion of the subtransaction.

(3) The site checks whether a completed subtransaction is the last subtransaction of the global transaction to terminate.

(3a) If the subtransaction is not the last to terminate, then the subtransactions waiting in the queue cannot be scheduled.

(3b) If the subtransaction is the last subtransaction of the global transaction to terminate, then other conflicting subtransactions can be scheduled. The subtransactions from the queue then follow the normal submission steps as discussed in Figure 11.3.

Explanation of Figure 11.4. The originator site of the global transaction is informed after any subtransaction completes execution. The global transaction,

---

Algorithm: Grid Concurrency Control Algorithm for termination phase

---

input ST: subtransaction of T_i at a site that completes execution

1. **Active_trans** = (**Active_trans** - T_i)
// removes the global transaction from active set of the site
2. **Conflict_Active_trans** = (**Conflict_Active_trans** - T_i)
3. **Database_accessed** [T_i] = (**Database_accessed** [T_i] - DB$_k$)
// the database where the subtransaction committed is removed from the set of database being accessed by the global transaction
4. if(**Database_accessed** [T_i]) = ϕ
   //subtransaction was last cohort of GT T_i
5.   resubmit subtransactions from queue for execution
      //from Figure 11.3
   else
6.   resubmit subtransactions to the queue
      // same as line (14) Figure 11.3

Figure 11.4   Grid concurrency control algorithm for termination phase

T_i, is then removed from the active transaction's set (line 1). This follows the earlier assumption that a global transaction can have only one subtransaction running at any site at any particular time. The conflicting active transaction's set is also adjusted accordingly (line 2). The database site where the subtransaction is completed is removed from the database accessed set (line 3). If the completed subtransaction is the last subtransaction of the global transaction, that is, the database accessed set is empty (line 4), other waiting subtransactions in the queue are submitted for execution (line 5). The normal transaction submission procedure from Figure 11.3 is followed thereafter. If the completed subtransaction is not the last subtransaction, then the queue is unaffected (line 6).

11.3.4 Revisiting the Earlier Example

Taking the same scenario as the earlier example, consider that global transactions T_1 and T_2 are submitted in quick succession. Since both the transactions need to access data from more than one site, they are forwarded to the middleware to check the metadata service and form subtransactions (eq. 11.1, 11.2, 11.3, and 11.4) (step 1 of the GCC protocol). As data from multiple sites are to be accessed, the transactions are added in the **Active_Trans** set (step 2 of the GCC protocol). Since subtransactions (eq. 11.1 and 11.2) belong to the same global transaction, T_1, the middleware appends same timestamp to both of them, say, timestamp $= 1$ (step 3 of the protocol). Similarly, subtransactions (eq. 11.3 and 11.4) belong to T_2, hence the same timestamp is appended to both of them, say, timestamp $= 2$ (step 3 of the protocol).

By looking at equation 11.5, we note that history produced at the database site DB_2 schedules the subtransaction of the global transaction T_1 before the subtransaction of T_2 (the history in equation 11.5 is serial, but it does not matter as long as H_2 is serializable, with serialization order $T_1 \prec T_2$ because the timestamp attached to T_1 by the middleware is less than T_2). Execution of equation 11.6 will be prohibited by line 14 (or step 4) of the algorithm, because T_1 and T_2 are conflicting global transactions and the serialization order is $T_2 \prec T_1$, which does not follow the timestamp sequence.

Hence, schedules H_2 and H_3 will be corrected by the GCC protocol as follows:

$$H_2 = r_{12}(O_1)r_{12}(O_2)w_{12}(O_1)C_{12}r_{22}(O_1)w_{22}(O_1)C_{22} \text{ (same as eq. 11.5)}$$
$$H_3 = w_{13}(O_3)C_{13}r_{23}(O_3)w_{23}(O_4)C_{23} \text{ (corrected execution order by the}$$
$$\text{GCC protocol)}$$

Thus in both schedules, $T_1 \prec T_2$. It is not required that the schedules be serial schedules, but only that the serializability order should be the same as that of the timestamp sequence from the middleware.

11.3.5 Comparison with Traditional Concurrency Control Protocols

Homogeneous distributed concurrency control protocols may be lock-based, timestamp-based, or hybrid protocols. The following discusses the lock-based protocol only, but the arguments hold for other protocols as well.

The homogeneous distributed concurrency control protocols can be broadly classified as (*i*) centralized and (*ii*) distributed. The lock manager and the global lock table are situated at a central site in a centralized protocol. The flow of control (sequence diagram) for centralized concurrency control protocols in distributed DBMS (e.g., centralized two-phase locking) is shown in Figure 11.5. All the global information is stored in a central site, which makes the central site a hotspot and prone to failure. To overcome the limitations of central management, a distributed concurrency protocol is used in distributed DBMSs. The flow of control messages is shown in Figure 11.6 for distributed concurrency control protocols (e.g., distributed two-phase locking).

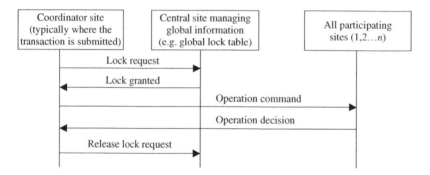

Figure 11.5 Operations of a general centralized locking protocol (e.g., centralized two-phase locking) in homogeneous distributed DBMS

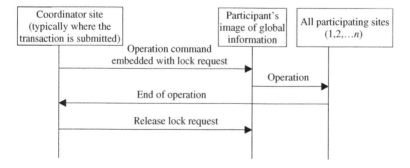

Figure 11.6 Operations of a general distributed locking protocol (e.g., decentralized two-phase locking) in homogeneous distributed DBMS

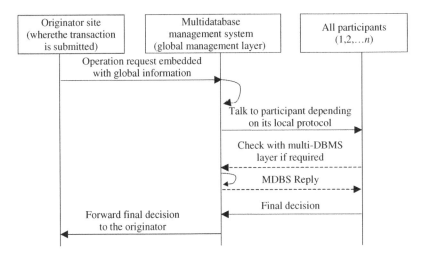

Figure 11.7   Operations of a general multi-DBMS protocol

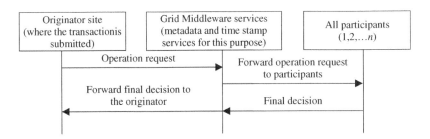

Figure 11.8   Operations of GCC protocol

Figure 11.7 shows the sequence of operations for heterogeneous distributed DBMS (e.g., multidatabase systems). Figure 11.8 shows the sequence of operations for the GCC protocol and highlights that the middleware's function is very lightweight in a Grid environment, as it acts only as the rerouting node for the global transaction (specifically from correctness perspective), unlike all other architectures. All other figures (Figs. 11.5–11.7) have a global image of the data and have more communication with the sites. It could be noted that the final decision in Figure 11.8 runs in a straight line from the participants to the originator via the middleware; this shows that there is no processing at the middleware and it acts only as a forwarding node. Conversely, Figure 11.7 shows a time lag after receiving the responses from the participants and before forwarding it to the originator, as the multi-DBMS layer has to map the responses in a protocol understandable to the originator.

The term "coordinator" is used in Figures 11.5 and 11.6 and "originator" in Figures 11.7 and 11.8. In both cases, the sites are where the global transaction is submitted. But the reason to distinguish between the two terms is that in Figures 11.5 and 11.6 the site also acts as the coordinator of the global transaction, while in Figures 11.7 and 11.8, because of site autonomy, the site acts only as the originator of the global transaction. But Figure 11.7 has far more communication compared with Figure 11.8, with the multi-DBMS layer, as it stores and processes all the global information.

11.4 CORRECTNESS OF GCC PROTOCOL

A Grid-serializable schedule is considered correct in the Grid environment for database systems. A concurrency control protocol conforming to theorem 11.1 is Grid-serializable, and is thus correct. Hence, to show the correctness of the GCC protocol, any schedule produced by the GCC protocol has the Grid-serializability property. Proposition 11.1 states the assumption that each DBMS can correctly schedule the transactions (local transactions and global subtransactions) submitted to its site.

Proposition 11.1: All local transactions and global subtransactions submitted to any local scheduler are scheduled in serializable order.

Because of the autonomy of sites, local schedulers cannot communicate with each other, and because of architectural limitations, the global scheduler cannot be implemented in a Grid environment. Because of the lack of communication among the local schedulers and the absence of a global scheduler, it becomes difficult to maintain consistency of the data. Thus the execution of global subtransactions at local database sites must be handled in such a way that data consistency is maintained. The additional requirement for Grid-serializability is stated in proposition 11.2.

Proposition 11.2: Any two global transactions having more than one subtransaction actively executing simultaneously must follow total-order.

Based on propositions 11.1 and 11.2, the following theorem shows that all schedules produced by GCC protocol are Grid-serializable.

Theorem 11.2: Every schedule produced by GCC protocol is Grid-serializable.

Proof: The types of possible schedules produced by the GCC are identified first, and then it can be shown that the schedules are Grid-serializable. Global transactions are broadly classified in two categories:

(a) *Global transactions having only one subtransaction*: Global transactions having a single subtransaction can be scheduled immediately and will always either precede or follow any of the conflicting transactions because they execute only on a single site. From proposition 11.1, local schedulers can schedule the transaction in serializable order.

(b) *Global transactions having more than one subtransaction*: Global transactions having more than one subtransaction may come under one of the following two cases:

(i) *Although the global transaction has multiple subtransactions, it conflicts with other active global transactions at only a single site*. This scenario is not a threat to data consistency, and thus the subtransactions could be scheduled immediately (Fig. 11.3, line 8). Local schedulers can correctly schedule transactions in this case.

(ii) *The global transaction has multiple transactions and conflicts with other global transactions at more than one site*: Local schedulers cannot schedule global transactions for this scenario. Hence, the GCC protocol submits all subtransactions in the queue and these subtransactions are executed strictly according to the timestamp attached at the Grid middleware. This ensures that if a subtransaction of any global transaction, GT_i, precedes a subtransaction of any other global transaction, GT_j, at any site, then subtransactions of GT_i will precede subtransactions of GT_j at all sites.

Thus for all cases: a, $b-i$ and $b-ii$ schedule conflicting global transactions in such a way that if any global transaction, GT_i, precedes any other global transaction, GT_j, at any site, then GT_i precedes GT_j at all sites. The type of schedules produced by GCC protocol is thus identified. Next, it is shown that these schedules are Grid-serializable.

To prove that schedules are Grid-serializable, the Grid-serializability graph must be acyclic and global transactions must be in total-order. Conflicts of the following types may occur:

- *Conflict between local and local transactions.* The local scheduler is responsible for scheduling local transactions. Total-order is required only for schedules where global subtransactions are involved. From proposition 11.1, local schedulers can schedule transactions in serializable order.

- *Conflict between global transaction and local transaction.* A local transaction executes only in one site. The subtransaction of the global transaction can only conflict with the local transaction in that site. Thus the local transaction and the subtransaction of global transaction are scheduled by the same scheduler. From proposition 11.1, these are scheduled in serializable order. Total-order is also maintained, as only one local scheduler is involved in the serialization process.

- *Conflict between global and global transactions.* Assume that an arc exists from $GT_i \rightarrow GT_j$ at any site DB_i. It will be shown that an arc from

$GT_j \rightarrow GT_i$ cannot exist in GCC. GT_j can either precede GT_i at the database site DB_i or at any other database site DB_n. Suppose GT_j precedes and conflicts with GT_i at data site DB_i. This contradicts with proposition 11.1. Thus GT_j cannot precede GT_i at DB_i. Suppose GT_j precedes and conflicts with GT_i at any other data site DB_n. If GT_j precedes GT_i at any other site, then total-order is not followed and it contradicts proposition 11.2. Figure 11.3 (line 14) of the GCC protocol prevents the occurrence of such a scenario. Thus schedules produced by the GCC protocol are Grid-serializable.

11.5 FEATURES OF GCC PROTOCOL

The concurrency control protocol helps to interleave operations of different transactions while maintaining the consistency of data in the presence of multiple users. The GCC protocol has the following main features:

(a) *Concurrency control in a heterogeneous environment*: The GCC protocol does not need to store global information regarding participating sites; e.g., in traditional distributed DBMS, a global lock table stores information of all locks being accessed by the global transaction. But in the Grid environment, all database sites might not be using the same concurrency control strategy (e.g., locking protocol). In the GCC protocol, individual subtransactions are free to execute the local concurrency control protocol of participating sites. The Grid middleware is used to monitor the execution order of the conflicting transactions.

(b) *Reducing the load from the originating site*: The centralized scheduling scheme and decentralized consensus-based policies intend to delegate the originating site of the transaction as the coordinator. Thus the coordinator site may become a bottleneck when a transaction has to access multiple sites simultaneously. The GCC protocol delegates the scheduling responsibility to the respective sites where the data resides without compromising the correctness of the data, and thus prevents the coordinator from becoming the bottleneck.

(c) *Reducing the number of messages in the internetwork*: Centralized and consensus-based decentralized scheduling schemes need to communicate with the coordinator to achieve correct schedules. The communication increases the number of messages in the system. Messages are one of the most expensive items to handle in any distributed infrastructure. The GCC protocol has fewer messages moving across the network to achieve concurrency.

Since the GCC protocol implements total-order on global transactions, the conflicting transactions will always proceed in one direction, thereby avoiding the problem of distributed deadlocks. Local deadlock management is the policy of the local database site. Because of autonomy restrictions, external interference in the local policy is not possible. Other concurrency control anomalies such as lost update, dirty read, and unrepeatable read are addressed at the local DBMS level.

The above-mentioned features are due to the architectural requirement of the Grid. But there is a serious architectural limitation of Grid architecture in concurrency control protocols. Because of the inability to install a global scheduler, it becomes difficult to monitor the execution of global subtransactions at different database sites. As a result, some valid interleaving of transactions cannot take place. Thus the resultant schedule becomes stricter than required.

11.6 SUMMARY

Grids are evolving as a new distributed computing infrastructure. Traditional distributed databases such as distributed database management systems and multidatabase management systems make use of globally stored information for concurrency control protocols. Centralized or decentralized consensus-based policies are mostly employed for these database systems. The Grid architecture does not support the storage of global information such as global lock tables, global schedulers, etc. Thus a new concurrency control protocol, called GCC, for Grid databases is needed.

The GCC protocol has several advantages: It operates in a heterogeneous environment; the load of the originator site is reduced compared with traditional distributed databases; and the number of messages in the network is reduced. But at the same time, because of the lack of global control and autonomy restrictions of the Grid architecture, it is difficult to optimize the scheduling process. In this chapter, the focus was the maintenance of data consistency during scheduling of the global transactions.

11.7 BIBLIOGRAPHICAL NOTES

Consistency and *isolation* are two of the ACID properties of transaction, which are the focus of this chapter. Most of the important work on concurrency control has been mentioned in the Bibliographical Notes section at the end of Chapter 10. This covers the work on parallel and grid transaction management by Brayner (*DEXA* 2001), Burger et al. (*BNCOD* 1994), Colohan et al. (*VLDB* 2005), 1993), Machado and Collet (*DASFAA* 1997), Wang et al. (*Parallel Computing* 1997), and Wiekum and Hasse (*VLDB J*).

11.8 EXERCISES

11.1. Explain how concurrency control helps to achieve the "C" and "I" of the ACID properties.

11.2. Explain why individual serializable schedules in each site of the Grid environment may not produce a serializable global schedule.

11.3. Explain the following terminologies:

    a. Total-order

    b. Grid-serial history

    c. Grid-serializable history

    d. Grid-serializability graph

    e. Grid-serializability theorem

11.4. Summarize the main features of the grid concurrency control (GCC) protocol, and explain how it solves the concurrency issues in the Grid.

11.5. Compare and contrast the difference between GCC and any other concurrency control protocols (e.g., distributed databases and multidatabase systems).

11.6. Discuss why the number of messages in the internetwork using GCC is reduced in comparison with other concurrency control protocols.

Chapter 12

Grid Transaction Atomicity and Durability

In this chapter, the "A" and "D" (atomicity and durability) of ACID properties of transactions running on Grid databases are explained. Atomic commitment protocols (ACPs) such as two-phase commit (2PC), three-phase commit (3PC), and other variants of these protocols are used for homogeneous and heterogeneous distributed DBMS. ACPs designed for homogeneous distributed DBMS are synchronous and tightly coupled between participating sites, while on the other hand, ACPs designed for heterogenous DBMS, for example, multidatabase systems, need a global management layer for monitoring the execution of global transactions. The former approach is unsuitable for a Grid database because communication among sites must be asynchronous, and the latter is unsuitable because sites in Grid databases are autonomous and cannot accept any functional/architectural changes due to external factors.

The purpose of this chapter is twofold. First, an ACP for a Grid database is described, that is, atomicity in a Grid database is addressed. Failures are unavoidable, and hence in the latter part of the chapter the effect of failure on transaction execution is discussed, including details of different types of logs stored in the originator and participant sites. The chapter is organized as follows. Section 12.1 presents the motivation for addressing atomic commitment in Grid databases. Section 12.2 describes the Grid-atomic commit protocol (Grid-ACP) and proves the correctness of the protocol. The Grid-ACP is extended to handle site failures in Section 12.3, including the comparison of the Grid-ACP with centralized and distributed recovery models. Correctness of the recovery protocol is also given.

High-Performance Parallel Database Processing and Grid Databases,
by David Taniar, Clement Leung, Wenny Rahayu, and Sushant Goel
Copyright © 2008 John Wiley & Sons, Inc.

12.1 MOTIVATION

2PC is the most widely accepted ACP in distributed data environments. 2PC is a consensus-based protocol, which needs to synchronize individual decisions of all participating sites to reach a global decision. It involves two phases, the *voting phase* and the *decision phase*. 2PC is also a blocking protocol. For n participants, 2PC needs $3n$ message and 3 rounds of message exchange to reach the final decision: (1) the coordinator broadcasts a request to vote, (2) participants reply with their vote, and (3) the coordinator broadcasts the decision. Many variations and optimizations have been proposed to increase the performance of 2PC. But homogeneity and synchronous communication among sites is the basic assumption behind the original and other variants of 2PC. Grid architecture is heterogeneous and autonomous; thus dependence on other sites and synchronous communication between sites is not a valid assumption.

Multi/federated database systems are heterogeneous, and they have been extensively studied during the last decade. Multi/federated database systems are mostly studied, designed, and optimized for short-lived and noncollaborative transactions. These database systems are designed in a bottom-up fashion, that is, the system designer knows the design requirements before the system is designed and deployed. On the other hand, a Grid database supports long-running collaborative transactions. Design requirements of Grid databases can vary rapidly as the system is more dynamic than the traditional distributed, multi/federated databases because sites should be able to join and leave the Grid dynamically without modifications to the database management systems. In addition, multidatabase systems have the leverage of a global management layer known as a multidatabase management system.

The transaction models developed for long-running transactions were designed with nested transaction structures. Hence, these models are not suitable for the collaborative environment of Grids. To summarize, the following points are noted:

(1) ACPs designed for homogeneous and synchronous distributed database systems cannot be implemented in Grid databases because of architectural limitations (Grid databases are heterogeneous and asynchronous).

(2) Multidatabase systems, being heterogeneous and autonomous in nature, are architecturally closer to the Grid environment. But they enjoy the leverage of a multidatabase management systems layer, which is absent in Grids. The multidatabase layer stores global information such as global lock table, global logs, etc. Because of site autonomy, Grids cannot store global information.

(3) A multidatabase employs redo, retry, and compensate approach for ACP. Redo and retry cannot be implemented in a Grid environment because both approaches make use of a global management layer. The compensate approach assumes that no other transaction should be serialized between the compensated-for transaction and the compensation transaction. This is impossible to implement in Grids because of the lack of a top-layer

management system and autonomy restrictions of sites. Grid databases need to operate in a loosely coupled service-oriented architecture.

Even from an architectural perspective (apart from a data consistency perspective), it is difficult to implement traditional ACPs in Grid environment. Grid databases will access data from globally separated data sites via WWW. Most of the distributed data architecture uses distributed objects for communication, for example, CORBA. CORBA has major limitations while operating on WWW. CORBA was not designed to work with HTTP, the standard web-based protocol. Thus there is a need to develop protocols that can be easily integrated into web services.

In this chapter, an ACP suitable for heterogeneous, autonomous, and asynchronous Grid databases is presented.

12.2 GRID ATOMIC COMMIT PROTOCOL (GRID-ACP)

The concept of compensating transactions is used in Grid-ACP. The execution of compensating transactions results in *semantic atomicity*. Semantic atomicity is defined as follows:

Definition 12.1: Let T_i be a global transaction and CT_i be a collection of local compensating subtransactions $\{CT_i^1, CT_i^2, \ldots, CT_i^n\}$, one for each site where T_i executes. T_i is semantically atomic if and only if either T_i is committed at all sites where T_i executes, or all CT_i^j (where $j = 1, 2 \ldots n$) are committed at all sites where T_i has committed.

12.2.1 State Diagram of Grid-ACP

Figure 12.1 shows the state diagram of the proposed grid-atomic commitment protocol (Grid-ACP). A *pre-abort* state is introduced in the originator, and two new states, the *sleep* and *compensate* states, are introduced in the participant's state diagram. The subtransaction will enter the "sleep" state when it has finished execution and is ready to release all acquired resources such as locks on data items, computing resources, etc. Because of the autonomy restriction in Grids, all resources must be released according to the participating site's requirement and cannot wait for the global decision. Thus the "sleep" state is an indication to transaction managers that the local subtransaction of the global transaction at the participating site has decided to commit. But the global decision is not yet made. At the time when the subtransaction enters into the "sleep" state, all computing and data resources can be released. All sites are autonomous and thus cannot hold resources for any external process.

If any of the other participating sites decide to abort any cohort of the global transaction, T_i, the originator site informs all the participating sites (in "sleep"

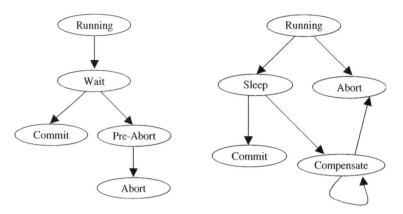

State diagram of transaction originator   State diagram of participating site

Figure 12.1 State diagram of Grid-ACP

state) of T_i to start the compensation. While the compensating transaction is executing, the site is in the compensate state. If the compensating transaction fails, it is re-executed until it is completed successfully. This raises the question as to whether the compensating transaction can keep on executing forever. The answer is "no," because the compensating transaction is the logical inverse of the committed subtransaction. Since the subtransaction decided to successfully commit and was in the "sleep" state, its logical inverse must also eventually commit. Once the compensating transaction successfully commits, the subtransaction is semantically aborted.

If the global transaction decides to commit, it can directly enter into the commit state. But if the global decision is to abort, the originator of the transaction cannot directly enter into the abort state. The originator must be assured that all participants have successfully compensated, that is, semantically aborted, and thus it enters in the pre-abort state. After receiving confirmation that all *sleep*ing subtransactions have been successfully aborted, the originator enters into the abort state.

12.2.2 Grid-ACP Algorithm

The Grid-ACP algorithm is as follows:

(1) Based on the information available at the middleware, the global transaction is divided into subtransactions and submitted to the participating database systems.

(2) The sites are autonomous in nature; hence after executing their portion of the subtransactions, participants go into the "sleep" state. The participants then inform the originator about the outcome of the subtransactions. Necessary information is logged. Details of log files are discussed in the following sections.

(3) The originator, after collecting responses from all participants, decides whether or not to commit or to abort the global transaction. If all participants decide to go into the "sleep" state, the decision is to commit, or else the decision is to abort. If the decision is to abort, the message is sent only to those participants who are in the sleep state. If the decision is to commit, the decision is sent to all participants.

(4) (a) If the participating site decides to commit and is in the "sleep" state and the global decision is also to commit, the subtransaction can go directly to the commit state because local and global decisions are the same.

(b) If the participating site decides to commit and is in the "sleep" state, but the final decision is to abort the global transaction, then the subtransaction, which is in the sleep state, must be aborted. But, as mentioned earlier, when the local site enters the sleep state it releases all locks on data items as well as all acquired resources. This makes abortion of the transaction impossible. Hence, a compensating transaction must be executed to reverse all the changes, using *compensation rules*, to restore the semantics of the database before executing the original subtransaction, thereby achieving *semantic autonomy*. If the compensating transaction fails, it is resubmitted until it commits. The compensating transaction must eventually commit, as it is a logical inverse of the "sleeping" transaction. We are not defining the compensation rules as they are out of the scope of this study.

Grid-ACP for the originator of the global transaction is shown in Figure 12.2. Grid-ACP for participants of the global transaction is shown in Figure 12.3.

Algorithm: Originator's algorithm for Grid-ACP

```
    submit subtransactions to participants;
    wait for response from all participants;
1.  if all response to sleep
2.     write commit record in log;
3.     send global_commit to all participants;
    else
4.     write abort record in log;
5.     send global_abort to participants, decided
       to commit;
6.     wait for response from these participants;
```

Figure 12.2   Originator's algorithm for Grid-ACP

Algorithm: Participant's algorithm for Grid-ACP

```
      received subtransaction from originator
      if participant decides to commit
         write sleep in log
         send commit decision to originator
1.       enter sleep state wait for decision from
         originator if decision is commit
            write commit in participant log
         else if decision is abort
            start compensating transaction for
            subtransaction
2.          if compensating transaction aborts
               restart compensating transaction until it
               commits
               write commit for compensating transaction
               send acknowledgement to originator
            else
               write commit for compensating transaction
      else if participant decides to abort
            write abort in log
            send abort decision to originator
```

Figure 12.3 Participant's algorithm for Grid-ACP

12.2.3 Early-Abort Grid-ACP

Step 3 of the Grid-ACP algorithm can be modified to improve the performance. The originator can decide to abort as soon as it receives the first abort from any of the participants. But with this strategy, the abort message has to be sent to all participants, not only to those who decided to commit. Thus there is a trade-off between saving the number of messages in the network and the processing time of those subtransactions that are still active and have not yet reached a decision. The participants' algorithm for *early-abort Grid-ACP* will be same as Figure 12.3, and hence the discussion of the participants' algorithm is omitted for the sake of brevity. Figure 12.4 shows the modified algorithm of the originator for the early-abort protocol.

The originator in the Grid-ACP algorithm waits until response from all participating sites is received (line 1, Fig. 12.2). Those participants who decided to abort would not be affected by the originator's decision. Thus if the global decision is to abort the transaction, the decision is only sent to participants that have decided to commit their subtransactions (and are in the "sleep" state). This strategy may sometimes become computationally expensive, for example, say a global transaction has n subtransactions. Suppose the first subtransaction returns an abort decision; then the final decision must be a global abort. Although the global decision can be made from available information, the originator still has

---

Algorithm: algorithm for early-abort Grid-ACP

```
   submit subtransactions to participants;
   wait for response from participants;
1. if any response is abort
2.     write abort record in log;
3.     send global_abort to all participants;
4.     wait for response from participants;
   else if all response to sleep then begin
5.     write commit record in log;
6.     send global_commit to all participants;
```

Figure 12.4 Originator's algorithm for early-abort Grid-ACP

to wait for other $(n-1)$ decisions to arrive from the participants. If all other participants decided to commit their subtransactions, effectively the computation is wasted, first in completing the subtransactions and then in compensating the subtransactions.

The originator's algorithm for the early-abort Grid-ACP can make the global decision as soon as the first abort decision from any participant is received (line 1, Fig. 12.4). An abort message to all participant sites can be sent immediately (line 3, Fig. 12.4), and the computation cost of other participants can be saved. Thus the overhead of compensation could also be reduced. If the last decision instead of the first one that was received from the participants is "abort," then the early-abort Grid-ACP reduces to a normal Grid-ACP because all the participants have already finished execution.

EXAMPLE

Let us consider a simple example to demonstrate the working of Grid-ACP. There is no subtransaction executing at the originator site in this case. Consider the following cases:

Case 1 (atomicity of a single transaction): Considering the execution of subtransactions of equations 11.1 and 11.2 from Chapter 11.

$$ST_{12} = r_{12}(O_1)r_{12}(O_2)w_{12}(O_1)C_{12}$$
$$ST_{13} = w_{13}(O_3)C_{13}$$

Subtransactions running to successful completion: Subtransactions will autonomously execute and enter into the "sleep" state (step 2 of Grid-ACP and line 1 of Fig. 12.3). Since ST_{12} and ST_{13} both decided to commit, the originator's decision is to "commit," which is communicated to the participants (step 3 of Grid-ACP and lines 1 to 3 of Fig. 12.2). As the global decision matches with the local ones, both subtransactions update their state from "sleep" to "commit" (step 4a of Grid-ACP, and *else* part of Fig. 12.3).

Any subtransaction decides to abort: Suppose ST_{13} decides to abort. The originator's decision will now be to abort the global transaction (lines 4 to 6 of Fig. 12.2). ST_{13} has unilaterally decided to abort, and the decision only needs to be sent to ST_{12} at site 2. Since

ST_{12} decided to commit, it starts the compensating procedure (step 4b of Grid-ACP and *else if* part of Fig. 12.3). Since the compensating transaction nullifies the effect of the ST_{12}, it may be of the following form:

CT_{12} (compensating transaction for global transaction 1 at site 2)

$$= w_{12} \text{ (old value of } O_1)$$

If CT_{12} aborts, it is reexecuted to successful completion, so that it reflects that ST_{12} has aborted. The acknowledgement is sent back to the originator.

Case 2 (atomicity in the presence of multiple transactions): Maintaining atomicity in the presence of multiple transactions is more complicated, because of the fact that other transactions may have read the values written by the "sleeping" transaction. If all the sub-transactions execute to completion, then the execution is similar to *case 1*. Therefore, we only discuss the case of aborting transactions. Consider global transactions, T_1 and T_2, from Chapter 11.

$$T_1 = r_1(O_1)r_1(O_2)w_1(O_3)w_1(O_1)C_1$$
$$T_2 = r_2(O_1)r_2(O_3)w_2(O_4)w_2(O_1)C_2$$

Consider the following history:

$$H_1 = r_{12}(O_1)r_{12}(O_2)w_{12}(O_1)S_{12}r_{22}(O_1)w_{22}(O_1)$$
$$(S_{12} \text{ means } ST_{12} \text{ is in sleep state})$$

In the above history H_1, ST_{12} is waiting for the global decision of T_2. Suppose the global decision is to abort T_2, then ST_{12} must also abort. Consequently, ST_{22} should also abort, as it has read from ST_{12}. This situation may lead to cascading aborts. Considering the autonomous behavior of Grids, this may be an unavoidable situation. If any database site implements a strict schedule, there will be no cascading aborts, but it is not in the control of the middleware. As a preventive measure, the following two options can be considered:

(a) After a transaction enters into "sleep" state, a ceiling or cap value can be defined to restrict the number of cascading aborts.

(b) A conflicting global transaction may not be submitted to a conflicting site until the originator has made the final decision on the already executing global transaction, so that cascading aborts may be avoided.

12.2.4 Discussion

The purpose of Grid-ACP and early-abort Grid-ACP is to deal with autonomy and heterogeneity between sites. Because of autonomy, synchronous communication between the originator and participants is not possible, and thus participants decide to commit unilaterally. Deciding to commit the transaction unilaterally and without consulting the originator does not come without a cost. The algorithm pays a price for releasing locks and resources early, which is unavoidable in an autonomous environment like the Grid. If the transaction releases the resources early, then other transactions may read the values written by this transaction. To handle this problem, traditional multidatabase systems implement a top layer of multidatabase management system. The top-layer management system enforces a criterion that prevents execution of any other global transaction between the compensated-for transaction and the compensating transaction.

Implementation of a top-layer management system is not possible in Grids for two reasons: (*i*) the autonomy of sites and (*ii*) the criterion becomes too restric tive in the Grid environment (heterogeneous). The absence of a global management layer increases the chances of *cascading aborts*. For example, any local transaction LT_i that reads data written by any global transaction T_s in the sleep state cannot decide to commit. If T_s has to abort from the sleep state, then the local transaction LT_i must also abort, thus having cascading aborts or compensating transactions. Hence, to avoid cascading aborts/compensation, any transaction that reads from values written by a transaction that is in the sleep state must also not commit until the "*sleep*ing" transaction commits. But, considering the heterogeneity and autonomy properties of the Grid architecture, cascading aborts/compensations are unavoidable. Thus the purpose of the "sleep" state becomes twofold. First, it acts as an intermediate step before the commit state to encounter autonomy of the archi- tecture, and second, the "sleep" state can be used by the application to cap the number of cascading aborts.

Implementing the "sleep" state does not need any modification to the local *transaction manager* module. The "sleep" state is defined in the interface, and hence no changes are required in any local modules. Thus the autonomy of the individual site is maintained.

12.2.5 Message and Time Complexity Comparison Analysis

The time and message complexity of the algorithm are described below.

Time Complexity Analysis

The Grid-ACP needs two rounds of messages under normal conditions: (1) the participant sends its decision to commit/abort and (2) the decision of the originator is communicated to participants. This gives an impression of 2PC, but the state of participants after sending the decision is different. While 2PC enters in wait state and holds all the resources, computing, and data, until the global decision is received, Grid-ACP releases all resources after sending the local decision and enters into a "sleep" state.

Message Complexity Analysis

Let the number of participants be n. Considering that the originator sends the final decision to all the sites, including those sites it has decided to abort, the number of messages in each round is n. Thus maximum number of messages required is $2n$ to reach a consistent decision under normal conditions. Early-abort Grid-ACP takes

Table 12.1   Message and time complexity of ACPs

Protocols	Messages	Rounds
2PC	$3n$	3
3PC	$5n$	5
Grid-ACP	$2n$	2
Grid-ACP for early abort	$(i + n)$, ith message is the abort decision	2

$(i + n)$ messages to reach a decision. Where $1 \leq i \leq n$, the ith message received is the abort decision from the subtransaction. The early-abort Grid-ACP behaves like a Grid-ACP if the last message received by the originator is the abort decision. If the global decision is to commit, then both protocols behave in a similar manner.

Table 12.1 shows the message and time complexity of Grid-ACP and compares it with 2PC and 3PC protocols.

12.2.6 Correctness of Grid-ACP

An atomic commitment algorithm ensures that all processes reach a decision such that:

$AC1$: All processes that reach a decision reach the same one.

$AC2$: A process cannot reverse its decision after it has reached one.

$AC3$: The commit decision can be reached only if all processes voted "yes".

$AC4$: If there are no failures and all processes voted "yes", then the decision will be to commit.

Grid-ACP meets the requirements mentioned above. Since the protocol does not use the *wait* state for the participants, condition $AC2$ is not valid for our discussion. $AC1$ is the main objective of the protocol. $AC3$ and $AC4$ will be proved while $AC1$ is proved.

Lemma 12.1: If one subtransaction aborts, all participating subtransactions also abort.

Proof: Referring to Step 3 of the algorithm, if even one participant decided to abort, the originator's decision is to abort. The decision is conveyed to all those participants who decided to commit and are in the "sleep" state. The abort decision is not required to send to those participants who decided to abort, because any participant deciding to abort may abort its subtransactions unilaterally. If there is no communication failure, all sites will eventually receive the message and are in a consistent state, that is, "abort" in this case.

Theorem 12.1: All participating sites reach the same final decision.

Proof: The theorem is proved in two parts: ***Part I*** for consistent commit and ***Part II*** for consistent abort.

   Part I: In this part, it is shown that when the global decision is to commit, all participants commit. From step 2 of the algorithm, it is clear that the participants execute autonomously. If the local decision is to commit, the information is logged in the stable storage and the subtransaction goes into the sleep state after sending a message to the originator. If the originator of the transaction finds a commit decision in the response, it sends the final commit to all participants. In this case, the participant is not required to perform any action, as all the resources were already released when the participant entered into the "sleep" state. The participant just has to mark the migration of the transaction's state from "sleep" to "commit."

   Part II: The participants have to do more computation to achieve atomicity if the global decision is to abort. In this part, it is shown that if the global decision is to abort, all participants decide to abort. From lemma 12.1, it is clear that all participants who decide to commit now receive an abort decision from the originator. Those participants deciding to abort have already aborted their subtransactions unilaterally. Those subtransactions that have decided to commit have already released locks on data items and cannot be aborted. Hence, compensating transactions are constructed using the *event-condition-action* or the *compensation rules*. These compensating transactions are then executed to achieve the semantic atomicity (step 4b of the algorithm). To achieve semantic atomicity, the compensating transaction must commit. If the compensating transaction aborts for some reason, it is re-executed until it commits. The compensating transaction must eventually commit, as it is a logical inverse of a committed transaction. This is shown in the state diagram by a self-referring compensate state (Fig. 12.1), and line 2 of the participant's algorithm (Fig. 12.3). Although the compensating transaction commits, the subtransaction semantically aborts. Thus all the participants terminate with a consistent decision.

12.3 HANDLING FAILURE OF SITES WITH GRID-ACP

In an earlier section, ACP for Grid databases in a failure-free environment was discussed. Failures are inevitable in real life. In this section, the earlier proposed Grid-ACP is extended to handle failures.

12.3.1 Model for Storing Log Files at the Originator and Participating Sites

Traditional distributed databases store global logs for failure recovery. As discussed above, because of architectural limitations, Grid databases cannot store global logs. In the absence of global logs, distributed data can become corrupted. Thus the interface of the sites must contain information in local logs in order to recover from these failures. Figure 12.5 shows the model for storing logs at various sites.

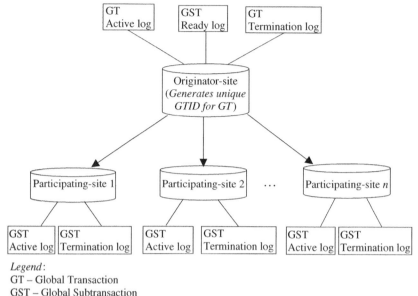

Legend:
GT – Global Transaction
GST – Global Subtransaction
GTID – Global Transaction Identifier

Figure 12.5 Model for storing log information at originator and participant sites

Any site can act as an originator or as a participant simultaneously, but for pedagogical simplicity in Figure 12.5 the originator site is distinguished from the participant sites. Figure 12.5 shows that the information for active global transactions must be stored at participants' sites as well as at the originator site. This log information is in addition to what is required by the sites to maintain local logs, and is implemented in the interface without any modifications to the local transaction managers.

12.3.2 Logs Required at the Originator Site

The following logs are required at each originator site (Fig. 12.5):

(1) *Global transaction active log:* When a global transaction is submitted to the originator, it is forwarded to the Grid middleware, which generates a globally unique identifier (GTID). The global transaction (GT) is then divided into subtransactions depending on the different distributed databases it has to access. Next, the global transaction active log at the originator is updated with GTID. Subtransactions are then submitted to respective database sites, and each database site is called a participant of the GT.

(2) *Global subtransaction ready log:* After the subtransaction has finished execution at the participating site, the originator is informed about the decision. If the participant's decision is to commit and the subtransaction is not the last

cohort of the GT, then the global subtransaction (GST) ready log is updated with the subtransaction's decision.

(3) *Global transaction termination log:* If the last subtransaction decides to commit along with all other subtransactions, then the originator also decides to commit. Global transaction termination log is updated for the respective GTID and sends the final decision to all participants. If any of the subtransactions decided to abort, then the global decision is "abort" and the GT termination log is accordingly updated.

12.3.3 Logs Required at the Participant Site

The following logs are required at each participating site (Fig. 12.5):

(1) *Global subtransaction active log:* As soon as the participant receives the subtransaction, it becomes active. The subtransaction is added in the *GST active log*. If the subtransaction executes successfully, it enters into the "sleep" state and the GST active log is updated.

(2) *Global subtransaction termination log:* If the subtransaction decides to abort, it can do so unilaterally, and hence the *GST termination log* is updated immediately. Otherwise, when the participant receives the global decision, the GST termination log is updated accordingly.

A global transaction can have one or more subtransaction(s). Participants do not need a ready log; this can be figured out from the combination of the GST active and GST termination logs. The "sleep" state is updated in the active log, which indicates that the local decision is to commit the subtransaction. Thus the ready log is not required for participants.

12.3.4 Failure Recovery Algorithm for Grid-ACP

Above in this chapter, various states of executing global transactions at the originator as well as at the participants' sites were outlined (Fig. 12.1). Sites may fail in any state during transaction execution. There could be different combinations of site failure, for example, failure of only the participants, failure of only the originator, and simultaneous failure of both participants and originator. In this section, *recovery procedures* for participants as well as for the originator are proposed. The recovery procedure can handle failure of global transactions executing in various states (from Fig. 12.1). Recovery algorithms for the originator and participants are discussed separately. There are two important points to make here, before we proceed. First, without loss of generality, participants and originators are distinguished, and second, global logs are not available for Grid databases.

Participant Recovery Procedure

The participant's recovery procedure is as follows.

Step 1:   Restart the participating DBMS.

Step 2:   Recover local transactions by using information stored in the log. Local transactions access only a single database site. Hence, local transactions can be recovered with the centralized database system's techniques.

Step 3:   The participating site then checks in the *global subtransaction active log*, whether it is executing a subtransaction of any global transaction.

> *Step 3A:*   If the site does not have any cohort of global transactions, then the site can recover independently by using local logs.

> *Step 3B:*   If the site is executing local subtransactions of any global transactions, the originator site of the respective global transaction is informed. The site is then in a global recovery mode, and normal access to the site is blocked until the recovery process is completed.

Case I Participating site failed in *running* state: The subtransaction is aborted, the GTID from the global subtransaction active log is removed, "abort" is appended to the global subtransaction termination log, and the originator is informed of the decision.

Case II Participating site failed during *compensate* state: This implies that the participant failed after the global decision was received but before the compensation was successfully executed. Hence, the subtransaction must be *semantically aborted*. After recovery, if the GST termination log contains abort but GTID still exists in the GST active log, then the participant knows it failed during the compensate state. The compensating transaction is then rerun to completion. After successful compensation, GTID is removed from the global subtransaction active log and acknowledgment is sent to the originator.

Case III Participating site failed during the *sleep* state: The participant in this state may not proceed unless it receives the decision from the originator. If GTID exists in the GST active log and no decision (*commit* or *abort*) can be found in the GST termination log regarding that GTID, then the participant knows that it failed during the *sleep* state.

> **(1)** The GT termination log at the originator contains *commit*: This implies that while the participant failed, all the other participants also decided to commit (the failed participant also decided to commit, as it is in *sleep* state). The originator replies with "commit," the participant recovers and updates the GST termination log and removes GTID from GST active log.

> **(2)** The GT termination log at the originator contains *abort*: This implies that although the failed participant decided to *commit*, some other participant or the originator itself must have

decided to abort the GT and thus the final decision was to *abort* the transaction. The originator replies with "abort," and the participant executes the compensating transaction. Successful completion of the compensating transaction semantically aborts the subtransaction. The GST termination log is then appended with "abort," and the GTID is removed from the GST active log.

(3) The GT is active (i.e., GT termination log has no information on transaction termination): If the GT is active, this implies that the originator is still waiting for the decision of other participants. The originator replies with "active," and the participant can safely recover to the state where it failed, i.e., *sleep*. No new entry in the participant's log is required.

(4) The GT termination log at originator contains *pre-abort*: This indicates that the global decision to abort has been made and the originator is waiting for acknowledgements. If "abort" is not found in the GST termination log at the participant, then it appends "abort" to GST termination log. The participant should then execute the compensation rules and acknowledge the abortion of the subtransaction and remove the GTID from the GST active log.

The originator makes the final decision as to when all subtransactions of the global transaction have the *ready* entry in the GST ready log or any of the subtransactions decide to abort.

Step 4: The decision is made depending on the message that the participant receives in *step 2* or *step 3* from the originator. Participants' logs are updated accordingly.

Step 5: The participating DBMS regains normal operations and starts accepting external requests.

Step 6: The participant's recovery process is terminated.

The algorithm first checks whether the site could recover locally, that is, whether no active subtransactions could be found at the participant (line 1 of Fig. 12.6, step 2 of the recovery procedure). If the participant had any active subtransaction at the time of failure (line 2), it checks the state of the global subtransaction. If the subtransactions executing at the participant is in the "running" state (line 3, step 3B (case I)), the decision is to abort the subtransaction and the originator is informed. If the subtransaction was in the "compensate" state during failure (line 4, step 3B (case II)), then the compensating transaction is rerun to completion. If the subtransaction was in the "sleep" state during failure (line 5, step 3B (case III)), then the participant checks the status of the originator before making any decision. The originator could be in commit (line 6), abort/pre-abort (line 7), or active state (line 8).

Algorithm: Recovery algorithm of Grid-ACP for
participant site

Variables used in the algorithm
TID: Transaction Identifier
GT_i: Global transaction submitted at originator site i
GST_{ij}: Subtransactions of GT_i executing at participant
site j
CT_i: Compensating transaction at site i.
ACK: Acknowledgement

// stores TID of active transaction
AL_{or}: Active Log stored at originator site

// stores acknowledgement from subtransactions
// eg. 'active', 'ready' etc.
RL_{or}: Ready Log stored at originator site

//stores final decision on TID
TL_{or}: Termination Log stored at originator site

// stores TID of respective subtransactions
AL_{pa}: Active Log stored at participating site

// decision of local subtransactions
TL_{pa}: Termination Log stored at participating site

Get_TID(*log_name*): Function that returns set of global
transaction ID's in *log_name* log.
Get_state (*log_name*, TID): Functions that returns
the state of TID in the respective site.
//states can be 'active', 'ready', etc.

Cardinality (X): returns number of element in set X

   begin recovery procedure   // recovery procedure
   for GT_i
1.   if Get_TID(AL_{pa}) $= \phi$
      recover locally
      //a subtransactions of global transaction, GT_i,
      found
2.   else if Get_TID(AL_{pa}) $\neq \phi$
3.   if $GST_{ij} \notin$Get_TID (TL_{pa})   // 'running' state
      abort GST_{ij} // subtransactions decides to abort
      send *abort* decision to originator
4.   if $GST_{ij} \in$Get_TID(TL_{pa})$\wedge$Get_state(TL_{pa}, TID) $=$
    '*compensate*'
      run CT_i
      send abort message to originator
      remove TID from AL_{pa}

Figure 12.6 Recovery algorithm of Grid-ACP for participant site

```
5.      if GSTᵢⱼ ∈ Get_TID (TLₚₐ) ∧ Get_state(TLₚₐ, TID) =
        'sleep'
6.          if Get_state(TLₒᵣ, TID) = 'commit'
                recover GSTᵢⱼ to values before is failed
                update TLₚₐ for GSTᵢⱼ to 'commit'
                remove TID from ALₚₐ
7.          if Get_state(TLₒᵣ, TID) = 'abort' ∨ 'pre-abort'
                run CTᵢ
                remove TID from ALₚₐ
8.          if Get_state(TLₒᵣ, TID) = 'active'
                recover GSTᵢⱼ to previous 'sleep' state
    end recovery procedure
```

Figure 12.6   (*Continued*)

Originator Recovery Procedure

The originator's recovery procedure is as follows:

Step 1:   Restart the originator site and restore the values from the log.

Step 2:   Determine the status of outstanding subtransactions executing in multiple participants.

Case I The originator is in the *running* state (subtransaction running at originator is active): If the subtransaction of the global transaction executing at the originator is active during the failure, the originator decides to abort, informs all participants to abort, and appends "abort" to GT termination log.

Case II The originator is in the *wait* state (subtransaction executing at the originator has successfully executed but waiting for response of other participants), that is, GTID can be found in the GT active log and no entry regarding the GTID in GT termination log. The number of "ready" entries in the GST ready log is also less than the number of subtransactions. The originator checks the status of participants before taking the final decision.

(i)   If all the participating subtransactions for the corresponding global transaction are in the running state, then the originator allows it to continue normally.

(ii)   If all the participating subtransactions are in the sleep state, then the originator decides to commit the global transaction. If some participants are running and some are in "sleep" state, then the originator records the information in the GST ready log for subtransactions in "sleep" state and lets the active subtransactions complete normal execution.

(iii)   If any of the participating sites are in either the "abort" or "compensate" state, then this signifies that the originator failed after the global decision to abort the transaction was made but could not update the log. The GT termination log is updated with "pre-abort". The originator then informs all participants, and it waits for acknowledgement from the participants.

(iv) If the originator does not receive any status information from the participant, then the originator assumes that the participating DBMS has failed and it is not operational. The recovery process is then blocked, and it waits for the participant to recover. For performance reasons, the originator may be designed to wait only for a predecided amount of time, that is, a *timeout* period is fixed. The originator starts the abort procedure if the participant does not recover during the specified timeout period.

Case III The originator is in the *commit* state, that is, the "commit" entry is found in the GT termination log, but the global transaction is still active, that is, GTID still exists in the GT active log. Since the originator decided to commit, this indicates that all subtransactions executed to successful completion. Hence, all subtransactions can only be in the *sleep* or *commit* state.

(i) If the participant is in the *sleep* state, then the originator instructs the participant about successful completion of the global transaction and updates the originator's log. The participant then enters the commit state.

(ii) If the participant is already in the *commit* state, then the originator only has to update its log.

After the response is sent to all participants, the GTID is removed from the GT active log. This case is also valid if the "commit" entry is not found in the GT termination log, but the number of "ready" entries in the GST ready log is equal to the number of executing subtransactions.

Case IV The originator is in the *pre-abort/abort* state, that is, a "pre-abort" or "abort" entry is found in the GT termination log. Since the originator decided to abort, this indicates that any of the subtransactions must have decided to abort. If the originator is in an "abort" state, then all participants must be in an "abort" state, since the originator enters the "abort" state only after receiving all acknowledgements.

If the originator is in the *pre-abort* state, then it is waiting for acknowledgment from some of the participants. Thus the participants can be either in the "sleep" or "abort" state.

(i) If the participant is in the "sleep" state, it communicates an "abort" decision to the originator. The participant then sends an acknowledgment to the originator after successful execution of the compensation procedure.

(ii) If the participant is in the "abort" state, acknowledgment from the participant is updated in the originator site. When all acknowledgments have been received from the participants, the originator moves from the "pre-abort" to "abort" state and the GTID is removed from the GT active log.

Step 3:   Depending on the above-mentioned scenario, responses from all participants are collected. If all participants' responses were to commit, i.e.
they are in the 'sleep' state, then the global decision is to commit, which
is conveyed to all participants. If any of the participants decided to abort,
then the global abort decision is conveyed to all participants. The GT
termination log is updated accordingly.

Step 4:   The global recovery process terminates.

A brief explanation of Figure 12.7 is as follows. If the global transaction is
active, that is, GTID is in GT active log and no termination decision is made (line
1), then the global transaction is active and thus the abort procedure is commenced.
If the termination log has a wait entry in the originator site and the transaction is
active (line 2), then the originator must check the status of subtransactions executing at all participants. All subtransactions of the global transaction could be active
and running (line 3); some or all of the subtransactions can be in a sleep state (line
4 and line 5); any of the subtransactions can be in an abort or pre-abort state (line
6); or there can be no reply from the participants (line 7). If the GTID exists in the
originator's termination log and the state of the global transaction was "commit"
(line 8), then the participants can be in either the "commit" or "sleep" state.

If the failure occurred during the pre-abort state of the global transaction (line
9), then participants can be in the "sleep" or "abort" state. If the transaction was
active and the termination log had an abort entry (line 10), then the site is recovered
to its earlier state. The transaction enters into an abort state only after receiving
acknowledgments from all participants. This implies that the failure occurred after
the global transaction was aborted, but before the GTID was removed from the
active log. Thus the GTID is removed from the active log after recovery (line 11).
Hence, the pre-abort state is important in Grid-ACP. The pre-abort state acts as an
intermediary state, while the global transaction receives acknowledgment from all
subtransactions.

12.3.5   Comparison of Recovery Protocols

This section compares the architecture of two centralized recovery models:
the recovery model for DBMS with global information (distributed and multidatabase), and the recovery model for DBMS without global information (Grid
database).

Figure 12.8 shows the recovery model for an individual database site. The stable
database storage may contain values written by uncommitted transactions, or might
not contain the values written by the actually committed transactions, because of
the buffering of data in the cache. After the system has recovered from the failure,
the recovery manager must be able to restore the committed state. Logs are updated
in the stable storage to help the recovery process. A typical entry in the log file
looks like $[T_i, o, v]$, which means that transaction T_i wrote the value v into the
data object o. The recovery manager also keeps the record of *active, committed*,
and *aborted* transactions in the log.

Algorithm: Recovery algorithm of Grid-ACP for
originator site

Variables used in the originator's algorithm are same as
that of participant's algorithm.
begin recovery procedure
// recovery process for Global Transaction GT_i
// global transaction is active
1. if $GT_i \in Get\_TID$ $(AL_{or}) \wedge$ $GT_i \notin Get\_TID$ (TL_{or})
      start abort procedure for GT_i
      remove GTID from AL_{or}
   else
2.   if $GT_i \in Get\_TID$ $(AL_{or}) \wedge$ Get_state $(TL_{or}$, TID$)$ = '$wait$'
          send request to check participants state
3.   if $\forall$ $GST_{ij} \notin Get\_TID$ (TL_{pa}) // All STs running
            recover originator to $wait$ state
4.   if $\exists$ $GST_{ij} \in Get\_TID(TL_{pa}) \wedge Get\_state(TL_{pa}, TID) = '$sleep$'
            for each cohort update TL_{or} to '$sleep$'
5.   if (Cardinality (Get_state $(TL_{pa}$, TID$)$)) =
            Cardinality (GST))
            // if all participants sleep, start commit
               start $commit$ procedure
               send message to all GST
6.   if $\exists GST_{ij} \in Get\_TID(TL_{pa}) \wedge (Get\_state(TL_{pa}$, TID$) = '$abort$'
         $\vee$'$pre\text{-}abort$'
            start global $abort$ procedure
            remove $\forall$GST from TL_{pa}
7.   if no response from participant
            wait till timeout period then start abort
8. if $GT_i \in Get\_TID$ $(TL_{or}) \wedge Get\_state(TL_{or}$, TID$) = '$commit$'
   // originator in commit state
      if Get_state $(TL_{pa}$, TID$)$ = '$commit$'
         send ACK of commit from participant to
         originator
      if Get_state $(TL_{pa}$, TID$)$ = '$sleep$'
         send message to participant to $commit$
9. if $GT_i \in Get\_TID$ $(TL_{or}) \wedge Get\_state$ $(TL_{or}$, TID$) = $ '$pre\text{-}abort$'
      if Get_state $(TL_{pa}$, TID$)$ = '$sleep$'
         send message to participant to $commit$
         run CT_i
      if Get_state $(TL_{pa}$, TID$)$ = '$abort$'
         send ACK of abort from participant to
         originator
10.if $GT_i \in$ Get_TID $(TL_{or}) \wedge$ Get_state $(TL_{or}$, TID$)$ = '$abort$'
11.   recover to state before failure. Remove GTID
       from AL_{or}

Figure 12.7 Recovery algorithm of Grid-ACP for originator site

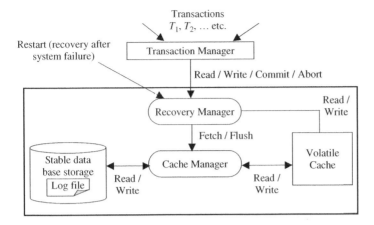

Figure 12.8   Recovery model in centralized DBMS

In distributed DBMS recovery manager architecture (shown in Fig. 12.9), a global log (stored in global stable storage) is also required in addition to the local logs. The global recovery manager stores critical information required to recover sites from failure. Similar to the centralized approach, the distributed DBMS also requires that only the effects of committed transactions be retained by *all* databases. A *single* global log is maintained on the global management layer's stable storage. The active completion and termination log of the global transactions, along with subtransactions, is stored in the global stable storage as shown in Figure 12.9.

The major architectural difference between the Grid database's recovery model (shown in Fig. 12.10) and the distributed DBMS recovery model (Fig. 12.9) is the absence of a global log. During the recovery process, the absence of global information may lead to an incorrect database state. Hence, additional information must be stored at individual database sites to maintain the consistency of data, as discussed in Figure 12.5. Also, in Figure 12.9 intermediate results can be stored during the execution of global transactions, but because of the autonomous sites, there is no provision for storing intermediate results in Figure 12.5 and Figure 12.10. The algorithms in Figure 12.6 and Figure 12.7 show the recovery process during various combinations of site failures with the help of independent recovery managers and local log entries using the "sleep" state.

12.3.6   Correctness of Recovery Algorithm

A recovery protocol is correct if it maintains the consistency of data and resumes the database state before failure. Assuming any of the database sites can fail, it is necessary to show that the recovery protocol is correct. Three possible combinations of failure are (*i*) only participant site failure (*ii*), only originator site

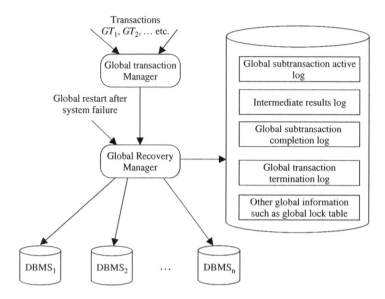

Figure 12.9 Recovery model for DBMSs with global recovery manager (distributed DBMS and multidatabase)

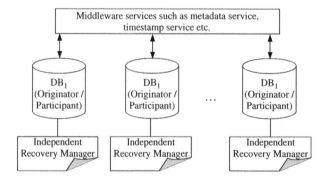

Figure 12.10 Recovery model for Grid database architecture

failure, and (*iii*) originator and participant failure simultaneously. These cases are discussed separately to prove the correctness of the recovery algorithm. The transaction submission procedure is discussed next, before the correctness of the protocol is explained.

Transaction Submission Procedure

(i) The log is updated with a *begin* operation upon the transaction's arrival. The global transaction is then subdivided into multiple logical subtransactions. A transaction identifier along with subtransaction identifier is also recorded in the active log.

(ii) The subtransactions are then submitted to the respective database sites. A subtransaction active log is updated at the participating site of the global transaction. The originator must wait if the subtransaction cannot be submitted, i.e., if the participant is not operational.

(iii) The decision to commit or abort the global transaction is made after responses from all participants have been gathered (similar to 2PC, but the participants do not wait for the global decision). If all participants' responses were positive, i.e., they are all in a "sleep" state, then the originator decides to commit, or else the decision is to abort. The decision is recorded in the global transaction termination log, and all sites participating in this global transaction are informed.

Correctness

Three possible cases of failure are discussed to prove the correctness of the algorithm.

Lemma 12.2: The effect of only the committed transaction is reflected in all databases. Uncommitted data is not reflected either in the participant(s) or in the originator after failure recovery.

Proof: To prove the correctness of the lemma, three different possibilities of failure have to be discussed separately.

Case I: *Only Participant Site Failure*: A participant's failure can leave the global transaction running at the originator, in any of the states shown in the state diagram, i.e., *running, wait, commit, pre-abort*, and *abort*. If the originator tries to submit a subtransaction to the failed participant, this implies that the global transaction is in the running state and has to wait until the participant has recovered (been taken care of by step ii of *transaction submission procedure*).

If the originator is *waiting* for a response from the participant, the originator is blocked until it receives a response from the participant (*step 3* of *participant recovery procedure*).

If the global transaction is in an "abort" state in the originator site, the participant can be either in a "sleep" or "running" state. So, when the DBMS recovers and contacts the originator, *step 3B (3-ii)* verifies the state of global transactions from the log and replies to the originator.

Similarly, the "commit" and "pre-abort" states of the global transaction at the originator can be verified in the log, and required messages can be communicated to the recovered participating DBMS (discussed in *step 3B-3* of the *participant recovery procedure*).

The subtransaction executing at a participant can be in the *running, compensate, sleep, commit*, or *abort* states. The first three states are handled in the participant recovery procedure (*step 3B-1 to 3*). Subtransactions in participating sites in the "abort" state at the time of failure will not affect the DBMS. Subtransactions move into the "abort" state, either by unilaterally aborting or after getting instructions from the originator. Since the participant has to acknowledge the abortion of transaction to the originator, it does not pose any threat to consistency of data stored in the database. The subtransactions that were in the "commit" state will have information stored in their log and may recover normally, similar to centralized DBMS. Since they failed in the commit state, it implies that the participant must have received a message to commit from the originator.

Case II: *Only Originator Site Failure*: The originator site failure may take place in any of the five states of global transaction, i.e., *running, wait, commit, pre-abort*, and *abort*. It is necessary to discuss each state of the global transaction and corresponding state of subtransactions at the participating sites.

The global transaction is aborted and logs are updated accordingly if the originator fails in the running state (*step 2, case I* in the *originator recovery procedure*). The originator then enters the *pre-abort* state, sends a message to all participants to abort their respective subtransactions, and waits for the acknowledgment (at this point we assume that the participant is operational; simultaneous failure of participants and originator is dealt with in case III).

If the global transaction at the originator is in the "wait" state, the participants can be in "running," "sleep," "abort," or "compensate" states (*step 2, case II* in *originator recovery procedure*). The participant cannot be in the "commit" state while the originator is in the "wait" state. The originator needs to arrive at a consensus before it can reach a final decision (step 3). The originator requests all participants to send their responses and then decides according to step 3 of the *originator recovery procedure*.

If the originator is in the "commit" state, then the participants can only be in the "commit" or "sleep" state. This situation is dealt with in *step 2, case III* of the *originator recovery procedure*.

While the originator is in the "abort" or "pre-abort" state, the participants can only be in either the "abort" state or "sleep" state. This situation is dealt with in *step 2, case IV* of the *originator recovery procedure*.

Case III: *Originator and Participant Fail Simultaneously*: Since all sites are autonomous, it is possible for the originator and one or more participants to fail simultaneously. At the same time, considering the sites are autonomous, all DBMS sites have the capability to recover independently from failure. Thus, with this architecture, the synchronization between recovery must be addressed. There could be two scenarios: (*i*) the participating site recovering before the originator site and (*ii*) the originator site recovering before the participant.

If the participating site recovers first, then it tries to contact the originator to get the recovery information. As discussed in *participant recovery procedure (step 3B)*, the site is in *global recovery mode* and normal access to the database is blocked. Since the originator is not operational, the participant is blocked and waits for the originator's recovery. After the originator has been repaired, it tries to collect status information from outstanding subtransactions as explained in *originator recovery procedure (step 2)*. At this stage, the communication between originator and participant is re-established, and normal recovery procedure continues. If more than one participant of the global transaction failed simultaneously, the originator waits until all participants are up and running.

If the originator recovers before the participant, then at *step 2* of *originator recovery procedure*, where the originator tries to collect status information from the participants, the recovery procedure is blocked. The recovery procedure again wakes up when the recovered participating site contacts the originator to gather recovery information. Normal global recovery procedure is followed thereafter.

Thus the proposed recovery protocol deals with all possible combinations of failure of sites and hence maintains the consistency of data during the recovery procedure.

12.4 SUMMARY

In this chapter, the atomicity property of transactions in Grid databases is addressed. It describes the Grid-atomic commit protocol for global transactions and demonstrates the correctness of the protocol. Failure is inevitable in distributed systems; thus the Grid-ACP is extended to handle site failures. It is assumed that if the message is sent by a participant to the originator or vice versa, it is eventually delivered. If the communication medium is not reliable, an additional round of acknowledgment messages should be introduced in the protocol.

Because of the autonomy of sites, participants cannot hold the resources until the originator makes the final decision. Hence, Grid-ACP implements the "sleep" state where the subtransactions can release the resources but are still aware that the global decision has not yet been received. In such an autonomous environment, cascading aborts are unavoidable, but the "sleep" state can be used to put a cap on cascading aborts. The traditional atomic commit protocol (2PC) can work in a homogeneous environment, that is, all sites must use a locking protocol. But Grids are a heterogeneous architecture, and hence 2PC cannot be implemented in the Grid environment. The Grid-ACP can work in a heterogeneous environment as the participants can release the resources autonomously without any dependence on other sites. Compensating transactions are a logical inverse of the subtransaction that has to abort from the sleep state. The execution of a compensating transaction semantically aborts the subtransaction at the participant's site. After execution of the compensating transactions, the database state is reinstated to the earlier state. For example, if booking of the hotel reservation is the subtransaction, then the compensating transaction may be to cancel the reservation and return the deposit after charging a processing fee for cancellation.

The summary of the chapter is as follows:

- An atomic commit protocol is described with a "sleep" state to encounter autonomy and heterogeneity of Grid database systems. The "sleep" state helps the database system to continue its operations without waiting for other external databases.

- A detailed failure recovery procedure of the sites is also discussed, so that the atomicity of the transaction is maintained.
- Correctness of both protocols (Grid-ACP and recovery algorithm for Grid-ACP) is discussed.

12.5 BIBLIOGRAPHICAL NOTES

Atomicity and *durability* are two of the ACID properties of transactions, which are the focus of this chapter. Most important works on transaction management normally cover these ACID properties, some of which have been mentioned in the Bibliographical Notes section at the end of the previous two chapters on Grid transaction management (Chapters 10 and 11).

12.6 EXERCISES

12.1. Discuss the reasons why the atomic commitment protocols in distributed databases and multidatabase systems may not be employed by the Grid.

12.2. Compare and contrast the state diagram between the Grid-ACP and traditional 2PC/3PC.

12.3. Outline the primary difference between Grid-ACP and early-abort Grid-ACP.

12.4. Discuss why the number of messages of 2PC and 3PC are higher than that of the Grid-ACP.

12.5. Describe how failure recovery is incorporated into the Grid-ACP, and outline the differences between failure recovery in Grid-ACP and other systems (e.g., distributed and multidatabase systems).

Chapter 13

Replica Management in Grids

Grid databases or data Grids operate on data-intensive complex applications. A large amount of data is stored in geographically distributed sites. Applications such as earth simulation, weather forecasting, study of global warming, and other collaborative works need to access the data from different sites. Shipping of data is computationally expensive. To avoid frequent movement of data across the network, data is replicated among a few sites. Various replication strategies such as ROWA, primary copy, quorum-based protocols, etc., are proposed for distributed databases. As discussed in earlier chapters, the heterogeneity and autonomy of sites in a Grid environment are the key differences between Grid databases and traditional distributed databases. Replica control protocols must manage the replicated data properly to ensure consistency of replicated copies of the data. In this chapter, the need to have write transactions operating in Grid databases is explained, and thus the importance of replica synchronization is discussed.

This chapter presents a replica synchronization protocol. The replica synchronization protocol is then extended to handle multiple network partitioning. In Section 13.1, the motivation is presented along with some use-case scenarios that emphasize the importance of one-copy serializability in the Grid environment. Section 13.2 presents the general architecture of replica management in Grid databases along with an example that identifies the problem of implementing the traditional replica management protocols in Grids. Section 13.3 describes the Grid replica access protocol (GRAP) and shows the correctness. Section 13.4 extends the GRAP to handle multiple partitioning with the concept of contingency quorums.

13.1 MOTIVATION

Recent research in Grid databases deals with replication of read-only files, therefore the problem of replica synchronization has not been well addressed. The

High-Performance Parallel Database Processing and Grid Databases,
by David Taniar, Clement Leung, Wenny Rahayu, and Sushant Goel
Copyright © 2008 John Wiley & Sons, Inc.

following two examples illustrate the need for a replica control protocol in the Grids. Early work on replica control protocol compromises the data consistency and supports only various levels of weaker consistency. It proposes a higher-level service rather than a lower-level protocol. Certain applications in Grids will modify the data and will require one-copy serializability (1SR). The following use-case examples show the need for 1SR.

Example 1: Consider a group of researchers gathering data to study global warming. The group is a collaboration of a number of diverse institutes and universities from all over the globe. Data for such a project can be best collected locally, but to run the experiment, access is required to the data collected by other organisations situated at globally distributed sites. Hence, individual organizations collect data in their databases locally and are connected to other organizations by the Grid infrastructure. Considering the huge amount of data gathered, databases are replicated at participating sites for performance reasons. It is assumed that security and authentication requirements are taken care of by other Grid services. If any site runs the experiment, then the result must be updated for all the participants in a synchronous manner. If the results of the global warming studies are not strictly synchronized (i.e., 1SR) between sites, other database sites may read incorrect values and take the wrong input for their experiments, thus producing undesirable and unreliable results.

Example 2: Any sort of collaborative computing (e.g., collaborative simulation or collaborative optimization process) needs to access up-to-date data. If a distributed optimization process does not have access to the latest data, it may lead to wastage of computing processes due to repeated iteration of the optimization process, or in some cases may even lead to incorrect results. Thus applications working in a collaborative computing environment need synchronous and strict consistency between distributed database sites. Strict consistency can be achieved by using 1SR.

Warning systems for natural disaster also need high accuracy. High-precision warning systems for cyclones, earthquakes, tsunamis, etc, can save thousands of lives. This chapter presents a replica synchronization protocol to maintain 1SR in the Grid environment. Replication is transparent to the user.

13.2   REPLICA ARCHITECTURE

13.2.1   High-Level Replica Management Architecture

The Grid database is a collection of autonomously evolved distributed database systems. Because of the autonomy of sites, protocols implemented in individual DBMS tend to be heterogeneous in nature. Grid middleware provides various services for communication between these heterogeneous, autonomous DBMSs. Figure 13.1 shows the general architecture of Grid database with specific emphasis on high-level replica management components.

Databases $DB_1, DB_2, \ldots, DB_n$ in Figure 13.1 are geographically distributed, autonomously evolved, and probably heterogeneous database systems. These

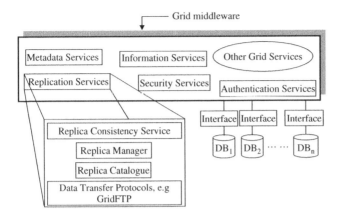

Figure 13.1   Grid database architecture with high-level replication management service

databases interact with each other with the help of Grid middleware. The Grid middleware provides various services like authentication, security, metadata, network communication, and replication with the help of the Globus toolkit. The focus of this chapter is maintaining the consistency of data in the presence of multiple replicas of data. Figure 13.1 shows the expanded version of a replication service. These services are at a higher level in the architecture.

Most of the Grid applications assume the execution of read-only queries. Hence, only the lower three layers, data transfer protocol, replica catalog, and replica manager (Fig. 13.1), would be sufficient for replica management. GridFTP is widely accepted as a data transfer protocol in the Grid community, and it deals with efficient data transfer between sites. Applications rely on replica catalogs to map logical file names to physical data locations, an important requirement in replicated databases. As the name suggests, the replica manager manages the replicas, that is, it creates, deletes, and moves replicas between sites and updates the replica catalog accordingly.

Only the lower three layers are incapable of maintaining consistency of distributed databases, if the applications update the data. Some existing works propose a consistency service on top of existing layers. This service is a high-level replication service that uses different levels of data consistency. Replica synchronization protocols (replica synchronization and replica control are used interchangeably) for a Grid environment assume the use of uniform protocols like two-phase locking (2PL) or 2PC. But as discussed earlier, because of the heterogeneous nature of sites, this may not be a valid assumption. Hence, this chapter focuses on a replica control protocol that deals with the heterogeneous (and autonomous) nature of Grids.

13.2.2 Some Problems

Considering their distributed nature, quorum-based replica control protocols are best suited for Grid databases. Hence, we use a quorum-based replica control protocol. The heterogeneity and autonomy of the Grid database limit communication between sites. Because of autonomy restrictions, a site cannot participate in a global decision of the database system. For example, for a global write transaction, some of the sites may decide to commit while some other local sites may decide to abort the subtransaction, as it is not possible to completely synchronize autonomous databases. The following scenario shows the problem of implementing the traditional replica control protocol in heterogeneous and autonomous Grid environments.

Example: Suppose there are three sites in a distributed Grid environment. Let the database, DB_1, be replicated in all three sites. Suppose the network is partitioned in two partitions, {site 1} in one partition and {site 2, site 3} in the other partition (as shown in Fig. 13.2 for partition P_1). The transaction T_i, which modifies an object in DB_1, is submitted at site 3. The value of write quorum is 2, and hence T_i can successfully obtain a write quorum from sites 2 and 3. T_i must write at both sites to satisfy the requirement of write quorum. Both sites initially decide to commit; thus the global decision to commit is made. But immediately after the global decision is made, site 2 decides to abort T_i because of some local conflict. In a homogeneous environment, this scenario is impossible because of the synchronous communication. Because of the autonomy of sites in a Grid architecture, it is impossible to track that site 2 has decided to abort due to local conflict after having decided to commit.

Now let us assume that partition P_1 is repaired and P_2 occurs with {site 1, site 2} in one partition and {site 3} in the other partition (Fig. 13.2). A transaction T_j arrives at site 1 to read the same data item. T_j can obtain the read quorum from site 1 and site 2. Unfortunately, both replicas have stale copy. The replicated systems have no means of finding out that site 2 had earlier decided to abort after the global decision to commit was made. Thus it can be seen that autonomy can lead to an inconsistent database state. For simplicity, without loss of generality, the database is chosen as the granule, and not an individual data item for discussion in this chapter.

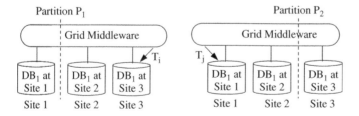

Read quorum (Q_R) = write quorum (Q_W) = 2
Vote of each site = 1

Figure 13.2   A replicated database at three sites in a Grid environment with traditional replica control protocol

13.3 GRID REPLICA ACCESS PROTOCOL (GRAP)

The scenario discussed in the previous section highlights that, because of the autonomy restriction, it is impossible to handle this problem at the individual site level. Hence, it has to be handled at the Grid middleware level. Fortunately, grid middleware also provides the metadata service, which is used in the protocol discussed here. The protocol is based on quorum consensus.

The metadata service of Grid middleware stores information of physical database sites connected to the Grid. It also stores the mapping details of logical to physical database. To implement the protocol, a pointer in metadata services is added that will point to the latest replica. The pointer is of the form *timestamp.site_id* (TS.SID). The timestamp helps in identifying the latest version of the replica, and *site_id* points to the site that has this copy. More than one site can have the latest copy, with a maximum up to the quorum size. At least one site must have the latest copy.

The *Grid replica access protocol* (GRAP) (Fig. 13.3) ensures consistency of data in an autonomous and heterogeneous Grid database environment. The following points are a reminder before proceeding with GRAP:

(1) Part of the distributed transaction (at local site) may decide to abort autonomously.

(2) TS.SID is updated only if the write quorum could be obtained.

(3) Local DB site is able to manage timestamps via the interface to Grid.

13.3.1 Read Transaction Operation for GRAP

GRAP is based on a quorum consensus protocol. Q_R is the read quorum and Q_W is write quorum. Majority consensus is used in GRAP, that is both $(2 \times Q_W)$ and $(Q_R + Q_W)$ should be greater than the total vote for the replica. The following steps are executed for read transactions in GRAP:

(1) If read quorum, Q_R, could not be collected for the read operation, the transaction must abort.

(2) If Q_R can be collected, then the transaction chooses, from the metadata service, the site that has the highest timestamp for the collected quorum.

(3) Corresponding site IDs for the highest timestamp in Q_R are then found from TS.SID.

(4) Data is read from the local site whose timestamp at Grid middleware matches the local timestamp of the replica.

It is possible that none of SIDs obtained from step 3 has matching timestamps in step 4. If the number of such SIDs is 0, then read cannot be performed immediately because all sites with the latest copy of replica may be down. Step 4 is important because some of the local replica may have decided to abort after the global commit decision. Hence, to obtain the latest replica, the timestamp of the

---

Algorithm: GRAP algorithm for read transaction

Q_a: Actual quorum collected by the transaction
Q_R: Read quorum required to read the data

TS.SID(D): TS is timestamp (at Grid's metadata
service) and SID is pointer to the site where latest
replica of data item D is stored. We will only
use TS.SID, since D is the only data item in concern.

TS_i: Timestamp of data item D at local site i
T_r: Read transaction
TS_G: Set of timestamps of sites in Q_R at Grid level
TS_L: Set of timestamp at local level

Q_a ← Collect quorum at metadata service to read data
item D //at Grid level

if ($Q_a \leq Q_R$)
   abort T_r
else
   // more than one site can have same max value,
   // but max value will be unique (at Grid level)
   TS_G ← {collect timestamp from TS.SID from all
   sites in Q_R} TS $_{max}$ ← {TS | TS is maximum in TS_G}
   TSG_{max} ←any element of TS $_{max}$//Max timestamp at
   Grid level SID ← {SID | SID is TS.SID for each
   timestamp ∈ TS $_{max}$} for each SID ∈ SID begin
     TS_L ← { TS_L ∪ TS_i} //set of timestamp at local
     site
   TSL_{max} ← Maximum of TS_L //maximum timestamp at
   local site
   if (TSG_{max} = TSL_{max}) then begin
     read data D from local site whose site ID =
     TSL_{max}
   else
     abort T_r //sites with latest timestamp are
     unreachable

Figure 13.3   GRAP algorithm for read transaction

metadata service and the local copy of the replica must match. This will be clearer when the algorithm for write transaction of GRAP is discussed.

13.3.2   Write Transaction Operation for GRAP

The algorithm for the write transaction of GRAP (Fig. 13.4) is explained as follows:

1. A submitted transaction tries to collect the write quorum (Q_W). If Q_W could not be collected, the transaction aborts.

2. If Q_W is obtained and the site where the transaction was submitted (originator) decides to commit, then the transaction finds the maximum timestamp from Q_W for that data in the metadata service (at Grid middleware).

3. The TS.SID for that replica is then updated in the metadata service, thereby reflecting the latest update in the data. The TS is set to a new maximum reflecting the latest replica of the data item, and SID is set to the site ID of the originator. The originator's local timestamp is also updated to match the metadata service's new timestamp.

4. Other sites (participants) in the quorum must also be monitored for their final decisions as, because of autonomy restrictions, the commitment of the coordinator does not mean participants' commitment. The following two cases are possible:

   a. *If the participant decides to commit:* The TS.SID is updated in the normal way, i.e., the TS will be set to the maximum timestamp decided by the metadata service for the originator, and the SID will be the site ID of the corresponding participant. The timestamp is updated at both locations, at the Grid middleware's metadata service as well as at the local participating site's replica.

   b. *If the participant decides to abort:* Because of any local conflict, if the participant decides to abort, it must be handled so that the replica is not corrupted. In this case, the timestamp (TS of TS.SID) of the middleware's metadata service is still updated as usual to reflect that the update of one of the replicas has taken place, but SID is updated to point to the originator site instead of pointing to the participant (which decided to abort). The local timestamp of the replica is also not updated. This helps the read transactions to avoid reading stale data in the future (as discussed in step 4 of the reading transaction algorithm, the metadata's timestamp and local replica's timestamp must match).

Step 4b helps the quorum-based system to operate correctly, even if some of the replica decides to abort, with the help of the TS.SID pointer. The quorum at Grid level is still valid because the timestamp at the metadata service has been updated to reflect successful completion of the transaction at the Grid. Thus the metadata information of the site that had to abort its local transaction points to the latest replica at the originator of the transaction and not to the participant site itself. This is the reason why, although the site may have participated in the quorum, it may still not have any matching timestamps in step 4 of the read transaction. Thus, if the participant aborts its subtransaction, the SID will point to the site having the latest replica, typically the originator. The transaction can successfully complete only if at least the originator commits successfully. If the originator aborts, then one participant cannot point to the other participant, because other participants may abort later because of local conflict.

Algorithm: GRAP algorithm for write transaction

Q_a: Actual quorum collected by the transaction
Q_W: Write quorum required to write the data
T_w: Write transaction

TS.SID(D): TS is the timestamp (at Grid's metadata service) and SID is pointer to the site where latest replica of data item D is stored.
ST_O: Subtransaction of T_w at originator site (local site where transaction originated)
ST_P: Subtransaction of T_w at participating site (all other replicas of data item D)
TSG_i: Timestamp for each replica at the metadata service (Grid level)
TSG_{max}: Maximum timestamp calculated at Grid level
//similar to read transaction
TSL_i: Timestamp for any participating site at local level

Q_a ← Collect quorum to write the data item D
//at Grid level
if ($Q_a \leq Q_W$)
    abort T_w
else
    if ST_O decides to abort then begin
        abort T_w
    else
        TSG_{max} ← maximum of {TSG_i for sites in Q_w}
        for each SID ∈ Q_w begin
            TSG_i ← (TSG_{max} +1)   //TS part of TS.ID
            (Grid level)
        // SID part of TS.SID
        SID of replica at Grid (for originator) ←
            SID of originator (local site)
        TSL_O ← (TSG_{max} +1)
        //set originator timestamp to reflect Grid level
        //update for participant site, if it decides
            to commit
        if ST_P decides to commit
            SID of replica at Grid (for participant) ←
                SID of participant (local site)
            TSL_p ← (TSG_{max} +1)
        // for participant site, if it decides to abort
        if ST_P decides to abort
        //if local site aborts the global SID pointer
        //points to the committed originator.
        //Thus latest value can be retrieved.
            SID of replica at Grid (for participant) ←
                SID of originator (local site)
            //local timestamp isn't updated.
            //avoids reading stale value
            TSL_p ← set as old value

Figure 13.4 GRAP algorithm for write transaction

The line-by-line explanation of algorithms (Figs. 13.3 and 13.4) is similar to the contingency GRAP algorithm discussed in the next section, and hence the description will become clear when Figure 13.6 is explained in detail.

13.3.3 Revisiting the Example Problem

The same scenario of Section 13.2 is discussed below, to demonstrate how GRAP prevents the reading of stale data.

Let us assume that the timestamp for all replicas is 0 in the beginning and the site IDs are 1,2,3 ... etc. Say a transaction, T_i, arrives at site 3 and wants to write a data item (Fig. 13.5). After obtaining the write quorum (step 1 of write transaction of GRAP), site 3 decides to commit but site 2 decides to abort its respective cohorts (same as Fig. 13.2). Since the quorum was obtained, the timestamp at Grid level, TS, will be increased to reflect the latest replica of the data (step 2 of write transaction of GRAP). Since site 3 has decided to commit, the local timestamp will also be increased to match the Grid TS and the SID is set to 3 (same as site ID). This confirms that the cohort of the transaction at site 3 is already committed (steps 3 and 4a of write transaction of GRAP). Thus the (*TS.SID, local timestamp*) for site 3 is (1.3, 1). This indicates that the maximum timestamp TS at the Grid middleware and the local timestamp are the same (i.e., 1); hence, the latest replica could be found at the same site. But as site 2 decided to abort its part of the transaction, the local timestamp is not changed and the SID points to the originator of the transaction (step 4b of write transaction of GRAP), that is, site 3. Now, say P_1 is repaired and partitioning P_2 occurs. T_j arrives during $P_2.T_j$ can obtain the read quorum (Q_R), as site 1 and site 2 are available (step 1 of read transaction of GRAP).

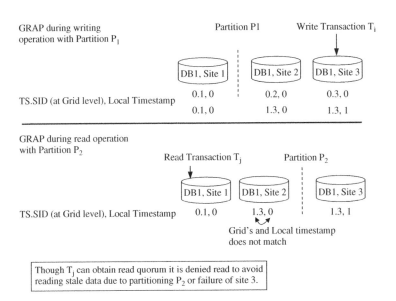

Figure 13.5 A replicated database using GRAP protocol

Algorithm: Contingency GRAP algorithm for write transaction operation

---

CQ_w: Contingency quorum for write operation
C-log: Log to maintain records when writes are processed in absence of quorum

Cardinality(X)
// returns number of elements in X
Update (D)
// checks for old value and updates with latest value of D
// Other variables used are same as write algorithm for GRAP
1. $Q_a \leftarrow$ Collect quorum to write the data item D
   //Grid level
2. if (($Q_a \leq Q_w$) $\wedge$ (network is not partitioned))
      abort T_w // No quorum is available for the data item
3. if (($Q_a \leq Q_w$) $\wedge$ (network is partitioned))
      $TSG_{max} \leftarrow$ maximum of {TSG_i for sites in Q_w}
      $TSL_{max} \leftarrow$ maximum of {TSL_i for sites in the partition where T_w initiated}
4.   if $TSG_{max} \neq TSL_{max}$ then begin
         abort T_w // Partition doesn't contain latest copy
5.   else
6.   if ST_O decides to abort
         abort T_w
7.   else
8.   for each SID $\in CQ_w$ // $CQ_w < Q_w$
               $TSG_i \leftarrow$ (TSG_{max} +1)   //TS part of TS.ID
               // for originator site
9.   SID of data at Grid (for originator) $\leftarrow$ SID of originator (local site)
            $TSL_O \leftarrow$ (TSG_{max} +1)
            C-log $\leftarrow$ C-log $\cup$ SID
            // SID where transaction is executing.
10.   if ST_p decides to commit
               SID of data at Grid (for participant) $\leftarrow$ SID of participant
               $TSL_p \leftarrow$ (TSG_{max} +1)
               C-log $\leftarrow$ C-log $\cup$ SID
            // for participant site, if it decides to abort
11.   if ST_p decides to abort
               SID of data at Grid (for participant)$\leftarrow$ SID of originator (local site)
               $TSL_p \leftarrow$ set as old value of site

Figure 13.6 Contingency GRAP algorithm for write transaction operation

The maximum timestamp at Grid level is 1, and it belongs to site 2 (step 2 of read transaction of GRAP). But site 2 has stale data. GRAP avoids reading the stale data at site 2 and redirects the transaction to obtain a quorum that has a site with the latest value of data as follows. The pair (TS.SID, local timestamp) for site 2 is (1.3, 0) (as shown in Fig. 13.5). The maximum timestamp at Grid middleware is found at site 2, which implies that site 2 had participated in the quorum for the latest update of the data item. But since the TS at the middleware do not match with the local timestamp, this indicates that site 2 does not contain the latest replica of the data item. SID at site 2 points to the site that contains the latest replica, namely, site 3 (step 3 of read transaction of GRAP). Site 3 could not be reached because of the network partitioning; hence, the transaction must either wait or abort (depending on application semantics). Thus GRAP prevents T_j from reading stale data. Under normal circumstances, since T_j had already obtained Q_R, it would have read the stale value of the replicated data.

13.3.4 Correctness of GRAP

The main objective of GRAP is to provide a consistent view of data. As discussed above in examples 1 and 2, some applications cannot have a lower level of consistency and must support one-copy serializability (1SR). In this section, it is shown that the proposed protocol, GRAP, conforms to 1SR.

Lemma 13.1: Two write transactions on any replica will be strictly ordered; avoid write-write conflict and the write quorum will always have the latest copy of the data item.

Proof: Let two transactions T_i and T_j write any replicated object O. To write O, both transactions need to obtain write quorum, Q_W. As discussed earlier, $(2 \times Q_W)$ should be greater than the total votes of all replicas of O. Hence, two transactions can never obtain Q_W simultaneously. Thus any two transactions will be strictly ordered and will avoid write-write conflict. After one of the transactions, say T_i, has committed, T_j obtains Q_W. Because of the nonempty property of two write quorum sets, there will be at least one replica of O that overlaps with T_i's quorum. Thus the write quorum will always have one latest copy of the replicated data item or will point to a site that contains the latest data item.

Lemma 13.2: Any transaction T_i will always read the latest copy of a replica.

Proof: Every read operation has to obtain a read quorum from available sites in the Grid middleware. From the obtained quorum, a set of sites with the largest timestamps is created. These timestamps are collected at the Grid level, and as discussed earlier, because of autonomy restrictions, may vary from local timestamps. Hence, the latest copy of the replica cannot be obtained only by collecting timestamps at Grid level. GRAP ensures that the maximum timestamp obtained from the Grid level matches with the local timestamp. The data can be read from any of the sites whose Grid timestamp and local timestamp are equal. It is not possible to not have any matching timestamp. This condition is prevented by step 3 of the write operation of GRAP, as at least the coordinator will have the latest local copy that is being reflected at Grid level. The nonempty property of the intersection between the read quorum and the write quorum ensures that the read quorum will have at least one latest replica.

Theorem 13.1: Grid replica access protocol (GRAP) produces one-copy serializable (1SR) schedules.

Proof: From lemmas 13.1 and 13.2 it could be concluded that GRAP supports one-copy view of the replicated databases. GRAP could be combined with the concurrency control protocol (e.g., GCC protocol discussed in the previous chapter) to extend one-copy view to one-copy serializability.

13.4   HANDLING MULTIPLE PARTITIONING

Considering the global nature of Grids, failures are inevitable. Hence, the network may become partitioned. Network partitioning is a phenomenon that prevents communication between two sets of sites in a distributed architecture.

Network partitioning limits the execution of transactions in replicated databases because a quorum cannot be obtained, or all sites may not be available for update. ROWA and ROWA-A protocols cannot handle network partitioning at all. The primary copy protocol can handle network partitioning only if the primary copy is in the partition where the transaction originated. Quorum-based protocols can best handle network partitioning, but only simple network partitioning (only 2 partitions). The majority of consensus quorums cannot handle multiple network partitioning because in the case of multiple network partitioning, basic quorum rules, $Q_R + Q_W > Q$ and $2 \times Q_W > Q$, cannot be satisfied.

For example, for a 7-site network, assume $Q_R = Q_W = 4$. If the network is partitioned in three partitions (1, 3, and 3 sites), then a quorum cannot be obtained and thus transactions will be forced to either wait or abort. In this section, the GRAP is modified to handle multiple partitioning (more than 2 partitions).

13.4.1   Contingency GRAP

To handle multiple partitioning, the concept of a contingency quorum is introduced. If there is no partitioning, then GRAP collects a normal quorum and operates in a normal mode, but as soon as any network partitioning is detected, where normal quorum cannot be obtained, GRAP collects a contingency quorum (*contingency GRAP*). Any partition needs to have at least one up-to-date copy of the data to serve the transaction. Read transactions have the following steps in Contingency GRAP in partitioned networks.

Read Transaction Operation for Contingency GRAP

The steps for read operation are as follows:

1. After the read transaction arrives at the site, it checks for the normal read quorum at Grid middleware. If the normal read quorum is obtained, normal GRAP operation continues.

2. If the normal read quorum cannot be obtained, then the transaction chooses the highest timestamp from the metadata service of Grid middleware (similar to step 2 of normal GRAP).

3. If the maximum timestamp at the metadata service does not match with any of the local replicas' timestamp in that partition for the data item where the transaction originated, the transaction must either wait or abort. This indicates that the partition does not have the latest version of the data item.

4. If the timestamp of any of the local replicas from that partition and the timestamp of metadata service match, then it can be assured that the latest copy of the replica is in the partition and that the replica is read.

The algorithm for contingency GRAP for a read transaction is very similar to the algorithm of GRAP for the read transaction (Fig. 13.3).

Write Transaction Operation for Contingency GRAP

Contingency GRAP allows the transaction to write fewer numbers of sites than required in the quorum and maintains a log to guarantee consistency of the data. The write transaction of contingency GRAP in a partitioned network has the following steps:

1. The transaction first tries to collect the normal write quorum; if obtained, normal GRAP continues. If a normal quorum cannot be obtained, then contingency GRAP starts.

2. Contingency GRAP chooses the highest timestamp from the metadata service and checks it against the sites in the partition. If the metadata service's timestamp cannot find any matching timestamp in the partition, then the write transaction has to abort or wait until the partition is repaired (this is an application-dependent decision). This implies that the latest copy of the data is not in the partition, and hence the transaction cannot write the data until the partition is fixed or the quorum is obtained.

3. If the matching timestamp between metadata service and any site's local timestamp in the partition is found, then the transaction can proceed with the update at the site where the two timestamps match because it is assured that the latest version of the replica is in the partition. If the timestamp does not match, but the SID points to a site that is in the same partition, even then the transaction can be assured to update the latest copy. The sites that are written/updated during the contingency GRAP are logged in the log file.

4. If the originator site decides to commit the transaction, it updates the TS.SID (at metadata service). The TS is increased to a new maximum, and SID points to the originator. The local timestamp of the site is also increased to match the TS of the Grid middleware.

5. Other replica sites in the partition (participants) also follow the same procedure if they decide to commit, i.e., the SID is set to the respective participant and the local timestamp is set to match the new TS at middleware. But the SID points to the originator and the local timestamp is not increased for any site that decides to locally abort the write transaction.

6. The number and detail of sites participating in the contingency update process are updated in the log. This is an important step, because the number of sites being updated does not form a quorum. Thus, after the partitioning has been repaired, the log is used to propagate updates to additional sites that will form a quorum. Once the quorum has been formed, normal GRAP operation can resume.

Figure 13.6 is explained as follows. The quorum is collected for the data item to be written (line 1). If the network is not partitioned and the collected quorum (Q_a) is less than the required write quorum (Q_w) (line 2), the transaction is aborted. But if the collected quorum is less than the required write quorum and the network is partitioned (line 3), then the protocol works under the contingency quorum, that is, the actual collected quorum. The maximum local timestamp at the partition where the transaction is submitted and the maximum timestamp at the Grid (for the respective replica) are obtained. If both the maximum values do not match, then the transaction is aborted (line 4). This implies that the partition does not have the latest replica. If both timestamps match (line 5) but the originator decides to abort (line 6), then the global transaction will abort.

If the originator decides to commit (line 7), then the transaction can continue the execution. For each site in the originator's partition (line 8), the middleware's timestamp is increased to a new maximum. The new site ID (SID) for the originator is set to point toward itself (line 9), which reflects that the originator decided to commit, and contains the latest replica. The local timestamp of the originator is also increased to a new maximum to match the Grid middleware's timestamp. Since the site is working under a contingency quorum, the site ID is added in the log.

If the participant site decides to commit (line 10), then the SID pointer is set to point toward itself, because that participant will also have the latest copy of the replica and the local timestamp of the participant is set to match with the originator's maximum value. The site ID of the participant is also added to the log. But if the participant decides to abort its cohort (line 11), then the SID pointer points to the originator and the local timestamp is unchanged. This ensures that the participant points to the latest replica of the data item. Since the participant decided to abort, it is not necessary to add the site ID to the log file.

The contingency GRAP helps in executing transactions even in the case of multiple partitioning. The partition that has the latest copy of the replica can continue.

It acts as a combination of quorum consensus protocol and primary copy protocol. The difference is that it updates all sites in the partition, not only a single site. Grid middleware's metadata service helps to find the most up-to-date copy of the replica.

13.4.2   Comparison of Replica Management Protocols

Based on the update mechanism, replication synchronization protocols can broadly be classified into two categories: (*i*) synchronous, also known as eager replication, and (*ii*) asynchronous, also known as lazy replication. Synchronous replication updates all replicas of the data object as a single transaction. An asynchronous replication protocol updates only one replica of the data, and the changes are propagated to other replicas later (*lazily*).

Synchronous protocols ensure strict consistency among replicated data, but a disadvantage is that they are slow and computationally expensive, as many messages are to be sent in the network. The response time of asynchronous replication protocols is less, compared with synchronous protocols, as they update the data only at one site. Asynchronous protocols do not guarantee strict consistency of data at distributed replica sites.

The choice of a synchronous or an asynchronous replica protocol is a trade-off between strict consistency and the response time of the application. On the one hand, some applications need high precision and demand strict consistency (engineering applications, earth simulator, etc.); on the other hand, some applications can relax the consistency requirements. GRAP meets strict consistency requirements.

A major requirement of replica control protocols is that the transactions should be able to execute even if some of the replicated data sites are unavailable. In the presence of failure, synchronous protocols cannot execute the update transactions. Because of the distributed nature of the Grid, the failure probability is higher compared with centralized systems. Synchronous replication is best implemented in small local area networks with short latencies. In synchronous replication, the deadlock increases as the third power of the number of sites in the network and the fifth power of the transaction size. Thus the performance of a synchronous protocol is unacceptable in a Grid environment, and asynchronous protocols are unsuitable for our purpose, as they do not ensure strict consistency of data. Hence, the quorum-based protocols are most suited for Grid database requirements. However, the quorum-based majority consensus protocol can handle only simple network partitioning. The contingency GRAP protocol can sustain multiple partitioning. Table 13.1 compares the characteristics of various replica management protocols with GRAP and contingency GRAP.

The ROWA and ROWA-A protocols cannot handle network partitioning. The ROWA protocol cannot sustain any site failure. ROWA-A can sustain site failure by writing only on available copies, but if the sites are operational and they cannot communicate because of network partitioning, the database may become inconsistent. The inconsistencies may be addressed by using manual or automatic

Table 13.1 Comparison of various replica control protocols

Protocol	Behavior				
	Simple Network Partitioning	Multiple Network Partitioning	Minimum Number of Sites Having latest Replica	Site Required to Read a Data Item	Site Required to Write a Data Item
ROWA	No	No	All replicas	Any replica	All replicas
ROWA-A	No	No	Number of available sites	Any replica	Available replicas
Primary Copy	Only if primary site is in the partition	Only if primary site is in the partition	1 (primary site)	1 (primary site)	1 (primary site)
Majority consensus	Only if quorum can be obtained	No	Size of write quorum	Size of read quorum	Size of write quorum
GRAP	Only if quorum can be obtained	No	Size of write quorum	Size of read quorum	Size of write quorum
Contingency GRAP	Operates same as GRAP in simple partition-ing	Yes	*Under normal operation and simple partition-ing*: Size of write quorum *Under multiple partition-ing*: Less than write quorum	*Under normal operation and simple partition-ing*: Size of read quorum *Under multiple partition-ing*: Less than read quorum, if the partition contains the latest replica	*Under normal operation and simple partition-ing*: Size of write quorum *Under multiple partition-ing*: Less than write quorum

reconciliation processes. Primary site protocols can handle network partitioning only if the partition contains the primary site.

In Table 13.1, the properties of GRAP look very similar to those of the majority consensus protocol. But the main difference between the two is that the majority consensus protocol can lead to an inconsistent database state because of the autonomy of Grid database sites, while GRAP is designed to support autonomous sites. Contingency GRAP can handle multiple network partitioning. While the network is partitioned (multiple), contingency GRAP updates fewer sites, required by the quorum, and keeps a record. Read operations can be performed at all partitions having the latest replica copy of the data (verified by the middleware).

13.4.3 Correctness of Contingency GRAP

The following lemmas are used to prove the correctness of contingency GRAP, on the same grounds as GRAP.

Lemma 13.3: Two write operations are ordered in the presence of multiple partitioning.

Proof: In the presence of multiple partitioning, there will never be a majority consensus. Consider two transactions, T_i and T_j, executing in two different partitions P_1 and P_2, respectively. The following cases are possible:

 (i) P_1 and P_2 do not have a copy of the latest replica: Step 2 of contingency GRAP for write transaction takes care of this case. T_i and T_j have to either abort their respective transactions or wait until the partitioning has been repaired.

 (ii) P_1 has the latest replica: Step 2 of contingency GRAP for write transaction will abort its transaction T_j. Step 4 will ensure that the metadata service's timestamp is updated to reflect the latest write transaction T_i of P_1. Step 3 and step 6 ensure the updating of the log of sites where T_i's effects are reflected. This is an important step since, because of multiple partitioning, the write quorum could not be updated.

(iii) P_1 and P_2 both have a copy of the latest replica: Assume that both T_i and T_j send a request to check the latest copy of the replica. Both partitions initially may get the impression that they have the latest replica. But steps 3, 4, and 6 of the algorithm prevent the occurrence of such a situation by updating the log. Also, the first transaction to update the data item will increase the timestamp at the metadata service, and thus any later transaction that reads the timestamp from the metadata service has to abort the transaction (because it could not find any matching local timestamp), although it had the impression of latest copy at the first instance.

Cases ii and iii write replicas of the data item even if the quorum could not be obtained, which can lead to inconsistency. But the metadata service's timestamp and log entry only allows transactions to proceed in one partition, thereby preventing the inconsistency. After the partitioning has been recovered, the log file is used to propagate values of the latest replicas to more sites to at least form the quorum (steps 3 and (6) of contingency GRAP). Thus data consistency is maintained of replicas in the presence of multiple partitioning.

Lemma 13.4: Any transaction will always read the latest copy of the replica.

Proof: Although because of failure of sites a read quorum cannot be obtained, the latest copy of the replica can be located with the help of the metadata service's timestamp. If the latest replica is in the partition, then the transaction reads the replica; otherwise, it has to either abort the transaction or wait until the partition has been repaired. Thus any transaction will always read the latest replica of the data (steps 3 and 4 of contingency GRAP for read transaction).

Theorem 13.2: Contingency GRAP produces 1SR schedules.

Proof: On similar grounds as theorem 13.1, lemma 13.3 and lemma 13.4 ensure one-copy view of the replicated database. Contingency GRAP can be combined (like GRAP) with GCC concurrency control protocol to ensure 1SR schedules.

13.5 SUMMARY

To increase system availability and performance, data is replicated at different sites in physically distributed data intensive applications. Traditional distributed databases are synchronized and tightly coupled in nature. Although various replica synchronization protocols for distributed databases, such as ROWA, ROWA-available, primary copy, etc., are available, because of the autonomy of the sites, it is not possible to implement traditional replica synchronization protocols in the Grid environment.

   In this chapter, a quorum-based replica management protocol (GRAP) is introduced, which can handle the autonomy of sites in the Grid environment. It makes use of the metadata service of Grid middleware and a pointer that points to the site containing the latest replica of the data item. Considering the distributed nature of applications and the flexible behavior of quorums, quorum-based protocols in GRAP are suitable. Quorum-based protocols have the drawback that they cannot obtain the quorum in case of multiple partitioning. A contingency quorum and log file are used to extend GRAP, in order to handle multiple network partitioning, so that the partition containing the latest replica of the data can continue its operation. Once multiple partitioning has been repaired and normal quorum obtained, the normal GRAP operation resumes.

   Replica control protocols studied for the Grid environment either are high-level services or are intended to relax the consistency requirement. But high-precision applications cannot afford to relax data consistency. Thus in this chapter the main focus is on a lower level protocol that does not compromise data consistency at replicated sites. This chapter may be summarized as follows:

- A replica synchronization protocol for an autonomous Grid environment is introduced. Because of the autonomy of sites, participants can reverse the global decision due to local conflicts. GRAP protocol ensures that a transaction reads the latest version of the data item.

- Contingency GRAP protocol is used to sustain multiple network partitioning. When considering the global nature of Grids, it is important to address multiple network partitioning issues.

- The correctness of GRAP and contingency GRAP are demonstrated to ensure that 1SR schedule is maintained.

13.6 BIBLIOGRAPHICAL NOTES

In recent years, there have been emerging conferences in the Grid areas, such as *GCC, CCGrid*, etc, that publish numerous papers on data replication in the Grid environment. In the *GCC* conference series, You et al. (2006) described a utility-based replication strategy in data grid. On the other hand, Rahman et al. (2005) introduced a multiobjective model through the use of *p*-median and *p*-center models to address the replica placement problem, and Park et al. (2003) proposed a dynamic replication that reduced data access time by avoiding network congestions in a data grid network achieved through a network-level locality

In the *CCGrid* conference series, Liu and Wu (2006) studied replica placement in data grid systems by proposing algorithms for selecting optimal locations for placing the replicas. Carman et al. (2002) used an economic model for data replication. An early work on data replication using the Globus Data Grid architecture was presented by Vazhkudai et al. (2001), who designed and implemented a high-level replica selection services.

Other parallel/distributed and high-performance computing conferences, such as *HiPC, Euro-Par, HPDC*, and *ICPADS*, have also attracted grid researchers to publish data replication research. Chakrabarti et al. (*HiPC* 2004) presented an integration of scheduling and replication in data grids, and Tang et al. (*Euro-Par* 2005) combined job scheduling heuristics with data replication in the grid. Consistency in data replication has also been the focus of Dullman et al. (*HPDC* 2001), whereas Lin et al. (*ICPADS* 2006) studied the minimum number of replicas to ensure the locality requirements.

13.7 EXERCISES

13.1. Explain why data replication in the Grid is more common than in any other database systems (e.g., parallel databases, distributed databases, and multidatabase systems).

13.2. Discuss why replication may be a problem in the Grid.

13.3. Describe the main features of the *Grid replica access protocol*.

13.4. Illustrate how the Grid replica access protocol may solve the replication problem in the Grid.

13.5. What is a 1SR (1-copy serializable) schedule? Discuss Theorem 13.1, which states that GRAP produce 1SR.

13.6. What is *contingency quorum*?

13.7. Describe the difference between *eager replication* and *lazy replication*.

13.8. Outline the primary difference between GRAP and contigency GRAP.

Chapter 14

Grid Atomic Commitment in Replicated Data

An atomic commitment protocol and a replica management protocol were explained in Chapters 12 and 13. Atomic commitment protocols are used to ensure the *all-or-nothing* property of a transaction that is executing in a distributed environment. A global transaction has multiple cohorts executing at different physically distributed data sites. If one site aborts its cohort (subtransaction), then all other sites must also abort their subtransactions to enforce the all-or-nothing property. Thus the computing resources at all other sites where the subtransactions decided to commit are wasted.

Multiple copies of data are stored at multiple sites in a replicated database to increase system availability and performance. The database can operate even though some of the sites have failed, thereby increasing the availability of the system, and a transaction is more likely to find the data it needs close to the transaction's home site, thereby increasing overall performance of the system.

The number of aborts can be high in the Grid environment while maintaining the atomicity of global transactions. In this chapter, replicas available at different sites are used to maintain atomicity. The protocol will help to reduce the number of aborts of global transactions and will reduce wastage of computing resources. Section 14.1 presents the motivation for using replication in the ACPs. Section 14.2 describes a modified version of the Grid-ACP. The modified Grid-ACP uses replication at multiple levels to reduce the number of aborts in Grid databases. Section 14.3 discusses how the ACID properties of a transaction are affected in a replicated Grid environment.

14.1 MOTIVATION

Transactions executing in the Grid architecture are long-running transactions. Thus aborting the whole global transaction, even if a single subtransaction aborts, will result in high computational loss. On the other hand, if the global transaction does not abort on abortion of any subtransaction, then it violates the atomicity property of the transaction. Therefore, the two are contradictory requirements.

As discussed in Chapter 12, any site that might have decided to commit its cohort of the global transaction and is in "sleep" state, should execute the compensating transaction if any of the subtransactions of the global transaction decides to abort. Effectively, the computational job done by the participants is lost. Considering the large volume of work done in Grid databases, this is undesirable.

14.1.1 Architectural Reasons

The following points constitute the major motivation, from an architectural perspective, for using replication to reduce the number of aborts in the Grid database:

(1) The Grid database handles comparatively larger volumes of data than traditional distributed databases. The nature of the transactions is long-running, and hence aborts are very expensive in the Grid environment. Therefore, the number of aborts in the Grid database needs to be reduced.

(2) Replication increases the availability of data, e.g., if a site with a replica is unavailable, then the transaction is redirected to another replica, thereby increasing availability. Replica control protocols do not explore replicated data once the transaction has submitted its subtransactions to local sites and these are already executing; e.g., if a subtransaction fails during the execution, then the whole transaction aborts.

This chapter explores the possibility of using replication to reduce aborts, after any subtransaction has aborted but while the global transaction is still active. Thus, if a subtransaction decides to abort, it looks for another replica of the data instead of aborting the entire global transaction.

(3) Replication of data is provided in Grid databases naturally for fast and easy access of data, close to the transaction's originator site. Thus it will incur fewer overheads.

14.1.2 Motivating Example

A scenario of a normal operation of an atomic commitment protocol, which does not make use of replicated data, is demonstrated below.

Scenario: Figure 14.1 shows the functioning of an atomic commit protocol (e.g., Grid-ACP). Assume a data item D is replicated at five sites $DB_1, DB_2, \ldots DB_5$. To satisfy the threshold conditions, the read quorum (Q_R) and write quorum (Q_W)

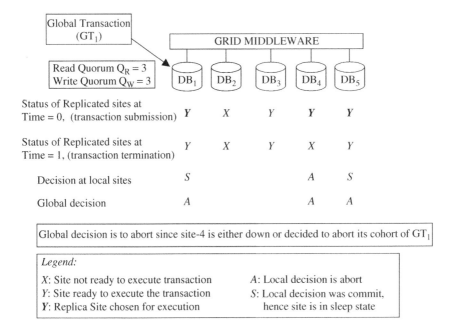

Figure 14.1 An ACP's operation without using replication

are equal to 3. Hence, any transaction must access three sites in order to read or write the data item.

In Figure 14.1, X denotes that the site is unable to fulfil the request at that time (i.e., either the site is down or the subtransaction's decision was to abort) and Y denotes that the database is ready to serve the request. Say that at time $T = 0$, GT_1 is submitted at database site DB_1. GT_1 intends to write data item D. Let us assume that all sites are active and working except DB_2. Q_W can be obtained from any three sites; let the chosen sites be DB_1, DB_4 and DB_5 (bold letters at time $= 0$). After execution, say at time $T = 1$, DB_1 and DB_5 decide to commit their respective subtransactions but DB_4 decides to abort its part of subtransaction because of some local dependencies (remember this is possible because of autonomy restriction among sites); to maintain atomicity of the global transaction, DB_1 and DB_5 must also abort their subtransactions. Thus the computing done at site 1 and site 5 is wasted. Furthermore, execution of the compensating transaction will consume more computing resources.

From Figure 14.1, it is clear that at time $T = 1$, when DB_4 decides to abort and consequently the global transaction also decides to abort, the quorum was still available in terms of DB_1, DB_3 and DB_5. But the transaction did not check the quorum at a later stage, and the global transaction was aborted. Thus the abortion of transaction wastes computing resources, which could have been avoided by exploring quorums at multiple levels.

14.2 MODIFIED GRID ATOMIC COMMITMENT PROTOCOL

In this section, the earlier Grid-ACP (from Chapter 12) is modified to explore multiple levels of checking of the quorums, so that the number of aborts could be reduced.

14.2.1 Modified Grid-ACP

As discussed earlier, atomic commitment protocols do not take advantage of data replication when any subtransaction decides to abort. Thus the advantage of data replication is only limited at the start of the transaction. Exploiting the benefits of replication other than at the beginning of a transaction can reduce aborts in the Grid environment.

Revisiting the Motivating Example

The same scenario explained in the previous section is discussed here, but this time the replication at multiple levels is explored, rather than only at the beginning of the transaction. Assume the same situation, at time $T = 0$, DB_1, DB_4 and DB_5 (Y in Fig. 14.2) being the chosen replicas for the quorum. At $T = 1$, DB_4 decides to abort and DB_1 and DB_5 decide to commit the subtransaction and hence are in the sleep state. Unlike the normal Grid-ACP, the modified Grid-ACP does not decide to abort the global transaction at this stage. Traditional ACPs, including Grid-ACP, exploit only level-1 operations (of Fig. 14.2) during the commit process. The Grid middleware is aware of other replica locations of the data item D. With the help of the *replica location service* of Grid middleware, the originator site, namely, DB_1, of global transaction GT_1 finds the other replica of D (site DB_3 in this case) and allocates the subtransaction to that database site.

In Figure 14.2, at $T = 2$, we see that DB_1 and DB_5 are in "sleep" state and DB_4 is in "abort" state. The replica location service chooses DB_3 as a new replica to satisfy the requirement of the write quorum (denoted as Y in Figure 14.2 at level-2 operations). DB_1 and DB_5 are in "sleep" state while DB_3 executes its subtransaction. If DB_3 executes successfully and decides to commit, then the originator (DB_1) can decide to commit the global transaction, because the requirement of the write quorum has been fulfilled from sites DB_1, DB_3, and DB_5 (instead of sites DB_1, DB_4, and DB_5). Thus the modified Grid-ACP explores more than one level of operation, during the commit procedure in order to reduce the number of aborts.

Modified Grid-ACP Algorithm

The procedure for modified Grid-ACP is explained as follows:

(1) Since the modified Grid-ACP uses the quorum-based replication strategy, it must collect the read/write quorum for data item D to be read/written.

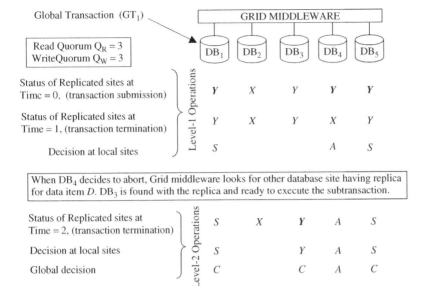

Figure 14.2   Modified Grid-ACP using replication at multiple levels

(2) If the required quorum could not be obtained, the global transaction is aborted and resubmitted at a later stage. If the quorum is obtained, the global transaction generates the set of subtransactions with the help of the Grid's metadata and replica management services. The subtransactions are then submitted to respective participating database sites. The site where the global transaction was submitted is known as the originator, and other sites are known as participants of the transaction.

(3) If no subtransaction aborts (i.e., $Na = 0$ in Fig. 14.3), then the global decision is to commit. The decision is logged in the originator's log before being communicated to all participants (similar to Grid-ACP).

(4) If any subtransaction aborts (i.e., $Na \neq 0$ in Fig. 14.3), then the coordinator checks with the Grid's metadata and replica management service as to whether the other replicas for data item D are available.

(i) If the number of other replicas available is more than the number of aborts (Na), then the aborted subtransactions are resubmitted to other

---

Algorithm: Modified Grid-ACP algorithm for
originator site

Q_a: Actual quorum collected by the transaction
Q_R/Q_W: Read/write quorum required to read/write the data
GT_i: Global transaction
N: Total num subtransactions GT_i executing on replicated
data Na: Num of local sites decided to abort
local subtransaction

```
       Qₐ ← Collect quorum at replica to read/write data
       item D
1. if (Qₐ > Q)        //Q could be either Q_R or Q_W
2.     create subtransactions
       N ← total number of subtransactions
3.     submit subtransactions to participants
4.     wait for response from all participants
5.     Na ← total number of abort response
6.     if Na = 0   // no subtransaction decides to abort
           write commit record in log
           send global_commit to all participants
           GTᵢ commits
7.     else          //check for other available replicas
       of GTᵢ
8          send check_available_replicas message to
               replica management service
9          if (Number_of_other_replicas ≥ Na)
               resubmit subtransaction to Na number of new
                   replica sites
10.            N ← total number of resubmitted
               subtransactions
11.            Goto Line 4
12.        else
               write abort record in log    // abort procedure
               send global_abort to participants to commit;
               wait for response from these participants
               GTᵢ aborts
13. else
           abort GTᵢ and resubmit later
```

Figure 14.3   Modified Grid-ACP algorithm for originator site

sites where the replica of the data is residing and waits for the response
from the newly submitted subtransaction. Importantly, the number of subtransactions (N) must be set to the new number of subtransactions being
submitted.

   (ii) If the available replicas are less than the number of aborts, Na, the originator then starts the abort procedure. The abort decision is sent only
   to those database sites that are in the "sleep" state. This procedure is

repeated until all replica sites have been explored. Thus the modified Grid-ACP exploits all replicas in order to reduce the number of aborts (Fig. 14.2 shows only two levels of operations for pedagogical simplicity).

The modified Grid-ACP algorithm is formally presented in Figure 14.3. A brief description of Figure 14.3 is as follows. The quorum (read or write) is collected for the data item being read/written. If the actual collected quorum is greater than the required read or write quorum (line 1), then the global transaction can proceed. If the collected quorum is less than the quorum required to read/write data, then the global transaction cannot proceed and must be aborted (line 13), and resubmitted later to obtain the quorum. Once the required quorum has been obtained, the Grid middleware's metadata service and replica management service are used to create the subtransactions (line 2). The total number of subtransactions is stored in a variable N. The subtransactions are then submitted to the respective participants (line 3). The originator waits for the participants' response (line 4).

The originator counts the number of participants whose responses were to abort and stores it in a variable Na (line 5). If all participants decide to commit (i.e., $Na = 0$) (line 6), then the normal Grid-ACP procedure can continue and the originator can send the global commit response to all the participants. If any participating site aborts (i.e., $Na > 0$) (line 7), then the originator checks the replica management service for other available replica of the data item (line 8). If the number of other available replicas (for a particular data item) is greater than, or equal to, the number of aborting subtransactions (i.e., Na) (line 9), then the subtransactions can again be submitted to Na number of other replicas, so that the quorum condition is maintained and the global transaction need not abort.

The number of subtransactions stored in the variable N is changed to the new number of subtransactions submitted to other replicas. This is an important step, because the originator will now wait only for the new value of N participants; at this stage, the control is set back to line 4 (line 11). The algorithm thus exploits all replicas at multiple levels in order to reduce aborts in case of site failure. If the originator cannot obtain the required number of replicas after participants responded to abort, then the originator has to abort the global transaction (line 12).

14.2.2 Correctness of Modified Grid-ACP

ACP Properties

As mentioned earlier, ACPs must have four properties. These properties are motivated from and modified to meet Grid database requirements. The properties are mentioned below:

AC1: All subtransactions of a global transaction must reach the same decision.

AC2: A subtransaction cannot reverse its decision unilaterally after it has reached one.

*AC*3: The commit decision by the originator can be reached only if all subtrans-actions decide to commit and are in the "sleep" state.

*AC*4: Any subtransaction can unilaterally decide to abort.

Next, the correctness of modified Grid-ACP is presented and is demonstrated to meet the abovementioned properties.

Correctness

*AC*1 is the main objective for any ACP because it ensures that all subtransactions will reach the same decision in a distributed environment to ensure atomicity of the global transaction. Correctness of the algorithm is proven with the help of the following theorems.

Lemma 14.1: All participants commit if the global decision is to commit.

Proof: Participants are heterogeneous in nature and cannot support the "wait" state; hence, if the subtransaction executes successfully, it informs the Grid inter-face and enters "sleep" state. The algorithm takes the global decision only after it has received response from all other participants. Step 3 of the modified Grid-ACP algorithm ensures that if no subtransaction aborts, that is, $Na = 0$, then the global decision is to commit. Meanwhile, the participants will be in a "sleep" state, after logging their decision in the log file, since they decided to commit. The log infor-mation will help in aborting the transaction at a later stage, if the subtransaction has to be compensated. The global decision is made after responses from all par-ticipants are received. If all responses are to commit, then the global decision is also to commit. The global decision is then communicated to all participants. Par-ticipants then enter into the "commit" state and are removed from the active log. Acknowledgment is sent to the originator.

It is easy to move from the "sleep" state to the "commit" state rather than from the "wait" state (traditional ACPs) to the "commit" state, because subtransactions in the "sleep" state do not hold any resources. Thus all participants reach a uniform decision of commit, and atomicity is maintained.

Lemma 14.2: All participants abort if global decision is to abort.

Proof: Step 4 of the algorithm checks if any of the subtransactions decide to abort. If yes, the traditional ACP decides to abort the global transaction at this stage, but the modified Grid-ACP does not abort the global transaction and checks whether any replica of the data item is available at any other data site. The modi-fied Grid-ACP does not make the global decision at this stage. Thus the modified Grid-ACP does not decide to abort the global transaction as soon as any subtransac-tion decides to abort, contrary to traditional ACPs. This is called level-1 operations. After the originator has received all responses from the participants at level 1, those participants who decided to commit are in a "sleep" state and those who decided to abort must have aborted locally, but the global decision is not yet made.

The originator, with the help of Grid middleware's metadata service and replica control service, finds other replicas for the respective data item. If the number of replicas found is at least equal to the number of participants who decided to abort (for the respective data item), then the subtransactions are submitted to new replica sites. The global decision has not yet been made; hence, those participants who decided to commit are still in the "sleep" state. Since the subtransactions are resubmitted, they enter level-2 operations. Consequently, the transaction can go up to n levels, until no further replicas are found. If the number of available replicas is less than the number of aborting participants, only then is the global decision made and the coordinator decides to abort. Step 4b (*else* part of the algorithm and *line 12* of Fig. 14.3) ensures this procedure. The global decision to abort is logged in log files, and the decision is communicated to those participants who have decided to commit and are in "sleep" state. Those participants then execute compensating transactions to semantically abort the *sleep*ing transactions. Thus, if the global decision is to abort, the effects of all subtransactions are either aborted or compensated from participating database sites (irrespective of the level of the operation). Atomicity, and thus atomicity property $AC1$, is maintained for global abort decisions.

Theorem 14.1: All participating sites reach the same final decision.

Proof: From lemmas 14.1 and 14.2, it can be deduced that all participants either commit or abort. Thus all sites reach the same final decision.

14.3 TRANSACTION PROPERTIES IN REPLICATED ENVIRONMENT

On the one hand, data replication can increase the performance and availability of the system, while on the other hand, if not designed properly, a replicated system can produce worse performance and availability. If the update must be applied and synchronized to all replicas, then it may lead to worse performance. And if all replicas are to be operational in order for any of them to be used, then it may lead to worse availability.

As discussed in earlier chapters, maintaining ACID properties in a middleware-based transaction system (e.g., Grid database) is more complicated than in traditional transaction systems. Traditional transaction systems (including central and distributed databases) execute a database transaction in a single (and central) DBMS. A middleware-based transaction system spans several sites in the Grid database. The middleware transaction system has to satisfy some message passing, locking, restart, and fault tolerance features.

In this section, the effect of replication on transactional properties (ACID) is discussed.

- *Atomicity:* For a nonreplicated environment, Grid-ACP is used. The atomic behavior of a transaction is complicated because of execution autonomy and heterogeneity of sites. Replication of data further complicates the atomic commitment issue. The atomic behavior of the transaction depends on the replication protocol (eager or lazy). If the replication protocol is eager and the replicated data should be strictly synchronized, then the transaction should be atomic. But if the replication protocol is lazy and the update can be lazily propagated to other replicas, then the transaction can update a subset of the replicas. The atomicity property also depends on the application requirement. Certain applications do not need atomic transactions, for example, workflows, business activities, etc.

- *Consistency and isolation:* Concurrency control issues are to be addressed if a replica is being modified. Different replicated sites may contain the replicated data in heterogeneous storage systems, for example, file systems, database systems etc. Thus in a distributed Grid environment it is very complicated to synchronize operations. In a nonreplicated environment, the GCC protocol relies on the timestamp provided by the middleware.

  The concurrency control issue in replicated sites is further complicated if the data is replicated and located at distributed directory systems and different process try to access multiple replicas. Replica synchronization protocols in Chapter 13 may be combined with concurrency control protocols in a replicated Grid environment.

  Similar to the atomicity property, many applications may not require the highest level of consistency. Different applications may need different levels of consistency. Consistency levels are used for a set of identical replicas and can be expressed by the time delay for keeping replicas identical. The update propagation to maintain a specified consistency level can either be automated or manual.

- *Durability:* The problem of durability in a Grid environment is quite similar to those in traditional distributed DBMSs. The important aspect is that all of the executing transactions must have the same view of all site failures and recoveries. An initial value must be stored in a replica copy, which is recovering from a failure. Say that a data item $D1$ is replicated at a database site 1 (represented as $D1_1$). On recovery, $D1_1$ must be updated with the latest version of $D1$; furthermore, middleware services should be made aware of $D1_1$'s recovery. The following example shows the problem that arises if the recovering site is not managed properly:

  Let us consider that $D1$ is replicated at two sites DB_1 and DB_2, represented as $D1_1$ and $D1_2$, respectively. DB_2 also has a replica of $D2$, represented as $D2_2$. The following transactions are submitted in the system for execution:

$$T_1 = r_1(D1_2)w_1(D1_1)c_1$$
$$T_2 = w_2(D1_2)w_2(D2_2)c_2$$
$$T_3 = r_3(D1_1)r_3(D2_2)c_3$$

T_1 is the transaction that reads the latest copy of $D1$ from DB_2 and updates the recovering replica. Now consider the following history:

$$H = r_1(D1_2)w_1(D1_1)c_1w_2(D1_2)w_2(D2_2)c_2r_3(D1_1)r_3(D2_2)c_3$$

The above history is not equivalent to the serial history $T_1T_2T_3$, because, in the serial history, T_3 will read the values of $D1$ and $D2$ written by transaction T_2. But in H, T_3 reads the value of $D1$ written by transaction T_1 and reads the value of $D2$ from T_2. This undesirable situation arises because transaction T_2 is not aware that the replica site at T_1 has already recovered. Thus the recovery protocols need special attention in a replicated Grid environment.

14.4 SUMMARY

Typical applications running on the Grid environment are distributed and long-running transactions. Transactions need to access data from physically distributed sites and thus have active subtransactions at multiple sites. Aborting such long-running distributed transactions can be a computationally expensive affair.

Data is naturally replicated in the Grid environment for availability and performance reasons. ACPs abort the global transaction (to maintain atomicity) even if one of the cohorts of the transaction decides to abort. If the global transaction has to access data from ten sites, then it will have ten subtransactions. For instance, if only one subtransaction out of ten decides to abort and the remaining nine subtransactions decide to commit, then to preserve atomicity all subtransactions must abort.

In this chapter, the ACP is modified to take advantage of replication to reduce the number of aborting transactions. The original ACP uses only one level of operations of the replicated database. The modified Grid-ACP checks for other available replicas (other than present quorum) of the data item to exploit replication at more than one level.

This chapter is summarized as follows:

- The modified Grid-ACP protocol is discussed, which uses multiple levels of operations in a replicated environment. Multiple levels of operations reduce the number of aborts in the system by exploiting all the available replicas.

- Correctness of the protocol is demonstrated to ensure that the data is not corrupted.

14.5 BIBLIOGRAPHICAL NOTES

Most of the important work on grid data replication has been mentioned in the Bibliographical Notes section at the end of Chapter 13. This covers the work that has been published in the Grid-related and parallel/distributed conferences, including *GCC*, *CCGrid*, *HiPC*, *Euro-Par*, *HPDC*, and *ICPADS*.

Specific work on atomic commitment has generally been included in the work on transaction management, including those that have been mentioned in the Bibliographical Notes section at the end of Chapter 10.

14.6 EXERCISES

14.1. What is a long-running transaction?

14.2. Describe why transactions in the grid are generally long-running transactions. What is the impact of long-running transactions on the atomic commitment in the Grid?

14.3. Discuss the four properties of ACP.

14.4. Describe why the Grid atomic commitment protocol (Grid-ACP) needs to be modified to accommodate replicated data in the Grid.

14.5. Discuss why execution autonomy and site heterogeneity make atomicity of transactions in the grid more complex. Describe how data replication even further complicates the atomic commitment.

14.6. Discuss the effect of replication on the ACID properties in the Grid.

Part V

Other Data-Intensive Applications

Chapter 15

Parallel Online Analytic Processing (OLAP) and Business Intelligence

The efficient and accurate management of data is not sufficient to enhance the performance of an organization. Data has to be to enhanced and harnessed so that profitable knowledge can be derived from it. Business Intelligence (BI) is concerned with transforming and enhancing data to support sound business and strategic decision making. In business intelligence applications, one is less concerned with the detailed accuracy of individual data items than with overall trends and global pictures of business performance. Such decision making aims to increase a company's profits, minimize risks, and improve Customer Relationship Management (CRM). One of the powerful tools used for Business Intelligence is Online Analytic Processing (OLAP).

Unlike Online Transaction Processing (OLTP), which is mostly concerned with updates, OLAP focuses mainly on *analysis*. The amount of data involved in an OLAP query tends to be very large, and the data level is highly aggregated. While OLTP focuses largely on current data, OLAP often must involve a significant degree of temporal and historical data processing. Because of its high data intensity and the need for flexible query processing, parallelism in OLAP is particularly beneficial.

Section 15.1 examines the parallel multidimensional analysis framework, and then we shall study how SQL queries for OLAP may be efficiently optimized and parallelized. In Section 15.2, we examine ROLLUP queries, while CUBE queries are examined in Section 15.3. The parallelization of Top-N and ranking queries are covered in Section 15.4, and CUME_DIST queries are covered in Section 15.5. This

High-Performance Parallel Database Processing and Grid Databases,
by David Taniar, Clement Leung, Wenny Rahayu, and Sushant Goel
Copyright © 2008 John Wiley & Sons, Inc.

is followed by the parallelization of NTILE and histogram queries in Section 15.6, and finally, we examine windowing queries in Section 15.7.

15.1 PARALLEL MULTIDIMENSIONAL ANALYSIS

In business intelligence, it is often valuable to be able to view information from a number of dimensions. A dimension is an attribute with which a numerical quantity is associated. Consider the sales volume of a business over a given number of years. Here the sales volume is the numerical quantity, while year can be regarded as a dimension, with different sales volumes being recorded for different years. In doing so, one would develop a conceptual representation of a multidimensional *hypercube*, which can have an arbitrary number of dimensions. Sometimes the terms *data cube* or simply *cube* are used interchangeably with hypercube, even though "cube" tends to suggest a three-dimensional, rather than an *n*-dimensional structure. Indeed, as we shall see later, the keyword CUBE is used in SQL for its OLAP computations. Figure 15.1 shows an example of a hypercube of sales volume. Here, the dimensions of Region, Product and Year are used, which result in a three-dimensional cube. In general, higher dimensions are possible but not so easily visualized.

Two common operations associated with OLAP are **rollup** and **drill-down**. Rollup involves the aggregation of a number of cells in order to obtain a bigger picture and a higher-level summary. Drill-down, on the other hand, is concerned with the breaking down of a numerical figure from a higher level to a lower level. Analysis of multidimensional data often requires the operations of *slicing* or *dicing* the data cube. Dicing is associated with drill-down operations where in the case of the above example, one focuses on the sales volume in a given region, for a given product, in a given year. This amounts to fixing each of the dimensions to a particular value so as to concentrate on the numerical figure in that cell. Similarly, slicing is the obtaining of a slice of the cube to determine some aggregated figure pertaining to that group of cells. Slicing involves fixing some, but not all, of the dimensions. For example, fixing on a region in the cube will give a slice of the sales volume by product and year for that region. A given operation may be regarded as rollup or drill-down depending on the point of view—slicing

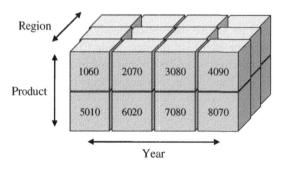

Figure 15.1   A data cube

is drill-down from the point of view of the entire cube, but it is rollup from the point of view of a single cell. While drilling down to the cell level may simply mean retrieving a single record with the dimension keys, other rollup or drill-down operations often require the aggregation of sums and, in particular, **subtotals**.

Because of the flexibility of these operations, potentially huge numbers of aggregations and calculations are required for analysis, which makes parallelization highly advantageous. For example, summarizing the quantities of different slices may be carried out in parallel.

Consider a two-dimensional slice of $m \times n$ cells, where $m < n$ (Fig. 15.2). Suppose we wish to find the subtotal of all the cells for this slice; then we can allocate each row to a separate processor that will be responsible for adding the values in that row (e.g., the second and last rows in Fig. 15.2 are allocated to two separate processors) to produce an intermediate result. After the parallel summing, all intermediate results will be aggregated to form the final subtotal for the entire slice. We call this scheme *row parallelism*, in which rows are parallelized. Likewise, we can adopt *column parallelism* by allocating each column to a separate processor (e.g., the lightly shaded columns in Fig. 15.2 are allocated to two separate processors) and perform similar processing. Let N be the number of processors, if

$$N \geq \max(m, n)$$

then, adopting either row parallelism or column parallelism will make little difference to parallel processing efficiency. Assuming that row parallelism is adopted, the processing time will be the time for processing n numbers (all m rows are processed concurrently, each requiring the addition of n values) plus the time for aggregating all the m partial sums. Thus the total processing time is that required for adding together $n + m$ values. Denoting by $T(r)$ the total processing time for processing r values, this processing time may be written as $T(n + m)$. On the other hand, if column parallelism is adopted, the processing time will be the time for processing m numbers (all n columns are processed concurrently) plus the time for aggregating all the n partial sums. Thus the total processing time is that required for adding together $m + n$ values, or $T(m + n)$.

Next, suppose $m < N < n$; then row parallelism should be adopted. Using the same reasoning as in the previous paragraph, the total processing time is that required for adding together $n + m$ values or $T(n + m)$. However, in adopting

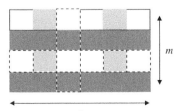

m

n

Figure 15.2   Parallelizing a slice

column parallelism in this situation, the total processing time will be

$$T\left(\left\lceil\frac{n}{N}\right\rceil m + n\right)$$

since not all the columns can be processed simultaneously because of not having enough processors. The above will reduce to the previous case of $T(m + n)$ when $n \leq N$. Thus, in general, the optimal parallelization strategy for this particular situation is selecting the minimum

$$\min\left\{T\left(\left\lceil\frac{n}{N}\right\rceil m + n\right), T\left(\left\lceil\frac{m}{N}\right\rceil n + m\right)\right\}$$

to effect parallel processing.

So far, we have been concerned with a two-dimensional slice. In general, a slice can be k-dimensional, with $m_1, \ldots, m_k$ cells for each dimension, respectively. Let us fix on the first dimension of this slice to obtain m_1 subslices of $(k - 1)$ dimensions, and we allocate a separate processor to each subslice. Thus each processor will add up in parallel

$$\prod_{i=2}^{k} m_i$$

values to obtain the partial sums, after which the partial sums will be aggregated to obtain the final subtotal for the entire slice. This will result in an overall subtotal time of

$$T(\prod_{i=2}^{k} m_i + m_1)$$

In general, fixing the jth dimension and assuming $m_j \leq N$, we have the following for the subtotal time for the slice

$$T(m_1 m_2 \ldots \hat{m}_j \ldots m_k + m_j)$$

where a "hat" over a symbol indicates that it is omitted. If $m_j > N$, we have for the overall subtotal time of the slice

$$T\left(\left\lceil\frac{m_j}{N}\right\rceil m_1 m_2 \ldots \hat{m}_j \ldots m_k + m_j\right)$$

Thus the optimal parallelization strategy is to choose a dimension j so that the above equation is minimized, that is,

$$T^* = \min_{1 \leq j \leq k}\left\{T\left(\left\lceil\frac{m_j}{N}\right\rceil m_1 m_2 \ldots \hat{m}_j \ldots m_k + m_j\right)\right\} \tag{15.1}$$

Useful bounds of the above may be obtained as follows. Let

$$m = \min(m_1, \ldots, m_k)$$
$$M = \max(m_1, \ldots, m_k)$$

Then an approximate upper bound for T^* is

$$T^* \leq T\left(\left\lceil \frac{m}{N} \right\rceil M^{k-1} + M\right) \tag{15.2}$$

This can be seen as follows. The product of the first term in equation 15.1 is largest when the smallest factor m is reduced by a factor of N. Moreover, the second term in equation 15.1 is bounded above by M. Thus, combining the maximum of each term respectively, these together establish the upper bound (equation 15.2). Likewise, a lower bound for T^* is

$$T^* \geq T\left(\left\lceil \frac{M}{N} \right\rceil m^{k-1} + m\right) \tag{15.3}$$

This follows by similarly observing that the product of the first term in equation 15.1 is smallest when the largest factor M is reduced by a factor of N, and that the second term in equation 15.1 is bounded below by m. Combining equations 15.2 and 15.3, we obtain

$$T\left(\left\lceil \frac{M}{N} \right\rceil m^{k-1} + m\right) \leq T^* \leq T\left(\left\lceil \frac{m}{N} \right\rceil M^{k-1} + M\right)$$

These provide reasonably tight bounds since they are attainable when

$$m_1 = m_2 = \ldots = m_k$$

In this case $m = M$, and

$$T^* = T\left(\left\lceil \frac{m}{N} \right\rceil m^{k-1} + m\right)$$

In the following sections, we shall consider the application of these techniques to concrete SQL OLAP aggregations.

15.2 PARALLELIZATION OF ROLLUP QUERIES

In SQL, the ROLLUP operation causes the computation of appropriate subtotals across a given set of dimensions. It rolls up from the most detailed level to an increasingly aggregated level, which makes use of a GROUP BY clause within a SELECT statement. Let us consider the following relation called Revenue (Table 15.1). Here, we have three dimensions: Year, District, and Product.

15.2.1 Analysis of Basic Single ROLLUP Queries

Consider the following ROLLUP query:

```
SELECT Year, District, Product, SUM (Earnings) AS Earnings
FROM Revenue
GROUP BY ROLLUP (Year, District, Product);
```

Table 15.1 Revenue

Year	District	Product	Earnings
2011	X	Book	76,000
2011	X	CD	75,000
2011	Y	Book	90,000
2011	Y	CD	116,000
2011	Z	Book	88,000
2011	Z	CD	87,000
2012	X	Book	83,000
2012	X	CD	86,000
2012	Y	Book	102,000
2012	Y	CD	138,000
2012	Z	Book	97,000
2012	Z	CD	98,000

This computes the union of four groupings of the Revenue relation:

{(Year, District, Product) , (Year, District), (Year), ()}.

The above notation signifies the following sets of subtotals:

- (Year, District, Product) corresponds to tuples where all the specific data values of Year, all the specific data values of District, and all the specific data values of Product are given explicitly, exhausting all combinations of the values of these three dimensions.

- (Year, District) corresponds to tuples where all the specific data values of Year and all the specific data values of District are given explicitly, exhausting all combinations of the values of these two dimensions, but the Earnings of all Products are summed. This is known as the first-level subtotal, as the values of only one dimension (i.e., Product) are summed.

- (Year) corresponds to tuples where all the specific data values of Year are given explicitly, but the Earnings of the other two dimensions are summed. This is known as the second-level subtotal, as the values of two dimensions (i.e., District and Product) are summed.

- () corresponds to a tuple where none of the specific data values of the three dimensions is given explicitly, giving a grand total of the Earnings of all three dimensions.

As we can see, the exact number of subtotals is determined by the cardinality (i.e., the number of different data values) of the underlying dimensions. The higher the cardinality, the greater is the number of subtotals that need to be computed.

Table 15.2   Rollup computations

Year (2)	District (3)	Product (2)	Earnings
2011	X	Book	76,000
2011	X	CD	75,000
2011	X	SUBTOTAL	151,000
2011	Y	Book	90,000
2011	Y	CD	116,000
2011	Y	SUBTOTAL	206,000
2011	Z	Book	88,000
2011	Z	CD	87,000
2011	Z	SUBTOTAL	175,000
2011	SUBTOTAL	SUBTOTAL	532,000
2012	X	Book	83,000
2012	X	CD	86,000
2012	X	SUBTOTAL	169,000
2012	Y	Book	102,000
2012	Y	CD	138,000
2012	Y	SUBTOTAL	240,000
2012	Z	Book	97,000
2012	Z	CD	98,000
2012	Z	SUBTOTAL	195,000
2012	SUBTOTAL	SUBTOTAL	604,000
SUBTOTAL	SUBTOTAL	SUBTOTAL	1,136,000

The execution of the above ROLLUP query yields Table 15.2, where we have additionally indicated the cardinality of each dimension in the column headings.

Here "SUBTOTAL" is indicated for clarity. In many SQL implementations, the actual output will indicate a blank instead of "SUBTOTAL" for the subtotals. More user-friendly explicit wordings may be produced by using a combination of the GROUPING function and the DECODE function. By using the cardinality information, we see that (Year, District, Product) produces $2 \times 3 \times 2 = 12$ tuples in the result, (Year, District) produces $2 \times 3 = 6$ subtotals in the result, (Year) produces 2 subtotals in the result, and () gives a single grand total tuple in the result. Thus we have $6 + 2 + 1 = 9$ additional subtotal rows compared with the base table.

In general, in executing ROLLUP $(C_1, \dots C_i, \dots, C_k)$, with $|C_i| = n_i$, that is each column C_i having cardinality n_i, then the number of subtotals is

$$n_1 \dots n_{k-1} + n_1 \dots n_{k-2} + n_1 \dots n_{k-3} + \dots + n_1 n_2 + n_1 + 1 \qquad (15.4)$$

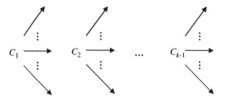

$C_1 \longrightarrow$ $C_2 \longrightarrow$ ... $C_{k-1} \longrightarrow$

Figure 15.3   Rollup partition tree

This can be seen by counting the SUBTOTALs successively, starting from the penultimate column of the relation (i.e., first-level subtotal). The first term in expression 15.4 corresponds to SUBTOTALs in the penultimate column, with the leftmost $k-1$ columns having definite values (these values would range over all possible combinations of values in these columns). The second term in expression 15.4 corresponds to having SUBTOTALs in the second and third columns from the right, with the leftmost $k-2$ columns having definite values (these values would range over all possible combinations of values in these columns), and so on. There are k terms in expression 15.4, each corresponding to a given level of subtotal.

As we can see, for any appreciable cardinality for the dimensions, the amount of computations associated with ROLLUP can be very high, and parallelization can bring considerable time savings. We may carry out the parallelization of ROLLUP $(C_1, \ldots C_i, \ldots, C_k)$, from left to right. First, we partition the relation, using the values of the leftmost column. Assuming for the moment that the number of processors N is greater than n_1, this will result in n_1 partitions, and we distribute these to n_1 separate processors. Thus each processor effectively contains a slice. If there are a large number of processors, then we may further partition the relation, using C_2. Upon the completion of this, the relation will have been partitioned into $n_1 n_2$ subrelations each of which will be allocated to a separate processor for computing the relevant subtotals. Thus the parallel processing will follow the rollup partition tree shown in Figure 15.3.

The above rollup partition tree can be fully expanded if $N \geq n_1 \ldots n_{k-1}$. In this case, all first level subtotals can be computed in parallel. In the above example, this means that all the different product earnings for each District and Year combination can be allocated to a separate processor, so that subtotaling for different combinations of District and Year values can all be carried out in parallel.

If, on the other hand, $N < n_1 \ldots n_{k-1}$, then the above rollup partition tree cannot be fully expanded, and the expansion will stop at column C_j, where a full partition of C_j will require more processors than are available. Assuming that a full expansion of C_j requires a total of n' processors, at such a stage of processor allocation, we have

$$n' = \prod_{i=1}^{j} n_i$$

Thus, whenever the condition $N < n'$ is encountered, we will then allocate multiple new branches of the expansion tree to a single processor. In such a situation, the load at each processor will not be uniform, although one should spread these branches as uniformly as possible over the available processors, and in so doing, the maximum completion time will be minimized.

15.2.2 Analysis of Multiple ROLLUP Queries

The basic ROLLUP command above admits a number of variations, which will cause the computation of different results. *Multiple* ROLLUP allows several ROLLUPs to be included in a single SELECT statement. Consider the following SQL query.

```
SELECT Year, District, Product, SUM (Earnings) AS Earnings
FROM Revenue
GROUP BY ROLLUP (Year), ROLLUP (District, Product);
```

This will generate the following set.

$$\{\text{Year}, ()\} \times \{(\text{District}, \text{Product}), (\text{District}), ()\}$$

$$= \{(\text{Year}, \text{District}, \text{Product}), (\text{Year}, \text{District}), (\text{Year}), (\text{District}, \text{Product}),$$

$$(\text{District}), ()\}$$

From the cardinalities of the dimensions, we can determine that this will produce $(2 \times 3) + 2 + (3 \times 2) + 3 + 1 = 18$ subtotals. The following gives the explicit result shown in Table 15.3.

Here, a reasonable parallelization strategy is to examine the product expression from which the output is generated:

$$\{(\text{Year}, \text{District}, \text{Product}), (\text{Year}, \text{District}), (\text{Year}),$$

$$(\text{District}, \text{Product}), (\text{District}), ()\}$$

We count the relative occurrence of a particular dimension in this expression, and we would expect that the more frequently it occurs in the expression, the less it is subtotaled, as a dimension's occurrence requires the inclusion of specific data values, rather than a subtotal. In the above expression, the most frequently occurred dimension is District, followed by Year, which in turn is followed by Product. Indeed, from Table 15.3, we see that there are 12 subtotals under the Product dimension, 10 subtotals under the Year dimension, and 3 subtotals under the District dimension. Since our aim is to have the subtotal computations performed in parallel, we would construct the partition tree in descending frequency of occurrence of the dimensions.

Such a heuristic strategy may be generalized as follows. For a table with k dimensions, if we have multiple ROLLUPs of the form:

$$\text{GROUP BY ROLLUP}(C_1, \ldots, C_i), \text{ROLLUP}(C'_1, \ldots, C'_j)$$

we first form the product

$$\{(C_1, \ldots, C_i), (C_1, \ldots, C_{i-1}), (C_1, \ldots, C_{i-2}), \ldots, ()\} \times$$

$$\{(C'_1, \ldots, C'_j), (C'_1, \ldots, C'_{j-1}), (C'_1, \ldots, C'_{j-2}), \ldots, ()\}$$

Table 15.3   Multiple rollups

Year	District	Product	Earnings
SUBTOTAL	X	Book	159,000
SUBTOTAL	X	CD	161,000
SUBTOTAL	X	SUBTOTAL	320,000
SUBTOTAL	Y	Book	192,000
SUBTOTAL	Y	CD	254,000
SUBTOTAL	Y	SUBTOTAL	446,000
SUBTOTAL	Z	Book	185,000
SUBTOTAL	Z	CD	185,000
SUBTOTAL	Z	SUBTOTAL	370,000
2011	X	Book	76,000
2011	X	CD	75,000
2011	X	SUBTOTAL	151,000
2011	Y	Book	90,000
2011	Y	CD	116,000
2011	Y	SUBTOTAL	206,000
2011	Z	Book	88,000
2011	Z	CD	87,000
2011	Z	SUBTOTAL	175,000
2011	SUBTOTAL	SUBTOTAL	532,000
2012	X	Book	83,000
2012	X	CD	86,000
2012	X	SUBTOTAL	169,000
2012	Y	Book	102,000
2012	Y	CD	138,000
2012	Y	SUBTOTAL	240,000
2012	Z	Book	97,000
2012	Z	CD	98,000
2012	Z	SUBTOTAL	195,000
2012	SUBTOTAL	SUBTOTAL	604,000
SUBTOTAL	SUBTOTAL	SUBTOTAL	1,136,000

Next, we count the occurrence of each dimension in the resultant product and then arrange these in *descending* order of occurrence. Let these be ordered as $D_1, \ldots, D_k$. Finally, we construct the partition tree as shown in Figure 15.4.

From this tree, we carry out processor allocation and parallelization as before.

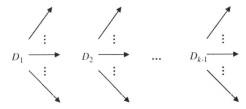

Figure 15.4   Multiple rollup partition tree

15.2.3   Analysis of Partial ROLLUP Queries

In addition to multiple rollup, *partial* ROLLUP is also commonly used in OLAP, where only selected subtotals will be calculated. Consider the following SQL query.

```
SELECT Year, District, Product, SUM (Earnings) AS Earnings
FROM Revenue
GROUP BY Year, Product, ROLLUP (District);
```

The result of this query is shown in Table 15.4. Here, only the District dimension is allowed to have "SUBTOTAL" under it, with Year and Product varying over all their possible values.

Table 15.4   Partial rollup

Year	District	Product	Earnings
2011	X	Book	76,000
2011	Y	Book	90,000
2011	Z	Book	88,000
2011	SUBTOTAL	Book	254,000
2011	X	CD	75,000
2011	Y	CD	116,000
2011	Z	CD	87,000
2011	SUBTOTAL	CD	278,000
2012	X	Book	83,000
2012	Y	Book	102,000
2012	Z	Book	97,000
2012	SUBTOTAL	Book	282,000
2012	X	CD	86,000
2012	Y	CD	138,000
2012	Z	CD	98,000
2012	SUBTOTAL	CD	322,000

The parallelization strategy for partial rollup can be carried out as in the situation for the single rollup, proceeding from left to right of the statement, partitioning in this case Year first, then Product, and then finally District to enable the parallel computation of the subtotals. Similarly, for a partial ROLLUP of the form:

$$\text{GROUP BY } C_1, \ldots, C_i, \text{ROLLUP}(C_{i+1}, \ldots, C_k)$$

we may carry out the partition in accordance with the partition tree in Figure 15.3.

15.2.4 Parallelization Without Using ROLLUP

ROLLUP is a powerful SQL operation in OLAP, as without ROLLUP, we need to compute the subtotals in separate SQL queries and then finally form a Union of the different results table, necessitating multiple passes of the table to perform the calculations. In general, for a k-column ROLLUP, we need to Union the results of $(k + 1)$ SELECT statements if we do not use ROLLUP, and the number of table accesses will increase from 1 to $(k + 1)$. Thus, in terms of table accesses, using ROLLUP gives a saving of $[(k + 1)-1)]/(k + 1) = k/(k + 1)$, which for large k will be very close to 100%.

The same observation, however, also suggests a method for computing the ROLLUP subtotals without using ROLLUP queries, such as in certain database management systems where the SQL dialect does not support ROLLUP. Here, we replicate the relation over $(k + 1)$ processors and carry out the SELECT in parallel. After this, we then Union all the SELECT outputs together to form the final results.

15.3 PARALLELIZATION OF CUBE QUERIES

The ROLLUP operation for multidimensional analysis in the previous section can be regarded as a selective form of rollup in OLAP, as it does not offer all possible combination of dimensions. The basic single ROLLUP, the multiple ROLLUP, and the partial ROLLUP only enable certain subtotals to be computed. Consider the operation

$$\text{ROLLUP}(C_1, C_2, \ldots, C_k)$$

The summing of numerical quantities associated with all values of C_i for a given value of C_j is not computed for $i < j$. Unlike ROLLUP, the CUBE operation allows subtotals to be computed for every dimension value combination plus an overall total where all dimensions are allowed to take on "SUBTOTAL" simultaneously. Thus the amount of computations involved in a CUBE query forms a superset of those in a ROLLUP query.

15.3.1 Analysis of Basic CUBE Queries

Consider the following SQL query.

```
SELECT Year, District, Product, SUM (Earnings) AS Earnings
FROM Revenue
GROUP BY CUBE (Year, District, Product);
```

This computes the union of eight different groupings of the Revenue relation:

$$\{(\text{Year, District, Product}),$$
$$(\text{Year, District}), (\text{Year, Product}), (\text{District, Product}),$$
$$(\text{Year}), (\text{District}), (\text{Product}),$$
$$()\}$$

From the cardinalities of the dimensions, we can determine that this will produce $(2 \times 3) + (2 \times 2) + (3 \times 2) + 2 + 3 + 2 + 1 = 24$ subtotals. Figure 15.5 compares the computations carried out by CUBE with those carried out by ROLLUP (the ones omitted by ROLLUP are shaded). Table 15.5 shows the actual output of the CUBE operation (again, the ones omitted by ROLLUP are shaded). A hypercube representation of this table is given in Figures 15.6 and 15.7. The hypercube is made up of two Year slices 2011 and 2012. A particular column of the slice results in subtotal by District, and a particular row of the slice results in subtotal by Product.

In the above example, we have $k = 3$ columns. In general, for k columns $(C_1, \ldots C_i, \ldots, C_k)$, with $|C_i| = n_i$, the number of subtotals is

$$S = \sum_{j=1}^{k} n_1 n_2 \ldots \hat{n}_j \ldots n_k + \sum_{i,j=1}^{k} n_1 n_2 \ldots \hat{n}_i \ldots \hat{n}_j \ldots n_k + \ldots + \sum_{i=1}^{k} n_i + 1$$

where a "hat" over a symbol indicates that it has been omitted. There are

$$\binom{k}{1}$$

terms in the first summation and

$$\binom{k}{2}$$

terms in the second summation, and so on. The total number of terms in calculating S is

$$\binom{k}{1} + \ldots + \binom{k}{k} = 2^k - 1$$

Now, assuming that the minimum number of values among all the columns is n, that is,

$$n = \min(n_1, \ldots, n_k)$$

```
SELECT Year, District,          SELECT Year, District,
Product,                        Product,
SUM (Earnings) AS Earnings      SUM (Earnings) AS Earnings
FROM Revenue                    FROM Revenue
GROUP BY CUBE (Year,            GROUP BY ROLLUP (Year,
District, Product);             District, Product);
```

{ (Year, District, Product),	{ (Year, District, Product),
(Year, District), (Year, Product),	(Year, District),
(District, Product),	(Year),
(Year), (District), (Product),	( ) }
( ) }	

Figure 15.5 Comparison of cube and rollup

then

$$S - 1 \geq \binom{k}{1} n^{k-1} + \ldots + \binom{k}{k-1} n \geq (2^k - 2)n$$

Thus

$$S \geq (2^k - 2)n + 1$$

and for reasonably large value of k, $2^k \rangle\rangle 1$, and so we have, approximately

$$S \geq n \times 2^k$$

For example, if $k = n = 10$, we have $S \geq 10,000$. If $k = n = 5$, we have $S \geq 160$. Thus we see that in executing the CUBE statement, even modest numbers of dimensions and cardinalities are highly computation intensive. This makes parallelization all the more beneficial.

In the ROLLUP operation, where only selected subtotals are computed, we can preferentially choose dimensions for allocation to processors to optimize subtotal computations. Here, all the dimensions are symmetrical in the sense that they all participate equally in the subtotal computations. In this situation, we will need to exploit the cardinality characteristics of the dimensions instead of the dimensions themselves. Thus the optimal parallelization strategy given in Section 15.1 can be used, where a useful heuristic method is to partition the dimensions with the smallest cardinalities first. Arranging the dimensions in ascending order of their cardinalities as $C_1^*, \ldots, C_k^*$, we carry out processor allocation based on the partition tree shown in Figure 15.8.

Table 15.5   Cube computations

Year	District	Product	Earnings
2011	X	Book	76,000
2011	X	CD	75,000
2011	X	SUBTOTAL	151,000
2011	Y	Book	90,000
2011	Y	CD	116,000
2011	Y	SUBTOTAL	206,000
2011	Z	Book	88,000
2011	Z	CD	87,000
2011	Z	SUBTOTAL	175,000
2011	SUBTOTAL	Book	254,000
2011	SUBTOTAL	CD	278,000
2011	SUBTOTAL	SUBTOTAL	532,000
2012	X	Book	83,000
2012	X	CD	86,000
2012	X	SUBTOTAL	169,000
2012	Y	Book	102,000
2012	Y	CD	138,000
2012	Y	SUBTOTAL	240,000
2012	Z	Book	97,000
2012	Z	CD	98,000
2012	Z	SUBTOTAL	195,000
2012	SUBTOTAL	Book	282,000
2012	SUBTOTAL	CD	322,000
2012	SUBTOTAL	SUBTOTAL	604,000
SUBTOTAL	X	Book	159,000
SUBTOTAL	X	CD	161,000
SUBTOTAL	X	SUBTOTAL	320,000
SUBTOTAL	Y	Book	192,000
SUBTOTAL	Y	CD	254,000
SUBTOTAL	Y	SUBTOTAL	446,000
SUBTOTAL	Z	Book	185,000
SUBTOTAL	Z	CD	185,000
SUBTOTAL	Z	SUBTOTAL	370,000
SUBTOTAL	SUBTOTAL	Book	536,000
SUBTOTAL	SUBTOTAL	CD	600,000
SUBTOTAL	SUBTOTAL	SUBTOTAL	1,136,000

2011 Year Slice

	X	Y	Z	
Book	76,000	90,000	88,000	Subtotal in Row 10 (254,000)
CD	75,000	116,000	87,000	Subtotal in Row 11 (278,000)
	Subtotal in Row 3 (151,000)	Subtotal in Row 6 (206,000)	Subtotal in Row 9 (175,000)	Subtotal in Row 12 (532,000)

Figure 15.6   Hypercube representations (2011 Year slice)

15.3.2   Analysis of Partial CUBE Queries

In addition to the basic CUBE operation, *partial* CUBE may be used, which limits the number of subtotals produced. Consider the following SQL query.

```
SELECT Year, District, Product,
SUM (Earnings) AS Earnings FROM sales
GROUP BY Year, CUBE (District, Product);
```

2012 Year Slice

	X	Y	Z	
Book	83,000	102,000	97,000	Subtotal in Row 22 (282,000)
CD	86,000	138,000	98,000	Subtotal in Row 23 (322,000)
	Subtotal in Row 15 (169,000)	Subtotal in Row 18 (240,000)	Subtotal in Row 21 (195,000)	Subtotal in Row 24 (604,000)

Figure 15.7   Hypercube representation (2012 Year slice)

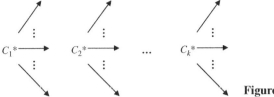

Figure 15.8 Cube partition tree

Here, the dimension Year is not allowed to have "SUBTOTAL" under it in the result, while CUBE (District, Product) follows the usual CUBE operations. This will generate the following set:

{Year } × {(District, Product), (District), (Product), ()}

= {(Year, District, Product), (Year, District), (Year, Product), (Year) }

Here, we may apply the heuristics of Section 15.2.2 and carry out partition in *descending* order of dimension occurrence. We will therefore partition Year first, as it occurs most often. Thus, in general, for a statement of the form

$$\text{GROUP BY} C_1, \ldots, C_i, \text{CUBE}(C_{i+1}, \ldots, C_k)$$

we first carry out the partition for dimensions that fall outside the CUBE brackets, before partitioning those that are within the CUBE brackets (since the former dimensions tend to occur more frequently in the product expression), and in both cases, we follow the rule of *ascending* cardinality.

15.3.3 Parallelization Without Using CUBE

CUBE is a more powerful SQL operation than ROLLUP, and without it or ROLLUP, we need to compute a large number of subtotals in separate SQL queries and then form a Union of the different results table, necessitating multiple passes of the table to perform the computations. More precisely, for a k-dimensional cube, 2^k SELECT statements are needed. Each SELECT statement requires a separate pass of the table, compared with a single pass from using CUBE. Thus, in terms of table accesses, using CUBE gives a saving of $(2^k - 1)/2^k = 1 - 1/2^k$, which even for moderate values of k will be close to 100%.

As in the case of ROLLUP, this also suggests a method of computing the CUBE subtotals without using CUBE queries, in database systems where CUBE is not directly supported. We replicate the relation over 2^k processors, and carry out the SELECT in parallel. If there are fewer than 2^k processors, then we will need to have two or more SELECTs performed by a single processor.

15.4   PARALLELIZATION OF TOP-*N* AND RANKING QUERIES

Top-N query is a common OLAP operation and is a query requesting the N largest or smallest values of a numerical column. While the SQL aggregation functions MAX and MIN simply determine the largest value and smallest value, respectively, within a numerical column, top-N queries require more complete ranking of these columns. The class of Top-N queries also includes bottom-N queries, as one can simply reverse the ordering of the numerical magnitude in the ranking process. Examples of top-N queries include "Who are the top five highest-paid executives in the company?" and "Who are the ten worst students in the class?"

SQL makes use of two ranking functions to effect the ranking of values

- RANK ()
- DENSE_RANK ()

Both functions use the integers $1, 2, 3, \ldots$ in allocating the rank. While DENSE_RANK () admits no gaps in these ranking integers, RANK () allows gaps to exist when there is a tie. For example, when there are two equal top salespersons, then the next one will be assigned a rank of 3 when using RANK () but will be assigned a rank of 2 when using DENSE_RANK (). Consider Table 15.6, concerning the performance of salespersons in the company.

From the following SQL query

```
SELECT EmployeeNo, Sales,
RANK ( ) OVER (ORDER BY Sales DESC) AS Position
FROM Performance;
```

we obtain result shown in Table 15.7.

To produce a ranking of a table based on a column, the table will need to be sorted based on that column. The parallelization of these queries may be carried out by using the techniques developed for parallel sorting in Chapter 4.

As a result of ranking, we can easily produce the answers to top-N queries through nesting. For example, we can issue the nested query

Table 15.6   Performance

EmployeeNo	Sales
E123	18,000
E234	19,000
E345	17,600
E456	11,000
E789	15,000

Table 15.7   Ranked performance

EmployeeNo	Sales	Position
E234	19,000	1
E123	18,000	2
E345	17,600	3
E789	15,000	4
E456	11,000	5

```
SELECT EmployeeNo FROM
 (SELECT EmployeeNo, Sales,
  RANK ( ) OVER (ORDER BY Sales DESC) AS Position
  FROM Performance)
WHERE Position < = 3;
```

to obtain the EmployeeNo of the top three salespersons.

15.5   PARALLELIZATION OF CUME_DIST QUERIES

The cumulative distribution function (CUME_DIST) orders a particular (often non-negative integral) numerical column, and determines the fraction of tuples, either within the relation or within a particular group of the relation, that have a numerical value not exceeding that of a tuple. Cumulative distribution is a construct from probability theory, where for a given numerical value x, the cumulative distribution function of x is given by

$$F(x) = \frac{1}{|R|} \sum_{k=0}^{x} r_k$$

where r_k is the number of tuples having the value k, and $|R|$ is the total number of tuples in the relation or appropriate group.

Using the data of Table 15.6, the cumulative distribution of sales can be obtained from the query:

```
SELECT EmployeeNo, Sales,
CUME_DIST ( ) OVER (ORDER BY Sales DESC) AS Cdf
FROM Performance;
```

which will result in Table 15.8. To compute the cumulative distribution function, we need to sort the tuples first based on the numerical column of interest, and then determine a tuple's position by counting the number of tuples either above or below it. Thus the parallel execution of CUME_DIST queries may be effected by exploiting the parallel sorting techniques given in Chapter 4.

Table 15.8   Cumulative distribution function

EmployeeNo	Sales	Cdf
E234	19,000	1
E123	18,000	0.8
E345	17,600	0.6
E789	15,000	0.4
E456	11,000	0.2

15.6 PARALLELIZATION OF NTILE AND HISTOGRAM QUERIES

The function NTILE(k) allocates a set of numerical values into k bins according to their magnitude. It places the tuples into k bins with (close to) an equal number of tuples in each bin. Using the data of Table 15.6, and supposing we set $k = 4$ (quartile), the SQL query

```
SELECT EmployeeNo, Sales,
NTILE(4) OVER (ORDER BY Sales DESC) AS Quartile
FROM Performance;
```

will give the result in Table 15.9.

Again, the execution of this query will require sorting, and thus the parallelization of NTILE queries can make use of the parallel sorting techniques in Chapter 4. Note, however, that it is not feasible to perform the NTILE allocations in parallel in different processors and then merge the results, since a value belonging to the top NTILE in one data set may belong to a different NTILE in another. This is because the values defining the bin boundaries are relative to the tuple values rather than fixed absolutely. In addition, the correct execution of the NTILE function depends on the global range, which cannot be determined locally at an individual processor. Thus a global sort needs to be performed first before bin boundaries are defined (Fig. 15.9).

On the other hand, histogram queries will benefit from concurrent processing by separate processors carried out on data fragments without needing to do a global sort first. Consider the set of marks in Table 15.10. A histogram may be constructed by using the SQL query

```
SELECT
SUM(CASE WHEN Mark BETWEEN 80 AND 100 THEN 1 ELSE 0 END) as A,
SUM(CASE WHEN Mark BETWEEN 70 AND 80 THEN 1 ELSE 0 END) as B,
SUM(CASE WHEN Mark BETWEEN 60 AND 70 THEN 1 ELSE 0 END) as C,
SUM(CASE WHEN Mark BETWEEN 50 AND 60 THEN 1 ELSE 0 END) as D,
SUM(CASE WHEN Mark BETWEEN 40 AND 50 THEN 1 ELSE 0 END) as E,
FROM Students;
```

which will give the histogram in Table 15.11: Unlike for NTILE queries, the boundary values of bins here are not relative but are fixed beforehand by the

Table 15.9   The NTILE function

EmployeeNo	Sales	Quartile
E234	19,000	1
E123	18,000	2
E345	17,600	2
E789	15,000	3
E456	11,000	4

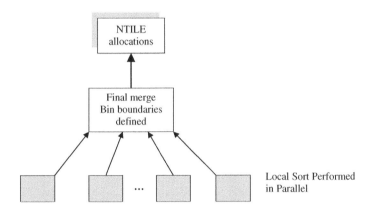

Figure 15.9   Parallelization of NTILE query

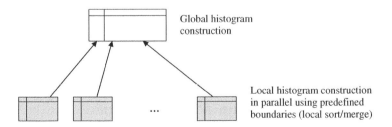

Figure 15.10   Parallelization of histogram query

query so that the parallel processing of data fragments for allocating values to bins can be performed by individual processors concurrently. This is illustrated in Figure 15.10.

After building the local histogram with the data in a given processor, the global histogram may be obtained by adding all the results from individual processors.

Table 15.10 Marks

Mark
93
61
47
88
73
65
58
68
51
79

Table 15.11 Histogram query

A	B	C	D	E
2	2	3	2	1

15.7 PARALLELIZATION OF MOVING AVERAGE AND WINDOWING QUERIES

Very often in dealing with time information in a data warehouse, data is presented in the form of a time series. A common operation to smooth out the fluctuations in a time series is to average out a set of consecutive values. Consider the time series in Table 15.12, which gives the estimated sale of a particular product.

If we wish to compute the moving average using three consecutive sales figures, we can use the SQL query:

```
SELECT Month, Sales,
AVG(Sales) OVER (ORDER BY Month ROWS 2 PRECEDING)
AS Moving_Avg
FROM Forecast;
```

which will average the current sales together with the two preceding sales figures, giving Table 15.13.

Note that the first two moving averages are computed on the basis of less than three values. In general, a moving average may involve averaging k values, and the first $(k - 1)$ average values are computed using less than k values because of the absence of certain preceding values.

In parallelizing the moving average or other windowing computations, one can divide the set of data among the available processors. The processors will then

Table 15.12   Forecast

Month	Sales
January 2018	100
February 2018	200
March 2018	300
April 2018	400
May 2018	500
June 2018	600
July 2018	700
August 2018	800
September 2018	900
October 2018	1000
November 2018	1100
December 2018	1200

Table 15.13   Moving average query

Month	Sales	Moving_Avg
January 2018	100	100
February 2018	200	150
March 2018	300	200
April 2018	400	300
May 2018	500	400
June 2018	600	500
July 2018	700	600
August 2018	800	700
September 2018	900	800
October 2018	1000	900
November 2018	1100	1000
December 2018	1200	1100

compute the corresponding moving average values in parallel. However, as we have noted above, the boundary values will require special attention. Since the first few moving averages are not the true moving average required from averaging k values, some tuples will need to be replicated on two processors. This is illustrated in Figure 15.11 for the case of three processors.

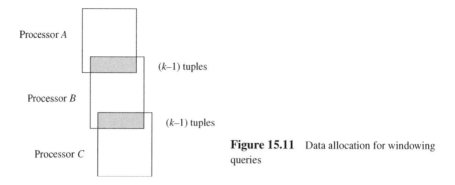

Figure 15.11 Data allocation for windowing queries

More precisely, if the computation is allocated to N processors, and if a windowing function involves k values, then $(k - 1) \times (N - 1)$ tuples will need to be replicated on two processors. This can be seen by suitably extending the number of processors in Figure 15.11.

15.8 SUMMARY

This chapter studies the parallelization of OLAP queries. We have looked at the multidimensional analysis framework and introduced heuristics for parallelizing slicing and dicing operations. Formulae and bounds for performance estimation have also been derived.

As OLAP operations are carried out by concrete queries, we have considered how different kinds of OLAP queries may be efficiently parallelized. These include:

- ROLLUP queries
- CUBE queries
- Top-N and Ranking queries
- CUME_DIST queries
- NTILE and Histogram queries
- Windowing queries

These analysis queries tend to be computation intensive, and their parallelization with the heuristics and techniques covered in this chapter is especially beneficial when huge volumes of data are being processed.

15.9 BIBLIOGRAPHICAL NOTES

Having laid down the criteria for evaluating truly relational database systems (Codd 1986), Codd proceeded to lay down 12 rules for OLAP (Codd 1993). In particular, to meet the requirements of rules 9 and 12, the deployment of parallel technology is essential. Most of the work in parallel data warehouses focuses on ROLAP, data cubes (constructions and queries), and query scheduling. The group led by Dehne (http://www.dehne.net) has published numerous papers in parallelization of ROLAP and data cubes. Dehne et al. (*DAPD* 2006) reported their cgmCube project, which designed and implemented a multiprocessor platform for data cube generation that targets the relational database model (ROLAP). Their earlier work published in *DAPD* proposed parallelization of data cube construction on a shared-disk architecture (Dehne et al. *DAPD* 2002) and on a shared-nothing architecture (Chen and Dehne et al. *DAPD* 2004). Two data partitioning strategies, one for top-down and the other for bottom-up cube algorithms, were reported in Dehne et al. (*ICDT* 2001).

Jin et al. in *IEEE TPDS* (2005) and *ICPP* (2003 and 2004) reported their work on parallel data cube construction. In *IEEE TPDS* (2005), Jin et al. presented an aggregation tree for parallel data cube construction, which focused on interprocessor communication. This was an extension of their previous work reported in *ICPP* (2003). Their other work presented in *ICPP* (2004) combined the use of tiling the input and output arrays on each processor and interprocessor communication in a data cube construction process.

In the area of OLAP queries, Li and Gao (*DEXA* 2004) presented a hierarchical data cube for range-sum queries. A more complete work on range-sum queries and dynamic updates was reported in 2005 (Gao and Li 2005). Datta et al. (*IEEE TKDE* 2002) proposed a storage structure, called DataIndexes, to vertically partition star schema. They also proposed a declustering strategy that incorporates both task and data partitioning for parallel star join.

In the area of query scheduling, Märtens et al. (2002 and 2003) proposed a dynamic query scheduling in parallel data warehouses, where they proposed a scheduling that considers both processors and disks for load balancing in a shared-disk architecture.

15.10 EXERCISES

15.1. Discuss the differences between *row parallelism* and *column parallelism* in two-dimensional data.

15.2. Outline the differences between rollup and drill-down. Use an example to highlight their differences.

15.3. Indicate the main difference between the following two GROUP BY ROLLUP clauses in SQL:

```
GROUP BY ROLLUP (Product, Branch);
```

and

```
GROUP BY ROLLUP (Branch, Product);
```

15.4. Multiple rollup uses multiple ROLLUP clauses in the GROUP BY. Describe the difference between the following single ROLLUP and multiple ROLLUP:

```
GROUP BY ROLLUP (Branch, Product, Season);
```

and

```
GROUP BY ROLLUP (Branch, Product), ROLLUP (Season);
```

15.5. What is a partial ROLLUP? Outline the main differences between partial ROLLUP and the other two ROLLUPs (i.e., single and multiple ROLLUPs).

15.6. Highlight the differences between ROLLUP and CUBE. What is the difference between:

```
GROUP BY ROLLUP (Branch, Product, Season);
```

and

```
GROUP BY CUBE (Branch, Product, Season);?
```

15.7. What is partial CUBE? Give an example.

15.8. Explain the main difference between the Rank() and Dense_Rank() functions in SQL. Illustrate your answer with an example.

15.9. What parallelization methods can be applied to CUME_DIST queries?

15.10. Describe the main differences between two NTile queries, one where the boundary values of bins are fixed and the other where the boundary values of bins are already predetermined.

15.11. To what degree is parallelization of moving average queries different from the parallelization of other queries?

Chapter 16

Parallel Data Mining—Association Rules and Sequential Patterns

This chapter focuses on *data mining*, another data-intensive application whereby parallelism can be used in order to achieve high performance. Data mining analyzes a large amount of data stored in databases to discover interesting knowledge in the form of patterns, association, changes, anomalies, significant structures, etc. Data mining is also known as *knowledge discovery*, or more precisely, knowledge discovery of data. Both terms are basically interchangeable. In this book, the term "data mining" is used throughout.

Data mining is considered a multidisciplinary area, covering machine learning, statistics, as well as databases. From a machine learning viewpoint, data mining uses learning techniques that generally exist in the machine learning domain, such as knowledge representation, classification, and structure. From a statistical point of view, it is obvious that data analysis requires some statistical techniques, such as correlation, clustering, outliers, etc. However, this book focuses on database and database processing and considers data mining processes from a database processing perspective. It covers commonly used data mining techniques, such as association rules, sequential patterns, clustering, and classification. This chapter focuses on association rules and sequential patterns, whereas Chapter 17 focuses on the other two data mining techniques: clustering and classification.

As discussed throughout the book, processing a large volume of data requires parallelism techniques in order to achieve high performance. Subsequently, it is also desirable to apply parallelism techniques to data mining processes. Therefore, the focus of the two chapters on parallel data mining (Chapters 16 and 17) is twofold:

High-Performance Parallel Database Processing and Grid Databases,
by David Taniar, Clement Leung, Wenny Rahayu, and Sushant Goel
Copyright © 2008 John Wiley & Sons, Inc.

first, to introduce data mining techniques, covering association rules, sequential patterns, clustering, and classification, and second, to describe parallelism opportunities in these data mining techniques.

This chapter will start with a road map that shows the historical evolution of data mining from databases (Section 16.1). The section reflects on what has been discussed in the previous chapters and examines how it can further evolve in the future. To become familiar with data mining, especially in the context of databases and data analysis, it is essential to understand the evolution of data mining, through databases and data warehousing, all of which have a common denominator called data or databases.

An overview of data mining is described in more detail in Section 16.2, covering basic data mining tasks, differences between data mining and database querying, and parallelism techniques for data mining algorithms. Following this, Sections 16.3 and 16.4 describe parallel association rules and parallel sequential patterns, respectively.

16.1 FROM DATABASES TO DATA WAREHOUSING TO DATA MINING: A JOURNEY

All three, *databases, data warehouses,* and *data mining,* deal with data. Therefore, it is necessary to understand the evolution of these data-intensive applications. Figure 16.1 illustrates this evolution.

Databases are commonly deployed in almost every organization. In a simple form, databases are referred to as data repositories. Although there are several database models, they serve a common purpose, that is, data repository. As already discussed, database processing can be divided into two main categories: (*i*) queries and (*ii*) transactions. Queries are basically retrievals. Or, in other words, database users need to ask the database to retrieve the required information. There is no point in storing something in a data repository if we do not need to retrieve it. So, querying has been one of the main purposes of databases. Earlier in this book,

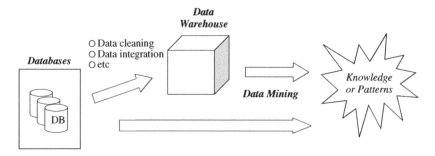

Figure 16.1 Evolution of data-intensive applications

especially in Parts II and III, parallelism is applied to queries in order to speed up the process. These queries are often known as *read-only* queries, since the queries retrieve (or read) only the requested data and do not change the data.

Transactions, on the other hand, are required by users because of the need to keep updating the data in the database as well as storing new information in the database. Since a database is shared by many users, effective management of transactions is critical; otherwise, it will end up with inconsistent data, which is undesirable. Therefore, transaction management and concurrency control are two other important elements of database processing. Parallelism of transaction management, particularly in a grid environment, is studied in Part IV, where grid concurrency control, focusing on the four main properties of transactions, namely atomicity, concurrency, isolation, and durability, is discussed in the context of grid databases. Replication has also been discussed, which is particularly important in a grid infrastructure. Since the main aim of a transaction is to update data, transactions are often known as *write* queries, which may include some updates, deletions, and insertions.

The bottom line of databases is that the data be active. The data contained in a database is normally operational data. The data is required for day-to-day operation of the organization. For example, in a banking scenario, users make withdrawals and deposits, management produces financial statements and reports, etc. To support all of these activities, the data, including bank account details, has to be active, and hence the data is called operational data.

Over time, the data piles up. Some of the data is no longer operational, but historical. For example, sales data from 5 years ago may be considered as historical data, since it might not affect the current operations, meaning that users no longer update this old data. Although this data is old and not currently used, obviously it cannot be discarded. Management may want to produce reports involving this data for decision support and for historical analysis. Business reports may often need to include old data.

Therefore, it is common sense to segregate this old data in a *data warehouse*. A data warehouse provides information from a historical perspective, whereas an operational database keeps data of current value. Figure 16.2 shows the transformation of data from operational data in a database into data warehousing data. The process involves data extraction, filtering, transforming, integrating from various sources, classifying the data, aggregating, and summarizing the data. The result is a data warehouse where the data is integrated, time-variant, nonvolatile, and commonly subject-oriented.

Since the data in the databases is operational, some of it needs to be filtered, extracted, and transformed into a suitable structure for a data warehouse. As already discussed in Chapter 15 on data warehousing and OLAP (online analytical processing), the data in a data warehouse is commonly aggregated or summarized, since for historical purposes only summarized data is needed, not the entire details. The full details of the data are in the operational database anyway.

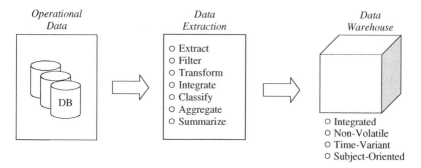

Figure 16.2 Building a data warehouse

A data warehouse is integrated and subject-oriented, since the data is already integrated from various sources through the cleaning process, and each data warehouse is developed for a certain domain of subject area in an organization, such as sales, and therefore is subject-oriented. The data is obviously nonvolatile, meaning that the data in a data warehouse is not update-oriented, unlike operational data. The data is also historical and normally grouped to reflect a certain period of time, and hence it is time-variant.

Once a data warehouse has been developed, management is able to perform some operation on the data warehouse, such as drill-down and rollup. Drill-down is performed in order to obtain a more detailed breakdown of a certain dimension, whereas rollup, which is exactly the opposite, is performed in order to obtain more general information about a certain dimension. Business reporting often makes use of data warehouses in order to produce historical analysis for decision support. Parallelism of OLAP has already been presented in Chapter 15.

As can be seen from the above, the main difference between a database and a data warehouse lies in the data itself: operational versus historical. However, any decision to support the use of a data warehouse has its own limitations. The query for historical reporting needs to be formulated similarly to the operational data. If the management does not know what information or pattern or knowledge to expect, data warehousing is not able to satisfy this requirement. A typical anecdote is that a manager gives a pile of data to subordinates and asks them to find something useful in it. The manager does not know what to expect but is sure that something useful and surprising may be extracted from this pile of data. This is not a typical database query or data warehouse processing. This raises the need for a data mining process.

Data mining, defined as a process to mine knowledge from a collection of data, generally involves three components: the data, the mining process, and the knowledge resulting from the mining process (see Fig. 16.1). The data itself needs to go through several processes before it is ready for the mining process. This preliminary process is often referred to as data preparation. Although Figure 16.1 shows that the data for data mining is coming from a data warehouse, in practice this may or may not be the case. It is likely that the data may be coming from any data repositories. Therefore, the data needs to be somehow transformed so that it becomes ready for the mining process.

Data preparation steps generally cover:

- Data selection: Only relevant data to be analyzed is selected from the database.
- Data cleaning: Data is cleaned of noise and errors. Missing and irrelevant data is also excluded.
- Data integration: Data from multiple, heterogeneous sources may be integrated into one simple flat table format.
- Data transformation: Data is transformed and consolidated into forms appropriate for mining by performing summary or aggregate operations.

Once the data is ready for the mining process, the mining process can start. The mining process employs an intelligent method applied to the data in order to extract data patterns. There are various mining techniques, including but not limited to association rules, sequential patterns, classification, and clustering. The results of this mining process are knowledge or patterns.

16.2 DATA MINING: A BRIEF OVERVIEW

As mentioned earlier, data mining is a process for discovering useful, interesting, and sometimes surprising knowledge from a large collection of data. Therefore, we need to understand various kinds of data mining tasks and techniques. Also required is a deeper understanding of the main difference between querying and the data mining process. Accepting the difference between querying and data mining can be considered as one of the main foundations of the study of data mining techniques. Furthermore, it is also necessary to recognize the need for parallelism of the data mining technique. All of the above will be discussed separately in the following subsections.

16.2.1 Data Mining Tasks

Data mining tasks can be classified into two categories:

- Descriptive data mining and
- Predictive data mining

Descriptive data mining describes the data set in a concise manner and presents interesting general properties of the data. This somehow summarizes the data in terms of its properties and correlation with others. For example, within a set of data, some data have common similarities among the members in that group, and hence the data is grouped into one cluster. Another example would be that when certain data exists in a transaction, another type of data would follow.

Predictive data mining builds a prediction model whereby it makes inferences from the available set of data and attempts to predict the behavior of new data sets. For example, for a class or category, a set of rules has been inferred from the available data set, and when new data arrives the rules can be applied to this new data to determine to which class or category it should belong. Prediction is made possible because the model consisting of a set of rules is able to predict the behavior of new information.

Either descriptive or predictive, there are various data mining techniques. Some of the common data mining techniques include class description or characterization, association, classification, prediction, clustering, and time-series analysis. Each of these techniques has many approaches and algorithms.

Class description or *characterization* summarizes a set of data in a concise way that distinguishes this class from others. Class characterization provides the characteristics of a collection of data by summarizing the properties of the data. Once a class of data has been characterized, it may be compared with other collections in order to determine the differences between classes.

Association rules discover association relationships or correlation among a set of items. Association analysis is widely used in transaction data analysis, such as a market basket. A typical example of an association rule in a market basket analysis is the finding of rule (*magazine* → *sweet*), indicating that if a magazine is bought in a purchase transaction, there is a likely chance that a sweet will also appear in the same transaction. Association rule mining is one of the most widely used data mining techniques. Since its introduction in the early 1990s through the Apriori algorithm, association rule mining has received huge attention across various research communities. The association rule mining methods aim to discover rules based on the correlation between different attributes/items found in the data set. To discover such rules, association rule mining algorithms at first capture a set of significant correlations present in a given data set and then deduce meaningful relationships from these correlations. Since the discovery of such rules is a computationally intensive task, many association rule mining algorithms have been proposed.

Classification analyzes a set of training data and constructs a model for each class based on the features in the data. There are many different kinds of classifications. One of the most common is the decision tree. A decision tree is a tree consisting of a set of classification rules, which is generated by such a classification process. These rules can be used to gain a better understanding of each class in the database and for classification of new incoming data. An example of classification using a decision tree is that a "fraud" class has been labeled and it has been identified with the characteristics of fraudulent credit card transactions. These characteristics are in the form of a set of rules. When a new credit card transaction takes place, this incoming transaction is checked against a set of rules to identify whether or not this incoming transaction is classified as a fraudulent transaction. In constructing a decision tree, the primary task is to form a set of rules in the form of a decision tree that correctly reflects the rules for a certain class.

Prediction predicts the possible values of some missing data or the value distribution of certain attributes in a set of objects. It involves the finding of the set of attributes relevant to the attribute of interest and predicting the value distribution based on the set of data similar to the selected objects. For example, in a time-series data analysis, a column in the database indicates a value over a period of time. Some values for a certain period of time might be missing. Since the presence of these values might affect the accuracy of the mining algorithm, a prediction algorithm may be applied to predict the missing values, before the main mining algorithm may proceed.

Clustering is a process to divide the data into clusters, whereby a cluster contains a collection of data objects that are similar to one another. The similarity is expressed by a similarity function, which is a metric to measure how similar two data objects are. The opposite of a similarity function is a distance function, which is used to measure the distance between two data objects. The further the distance, the greater is the difference between the two data objects. Therefore, the distance function is exactly the opposite of the similarity function, although both of them may be used for the same purpose, to measure two data objects in terms of their suitability for a cluster. Data objects within one cluster should be as similar as possible, compared with data objects from a different cluster. Therefore, the aim of a clustering algorithm is to ensure that the intracluster similarity is high and the intercluster similarity is low.

Time-series analysis analyzes a large set of time series data to find certain regularities and interesting characteristics. This may include finding sequences or sequential patterns, periodic patterns, trends, and deviations. A stock market value prediction and analysis is a typical example of a time-series analysis.

16.2.2   Querying vs. Mining

Although it has been stated that the purpose of mining (or data mining) is to discover knowledge, it should be differentiated from querying (or database querying), which simply retrieves data. In some cases, this is easier said than done. Consequently, highlighting the differences is critical in studying both database querying and data mining. The differences can generally be categorized into *unsupervised* and *supervised* learning.

Unsupervised Learning

The previous section gave the example of a pile of data from which some knowledge can be extracted. The difference in attitude between a data miner and a data warehouse reporter was outlined, albeit in an exaggerated manner. In this example, no direction is given about where the knowledge may reside. There is no guideline of where to start and what to expect. In a machine learning term, this is called *unsupervised* learning, in which the learning process is not guided, or even dictated, by the expected results. To put it in another way, unsupervised learning does not require a hypothesis. Exploring the entire possible space in the jungle of data might be overstating, but can be analogous that way.

Using the example of a supermarket transaction list, a data mining process is used to analyze all transaction records. As a result, perhaps, a pattern, such as the majority of people who bought milk will also buy cereal in the same transaction, is found. Whether this is interesting or not is a different matter. Nevertheless, this is data mining, and the result is an association rule. On the contrary, a query such as "What do people buy together with milk?" is a database query, not a data mining process.

If the pattern *milk* → *cereal* is generalized into $X \rightarrow Y$, where X and Y are items in the supermarket, X and Y are not predefined in data mining. On the other hand, database querying requires X as an input to the query, in order to find Y, or vice versa. Both are important in their own context. Database querying requires some selection predicates, whereas data mining does not.

Definition 16.1 (association rule mining vs. database querying): Given a database D, association rule mining produces an association rule $Ar(D) = X \rightarrow Y$, where $X, Y \in D$. A query $Q(D, X) = Y$ produces records Y matching the predicate specified by X.

The pattern $X \rightarrow Y$ may be based on certain criteria, such as:

- Majority
- Minority
- Absence
- Exception

The *majority* indicates that the rule $X \rightarrow Y$ is formed because the majority of records follow this rule. The rule $X \rightarrow Y$ indicates that if a person buys X, it is 99% likely that the person will also buy Y at the same time, and both items X and Y must be bought frequently by all customers, meaning that items X and Y (separately or together) must appear frequently in the transactions.

Some interesting rules or patterns might not include items that frequently appear in the transactions. Therefore, some patterns may be based on the *minority*. This type of rules indicates that the items occur very rarely or sporadically, but the pattern is important. Using X and Y above, it might be that although both X and Y occur rarely in the transactions, when they both appear together it becomes interesting.

Some rules may also involve the *absence* of items, which is sometimes called *negative association*. For example, if it is true that for a purchase transaction that includes coffee it is very likely that it will NOT include tea, then the items tea and coffee are negatively associated. Therefore, rule $X \rightarrow \sim Y$, where the $\sim$ symbol in front of Y indicates the absence of Y, shows that when X appears in a transaction, it is very unlikely that Y will appear in the same transaction.

Other rules may indicate an *exception*, referring to a pattern that contradicts the common belief or practice. Therefore, pattern $X \to Y$ is an exception if it is uncommon to see that X and Y appear together. In other words, it is common to see that X or Y occurs just by itself without the other one.

Regardless of the criteria that are used to produce the patterns, the patterns can be produced only after analyzing the data globally. This approach has the greatest potential, since it provides information that is not accessible in any other way. On the contrary, database querying relies on some directions or inputs given by the user in order to retrieve suitable records from the database.

Definition 16.2 (sequential patterns vs. database querying): Given a database D, a sequential pattern $Sp(D) = O : X \to Y$, where O indicates the owner of a transaction and $X, Y \in D$. A query $Q(D, X, Y) = O$, or $Q(D, aggr) = O$, where *aggr* indicates some aggregate functions.

Given a set of database transactions, where each transaction involves one customer and possibly many items, an example of a sequential pattern is one in which a customer who bought item X previously will later come back after some allowable period of time to buy item Y. Hence, $O : X \to Y$, where O refers to the customer sets.

If this were a query, the query could possibly request "Retrieve customers who have bought a minimum of two different items at different times." The results will not show any patterns, but merely a collection of records. Even if the query were rewritten as "Retrieve customers who have bought items X and Y at different times," it would work only if items X and Y are known *a priori*. The sequential pattern $O : X \to Y$ obviously requires a number of steps of processes in order to produce such a rule, in which each step might involve several queries including the query mentioned above.

Definition 16.3 (clustering vs. database querying): Given database D, a clustering $Cl(D) = \sum_{i=1}^{n} \{X_{i1}, X_{i2}, \ldots\}$, where it produces n clusters each of which consists of a number of items X. A query $Q(D, X_1) = \{X_2, X_3, X_4, \ldots\}$, where it produces a list of items $\{X_2, X_3, X_4, \ldots\}$ having the same cluster as the given item X_1.

Given a movement database consisting of mobile users and their locations at a specific time, a cluster containing a list of mobile users $\{m_1, m_2, m_3, \ldots\}$ might indicate that they are moving together or being at a place together for a period of time. This shows that there is a cluster of users with the same characteristics, which in this case is the location.

On the contrary, a query is able to retrieve only those mobile users who are moving together or being at a place at the same time for a period of time with the given mobile user, say m_1. So the query can be expressed to something like: "Who are mobile users usually going with m_1?" There are two issues here. One is whether or not the query can be answered directly, which depends on the data itself and whether there is explicit information about the question in the query. Second, the records to be retrieved are dependent on the given input.

Supervised Learning

Supervised learning is naturally the opposite of unsupervised learning, since supervised learning starts with a direction pointing to the target. For example, given a list of top salesmen, a data miner would like to find the other properties that they have in common. In this example, it starts with something, namely, a list of top salesmen. This is different from unsupervised learning, which does not start with any particular instances.

In data warehousing and OLAP, as explained in Chapter 15, we can use drill-down and rollup to find further detailed (or higher level) information about a given record. However, it is still unable to formulate the desired properties or rules of the given input data. The process is complex enough and looks not only at a particular category (e.g., top salesmen), but all other categories. Database querying is not designed for this.

Definition 16.4 (decision tree classification vs. database querying): Given database D, a decision tree $Dt(D, C) = P$, where C is the given category and P is the result properties. A query $Q(D, P) = R$ is where the property is known in order to retrieve records R.

Continuing the above example, when mining all properties of a given category, we can also find other instances or members who also possess the same properties. For example, find the properties of a good salesman and find who the good salesman are. In database querying, the properties have to be given so that we can retrieve the names of the salesmen. But in data mining, and in particular decision tree classification, the task is to formulate such properties in the first place.

16.2.3 Parallelism in Data Mining

Like any other data-intensive applications, parallelism is used purely because of the large size of data involved in the processing, with an expectation that parallelism will speed up the process and therefore the elapsed time will be much reduced. This is certainly still applicable to data mining. Additionally, the data in the data mining often has a high dimension (large number of attributes), not only a large volume of data (large number of records). Depending on how the data is structured, high-dimension data in data mining is very common. Processing high-dimension data produces some degree of complexity, not previously found or applicable to databases or even data warehousing. In general, more common in data mining is the fact that even a simple data mining technique requires a number of iterations of the process, and each of the iterations refines the results until the ultimate results are generated.

Data mining is often needed to process complex data such as images, geographical data, scientific data, unstructured or semistructured documents, etc. Basically, the data can be anything. This phenomenon is rather different from databases and data warehouses, whose data follows a particular structure and model, such as relational structure in relational databases or star schema or data cube in data warehouses. The data in data mining is more flexible in terms of the structures, as it is not confined to a relational structure only. As a result, the processing of complex data also requires parallelism to speed up the process.

The other motivation is due to the widely available multiple processors or parallel computers. This makes the use of such a machine inevitable, not only for data-intensive applications, but basically for any application.

The objectives of parallelism in data mining are not uniquely different from those of parallel query processing in databases and data warehouses. Reducing data mining time, in terms of speed up and scale up, is still the main objective. However, since data mining processes and techniques might be considered much more complex than query processing, parallelism of data mining is expected to simplify the mining tasks as well. Furthermore, it is sometimes expected to produce better mining results.

There are several forms of parallelism that are available for data mining. Chapter 1 described various forms of parallelism, including: interquery parallelism (parallelism among queries), intraquery parallelism (parallelism within a query), intraoperation parallelism (partitioned parallelism or data parallelism), interoperation parallelism (pipelined parallelism and independent parallelism), and mixed parallelism. In data mining, for simplicity purposes, parallelism exists in either

- Data parallelism or
- Result parallelism

If we look at the data mining process at a high level as a process that takes data input and produces knowledge or patterns or models, *data parallelism* is where parallelism is created due to the fragmentation of the input data, whereas *result parallelism* focuses on the fragmentation of the results, not necessarily the input data. More details about these two data mining parallelisms are given below.

Data Parallelism

In *data parallelism*, as the name states, parallelism is basically created because the data is partitioned into a number of processors and each processor focuses on its partition of the data set. After each processor completes its local processing and produces the local results, the final results are formed basically by combining all local results.

Since data mining processes normally exist in several iterations, data parallelism raises some complexities. In every stage of the process, it requires an input and produces an output. On the first iteration, the input of the process in each processor is its local data partitions, and after the first iteration, completes each processor will produce the local results. The question is: What will the input be for the subsequent iterations? In many cases, the next iteration requires the global picture of the results from the immediate previous iteration. Therefore, the local results from each processor need to be reassembled globally. In other words, at the end of each iteration, a global reassembling stage to compile all local results is necessary before the subsequent iteration starts.

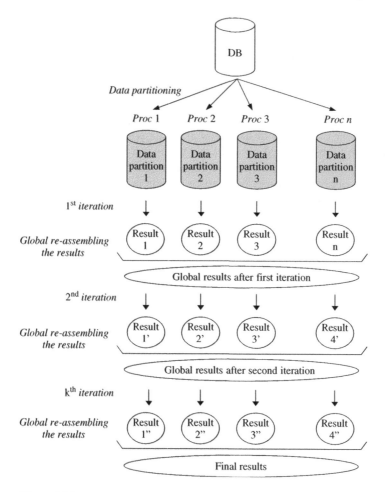

Figure 16.3   Data parallelism for data mining

This situation is not that common in database query processing, because for a primitive database operation, even if there exist several stages of processing each processor may not need to see other processors' results until the final results are ultimately generated.

Figure 16.3 illustrates how data parallelism is achieved in data mining. Note that the global temporary result reassembling stage occurs between iterations. It is clear that parallelism is driven by the database partitions.

Result Parallelism

Result parallelism focuses on how the target results, which are the output of the processing, can be parallelized during the processing stage without having produced any results or temporary results. This is exactly the opposite of data parallelism, where parallelism is created because of the input data partitioning. Data parallelism might be easier to grasp because the partitioning is done up front, and then parallelism occurs. Result parallelism, on the other hand, works by partitioning the target results, and each processor focuses on its target result partition.

The way result parallelism works can be explained as follows. The target result space is normally known in advance. The target result of an association rule mining is frequent itemsets in a lexical order. Although we do not know the actual instances of frequent itemsets before they are created, nevertheless, we should know the range of the items, as they are confined by the itemsets of the input data. Therefore, result parallelism partitions the frequent itemset space into a number of partitions, such as frequent itemset starting with item A to I will be processed by processor 1, frequent itemset starting with item H to N by the next processor, and so on. In a classification mining, since the target categories are known, each target category can be assigned a processor.

Once the target result space has been partitioned, each processor will do whatever it takes to produce the result within the given range. Each processor will take any input data necessary to produce the desired result space. Suppose that the initial data partition 1 is assigned to processor 1, and if this processor needs data partitions from other processors in order to produce the desired target result space, it will gather data partitions from other processors. The worst case would be one where each processor needs the entire database to work with.

Because the target result space is already partitioned, there is no global temporary result reassembling stage at the end of each iteration. The temporary local results will be refined only in the next iteration, until ultimately the final results are generated. Figure 16.4 illustrates result parallelism for data mining processes.

Contrasting with the parallelism that is normally adopted by database queries, query parallelism to some degree follows both data and result parallelism. Data parallelism is quite an obvious choice for parallelizing query processing. However, result parallelism is inherently used as well. For example, in a disjoint partitioning parallel join, each processor receives a disjoint partition based on a certain partitioning function. The join results of a processor will follow the assigned partitioning function. In other words, result parallelism is used. However, because disjoint partitioning parallel join is already achieved by correctly partitioning the input data, it is also said that data parallelism is utilized. Consequently, it has never been necessary to distinguish between data and result parallelism.

The difference between these two parallelism models is highlighted in the data mining processing because of the complexity of the mining process itself, where there are multiple iterations of the entire process and the local results may need to be refined in each iteration. Therefore, adopting a specific parallelism model becomes necessary, thereby emphasizing the difference between the two parallelism models.

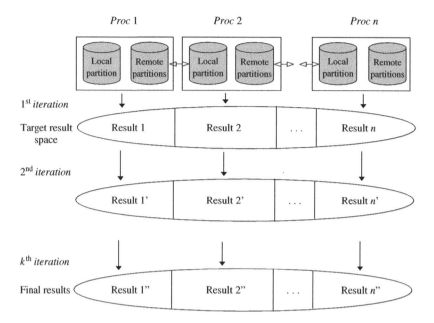

Figure 16.4 Result parallelism for data mining

16.3 PARALLEL ASSOCIATION RULES

Association rule mining is one of the most widely used data mining techniques. The association rule mining methods aim to discover rules based on the correlation between different attributes/items found in the data set. To discover such rules, association rule mining algorithms at first capture a set of significant correlations present in a given data set and then deduce meaningful relationships from these correlations. Since discovering such rules is a computationally intensive task, it is desirable to employ a parallelism technique.

Association rule mining algorithms generate association rules in two phases: (*i*) phase one: discover frequent itemsets from a given data set and (*ii*) phase two: generate a rule from these frequent itemsets. The first phase is widely recognized as being the most critical, computationally intensive task. Upon enumerating support of all frequent itemsets, in the second phase association rule methods association rules are generated. The rule generation task is straightforward and relatively easy.

Since the frequent itemset generation phase is computationally expensive, most work on association rules, including parallel association rules, have been focusing on this phase only. Improving the performance of this phase is critical to the overall performance.

This section, focusing on parallel association rules, starts by describing the concept of association rules, followed by the process, and finally two parallel algorithms commonly used by association rule algorithms.

16.3.1 Association Rules: Concepts

Association rule mining can be defined formally as follows: let $I = \{I_1, I_2, \ldots, I_m\}$ be a set of attributes, known as *literals*. Let D be the databases of transactions, where each transaction $t \in T$ has a set of items and a unique transaction identifier (*tid*) such that $t = (tid, I)$. The set of items X is also known as an *itemset*, which is a subset of I such that $X \subseteq I$. The number of items in X is called the length of that *itemset* and an itemset with k items is known as a k-itemset. The *support* of X in D, denoted as $sup(X)$, is the number of transactions that have itemset X as subset.

$$sup(X) = |\{I : X \in (tid, I)\}|/|D| \qquad (16.1)$$

where $|S|$ indicates the cardinality of a set S.

Frequent Itemset: An itemset X in a dataset D is considered as frequent if its support is equal to, or greater than, the minimum support threshold *minsup* specified by the user.

Candidate Itemset: Given a database D and a minimum support threshold *minsup* and an algorithm that computes $F(D, minsup)$, an itemset I is called a *candidate* for the algorithm to evaluate whether or not itemset I is frequent.

An *association rule* is an implication of the form $X \rightarrow Y$, where $X \subseteq I, Y \subseteq I$ are *itemset*, and $X \cap Y = \phi$ and its support is equal to $X \cup Y$. Here, X is called *antecedent*, and Y *consequent*.

Each association rule has two measures of qualities such as *support* and *confidence* as defined as:

The support of association rule $X \rightarrow Y$ is the ratio of a transaction in D that contains itemset $X \cup Y$.

$$sup(X \cup Y) = |\{X \cup Y \in (tid, I)|X \cup Y \subseteq I\}|/|D| \qquad (16.2)$$

The confidence of a rule $X \rightarrow Y$ is the conditional probability that a transaction contains Y given that it also contains X.

$$conf(X \rightarrow Y) = \{X \cup Y \in (tid, I)|X \cup Y \subseteq I\}/\{X \in (tid, I)|X \subseteq I\} \quad (16.3)$$

We note that while $sup(X \cup Y)$ is symmetrical (i.e., swapping the positions of X and Y will not change the support value) $conf(X \rightarrow Y)$ is not symmetrical, which is evident from the definition of confidence.

Association rules mining methods often use these two measures to find all association rules from a given data set. At first, these methods find frequent itemsets, then use these frequent itemsets to generate all association rules. Thus, the task of mining association rules can be divided into two subproblems as follows:

Itemset Mining: At a given user-defined support threshold *minsup*, find all itemset I from data set D that have support greater than or equal to *minsup*. This generates all frequent itemsets from a data set.

Association Rules: At a given user-specified minimum confidence threshold *minconf*, find all association rules R from a set of frequent itemset F such that each of the rules has confidence equal to or greater than *minconf*.

Although most of the frequent itemset mining algorithms generate candidate itemsets, it is always desirable to generate as few candidate itemsets as possible. To minimize candidate itemset size, most of the frequent itemset mining methods utilize the anti-monotonicity property.

Anti-monotonicity: Given data set D, if an itemset X is frequent, then all the subsets are such that $x_1, x_2, x_3 \ldots x_n \subseteq X$ have higher or equal support than X.

Proof: Without loss of generality, let us consider x_1. Now, $x_1 \subseteq X$ so that $|X \in (tid, I)| \subseteq |x_1 \in (tid, I)|$, thus, $sup(x_1) \geq sup(X)$. The same argument will apply to all the other subsets.

Since support of a subset itemset of a frequent itemset is also frequent, if any itemset is infrequent, subsequently this implies that the support of its superset itemset will also be infrequent. This property is sometimes called anti-monotonicity. Thus the candidate itemset of the current iteration is always generated from the frequent itemset of the previous iteration. Despite the above downward closure property, the size of a candidate itemset often cannot be kept small. For example, suppose there are 500 frequent 1-itemsets; then the total number of candidate itemsets in the next iteration is equal to $(500) \times (500-1)/2 = 124{,}750$ and not all of these candidate 2-itemsets are frequent.

Since the number of frequent itemsets is often very large, the cost involved in enumerating the corresponding support of all frequent itemsets from a high-dimensional dataset is also high. This is one of the reasons that parallelism is desirable.

To show how the support confidence-based frameworks discover association rules, consider the example below:

EXAMPLE

Consider a data set as shown in Figure 16.5. Let item $I = \{bread, cereal, cheese, coffee, milk, sugar, tea\}$ and transaction ID $TID = \{100, 200, 300, 400 \ and \ 500\}$.

Each row of the table in Figure 16.5 can be taken as a transaction, starting with the transaction ID and followed by the items bought by customers. Let us

Transaction ID	Items Purchased
100	bread, cereal, milk
200	bread, cheese, coffee, milk
300	cereal, cheese, coffee, milk
400	cheese, coffee, milk
500	bread, sugar, tea

Figure 16.5 Example dataset

Frequent Itemset	Support
bread	60%
Cereal	40%
Cheese	60%
Coffee	60%
Milk	80%
bread, milk	40%
cereal, milk	40%
cheese, coffee	60%
cheese, milk	60%
coffee, milk	60%
cheese, coffee, milk	60%

Figure 16.6   Frequent itemset

now discover association rules from these transactions at 40% support and 60% confidence thresholds.

As mentioned earlier, the support-based and confidence-based association rule mining frameworks have two distinct phases: First, they generate those itemsets that appeared 2 (i.e., 40%) or more times as shown. For example, item "*bread*" appeared in 3 transactions: transaction IDs 100, 200 and 500; thus it satisfies the minimum support threshold. In contrast, item "*sugar*" appeared only in one transaction, that is transaction ID 500; thus the support of this item is less than the minimum support threshold and subsequently is not included in the frequent itemsets as shown in Figure 16.6. Similarly, it verifies all other itemsets of that data set and finds support of each itemset to verify whether or not that itemset is frequent.

In the second phase, all association rules that satisfy the user-defined confidence are generated using the frequent itemset of the first phase. To generate association rule $X \rightarrow Y$, it first takes a frequent itemset XY, finds two subset itemsets X and Y such that $X \cap Y = \phi$. If the confidence of $X \rightarrow Y$ rule is higher than or equal to the minimum confidence, then it includes that rule in the resultant rule set. To generate confidence of an association rule, consider the frequent itemset shown in Figure 16.6. For example, "*bread, milk*" is a frequent itemset and *bread* $\rightarrow$ *milk* is an association rule. To find confidence of this rule, use equation 16.2, which will return 100% confidence (higher than the minimum confidence threshold of 60%). Thus the rule *bread* $\rightarrow$ *milk* is considered as a valid rule as shown in Figure 16.7.

On the contrary, although '*bread, milk*' is a frequent itemset, the rule *milk* $\rightarrow$ *bread* is not valid because its confidence is below the minimum confidence threshold and thus is not included in the resultant rule set. Similarly, one can generate all other valid association rules as illustrated in Figure 16.7.

Association Rules	Confidence
bread→milk	67%
cereal→milk	100%
cheese→coffee	100%
cheese→milk	100%
coffee→milk	100%
coffee→cheese	100%
milk→cheese	75%
milk→coffee	75%
cheese, coffee→milk	100%
cheese, milk→coffee	100%
coffee, milk→cheese	100%
cheese→coffee, milk	100%
coffee→cheese, milk	100%
milk→cheese, coffee	75%

Figure 16.7   Association rules

16.3.2 Association Rules: Processes

The details of the two phases of association rules, frequent itemset generation and association rules generation, will be explained in the following sections.

Frequent Itemset Generation

The most common frequent itemset generation searches through the dataset and generates the support of frequent itemset levelwise. It means that the frequent itemset generation algorithm generates frequent itemsets of length 1 first, then length 2, and so on, until there are no more frequent itemsets. The Apriori algorithm for frequent itemset generation is shown in Figure 16.8.

At first, the algorithm scans all transactions of the data set and finds all frequent 1-itemsets. Next, a set of potential frequent 2-itemsets (also known as candidate 2-itemsets) is generated from these frequent 1-itemsets with the *apriori_gen*() function (where it takes the frequent itemset of the previous iteration and returns the candidate itemset for the next iteration). Then, to enumerate the exact support of frequent 2-itemsets, it again scans the data set. The process continues until all frequent itemset are enumerated. To generate frequent itemsets, the Apriori involves three tasks: (1) generating candidate itemset of length k using the frequent itemset of $k - 1$ length by a self-join of F_{k-1}; (2) pruning the number of candidate itemsets by employing the anti-monotonicity property, that is, the subset of all frequent

---

Algorithm: Apriori

```
1. F₁ = {frequent 1-itemset}
2. k = 2
3. While Fₖ₋₁ ≠ {} do
       //Generate candidate itemset
4.     Cₖ = apriori_gen(Fₖ₋₁)
5.     For transaction t∈ T
6.         Cₜ = subset(Cₖ, t)
7.         For candidate itemset X∈ Cₜ
8.             X.support++
       //Extract frequent itemset
9.     Fₖ = {X∈ Cₖ|X.support ≥ minsup }
10.    k++
11.Return ⋃Fₖ
          k
```

Figure 16.8   The Apriori algorithm for frequent itemset generation

itemsets is also frequent; and (3) extracting the exact support of all candidate itemsets of any level by scanning the data set again for that iteration.

EXAMPLE

Using the data set in Figure 16.5, assume that the minimum support is set to 40%. In this example, the entire frequent itemset generation takes three iterations (see Fig. 16.9).

- ○ In the first iteration, it scans the data set and finds all frequent 1-itemsets.
- ○ In the second iteration, it joins each frequent 1-itemset and generates candidate 2-itemset. Then it scans the data set again, enumerates the exact support of each of these candidate itemsets, and prunes all infrequent candidate 2-itemsets.
- ○ In the third iteration, it again joins each of the frequent 2-itemsets and generates the following potential candidate 3-itemsets {*bread coffee milk*, *bread cheese milk*, and *cheese coffee milk*}. Then it prunes those candidate 3-itemsets that do not have a subset itemset in F_2. For example, itemsets "*bread coffee*" and "*bread cheese*" are not frequent and are pruned. After pruning, it has a single candidate 3-itemset {*cheese coffee milk*}. It scans the data set and finds the exact support of that candidate itemset. It finds that this candidate 3-itemset is frequent. In the joining phase, the *apriori_gen()* function is unable to produce any candidate itemset for the next iteration, indicating that there are no more frequent itemsets at the next iteration.

Association Rules Generation

Once a frequent itemset has been generated, the generation of association rules begins. As mentioned earlier, rule generation is less computationally expensive

Dataset

Transaction ID	Items Purchased
100	bread, cereal, milk
200	bread, cheese, coffee, milk
300	cereal, cheese, coffee, milk
400	cheese, coffee, milk
500	bread, sugar, tea

scan d_1

C_1

Candidate Itemset	Support Count
bread	3
cereal	2
cheese	3
coffee	3
milk	4
sugar	1
tea	1

F_1

Frequent Itemset	Support Count
bread	3
cereal	2
cheese	3
coffee	3
milk	4

scan d_2

C_2

Candidate Itemset	Support Count
bread, cereal	1
bread, cheese	1
bread, coffee	1
bread, milk	2
cereal, cheese	1
cereal, coffee	1
cereal, milk	2
cheese, coffee	3
cheese, milk	3
coffee, milk	3

F_2

Frequent Itemset	Support Count
bread, milk	2
cereal, milk	2
cheese, coffee	3
cheese, milk	3
coffee, milk	3

scan d_3

C_3

Candidate Itemset	Support Count
cheese, coffee, milk	3

F_3

Candidate Itemset	Support Count
cheese, coffee, milk	3

Figure 16.9 Example of the Apriori algorithm

compared with frequent itemset generation. It is also simpler in terms of its complexity.

The rule generation algorithm takes every frequent itemset F that has more than one item as an input. Given that F is a frequent itemset, at first the rule generation algorithm generates all rules from that itemset, which has a single item in the consequent. Then, it uses the consequent items of these rules and employs the *apriori_gen*() function as mentioned above to generate all possible consequent

---

Algorithm: Association rule generation

```
1.  For all I∈ Fₖ such that k≥2
2.      C₁ = {{i}|i∈ I}
3.      k = 1
4.      While Cₖ ≠ {} do
            //confidence of each rule
5.          Hₖ = {X ∈ Cₖ | σ (I)/σ(X) ≥ minconf}
6.          Cₖ₊₁ = apriori_gen(Hₖ)
7.          k++
8.      R = R ∪ {(I− X) → (X)/X ∈ H₁ ∪ H₂ ∪ ··· ∪ Hₖ }
```

Figure 16.10   Association rule generation algorithm

2-itemsets. And finally, it uses these consequent 2-itemsets to construct rules from that frequent itemset F. It then checks the confidence of each of these rules. The process continues, and with each iteration the length of the candidate itemset increases until it is no longer possible to generate more candidates for the consequent itemset. The rule generation algorithm is shown in Figure 16.10.

EXAMPLE

Suppose "$ABCDE$" is a frequent itemset and $ACDE → B$ and $ABCE → D$ are two rules that, having one item in the consequent, satisfy minimum confidence threshold.

- At first it takes the consequent items "B" and "D" as input of the *apriori_gen*() function and generates all candidate 2-itemsets. Here "BD" turns out to be the only candidate 2-itemset, so it checks the confidence of the rule $ACE → BD$.

- Suppose the rule $ACE → BD$ has a user-specified minimum confidence threshold; however it is unable to generate any rule for the next iteration because there is only a single rule that has 2 items in the consequent. The algorithm will not invoke the *apriori_gen*() function any further, and it stops generating rules from the frequent itemset "$ABCDE$".

EXAMPLE

Using the frequent itemset {*cheese coffee milk*} in Figure 16.9, the following three rules hold, since the confidence is 100%:

$$cheese, coffee → milk$$
$$cheese, milk → coffee$$
$$coffee, milk → cheese$$

Then we use the *apriori_gen()* function to generate all candidate 2-itemsets, resulting in {*cheese milk*} and {*coffee milk*}. After confidence calculation, the following two rules hold:

$$coffee \rightarrow cheese, milk \qquad \text{(confidence} = 100\%)$$
$$cheese \rightarrow coffee, milk \qquad \text{(confidence} = 75\%)$$

Therefore, from one frequent itemset {*cheese coffee milk*} alone, five association rules shown above have been generated. For the complete association rule results, refer to Figure 16.7.

16.3.3 Association Rules: Parallel Processing

There are several reasons that parallelism is needed in association rule mining. One obvious reason is that the data set (or the database) is big (i.e., the data set consists of a large volume of record transactions). Another reason is that a small number of items can easily generate a large number of frequent itemsets. The mining process might be prematurely terminated because of insufficient main memory. I/O overhead due to the number of disk scans is also known to be a major problem. All of these motivate the use of parallel computers to not only speed up the entire mining process but also address some of the existing problems in the uniprocessor system.

Earlier in this chapter, two parallelism models for data mining were described. This section will examine these two parallelism models for association rule mining. In the literature, *data parallelism* for association rule mining is often referred to as *count distribution*, whereas *result parallelism* is widely known as *data distribution*.

Count Distribution (Based on Data Parallelism)

Count distribution-based parallelism for association rule mining is based on data parallelism whereby each processor will have a disjoint data partition to work with. Each processor, however, will have a complete candidate itemset, although with partial support or support count.

At the end of each iteration, since the support or support count of each candidate itemset in each processor is incomplete, each processor will need to "*redistribute*" the count to all processors. Hence, the term "*count distribution*" is used. This global result reassembling stage is basically to redistribute the support count, which often means global reduction to get global counts. The process in each processor is then repeated until the complete frequent itemset is ultimately generated.

Using the same example shown in Figure 16.9, Figure 16.11 shows an illustration of how count distribution works. Assume in this case that a two-processor system is used. Note that after the first iteration, each processor will have an incomplete count of each item in each processor. For example, processor 1 will have only two breads, whereas processor 2 will only have one bread. However, after the global count reduction stage, the counts for bread are consolidated, and hence each processor will get the complete count for bread, which in this case is equal to three.

Original dataset

Transaction ID	Items Purchased
100	bread,cereal,milk
200	bread,cheese,coffee,milk
300	cereal, cheese, coffee, milk
400	cheese,coffee,milk
500	bread, sugar, tea

Processor 1

TID	Items Purchased
100	bread, cereal, milk
200	bread, cheese, coffee, milk

Processor 2

TID	Items Purchased
300	cereal, cheese, coffee, milk
400	cheese,coffee,milk
500	bread, sugar,tea

Candidate Itemset	Support Count
bread	2
cereal	1
cheese	1
coffee	1
milk	2
sugar	0
tea	0

Candidate Itemset	Support Count
bread	1
cereal	1
cheese	2
coffee	2
milk	2
sugar	1
tea	1

Global reduction of counts

Processor 1

Processor 2

Candidate Itemset	Support Count
bread	3
cereal	2
cheese	3
coffee	3
milk	4
sugar	1
tea	1

Candidate Itemset	Support Count
bread	3
cereal	2
cheese	3
coffee	3
milk	4
sugar	1
tea	1

The process continues to generate 2-frequent itemset...

Figure 16.11   Count distribution (data parallelism for association rule mining)

After each processor receives the complete count for each item, the process continues with the second iteration. For simplicity, the example in Figure 16.11 shows only the results up to the first iteration. Readers can work out the rest in order to complete this exercise. As a guideline to the key solution, the results in Figure 16.9 can be consulted.

Data Distribution (Based on Result Parallelism)

Data distribution-based parallelism for association rule mining is based on result parallelism whereby parallelism is created because of the partition of the result, instead of the data. However, the term "data distribution" might be confused with data parallelism (count distribution). To understand why the term "data distribution" is used, we need to understand how data distribution works.

In data distribution, a candidate itemset is distributed among the processors. For example, a candidate itemset starting with "*b*" like *bread* is allocated to the first processor, whereas the rest are allocated to the second processor. Initially, the data set has been partitioned (as in count distribution—see Fig. 16.11). In this case, processor 1 will get only the first two records, whereas the last three records will go to processor 2. However, each processor needs to have not only its local partition but all other partitions from other processors. Consequently, once local data has been partitioned, it is broadcasted to all other processors; hence the term "*data distribution*" is used.

At the end of each iteration, where each processor will produce its own local frequent itemset, each processor will also need to send to all other processors its frequent itemset, so that all other processors can use this to generate their own candidate itemset for the next iteration. Therefore, "*data distribution*" is applied not only in the beginning of the process where the data set is distributed, but also along the way in the process such that at the end of each iteration, the frequent itemset is also distributed. Hence, the term "*data distribution*" appropriately reflects the case.

With a data distribution model, it is expected that high communication cost will occur because of the data movement (i.e., data set as well as frequent itemset movements). Also, redundant work due to multiple traversals of the candidate itemsets can be expected.

Figure 16.12 gives an illustration of how data distribution works in parallel association rule mining. Note that at the end of the first iteration, processor 1 has one itemset {*bread*}, whereas processor 2 has all other itemsets (items *sugar* and *tea* in processor 2—the dark shaded cells—will be eliminated because of a low support count).

Then frequent itemsets are redistributed to all processors. In this case, processor 1 that has *bread* in its 1-frequent itemset will also see other 1-frequent itemset. With this combine information, 2-candidate itemsets in each processor can be generated.

16.4 PARALLEL SEQUENTIAL PATTERNS

Sequential patterns, also known as *sequential rules*, are very similar to association rules. They form a causal relationship between two itemsets, in the form of $X \rightarrow Y$, where because X occurs, it causes Y to occur with a high probability. Although both sequential patterns and association rules have been used in the market basket

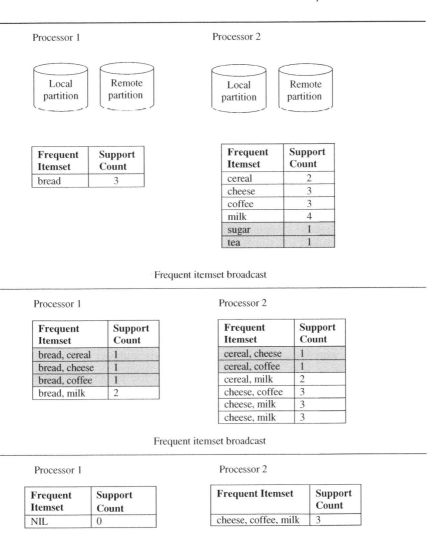

Figure 16.12   Data distribution (result parallelism for association rule mining)

analysis, the concepts are certainly applicable to any transaction-based applications.

Despite the similarities, there are two main differences between sequential patterns and association rules:

Association rules are *intratransaction* patterns or sequences, where the rule $X \rightarrow Y$ indicates that both items X and Y must exist in the same transaction. As

TID	Items
1	A B C G X R T Y
2	
3	*Sequential pattern*
4	
5	J K M N

Association rule

Figure 16.13 Sequential patterns
vs. association rules

the opposite, sequential patterns are *intertransaction* patterns or sequences. The same rule above indicates that since item X exists, this will lead to the existence of item Y in the near future transaction.

The transaction record structure in an association rule simply consists of the transaction ID (TID) and a list of items purchased, similar to what is depicted in Figure 16.5. In a sequential pattern, because the rule involves multiple transactions, the transactions must belong to the same customer (or owner of the transactions). Additionally, it is assumed that each transaction has a timestamp. In other words, a sequential pattern $X \rightarrow Y$ has a temporal property.

Figure 16.13 highlights the difference between sequential patterns and association rules. If one transaction is horizontal, then association rules are horizontal-based, whereas sequential patterns are vertical-based.

If the association rule algorithms focus on frequent itemset generation, sequential pattern algorithms focus on frequent sequence generation. In this section, before parallelism models for sequential patterns are described, the basic concepts and processes of sequential patterns will first be explained.

16.4.1 Sequential Patterns: Concepts

Mining sequential patterns can be formally defined as follows:

Definition: Given a set of transactions D each of which consists of the following fields, customer ID, transaction time, and the items purchased in the transaction, mining sequential patterns is used to find the intertransaction patterns/sequences that satisfy minimum support *minsup*, minimum gap *mingap*, maximum gap *maxgap*, and window size *wsize* specified by the user.

Figure 16.14 shows a sample data set of sequences for customer ID 10.

In sequential patterns, as the name implies, a sequence is a fundamental concept. If two sequences occur, one sequence might totally contain the other.

Definition: A *sequence s* is an ordered list of itemsets i. We denote itemset i as $(i_1, i_2, \ldots, i_m)$ and a sequence s by $<s_1, s_2, \ldots, s_n>$ where $s_j \subseteq i$.

For example, a customer sequence is a set of transactions of a customer ordered by increasing transaction time t. Given a set of itemsets i for a customer

Cust ID	Timestamp	Items
10	20-Apr	Oreo, Aqua, Bread
10	28-Apr	Canola oil, Chicken, Fish
10	5-May	Chicken wing, Bread crumb

Figure 16.14   Sequences for customer ID 10

that is ordered by transaction time $t_1, t_2, \ldots, t_n$, the customer sequence is $<i(t_1), i(t_2), \ldots, i(t_n)>$. Note that a sequence is denoted by the sharp brackets $<>$, where as the itemsets in a sequence use a round bracket $<>$ to indicate that they are sets. Using the example shown in Figure 16.14, the sequence may be written as <(Oreo, Aqua, Bread), (Canola oil, Chicken, Fish), (Chicken wing, Bread crumb)>.

Definition 16.5: A sequence $s<s_1, s_2, \ldots, s_n>$ is *contained* in another sequence $s'<s'_1, s'_2, \ldots, s'_m>$, if there exist integers $j_1 < j_2 < \ldots < j_n$ that $s_1 \subseteq s'_{j1}, s_2 \subseteq s'_{j2}, \ldots, s_n \subseteq s'_{jn}$, for $jn \leq m$.

In other words, s is subsequence of s', if s' contained s.

EXAMPLE

<(5 6) (7)> is contained in <(4 5) (4 5 6 7) (7 9 10)>, because (5 6) $\subseteq$ (4 5 6 7) and (7) $\subseteq$ (7 9 10), whereas <(3 5)> is not contained in <(3) (5)>.

As stated in the definition of mining sequential pattern problem, there are four important parameters in mining sequential patterns, namely:

○ Support,
○ Window size,
○ Minimum gap, and
○ Maximum gap

The concept of support in sequential patterns is related to the length of a sequence. The length of a sequence is the number of items in the sequence. Hence, a sequence of length k is called a k-sequence.

Definition 16.6: Given a set of customer sequence D, the *support* of a sequence s is the fraction of total D that contains s. A *frequent sequence* (*fseq*) is the sequence that has minimum support (*minsup*).

Definition 16.7: *Window size* is the maximum time span between the first and the last itemset in an element, where an element consists of one or more itemsets.

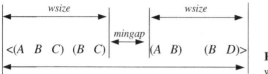

Figure 16.15 Time and sliding windows

Definition 16.8: *Minimum gap* is the minimum time gap between consecutive itemsets in a sequence.

Definition 16.9: *Maximum gap* is the maximum time gap between the first itemset of the previous.

Figure 16.15 shows an illustration of window size and minimum and maximum gap. The two windows in the sequence are clearly drawn, and there is a gap (minimum gap) between the two windows. The overall time span between the two windows defines the maximum gap.

Figure 16.16 shows an example of the use of *minsup* and *wsize* in determining frequent k-sequence. In this example, *minsup* count is set to 2, meaning that the database must contain at least two subsequence customers. Since there are only 3 customers in the data set, *minsup* = 67%.

The first example in Figure 16.16 uses no window, meaning that all the items bought by a customer are treated individually. When no windowing is used, if we see that all transactions from the same customer are treated as one transaction, then sequential patterns can be seen as association rules, and the three customer transactions in this example can be rewritten as:

$$100 \ <(A) \ (C) \ (B) \ (C) \ (D) \ (C) \ (D)>$$
$$200 \ <(A) \ (D) \ (B) \ (D)>$$
$$300 \ <(A) \ (B) \ (B) \ (C)>$$

With this structure, sequence $<(A) \ (B)>$, for example, appears in all of the three transactions, whereas sequence $<(A) \ (C)>$ appears in the first and the last transactions only. If the user threshold *minsup* = 2 is used, sequences $<(B) \ (D)>$ and $<(C) \ (D)>$ with support 1 are excluded from the result. Example 1 from Figure 16.16 shows that it only includes four frequent 2-sequences, which are: $<(A) \ (B)>$, $<(A) \ (C)>$, $<(A) \ (D)>$, and $<(B) \ (C)>$.

In the second example in Figure 16.16, window size *wsize* = 3. This means that all transactions within the 3-days window are grouped into one, and patterns will be derived only among windows, not within a window. With *wsize* = 3, two transactions from customer 200 are only 2 days apart and are below the threshold of *wsize* = 3. As a result, the two transactions will be grouped into one window, and there will be no frequent sequence from this customer.

Looking at customer 100 with 3 transactions on days 1, 3, and 7, the first two transactions (days 1 and 3) will be grouped into one window, and the third transaction (day 7) will be another window. For customer 300, the 2 transactions on

Customer transactions

Customer ID	Transaction time (days)	Items bought
100	1	(A C)
	3	(B C D)
	7	(C D)
200	2	(A D)
	4	(B D)
300	4	(A B)
	8	(B C)

The above table can be written as follows:
   100 <(A C) (B C D) (C D)>
   200 <(A D) (B D)>
   300 <(A B) (B C)>

minsup = 2

Example 1: *wsize* = 0

Frequent 2-sequence	Support count (Support)
<(A) (B)>	3 (100%)
<(A) (C)>	2 (67%)
<(A) (D)>	2 (67%)
<(B) (C)>	2 (67%)

Example 2: *wsize* = 3

Frequent 2-sequence	Support count (Support)
<(A) (C)>	2 (67%)
<(B) (C)>	2 (67%)

Figure 16.16   *minsup* and *wsize* examples

days 4 and 8 will remain two transactions. The two customers' transactions can be rewritten as follows:

$$100 <(A\ C\ B\ C\ D)\ (C\ D)>$$

$$300 <(A\ B)\ (B\ C)>$$

As s result, two frequent 2-sequences $<(A)\ (C)>$ and $<(B)\ (C)>$ are generated, both with support = 2 from the two customers. The sequence $<(A)\ (C)>$ has item A from the first window and C from the second window—from both transactions. The sequence $<(B)\ (C)>$ is also the same, where item B is from the first window and item C from the second. Note that in the above customers' transaction list, the items that appeared in the frequent 2-sequences are printed in bold.

Note that the examples in Figure 16.16 have not yet used the time gap constraints (i.e., *mingap* and *maxgap*).

Algorithm: Mining sequential patterns

---

1. **pass $k=1$**
   a. Find all frequent 1-sequences

2. **pass $k>1$**
   a. Generate candidate sequences C_k from freq $(k\text{-}1)$
      sequences
   b. Count supports for candidate sequences C_k
   c. Get frequent k-sequences
   d. Prune frequent k-sequences where some $(k\text{-}1)$
      contiguous subsequences is not in frequent $(k\text{-}1)$
      sequences

Figure 16.17   Mining sequential pattern algorithm

16.4.2   Sequential Patterns: Processes

The algorithm for a sequential pattern is decomposed into two phases: phase one is when $k = 1$, and phase two is applied to $k > 1$. This multiple passes algorithm is similar to the Apriori algorithm for mining association rules. Hence, the algorithm for mining sequential pattern is also based on Apriori. Figure 16.17 shows the algorithm for mining sequential patterns.

Finding all frequent 1-sequences is rather straightforward, applying the four parameters, namely, *minsup*, *wsize*, *mingap*, and *maxgap*. The main process is in the second phase where $k > 1$. In the second phase, there are two main important processes, specifically, generating candidate sequences from the previous iteration of frequent sequences (step 2a) and the pruning phases (step 2d).

In the original Apriori algorithm for mining association rules, step 2a corresponds to the joining phase, where the previous iteration frequent itemset is self-joined to produce a candidate itemset for the current iteration. Self-join in frequent itemsets in association rules is rather straightforward, because there is no notion of sequences. In sequential patterns, the joining phase is rather complex because of the notion of sequences. To understand the joining phase in sequences, or sequences join, we need to understand the concept of contiguity.

Definition 16.10: Let F_k denote the set of all frequent k-sequences, and C_k the set of candidate k-sequences.

Definition 16.11: Given a sequence $s = <s_1, s_2, \ldots, s_n>$ and subsequence s', subsequence s' is a *contiguous* subsequence of s if:

- Subsequence s' is derived from sequence s by dropping an item(s) from either s_1 or s_n, or

○ Subsequence s' is derived from sequence s by dropping an item from an element s_i that has at least 2 items, or

○ Subsequence s' is a contiguous subsequence of s'' and s'' is a contiguous subsequence of s.

EXAMPLE

Given $s = <(1\ 3)\ (4)\ (5\ 6)\ (7\ 8)>$

$$<(1)\ (4)\ (5\ 6)\ (7)>,\ <(4)\ (5)>,\ \text{and}\ <(3)\ (4)\ (6)>$$

are contiguous subsequence of s.

In contrast,

$$<(1\ 3)\ (5)\ (8)>,\ \text{and}\ <(1)\ (4)\ (8)>$$

are not.

In the first part of the above example, subsequence $<(1)\ (4)\ (5\ 6)\ (7)>$ is contiguous because it is derived by dropping an element from both the first and the last itemsets (e.g., item 3 is drop from (1 3), and element 8 is dropped from (7 8)).

The second subsequence $<(4)\ (5)>$ is also contiguous because it is derived by dropping an element that has 2 items (e.g., dropping an element from all 2 itemsets) as well as dropping an item from the first and last itemsets.

The third subsequence $<(3)\ (4)\ (6)>$ is derived in a similar manner to the second subsequence, except that it does not drop an additional item from the first itemset.

In the second part of the above example, the subsequences are not contiguous because (4) is missing from the first subsequence $<(1\ 3)\ (5)\ (8)>$, and (5 6) is missing from the second subsequence $<(1)\ (4)\ (8)>$. We cannot drop (4) because it is a single-element item, and we cannot drop two elements within an itemset (5 6) either. Hence, the two subsequences are not contiguous of sequence s.

Join Phase

In the joining phase, all sequences from frequent $k - 1$ sequences are joined to create candidate k-sequences. The joining conditions are as follows:

○ For all $s_1 \in F_{k-1}$ and $s_2 \in F_{k-1}$, join s_1 and s_2 if the subsequence obtained by dropping the first item of s_1 is the same as the subsequence obtained by dropping the last item of s_2.

○ Given x the last element of s_1, and y the last item of s_2, the new candidate is $<s_1, (y)>$ if y is a single item element, or add y to x otherwise.

○ For candidate 2-sequences, for all $x \in F_1$ and $y \in F_1$, join x and y to become $<(x)(y)>$ and $<(xy)>$.

Pruning Phase

The pruning phase in mining sequential patterns has a concept similar to the pruning phase in the association rule frequent mining, where the anti-monotone property is used. The pruning phase in mining sequential patterns is described as follows:

- Delete candidate subsequences C_k that have a contiguous $(k - 1)$ subsequence that is not in frequent subsequence F_{k-1}.
- If there is no *maxgap* constraint, we also delete candidate sequences C_k that have any subsequence not in F_{k-1}.

Figure 16.18 shows an example of candidate generation. The table gives frequent 3-sequences, and we would like to use the joining and pruning to create candidate 4-sequences.

By joining the first sequence <(1 2) (3)> and the fifth sequence <(2) (3 4)>, we get <(1 2) (3 4)>. The two subsequences are joinable because we drop the first item (1) from the first sequence and drop the last item (4) from the other sequence, and both subsequences are the same, that is, <(2) (3)>. The result of the join is sequence <(1 2) (3 4)>, that is, the complete first sequence <(1 2) (3)> plus the last item (4) of the other sequence, making <(1 2) (3 4)>.

By joining the first sequence <(1 2) (3)> and the sixth sequence <(2) (3) (5)>, we obtained <(1 2) (3) (5)>. The first item (1) is dropped from the first sequence, and the last item (5) is dropped from the last sequence. Both subsequences are identical and hence joinable. The result of the join is sequence <(1 2) (3) (5)>, whereby (5) is a single element item from the sixth sequence, which is then added to the end of the first sequence, making <(1 2) (3) (5)>.

Other frequent 3-sequences are not joinable because they do not meet the constraints stated in the joining phase. Hence, only two sequences are generated after the join phase.

In the pruning phase, we need to check whether all subsequences exist in the frequent 3-sequences. So, first we need to work out all subsequences of the two sequences produced by the join phase.

No	Frequent 3-sequences	After join	After prune
1	<(1 2) (3)>	<(1 2) (3 4)>	<(1 2) (3 4)>
2	<(1 2) (4)>	<(1 2) (3) (5)>	
3	<(1) (3 4)>		
4	<(1 3) (5)>		
5	<(2) (3 4)>		
6	<(2) (3) (5)>		

Figure 16.18   Example of the joining and pruning phases

The sequence <(1 2) (3 4)> has the following subsequences:

$$<(1) (3 4)>,$$
$$<(2) (3 4)>,$$
$$<(1 2) (3)>, \text{ and}$$
$$<(1 2) (4)>$$

All of the subsequences exist in the frequent 3-sequences. Hence, we keep sequence <(1 2) (3 4)>.

The second sequence produced by the join phase <(1 2) (3) (5)> has the following contiguous subsequences:

$$<(1) (3) (5)>, <(1 2) (3)> \text{ and}$$
$$<(2) (3) (5)>$$

Unfortunately, because subsequence <(1) (3) (5)> does not exist in the frequent 3-sequences, sequence <(1 2) (3) (5)> has to be pruned out.

16.4.3 Sequential Patterns: Parallel Processing

Parallel algorithms for mining sequential patterns are very similar to those of mining association rules, which are based on *count distribution* and *data distribution*.

Count Distribution

Similar to the parallel association rule algorithm, count distribution is basically *data parallelism*, where parallelism is created due to the partitioning of the initial data set. The count distribution algorithm for mining sequential patterns is listed in Figure 16.19.

Note that data partitioning is done in steps 1–2. Local processing is done in steps 3 and 4a–c. The global reduction step to exchange local support count is done in step 4d. The last step, step 4e, makes the complete frequent k-sequences available to all processors. The process of step 4 is repeated from the next k.

Data Distribution

Data distribution is based on *result parallelism* and is similar to the data distribution model for parallel frequent itemsets generation in association rules. The data distribution model involves partitioning both the data and the candidate sequences.

The algorithm is shown in Figure 16.20. When $k = 1$, the process is identical to count distribution. Counting the support for single items is straightforward, and frequent 1-sequence is generated.

For $k > 1$, after each processor generates candidate sequences, it partitions them into a number of processors according to some partitioning rule. This is

---

Algorithm: Count Distribution Sequential Pattern Mining

---

1. Partition dataset into p partitions
   where p is the total number of processors
2. Allocate each partition to a processor

3. pass $k=1$
   a. Each processor P_i asynchronously finds 1-sequence
      support count from its local partition
   b. Synchronous to exchange local sequence support
      count
   c. Each processor P_i finds the same set frequent
      1-sequences

4. pass $k>1$
   a. Generate candidate sequences C_k from freq (k-1)
      sequences
   b. Add all candidate k-sequences C_k into hash tree
   c. Processor P_i scans its local partition to update
      support count for C_k
   d. Synchronous all processors and exchange with all
      other processors their C_k local support count
   e. Each processor gets frequent k-sequences from C_k.

Figure 16.19   Count distribution algorithm for parallel mining sequential patterns

---

Algorithm: Data Distribution Sequential Pattern Mining

---

1. pass $k=1$
   a. Similar to Count Distribution

2. pass $k>1$
   a. Generate candidate sequences using previous
      iteration frequent sequences. Divide $1/P$ of them
      to each processor
   b. Use local and received data sequences to update
      candidate sequences support counts
   c. Get frequent sequences
   d. Gather all frequent sequences from all processors

Figure 16.20   Data distribution algorithm for parallel mining sequential patterns

the manifestation of *result parallelism*, which in this case is reflected by the partitioning of the candidate sequences. After the local candidate sequences have been updated and local frequent sequences have been produced, before the next iteration starts, similarly to data distribution for association rule mining, we need to gather frequent sequences from all other processors. The iteration is then repeated for the next k, until no more iteration can be done.

16.5 SUMMARY

This chapter introduces another type of data-intensive application, namely data mining. Data mining analyzes data and produces patterns, rules, clusters, and other forms of knowledge. There are various data mining techniques. This chapter concentrates on the two most common data mining techniques in the form of pattern discovery, association rules and sequential patterns.

Parallelism for data mining techniques, including *data parallelism* and *result parallelism*, was introduced. These two parallelism methods are also applied to association rules and sequential patterns. Data parallelism in association rules and sequential patterns is often known as *count distribution*, where the counts of candidate itemsets in each iteration are shared and distributed to all processors. Hence, there is a synchronization phase. Result parallelism, on the other hand, is parallelization of the results (i.e., frequent itemset and sequence itemset). This parallelism model is often known as *data distribution*, where the data set and frequent itemsets are distributed and moved from one processor to another at the end of each iteration.

16.6 BIBLIOGRAPHICAL NOTES

The work on parallel data mining, especially focusing on parallel association rules, started in the late 1990s. One of the early works on parallel association rule was by Zaki et al. (*DMKD* 1997). M.J. Zaki, who pioneered parallel data mining, then published a number of important articles on parallel association rules and parallel sequential patterns, such as Parthasarathy and Zaki et al. (1998, 2001), which thoroughly discussed parallel association rule mining, and Zaki (1999, 2001), which introduced parallel sequence mining, especially for shared-memory architecture. There was also a journal special issue on parallel and distributed data mining edited by Zaki and Pan (*DAPD* 2002). Another important work on parallel association rule mining is that by Zaïane et al. (*ICDM* 2001), who proposed parallel association rule mining without candidate generation.

The work on parallel data mining using PC clusters has been reported in a number of research articles, such as Jin and Ziavras (*IEEE TPDS* 2004), Senger et al. (2004), Kitsuregawa and Pramudiono (2003), Goda et al. (*DEXA* 2002), and Oguchi and Kitsuregawa (*Cluster Comp* 2000).

The work on parallel sequential patterns includes that of Cong et al. (*KDD* 2005) and Demiriz (*ICDM* 2002).

Recently, there have emerged works on grid data mining. Wang and Helian (Euro-Par 2005) used Oracle Grid for global association rule mining. Li and Bollinger (2004) and Congiusta et al. (2005) introduced parallel data mining on the Grid.

16.7 EXERCISES

16.1. Outline the main differences between:

    a. Querying and association rules,

    b. Querying and sequential patterns,

    c. Querying and clustering, and

    d. Querying and classification.

    Use examples to highlight your points.

16.2. Discuss the differences between *OLAP* and *OLTP*. Illustrate your answer with an example.

16.3. *Anti-monotonicity* property is one of the features in many frequent itemset mining algorithms. Explain this property and illustrate your answer with an example.

16.4. During the frequent itemset generation in association rule mining, to generate frequent candidate itemset of length k, the frequent itemset of $k - 1$ length is *self-join*ed. Explain this process and illustrate your answer with an example.

16.5. Association rule mining exercises:

Transaction #	Item Purchased
1	bread, milk, toothpaste
2	bread, cheese, milk
3	cereal, coffee, cheese, milk
4	beef, coffee, milk
5	bread, sugar, tea
6	milk, potatoes, sugar
7	cheese, tea
8	bread, coffee, cheese, milk, pasta, sugar
9	beef, coffee, pasta
10	bread, sugar, tea
11	rice, soap, toy
12	battery, beef, potatoes, rice

    a. Using the above data set, show a walk-through of how frequent itemset is constructed the Apriori algorithm. Use 25% for the support threshold.

    b. Then apply the association rule generation algorithm to this frequent itemset to generate the association rules. Use 60% as the confidence threshold.

    c. Using three available processors, trace the results of frequent itemset generation with the *count distribution* association rule mining algorithm.

    d. Now apply the *data distribution* association rule mining algorithm.

16.6. What are *minimum* and *maximum gaps* in sequential pattern mining, and what is the relationship between minimum gap and *window size*? Illustrate your answer with an example.

16.7. Given a subsequence $s = <(1\ 2\ 3)\ (4\ 5)\ (6)\ (7\ 8\ 9)>$, give some examples of *contiguous subsequences* and *noncontiguous subsequences*.

16.8. Given the following frequent 3-sequences:

No	Frequent 3-sequences
1	$<(A)\ (B)\ (C)>$
2	$<(A)\ (B\ E)>$
3	$<(A)\ (E)\ (C)>$
4	$<(B)\ (C)\ (D)>$
5	$<(B)\ (D)\ (E)>$
6	$<(B\ E)\ (C)>$
7	$<(E)\ (C\ D)>$

    a. Show the results of the joining phase.

    b. Show the results of the pruning phase.

Chapter 17

Parallel Clustering and Classification

This chapter continues the discussion of parallel data mining from Chapter 16, but focuses on *clustering* and *classification*. There are many different techniques for clustering and classification. For this chapter, we have chosen k-means and decision tree for clustering and classification, respectively. Parallelism models for k-means and decision tree are also based on data parallelism and result parallelism introduced in the previous chapters.

Section 17.1 briefly introduces clustering and classification. Sections 17.2 and 17.3 describe parallelism models for clustering and classification, respectively. Because a thorough understanding of the main concepts of clustering and classification is important in order to understand their parallelism models, Sections 17.2 and 17.3 will also discuss basic concepts and algorithms for clustering and classification.

17.1 CLUSTERING AND CLASSIFICATION

17.1.1 Clustering

Clustering is a data mining technique to find groups in data. The formed groups are normally called a "cluster." A cluster comprises a number of "*similar*" objects or data. Members or objects within a cluster are considered to be closer or similar. This also implies that a member is closer to another member within the same group than to a member of a different group. The group does not have a category label that tags the cluster with prior identifiers. Hence, clustering is an unsupervised learning, where the target label of a training data is unknown. The clustering algorithm tries to form groups from the data characteristics, not based on cluster labels.

High-Performance Parallel Database Processing and Grid Databases,
by David Taniar, Clement Leung, Wenny Rahayu, and Sushant Goel
Copyright © 2008 John Wiley & Sons, Inc.

The following are a couple of clustering examples:

- Cluster customers according to their buying behaviors. In this example, we assume that each customer has a number of attributes containing his/her buying records, and in the database there is a large volume of customers. Clustering is used to form groups of customers whereby customers within a group (or cluster) have similar buying habits. It does not matter what the cluster is. The most important thing is the membership of the cluster. After obtaining the clusters and understanding the members of each cluster, we may identify each cluster with a label. But this is not the point of clustering. Clustering deals with cluster formation by using the characteristics of its potential members.

- Cluster students based on their examination marks, gender, heights, nationality, etc. The cluster task is to form groups of students, where students within a group are more similar than those from a different group. Again, the groups do not have a prelabel. The grouping is based purely on the characteristics of each student. At the end, it might turn out that it is difficult to give a label to the groups, but this is acceptable. The important point is that groups are formed and the members within each group are identified.

Sometimes it is easier to understand the clustering results if the clusters are visually presented, such as in Figure 17.1. In this example, each record is presented by two attributes: age and salary. From the figure, it is clear that the available records are grouped into three clusters.

In the clustering process, after the data has been initially clustered, the clusters are further refined until final cluster composition is formed. It is not uncommon for the process to undergo several iterations, making clustering an intensive data processing job. Parallel algorithms become desirable in order to speed up the entire clustering process.

17.1.2 Classification

Classification is predictive data mining. After a model has been built consisting of the predefined classes, it can be used to predict the class to which an incoming

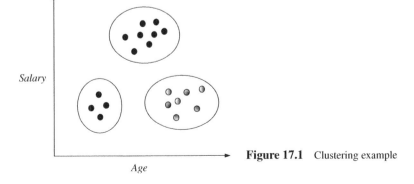

Figure 17.1   Clustering example

instance will be assigned. Classification is the process of assigning new instances (or objects) to predefined categories or classes. There are many different techniques for classification. A *decision tree* is one of the most popular tools for classification because of its comprehensible result in the form of a decision tree. Other classification tools are neural networks, statistical models, and genetic models. In this chapter, we focus on the decision tree.

In a decision tree, the objective is to create a set of rules that could be used to differentiate one target class from another. The target class is labeled with categorical values (e.g., animal classes like: Amphibian, Bird, Fish, Insect, Mammal, Worm), binary values (e.g., Yes or No), or any categorizable values.

The data used to build a decision tree are a collection of records, each containing attributes and corresponding target class. Using this data, often called a *training data set*, a classifier algorithm builds a classification model, which in this case is a decision tree. To test the correctness of the decision tree model, another set of data, known as a *testing data set*, is used to apply the rules to the decision tree model to check whether the correct class or category of each record in the testing data set has been correctly produced by the model. Hence, after a set of decision rules has been constructed, it can be used to help decision makers in decision-making or estimation.

To some degree, there are similarities between classification and clustering. Both seem to group the input data set into groups or categories or classes. In clustering, records from the input data set, which are grouped together in one cluster, are said to be more similar to each other than records from a different cluster. In classification, records from the training data set fall into the same class or category, if they possess the same features. Thus these records can be seen as forming a group of the class or the category. So both methods form groups or clusters.

Nonetheless, they have distinct differences, which are outlined as follows:

○ In *classification*, the label for each class or category is predefined. The aim of the classifier is to form a set of rules to identify records that will fall into a predefined class or category. In *clustering*, the label for each cluster is not predefined. After the clusters are formed, we may or may not have a label for each cluster. Hence, labeling that identifies the clusters is not the main issue in clustering. In contrast, labels (or class/category names) are the input to the classifier.

○ In *classification*, especially in decision trees, a record that falls into a certain class or category is identifiable through its features or attributes. The records from the same class or category are grouped or clustered in the same class or category because their attribute values satisfy the criteria or rules specified in the decision tree. In other words, because each record satisfies all the rules of a class, they are grouped together in a class. In *clustering*, records are grouped within a cluster because they are "*similar*" to each other, without necessarily knowing what their common properties are. Most important is the fact that if a record is clustered in a cluster with another record, they must be quite similar. In clustering, we are not interested in finding out the criteria of cluster membership.

○ Based on the training data set, a set of rules in the form of a decision tree is built, which is then used to "*predict*" to which class the incoming data will fall. Consequently, a classification model is used for prediction, and hence the *classification* technique is a predictive data mining technique. In contrast, in *clustering* records from the input data set are analyzed to determine how close/far they are from each other. The clustering process is used to describe the input data set, and hence clustering is a descriptive data mining technique.

○ From a learning point of view, *classification* is supervised, as the process is guided toward the stated goals that are the predefined classes or categories. In contrast, *clustering* is unsupervised, because the exploration during the clustering process is not guided in relation to which direction it should take as the target clusters is not predefined.

The motivation for parallelism in classification is quite similar to that of clustering, that is, classification needs to handle large data sets. Memory limitation of sequential computers cause sequential algorithms to make multiple expensive I/O passes over the data set on the disk. The main objective has been to have scalable, efficient, and fast data mining computation.

17.2 PARALLEL CLUSTERING

17.2.1 Clustering: Concepts

Assuming that each data record is represented as a data point in a high-dimensional space. The clustering problem can then be defined as follows:

Definition 17.1: Given a set of data points, each having a set of attributes, and a similarity measure among them, a clustering problem is to find clusters such that

○ Data points in the same cluster are more similar to one another.

○ Data points in separate clusters are less similar to one another.

Based on the above definition, one of the key factors in clustering is the similarity measure. A similarity measure can then be used to determine the degree of similarity between data points.

Similarity Measures

All clustering algorithms must use some kind of similarity measure between two data points. A *similarity measure* measures the degree of similarity between two data points. The more similar the two data points, the higher the similarity measure.

Another way to determine the similarity between two data points is by calculating the distance between the two data points. With a *distance measure*, the shorter the distance, the more similar are the two data points (in other words, a zero distance means identical). In this context, the similarity measure is the opposite of the distance measure, although both can be used to achieve the same objective, that is, to identify the closeness of, or the distance, between two data points.

One of the most common distance measurements is the *Euclidean distance*. Equation 17.1 calculates the distance between two data points x_i and x_j using the Euclidean distance. The two data points x_i and x_j have h dimensions. The distance between the two data points in each dimension is calculated by subtraction.

$$dist(x_i, x_j) = \sqrt{\sum_{k=1}^{h} \left(x_{ik} - x_{jk}\right)^2} \tag{17.1}$$

Euclidean distance is good for attributes that are continuous. For other types of data, other problem-specific measures may be used.

Clustering Techniques

The main goal of clustering is to maximize intracluster similarity and minimize intercluster similarity. To achieve this goal, there are various clustering techniques. Clustering techniques can be broadly classified into two categories: *hierarchical* and *partitional* clustering.

A *hierarchical* clustering is a sequence of partitions in which each partition is nested into the next partition in the sequence. From this view, hierarchical clustering can be bottom-up or top-down. An *agglomerative* clustering uses a bottom-up approach. Agglomerative hierarchical clustering starts by placing each data object in its own cluster, and then merges these atomic clusters into larger and larger clusters until all data objects are in a single cluster. In contrast, *divisive* clustering uses a top-down approach. It reverses the process by starting with all data objects in one cluster and subdividing into smaller pieces, until each data object forms an individual cluster. In short, hierarchical cluster methods construct the cluster either by merging (agglomerative) the clusters or by splitting (divisive) the clusters in successive steps.

Partitional clustering partitions the data objects based on a clustering criterion and places the data objects into clusters such that the data objects in a cluster are more similar to each other than to data objects in different clusters. Partitional clustering is an iterative method with a stopping criterion. It starts with initial clusters and assigns each data object to a cluster. At each iteration, the cluster's centroids are updated and the data objects are reassigned to the nearest cluster.

Therefore, the main difference between hierarchical and partitional clustering is that the hierarchical does not construct k clusters, but deals with all values of k in the same run; that is, the partition with $k = 1$ cluster is part of the output, and also the situation with $k = n$ clusters where n is the number of data objects. On the other hand, partitional clustering focuses on k clusters, where the value of k might be given or discovered during the clustering process.

17.2.2   *k*-Means Algorithm

One of the basic and common partitional clustering techniques is k-means, which is the focus of this chapter. It is the simplest and most commonly used algorithm

---

Algorithm: k-means

```
Input:
    D = {x₁, x₂, ..., xₙ}        //Data objects
    k                            //Number of desired clusters
Output:
    K                            //Set of clusters
1. Assign initial values for means m₁, m₂, ..., mₖ
2. Repeat
3.    Assign each data object xᵢ to the cluster
      which has the closest mean
4.    Calculate new mean for each cluster
5. Until convergence criteria is met
```

Figure 17.2 k-Means algorithm

employing a squared error criterion with a complexity of $O(n)$ where n is the number of data objects. k-Means is an iterative algorithm until a convergence criterion is met. The aim is to minimize total squared error in each iteration.

Figure 17.2 describes the k-means algorithm. First, the algorithm specifies k number of clusters, and guesses the k seed cluster centroid. It then iteratively looks at each data point and assigns it to the closest centroid. Because of the addition of new members coming from other clusters and the loss of members to other clusters, each cluster must then recalculate the mean (the mean of a cluster being the centroid of that cluster). This process is repeated until the cluster membership composition becomes stable or a fixed number of iterations have been performed.

The following gives an example to show how the k-means clustering algorithm works. Given data set D with twenty data points and k as follows:

$$D = \{5, 19, 25, 21, 4, 1, 17, 23, 8, 7, 6, 10, 2, 20, 14, 11, 27, 9, 3, 16\}$$
$$k = 3$$

Suppose the initial centroids chosen from D are $m_1 = 8$, $m_2 = 7$, and $m_3 = 6$, the three data points in the middle of data set D.

The first three clusters $C_1 = \{1, 2, 3, 4, 5, 6\}$, $C_2 = \{7\}$, and $C_3 = \{8, 9, 10, 11, 14, 16, 17, 19, 20, 21, 23, 25, 27\}$ are determined based on the initial means. The distance of each data point and the centroid (or mean) is calculated using Euclidean distance. Based on these three clusters, the new means are calculated as $m_1 = 3.5$, $m_2 = 7$, and $m_3 = 16.9$.

In the second iteration, because of the new means, the distance between each member of the cluster and the new mean must be recalculated, to see whether it is closer to its own cluster centroid or to another cluster's centroid. If it is closer to its own cluster centroid, obviously the data member stays in its own cluster, otherwise it has to move out to a new cluster. In the second iteration, data point 6 from C_1 moves to C_2, and data points 8, 9, 10, and 11 from C_3 moves to C_2. Because of some data points moving out and some moving in, each cluster must recalculate its centroid or mean, and a new set of means is generated, which in this case is: $m_1 = 3, m_2 = 8.5$, and $m_3 = 20.2$.

In the third iteration, only one data point, which is 14 from C_3, moves to C_2. New means are calculated as follows: $m_1 = 3, m_2 = 9.29$, and $m_3 = 21$. Note that the mean of cluster C_1 remans unchanged, because C_1 membership composition does not change either.

In the fourth iteration, data point 6 from C_2 is now back to C_1. Others stay where they are. The new means for C_1 and C_2 are $m_1 = 3.5$ and $m_2 = 9.83$. m_3 is unchanged because C_3 is unchanged.

In the fifth iteration, there is no data movement and each cluster remains the same. Because of this, the iteration stops, and the final three clusters are produced as the final results.

Figure 17.3 gives a table showing the clusters composition and the means in each iteration. The final clusters are produced at the end of final iteration.

Here are a few observations from the k-means process.

- The number of clusters k is predefined. The algorithm does not discover the ideal number of clusters. During the process, the number of clusters remains fixed—it does not shrink nor expand.

- The final composition of clusters is very sensitive to the choice of initial centroid values. Different initialisations may result in different final clusters composition.

  For example, if the first three data points 5, 19, and 25 were chosen as the initial means, the process would terminate in just two iterations with

$$C_1 = \{1, 2, 3, 4, 5, 6, 7, 8, 9, 10, 11\},$$
$$C_2 = \{14, 16, 17, 19, 20, 21\}, \text{ and}$$
$$C_3 = \{23, 25, 27\}.$$

If instead, the last three data points in D, 9, 3 and 16 were chosen, after four iterations only, the final three clusters would be the same as those in Figure 17.3.

m_1	m_2	m_3	C_1	C_2	C_3
6	7	8	1, 2, 3, 4, 5, 6	7	8, 9, 10, 11, 14, 16, 17, 19, 20, 23, 25, 27
3.5	7	16.9	1, 2, 3, 4, 5	6, 7, 8, 9, 10, 11	14, 16, 17, 19, 20, 21, 23, 25, 27
3	8.5	20.2	1, 2, 3, 4, 5	6, 7, 8, 9, 10, 11, 14	16, 17, 19, 20, 21, 23, 25, 27
3	9.29	21	1, 2, 3, 4, 5, 6	7, 8, 9, 10, 11, 14	16, 17, 19, 20, 21, 23, 25, 27
3.5	9.83	21	1, 2, 3, 4, 5, 6	7, 8, 9, 10, 11, 14	16, 17, 19, 20, 21, 23, 25, 27

Figure 17.3 k-Means example

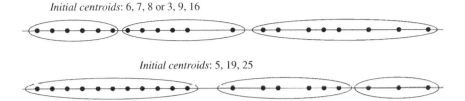

Initial centroids: 6, 7, 8 or 3, 9, 16

Initial centroids: 5, 19, 25

Figure 17.4   Different clustering results for different initial centroids

If the twenty data points are drawn on a one-dimensional space, such as in Figure 17.4, we can easily visualize the two versions of the clustering results for different initial sets of centroids. One might question whether the choice of $k = 3$ is the right one. Nevertheless, the k-means algorithm does not decide the best value for k, but rather forms k clusters.

- Each data point is treated equally. Each data point contributes equally to the centroid (mean) calculation. Because of this property, k-means cannot handle outliers well.

- k-Means does not work with categorical data, because it needs to calculate the mean of each cluster, which is applicable only to numerical data. Hence, k-means works well with continuous attributes. For categorical data, k-modes can be used in lieu of k-means, where it uses *modes*, instead of *means*.

- Although k-means often produces good results, because k-means relies on the mean, which becomes the centroid of each cluster, only convex-shaped clusters are generated.

- Performance of k-means might not be ideal. Note that in each iteration the distance between each data point and the new centroid needs to be calculated. Without any conceptual revisions to improve the performance, such as carefully selecting the initial clusters and means, or allowing clusters to split and merge, parallel processing may offer performance improvement over the original k-means clustering algorithm.

17.2.3   Parallel *k*-Means Clustering

The two parallelism models available for data mining techniques as described earlier in this chapter are applicable to parallel k-means clustering. The two parallelism models are *data parallelism* and *result parallelism*. Data parallelism, which is obvious, creates parallelism from the beginning because of the partition of the data set. Result parallelism, on the other hand, is based on the target clusters.

The difference between data and result parallelism, especially in parallel clustering, is highlighted as follows. Suppose $k = 3$, and three processors are used in parallel processing.

Using data parallelism, after the data set has been partitioned into three partitions where each processor gets a partition, each processor will work independently to create three clusters. The final clusters from each processor are respectively united. For example, all first clusters from each processor are united to form the first cluster, all second clusters are joined to form the second cluster, and so on.

Using result parallelism, the first cluster is targeted by the first processor, the second cluster by the second processor, and so on. From the beginning, the first processor will produce only one cluster assigned to it, namely cluster 1. During the iteration, the memberships of cluster 1 are likely to change. This requires some data points to move from a different cluster (different processor) to cluster 1 (processor 1). Hence, data movement is inevitable. Nevertheless, each processor is already assigned some clusters to be generated, and a cluster is produced by only one processor. If the number of clusters is larger than the available processors, it is likely that each processor may be allocated more than one cluster to work with.

Figure 17.5 illustrates the difference between data parallelism and result parallelism in parallel clustering.

Data Parallelism Parallel k-Means

Like count distribution in parallel association rules and parallel sequential patterns, *data parallelism* in parallel k-means has a global information exchange at the end of each iteration. In count distribution parallel association rules, support count of frequent itemsets in each processor is globally collected so that each processor will have the global support count for each of the frequent itemsets that it has.

In data parallelism parallel k-means, at the end of each iteration, we collect information about the sum and the count of data points in the local clusters. We need both sum and count of data points in order to correctly calculate the new means. Averaging all means will not produce a correct new mean.

Figure 17.6 shows an algorithm for data parallelism parallel k-means.

Using the same example as in Figure 17.3 with twenty data points, assume that three processors are employed. The twenty data points are distributed to the three processors with a round-robin data partitioning. As in the example in Figure 17.3, the three initial centroids are 6, 7, and 8. Figure 17.7 shows the first two iterations. As noted in Figure 17.3, the entire process will complete in five iterations.

Note that in Figure 17.7, there are several "data point movements" among different clusters within each processor. The data does not move among processors. It stays where it was allocated initially and remains in that processor until the end. In this example, data point 11 in processor 1 moves from cluster 3 to cluster 2 after one iteration. In processor 2, data point 6 moves from cluster 1 to 2. In processor 3, data points 8 and 9 move from cluster 3 to cluster 2.

Also, note that the mean of the same cluster number from different processors is the same for the same iteration. For example, cluster 3 in iteration 2 has a mean of 16.92 across all the three processors. This is because of the global sum/count distribution at the end of each iteration, whereby the mean of a cluster number is recalculated based on the global sum and count.

(a) Data Parallelism *k*-means

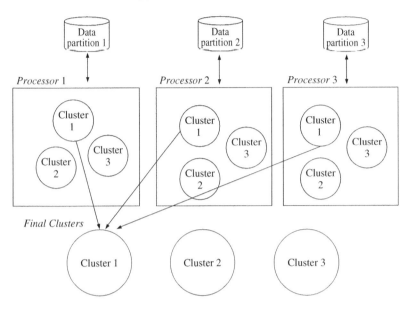

(b) Result Parallelism *k*-means

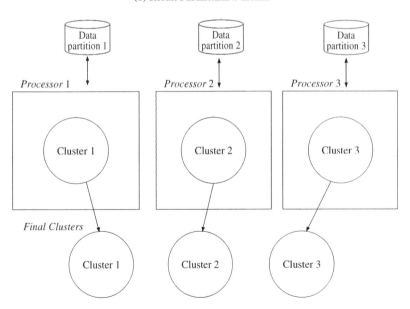

Figure 17.5   Data parallelism vs. result parallelism in parallel *k*-means clustering

---

Algorithm: Data parallelism parallel k-means

Input:
    $D=\{x_1,\ x_2,\ \ldots,\ x_n\}$ //Data objects
    k //Number of desired clusters
    $P=\{P_1,\ P_2,\ \ldots,\ P_m\}$ //Processors
Output:
    K //Set of clusters
// Initialization
1. Divide dataset D among P processors
2. Replicate the initial means m_1, m_2, ..., m_k to each proc P
// In each processor:
3. Compute distance of each local data points to the centroids
4. Construct local clusters C_{ij} for processor P_i where j indicates the cluster number $1 \le j \le k$ by assigning local data points to closest centroid
5. Maintain a sum and a count of each local cluster C_{ik}
6. At each iteration, the master process computes the new means and sends them to all processors
7. Repeat steps 3-6 until convergence
8. The master process collate local clusters C_{ij} from processor P_i to form global clusters C_j where $1 \le j \le k$
9. Return clusters $K=\{C_1,\ C_2,\ \ldots,\ C_k\}$

Figure 17.6   Data parallelism parallel k-means algorithm

At the end of five iterations, the clusters composition in each processor is unchanged and the entire process is finished. The results from each processor are:

                 Processor 1: Cluster 1 = 2, 3, 5
                              Cluster 2 = 7, 11
                              Cluster 3 = 17, 21
                 Processor 2: Cluster 1 = 4, 6
                              Cluster 2 = NIL
                              Cluster 3 = 16, 19, 20, 23, 27
                 Processor 3: Cluster 1 = 1
                              Cluster 2 = 8, 9, 10, 14
                              Cluster 3 = 25

Clusters having the same number from each processor will be collated to form the final cluster results, which are as follows:

Cluster 1 = 1, 2, 3, 4, 5, 6

Initial dataset: 5, 19, 25, 21, 4, 1, 17, 23, 8, 7, 6, 10, 2, 20, 14, 11, 27, 9, 3, 16

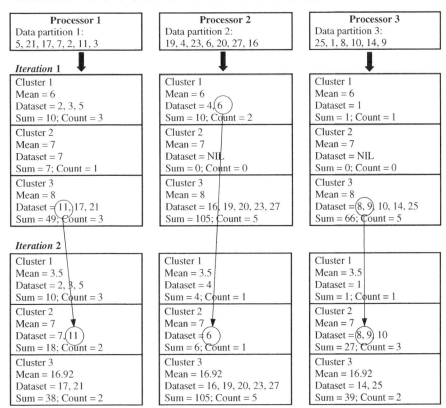

Figure 17.7 An example of data parallelism parallel k-means

Cluster 2 = 7, 8, 9, 10, 11, 14

Cluster 3 = 16, 17, 19, 20, 21, 23, 25, 27

This result is the same as that shown earlier in Figure 17.3.

Result Parallelism Parallel k-Means

Like data distribution in parallel association rules and parallel sequential patterns, *result parallelism* in parallel k-means focuses on the result partitioning, which in clustering is clusters partitioning. The data points may move from one processor to another at each iteration only to join a cluster in a different processor. As a result, data movement among processors becomes frequent, whereas in data parallelism the data never moves out from a processor.

Another difference between data parallelism and result parallelism for parallel clustering is that in result parallelism a cluster is not replicated as in data parallelism. A cluster with the same identification number, say cluster 1, exists in

---

Algorithm: Result parallelism parallel *k*-means

Input:
    $D = \{x_1, x_2, \ldots, x_n\}$ //Data objects
    k //Number of desired clusters
    $P = \{P_1, P_2, \ldots, P_m\}$ //Processors
Output:
    K //Set of clusters
// Initialization
1. Divide dataset D among P processors, and
   sort the data within each processor
2. Divide the initial means $m_1, m_2, \ldots, m_k$ among P
   processors
3. Allocate data points to the nearest cluster centroid
// In each processor:
4. For each cluster, calculate the distance between each
   local data point and the cluster centroid
5. For extreme low and high data points in each cluster,
6. If they are closer to centroid of other cluster of
   the same processor, then move these data points into
   the new cluster
7. If they are closer to centroid of other cluster of
   different processor, then move these data points into
   a new processor
8. Repeat steps 4-7 until convergence
9. Return clusters K consisting of all local clusters
   from processor P

Figure 17.8 Result parallelism parallel *k*-means algorithm

only one processor. In contrast, clusters with the same number (e.g., cluster 1) are replicated in data parallelism, making global consolidation necessary at the end of the entire clustering process. This additional process is not needed in result parallelism. Figure 17.8 shows an algorithm for result parallelism parallel *k*-means.

The example in Figure 17.9 shows that initially the twenty data points are partitioned to the three processors with a round-robin partitioning. Since there are only three clusters and three processors, each processor is allocated only one cluster. This means that the three initial means are distributed among the three processors, where processor 1 processes cluster 1 with an initial mean of 6, processor 2 with initial mean = 7, and processor 3 with initial mean = 8.

Figure 17.9 shows the results of the first two iterations. After the first iterations, there are data movements among processors. In this example, data point 6 is moved from cluster 1 (processor 1) to cluster 2 (processor 2), whereas data points 8, 9, 10, and 11 move from cluster 3 (processor 3) to cluster 2 (processor 2).

Since a cluster is processed by one processor, calculating the mean is straightforward because all the data points within a cluster are located at the same

Initial dataset: 5, 19, 25, 21, 4, 1, 17, 23, 8, 7, 6, 10, 2, 20, 14, 11, 27, 9, 3, 16

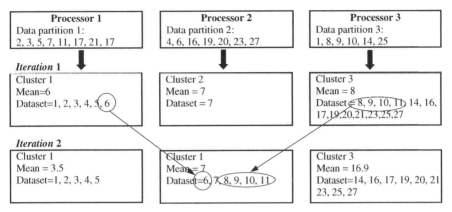

Figure 17.9   An example of result parallelism parallel k-means

processor. However, at the start of the next iteration, the neighboring processor needs to check its cluster members and determine whether it is more desirable to move the data to other neighboring processors. For example, after the first iteration, data point 6 from processor 1 is closer to the mean of cluster 2, and hence it is desirable to move data point 6 to cluster 2. In this case, we need to check only the bordering data points. Since data point 5 from cluster 1 is not moved to cluster 2 (unlike data point 6), there is no need to check other data points in cluster 1, because they are even further from the centroid of cluster 2.

At the end of the process, because each cluster is not replicated to processors, the final cluster result is basically the union of all local clusters from each processor. In this case, the results are:

Processor 1 cluster 1 = 1, 2, 3, 4, 5, 6
Processor 2 cluster 2 = 7, 8, 9, 10, 11, 14
Processor 3 cluster 3 = 16, 17, 19, 20, 21, 23, 25, 27

17.3 PARALLEL CLASSIFICATION

17.3.1 Decision Tree Classification: Structures

The term "*decision tree*" comes from the treelike structure constructed from the training data set. The other important structure in decision tree classification is the training/testing data set structure itself. The two structures, decision tree and data set, are discussed in the following:

Decision Tree Structure

A *decision tree* is usually a directed graph consisting of nodes and directed arcs. Like any other trees, nodes can be nonleaf (or internal) nodes or leaf nodes. An internal node frequently corresponds to a question or a test on an attribute (or a feature), whereas an arc (or a branch) represents an outcome of the test (e.g., weather = shower). A leaf node contains a final decision or target class for a decision tree. A nonleaf node generally can have as many branches as possible according to the possible values of the question at that node. Some decision tree nodes contain only a maximum of two child nodes (in a binary tree). A node is assigned as a leaf node when all the records at that node belong to the same class or the majority of records belong to a class.

Figure 17.10 shows an example that illustrates a decision tree structure. Each nonleaf node asks a question stated by the node label, whereas the answers are indicated by the branches that come out from the node. For example, the root node asks how the weather is, whether it is "*fine*", "*shower*", or "*thunderstorm*". The next question will depend on the answer to the current question. For example, if the weather is fine, then what is the temperature: "*hot*", "*mild*", or "*cool*"?

At the leaf node, it shows the class or category, which in this case is a binary class: class "*Yes*" or class "*No*". The decision tree shown in Figure 17.10 is an example of whether "*to jog*" or "*not to jog*" (class "*Yes*" or class "*No*", respectively), depending on several indicators, such as the weather, temperature, weekday or weekend, and time of day.

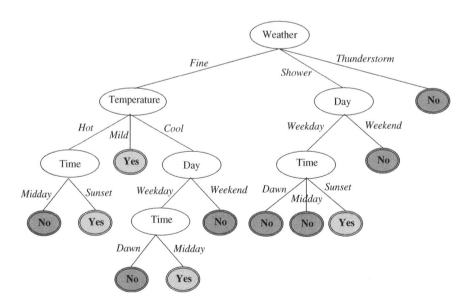

Figure 17.10   A decision tree

Following the left-most branches, if the weather is fine, the temperature is hot, and the time of day is midday, then the decision is not to jog, whereas if the weather is fine and the temperature is mild, regardless of the time of day, the decision is to jog. On the right-most branch, if the weather is thunderstorm, we definitely decide not to jog. Note that each decision (the class label in each leaf node) does not have to meet all the four criteria (e.g., weather, temperature, time of day, weekday/weekend). Moreover, some criteria might not be used in a decision tree at all.

Although a decision tree is shown in a treelike structure, a decision tree basically comprises a set of rules with the nonleaf nodes and branches as the antecedent and the class label as the consequence. Using the above example, some of the rules can be expressed as follows:

[Weather $= Fine$, Temperature $= Hot$, Time $= Midday$] $\rightarrow$ Jog $= No$

[Weather $= Fine$, Temperature $= Mild$] $\rightarrow$ Jog $= Yes$

. . .

. . .

[Weather $= Thunderstorm$] $\rightarrow$ Jog $= No$

Hence, a decision tree is perfectly written in the format of a set of rules, which is equivalent to the tree structure.

A decision tree is constructed based only on the given training data set. It is not based on a universal belief. The decision of whether to jog or not to jog as shown in Figure 17.10, is based on the given training data set, which might be limited. If a different training data set is given, it is likely that the result will be different. Even for the same training data set, it is most likely that there are several possible equivalent decision trees that can look very different, but all of which correctly summarize the decision rules of the training data set and can be used to correctly classify the training data set. Therefore, the question of which attribute is used to represent a node (or a question) is critical. Choosing a different attribute as a leaf node at any level of the decision tree will ultimately produce a different tree structure.

Data Set Structure

Each record in the data set, whether it is within the training or testing data set, consists of several attributes and one class or category attribute. The class/category attribute is used to identify the classes/categories in the decision tree. This is also called the target class attribute, whereas all the other attributes are feature attributes that will be used as internal nonleaf nodes in the decision tree. To simplify, the class/category attribute is called the target class, whereas the others are just known as attributes.

The attributes can be categorical or continuous. In the example shown in Figure 17.10, the attributes (e.g., weather, temperature, time, and day) are all categorical (countable), where each attribute has a number of distinct countable values. For example, the possible values for weather are fine, shower, and

Rec#	Weather	Temperature	Time	Day	Jog *(Target Class)*
1	Fine	Mild	Sunset	Weekend	Yes
2	Fine	Hot	Sunset	Weekday	Yes
3	Shower	Mild	Midday	Weekday	No
4	Thunderstorm	Cool	Dawn	Weekend	No
5	Shower	Hot	Sunset	Weekday	Yes
6	Fine	Hot	Midday	Weekday	No
7	Fine	Cool	Dawn	Weekend	No
8	Thunderstorm	Cool	Midday	Weekday	No
9	Fine	Cool	Midday	Weekday	Yes
10	Fine	Mild	Midday	Weekday	Yes
11	Shower	Hot	Dawn	Weekend	No
12	Shower	Mild	Dawn	Weekday	No
13	Fine	Cool	Dawn	Weekday	No
14	Thunderstorm	Mild	Sunset	Weekend	No
15	Thunderstorm	Hot	Midday	Weekday	No

Figure 17.11 Training data set

thunderstorm, whereas the possible values for temperature are hot, mild, and cool. Continuous values are real numbers (e.g., heights of a person in centimetres).

Figure 17.11 shows the training data set for the decision tree shown previously. This training data set consists of only 15 records. For simplicity, only categorical attributes are used in this example. Examining the first record and matching it with the decision tree in Figure 17.10, the target is a Yes for fine weather and mild temperature, disregarding the other two attributes. This is because all records in this training data set follow this rule (see records 1 and 10). Other records, such as records 9 and 13 use all the four attributes.

17.3.2 Decision Tree Classification: Processes

Decision Tree Algorithm

There are many different algorithms to construct a decision tree, such as ID3, C4.5, Sprint, etc. Constructing a decision tree is generally a recursive process. At the start, all training records are at the root node. Then it partitions the training records recursively by choosing one attribute at a time. The process is repeated for the partitioned data set. The recursion stops when a stopping condition is reached, which is when all of the training records in the partition have the same target class label.

Figure 17.12 shows an algorithm for constructing a decision tree. The decision tree construction algorithm uses a divide-and-conquer method. It constructs the tree using a depth-first fashion. Branching can be binary (only 2 branches) or multiway (≥ 2 branches).

Algorithm: Decision Tree Construction

Input: training dataset D
Output: decision tree T
Procedure **DTConstruct**(D):
1. $T=\emptyset$
2. Determine best splitting attribute
3. T=create root node and label with splitting attribute
4. T=add arc to root node for each split predicate with label
5. For each arc do
6. D=dataset created by applying splitting predicate to D
7.   If stopping point reached for this path Then
8.   T'=create leaf node and label with appropriate class
9.   Else
10.   T'=**DTConstruct**(D)
11. T=add T' to arc

Figure 17.12 Decision tree algorithm

Note that in the algorithm shown in Figure 17.12, the key element is the splitting attribute selection (line 2). The splitting attribute is the attribute chosen to split the training data set into a number of partitions. The splitting attribute step is also often known as feature selection, because the algorithm needs to select a feature (or an attribute) of the training data set to create a node. As mentioned earlier, choosing a different attribute as a splitting attribute will cause the result decision to be different. The difference in the decision tree produced by an algorithm lies in how to position the features or input attributes. Hence, choosing a splitting attribute, which will result in an optimum decision tree, is desirable. The way by which a splitting node is determined will be described in greater detail in the following.

Splitting Attributes or Feature Selection

When constructing a decision tree, it is necessary to have a means of determining the importance of the attributes for the classification. Hence, calculation is needed to find the best splitting attribute at a node. All possible splitting attributes are evaluated with a feature selection criterion to find the best attribute. Although the feature selection criterion still does not guarantee the best decision tree, nevertheless, it also relies on the completeness of the training data set and whether or not the training data set provides enough information.

The main aim of feature selection or choosing the right splitting attribute at some point in a decision tree is to create a tree that is as simple as possible and gives the correct classification. Consequently, poor selection of an attribute can result in a poor decision tree.

At each node, available attributes are evaluated on the basis of separating the classes of the training records. For example, looking at the training records in Figure 17.11, we note that if Time = *Dawn*, then the answer is always *No* (see records 4, 7, 11–13). It means that if Time is chosen as the first splitting attribute, at the next stage, we do not need to process these 5 records (records 4, 7, 11–13). We need to process only those records with Time = *Sunset* or *Midday* (10 records altogether), making the gain for choosing attribute Time as a splitting attribute quite high and hence, desirable.

Let us look at another possible attribute, namely, Weather. Also notice that when the Weather = *Thunderstorm*, the target class is always *No* (see records 4, 8, 14–15). If attribute Weather is chosen as a splitting attribute in the beginning, in the next stage, these four records (records 4, 8, 14–15) will not be processed—we need to process only the other 11 records. So, the gain in choosing attribute Weather as a splitting attribute is not that bad, but not as good as the attribute Time, because a higher number of records are pruned out.

Therefore, the main goal for choosing the best splitting attribute is to choose the attribute that will prune out as many records as possible at the early stage, so that fewer records need to be processed in the subsequent stages. We can also say that the best splitting attribute is the one that will result in the smallest tree.

There are various kinds of feature selection criteria for determining the best splitting attributes. The basic feature selection criterion is called *gain criterion*, which was designed for the one of the original decision tree algorithm (i.e., ID3/C4.5). Heuristically, the best splitting attribute will produce the "purest" nodes. A popular impurity criterion is information gain. Information gain increases with the average purity of the subsets that an attribute produces. Therefore, the strategy is to choose an attribute that results in greatest information gain.

The *gain criterion* basically consists of four important calculations.

- ○ Given a probability distribution, the information required to predict an event is the distribution's entropy. Entropy for the given probability of the target classes, $p_1, p_2, \ldots, p_n$ where $\sum_{i=1}^{n} p_i = 1$, can be calculated as follows:

$$entropy(p_1, p_2, \ldots, p_n) = \sum_{i=1}^{n} (p_i \log(1/p_i)) \qquad (17.2)$$

Let us use the training data set in Figure 17.11. There are two target classes: *Yes* and *No*. With 15 records in the training data set, 5 records have target class *Yes* and the other 10 records have target class *No*. The probability of falling into a *Yes* is 5/15, whereas the *No* probability is 10/15. Entropy for the given probability of the two target classes is then calculated as follows:

$$entropy(Yes, No) = 5/15 \times \log(15/5) + 10/15 \times \log(15/10)$$
$$= 0.2764 \qquad (17.3)$$

At the next iteration, when the training data set is partitioned to a smaller subset, we need to calculate the entropy based on the number of training records in the partition, not the total number of records in the original training data set.

○ For each of the possible attributes to be chosen as a splitting attribute, we need to calculate the entropy value for each of the possible values of that particular attribute. Equation 17.2 can be used, but the number of records is not the total number of training records but rather the number of records possessing the attribute value of the entropy of a particular attribute:

For example, for Weather = *Fine*, there are 4 records with target class *Yes* and 3 records with *No*. Hence the entropy for Weather = *Fine* is:

$$entropy(\text{Weather} = Fine) = 4/7 \times \log(7/4) + 3/7 \times \log(7/3)$$
$$= 0.2966 \qquad (17.4)$$

For example, for Weather = *Shower*, there is only 1 record with target class *Yes* and 3 records with *No*. Hence the entropy for Weather = *Shower* is:

$$entropy(\text{Weather} = Shower) = 1/4 \times \log(4/1) + 3/4 \times \log(4/3)$$
$$= 0.2442 \qquad (17.5)$$

Note that the entropy calculation for both examples above uses a different total number of records. In Weather = *Fine* the number of records is 7, whereas in Weather = *Shower* the number of records is only 4. This number of records is important, because it affects the probability of having a target class. For example, for target class *Yes* in *Fine* weather the probability is 4/7, whereas the same target class *Yes* in *Shower* weather the probability is only 1/4.

For each of the attribute values, we need to calculate the entropy. In other words, for attribute Weather, because there are three attribute values (e.g., *Fine, Shower,* and *Thunderstorm*), each of these three values must have an entropy value. For attribute Temperature, for instance, we need an entropy calculated for values *Hot, Mild,* and *Cool*.

○ The entropy values for each attribute must be summed with a weighted sum. The aim is that each attribute must have one entropy value. Because each attribute value has an individual entropy value (e.g., attribute Weight has three entropy values, one for each weather), and the entropy of each attribute value is based on a different probability distribution, when we combine all the entropy values from the same attributes, their individual weight must be considered.

To calculate the weighted sum, each entropy value must be multiplied with the probability of each value of the total number of training records in the partition. For example, the weighted entropy value for *Fine* weather is 7/15 × 0.2966.

There are 7 records out of 15 records with *Fine* weather, and the entropy for *Fine* weather is 0.2966 as calculated earlier (see equation 17.4).

Using the same method, the weighted sum for *Shower* weather is $4/15 \times 0.2442$, as there are only 4 records out of the 15 records in the training dataset with *Shower* weather, and the original entropy for *Shower* as calculated in equation 17.5 is 0.2442.

After each individual entropy value has been weighted, we can sum them for each individual attribute. For example, the weighted sum for attribute *Weather* is:

$$
\begin{aligned}
\text{Weighted sum entropy } (Weather) &= \text{Weighted entropy } (Fine) \\
&\quad + \text{Weighted entropy } (Shower) \\
&\quad + \text{Weighted entropy } (Thunderstorm) \\
&= 7/15 \times 0.2966 + 4/15 \times 0.2442 + 4/15 \times 0 \\
&= 0.2035
\end{aligned}
\tag{17.6}
$$

- Finally, the gain for an attribute can be calculated by subtracting the weighted sum of the attribute entropy from the overall entropy. For example, the gain for attribute *Weather* is:

$$
\begin{aligned}
gain(Weather) &= entropy(\text{training dataset} D) - entropy(\text{attribute} Weather) \\
&= 0.2764 - 0.2035 \\
&= 0.0729
\end{aligned}
\tag{17.7}
$$

The first part of equation 17.7 was previously calculated from equation 17.3, whereas the second part of the equation is from equation 17.6

After all attributes have their gain values, the attribute that has the highest gain value is chosen as the splitting attribute.

After an attribute has been chosen as a splitting attribute, the training data set is partitioned into a number of partitions according to the number of distinct values in the splitting attribute. Once the training data set has been partitioned, for each partition, the same process as above is repeated, until all records at the same partition fall into the same target class, and then the process for the partition terminates (refer to Fig. 17.12 for the algorithm).

A Walk-Through Example

Using the sample training data set in Figure 17.11, the following gives a complete walk-through of the process to create a decision tree.

Step 1: Calculate entropy for the training data set in Figure 17.11. The result is previously calculated as 0.2764 (see equation 17.3).

Step 2: Process attribute *Weather*

○ Calculate weighted sum entropy of attribute *Weather*:

$entropy(Fine) = 0.2966$ (equation 17.4)

$entropy(Shower) = 0.2442$ (equation 17.5)

$entropy(Thunderstorm) = 0 + 4/4 \times \log(4/4) = 0$

weighted sum entropy(Weather) $= 0.2035$ (equation 17.6)

○ Calculate information gain for attribute *Weather*:

gain (Weather) $= 0.0729$ (equation 17.7)

Step 3: Process attribute *Temperature*

○ Calculate weighted sum entropy of attribute *Temperature*:

$entropy(Hot) = 2/5 \times \log(5/2) + 3/5 \times \log(5/3) = 0.2923$

$entropy(Mild) = entropy(Hot)$

$entropy(Cool) = 1/5 \times \log(5/1) + 4/5 \times \log(5/4) = 0.2173$

weighted sum entropy(Temperature) $= 5/15 \times 0.2923 + 5/15$
    $\times\ 0.2173 = 0.2674$

○ Calculate information gain for attribute *Temperature*:

$$gain\ (Temperature) = 0.2764 - 0.2674 = 0.009 \qquad (17.8)$$

Step 4: Process attribute *Time*

○ Calculate weighted sum entropy of attribute *Time*:

$entropy(Dawn) = 0 + 5/5 \times \log(5/5) = 0$

$entropy(Midday) = 2/6 \times \log(6/2) + 4/6 \times \log(6/4) = 0.2764$

$entropy(Sunset) = 3/4 \times \log(4/3) + 1/4 \times \log(4/1)$
    $= 0.2443$

weighted sum entropy (Time) $= 0 + 6/15 \times 0.2764 + 4/15$
    $\times 0.2443 = 0.1757$

○ Calculate information gain for attribute *Time*:

$$gain(Temperature) = 0.2764 - 0.1757 = 0.1007 \qquad (17.9)$$

Step 5: Process attribute *Day*

○ Calculate weighted sum entropy of attribute *Day*:

$entropy(Weekday) = 4/10 \times \log(10/4) + 6/10 \times \log(10/6)$
    $= 0.2923$

$entropy(Weekend) = 1/5 \times \log(5/1) + 4/5 \times \log(5/4)$
    $= 0.2173$

weighted sum entropy (Day) $= 10/15 \times 0.2923 + 5/15$
    $\times 0.2173 = 0.2674$

○ Calculate information gain for attribute *Day*:

$$gain(Temperature) = 0.2764 - 0.2674 = 0.009 \qquad (17.10)$$

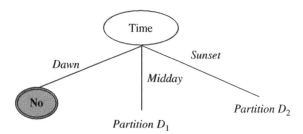

Figure 17.13   Attribute *Time* as the root node

Comparing equations 17.7, 17.8, 17.9, and 17.10 ,and 17.10 for the gain of each other attributes (Weather, Temperature, Time, and Day), the biggest gain is *Time*, with gain value $= 0.1007$ (see equation 17.9), and as a result, attribute *Time* is chosen as the first splitting attribute. A partial decision tree with the root node *Time* is shown in Figure 17.13.

The next stage is to process partition D_1 consisting of records with Time $=$ *Midday*. Training dataset partition D_1 consists of 6 records with record numbers 3, 6, 8, 9, 10, and 15. The next task is to determine the splitting attribute for partition D_1, whether it is *Weather*, *Temperature*, or *Day*. The process similar to the above to calculate the entropy and information gain, is summarized as follows:

Step 1:   Calculate entropy for the training dataset partition D_1.

$$entropy(D_1) = 2/6 \log(6/2) + 4/6 \log(6/4) = 0.2764 \qquad (17.11)$$

Step 2:   Process attribute *Weather*

- Calculate weighted sum entropy of attribute *Weather*
  $entropy(Fine) = 2/3 \times \log(6/2) + 1/3 \times \log(3/1) = 0.2764$
  $entropy(Shower) = entropy(Thunderstorm) = 0$
  $weighted\ sum\ entropy\ (Weather) = 3/5 \times 0.2764 = 0.1382$
- Calculate information gain for attribute *Weather*:

$$gain(Weather) = 0.2764 - 0.1382 = 0.1382 \qquad (17.12)$$

Step 3:   Process attribute *Temperature*

- Calculate weighted sum entropy of attribute *Temperature*
  $entropy(Hot) = 0$
  $entropy(Mild) = entropy(Cool) = 1/2 \times \log(2/1) + 1/2$
  $\times \log(2/1) = 0.3010$
  $weighted\ sum\ entropy\ (Temperature) = 2/6 \times 0.3010 + 2/6$
  $\times 0.3010 = 0.2006$
- Calculate information gain for attribute *Temperature*:

$$gain(Temperature) = 0.2764 — 0.2006 = 0.0758 \qquad (17.13)$$

Step 4:   Process attribute *Day*
- Calculate weighted sum entropy of attribute *Day*:
  $entropy(Weekday) = 2/6 \times \log(6/2) + 4/6 \times \log(6/4) = 0.2764$
  $entropy(Weekend) = 0$
  $weighted\ sum\ entropy\ (Day) = 0.2764$
- Calculate information gain for attribute *Day*:

$$gain(Temperature) = 0.2764 - 0.2764 = 0 \qquad (17.14)$$

The best splitting node for partition D_2 is attribute Weather with information gain value of 0.1382 (see equation 17.12). Continuing from Figure 17.13, Figure 17.14 shows the temporary decision tree.

For partition D_2, the splitting attribute is also *Weather*. The entropy and information gain calculations are summarized as follows:

$$entropy\ (D_2) = 0.2443$$
$$weighted\ sum\ entropy\ (Weather) = 0$$
$$gain\ (Weather) = 0.2443 \Rightarrow\ Highest\ information\ gain$$
$$weighted\ sum\ entropy\ (Temperature) = 0.1505$$
$$gain\ (Temperature) = 0.0938$$
$$weighted\ sum\ entropy\ (Day) = 0.1505$$
$$gain\ (Day) = 0.0938$$

And for partition D_{11}, the splitting attribute is *Temperature*. The entropy and information gain calculations are summarized as follows:

$$entropy\ (D_{11}) = 0.2546$$
$$weighted\ sum\ entropy\ (Temperature) = 0$$

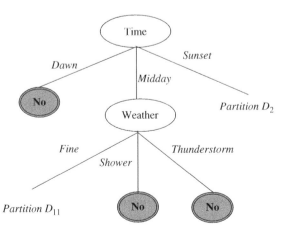

Figure 17.14   Attribute *Weather* as next splitting attribute

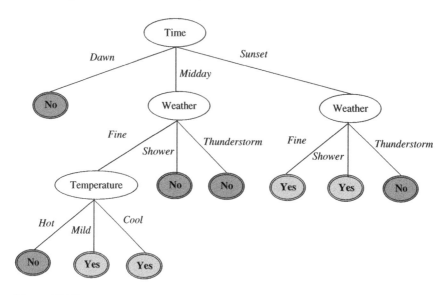

Figure 17.15 Final decision tree

$$gain\ (Temperature) = 0.2546 \Rightarrow Highest\ information\ gain$$
$$weighted\ sum\ entropy\ (Day) = 0.2546$$
$$gain\ (Day) = 0$$

Because each of the partitions has branches that reach the target class node, a complete decision tree is generated. Figure 17.15 shows the final decision tree. Note that the decision tree in Figure 17.15 looks different from the decision tree in Figure 17.10, and yet both correctly represent all rules from the training data set in Figure 17.11. The decision tree in Figure 17.15 looks more compact and is better than the one previously shown in Figure 17.10. Also note that Figure 17.15 does not use attribute *Day* as a splitting attribute at all (as the training data set is limited) and all rules can be generated without the need for attribute *Day*.

17.3.3 Decision Tree Classification: Parallel Processing

Since the structure of a decision tree is similar to query tree optimization, parallelization of a decision tree would be quite similar to subqueries execution scheduling in parallel query optimization (refer to Chapter 9). In subqueries execution scheduling for query tree optimization, there are *serial subqueries execution scheduling* and *parallel subqueries execution scheduling*, whereas for parallel data mining, this chapter introduces *data parallelism* and *result parallelism*. A parallel decision tree combines both concepts, subqueries execution scheduling and parallel data mining, because both deal with tree parallelism. Data parallelism for a decision tree is basically similar to serial subqueries execution scheduling, whereas result parallelism is identical to parallel subqueries execution scheduling. Both data parallelism and result parallelism for a decision tree are described below.

Data Parallelism for Decision Tree

There are many terms used to describe *data parallelism* for a decision tree, including *synchronous tree construction*, *feature/attribute partitioning*, or *intratree node parallelism*. All of these basically describe data parallelism from a different angle. As we discuss data parallelism for a decision tree, we will then note how other names would occur.

Data parallelism is created because of data partitioning. Previously, particularly in parallel association rules, parallel sequential patterns, and parallel clustering, data parallelism employed horizontal data partitioning, whereby different records from the data set are distributed to different processors. Each processor will have a disjoint partitioned data set, each of which consists of a number of records with the complete attributes.

Data parallelism for decision making employs another type of data partitioning, namely vertical data partitioning. Note that basic data partitioning, covering horizontal and vertical data partitioning, was explained in Chapter 3 on parallel searching operation (or parallel selection operation). For a parallel decision tree using data parallelism, the training data set is vertically partitioned, so that each partition will have one or more feature attributes, the target class, and the record number. In other words, the feature attributes are vertically partitioned, but the record number and target class are replicated to all partitions. Figure 17.16 illustrates the vertical data partitioning of a training data set.

The target class needs to be replicated to all partitions because only by having the target class can the partitions be glued together. The record numbers will be used in the subsequent iterations in building the tree, as the partition size will be shrunk because of further partitioning of each partition.

In data parallelism for a decision tree, like any other data parallelism, the complete temporary result, in this case the decision tree, will be maintained in each processor. In other words, at the end of each stage of building the decision tree, the same temporary decision tree will exist in all processors. This is the same as any other data parallelism, like data parallelism for association rules, where in count distribution, at the end of each iteration, the frequent itemset is the same for each processor. This is also the same in data parallelism for k-means clustering, where each processor will have the same clusters at the end of each iteration.

Figure 17.17 shows an illustration of data parallelism for a decision tree. At level 1, the root node is processed and determined. At the end of level 1, each processor will have the same root node.

At level 2, if the root node has n branches, there will be n level 2s. In the example shown in Figure 17.17, there are 3 branches from the root node. Consequently, there will be levels 2a, 2b, and 2c. Each sublevel of level 2 will be

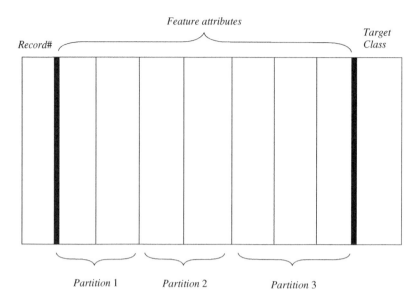

Figure 17.16 Vertical data partitioning of training data set

processed one after another, but when processing a sublevel of level 2, parallel processors are employed. In this sense, it is similar to the *serial subqueries execution scheduling*. Parallelism is within a node, and hence it is an *intratree node parallelism*.

The sublevel processing is also applied to the subsequent levels. For example, Figure 17.17 shows the processing of level 3a. To highlight that a node is currently being processed within a sublevel, the node in the decision tree in Figure 17.17 is filled in black to indicate the node currently being processed. All other nodes are not filled.

Using the training data set in Figure 17.11, assume that there are 2 processors to be employed in the parallel decision tree construction. As there are four feature attributes, these attributes are vertically partitioned into the two processors: processor 1 receives the first two attributes, *Weather* and *Temperature*, whereas processor 2 receives the other two attributes, *Time* and *Day*. Figure 17.18 shows the parallel processing.

At the level 1 stage (processing the root node), each processor focuses solely on their partitions in order to calculate the entropy value for each attribute.

After each processor completes the entropy calculation of each attribute, each processor needs to share with other processors the target class counts in order to calculate the entropy of the training data set. This value, together with the individual entropy value for each attribute, is needed to determine the best splitting attribute. Once the splitting attribute has been determined, we need to identify which records to include in the subsequent partitions, and hence the distribution of record numbers is carried out. All of these activities are information sharing

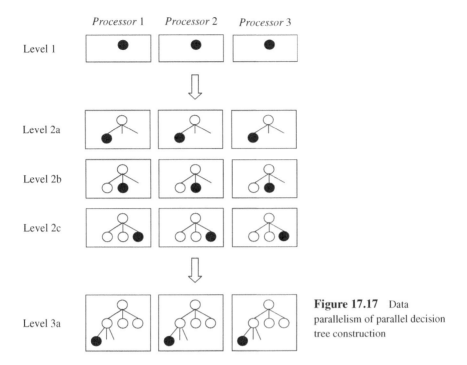

Figure 17.17 Data parallelism of parallel decision tree construction

activities—similar to count distribution in parallel association rules. In a parallel decision tree, these information sharing activities can be thought of as a mean to "*synchronize*" the decision tree, and hence data parallelism for a parallel decision tree is also known as a *synchronous tree construction* approach.

Once the tree has been synchronized, each processor will have the same decision tree. Then the next stage (i.e., level 2a) starts. Note that each partition has a smaller number of records (i.e., only 6 records in each partition). Furthermore, because attribute *Time* is already processed, this attribute is then eliminated from the partition (see the shaded *Time* attribute in Fig. 17.18). In this case, processor 2 will have only one feature attribute (e.g., Day) to process, whereas processor 1 has the original two feature attributes (e.g., Weather and Temperature).

If all of the feature attributes from one partition (one processor) have been processed in the previous stages, then there are two options. Option one is to leave the processor idle, and option two is to request other processors to send or to share one of their feature attributes. The latter is the subject of load balancing, which has been discussed in Chapter 9 on parallel query optimization. So, although theoretically data parallelism does not require any data movements, in some cases where load balancing needs to be performed, data movement among processors may happen.

If, in the first place, the number of processors is more than the available number of feature attributes, then a few processors may share the same feature attribute.

Level 1 (Root Node):

Processor 1

Rec#	Weather	Temperature	Target Class
1			
2			
...			
15			

Processor 2

Rec#	Time	Day	Target Class
1			
2			
...			
15			

Locally calculate the information gain
values for: *Weather* and *Temperature*

Locally calculate the information gain
values for: *Time* and *Day*

Global information sharing stage:
  a. Share target class counts to calculate dataset entropy value
  b. Exchange dataset entropy value to determine splitting attribute
     (e.g. Time attribute is decided to be the splitting attribute)
  c. Distribute selected records# to all processor for the next phase
     (e.g. records 3, 6, 8, 9, 10, 15 for Time *Midday*, and
     records 1, 2, 5, 14 for Time *Sunset*)

Decision tree for Level 1:

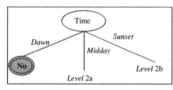
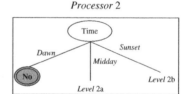

Figure 17.18 Data parallelism in decision tree

Once level 2a processing starts, each processor will work independently, and afterward information sharing or tree synchronization is carried out. The process is repeated for all nodes. In this case, level 2b will commence once level 2a has completed its task.

Result Parallelism for Decision Tree

As opposed to data parallelism, where the parallelism is intratree node, the *result parallelism* for the decision tree is *intertree node parallelism*. Hence, if there are multiple nodes on a level, parallelism is achieved through processing nodes concurrently by several processors.

Analogous to subqueries execution scheduling in parallel query optimization, if data parallelism is serial subqueries execution scheduling, result parallelism is *parallel subqueries execution scheduling*. So, there is some degree of similarity between parallel decision tree construction and parallel query tree optimization.

Level **2a:**

	Processor 1					Processor 2		

Rec#	Weather	Temperature	TargetClass
3			
6			
8			
9			
10			
15			

Rec#	Time	Day	TargetClass
3			
6			
8			
9			
10			
15			

Locally calculate the information gain
values for:*Weather* and *Temperature*

Locally calculate the information
gain values for: *Day*

Global information sharing stage:

    a.   Share target class counts of each partition to calculate dataset entropy value

    b.   Exchange dataset entropy value to determine splitting attribute
        (e.g. Weather attribute is decided to be the splitting attribute)

    c·   Distribute selected records# to all processor for the next phase

***Result decision tree for Level* 2**:

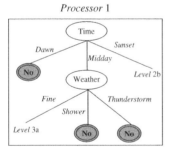   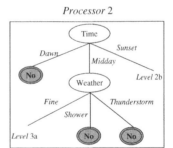

Level **2b: to continue…**

Figure 17.18   *(Continued)*

Basically, result parallelism focuses on the result—the decision tree. Hence, the tree itself is parallelized or partitioned, and that's why result parallelism for parallel decision tree is also known as *"partitioned tree construction."* Figure 17.19 gives an illustration of how a decision tree is partitioned. Logically, partitioning a decision tree is similar to the *partially replicated index (PRI)* described in Chapter 7 on parallel indexing. The main rule is that the processor that processes a child node in a tree will also process its parent nodes. Consequently, the root node is processed by all processors.

Figure 17.19 shows that at the root node level the root node processing is shared by all the three processors. On level 2, the three nodes below the root

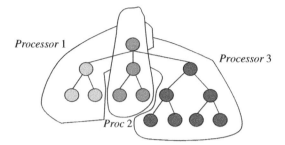

Figure 17.19 Tree partitioning in result parallelism

node are processed independently by the three processors—resulting in internode parallelism. On level 3, since the number of nodes is greater than the available processors, the processors need to take on more nodes. For example, processor 1 processes 2 nodes, and so does processor 2. Processor 3 takes not only the two nodes on level 3, but all the child nodes in the subsequent level.

In summary, if the number of processors is less than the number of nodes, an intranode parallelism is applied. If not, then an internode parallelism is employed.

The decision tree partitioning in Figure 17.19 can be redrawn to Figure 17.20, emphasizing the load of each processor. The dark shaded nodes indicate the node being processed by the processor at a particular level.

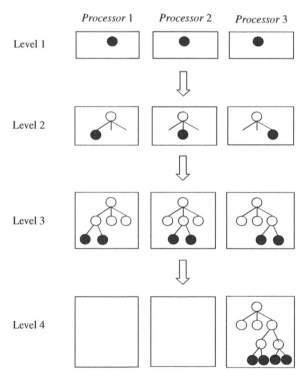

Figure 17.20 Result parallelism of parallel decision tree construction

Using the training dataset in Figure 17.11, again assume that 2 processors are used. If in data parallelism, vertical data partitioning is used; in result parallelism, a horizontal data partitioning is used to partition the training data set. In this example, we simply split the training data set into 2 partitions, where processor 1 gets the first 8 records, and processor 2 the last 7 records.

Since entropy and information gain calculations need global information from the entire training data set, each processor needs to exchange counts with other processors, and this is global information exchange. Once each processor receives the necessary information to calculate the entropy and information gain values, it decides the best splitting attribute.

Before level 2 processing starts, each processor needs to know which records are to be processed next. In this case, processor 1 will process the node pointed by the *Midday* time arc, whereas processor 2 will process the node pointed by the *Sunset* time arc. Processor 1 needs to know which records to process, and so does processor 2. In this example, processor 1 will obtain a data set partition containing records 3, 6, 8, 9, 10, and 15, whereas processor 2 will obtain records 1, 2, 5, and 14. At this stage, there will be record movement from one processor to the other, since each processor may require records from other processors to process the node allocated to it. For example, processor 1 now needs record 15, which was initially located in partition 2 (processor 2). Once data movement is complete, level 2 processing can commence.

Note that the decision tree from level 1 is shown in each processor. The dotted line indicates that this path is processed by another processor. Arc *Sunset* dotted in processor 1 means that this arc is processed by processor 2, and on the other hand, the arc *Midday*, which is dotted line in processor 2, refers to the path being processed by processor 1.

During level 2 processing, global information sharing is also needed, as in level 1 processing. The global information sharing is needed to calculate the entropy and information gain values in order to determine the next splitting attribute. After the splitting attribute has been determined, the records need to be redistributed again.

In our example in Figure 17.21, level 3 processing requires only processor 1 to work. This is because processor 2 has completed its part and all the necessary target class nodes have been generated. Processor 1 on level 3 processing will obtain records 6, 9, and 10, which are a subset of the previous partition in level 2.

Figure 17.21 shows the entire process of result parallelism of the parallel decision tree.

17.4 SUMMARY

This chapter presents two more data mining techniques, namely clustering and classification. For clustering, the k-means method is chosen, whereas for classification, the decision tree method is used.

Parallel k-means and the parallel decision tree adopt data parallelism and result parallelism. Data parallelism in clustering is based on data partitioning whereby

Horizontal Data Partitioning:

Processor 1						*Processor 2*				

Rec#	Weather	Temp	Time	Day	Target Class	Rec#	Weather	Temp	Time	Day	Target Class
1						9					
2						10					
…						…					
8						15					

Level **1 (Root Node):**

   a. Count target class on each partition

   b. Perform intra-nod eparallelism the same as for data parallelism to share target class counts to calculate dataset entropy value, exchange dataset entropy value todetermine splitting attribute, and distribute selected records# to all other processors for the next phase)

Decision tree for Level **1**:

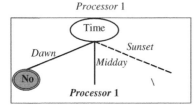
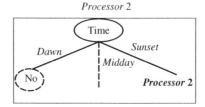

Level **2:**

Processor 1						*Processor 2*				

Rec#	Weather	Temp	Time	Day	Target Class	Rec#	Weather	Temp	Time	Day	Target Class
3						1					
6						2					
8						5					
9						14					
10											
15											

Global information sharing stage:

   a. Count target class on each partition

   b. Perform intra-node parallelism the same as for data parallelism to share target class counts to calculate dataset entropy value, exchange dataset entropy value to determin esplitting attribute,and distribute selected records# to allother processors for the next phase)

Figure 17.21   Result parallelism in decision tree

Result decision tree for Level **2**:

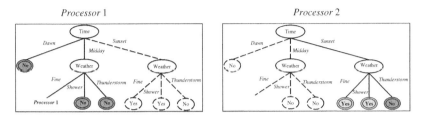

Level **3**: **WeatherTempTime**

Processor 1					
Rec#	Weather	Temp	Time	Day	Target Class
6					
9					
10					

Processor 2					
Rec#	Weather	Temp	Time	Day	Target Class

Global information sharing stage:... as like in Level 2 ...
Result decision tree for Level **3**:

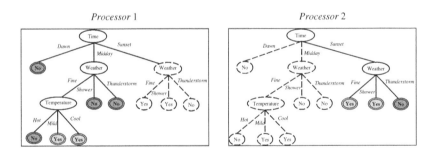

Figure 17.21 (*Continued*)

each processor builds local clusters based on its data partition, whereas result parallelism in clustering is based on allocating different final clusters into different processors to construct them.

Data parallelism in a decision tree is based on vertical data partitioning, as opposed to horizontal data partitioning commonly used by other data parallelism models (e.g., data parallelism of association rules, data parallelism of clustering, etc). Vertical data partitioning in a decision tree is necessary so that each processor may focus on different feature attributes of the training data set. Result parallelism in a decision tree is based on tree partitioning. This resembles parallel index partitioning explained in Chapter 7. Both data parallelism and result parallelism for decision tree have a similar concept with subqueries execution scheduling explained in Chapter 9 on parallel query optimization.

All parallelism methods for various data mining techniques show some similarities with those of query processing, indexing partitioning, and query optimization. All of these parallelism methods are designed for data-intensive applications, including database query processing, data warehousing, and OLAP, as well as data mining.

17.5 BIBLIOGRAPHICAL NOTES

Zaki et al. (*ICDE* 1999), who pioneered the work on parallel data mining, proposed parallel classification for shared-memory architecture. Jin and Agrawal (*Euro-Par* 2002) also used shared-memory architecture in their parallelization of decision trees. Eitrich and Lang (2006) used the parallel support vector machine (SVM) for classification.

Foti et al. (2000) presented parallel clustering for multicomputers. Recent work on parallel clustering includes that of Qiang et al. (2005), who proposed a window-based incremental parallel clustering method, and Fiolet and Toursel (2005), who also described progressive clustering, but for the Grid. Kim et al. (*WAIM* 2006) also focused on clustering algorithms for the Grid.

17.6 EXERCISES

17.1. One of the main differences between clustering and classification is that in classification each class or category is predefined, whereas in clustering the label of each cluster is not predefined. Elaborate this concept with an example.

17.2. One of the main differences between clustering and decision trees is that in decision trees a record that falls into a certain class or category is identifiable through its features or attributes, whereas in clustering records are grouped within a cluster because they are "*similar*" to each other, without necessarily knowing what their common properties are. Elaborate this concept with an example.

17.3. Clustering exercises:

    a. Given a data set $D = \{55, 30, 68, 39, 1, 4, 49, 90, 34, 76, 82, 56, 31, 25, 78, 56,$ $38, 32, 88, 9, 44, 98, 11, 70, 66, 89, 99, 22, 23, 26\}$, use the k-means *serial* algorithm to cluster the data in three clusters.

    b. Now choose a different set of centroid values, and perform the k-means clustering again. Analyze whether the clusters are different as a result of choosing different centroid values.

    c. Use the k-means *serial* algorithm to cluster the data above in four clusters. Observe the clusters' composition and how they differ should there only be three clusters.

    d. Use the k-means *data parallelism* algorithm to cluster the data in three clusters using three processors.

e. Now use the *k*-means *result parallelism* algorithm to cluster the data in three clusters using three processors.

17.4. Classification exercises:

Rec#	Employment	Marital	Gender	Age	Approved (*Target Class*)
1	Full-Time	Single	M	Teen	No
2	Full-Time	Single	F	20–50	No
3	Self Employed	Single	M	Above 50	Yes
4	Part-Time	Single	F	Above 50	Yes
5	Self Employed	Single	F	20–50	Yes
6	Self Employed	Married	M	20–50	Yes
7	Self Employed	Married	M	Above 50	Yes
8	Full-Time	Married	F	Teen	No
9	Full-Time	Married	F	20–50	Yes
10	Part-Time	Married	F	Above 50	Yes
11	Part-Time	Single	M	Teen	No
12	Full-Time	Single	M	Above 50	No
13	Full-Time	Married	M	20–50	Yes
14	Full-Time	Single	M	20–50	No
15	Part-Time	Married	M	20–50	Yes

a. Using the this data set, show a walk-through of how a decision tree is built with a *serial* decision tree algorithm.

b. Assuming that there are three available processors, demonstrate with a walk-through how a decision tree is built with a *data parallelism* decision tree algorithm.

c. Now use a *result parallelism* decision tree algorithm to build the decision tree.

Permissions

CHAPTER 4: PARALLEL SORT AND GROUP-BY

Some parts of this chapter have appeared in our early publications:

[1] David Taniar, Wenny Rahayu: Parallel database sorting. *Inf. Sci.* 146(1–4): 171–219, 2002 (©2002 Elsevier)

[2] David Taniar, Wenny Rahayu: Parallel group-by query processing in a cluster architecture. *Comput. Syst. Sci. Eng.* 17(1): 23–39, 2002 (©2002 CRL Publishing)

[3] David Taniar, Wenny Rahayu: Sorting in parallel database systems, *HPC-Asia* (2) 2000: 830–835 (©2000 IEEE)

Sections 4.2, 4.3, and 4.5 contain materials from [1] with kind permission from Elsevier. Sections 4.4 and 4.6 contain materials from [2] with kind permission from CRL Publishing.

Figures 4.1–4.9 have been reproduced from [1] with kind permission from Elsevier. Figures 4.3–4.4 and 4.6–4.9 have been reproduced from [3] with kind permission from IEEE. Figures 4.12–4.13 have been reproduced from [3] with kind permission from CRL Publishing.

Table 4.1 has been reproduced from [1] with kind permission from Elsevier.

CHAPTER 6: PARALLEL GROUP-BY JOIN

Some parts of this chapter have appeared in our early publications:

[4] David Taniar, Wenny Rahayu, Hero Ekonomosa: Performance Evaluation of Parallel GroupBy-Before-join Query Processing in High Performance Database Systems. *HPCN Europe* 2001: 241–250, Lecture Notes in Computer Science 2110 (©2001 Springer)

[5] David Taniar, Wenny Rahayu: Parallel Processing of "GroupBy-Before-Join" Queries in Cluster Architecture. *CCGrid* 2001: 178–185 (©2001 IEEE)

[6] David Taniar, Wenny Rahayu: Parallel "GroupBy-Before-Join" Query Processing for High Performance Parallel/Distributed Database Systems. *AINA* (1) 2006: 693–700 (© 2006 IEEE)

[7] David Taniar Rebecca Boon-Noi Tan: Parallel Processing of Multi-Join Expansion_aggregate Data Cube Query in High Performance Database Systems. *ISPAN* 2002 (© 2002 IEEE)

[8] David Taniar, Yi Jiang, Kevin Liu, Clement H.C. Leung: Aggregate-join query processing in parallel database systems, *HPC-Asia* (2) 2000: 824–829 (© 2000 IEEE)

[9] David Taniar, Rebecca Boon-Noi Tan, Clement H. C. Leung, Kevin H. Liu: Performance analysis of "Groupby-After-Join" query processing in parallel database systems. *Inf. Sci.* 168(1–4): 25–50, 2004 (© 2004 Elsevier)

[10] David Tania, Yi Jian, Kevin H. Liu, Clement H. C. Leung: Parallel Aggregate-Join Query Processing. *Informatica* (Slovenia) 26(3), 2002

Section 6.1 contains materials from [9] with kind permission from Elsevier, from [5,8] with kind permission from IEEE. Section 6.2 contains materials from [5] with kind permission from IEEE, and from [4] with kind permission from Springer. Section 6.3 contains materials from [8, 9] with kind permissions from IEEE and Elsevier. Section 6.5 contains materials from [6] with kind permission from IEEE. Section 6.6 contains materials from [9] with kind permissions from Elsevier.

Figures 6.1–6.3 have been reproduced from [4,5,7] with kind permissions from Springer and IEEE. Figures 6.4–6.5 have been reproduced from [8,9] with kind permissions from IEEE and Elsevier.

CHAPTER 7: PARALLEL INDEXING

Some parts of this chapter have appeared in our early publications:

[11] David Taniar, J. Wenny Rahayu: Global parallel index from multiprocessors database systems. *Inf. Sci.* 165 (1–2): 103–127, 2004 (© 2004 Elsevier)

[12] David Taniar, J. Wenny Rahayu: A Taxonomy of Indexing Schemes for Parallel Database Systems. *Distributed and Parallel Databases* 12(1): 73–106, 2002 (© 2002 Kluwer Springer)

[13] David Taniar, Wenny Rahayu: Global B+ Tree Indexing in Parallel Database Systems. *IDEAL* 2003: 701–708, Lecture Notes in Computer Science 2690 (© 2003 Springer)

[14] David Taniar, Wenny Rahayu, Rebecca Boon-Noi Tan: Parallel algorithms for selection query processing involving index in parallel database systems. *Comput. Syst. Sci. Eng.* 19(2): 95–114, 2004 (© 2004 CRL Publishing)

[15] Wenny Rahayu, David Taniar: Parallel Selection Query Processing Involving Index in Parallel Database Systems. *ISPAN* 2002: 309–314 (© 2002 IEEE)

Sections 7.1–7.5 contain materials from [12] with kind permission from Springer. Section 7.2 contains materials from [11, 12, 13, 14] with kind permissions from Elsevier, Springer, and CRL Publishing. Sections 7.5–7.7 contain materials from [11, 13, 14, 15] with kind permissions from Elsevier, CRL Publishing and IEEE.

Figure 7.1 has been reproduced from [11, 12] with kind permissions from Elsevier and Springer. Figure 7.2 has been reproduced from [12] with kind permission from Springer. Figures 7.3–7.17 have been reproduced from [11, 12, 13, 14, 15] with kind permissions from Elsevier, Springer, CRL Publishing, and IEEE. Figures 7.18–7.27 have been reproduced from [13, 14, 15] with kind permissions from Springer, CRL Publishing, and IEEE.

CHAPTER 8: PARALLEL UNIVERSAL QUANTIFICATION – COLLECTION JOIN QUERIES

Some parts of this chapter have appeared in our early publications:

[16] David Taniar, Wenny Rahayu: Parallel sort-merge object-oriented collection join algorithms. *Comput. Syst. Sci. Eng.* 17(3): 145–158, 2002 (© 2002 CRL Publishing)

[17] David Taniar, Wenny Rahayu: Parallel sort-hash object-oriented collection join algorithms for shared-memory machines. *Parallel Algorithms Appl.* 17(2): 85–126, 2002 (© 2002 Taylor & Francis)

[18] David Taniar, Wenny Rahayu: Parallel Collection Equi-Join Algorithms for Object-Oriented Databases. *IDEAS* 1998: 159–168 (© 1998 IEEE)

[19] David Taniar, Wenny Rahayu: Parallel double sort-merge algorithm for object-oriented collection join queries, *HPC-Asia* 1997: 122-127 (© 1997 IEEE)

[20] David Taniar, Wenny Rahayu: Divide and Partial Broadcast Method for Parallel Collection Join Queries. *HPCN Europe* 1998: 937–939, Lecture Notes in Computer Science 1401 (© 1998 Springer)

[21] David Taniar: Toward an Ideal Data Placement Scheme for High Performance Object-Oriented Database Systems. *HPCN Europe* 1998: 508–517, Lecture Notes in Computer Science 1401 (© 1998 Springer)

[22] David Taniar, Wenny Rahayu: Collection-Intersect Join Algorithms for Parallel Object-Oriented Database Systems. *Euro-Par* 1998: 505–512, Lecture Notes in Computer Science 1470 (© 1998 Springer)

[23] David Taniar, Wenny Rahayu: Parallel Sub-Collection Join Algorithm for High Performance Object-Oriented Databases. *BNCOD* 1998: 173–174, Lecture Notes in Computer Science 1405 (© 1998 Springer)

[24] David Taniar, Wenny Rahayu: Parallel Sub-collection Join Query Algorithms for a High Performance Object-Oriented Database Architecture. *ACPC* 1999: 559–569, Lecture Notes in Computer Science 1557 (© 1999 Springer)

Sections 8.1, 8.2, 8.4–8.6 contain some materials form [16, 17, 18, 20–24] with kind permission from CRL Publishing, Taylor & Francis, IEEE, and Springer.

Figures 8.1, 8.3–8.6, 8.12, 8.20, 8.23 have been reproduced from [16] with kind permission from CRL Publishing. Figure 8.1, 8.3–8.5, 8.7–8.8, 8.11–8.12, 8.20–8.25 have been reproduced from [17] with kind permission from Taylor & Francis. Figures 8.1, 8.3, 8.6–8.8 have been reproduced from [18] with kind permission from IEEE.

CHAPTER 9: PARALLEL QUERY SCHEDULING AND OPTIMIZATION

Some parts of this chapter have appeared in our early publications:

[25] David Taniar, Yi Jiang: A High Performance Object-Oriented Distributed Parallel Database Architecture. *HPCN Europe* 1998: 498–507, Lecture Notes in Computer Science 1401 (© 1998 Springer)

[26] David Taniar, Clement H. C. Leung: Query execution scheduling in parallel object-oriented databases. *Information & Software Technology* 41(3): 163–178, 1999 (© 1999 Elsevier)

[27] Yi Jiang, David Taniar, Clement H. C. Leung: High performance distributed parallel query processing. *Comput Syst. Sci. Eng.* 16(5): 277–289, 2001 (© 2001 CRL Publishing)

[28] David Taniar, Clement H. C. Leung: The impact of load balancing to object-oriented query execution scheduling in parallel machine environment. *Inf. Sci.* 157: 33–71, 2003 (© 2003 Elsevier)

Sections 9.2–9.3 contain materials from [26,28] with kind permission from Elsevier. Section 9.4 contains materials from [26] with kind permission from Elsevier. Sections 9.5–9.7 contain materials from [27] with kind permission from CRL Publishing.

Figure 9.2 has been reproduced from [25] courtesy of Springer. Figures 9.3, 9.5 and 9.6 have been reproduced from [28] with kind permission from Elsevier. Figures 9.4 and 9.7–9.9 have been reproduced from [26] with kind permission from Elsevier. Figures 9.10–9.15 have been reproduced from [27] with kind permission from CRL Publishing.

CHAPTER 10: TRANSACTIONS IN DISTRIBUTED AND GRID DATABASES

Some parts of this chapter have appeared in our early publications:

[29] Sushant Goel, Hema Sharda, David Taniar: Multi-scheduler Concurrency Control for Parallel Database Systems. *APPT* 2003: 643–654, Lecture Notes in Computer Science volume 2834 (© 2003 Springer)

[30] Sushant Goel, Hema Sharda, David Taniar: Transaction Management in Distributed Scheduling Environment for High Performance Database

Applications. *IWDC* 2003: 120–130, Lecture Notes in Computer Science volume 2918 (© 2003 Springer)

[31] Sushant Goel, Hema Sharda, David Taniar: Distributed scheduler for high performance data-centric systems, *TENCON* (3) 2003: 1157–1161 (© 2003 IEEE)

Section 10.3 contains materials from [29, 31] courtesy of Springer and with kind permission from IEEE.

CHAPTER 11: GRID CONCURRENCY CONTROL

Some parts of this chapter have appeared in our early publications:

[32] David Taniar, Sushant Goel: Concurrency control issues in Grid databases. *Future Generation Comp. Syst.* 23(1): 154–162, 2007 (© 2007 Elsevier)

[33] Sushant Goel, Hema Sharda, David Taniar: Preserving Data Consistency in Grid Databases with Multiple Transactions. *GCC* (2) 2003: 847–854, Lecture Notes in Computer Science volume 3033 (© 2003 Springer)

Sections 11.2–11.4 contain some materials from [32] with kind permission from Elsevier. Sections 11.3–11.4 contain some material from [33] courtesy of Springer. Figures 11.3–11.4 have been reproduced from [32] with kind permission from Elsevier.

CHAPTER 12: GRID TRANSACTION ATOMICITY AND DURABILITY

Some parts of this chapter have appeared in our early publications:

[34] Sushant Goel, Hema Sharda, David Taniar: Atomic Commitment in Grid Database Systems. *NPC* 2004: 22–29, Lecture Notes in Computer Science volume 3222 (© 2004 Springer)

[35] Sushant Goel, Hema Sharda, David Taniar: Failure Recovery in Grid Database Systems, *IWDC* 2004: 75–81, Lecture Notes in Computer Science volume 3326 (© 2004 Springer)

Sections 12.1–12.2 contain some materials from [34] courtesy of Springer. Section 12.3 contains some materials from [35] courtesy of Springer.

Figures 12.1–12.3 have been reproduced from [34] courtesy of Springer. Figure 12.5 has been reproduced from [35] courtesy of Springer.

List of Conferences and Journals

Important conferences and journals mentioned in the Bibliographical Notes at the end of each chapter are listed below.

- *Database Conferences.*

  SIGMOD (ACM)—International Conference on Management of Data
  DBLP URL: http://www.informatik.uni-trier.de/~ley/db/conf/sigmod/index.html
  ACM SIGMOD URL: http://www.sigmod.org/

  PODS—International Symposium on Principles of Database Systems (normally collocated with ACM SIGMOD)
  DBLP URL: http://www.informatik.uni-trier.de/~ley/db/conf/pods/index.html
  ACM SIGMOD URL: http://www.sigmod.org/

  VLDB—International Conference on Very Large Data Bases
  URL: http://www.informatik.uni-trier.de/~ley/db/conf/vldb/index.html
  VLDB URL: http://www.vldb.org/

  ICDE—International Conference on Data Engineering
  DBLP URL: http://www.informatik.uni-trier.de/~ley/db/conf/icde/index.html

  ICDT—International Conference on Database Theory
  DBLP URL: http://www.informatik.uni-trier.de/~ley/db/conf/icdt/index.html

  EDBT—International Conference on Extending Database Technology
  A database conference based in Europe.
  DBLP URL: http://www.informatik.uni-trier.de/~ley/db/conf/edbt/index.html

  ADBIS—International Conf. on Advances in Databases and Information Systems
  Like EDBT, ADBIS is also based in Europe.
  DBLP URL: http://www.informatik.uni-trier.de/~ley/db/conf/adbis/index.html

  DASFAA—International Conf. on Database Systems for Advanced Applications
  This conference is based in Asia.
  DBLP URL: http://www.informatik.uni-trier.de/~ley/db/conf/dasfaa/index.html

  BNCOD—British National Conference on Databases
  DBLP URL: http://www.informatik.uni-trier.de/~ley/db/conf/bncod/index.html

  DEXA—International Conference on Database and Expert Systems Applications

High-Performance Parallel Database Processing and Grid Databases,
by David Taniar, Clement Leung, Wenny Rahayu, and Sushant Goel
Copyright © 2008 John Wiley & Sons, Inc.

An applied database conference normally held in Europe.
DBLP URL: http://www.informatik.uni-trier.de/~ley/db/conf/dexa/index.html
DEXA URL: http://www.dexa.org/

CIKM—International Conference on Information and Knowledge Management
DBLP URL: http://www.informatik.uni-trier.de/~ley/db/conf/cikm/index.html
CIKM URL: http://www.cikm.org/

○ *Other Data-Related (Data Warehousing, Data Mining, and the Web) Conferences.*

DaWaK—International Conference on Data Warehousing and Knowledge Discovery
Normally held in conjunction with DEXA.
DBLP URL: http://www.informatik.uni-trier.de/~ley/db/conf/dawak/index.html
DEXA URL: http://www.dexa.org/

ICDM—IEEE International Conference on Data Mining
DBLP URL: http://www.informatik.uni-trier.de/~ley/db/conf/incdm/index.html
ICDM URL: http://www.cs.uvm.edu/~icdm/

KDD (also known as ACM SIGKDD)—Knowledge Discovery and Data Mining
DBLP URL: http://www.informatik.uni-trier.de/~ley/db/conf/kdd/index.html
ACM SIGKDD URL: http://www.acm.org/sigs/sigkdd/

APWeb—Asia-Pacific Web Conference
DBLP URL: http://www.informatik.uni-trier.de/~ley/db/conf/apweb/index.html

WAIM—International Conference on Web-Age Information Management
Often regarded as the Asian version of VLDB.
DBLP URL: http://www.informatik.uni-trier.de/~ley/db/conf/waim/index.html

○ *Parallel/Distributed, High-Performance, and Grid Computing Conferences.*

ICPP—International Conference on Parallel Processing
DBLP URL: http://www.informatik.uni-trier.de/~ley/db/conf/icpp/index.html

ICPADS—International Conference on Parallel and Distributed Systems
DBLP URL: http://www.informatik.uni-trier.de/~ley/db/conf/icpads/index.html

IPDPS—International Parallel and Distributed Processing Symposium
DBLP URL: http://www.informatik.uni-trier.de/~ley/db/conf/ipps/index.html

CCGrid—IEEE/ACM International Symposium on Cluster Computing and the Grid
DBLP URL: http://www.informatik.uni-trier.de/~ley/db/conf/ccgrid/index.html
CCGrid URL: http://www.buyya.com/ccgrid/

GCC—International Conference on Grid and Cooperative Computing
DBLP URL: http://www.informatik.uni-trier.de/~ley/db/conf/gcc/index.html

HPDC—IEEE International Symp. on High-Performance Distributed Computing
DBLP URL: http://www.informatik.uni-trier.de/~ley/db/conf/hpdc/index.html
HPDC URL: http://www.hpdc.org/

Euro-Par—European Conference on Parallel Processing
DBLP URL: http://www.informatik.uni-trier.de/~ley/db/conf/europar/index.html
Euro-Par URL: http://www.euro-par.org/

○ *Database journals.*

IEEE TKDE—*IEEE Transactions on Knowledge and Data Engineering*
DBLP URL: http://www.informatik.uni-trier.de/~ley/db/journals/tkde/index.html
TKDE URL: http://www.computer.org/tkde

ACM TODS—*ACM Transactions on Database Systems*
DBLP URL: http://www.informatik.uni-trier.de/~ley/db/journals/tods/index.html
TODS URL: http://www.acm.org/tods/

DAPD—*Distributed and Parallel Databases*
DBLP URL: http://www.informatik.uni-trier.de/~ley/db/journals/dpd/index.html
DAPD URL: http://www.springerlink.com/content/100257/

VLDB J—*The VLDB Journal*
DBLP URL: http://www.informatik.uni-trier.de/~ley/db/journals/vldb/index.html

DKE—*Data & Knowledge Engineering*
DBLP URL: http://www.informatik.uni-trier.de/~ley/db/journals/dke/index.html
DKE Science Direct URL: http://www.sciencedirect.com/science/journal/0169023X

○ *Other Data-Related Journals.*

DMKD—*Data Mining and Knowledge Discovery*
DBLP   URL: http://www.informatik.uni-trier.de/~ley/db/journals/datamine/index.
  html
DMKD URL: http://www.springerlink.com/content/100254/

○ *Parallel/Distributed, High-Performance, and Grid Computing Journals.*

IEEE TPDS—*IEEE Transactions on Parallel and Distributed Systems*
DBLP URL: http://www.informatik.uni-trier.de/~ley/db/journals/tpds/index.html
TPDS URL: http://computer.org/tpds/

IEEE TC—*IEEE Transactions on Computers*
DBLP URL: http://www.informatik.uni-trier.de/~ley/db/journals/tc/index.html
TC URL: http://www.computer.org/tc

FGCS—*Future Generation Computer Systems*
DBLP URL: http://www.informatik.uni-trier.de/~ley/db/journals/fgcs/index.html
FGCS Science Direct URL: http://www.sciencedirect.com/science/journal/0167739X

Cluster Computing
DBLP URL: http://www.informatik.uni-trier.de/~ley/db/journals/cluster/index.html
Cluster Computing URL: http://www.springerlink.com/content/101766/

Parallel Computing
DBLP URL: http://www.informatik.uni-trier.de/~ley/db/journals/pc/index.html
ParCo Science Direct URL: http://www.sciencedirect.com/science/journal/01678191

Concurrency and Computation—*Concurrency and Computation: Practice and Experience*
DBLP URL: http://www.informatik.uni-trier.de/~ley/db/journals/concurrency

○ *General Computing Journals.*

CACM—*Communications of the ACM*
DBLP URL: http://www.informatik.uni-trier.de/~ley/db/journals/cacm/index.html
CACM URL: http://www.acm.org/pubs/cacm/

ACM Comp Surv—*ACM Computing Surveys*
DBLP URL: http://www.informatik.uni-trier.de/~ley/db/journals/csur/index.html
ACM Survey URL: http://www.acm.org/pubs/surveys/

Bibliography

CHAPTER 1: PARALLEL DATABASES AND GRID DATABASES

Almasi, G. and Gottlieb, A., *Highly Parallel Computing*, Second edition, The Benjamin/Cummings Publishing Company Inc., 1994.

Antonioletti, M., et al., "The design and implementation of Grid database services in OGSA-DAI", *Concurrency—Practice and Experience*, **17**(2–4):357–376, 2005.

Atkinson, M.P., "Databases and the Grid: Who Challenges Whom?", *Proceedings of British National Conference on Databases (BNCOD)*, pp. 1–2, 2003.

Bergsten, B., Couprie, M., and Valduriez, P., "Overview of Parallel Architecture for Databases", *The Computer Journal*, **36**(8):734–740, 1993.

Bhalla, S., "Improving Parallelism in Asynchronous Reading of an Entire Database", *Proceedings of High Performance Computing (HiPC)*, pp. 377–384, 2000.

Boral, H. and DeWitt, D.J., "Database Machines: An Idea Whose Time Passed? A Critique of the Future of Database Machines", *Proceedings of International Workshop on Data Machines (IWDM)*, pp. 166–187, 1983.

Burger, A., "Developing Scientific Database Applications in a Grid Environment", *Proceedings of Statistical and Scientific Database Management (SSDBM)*, pp. 187, 2002.

Chandrasekaran, S. and Bamford, R., "Shared Cache—The Future of Parallel Databases", *Proceedings of International Conference on Data Engineering (ICDE)*, pp. 840–850, 2003.

Chen, H., Wu, Z., and Mao, Y., "Q3: A Semantic Query Language for Dart Database Grid", *Proceedings of Grid and Cooperative Computing (GCC)*, pp. 372–380, 2004.

Chen, H., Wu, Z., Mao, Y., and Zheng, G., "DartGrid: a semantic infrastructure for building database Grid applications", *Concurrency and Computation: Practice and Experience*, **18**(14):1811–1828, 2006.

Cruanes, T., Dageville, B., and Ghosh, B., "Parallel SQL Execution in Oracle 10g", *Proceedings of the ACM SIGMOD International Conference on Management of Data*, pp. 850–854, 2004.

DeWitt, D.J. and Gray, J., "Parallel Database Systems: The Future of High Performance Database Systems", *Communication of the ACM*, **35**(6):85–98, 1992.

DeWitt, D., et al., "The Gamma Database Machine Project", *IEEE Transaction on Knowledge and Data Engineering*, **2**(1):44–62, 1990.

DeWitt, D.J., Gerber, R.H., Graefe, G., Heytens, M.L., Kumar, K.B., and Muralikrishna, M., "GAMMA—A High Performance Dataflow Database Machine", *Proceedings of Very Large Data Bases (VLDB)*, pp. 228–237, 1986.

High-Performance Parallel Database Processing and Grid Databases,
by David Taniar, Clement Leung, Wenny Rahayu, and Sushant Goel
Copyright © 2008 John Wiley & Sons, Inc.

511

Fu, X., Xu, H., Hou, W., Lu, Y., and Chen, B., "Research of the Access and Integration of Grid Database", *Proceedings of the 10th International Conference on Computer Supported Cooperative Work in Design (CSCWD)*, pp. 1071–1076, 2006.

Gançarski, S., Naacke, H., Pacitti, E., and Valduriez, P., "Parallel Processing with Autonomous Databases in a Cluster System", *Proceedings of CoopIS/DOA/ODBASE*, pp. 410–428, 2002.

Gottemukkala, V., Jhingran, A., and Padmanabhan, S., "Interfacing Parallel Applications and Parallel Databases", *Proceedings of International Conference on Data Engineering (ICDE)*, pp. 355–364, 1997.

Grabs, T., Böhm, K., and Schek, H., "High-level Parallelism in a Database Cluster: A Feasibility Study Using Document Services", *Proceedings of International Conference on Data Engineering (ICDE)*, pp. 121–130, 2001.

Graefe, G. and Davison, D.L., "Encapsulation of Parallelism and Architecture-Independence in Extensible Database Query Execution", *IEEE Trans. Software Eng.*, **19**(8):749–764, 1993.

Hameurlain, A. and Morvan, F., "Parallel Relational Database Systems: Why, How and Beyond", *Proceedings of Database and Expert Systems Applications (DEXA)*, pp. 302–312, 1996.

Haran, B., et al., "Prototyping Bubba, A Highly Parallel Database System", *IEEE Transaction on Knowledge and Data Engineering*, **2**(1):4–24, 1990.

Hawthorn, P.B., "Database Machines". *Proceedings of the Very Large Data Bases (VLDB)*, pp. 393–395, 1980.

Hawthorn, P.B., "People Who Need Large Parallel Databases", *Proceedings of Conference on Parallel and Distributed Information Systems (PDIS)*, p. 192, 1993.

Hoschek, W., Martinez, J.J., Samar, A.S., Stockinger, H., and Stockinger, K., "Data management in an international data grid project." *ACM International Workshop on Grid Computing (GRID-00)*, pp. 77–90, 2000.

Hsiao, D.K., "Database Machines are Coming, Database Machines are Coming!" *IEEE Computer* **12**(3), 1979.

Hua, K.A and Lee, C., "Interconnecting Shared-Everything Systems for Efficient Parallel Query Processing", *Proceedings of the 1st International Conference on Parallel and Distributed Information Systems PDIS'91*, Miami Beach, pp. 262–270, 1991.

Jeffery, K.G., "Database Research Issues in a WWW and GRIDs World", *Proceedings of Conference on Current Trends in Theory and Practice of Informatics (SOFSEM)*, pp. 9–21, 2004.

Jeffery, K.G., "GRIDS, Databases, and Information Systems Engineering Research", *Proceedings of Extending Database Technology (EDBT)*, pp. 3–16, 2004.

Johnston, W.E., Gannon, D., Nitzberg, B., Tanner, L.A., Thigpen, B., and Woo, A., "Computing and Data Grids for Science and Engineering", *Proceedings of the ACM/IEEE Conference on Supercomputing*, Dallas, November 2000.

Langdon Jr., G.G., "Database Machines: An Introduction", *IEEE Trans. Computers* **28**(6):381–383, 1979.

Leung, C.H.C. and Ghogomu, H.T., "A High-Performance Parallel Database Architecture", *Proceedings of International Conference on Supercomputing*, pp. 377–386, 1993.

Liu, D.T., Franklin, M.J., and Parekh, D., "GridDB: A relational interface for the Grid", *Proceedings of the ACM SIGMOD International Conference on Management of Data*, June 2003.

Majkic, Z., "Massive Parallelism for Query Answering in Weakly Integrated P2P Systems", *Proceedings of Database and Expert Systems Applications DEXA Workshop*, pp. 524–528, 2004.

Malaika, S., Eisenberg, A., and Melton, J., "Standards for Databases on the Grid", *ACM SIGMOD Record*, **32**(3):92–100, 2003.

Mehta, M. and DeWitt, D.J., "Managing Intra-operator Parallelism in Parallel Database Systems", *Proceedings of Very Large Data Bases (VLDB)*, pp. 382–394, 1995.

Miller, S.S., "Parallel Databases", *Proceedings of High-Performance Web Databases*, pp. 653–659, 2001.

Narayanan, S., Kurç, T.M., Çatalyürek, Ü.V., and Saltz, J.H., "Database Support for Data-Driven Scientific Applications in the Grid", *Parallel Processing Letters*, **13**(2):245–271, 2003.

Nieto-Santisteban, M.A., Gray, J., Szalay, A.S., Annis, J., Thakar, A.R., and O'Mullane, W., "When Database Systems Meet the Grid", *Proceedings of Conference on Innovative Data Systems Research (CIDR)*, pp. 154–161, 2005.

Ozkarahan, E., *Database Machines and Database Management*, Prentice-Hall, 1986.

Patterson, D.A and Hennessy, J.L., *Computer Organization & Design: The Hardware/Software Interface*, Morgan Kaufmann, 1994.

Poess, M. and Othayoth, R., "Large Scale Data Warehouses on Grid: Oracle Database 10g and HP ProLiant Systems", *Proceedings of Very Large Data Bases (VLDB)*, pp. 1055–1066, 2005.

Sion, R., Natarajan, R., Narang, I., and Phan, T., "XG: A Grid-Enabled Query Processing Engine", *Proceedings of Extending Database Technology (EDBT)*, pp. 1115–1120, 2006.

Soares, T., "Deductive Databases: Implementation, Parallelism and Applications", *Proceedings of International Conference on Logic Programming (ICLP)*, pp. 467–468, 2006.

Song, S.W., "A Survey and Taxonomy of Database Machines", *IEEE Database Eng. Bull.*, **4**(2):3–13, 1981.

Stockinger, H., "Distributed Database Management Systems and the Data Grid", *18th IEEE Symposium on Mass Storage Systems and 9th NASA Goddard Conference on Mass storage Systems and Technologies*, April 2001.

Su, S.Y.W., "Database Machines", *Proceedings of the ACM SIGMOD International Conference on Management of Data*, pp. 157–158, 1978.

Valduriez, P., "Parallel Database Systems: Open Problems and New Issues", *Distributed and Parallel Databases 1*, pp. 137–165, 1993.

Valduriez, P., "Parallel Database Systems: The Case for Shared-Something", *Proceedings of the International Conference on Data Engineering (ICDE)*, pp. 460–465, 1993.

Wang, J., Miyazaki, M. and Li, J., "A Technique for Upgrading Database Machines Online", *Proceedings of Advances in Information Systems (ADVIS)*, pp. 82–91, 2000.

Watson, P., "Databases and the Grid", *UK e-Science Programme Technical Report, UKeS-2002-01, National e-Science Centre*; *Technical Report, CS-TR-755*, University of Newcastle, 2002.

Weikum, G., "Tutorial on Parallel Database Systems", *Proceedings of the Fifth International Conference on Database Theory ICDT'95*, Prague, pp. 33–37, 1995.

Weininger, A., "Handling Very Large Databases with Informix Extended Parallel Server", *Proceedings of the ACM SIGMOD International Conference on Management of Data*, pp. 548–549, 2000.

Winters, V.G., "Parallelism For High Performance Query Processing", *Proceedings of Extending Database Technology (EDBT)*, pp. 344–356, 1992.

Wu, Z., Chen, H., Changhuang, C., Zheng, G., and Xu, J., "DartGrid: Semantic-Based Database Grid", *Proceedings of International Conference on Computational Science*, pp. 59–66, 2004.

Wu, Z., Chen, H., Mao, Y., and Zheng, G., "Dart Database Grid: A Dynamic, Adaptive, RDF-Mediated, Transparent Approach to Database Integration for Semantic Web", *Proceedings of Asia-Pacific Web Conference (APWeb)*, pp. 1053–1057, 2005.

CHAPTER 2: ANALYTICAL MODELS

Bogdanowicz, R., Crocker, M., Hsiao, D.K., Ryder, C., Stone, V., and Strawser, P., "Experiments in Benchmarking Relational Database Machines", *Proceedings of International Workshop on Digital Mammography (IWDM)*, pp. 106–134, 1983.

Dietrich, S.W., Brown, M., Cortes-Rello, E., and Wunderlin, S., "A Practitioner's Introduction to Database Performance Benchmarks and Measurements", *Comput. J.*, **35**(4):322–331, 1992.

Englert, S., Gray, J., Kocher, T., and Shah, P., "A Benchmark of NonStop SQL Release 2 Demonstrating Near-Linear Speedup and Scaleup on Large Databases", *Proceedings of Measurement and Modeling of Computer Systems (SIGMETRICS)*, pp. 245–246, 1990.

Ganguly, S., Goel, A., and Silberschatz, A., "Efficient and Acurate Cost Models for Parallel Query Optimization", *Proceedings of Symposium on Principles of Database Systems (PODS)*, pp. 172–181, 1996.

Graefe, G. and Cole, R.L., "Fast Algorithms for Universal Quantification in Large Databases", *ACM Trans. Database Syst.*, **20**(2):187–236, 1995.

Gray, J., *The Benchmark Handbook for Database and Transaction Systems*, Second edition, Morgan Kaufmann, 1993.

Hameurlain, A. and Morvan, F., "A Cost Evaluator for Parallel Database Systems", *Proceedings of Database and Expert Systems Applications (DEXA)*, pp. 146–156, 1995.

Hennessy, J.L. and Patterson, D.A., *Computer Architecture: A Quantitative Approach*, Morgan Kaufmann, 1990.

Jain, R., *The Art of Computer Systems Performance Analysis: Techniques for Experimental Design, Measurement, Simulation, and Modeling*, John Wiley & Sons, 1991.

Jelly, I., Kerridge, J.M., and Bates, C., "Benchmarking Parallel SQL Database Machines", *Proceedings of British National Conference on Databases (BNCOD)*, pp. 105–120, 1994.

Leung, C.H.C., *Quantitative Analysis of Computer Systems*, John Wiley & Sons, 1988

O'Neil, P. E., *The Set Query Benchmark*, The Benchmark Handbook, 1993.

Orji, C.U., "A Methodology for Benchmarking Distributed Database Management Systems", *Proceedings of International Conference on Data Engineering (ICDE)*, pp. 612–619, 1991.

Poess, M., "Controlled SQL query evolution for decision support benchmarks", *Proceedings of Workshop on Software and Performance (WOSP)*, pp. 38–41, 2007.

Sampaio, S., Paton, N.W., Smith, J., and Watson, P., "Validated Cost Models for Parallel OQL Query Processing", *Proceedings of Object Oriented Information Systems (OOIS)*, pp. 60–75, 2002.

Shatdal, A. and Naughton, J.F., "Adaptive Parallel Aggregation Algorithms", *Proceedings of the ACM SIGMOD International Conference on Management of Data*, pp. 104–114, 1995.

Slimani, Y., Najjar, F., and Mami, N., "An Adaptive Cost Model for Distributed Query Optimization on the Grid", *Proceedings of OnTheMove (OTM) Workshops*, pp. 79–87, 2004.

Zipf, G.K., *Human Behaviour and the Principle of Least Effort*, Addison Wesley, 1949.

CHAPTER 3: PARALLEL SELECTION/SEARCH AND DATA PARTITIONING/PLACEMENT

Bell, D., "Difficult Data Placement Problems", *The Computer Journal*, **27**(4):315–320, 1984.

Copeland, G. et. al., "Data Placement in Bubba", *Proceedings of the ACM SIGMOD International Conference on Management of Data*, pp. 99–108, 1988.

Dikenelli, O., Ünalir, M.O., and Ozkarahan, E.A., "BLOCKER: A Variable & Multiattribute Declustering for Parallel Database Machines", *Proceedings of Euro-Par*, Vol. II, pp. 892–895, 1996.

Duan, G., Suzuki, Y. and Kawagoe, K., "Grid Representation for Efficient Similarity Search in Time Series Databases", *Proceedings of the International Conference on Data Engineering (ICDE) Workshops*, pp. 123, 2006.

Feelifl, H. and Kitsuregawa, M., "RING: A Strategy for Minimizing the Cost of Online Data Placement Reorganization for Btree Indexed Database over Shared-Nothing Machines", *Proceedings of Database Systems for Advanced Applications (DASFAA)*, pp. 190–199, 2001.

Furtado, P., "Experimental evidence on partitioning in parallel data warehouses", *Proceedings of International Workshop on Data Warehousing and OLAP (DOLAP)*, pp. 23–30, 2004.

Gao, Y., Chen, L., Chen, G., and Chen, C., "Efficient Parallel Processing for K-Nearest-Neighbor Search in Spatial Databases", *Proceedings of Computational Science and Its Applications (ICCSA)*, pp. 39–48, 2006.

García, M.B. et al., "Multi-dimensional Declustering Methods for Parallel Database Systems", *Proceedings of Euro-Par*, pp. 866–871, 1996.

Geisler, S., "Efficient Parallel Search in Video Databases with Dynamic Feature Extraction", *Proceedings of Parallel Computing (PARCO)*, pp. 431–438, 2003.

Ghandeharizadeh, S. and DeWitt, D.J., "MAGIC: A Multiattribute Declustering Mechanism for Multiprocessor Database Machines". *IEEE Trans. Parallel Distrib. Syst*, **5**(5):509–524, 1994.

Ghandeharizadeh, S. et. al., "A Performance Analysis of Alternative Multi-Attribute Declustering Strategies, *Proceedings of the ACM SIGMOD International Conference on Management of Data*, pp. 29–38, 1992.

Ghandeharizadeh, S. and DeWitt, D., "Hybrid-Range Partitioning Strategy: A New Declustering Strategy for Multiprocessor Database Machines", *Proceedings of the 16th Very Large Data Bases (VLDB) Conference, Brisbane*, pp.481–492, 1990.

Golubchik, L., Khanna, S., Khuller, S., Thurimella, R. and Zhu, A., "Approximation algorithms for data placement on parallel disks", *Proceedings of Symposium on Discrete Algorithms (SODA)*, pp. 223–232, 2000.

Guha, S. and Munagala, K., "Improved algorithms for the data placement problem", *Proceedings of Symposium on Discrete Algorithms (SODA)*, pp. 106–107, 2002.

Hababeh, I.O., Ramachandran, M. and Bowring, N., "A high-performance computing method for data allocation in distributed database systems", *The Journal of Supercomputing*, **39**(1):3–18, 2007.

Hua, K.A. and Lee, C., "An Adaptive Data Placement Scheme for Parallel Database Computer Systems", *Proceedings of the Very Large Data Bases (VLDB)*, pp. 493–506, 1990.

Ibáñez-Espiga, M. and Williams, M.H., "Data Placement Strategy for a Parallel Database System", *Proceedings of Database and Expert Systems Applications (DEXA)*, pp. 48–54, 1992.

Joshi, R. and Aslandogan, Y.A., "Concept-based web search using domain prediction and parallel query expansion", *Proceedings of Information Reuse and Integration (IRI)*, pp. 166–171, 2006.

Kido, K., Amagasa, T., and Kitagawa, H., "Processing XPath Queries in PC-Clusters Using XML Data Partitioning", *Proceedings of ICDE Workshops*, pp. 114, 2006.

Knuth, D.E., *The Art of Computer Programming, Volume III: Sorting and Searching*, Addison-Wesley, 1973.

Layer, C. and Pfleiderer, H., "High Performance Associative Coprocessor Architecture for Advanced Database Searching", *Proceedings of Databases and Applications (DBA)*, pp. 87–92, 2004.

Lee, M., Kitsuregawa, M., Ooi, B.C., Tan, K., and Mondal, A., "Towards Self-Tuning Data Placement in Parallel Database Systems", *Proceedings of the ACM SIGMOD International Conference on Management of Data*, pp. 225–236, 2000.

Märtens, H., "On Disk Allocation of Intermediate Query Results in Parallel Database Systems", *Proceedings of Euro-Par*, pp. 469–476, 1999.

Ndiaye, Y., Diene, A.W., Litwin, W., and Risch, T., "Scalable Distributed Data Structures for High-Performance Databases", *Proceedings of Workshop on Distributed Data and Structures (WDAS)*, pp. 45–69, 2000.

Nguyen, K.Q., Thompson, T., and Bryan, G., "An Enhanced Hybrid Range Partitioning Strategy for Parallel Database Systems", *Proceedings of DEXA Workshop*, pp. 289–294, 1997.

No, J., Thakur, R., and Choudhary, A.N., "Integrating Parallel File I/O and Database Support for High-Performance Scientific Data Management", *Proceedings of Supercomputing Conference (SC)*, 2000.

Qiao, J., Ye, Y., and Zhang, C., "Parallelization of Similarity Search in Large Time Series Databases", *Proceedings of International Multi-Symposium of Computer and Computational Sciences (IMSCCS)*, pp. 355–362, 2006.

Schmidt, B., Schröder, H., and Schimmler, M., "Scanning Biosequence Databases on a Hybrid Parallel Architecture", *Proceedings of Euro-Par*, pp. 360–370, 2001.

Stöhr, T. and Rahm, E., "WARLOCK: A Data Allocation Tool for Parallel Warehouses", *Proceedings of Very Large Data Bases (VLDB)*, pp. 721–722, 2001.

Stöhr, T., Märtens, H., and Rahm, E., "Multi-Dimensional Database Allocation for Parallel Data Warehouses", *Proceedings of Very Large Data Bases (VLDB)*, pp. 273–284, 2000.

Sun, J. and Grosky, W.I., "Dynamic Maintenance of Multidimensional Range Data Partitioning for Parallel Data Processing", *Proceedings of International Workshop on Data Warehousing and OLAP (DOLAP)*, pp. 72–79, 1998.

Tamura, K., Nakano, Y., Kaneko, K., and Makinouchi, A., "The Parallel Processing of Spatial Selection for Very Large Geo-Spatial Databases", *Proceedings of International Conference on Parallel and Distributed Systems (ICPADS)*, pp. 721–726, 2001.

Tang, N., Wang, G., Yu, J.X., Wong, K., and Yu, G., "WIN: An Efficient Data Placement Strategy for Parallel XML Databases", *Proceedings of International Conference on Parallel and Distributed Systems (ICPADS)*, pp. 349–355, 2005.

Veitch, A.C., Riedel, E., Towers, S.J., and Wilkes, J., "Towards Global Storage Management and Data Placement", *Proceedings of Workshop on Hot Topics in Operating Systems (HotOS)*, pp. 184, 2001.

Watson, P., "Databases in Grid Applications: Locality and Distribution", *Proceedings of British National Conference on Databases (BNCOD)*, pp. 1–16, 2005.

Yang, G., Jin, R., and Agrawal, G., "Impact of Data Distribution, Level of Parallelism, and Communication Frequency on Parallel Data Cube Construction", *Proceedings of International Parallel and Distributed Processing Symposium (IPDPS)*, pp. 66, 2003.

Yu, Y., Wang, G., Yu, G., Wu, G., Hu, J., and Tang, N., "Data Placement and Query Processing Based on RPE Parallelisms", *Proceedings of International Computer Software and Applications Conference (COMPSAC)*, 2003.

Zhu, Y. and Lü, K., "An Effective Data Placement Strategy for XML Documents", *Proceedings of British National Conference on Databases (BNCOD)*, pp. 43–56, 2001.

CHAPTER 4: PARALLEL SORTING

Baugst, B.A.W. and Greipsland, J.F., "Parallel Sorting Methods for Large Data Volumes on a Hypercube Database Computer", *Proceedings of International Workshop on Digital Mammography (IWDM)*, pp. 127–141, 1989.

Bitton, D., et al, "A Taxonomy of Parallel Sorting", *ACM Comp. Surv.*, **16**(3), pp. 287–318, 1984.

Cérin, C., Koskas, M., Fkaier, H., and Jemni, M., "Sequential in-core sorting performance for a SQL data service and for parallel sorting on heterogeneous clusters", *Future Generation Comp. Syst.*, **22**(7):776–783, 2006.

Cérin, C., Dubacq, J., and Roch, J., "Methods for Partitioning Data to Improve Parallel Execution Time for Sorting on Heterogeneous Clusters", *Proceedings of Advances in Grid and Pervasive Computing (GPC)*, pp. 175–186, 2006.

Dementiev, R. and Sanders, P., "Asynchronous parallel disk sorting", *Proceedings of ACM Symposium on Parallel Algorithms and Architectures (SPAA)*, pp. 138–148, 2003.

DeWitt, D.J., Naughton, J.F., Schneider, D.A., and Seshadri, S., "Practical Skew Handling in Parallel Joins", *Proceedings of Very Large Data Bases (VLDB)*, pp. 27–40, 1992.

Govindaraju, N.K., Gray, J., Kumar, R., and Manocha, D., "GPUTeraSort: high performance graphics co-processor sorting for large database management", *Proceedings of the ACM SIGMOD International Conference on Management of Data,* pp. 325–336, 2006.

Iyer, B.R. and Dias, D.M., "System Issues in Parallel Sorting for Database Systems", *Proceedings of International Conference on Data Engineering (ICDE)*, pp. 246–255, 1990.

Jeon, M. and Kim, D., "Distribution-Insensitive Parallel External Sorting on PC Clusters", *Proceedings of International Symposium High Performance Computing (ISHPC)*, pp. 202–213, 2003.

Knuth, D.E., *The Art of Computer Programming, Volume III: Sorting and Searching*, Addison-Wesley, 1973.

Levcopoulos, C., "On Optimal Parallel Algorithm for Sorting Presorted Files", *Proceedings of Foundations of Software Technology and Theoretical Computer Science (FSTTCS)*, pp. 154–160, 1988.

Lo, Y. and Huang, Y., "Effective Skew Handling for Parallel Sorting in Multiprocessor Database Systems", *Proceedings of International Conference on Parallel and Distributed Systems (ICPADS)*, pp. 151–156, 2002.

Lorie, R.A. and Young, H.C., "A Low Communication Sort Algorithm for a Parallel Database Machine", *Proceedings of Very Large Data Bases (VLDB)*, pp. 125–134, 1989.

Maekawa, M., "Parallel Join and Sorting Algorithms", *Proceedings of Data Base Design Techniques II*, pp. 266–298, 1979.

Pawlowski, M. and Bayer, R., "Parallel Sorting of Large Data Volumes on Distributed Memory Multiprocessors", *Proceedings of Parallel Computer Architectures*, pp. 246–264, 1993.

Yamane, Y. and Take, R., "Parallel Partition Sort for Database Machines", *Proceedings of International Workshop on Digital Mammography (IWDM)*, pp. 117–130, 1987.

Young, H.C. and Swami, A.N., "The parameterized Round-Robin partitioned algorithm for parallel external sort", *Proceedings of International Parallel Processing Symposium (IPPS)*, 1995.

Zhao, X., Martin, N.J. and Johnson, R.G., "PPS—A Parallel Partition Sort Algorithm for Multiprocessor Database Systems", *Proceedings of DEXA Workshop,* pp. 635–646, 2000.

CHAPTER 5: PARALLEL JOIN

Aguilar-Saborit, J., Muntés-Mulero, V., Zuzarte, C., and Larriba-Pey, J., "Ad Hoc Star Join Query Processing in Cluster Architectures", *Proceedings of Data Warehousing and Knowledge Discovery (DaWaK)*, pp. 200–209, 2005.

Alsabti, K., Ranka, S., and Singh, V., "An Efficient Parallel Algorithms for High Dimensional Similarity Join", *Proceedings of the International Parallel Processing Symposium/Symposium on Parallel and Distributed Processing (IPPS/SPDP)*, pp. 556–560, 1998.

Bamha, M. and Exbrayat, M., "Pipelined parallelism for multi-join queries on shared nothing machines", *Proceedings of Parallel Computing (PARCO)*, pp. 47–54, 2003.

Ben-Asher, Y., Berkovsky, S., Tammam, A., and Shmueli, E., "Using a J2EE Cluster for Parallel Computation of Join Queries in Distributed Databases", *Proceedings of the Third International Symposium on Parallel and Distributed Computing/the Third International Workshop on Algorithms, Models and Tools for Parallel Computing on Heterogeneous Networks (ISPDC/HeteroPar)*, pp. 58–63, 2004.

Chung, S.M. and Yang, J., "A Parallel Distributive Join Algorithm for Cube-Connected Multiprocessors", *IEEE Trans. Parallel Distrib. Syst.*, 7(2):127–137, 1996.

Chung, S.M. and Chatterjee, A., "Adaptive Parallel Distributive Join Algorithm for Skewed Data", *Proceedings of International Conference on Parallel and Distributed Systems (ICPADS)*, pp. 15–22, 2001.

Chen, S.D., Shen, H., and Topor, R.W., "Efficient Parallel Permutation-Based Range-Join Algorithms on Mesh-Connected Computers", *Proceedings of Asian Computing Science Conference (ASIAN)*, pp. 225–238, 1995.

Chung, W., Park, S., and Bae, H., "Efficient Parallel Spatial Join Processing Method in a Shared-Nothing Database Cluster System", *Proceedings of Int. Conf. on Embedded Software and Systems (ICESS)*, pp. 81–87, 2004.

DeWitt, D.J., Naughton, J.F., Schneider, D.A., and Seshadri, S., "Practical Skew Handling in Parallel Joins", *Proceedings of Very Large Data Bases (VLDB)*, pp. 27–40, 1992.

Esquivel, J.A. and Chan, P., "An Algorithm for Resolving the Join Component Selection Problem in Parallel Join Optimization", *Proceedings of International Symposium on Parallel Architectures, Algorithms and Networks (I-SPAN)*, pp. 45–50, 2002.

Harada, L. and Kitsuregawa, M., "Dynamic Join Product Skew Handling for Hash-Joins in Shared-Nothing Database Systems", *Proceedings of Database Systems for Advanced Applications (DASFAA)*, pp. 246–255, 1995.

Hua, K.A. and Lee, C., "Handling Data Skew in Multiprocessor Database Computers Using Partition Tuning", *Proceedings of the 17th International Conference on Very Large Data Bases (VLDB)*, Barcelona, pp. 525–535, 1991.

Hua, K.A., Lee, C., and Hua, C.M., "Dynamic Load Balancing in Multicomputer Database Systems Using Partition Tuning", *IEEE Transactions on Knowledge and Data Engineering*, **7**(6):968–983, December 1995.

Jiang, Y. and Makinouchi, A., "A parallel hash-based join algorithm for a networked cluster of multiprocessor nodes", *Proceedings of International Computer Software and Applications Conference (COMPSAC)*, pp. 678–, 1997.

Kang, M., Ko, S., Koh, K., and Choy, Y., "A Parallel Spatial Join Processing for Distributed Spatial Databases", *Proceedings of Flexible Query-Answering Systems (FQAS)*, pp. 212–225, 2002.

Kim, J. and Hong, B., "Parallel Spatial Joins Using Grid Files", *Proceedings of International Conference on Parallel and Distributed Systems (ICPADS)*, pp. 531–536, 2000.

Kitsuregawa, M. and Ogawa, Y., "Bucket Spreading Parallel Hash: A New, Robust, Parallel Hash Join Method for Data Skew in the Super Database Computer (SDC)", *Proceedings of Very Large Data Bases (VLDB)*, pp. 210–221, 1990.

Kitsuregawa, M., Tsudaka, S., and Nakano, M., "Parallel GRACE Hash Join on Shared-Everything Multiprocessor: Implementation and Performance Evaluation on Symmetry S81", *Proceedings of International Conference on Data Engineering (ICDE)*, pp. 256–264, 1992.

Lakshmi, M.S. and Yu, P.S., "Effectiveness of Parallel Joins", *IEEE Transactions of Knowledge and Data Engineering*, **2**(4):410–424, December 1990.

Li, J., Sun, W., and Li, Y., "Parallel Join Algorithms based on Parallel B + -trees", *Proceedings of International Symposium on Cooperative Database Systems for Advanced Applications (CODAS)*, pp. 197–204, 2001.

Li, W., Gao, D., and Snodgrass, R.T., "Skew handling techniques in sort-merge join", *Proceedings of the ACM SIGMOD International Conference on Management of Data*, pp. 169–180, 2002.

Lifschitz, S. and Sá, M., "Competitive Online Comparison for Parallel Joins", *Proceedings of Brazilian Symposium on Databases (SBBD)*, pp. 151–165, 2002.

Lima, A., Esperança, C., and Mattoso, M., "A Parallel Spatial Join Framework Using PMR-Quadtrees", *Proceedings of DEXA Workshop*, pp. 889–893, 2000.

Liu, B. and Rundensteiner, E.A., "Revisiting Pipelined Parallelism in Multi-Join Query Processing", *Proceedings of Very Large Data Bases (VLDB)*, pp. 829–840, 2005.

Lu, H., Shan, M-C., and Tan, K-L., "Optimization of Multi-Way Join Queries for Parallel Execution", *Proceedings of Very Large Data Bases (VLDB)*, pp. 549–560, 1991.

Luo, G., Naughton, J.F., and Ellmann, C., "A Non-Blocking Parallel Spatial Join Algorithm", *Proceedings of International Conference on Data Engineering (ICDE)*, pp. 697–705, 2002.

Luo, G., Naughton, J.F., Ellmann, C., and Watzke, M., "A Comparison of Three Methods for Join View Maintenance in Parallel RDBMS", *Proceedings of International Conference on Data Engineering (ICDE)*, pp. 177–188, 2003.

Mishra, P. and Eich, M. H., "Join Processing in Relational Databases", *ACM Comput. Surv.*, **24**(1):63–113, 1992.

Mohammed, S. and Zhou, P.L., "Efficient Parallel Join Algorithms for Skewed Multidimensional Data", *Proceedings of Parallel and Distributed Processing Techniques and Applications (PDPTA)*, pp. 1103–1112, 2006.

Moon, A., Oh, K., and Cho, H., "Performance of Dynamic Load Balanced Join Algorithms in Shared Disk Parallel Database Systems", *Proceedings of Future Trends of Distributed Computer Systems (FTDCS)*, pp. 176–184, 1999.

Moon, A. and Cho, H., "Parallel Hash Join Algorithms for Dynamic Load Balancing in a Shared Disks Cluster", *Proceedings of Computational Science and Its Applications (ICCSA)*, pp. 214–223, 2006.

Nakano, M., Imai, H., and Kitsuregawa, M., "Performance Analysis of Parallel Hash Join Algorithms on a Distributed Shared Memory Machine: Implementation and Evaluation on HP Exemplar SPP 1600", *Proceedings of International Conference on Data Engineering (ICDE)*, pp. 76–85, 1998.

Patel, J.M. and DeWitt, D.J., "Clone join and shadow join: two parallel spatial join algorithms", *Proceedings of ACM International Symposium on Advances in Geographic Information Systems (ACM-GIS)*, pp. 54–61, 2000.

Schikuta, E., "Modeling and Analysis of a Parallel Nested Loop Join on Cluster Architectures", *Proceedings of International Symposium on Parallel and Distributed Processing and Applications (ISPA)*, pp. 33–38, 2005.

Schikuta, E., "Performance Analysis of a Parallel Sort Merge Join on Cluster Architectures", *Proceedings of International Conference on Algorithms and Architectures for Parallel Processing (ICA3PP)*, pp. 277–286, 2005.

Schneider, D. and DeWitt, D.J., "A Performance Evaluation of Four Parallel Join Algorithms in a Shared-Nothing Multiprocessor Environment", *Proceedings of the ACM SIGMOD International Conference on Management of Data*, pp. 110–121, 1989.

Schneider, D.A. and DeWitt, D.J., "Tradeoffs in Processing Complex Join Queries via Hashing in Multiprocessor Database Machines", *Proceedings of the 16th Very Large Data Bases (VLDB) Conference*, pp. 469–480, Brisbane, Australia, 1990.

Shum, C., "Parallel Implementations of Exclusion Joins", *Proceedings of Symposium on Parallel and Distributed Processing (SPDP)*, pp. 742–747, 1993.

Walton, C.B. et al., "A Taxonomy and Performance Model of Data Skew Effects in Parallel Joins", *Proceedings of the 17th International Conference on Very Large Data Bases (VLDB)*, Barcelona, pp. 537–548, 1991.

Wilschut, A.N., Flokstra, J., and Apers, P.M.G., "Parallel Evaluation of Multi-Join Queries", *Proceedings of the ACM SIGMOD International Conference on Management of Data*, pp. 115–126, 1995.

Wilschut, A.N., Flokstra, J., and Apers, P.M.G., "Parallel Evaluation of Multi-join Queries", *Proceedings of Third International ACPC Conference with Special Emphasis on Parallel Databases and Parallel I/O (ACPC)*, pp. 90–97, 1996.

Wolf, J.L. et al., "A Parallel Hash Join Algorithm for Managing Data Skew", *IEEE Transactions on Parallel and Distributed Systems*, **4**(12):1355–1371, 1993.

Wolf, J.L., Dias, D.M., and Yu, P.S., "A Parallel Sort Merge Join Algorithm for Managing Data Skew", *IEEE Transactions on Parallel and Distributed Systems*, **4**(1):70–86, 1993.

Zhang, X., Kurç, T.M., Pan, T., Çatalyürek, Ü.V., Narayanan, S., Wyckoff, P., and Saltz, J.H., "Strategies for Using Additional Resources in Parallel Hash-Based Join Algorithms", *Proceedings of IEEE International Symposium on High Performance Distributed Computing (HPDC)*, pp. 4–13, 2004.

CHAPTER 6: PARALLEL GROUPBY-JOIN

Albrecht, J. and Sporer, W., "Aggregate-Based Query Processing in a Parallel Data Warehouse Server", *Proceedings of DEXA Workshop*, pp. 40–44, 1999.

Bhargava, G., Goel, P., and Iyer, B.R., "Efficient Processing of Outer Joins and Aggregate Functions", *Proceedings of International Conference on Data Engineering (ICDE)*, pp. 441–449, 1996.

Bultzingsloewen, G., "Translating and optimizing SQL queries having aggregate", *Proceedings of the 13th International Conference on Very Large Data Bases*, 1987.

Cohen, S., Nutt, W., and Serebrenik, A., "Algorithms for Rewriting Aggregate Queries Using Views", *Proceedings of East-European Conference on Advances in Databases and Information Systems Held Jointly with International Conference on Database Systems for Advanced Applications (ADBIS-DASFAA)*, pp. 65–78, 2000.

Deutsch, A., Papakonstantinou, Y., and Xu, Y., "Minimization and Group-By Detection for Nested XQueries", *Proceedings of International Conference on Data Engineering (ICDE)*, pp. 839, 2004.

Dobra, A., "Histograms revisited: when are histograms the best approximation method for aggregates over joins?", *Proceedings of the Twenty-fourth ACM SIGACT-SIGMOD-SIGART Symposium on Principles of Database Systems*, pp. 228–237, 2005.

Ganguly, S., Garofalakis, M.N., Kumar, A., and Rastogi, R., "Join-distinct aggregate estimation over update streams", *Proceedings of Symposium on Principles of Database Systems (PODS)*, pp. 259–270, 2005.

Ganguly, S., Garofalakis, M.N., and Rastogi, R., "Processing Data-Stream Join Aggregates Using Skimmed Sketches", *Proceedings of Extending Database Technology (EDBT)*, pp. 569–586, 2004.

Gao, D., Gendrano, J.A.G., Moon, B., Snodgrass, R.T., Park, M., Huang, B.C., and Rodrigue, J.M., "Main Memory-Based Algorithms for Efficient Parallel Aggregation for Temporal Databases", *Distributed and Parallel Databases*, **16**(2):123–163, 2004.

Gray, P.M.D., "The "Group By" Operation in Relational Algebra", *Proceedings of the First British National Conference on Databases (BNCOD)*, pp. 80–93, 1981.

Gray, J., Bosworth, A., Layman, A., and Pirahesh, H., "Data Cube: A Relational Aggregation Operator Generalizing Group-By, Cross-Tab, and Sub-Total", *Proceedings of International Conference on Data Engineering (ICDE)*, pp. 152–159, 1996.

Hassan, M.A.H. and Bamha, M., "Parallel processing of "group-by join" queries on shared nothing machines", *Proceedings of International Conference on Software and Data Technologies (ICSOFT)*, pp. 301–307, 2006.

Jiang, Z., Luo, C., Hou, W., Yan, F., and Zhu, Q., "Estimating Aggregate Join Queries over Data Streams Using Discrete Cosine Transform", *Proceedings of Database and Expert Systems Applications (DEXA)*, pp. 182–192, 2006.

Lee, Y., Loh, W., Moon, Y., Whang, K., and Song, I., "An Efficient Algorithm for Computing Range-Groupby Queries", *Proceedings of Database Systems for Advanced Applications (DASFAA)*, pp. 483–497, 2006.

Li, H., Yu, H., Agrawal, D., and Abbadi, A.E., "Progressive Ranking of Range Aggregates", *Proceedings of Data Warehousing and Knowledge Discovery (DaWaK)*, pp. 179–189, 2005.

Liang, W. and Orlowska, M.E., "Computing Multidimensional Aggregates in Parallel", *Informatica (Slovenia)*, **24**(1), 2000.

Liu, K. and Lochovsky, F.H., "Efficient Computation of Aggregate Structural Joins", *Proceedings of Web Information Systems Engineering (WISE)*, pp. 21–30, 2003.

Luo, G., Naughton, J.F., Ellmann, C., and Watzke, M., "Locking Protocols for Materialized Aggregate Join Views", *Proceedings of Very Large Data Bases (VLDB)*, pp. 596–607, 2003.

Luo, G., Naughton, J.F., Ellmann, C.J. and Watzke, M., "Locking Protocols for Materialized Aggregate Join Views", *IEEE Trans. Knowl. Data Eng.*, **17**(6):796–807, 2005.

Kim, J., Kim, Y., Kim, S. and Ok, S., "An Efficient Processing of Queries with Joins and Aggregate Functions in Data Warehousing Environment", *Proceedings of DEXA Workshops*, pp. 785–794, 2002.

Kiviniemi, J., Wolski, A., Pesonen, A. and Arminen, J., "Lazy Aggregates for Real-Time OLAP", *Proceedings of Data Warehousing and Knowledge Discovery (DaWaK)*, pp. 165–172, 1999.

Mandawat, P. and Tsotras, V.J., "Indexing Schemes for Efficient Aggregate Computation over Structural Joins", *Proceedings of International Workshop on the Web and Databases (WebDB)*, pp. 55–60, 2005.

Muralikrishna, M., "Improved Unnesting Algorithms for Join Aggregate SQL Queries", *Proceedings of Very Large Data Bases (VLDB)*, pp. 91–102, 1992.

Pourabbas, E. and Shoshani, A., "Answering Joint Queries from Multiple Aggregate OLAP Databases", *Proceedings of Data Warehousing and Knowledge Discovery (DaWaK)*, pp. 24–34, 2003.

Shatdal, A. and Naughton, J.F., "Adaptive Parallel Aggregation Algorithms", *Proceedings of the ACM SIGMOD International Conference on Management of Data*, pp. 104–114, 1995.

Spiliopoulou, M., Hatzopoulos, M. and Cotronis, Y., "Parallel Optimization of Large Join Queries with Set Operators and Aggregates in a Parallel Environment Supporting Pipeline", *IEEE Trans. Knowl. Data Eng*, **8**(3):429–445, 1996.

Wang, W., Li, J., Zhang, D. and Guo, L., "Processing Sliding Window Join Aggregate in Continuous Queries over Data Streams", *Proceedings of Advances in Databases and Information Systems (ADBIS)*, pp. 348–363, 2004.

Yan, W.P. and Larson, P., "Performing Group-By before Join", *Proceedings of International Conference on Data Engineering (ICDE)*, pp. 89–100, 1994.

Yan, W.P., "Interchanging group-by and join in distributed query processing", *Proceedings of the 1993 Conference of the Centre for Advanced Studies on Collaborative Research (CASCON)*, pp. 823–831, 1993.

CHAPTER 7: PARALLEL INDEXING

Achyutuni, K.J., Omiecinski, E., and Navathe, S.B., "Two Techniques for On-Line Index Modification in Shared Nothing Parallel Databases", *Proceedings of the ACM SIGMOD International Conference on Management of Data*, pp. 125–136, 1996.

Ali, M.H., Saad, A.A., and Ismail, M.A., "The PN-Tree: A Parallel and Distributed Multidimensional Index", *Distributed and Parallel Databases*, **17**(2):111–133, 2005.

An, J., Chen, H., Furuse, K., Ohbo, N., and Keogh, E.J., "Grid-Based Indexing for Large Time Series Databases", *Proceedings of Intelligent Data Engineering and Automated Learning (IDEAL)*, pp. 614–621, 2003.

Berchtold, S., Böhm, C., and Kriegel, H., "Improving the Query Performance of High-Dimensional Index Structures by Bulk-Load Operations", *Proceedings of Extending Database Technology (EDBT)*, pp. 216–230, 1998.

Bok, K.S., Seo, D.M., Song, S.I., Kim, M., and Yoo, J.S., "An Index Structure for Parallel Processing of Multidimensional Data", *Proceedings of Web-Age Information Management (WAIM)*, pp. 589–600, 2005.

Bok, K.S., Song, S.I., and Yoo, J.S., "Efficient k-Nearest Neighbor Searches for Parallel Multidimensional Index Structures", *Proceedings of Database Systems for Advanced Applications (DASFAA)*, pp. 870–879, 2006.

Cambazoglu, B.B., Catal, A., and Aykanat, C., "Effect of Inverted Index Partitioning Schemes on Performance of Query Processing in Parallel Text Retrieval Systems", *Proceedings of International Symposium on Computer and Information Sciences (ISCIS)*, pp. 717–725, 2006.

Chang, J., Kim, Y., and Kim, Y., "Parallel High-Dimensional Index Structure Using Cell-Based Filtering for Multimedia Data", *Proceedings of International Symposium on Parallel and Distributed Processing and Applications (ISPA) Workshops*, pp. 781–790, 2006.

Chen, W., Tseng, S., Chang, L., Hong, T., and Jiang, M., "A parallelized indexing method for large-scale case-based reasoning", *Expert Syst. Appl.*, **23**(2):95–102, 2002.

Cooper, B.F., Sample, N., and Shadmon, M., "A parallel index for semi-structured data", *Proceedings of Symposium on Applied Computing (SAC)*, pp. 890–896, 2002.

Dehne, F., Eavis, T., and Rau-Chaplin, A., "Parallel Multi-Dimensional ROLAP Indexing", *Proceedings of Cluster Computing and the Grid (CCGRID)*, 2003.

Ding, C.H.Q., "An Optimal Index Reshuffle Algorithm for Multidimensional Arrays and Its Applications for Parallel Architectures", *IEEE Trans. Parallel Distrib. Syst.*, **12**(3):306–315, 2001.

Elmasri, R. and Navathe, S.B., *Fundamentals of Database Systems*, 5th edition, Addison-Wesley, 2007.

Feelifl, H., Kitsuregawa, M., and Ooi, B.C., "A Fast Convergence Technique for Online Heat-Balancing of B tree Indexed Database over Shared-Nothing Parallel Systems", *Proceedings of Database and Expert Systems Applications (DEXA)*, pp. 846–858, 2000.

Fu, X., Wang, D., and Zheng, W., "GPR-Tree: A Global Parallel Index Structure for Multi-attribute Declustering on Cluster of Workstations", *Proceedings of Advances in Parallel and Distributed Computing (APDC)*, pp. 300–306, 1997.

Honishi, T., Satoh, T., and Inoue, U., "An Index Structure for Parallel Database Processing", *Proceedings of Research Issues on Data Engineering—Transaction and Query Processing (RIDE-TQP)*, pp. 224–225, 1992.

Lee, C. and Chang, Z., "Utilizing Page-Level Join Index for Optimization in Parallel Join Execution", *IEEE Trans. Knowl. Data Eng.* **7**(6):900–914, 1995.

Omiecinski, E. and Shonkwiler, R., "Parallel Join Processing Using Nonclustered Indexes for a Shared Memory Multiprocessor", *Proceedings of Symposium on Parallel and Distributed Processing (SPDP)*, pp. 144–151, 1990.

Premchaiswadi, W., Premchaiswadi, N., and Patnasirivakin, T., Chimlek, S. and Narita, S., "Image Indexing Technique and Its Parallel Retrieval on PVM", *Proceedings of Digital Image Computing: Techniques and Applications (DICTA)*, pp. 289–298, 2003.

Ramakrishnan, R. and Gehrke, J., *Database Management Systems*, 2nd edition, McGraw Hill, 2000.

Tsuji, T., Vreto, A., Higuchi, K., and Hochin, T., "A Two Dimensional Parallel Indexing Scheme for Complex Objects", *I. J. Comput. Appl.*, **9**(2):67–78, 2002.

CHAPTER 8: PARALLEL UNIVERSAL QUANTIFICATION, OBJECT-ORIENTED AND OBJECT-RELATIONAL DATABASES

Carvalho, S., Lerner, A., and Lifschitz, S., "An Object-Oriented Framework for the Parallel Join Operation", *Proceedings of DEXA Workshop*, pp. 34–38, 1999.

Fang, Q., Wang, G., Yu, G., Kaneko, K., and Makinouchi, A., "Design and Performance Evaluation of Parallel Algorithms for Path Expressions in Object Database Systems on NOW", *Proceedings of Database Applications in Non-Traditional Environments (DANTE)*, pp. 395–402, 1999.

Graefe, G. and Cole, R.L., "Fast Algorithms for Universal Quantification in Large Databases", *ACM Trans. Database Syst.*, **20**(2):187–236, 1995.

Hahn, K., Reiner, B., and Höfling, G., "Parallel Query Support for Multidimensional Data: Intra-object Parallelism", *Proceedings of Database and Expert Systems Applications (DEXA)*, pp. 212–222, 2003.

Hahn, K., Reiner, B., Höfling, G., and Baumann, P., "Parallel Query Support for Multidimensional Data: Inter-object Parallelism", *Proceedings of Database and Expert Systems Applications (DEXA)*, pp. 820–830, 2002.

Horie, T., Ukon, T., Tsuji, T., and Higuchi, K., "An Efficient Parallel Retrieval for Complex Object Index", *Proceedings of ICDE Workshops*, 2005.

Hyun, S.J. and Su, S.Y.W., "Parallel Query Processing Strategies for Object-Oriented Temporal Databases", *Proceedings of Conference on Parallel and Distributed Information Systems (PDIS)*, pp. 232–245, 1996.

Jaedicke, M., *New Concepts for Parallel Object-Relational Query Processing*, Springer, 2001.

Kaczmarski, K., Habela, P., Kozankiewicz, H., Stencel, K., and Subieta, K., "Transparency in Object-Oriented Grid Database Systems", *Proceedings of Parallel Processing and Applied Mathematics (PPAM)*, pp. 675–682, 2005.

Khoshafian, S., Valduriez, P., and Copeland, G.P., "Parallel Query Processing for Complex Objects", *Proceedings of the International Conference on Data Engineering (ICDE)*, pp. 202–209, 1988.

Kim, K-C., "Parallelism in Object-Oriented Query Processing", *Proceedings of the International Conference on Data Engineering*, pp. 209–217, 1990.

Kuliberda, K., Wislicki, J., Adamus, R., and Subieta, K., "Object-Oriented Wrapper for Relational Databases in the Data Grid Architecture", *Proceedings of OnTheMove (OTM) Workshops*, pp. 367–376, 2005.

Leung, C. and Taniar, D., "Parallel Query Processing in Object-Oriented Database Systems". *Proceedings of Australasian Database Conference,* pp. 119–131, 1995.

Mendes, S.F. and Sampaio, P.R.F., "Rule-Based Parallel Query Optimization for OQL Using a Parallelism Extraction Technique", *Proceedings of DEXA Workshop,* pp. 705–710, 1998.

Sampaio, S., Paton, N.W., Watson, P., and Smith, J., "A Parallel Algebra for Object Databases", *Proceedings of DEXA Workshop,* pp. 56–60, 1999.

Sampaio, S., Smith, J., Paton, N.W., and Watson, P., "An Experimental Performance Evaluation of Join Algorithms for Parallel Object Databases", *Proceedings of Euro-Par*, pp. 280–290, 2001.

Sampaio, S, Smith, J., Paton, N.W., and Watson, P., "Experimenting with Object Navigation in Parallel Object Databases", *Proceedings of DEXA Workshop,* pp. 103–109, 2001.

Smith, J., Watson, P., Sampaio, S., and Paton, N.W., "Polar: An Architecture for a Parallel ODMG Compliant Object Database", *Proceedings of International Conference on Information and Knowledge Management (CIKM),* pp. 352–359, 2000.

Taniar, D. and Rahayu, J.W. "Performance Analysis of Parallelization Models for Path Expression Queries", *Inf. Sci.* **117**(1–2):107–142, 1999.

Wang, G., Yu, G., Kaneko, K., and Makinouchi, A., "Comparison of Parallel Algorithms for Path Expression Query in Object Database Systems", *Proceedings of Database Systems for Advanced Applications (DASFAA)*, pp. 250–258, 2001.

CHAPTER 9: PARALLEL AND GRID QUERY OPTIMIZATION AND SCHEDULING

Andrade, H., Kurç, T.M., Sussman, A., and Saltz, J.H., "Active Proxy-G: optimizing the query execution process in the grid", *Proceedings of Supercomputing (SC)*, pp. 1–15, 2002.

Andrade, H., Kurç, T.M., Sussman, A., and Saltz, J.H., "Scheduling Multiple Data Visualization Query Workloads on a Shared Memory Machine", *Proceedings of International Parallel and Distributed Processing Symposium (IPDPS)*, pp. 11–18, 2002.

Baboo, S.S., Subashini, P., and Easwarakumar, K.S., "Parallel Query Processing Using Warp Edged Bushy Trees in Multimedia Databases", *Proceedings of International Conference on Enterprise Information Systems (ICEIS)*, pp. 273–276, 2006.

Biscondi, N., Flory, A., and Brunie, L., "Parallel Databases: Structured Query Optimization", *Proceeding of Advances in Databases and Information Systems (ADBIS)*, pp. 146–152, 1996.

Bonneau, S. and Hameurlain, A., "Hybrid Simultaneous Scheduling and Mapping in SQL Multi-query Parallelization", *Proceedings of Database and Expert Systems Applications (DEXA)*, pp. 88–99, 1999.

Bültzingsloewen, G.v., "Optimizing SQL Queries for Parallel Execution", *SIGMOD Records*, **18**(4):17–22, 1989.

Chekuri, C., Hasan, W., and Motwani, R., "Scheduling Problems in Parallel Query Optimization", *Proceedings of Symposium on Principles of Database Systems (PODS)*, pp. 255–265, 1995.

Chen, M., Yu, P.S., and Wu, K., "Scheduling and Processor Allocation for Parallel Execution of Multi-Join Queries", *Proceedings of International Conference on Data Engineering (ICDE)*, pp. 58–67, 1992.

Drews, F., Ecker, K.H., Kao, O., and Schomann, S., "A Stimulated Annealing Strategy for Workload Balancing in Parallel Image Databases", *Proceedings of Parallel and Distributed Processing Techniques and Applications (PDPTA)*, pp. 734–740, 2002.

Frieder, O. and Baru, C.K., "Site and Query Scheduling Policies in Multicomputer Database Systems", *IEEE Trans. Knowl. Data Eng.*, **6**(4):609–619, 1994.

Furtado, P., "Workload-Based Placement and Join Processing in Node-Partitioned Data Warehouses", *Proceedings of Data Warehousing and Knowledge Discovery (DaWaK)*, pp. 38–47, 2004.

Gounaris, A., Paton, N.W., Sakellariou, R., and Fernandes, A., "Adaptive Query Processing and the Grid: Opportunities and Challenges", *Proceedings of DEXA Workshops*, pp. 506–510, 2004.

Gounaris, A., Paton, N.W., Sakellariou, R., Fernandes, A., Smith, J., and Watson, P., "Practical Adaptation to Changing Resources in Grid Query Processing", *Proceedings of International Conference on Data Engineering (ICDE)*, pp. 165–166, 2006.

Gounaris, A., Sakellariou, R., Paton, N.W., and Fernandes, A., "A novel approach to resource scheduling for parallel query processing on computational grids", *Distributed and Parallel Databases*, **19**(2–3):87–106, 2006.

Gounaris, A., Sakellariou, R., Paton, N.W., and Fernandes, A., "Resource Scheduling for Parallel Query Processing on Computational Grids", *Proceedings of International Workshop on Grid Computing (GRID)*, pp. 396–401, 2004.

Gounaris, A., Smith, J., Paton, N.W., Sakellariou, R., Fernandes, A., and Watson, P., "Adapting to Changing Resource Performance in Grid Query Processing", *Proceedings of Data Management in Grids (DMG)*, pp. 30–44, 2005.

Graefe, G., "Encapsulation of Parallelism in the Volcano Query Processing System". *Proceedings of the ACM SIGMOD International Conference on Management of Data*, pp. 102–111, 1990.

Graefe, G., "Query Evaluation Techniques for Large Databases", *ACM Computing Survey*, **25**(2), pp. 73–170, 1993.

Graefe, G. et al., "Extensible Query Optimization and Parallel Execution in Volcano", *Query Processing For Advanced Database Systems*, J.C. Freytag et al. (eds.), Morgan Kaufmann, pp. 305–335, 1994.

Hameurlain, A. and Morvan, F., "CPU and incremental memory allocation in dynamic parallelization of SQL queries", *Parallel Computing*, **28**(4):525–556, 2002.

Hameurlain, A. and Morvan, F., "Invited Address: An Overview of Parallel Query Optimization in Relational Systems", *Proceedings of Database and Expert Systems Applications DEXA Workshop*, pp. 629–634, 2000.

Hameurlain, A. and Morvan, F., "A Parallel Scheduling Method for Efficient Query Processing", *Proceedings of International Conference on Parallel Processing (ICPP)*, pp. 258–262, 1993.

Hameurlain, A. and Morvan, F., "Exploiting Inter-Operation Parallelism for SQL Query Optimization", *Proceedings of Database and Expert Systems Applications (DEXA)*, pp. 759–768, 1994.

Hameurlain, A. and Morvan, F., "Scheduling and Mapping for Parallel Execution of Extended SQL Queries", *Proceedings of International Conference on Information and Knowledge Management (CIKM)*, pp. 197–204, 1995.

Heichler, J. and Keller, J., "A Distributed Query Structure to Explore Random Mappings in Parallel", *Proceedings of the 14th Euromicro International Conference on Parallel, Distributed, and Network-Based Processing (PDP'06)*, pp. 173–177, 2006.

Hong, W. and Stonebraker, M., "Optimization of Parallel Execution Plans in XPRS", *Proceedings of the First International Conference on Parallel and Distributed Information Systems PDIS'91*, Florida, pp. 218–225, 1991.

Hong, W. and Stonebraker, M., "Optimization of Parallel Query Execution Plans in XPRS", *Distributed and Parallel Databases 1*, pp. 9–32, 1993.

Hong, W., "Exploiting Inter-Operation Parallelism in XPRS", *Proceedings of the ACM SIGMOD International Conference on Management of Data*, pp. 19–28, 1992.

Langer, U.J. and Meyer, H., "Join Sequence Optimization in Parallel Query Plans", *Proceedings of DEXA Workshop*, pp. 506–513, 1996.

Li, J., Cai, Z. and Chen, S., "Multi-Weighted Tree Based Query Optimization Method for Parallel Relational Database Systems", *Proceedings of International Symposium on Cooperative Database Systems for Advanced Applications (CODAS)*, pp. 205–212, 2001.

Li, W., Altintas, K., and Kantarcioglu, M., "On demand synchronization and load distribution for database grid-based Web applications", *Data Knowl. Eng.*, **51**(3):295–323, 2004.

Lin, E.T., Omiecinski, E. and Yalamanchili, S., "Parallel Optimization and Execution of Large Join Queries", *Proceedings of Fifth Generation Computer Systems (FGCS)*, pp. 907–914, 1992.

Lu, H., Shan, M. and Tan, K., "Optimization of Multi-Way Join Queries for Parallel Execution", *Proceedings of Very Large Data Bases (VLDB)*, pp. 549–560, 1991.

Lu, H. and Tan, K-L., "Dynamic and Load-balanced Task-Oriented Database Query Processing in Parallel Systems", *Proceedings of Extending Database Technology (EDBT)*, pp. 357–372, 1992.

Mayr, T., Bonnet, P., Gehrke, J., and Seshadri, P., "Leveraging Non-Uniform Resources for Parallel Query Processing", *Proceedings of Cluster Computing and the Grid (CCGRID)*, 2003.

Miranda, B., Lima, A.A.B., Valduriez, P., and Mattoso, M., "Apuama: Combining Intra-query and Inter-query Parallelism in a Database Cluster", *Proceedings of Extending Database Technology Extending Database Technology (EDBT) Workshops*, pp. 649–661, 2006.

Morvan, F. and Hameurlain, A., "Dynamic memory allocation strategies for parallel query execution", *Proceedings of Symposium on Applied Computing (SAC)*, pp. 897–901, 2002.

Nafjan, K.A. and Kerridge, J.M., "Large Join Order Optimization on Parallel Shared-Nothing Database Machines Using Genetic Algorithms", *Proceedings of Euro-Par*, pp. 1159–1163, 1997.

Rahm, E., "Parallel Query Processing in Shared Disk Database Systems", *Proceedings of High Performance Transaction Systems (HPTS)*, 1993.

Silva, V.F.V.d., Dutra, M.L., Porto, F., Schulze, B., Barbosa, Á.C.P., and Oliveira, J.C.d., "An adaptive parallel query processing middleware for the Grid", *Concurrency and Computation: Practice and Experience*, **18**(6):621–634, 2006.

Smith, J., Gounaris, A., Watson, P., Paton, N.W., Fernandes, A.A.A., and Sakellariou, R., "Distributed Query Processing on the Grid", *Proceedings of International Workshop on Grid Computing (GRID)*, pp. 279–290, 2002.

Soe, K.M., Aung, T.N., Nwe, A.A., Naing, T.T., and Thein, N., "A Framework for Parallel Query Processing on Grid-Based Architecture", *Proceedings of International Conference on Enterprise Information Systems (ICEIS)*, pp. 203–208, 2005.

Sokolinsky, L.B., "Organization of Parallel Query Processing in Multiprocessor Database Machines with Hierarchical Architecture", *Programming and Computer Software*, **27**(6):297–308, 2001.

Soleimany, C. and Dandamudi, S.P., "Distributed Parallel Query Processing on Networks of Workstations", *Proceedings of the International Conference on High-Performance Computing and Networking (HPCN) Europe*, pp. 427–436, 2000.

Soleimany, C. and Dandamudi, S.P., "Performance of a distributed architecture for query processing on workstation clusters", *Future Generation Comp. Syst.*, **19**(4):463–478, 2003.

Wolf, J.L. et al., "A Hierarchical Approach to Parallel Multiquery Scheduling", *IEEE Transactions on Parallel and Distributed Systems*, 6(6):578–589, 1995.

Woo, S. and Yang, S., "An improved network clustering method for I/O-efficient query processing", *Proceedings of the ACM International Symposium on Advances in Geographic Information System (ACM-GIS)*, pp. 62–68, 2000.

Wu, J., Chen, J., Hsueh, C., and Kuo, T., "Scheduling of Query Execution Plans in Symmetric Multiprocessor Database Systems", *Proceedings of International Parallel and Distributed Processing Symposium (IPDPS)*, pp. 113–118, 2004.

Zheng, X., Chen, H., Wu, Z., and Mao, Y., "Dynamic Query Optimization Approach for Semantic Database Grid", *J. Comput. Sci. Technol.*, 21(4):597–608, 2006.

Zheng, X., Chen, H., Wu, Z., and Mao, Y., "Query Optimization in Database Grid", *Proceedings of Grid and Cooperative Computing (GCC)*, pp. 486–497, 2005.

Ziane, M., Zaït, M., and Quang, H.H., "The Impact of Parallelism on Query Optimization", *Proceedings of Workshop on Foundations of Models and Languages for Data and Objects (FMLDO)*, pp. 127–138, 1993.

CHAPTERS 10, 11, 12: PARALLEL AND GRID TRANSACTION PROCESSING

Bhalla, S. and Hasegawa, M., "Parallelizing Serializable Transactions Within Distributed Real-Time Database Systems", *Proceedings of Embedded and Ubiquitous Computing (EUC)*, pp. 203–213, 2005.

Bhalla, S. and Hasegawa, M., "Parallelizing serializable transactions using transaction classification in real-time database systems", *Proceedings of the 10th ISPE International Conference on Concurrent Engineering (ISPE CE 2003)*, pp. 1051–1057, 2003.

Bhalla, S., "Parallel Concurrency Control Activity for Transaction Management in Real-time Database Systems", *The Journal of Supercomputing*, 28(3):345–369, 2004.

Brayner, A., "Lock Downgrading: An Approach to Increase Inter-transaction Parallelism in Advanced Database Applications", *Proceedings of Database and Expert Systems Applications (DEXA)*, pp. 330–339, 2001.

Burger, A. and Thanisch, P., "Branching Transactions: A Transaction Model for Parallel Database Systems", *Proceedings of British National Conference on Databases (BNCOD)*, pp. 121–136, 1994.

Coghlan, B.A., Walsh, J., Quigley, G., O'Callaghan, D., Childs, S., and Kenny, E., "Principles of Transactional Grid Deployment", *Proceedings of European Grid Conference (EGC)*, pp. 88–97, 2005.

Colohan, C.B., Ailamaki, A., Steffan, J.G., and Mowry, T.C., "Optimistic Intra-Transaction Parallelism on Chip Multiprocessors", *Proceedings of Very Large Data Bases (VLDB)*, pp. 73–84, 2005.

Hammond, L., Carlstrom, B.D., Wong, V., Chen, M.K., Kozyrakis, C., and Olukotun, K., "Transactional Coherence and Consistency: Simplifying Parallel Hardware and Software", *IEEE Micro*, 24(6):92–103, 2004.

Hwang, J., Aravamudham, P., Liddy, E.D., Stanton, J., and MacInnes, I., "IRTL (Information Resource Transaction Layer) Middleware Design for P2P and Open GRID Services", *Proceedings of Hawaii International Conference on System Sciences (HICSS)*, pp. 218, 2003.

Ibrahim, H., "Checking Integrity Constraints—How it Differs in Centralized, Distributed and Parallel Databases", *Proceedings of DEXA Workshops*, pp. 563–568, 2006.

Ibrahim, H., "Parallel Execution of Transaction and Integrity Rules for Maintaining Database Integrity", *Proceedings of Parallel and Distributed Processing Techniques and Applications (PDPTA)*, pp. 1809–1818, 2003.

Jiang, J., Yang, G., and Shi, M., "A Transaction Model for Service Grid Environment and Implementation Considerations", *Proceedings of International Conference on Web Services (ICWS)*, pp. 949–950, 2006.

Jiang, J., Yang, G., and Shi, M., "Towards a Transaction Model for Services in Grid Environment", *Proceedings of Web Intelligence*, pp. 625–628, 2006.

Kim, I.K. and Lee, J.S., "Resource Demand Prediction-Based Grid Resource Transaction Network Model in Grid Computing Environment", *Proceedings of Computational Science and Its Applications (ICCSA)*, pp. 1–9, 2006.

Kuo, T-W., Wu, J., and Hsih, H-C., "Real-Time Concurrency Control in Multiprocessor Environment", *IEEE Transactions on Parallel and Distributed Systems*, **13**(6):659–671, 2002.

Lang, F. and Bodendorf, F., "Agent Based Transaction Support in Commercial Grid", *Proceedings of Joint International Conference on Autonomic and Autonomous Systems and International Conference on Networking and Services (ICAS/ICNS)*, pp. 88, 2005.

Leymann, F. and Güntzel, K., "The Business Grid: Providing Transactional Business Processes via Grid Services", *Proceedings of International Conference on Service Oriented Computing (ICSOC)*, pp. 256–270, 2003.

Li, J., Wang, J., and Kameda, H., "Performance Studies of Shared-Nothing Parallel Transaction Processing Systems", *Proceedings of Parallel Computing Technologies (PaCT)*, pp. 235–247, 1999.

Liu, B., Chen, S., and Rundensteiner, E.A., "A Transactional Approach to Parallel Data Warehouse Maintenance", *Proceedings of Data Warehousing and Knowledge Discovery (DaWaK)*, pp. 307–316, 2002.

Machado, J. and Collet, C., "A Parallel Execution Model for Database Transactions", *Proceedings of Database Systems for Advanced Applications (DASFAA)*, pp. 511–520, 1997.

Pan, Y. and Lu, Y., "A Study on Parallel Real-Time Transaction Scheduling", *Proceedings of the Fourth International Conference on Computer and Information Technology (CIT)*, pp. 701–706, 2004.

Qi, Z., Fu, C., Shi, D., You, J., and Li, M., "Membrane Calculus: A Formal Method for Grid Transactions", *Proceedings of Grid and Cooperative Computing (GCC)*, pp. 73–80, 2004.

Qi, Z., Li, M., Fu, C., Shi, D., and You, J., "Membrane Calculus: a Formal Method for Grid transactions", *Concurrency and Computation: Practice and Experience*, **18**(14):1799–1809, 2006.

Qi, Z., Xie, X., Zhang, B., and You, J., "Integrating X/Open DTP into Grid Services for Grid Transaction Processing", *Proceedings of Future Trends of Distributed Computer Systems (FTDCS)*, pp. 128–134, 2004.

Qi, Z., You, J., Jin, Y., and Tang, F., "GridTP Services for Grid Transaction Processing", *Proceedings of Grid and Cooperative Computing (GCC)*, pp. 891–894, 2003.

Salvadores, M., Herrero, P., Pérez, M.S., and Robles, V., "DCP-Grid, a Framework for Conversational Distributed Transactions on Grid Environments", *Proceedings of International Conference on Computational Science*, pp. 171–178, 2005.

Tang, F., Li, M., and Cao, J., "A Transaction Model for Grid Computing", *Proceedings of Advanced Parallel Programming Technologies (APPT)*, pp. 382–386, 2003.

Tang, F., Li, M., and Huang, J.Z., "Automatic Transaction Compensation for Reliable Grid Applications", *J. Comput. Sci. Technol.*, 21(4):529–536, 2006.

Tang, F., Li, M., Cao, J., and Deng, Q., "Coordinating Business Transaction for Grid Service", *Proceedings of Grid and Cooperative Computing (GCC)*, pp. 108–114, 2003.

Tang, F., Li, M., Huang, J.Z., Cao, L., and Wang, Y., "A Real-Time Transaction Approach for Grid Services: A Model and Algorithms", *Proceedings of Network and Parallel Computing (NPC)*, pp. 57–64, 2004.

Tang, F., Li, M., Huang, J.Z., Wang, C., and Luo, Z., "Petri-Net-Based Coordination Algorithms for Grid Transactions", *Proceedings of International Symposium on Parallel and Distributed Processing and Applications (ISPA)*, pp. 499–508, 2004.

Türker, C., Haller, K., Schuler, C., and Schek, H., "How can we support Grid Transactions? Towards Peer-to-Peer Transaction Processing", *Proceedings of Conference on Innovative Data Systems Research (CIDR)*, pp. 174–185, 2005.

Wang, J., Li, J., and Kameda, H., "Scheduling Algorithms for Parallel Transaction Processing Systems", *Proceedings of Parallel Computing Technologies (PaCT)*, pp. 283–297, 1997.

Wang, J., Li, J., and Kameda, H., "Simulation Studies on Concurrency Control in Parallel Transaction Processing Systems", *Parallel Computing*, 23(6):755–775, 1997.

Wang, J., Miyazaki, M., Kameda, H., and Li, J., "Improving Performance of Parallel Transaction Processing Systems by Balancing Data Load on Line", *Proceedings of International Conference on Parallel and Distributed Systems (ICPADS)*, pp. 331–338, 2000.

Weikum, G. and Hasse, C., "Multi-Level Transaction Management for Complex Objects: Implementation, Performance, Parallelism", *VLDB J.*, 2(4):407–453, 1993.

Yali, Z., Hong, L., and Yonghua, W., "A Transaction Model and Implementation Based on Message Exchange for Grid Computing", *Proceedings of Web Information Systems and Technologies (WEBIST)*, pp. 225–228, 2006.

Yu, J., Li, M., Tang, F., Li, Y., and Hong, F., "A Framework for Implementing Transactions on Grid Services", *Proceedings of International Conference on Computer and Information Technology (CIT)*, pp. 375–379, 2004.

CHAPTERS 13 AND 14: GRID DATA REPLICATION

Carman, M., Zini, F., Serafini, L., and Stockinger, K., "Towards an Economy-Based Optimisation of File Access and Replication on a Data Grid", *Proceedings of Cluster Computing and the Grid (CCGRID)*, pp. 340–345, 2002.

Chakrabarti, A., Dheepak, R.A., and Sengupta, S., "Integration of Scheduling and Replication in Data Grids", *Proceedings of High Performance Computing (HiPC)*, pp. 375–385, 2004.

Chen, C. and Cheng, C.T., "Replication and retrieval strategies of multidimensional data on parallel disks", *Proceedings of International Conference on Information and Knowledge Management (CIKM)*, pp. 32–39, 2003.

Coulon, C., Pacitti, E., and Valduriez, P., "Consistency Management for Partial Replication in a High Performance Database Cluster", *Proceedings of International Conference on Parallel and Distributed Systems (ICPADS)*, pp. 809–815, 2005.

Dullmann, D., Hosckek, W., Jaen-Martinez, J., Segal, B., Samar, A., Stockinger, H., and Stockinger, K., "Models for Replica Synchronisation and Consistency in a Data Grid", *Proceedings of 10th IEEE International Symposium on High Performance and Distributed Computing (HPDC)*, pp. 67–75, August 2001.

Honicky, R.J. and Miller, E.L., "A Fast Algorithm for Online Placement and Reorganization of Replicated Data", *Proceedings of International Parallel and Distributed Processing Symposium (IPDPS)*, pp. 57, 2003.

Huang, C., Xu, F., and Hu, X., "Massive Data Oriented Replication Algorithms for Consistency Maintenance in Data Grids", *Proceedings of International Conference on Computational Science*, pp. 838–841, 2006.

Lamehamedi, H., Shentu, Z., Szymanski, B.K., and Deelman, E., "Simulation of Dynamic Data Replication Strategies in Data Grids", *Proceedings of International Parallel and Distributed Processing Symposium (IPDPS)*, pp. 100, 2003.

Lei, M. and Vrbsky, S.V., "A Data Replication Strategy to Increase Data Availability in Data Grids", *Proceedings of the International Conference on Grid Computing & Applications (GCA)*, pp. 221–227, 2006.

Lin, Y., Liu, P., and Wu, J., "Optimal Placement of Replicas in Data Grid Environments with Locality Assurance", *Proceedings of International Conference on Parallel and Distributed Systems (ICPADS)*, pp. 465–474, 2006.

Liu, P. and Wu, J., "Optimal Replica Placement Strategy for Hierarchical Data Grid Systems", *Proceedings of Cluster Computing and the Grid (CCGRID)*, pp. 417–420, 2006.

Park, S., Kim, J., Ko, Y., and Yoon, W., "Dynamic Data Grid Replication Strategy Based on Internet Hierarchy", *Proceedings of Grid and Cooperative Computing (GCC)*, pp. 838–846, 2003.

Rahman, R.M., Barker, K., and Alhajj, R., "Replica Placement in Data Grid: A Multi-objective Approach", *Proceedings of Grid and Cooperative Computing (GCC)*, pp. 645–656, 2005.

Ranganathan, K. and Foster, I.T., "Identifying Dynamic Replication Strategies for a High-Performance Data Grid", *Proceedings of International Workshop on Grid Computing (GRID)*, pp. 75–86, 2001.

Sithole, E., Parr, G.P., and McClean, S.I., "Data grid performance analysis through study of replication and storage infrastructure parameters", *Proceedings of Cluster Computing and the Grid (CCGRID)*, pp. 293–300, 2005.

Stockinger, H., Samar, A., Holtman, K., Allcock, W.E., Foster, I.T., and Tierney, B., "File and Object Replication in Data Grids", *Proceedings of IEEE International Symposium on High Performance Distributed Computing (HPDC)*, pp. 76–86, 2001.

Tang, M., Lee, B., Tang, X., and Yeo, C.K., "Combining Data Replication Algorithms and Job Scheduling Heuristics in the Data Grid", *Proceedings of Euro-Par*, pp. 381–390, 2005.

Tao, J. and Williams, J., "Concurrency Control and Data Replication Strategies for Large-scale and Wide-distributed Databases", *Proceedings of Database Systems for Advanced Applications (DASFAA)*, 2001.

Vazhkudai, S., Tuecke, S., and Foster, I., "Replica Selection in the Globus Data Grid", *Proceedings of the 1st IEEE/ACM International Conference on Cluster Computing and the Grid (CCGrid)*, pp. 106–113, May 2001.

You, X., Chang, G., Chen, X., Tian, C., and Zhu, C., "Utility-Based Replication Strategies in Data Grids", *Proceedings of Grid and Cooperative Computing (GCC)*, pp. 500–507, 2006.

CHAPTER 15: PARALLEL OLAP AND BUSINESS INTELLIGENCE

Akal, F., Böhm, K., and Schek, H., "OLAP Query Evaluation in a Database Cluster: A Performance Study on Intra-Query Parallelism", *Proceedings of Advances in Databases and Information Systems (ADBIS)*, pp. 218–231, 2002.

Azharul Hasan, K.M., Tsuji, T., and Higuchi, K., "A Parallel Implementation Scheme of Relational Tables Based on Multidimensional Extendible Array", *International Journal of Data Warehousing and Mining*, 2(4):66–85, 2006.

Chen, Y., Dehne, F., Eavis, T., and Rau-Chaplin, A., "Building Large ROLAP Data Cubes in Parallel", *Proceedings of International Database Engineering and Application Symposium (IDEAS)*, pp. 367–377, 2004.

Chen, Y., Dehne, F., Eavis, T., and Rau-Chaplin, A., "Improved data partitioning for building large ROLAP data cubes in parallel", *Journal of Data Warehousing and Mining*, 2(1):1–26, 2006.

Chen, Y., Dehne, F., Eavis, T., and Rau-Chaplin, A., "Parallel ROLAP Data Cube Construction On Shared-Nothing Multiprocessors", *Proceedings of International Parallel and Distributed Processing Symposium (IPDPS)*, pp. 70, 2003.

Chen, Y., Dehne, F., Eavis, T., and Rau-Chaplin, A., "Parallel ROLAP Data Cube Construction on Shared-Nothing Multiprocessors", *Distributed and Parallel Databases*, 15(3):219–236, 2004.

Chen, Y., Dehne, F., Eavis, T., and Rau-Chaplin, A., "PnP: Parallel And External Memory Iceberg Cubes", *Proceedings of International Conference on Data Engineering (ICDE)*, pp. 576–577, 2005.

Chen, Y., Rau-Chaplin, A., Dehne, F., Eavis, T., Green, D., and Sithirasenan, E., "cgmO-LAP: Efficient Parallel Generation and Querying of Terabyte Size ROLAP Data Cubes", *Proceedings of International Conference on Data Engineering (ICDE)*, pp. 164–165, 2006.

Codd, E. F. "An evaluation scheme for database management systems that are claimed to be relational", *Proceedings of International Conference on Data Engineering (ICDE)*, pp. 720–729, 1986.

Codd, E.F. et. al. "Providing OLAP to User-Analysts: An IT Mandate", http://dev.hyperion. com/resource_library/white_papers/providing_olap_to_user_analysts.pdf, 1993.

Datta, A., VanderMeer, D.E., and Ramamritham, K., "Parallel Star Join + DataIndexes: Efficient Query Processing in Data Warehouses and OLAP", *IEEE Trans. Knowl. Data Eng.*, 14(6):1299–1316, 2002.

Dehne, F., Eavis, T., and Rau-Chaplin, A., "A Cluster Architecture for Parallel Data Warehousing", *Proceedings of Cluster Computing and the Grid (CCGRID)*, pp. 161–168, 2001.

Dehne, F., Eavis, T., and Rau-Chaplin, A., "Coarse Grained Parallel On-Line Analytical Processing (OLAP) for Data Mining", *Proceedings of International Conference on Computational Science*, pp. 589–598, 2001.

Dehne, F., Eavis, T., and Rau-Chaplin, A., "Computing Partial Data Cubes for Parallel Data Warehousing Applications", *Proceedings of the 8th European PVM/MPI Users' Group*

Meeting on Recent Advances in Parallel Virtual Machine and Message Passing Interface, pp. 319–326, 2001.

Dehne, F., Eavis, T., and Rau-Chaplin, A., "Parallel querying of ROLAP cubes in the presence of hierarchies", *Proceedings of International Workshop on Data Warehousing and OLAP (DOLAP)*, pp. 89–96, 2005.

Dehne, F., Eavis, T., and Rau-Chaplin, A., "The cgmCUBE project: Optimizing parallel data cube generation for ROLAP", *Distributed and Parallel Databases*, 19(1):29–62, 2006.

Dehne, F., Eavis, T., Hambrusch, S.E., and Rau-Chaplin, A., "Parallelizing the Data Cube", *Distributed and Parallel Databases*, 11(2):181–201, 2002.

Dehne, F., Eavis, T., Hambrusch, S.E., and Rau-Chaplin, A., "Parallelizing the Data Cube", *Proceedings of International Conference on Database Theory (ICDT)*, pp. 129–143, 2001.

Fiser, B., Onan, U., Elsayed, I., Brezany, P., and Tjoa, A.M., "On-Line Analytical Processing on Large Databases Managed by Computational Grids", *Proceedings of DEXA Workshops*, pp. 556–560, 2004.

Gao, H. and Li, J., "Parallel Data Cube Storage Structure for Range Sum Queries and Dynamic Updates", *J. Comput. Sci. Technol.*, 20(3):345–356, 2005.

Gorawski, M. and Chechelski, R., "Parallel Telemetric Data Warehouse Balancing Algorithm", *Proceedings of the 5th International Conference on Intelligent Systems Design and Applications (ISDA)*, pp. 387–392, 2005.

Gorawski, M. and Marks, P., "Resumption of Data Extraction Process in Parallel Data Warehouses", *Proceedings of Parallel Processing and Applied Mathematics (PPAM)*, pp. 478–485, 2005.

Gorawski, M. and Stachurski, K., "On Efficiency and Data Privacy Level of Association Rules Mining Algorithms within Parallel Spatial Data Warehouse", *Proceedings of the First International Conference on Availability, Reliability and Security (ARES)*, pp. 936–943, 2006.

Hallmark, G., "Oracle Parallel Warehouse Server", *Proceedings of International Conference on Data Engineering (ICDE)*, pp. 314–320, 1997.

Hu, K., Ling, C., Jie, S., Qi, G., and Tang, X., "Computing High Dimensional MOLAP with Parallel Shell Mini-cubes", *Proceedings of Fuzzy Systems and Knowledge Discovery (FSKD)*, pp. 1192–1196, 2005.

Jin, R., Vaidyanathan, K., Yang, G., and Agrawal, G., "Communication and Memory Optimal Parallel Data Cube Construction", *IEEE Trans. Parallel Distrib. Syst.*, 16(12):1105–1119, 2005.

Jin, R., Vaidyanathan, K., Yang, G., and Agrawal, G., "Using Tiling to Scale Parallel Data Cube Construction", *Proceedings of International Conference on Parallel Processing (ICPP)*, pp. 365–372, 2004.

Jin, R., Yang, G., and Agrawal, G., "Parallel Data Cube Construction: Algorithms, Theoretical Analysis, and Experimental Evaluation", *Proceedings of High Performance Computing (HiPC)*, pp. 74–84, 2003.

Jin, R., Yang, G., Vaidyanathan, K., and Agrawal, G., "Communication and Memory Optimal Parallel Data Cube Construction", *Proceedings of International Conference on Parallel Processing (ICPP)*, pp. 573–580, 2003.

Kim, J., Lee, B.S., Moon, Y., Ok, S., and Lee, W., "Parallel Consistency Maintenance of Materialized Views Using Referential Integrity Constraints in Data Warehouses", *Proceedings of Data Warehousing and Knowledge Discovery (DaWaK)*, pp. 146–156, 2005.

Lawrence, M. and Rau-Chaplin, A., "The OLAP-Enabled Grid: Model and Query Processing Algorithms", *Proceedings of International Symposium on High Performance Computing Systems (HPCS)*, pp. 4, 2006.

Li, J. and Gao, H., "Parallel Hierarchical Data Cube for Range Sum Queries and Dynamic Updates", *Proceedings of Database and Expert Systems Applications (DEXA)*, pp. 339–348, 2004.

Lima, A., Mattoso, M., and Valduriez, P., "OLAP Query Processing in a Database Cluster", *Proceedings of Euro-Par*, pp. 355–362, 2004.

Liu, B., Chen, S., and Rundensteiner, E.A., "A Transactional Approach to Parallel Data Warehouse Maintenance", *Proceedings of Data Warehousing and Knowledge Discovery (DaWaK)*, pp. 307–316, 2002.

Lu, H., Yu, J.X., Feng, L., and Li, Z., "Fully Dynamic Partitioning: Handling Data Skew in Parallel Data Cube Computation", *Distributed and Parallel Databases*, **13**(2):181–202, 2003.

Märtens, H., Rahm, E., and Stöhr, T., "Dynamic query scheduling in parallel data warehouses", *Concurrency and Computation: Practice and Experience*, **15**(11–12):1169–1190, 2003.

Märtens, H., Rahm, E., and Stöhr, T., "Dynamic Query Scheduling in Parallel Data Warehouses", *Proceedings of Euro-Par*, pp. 321–331, 2002.

Monteiro, A.M.C. and Furtado, P., "Data Skew-Handling in Parallel MDIM Data Warehouses", *Proceedings of Databases and Applications*, pp. 157–162, 2005.

Nguyen, T. M., Brezany, P., Tjoa, A. M., and Weippl, E., "Toward a Grid-Based Zero-Latency Data Warehousing Implementation for Continuous Data Streams Processing", *International Journal of Data Warehousing and Mining*, **1**(4):22–55, 2005.

Saeki, S., Bhalla, S., and Hasegawa, M., "Parallel Generation of Base Relation Snapshots for Materialized View Maintenance in Data Warehouse Environment", *Proceedings of the 2002 International Conference on Parallel Processing Workshops (ICPPW)*, pp. 383–390, 2002.

CHAPTERS 16 AND 17: PARALLEL AND GRID DATA MINING

Brezany, P., Kloner, C., and Tjoa, A.M., "Development of a Grid Service for Scalable Decision Tree Construction from Grid Databases", *Proceedings of Parallel Processing and Applied Mathematics (PPAM)*, pp. 616–624, 2005.

Christen, P., Hegland, M., Nielsen, O.M., Roberts, S., Strazdins, P.E., Semenova, T., Altas, I., and Hancock, T., "Towards a Parallel Data Mining Toolbox", *Proceedings of International Parallel and Distributed Processing Symposium (IPDPS)*, pp. 156, 2001.

Chung, S.M. and Mangamuri, M., "Mining Association Rules from Relations on a Parallel NCR Teradata Database System", *Proceedings of Information Technology: Coding and Computing (ITCC)*, pp. 465–470, 2004.

Chung, S.M. and Mangamuri, M., "Mining Association Rules from the Star Schema on a Parallel NCR Teradata Database System", *Proceedings of Information Technology: Coding and Computing (ITCC)*, pp. 206–212, 2005.

Cong, S., Han, J., and Padua, D.A., "Parallel mining of closed sequential patterns", *Proceedings of Knowledge Discovery and Data Mining (KDD)*, pp. 562–567, 2005.

Congiusta, A., Talia, D., and Trunfio, P., "Parallel and Grid-Based Data Mining - Algorithms, Models and Systems for High-Performance KDD", *Proceedings of the Data Mining and Knowledge Discovery Handbook*, pp. 1017–1041, 2005.

Dehne, F., Eavis, T., and Rau-Chaplin, A., "Coarse Grained Parallel On-Line Analytical Processing (OLAP) for Data Mining", *Proceedings of International Conference on Computational Science*, pp. 589–598, 2001.

Demiriz, A., "webSPADE: A Parallel Sequence Mining Algorithm to Analyze Web Log Data", *Proceedings of IEEE International Conference on Data Mining (ICDM)*, pp. 755–758, 2002.

Eitrich, T. and Lang, B., "Data Mining with Parallel Support Vector Machines for Classification", *Proceedings of Advances in Information Systems (ADVIS)*, pp. 197–206, 2006.

El-Hajj, M. and Zaïane, O.R., "Parallel Association Rule Mining with Minimum Inter-Processor Communication", *Proceedings of DEXA Workshops*, pp. 519–523, 2003.

El-Hajj, M. and Zaïane, O.R., "Parallel Leap: Large-Scale Maximal Pattern Mining in a Distributed Environment", *Proceedings of International Conference on Parallel and Distributed Systems (ICPADS)*, pp. 135–142, 2006.

Fiolet, V. and Toursel, B., "Progressive Clustering for Database Distribution on a Grid", *Proceedings of the 4th International Symposium on Parallel and Distributed Computing (ISPDC)*, pp. 282–289, 2005.

Foti, D., Lipari, D., Pizzuti, C., and Talia, D., "Scalable Parallel Clustering for Data Mining on Multicomputers", *Proceedings of the 15 IPDPS 2000 Workshops on Parallel and Distributed Processing*, pp. 390–398, 2000.

Garcke, J. and Griebel, M., "On the Parallelization of the Sparse Grid Approach for Data Mining", *Proceedings of Large-Scale Scientific Computing (LSSC)*, pp. 22–32, 2001.

Glimcher, L., Zhang, X., and Agrawal, G., "Scaling and Parallelizing a Scientific Feature Mining Application Using a Cluster Middleware", *Proceedings of International Parallel and Distributed Processing Symposium (IPDPS)*, 2004.

Goda, K., Tamura, T., Oguchi, M., and Kitsuregawa, M., "Run-Time Load Balancing System on SAN-connected PC Cluster for Dynamic Injection of CPU and Disk Resource - A Case Study of Data Mining Application", *Proceedings of Database and Expert Systems Applications (DEXA)*, pp. 182–192, 2002.

Gorawski, M. and Stachurski, K., "On Efficiency and Data Privacy Level of Association Rules Mining Algorithms within Parallel Spatial Data Warehouse", *Proceedings of the First International Conference on Availability, Reliability and Security (ARES)*, pp. 936–943, 2006.

Guralnik, V., Garg, N., and Karypis, G., "Parallel Tree Projection Algorithm for Sequence Mining", *Proceedings of Euro-Par*, pp. 310–320, 2001.

Holt, J.D. and Chung, S.M., "Parallel Mining of Association Rules from Text Databases on a Cluster of Workstations", *Proceedings of International Parallel and Distributed Processing Symposium (IPDPS)*, 2004.

Inoue, H. and Narihisa, H., "Parallel and Distributed Mining with Ensemble Self-Generating Neural Networks", *Proceedings of International Conference on Parallel and Distributed Systems (ICPADS)*, pp. 423–428, 2001.

Ishikawa, H., Shioya, Y., Omi, T., Ohta, M., and Katayama, K., "A Peer-to-Peer Approach to Parallel Association Rule Mining", *Proceedings of Knowledge-Based Intelligent Information & Engineering Systems (KES)*, pp. 178–188, 2004.

Jin, D. and Ziavras, S.G., "A Super-Programming Approach for Mining Association Rules in Parallel on PC Clusters", *IEEE Trans. Parallel Distrib. Syst.*, **15**(9):783–794, 2004.

Jin, R. and Agrawal, G., "Shared Memory Parallelization of Decision Tree Construction Using a General Data Mining Middleware", *Proceedings of Euro-Par*, pp. 346–354, 2002.

Jinlan, T., et al., "Parallelism of Association Rules Mining and Its Application in Insurance Operations", *Proceedings of International Conference on Computational Science*, pp. 907–914, 2004.

Kim, H.S., Gao, S., Xia, Y., Kim, G.B., and Bae, H., "DGCL: An Efficient Density and Grid Based Clustering Algorithm for Large Spatial Database", *Proceedings of Web-Age Information Management (WAIM)*, pp. 362–371, 2006.

Kitsuregawa, M. and Pramudiono, I., "PC Cluster Based Parallel Frequent Pattern Mining and Parallel Web Access Pattern Mining", *Proceedings of Databases in Networked Information Systems (DNIS)*, pp. 172–176, 2003.

Kitsuregawa, M., Pramudiono, I., Takahashi, K., and Prasetyo, B., "Web Mining Is Parallel", *Proceedings of High Performance Computing (HiPC)*, pp. 385–398, 2001.

Kitsuregawa, M., Shintani, T., Yoshizawa, T., and Pramudiono, I., "Web Log Mining and Parallel SQL Based Execution", *Proceedings of Databases in Networked Information Systems (DNIS)*, pp. 20–32, 2000.

Kuntraruk, J. and Pottenger, W.M., "Massively Parallel Distributed Feature Extraction in Textual Data Mining Using HDDI(tm)", *Proceedings of IEEE International Symposium on High Performance Distributed Computing (HPDC)*, pp. 363–370, 2001.

Leung, C.K., "Efficient Parallel Mining of Constrained Frequent Patterns", *Proceedings of International Symposium on High Performance Computing Systems (HPCS)*, pp. 73–82, 2004.

Li, E., Li, W., Wang, T., Di, N., Dulong, C., and Zhang, Y., "Towards the Parallelization of Shot Detection—a Typical Video Mining Application Study", *Proceedings of International Conference on Parallel Processing (ICPP)*, pp. 585–592, 2006.

Li, T. and Bollinger, T., "Distributed and Parallel Data Mining on the Grid", *Proceedings of International Conference Architecture of Computing Systems (ARCS) Workshops*, pp. 370–379, 2004.

Li, X., Jin, R., and Agrawal, G., "Compiler and Runtime Support for Shared Memory Parallelization of Data Mining Algorithms", *Proceedings of Languages and Compilers for Parallel Computing (LCPC)*, pp. 265–279, 2002.

Liu, Z., Kamohara, S., and Guo, M., "A Scheme of Interactive Data Mining Support System in Parallel and Distributed Environment", *Proceedings of International Symposium on Parallel and Distributed Processing and Applications (ISPA)*, pp. 263–272, 2003.

Ma, C. and Li, Q., "Parallel Algorithm for Mining Frequent Closed Sequences", *Proceedings of International Workshop on Autonomous Intelligent Systems: Agents and Data Mining (AIS-ADM)*, pp. 184–192, 2005.

Melab, N. and Talbi, E., "A Parallel Genetic Algorithm for Rule Mining", *Proceedings of International Parallel and Distributed Processing Symposium (IPDPS)*, p. 133, 2001.

Melab, N., Cahon, S., Talbi, E., and Duponchel, L., "Parallel GA-Based Wrapper Feature Selection for Spectroscopic Data Mining", *Proceedings of International Parallel and Distributed Processing Symposium (IPDPS)*, pp. 201–208, 2002.

Oguchi, M. and Kitsuregawa, M., "Optimizing transport protocol parameters for large scale PC cluster and its evaluation with parallel data mining", *Cluster Computing*, 3(1):15–23, 2000.

Oguchi, M. and Kitsuregawa, M., "Parallel Data Mining on ATM-Connected PC Cluster and Optimization of Its Execution Environments", *Proceedings of International Parallel and Distributed Processing Symposium (IPDPS) Workshops*, pp. 366–373, 2000.

Oguchi, M. and Kitsuregawa, M., "Using Available Remote Memory Dynamically for Parallel Data Mining Application on ATM-Connected PC Cluster", *Proceedings of International Parallel and Distributed Processing Symposium (IPDPS)*, pp. 411–420, 2000.

Parthasarathy, S., Zaki, M.J., and Li, W., "Memory Placement Techniques for Parallel Association Mining", *Proceedings of Knowledge Discovery and Data Mining (KDD)*, pp. 304–308, 1998.

Parthasarathy, S., Zaki, M.J., Ogihara, M., and Li, W., "Parallel Data Mining for Association Rules on Shared-Memory Systems", *Knowl. Inf. Syst.* **3**(1):1–29, 2001.

Pramudiono, I. and Kitsuregawa, M., "Parallel Web Access Pattern Mining on PC Cluster", *Proceedings of International Conference on Internet Computing*, pp. 70–76, 2003.

Pramudiono, I. and Kitsuregawa, M., "Tree Structure Based Parallel Frequent Pattern Mining on PC Cluster", *Proceedings of Database and Expert Systems Applications (DEXA)*, pp. 537–547, 2003.

Qiang, Z., Zheng, Z., Wei, S.Z., and Daley, E., "WINP: A Window-Based Incremental and Parallel Clustering Algorithm for Very Large Databases", *Proceedings of International Conference on Tools with Artificial Intelligence (ICTAI)*, pp. 169–176, 2005.

Rana, O.F., Walker, D.W., Li, M., Lynden, S.J., and Ward, M., "PaDDMAS: Parallel and Distributed Data Mining Application Suite", *Proceedings of International Parallel and Distributed Processing Symposium (IPDPS)*, pp. 387–392, 2000.

Sarker, B.K., Mori, T., Hirata, T., and Uehara, K., "Parallel Algorithms for Mining Association Rules in Time Series Data", *Proceedings of International Symposium on Parallel and Distributed Processing and Applications (ISPA)*, pp. 273–284, 2003.

Sarker, B.K., Uehara, K., and Yang, L.T., "Exploiting Efficient Parallelism for Mining Rules in Time Series Data", *Proceedings of the International Conference on High Performance Computing and Communications (HPCC)*, pp. 845–855, 2005.

Senger, H., Hruschka, E.R., Silva, F.A.B.d., Sato, L.M., Bianchini, C.D.P., and Esperidião, M.D., Inhambu: Data Mining Using Idle Cycles in Clusters of PCs, *Proceedings of Network and Parallel Computing (NPC)*, pp. 213–220, 2004.

Shi, L., Niu, C., Zhou, M., and Gao, J., "A DOM Tree Alignment Model for Mining Parallel Data from the Web", *Proceedings of Meeting of the Association for Computational Linguistics (ACL)*, pp. 489–496, 2006.

Sterritt, R., Adamson, K., Shapcott, M., and Curran, E.P., "Parallel Data Mining of Bayesian Networks from Telecommunications Network Data", *Proceedings of IPDPS Workshops*, pp. 415–426, 2000.

Talaie, S., Leigh, R., Louis, S.J., and Raines, G.L., "Predicting mining activity with parallel genetic algorithms", *Proceedings of Genetic and Evolutionary Computation Conference (GECCO)*, pp. 2149–2155, 2005.

Valdés, J.J. and Barton, A.J., "Mining Multivariate Time Series Models with Soft-Computing Techniques: A Coarse-Grained Parallel Computing Approach", *Proceedings of Computational Science and Its Applications (ICCSA)*, pp. 259–268, 2003.

Veloso, A., Otey, M.E., Parthasarathy, S. and Meira Jr. W., "Parallel and Distributed Frequent Itemset Mining on Dynamic Datasets", *Proceedings of High Performance Computing (HiPC)*, pp. 184–193, 2003.

Wang, F. and Helian, N., "Mining Global Association Rules on an Oracle Grid by Scanning Once Distributed Databases", *Proceedings of Euro-Par*, pp. 370–378, 2005.

Wang, H., Xiao, Z., Zhang, H. and Jiang, S., "Parallel Algorithm for Mining Maximal Frequent Patterns", *Proceedings of Advanced Parallel Programming Technologies (APPT)*, pp. 241–248, 2003.

Wu, M., Chung, M. and Moonesinghe, H.D.K., "Parallel Implementation of WAP-Tree Mining Algorithm", *Proceedings of International Conference on Parallel and Distributed Systems (ICPADS)*, 2004.

Zaïane, O.R., El-Hajj, M. and Lu, P., "Fast Parallel Association Rule Mining without Candidacy Generation", *Proceedings of IEEE International Conference on Data Mining (ICDM)*, pp. 665–668, 2001.

Zaki, M.J. and Pan, Y., "Introduction: Recent Developments in Parallel and Distributed Data Mining", *Distributed and Parallel Databases* **11**(2):123–127, 2002.

Zaki, M.J. Parthasarathy, S., Ogihara, M., and Li, W., "Parallel Algorithms for Discovery of Association Rules", *Data Min. Knowl. Discov.* **1**(4): 343–373, 1997.

Zaki, M.J., "Parallel Sequence Mining on Shared-Memory Machines", *J. Parallel Distrib. Comput.* **61**(3):401–426, 2001.

Zaki, M.J., Ho, C-T. and Agrawal, R., "Parallel Classification for Data Mining on Shared-Memory Multiprocessors", *Proceedings of the International Conference on Data Engineering (ICDE)*, pp. 98–205, 1999.

Zaki, M.J., "Parallel Sequence Mining on Shared-Memory Machines", *Proceedings of Large-Scale Parallel KDD Systems*, pp. 161–189, 1999.

Zhao, B., Vogel, S., "Adaptive Parallel Sentences Mining from Web Bilingual News Collection", *Proceedings of IEEE International Conference on Data Mining (ICDM)*, 2002.

ADDITIONAL READING: FUTURE PARALLEL/GRID DATA-INTENSIVE APPLICATIONS

Chervenak, A., Foster, I., Kesselman, C., Salisbury, C., Tuecke, S., "The Data Grid: Towards an architecture for the Distributed Management and Analysis of Large Scientific Datasets", *Journal of Network and Computer Applications*, **23**(3):187–200, 2001.

Chung, Y., "Parallel Information Retrieval with Query Expansion", *Proceedings of the 6th International Conference on Applied Parallel Computing Advanced Scientific Computing (PARA)*, pp. 195–202, 2002.

Deloch, S., "Databases, Web Services, and Grid Computing—Standards and Directions", *Proceedings of Euro-Par*, pp. 3, 2003.

Koparanova, M.G. and Risch, T., "High-Performance GRID Stream Database Manager for Scientific Data", *Proceedings of European Across Grids Conference*, pp. 86–92, 2003.

Lü, K., Zhu, Y., and Sun, W., "Parallel Processing XML Documents", *Proceedings of International Database Engineering and Application Symposium (IDEAS)*, pp. 96–105, 2002.

Matsuda, H., "A Grid Environment for Data Integration of Scientific Databases", *Proceedings of e-Science*, pp. 3–4, 2005.

Qin, J., Yang, S., and Dou, W., "Parallel Storing and Querying XML Documents Using Relational DBMS", *Proceedings of Advanced Parallel Programming Technologies (APPT)*, pp. 629–633, 2003.

Sun, W. and Lü, K., "Parallel Query Processing Algorithms for Semi-structured Data", *Proceedings of Conference on Advanced Information Systems Engineering (CAiSE)*, pp. 770–773, 2002.

Trujillo, R., "Application-Specific XML Processing: A Parallel Approach for Optimum Performance", *Proceedings of Parallel and Distributed Processing Techniques and Applications (PDPTA)*, pp. 959–964, 2005.

Zaki, M.J. and Aggarwal, C.C., "XRules: An effective algorithm for structural classification of XML data", *Machine Learning* **62**(1–2):137–170, 2006.

Index

High-Performance Parallel Database Processing and Grid Databases,
by David Taniar, Clement Leung, Wenny Rahayu, and Sushant Goel
Copyright © 2008 John Wiley & Sons, Inc.

WILEY SERIES ON PARALLEL AND DISTRIBUTED COMPUTING

Series Editor: Albert Y. Zomaya

Parallel and Distributed Simulation Systems / Richard Fujimoto

Mobile Processing in Distributed and Open Environments / Peter Sapaty

Introduction to Parallel Algorithms / C. Xavier and S. S. Iyengar

Solutions to Parallel and Distributed Computing Problems: Lessons from Biological Sciences / Albert Y. Zomaya, Fikret Ercal, and Stephan Olariu (*Editors*)

Parallel and Distributed Computing: A Survey of Models, Paradigms, and Approaches / Claudia Leopold

Fundamentals of Distributed Object Systems: A CORBA Perspective / Zahir Tari and Omran Bukhres

Pipelined Processor Farms: Structured Design for Embedded Parallel Systems / Martin Fleury and Andrew Downton

Handbook of Wireless Networks and Mobile Computing / Ivan Stojmenović (*Editor*)

Internet-Based Workflow Management: Toward a Semantic Web / Dan C. Marinescu

Parallel Computing on Heterogeneous Networks / Alexey L. Lastovetsky

Performance Evaluation and Characteization of Parallel and Distributed Computing Tools / Salim Hariri and Manish Parashar

Distributed Computing: Fundamentals, Simulations and Advanced Topics, *Second Edition* / Hagit Attiya and Jennifer Welch

Smart Environments: Technology, Protocols, and Applications / Diane Cook and Sajal Das

Fundamentals of Computer Organization and Architecture / Mostafa Abd-El-Barr and Hesham El-Rewini

Advanced Computer Architecture and Parallel Processing / Hesham El-Rewini and Mostafa Abd-El-Barr

UPC: Distributed Shared Memory Programming / Tarek El-Ghazawi, William Carlson, Thomas Sterling, and Katherine Yelick

Handbook of Sensor Networks: Algorithms and Architectures / Ivan Stojmenović (*Editor*)

Parallel Metaheuristics: A New Class of Algorithms / Enrique Alba (*Editor*)

Design and Analysis of Distributed Algorithms / Nicola Santoro

Task Scheduling for Parallel Systems / Oliver Sinnen

Computing for Numerical Methods Using Visual C++ / Shaharuddin Salleh, Albert Y. Zomaya, and Sakhinah A. Bakar

Architecture-Independent Programming for Wireless Sensor Networks / Amol B. Bakshi and Viktor K. Prasanna

High-Performance Parallel Database Processing and Grid Databases / David Taniar, Clement Leung, Wenny Rahayu, and Sushant Goel

Algorithms and Protocols for Wireless and Mobile Ad Hoc Networks / Azzedine Boukerche (*Editor*)

Algorithms and Protocols for Wireless Sensor Networks / Azzedine Boukerche (*Editor*)